CHINESE LEXICOLOGY AND LEXICOGRAPHY

Chinese Lexicology and Lexicography
A Selected and Classified Bibliography

中國詞彙學及辭典學分類參考書目

Paul Fu-mien Yang, S.J.

楊福綿編著

The Chinese University Press
Hong Kong

International Standard Book Number: 962-201-312-0

The Chinese University Press
The Chinese University of Hong Kong
SHATIN, N. T., HONG KONG

Typesetting by Oceanset Typographers Limited
Printing by Hoi Kwong Printing Co.

In Memory of My Beloved Aunt
Sister Mary Ts'ui Ching-feng (1897–1982)
Who Was My First Teacher of Linguistics

Contents

7. SET-PHRASES, PROVERBS, *HSIEH-HOU-YÜ* AND WITTICISMS (1854–2748)

Foreword

Father Paul Fu-mien Yang received his M.A. degree from the University of Tokyo in 1964. At that time, I was teaching graduate courses on Classical Chinese and Chinese linguistics; Father Yang was one of the most brilliant and active young students. Later, he went to the United States of America, and received his Ph.D. degree in 1967 from Georgetown University, where he has been teaching Chinese linguistics until now. Fully utilizing this setting, he was able to publish two bibliographies on Chinese linguistics and Chinese dialectology. Recently, he compiled this *Chinese Lexicology and Lexicography: A Selected and Classified Bibliography,* which is divided into two parts: Chinese lexicology and Chinese lexicography, including more than four thousand bibliographical entries collected from Chinese, Japanese, and various European languages.

In recently years, the field of Chinese studies has expanded extensively and has rapidly advanced. A great number of lexicological and lexicographical works have appeared. Without a good guide, however, it would be very difficult for the general public and students to begin their studies on this subject. To answer this need, Father Yang has published this book. To my knowledge, this comprehensive and analytical bibliography is the first of its kind. It surely will become a standard reference guide for the general public and students, as well as for scholars, and will be a very important contribution to the field of Chinese lexicology and lexicography. Thus, I recommend this book to all serious scholars and students of Chinese language and linguistics, and I wish the author continued success in his advancement in the scholarly world.

Akiyasu Tōdō
Visiting Professor of Waseda University
and Director of the Japanese-Chinese Institute

March 1, 1984

Preface

My interest in Chinese lexicology and lexicography goes back to 1971 when I first offered the graduate course Chinese Lexicology at Georgetown University. For that particular course, I put together a basic working bibliography. Ever since then, I have gathered materials inchmeal with a view to ultimately compile a reference work on that subject. My intensive work on that subject, however, did not begin until after the publication of my *Chinese Dialectology: A Selected and Classified Bibliography* in 1981. By the summer of 1982, I had completed a preliminary draft of the bibliography here. At that time, there were only 2,000 entries. Later, during my sabbatical leave of 1982–1983 from Georgetown University, I made a trip to the Far East where I was able to collect additional materials and, thus, make this final draft containing more than double the number of entries included in that preliminary draft.

Thus far, to the best of my knowledge, except for either partial or fragmentary listings of works on certain aspects of Chinese lexicology and lexicography, there has not been a similar work of the present type published in any language; this work, being a comprehensive and independent study, then, is the first of its kind. In the compilation of this bibliography, the most difficult task was the classification of topics; in other words, devising a comprehensive and sound scheme that would systematically cover all important aspects of the field. Being without a similar previously published work that could serve as a guide, I had to consult various books and articles dealing with Chinese and foreign lexicology and lexicography; my classification of topics, then, is to be considered synthetic. Once this was done, my next task was to classify all the collected materials within the determined topics. The classification of collected materials was itself complicated by limitations on the amount of available published materials on certain topics; sometimes, it occurred that there were either no or very few publications to be found on certain topics. Although inclusion of headings for such topics could be argued for from a pedagogical point of view, I, nevertheless, did not want to establish empty or near empty headings. Consequently, in the end, my policy was there had to be at least two available published works on a certain topic before a heading was established. Another difficulty, from the perspective of overall layout, was how to balance the number of headings so as to give due consideration to symmetrics and aesthetics. As regards this, I made four the maximum number of digits for any heading. I do realize that in doing so, however, it was sometimes necessary to further divide some broad headings into narrower ones; therefore, the establishment of some headings was more practical than strictly logical.

Chinese lexicology, as a relatively new discipline, shares some of the same areas as the domain of other branches of Chinese linguistics. For example, the study of words and word formation is also a part of Chinese morphology; the history and development of Chinese lexicons is also a part of the history of the Chinese language; etc. Chinese traditional semantics or *hsün-ku-hsüeh* (訓詁學) is a branch of Chinese philology which deals with the explanations and interpretations of the forms, sounds, and meanings of words and phrases found in ancient Chinese texts. It became an independent discipline in the field of Sinology as early as the Han dynasty; yet, as it deals with the study of Chinese words and lexical meanings, it should properly be considered as a part of Chinese lexicology too.

The selection of entries in this bibliography was intended to be both theoretical and also practical. From a theoretical standpoint, selection included important linguistic studies and discussions; from a practical standpoint, it included listings of character and word books, vocabularies, and dictionaries on various topics. In the section on Lexicon of Modern Chinese, I have included general vocabulary, basic vocabulary, dialect vocabulary, loan-words, new terms, scientific and technical terms, etc. However, in that section, for dialect vocabulary, I have only included a few multi-dialectal dictionaries; for dictionaries of individual dialects, the reader is invited to consult my *Chinese Dialectology: A Selected and Classified Bibliography* (see #0034); for scientific and technical terms, I have only included a few general dictionaries; for dictionaries on specialized terms in science and technology, the reader is urged to consult the *Chinese Dictionaries* compiled by Thomas Creamer and others (see #2871).

For the convenience of readers who are less familiar with the Chinese, Japanese, Russian, and Latin languages, titles of works published in those languages are translated into English. Efforts were made to translate those titles as close to the original meanings as possible; my translations, thus, are more literal than free. Since many lexicological and lexicographical terms are not yet unified either in Chinese or in English translations, sometimes, translations were forced, and, on the other hand, sometimes, it was difficult or even impossible to find good English equivalents. For example, the Chinese terms *yen-yü* (諺語), *su-yü* (俗語), and *su-hua* (俗話) can all be translated as 'proverb.' However, since *yen-yü* is the standard Chinese term for 'proverb,' I translated *su-yü* and *su-hua* literally as 'popular saying.' Also, in Chinese lexicography, originally the term *tzu-tien* (字典) meant 'character dictionary' and the term *tz'u-tien* (辭典) meant 'word dictionary'; but, quite often the term *tzu-tien* is also used for both 'character dictionary' and 'word dictionary.' In this bibliography the two terms were both generally translated as 'dictionary.' However, the original distinction was kept whenever there was a clear contrast between the two terms. In certain cases, the term *tzu-tien* was translated as '(character) dictionary' with the word 'character' in parentheses, meaning the term could also include 'word dictionary.' Also, the term *hsieh-hou-yü* (歇後語) does not have a good English equivalent. Lin Yutang's translation is 'have the last word of a well-known phrase understood and not spoken.' Liang Shih-ch'iu's translation is 'to omit the last part of a common expression; a riddle thus made.' *Han-Ying tz'u-tien*'s translation is 'a two-part allegorical saying, of which the first part, always stated, is descriptive, while the second part, sometimes unstated, carries the message.' All these are explanations rather than translations. Therefore, I have followed the practice of some authors and used the romanized form *hsieh-hou-yü*.

During the compilation of this work, I was assisted by Mr. James R. Jennings, Ph.D. candidate in Chinese and my teaching assistant at Georgetown University. Mr. Jennings was especially helpful in proofreading and in compiling the index of authors. Without his devoted assistance, the publication of this work would have been delayed. To him, I would like to express my special thanks and appreciation. I am also indebted to many colleagues and friends for providing me with bibliographical materials: I would like to express my sincerest thanks and appreciation to Professor Yeh Hsiang-ling, Nanjing Normal College, for checking the paginations of many periodical articles not available to me; to Mr. Chu Chieh-fan, well-known and prolific writer, who generously allowed me to consult his collected works on Chinese proverbs; to Mr. Ts'ao Yung-ho, National Taiwan University Library, for providing me with bibliographical information on Taiwan proverbs; to Professor Hatano Tarō, Yokohama Municipal University, for his help in locating many out-of-print Chinese and Japanese publications; to Professor Hirayama Hisao, University of Tokyo, for always being kind enough during the past twenty years to provide me with bibliographical information both for my previous works on Chinese linguistics and for this present work. There are also many other colleagues and friends who in one way or another helped me during the compilation of this work. Although I am unable to list them all by name, I do sincerely thank all of them for their generous assistance. I would like to also thank Mr. Richard Lai, former Director of The Chinese University Press, Mr. T.L. Tsim, current Director of the Press, and Mr. Ho Chun-chung, manuscript Editor of the Press, for their arrangements and assistance in producing this work. Last, but not least, I would like to express my deepest gratitude and sincerest thanks to Professor Tōdō Akiyasu, my former teacher at the University of Tokyo, for teaching me a lot about Chinese linguistics and who is now so kind as to write a foreword to this work.

Despite the numerous proofreadings and corrections to which this bibliography was subjected, errors and omissions may still be present. Criticism and suggestions will be gratefully accepted and appreciated.

In fond memory of my aunt, Sister Mary Ts'ui Ching-feng (崔景峯) who taught me the Chinese Phonetic Symbols when I was six years old and inspired me to pursue study in the field of Chinese linguistics, this book is gratefully dedicated.

Paul Fu-mien Yang, S.J.
Georgetown University
Washington, D.C.
October 16, 1983

Explanatory Notes

I. AUTHORS AND TRANSLATORS

1. The order followed is surname first, then given name. In case of pseudonyms, the real name, if known, follows in square brackets [ ].
2. Unknown authors are indicated by the term *Anonymous*.
3. Proper names following the term *Transl. by* indicate the translator.
4. Names of book revisors and reviewers follow usual signature order for Western names, but surname first, then given name, for East Asian names.

II. TITLES OF BOOKS AND ARTICLES

1. A colon separates the author's name from the title of his work.
2. Book titles are in italics, but article titles in Roman type.

III. PLACE OF PUBLICATION AND NAME OF PUBLISHERS

1. A period and a dash (.—) separate book titles from place of publication.
2. Place of publication is given in English spelling or in romanization for East Asian place names, followed by a colon.
3. The name of the publisher and the year of publication separated by a comma, follow the place of publication. The term *Ditto* indicates that the publisher is the same as the author or editor.
4. For the name of publishers and place of publication in respective East Asian languages, see List of Chinese and Japanese Publishers (pp. 301-317).

IV. PAGINATION OF BOOKS

1. Pagination of books follows the year of publication, separated by a comma.
2. The combination of small Roman numerals (for preface, table of contents, etc.) and of Arabic numerals (for the main text) is indicated if found in the work itself. Otherwise, Arabic numerals alone, separated by commas, are used. If relevant for a book, starting and ending pagination is linked by a hyphen.
3. In multi-volume works, pagination for each volume is given in succession, separated by a semi-colon.
4. Books of note found cited in works examined but which gave no pagination and as yet not themselves seen by this bibliographer are indicated by the term (not seen).

V. TITLE, VOLUME, NUMBER, YEAR AND PAGINATION OF PERIODICALS

1. Periodical titles follow article titles, separated by a period and a dash (.—). Periodical titles in italics are usually abbreviated. See List of Periodicals (pp. xxxvii-xlvi).
2. Volume of a periodical is given immediately after its title, without any mark of separation, next its issue number follows, separated by a colon, then the year, separated by a comma. But issue numbers, either published within a given year or coinciding with the twelve months of the calendar year, follow the year.
3. Pagination of an article is given after the year or the issue number, whatever be the case, separated by a comma. Starting and ending pagination is linked by a hyphen. In some Chinese periodicals (for example, the *CKYW*), the concluding part of an article may be found either on a preceding page or on a succeeding page, and thus be separated from the main body

of the article. In such cases, the main successive pagination is given first, then the concluding pagination.

4. Articles of note found cited in works examined but which gave no pagination and as yet themselves not seen by this bibliographer are indicated by the term (not seen).

IV.   ADDITIONAL REMARKS AND REVIEWS

1. Additional remarks as well as reviews of book or article follow the main entry, separated by a diagonal (/). Among the additional remarks is information concerning bibliography and contents, series and collection titles, etc.

2. Reviews of the book or article follow the same format of an article entry except that the names of reviews follow the order stated in I.4, and occur as final information given for reviews.

VII.   TRANSLATION OF TITLES

1. Chinese, Japanese, Korean, Latin, and Russian titles are translated into English and are given in square brackets.

2. A book or article that is a translation follows the format already outlined. The original title of the translated work is likewise given in square brackets.

VIII.   USE OF CHINESE, JAPANESE, AND KOREAN CHARACTERS

1. At the end of those entries indicating books or articles written by Chinese, Japanese, or Korean scholars, the respective characters follow: proper name first, then the title of the book or article. Characters for reviewers' names follow the title, separated by a diagonal.

2. Double quotation marks (「 」) in the title of an article indicate either titles of books or specific terms. Single quotation marks (「 」) indicate titles of a series or a collection. Book titles within a book are unmarked.

IX.   ROMANIZATION, TRANSCRIPTION, AND ENTRY ORDER

1. Chinese, Japanese, Korean, and Russian titles are romanized according to the following systems: Wade-Giles for Chinese; Hepburn for Japanese; McCune-Reischauer for Korean; and Library of Congress for Russian, with omission of diacritical mark (⌢).

2. The order of entries in the main body of the text, List of Periodicals, List of Chinese and Japanese Publishers, and Romanized Index of Authors is according to standard alphabetical order. For the convenience of arrangement, the order of spelling for Wade-Giles romanization is also adapted to the standard alphabetical order.

X.   ROMANIZATION OF PLACE NAMES

1. European, American, and Asian place names are found in standard English forms.

2. Well-known Chinese place names are transcribed according to accepted English forms. Other Chinese place names are transcribed according to Wade-Giles spelling without hyphens and mark of aspiration.

XI.   CROSS REFERENCES

1. Cross references to a book or an article appearing in this bibliography are indicated by their entry numbers in parentheses.

2. Reference to an original title of a translated work is indicated the same way.

List of Periodicals

AA American Anthropologist. Washington, D.C. 1888–

AAHG Anzeiger für die Altertumswissenschaft. Imsbruck. 1928–

AATS Ajia-Afurika Gengo Bunka Kenkyūjo Tsūshin. Tokyo. 1966–
アジア・アフリカ言語文化研究所通信　東京

AcOr Acta Orientalia. Copenhagen. 1922–

ADKK Ajia Daigaku Kyōyōbu Kiyō. Tokyo. 1975–
亞細亞大學教養部紀要　東京

AGDR Aichi Gakuin Daigaku Ronsō. Nagoya. 1961–
愛知學院大學論叢　名古屋

AHST An-hui shih-ta hsüeh-pao. Wuhu. 1973–
安徽師大學報　蕪湖

AHSY An-hui shih-fan hsüeh-yüan hsüeh-pao. Hofei. 1959–
安徽師範學院學報　合肥

AHTH An-hui ta-hsüeh hsüeh-pao. Hofei. 1960–1962; 1964–
安徽大學學報　合肥

AM Asia Major, new series. London. 1949–

Annales de l'Estrême-Orient et de l'Afrique. Paris. 1878–

Anthropos. International Review of Ethnology and Linguistics. Freiburg. 1906–

AO Archiv Orientální. Prague. 1933–

AOH Acta Orientalia Academiae Scientiarum Hungaricae. Budapest. 1950–

Archiv für Ostasien. Düsseldorf. 1948–

Archiv für Schreib-und Buchwessen. Wollenbüttel. 1927–

Asian Affairs. Honolulu; Vancouver. 1928–

Asian Survey. Berkeley. 1961–

Asie du Sud-est et Monde Insulindien. Paris. 1978–

Association for Literary and Linguistic Computing. Cambridge. 1973–

Babel. Revue International de la Traduction. Amsterdam. 1955–

BAEO Boletin de la Asociacion Española de Orientalistas. Madrid.

Baessler-Archiv. Basel. 1941.

BCUP Bulletin of the Catholic University of Peking. Peiping. 1926–1934.

BEFEO Bulletin de l'École Française d'Extrême-Orient. Hanoi; Saigon. 1901–

BGRS Bungaku Ronshū. Fukuoka. 1953–
文學論輯　福岡

Bibliografiia Vostoka. Leningrad. 1932–

Biburia. Tenri. 1949–
ビブリア　天理

BIE Bulletin of the Institute of Ethnology, Academia Sinica. Taipei. 1956–
中央研究院民族學研究所集刊　臺北

BIHP Bulletin of the Institute of History and Philology, Academia Sinica. Canton; Peking; Shanghai; Kunming; Chungking; Taipei. 1928–
中央研究院歷史語言研究所集刊　臺北

BIHPEV Bulletin of the Institute of History and Philology, Extra Volume, Academia Sinica. Taipei. 1928–
中央研究院歷史語言研究所集刊　外編

BMFEA Bulletin of the Museum of Far Eastern Antiquities. Stockholm. 1929–

BSL Bulletin de la Société de Linguistique de Paris. Paris. 1869–

BSOAS Bulletin of the School of Oriental and African Studies. London. Formerly *BSOS.*

BSOS Bulletin of the School of Oriental Studies. London. 1917–

BUA Bulletin de l'Université l'Aurore. 3rd series. Shanghai. 1940–1949.

Bulletin of Visiting Scholars Association, China Branch. Cambridge, Mass. 1962.

Bulletin, Société Belge d'Études Coloniales. Brussels. 1894–1925.

Bungaku. Tokyo. 1945–
文學　京都

CAAAL Computational Analysis of Asian and African Languages. Tokyo. 1975–
アジア・アフリカ語の計數研究　東京

CAJ Central Asiatic Journal. The Hague and Wiesbaden. 1955–

CBH Chūgoku Bungakuhō. Kyoto. 1954–
中國文學報　京都

CBKK Chūbun Kenkyū. Tenri. 1961–
中文研究　天理

CCCY Che-chiang chiao-yü hsing-cheng chou-k'an. Hangchow. 1932–
浙江教育行政周刊　杭州

CCS Collectanea Commissionis Synodalis. Peiping. 1928–1947.
公教教育叢刊　北平

CCSY Che-chiang shih-yüan hsüeh-pao. Hangchow. 1955–
浙江師院學報　杭州

CCTH (Kuo-li) Cheng-chih ta-hsüeh hsüeh-pao. Taipei. 1960–
National Chengchi University Journal.
（國立）政治大學學報　臺北

CCWH Ch'ao-chou wen-hsien. Taipei. 1974–
潮州文獻　臺北

CFHY Chung-Fa Han-hsüeh yen-chiu-so t'u-shu-kuan kuan-k'an. Peiping. 1945–
中法漢學研究所圖書館館刊　北平

CFTH Chung-fa ta-hsüeh yüeh-k'an. Peiping. 1945–1946.
Revue de l'Université Franco-Chinoise.
中法大學月刊　北平

CGGG Chūgoku Gogaku. Tokyo. 1947–
Bulletion of the Chinese Language Society of Japan.
中國語學　東京

CGGK Chūgokugo Kenkyū. Tokyo. 1981–
中國語研究　東京

CGKK Chūgoku Gogaku Kenkyūkai Kaihō. Tokyo. 1951–1954.
中國語學研究會會報　東京

CGKR Chūgoku Gogaku Kenkyūkai Ronshū. Nara. 1953.
中國語學研究會論集　奈良

CGKS Chūgoku Gogaku Kenkyūkai Shūkan. Tokyo. 1960.
中國語學研究會集刊　東京

CGZS Chūgokugo Zasshi. Tokyo. 1947–
中國語雜誌　東京

Ch'a-ho-erh wen-hsien. Taipei. 1977.
察合爾文獻　臺北

Ch'ang liu. Taipei. 1950–
暢流（半月刊）　臺北

CHCK Ch'ing-hua chou-k'an. Peiping. 1921–1937.
清華周刊　北平

CHCY Chiang-hsi chiao-yü yüeh-k'an. Nanchang. 1934–1937.
江西教育月刊　南昌

CHCYC Chung-hua chiao-yü chieh. Shanghai. 1913–1937; 1947–1949.
中華教育界（月刊）　上海

Che-chiang hsüeh-k'an. Hangchow. 1963–
浙江學刊（雙月刊）　杭州

Che-chiang ta-hsüeh wen-hsüeh-yüan chi-k'an. Hangchow. 1941–1944.
浙江大學文學院集刊　杭州

Che-chiang yüeh-k'an. Taipei. 1968–
浙江月刊　臺北

Chen-chih hsüeh-pao. Nanking. 1942.
眞知學報　南京

Cheng-feng yüeh-k'an. Tsaotien (Hupei). 1944–1945.
正風月刊　草店（湖北）

CHHK Chiang-hai hsüeh-k'an. Nanking. 1958–1963.
江海學刊（月刊）　南京

CHHP Ch'ing-hua hsüeh-pao. Peiping. 1924–1948; Hsinchu, New series, 1956–

Tsing Hua Journal of Chinese Studies.
清華學報　北平；新竹

CHHY Chung-hua hsüeh-yüan. Taipei. 1968–
Journal of Chinese Arts'.
中華學苑　臺北

Chi-Lin. Princeton. 1968–
Unicorn.
麒麟

Chi-nan ta-hsüeh wen-hsüeh-yüan chi-k'an. Shanghai. 1930–
暨南大學文學院集刊　上海

Chia-i wen-hsien. Chiayi (Taiwan). 1961–
嘉義文獻（半年刊）　嘉義（臺灣）

Chiang-hsi ta-hsüeh hsüeh-pao. Nanchang. 1963–
江西大學學報　南昌

Chiang-hsi wen-hsien. Taipei. 1966–
Documents of Kiangsi Province.
江西文獻（季刊）　臺北

Chiang-huai hsüeh-pao. Hofei. 1962–
江淮學刊（雙月刊）　合肥

Chiang-su hsün-k'an. Chenkiang. 1930.
江蘇旬刊　鎮江

Chiang-su wen-hsien. Taipei. 1963–
江蘇文獻　臺北

Chiao-hsüeh yü yen-chiu. Taipei. 1981–
教學與研究　臺北

Chiao-yü chin-yü tsa-chih. Tokyo. 1910–1911.
教育今語雜識　東京

Chiao-yü t'ung-hsün. Taipei. 1946–1954.
教育通訊（半月刊）　臺北

Chiao-yü yü k'o-hsüeh. Kunming. 1937–
教育與科學（半年刊）　昆明

Chiao-yü yü yen-chiu. Chinhua. 1972–
教育與研究　金華

Chien-kuo yü-wen yüeh-k'an. Chengku (Shensi). 1942–
建國語文月刊　城固（陝西）

Chien-she. Taipei. 1952–
The Reconstruction Magazine.
建設　臺北

Chih-hsüeh yüeh-k'an. Chengtu. 1942–
志學月刊　成都

Chih-yen. Soochow. 1935–1940.
制言（半月刊）　蘇州

Chin-jih Chung-kuo. Taipei. 1952–
今日中國　臺北

Chin-jih p'ing-lun. Kunming. 1939–
今日評論（週刊）　昆明

Chin-yang hsüeh-k'an. Taiyüan. 1980–
晉陽學刊（雙月刊）　太原

China Quarterly. Paris; London. 1960–

Chinese and Japanese Repository. London. 1863–

Chinese Culture. Yangmingshan. 1957–
中國文化季刊　陽明山

Chinese Repository. Canton. 1832–1951.

Ching shih. Nanking. 1937–
經世（半月刊）　南京

ChinRec Chinese Recorder. Foochow; Shanghai. 1868–1940.

CHN Chung-kuo hsüeh-shu nien-k'an. Taipei. 1977–
Annual Journal of Chinese Studies.
中國學術年刊　臺北

Chou-lun. Peiping. 1948–
周論　北平

CHP Chiang-han hsüeh-pao. Wuhan. 1961–1963.
江漢學報　武漢

CHS Chung-hsüeh sheng. Shanghai. 1930–
中學生（月刊）　上海

CTHP Cheng-chou ta-hsüeh hsüeh-pao. Chengchow. 1962–
鄭州大學學報　鄭州

Chu-i yü kuo-ts'e. Taipei. 1955–
主義與國策　臺北

Ch'u-pan chou-k'an (hsin). Shanghai. 1934–
出版週刊（新）　上海

Chūgoku Bunka. Kyoto. 1947–
中國文化　京都

Chūgokugo. Tokyo. 1955–
中國語（月刊）　東京

Chūgokugo (Zhongguoyu). Tokyo. 1968–
中國語 東京

Chūken Nōto. Osaka. 1960.
中研ノート 大阪

Chung-hsüeh yü-wen chiao-hsüeh. Peking. 1980–
中學語文教學 北京

Chung-hua chiao-yü chieh. Shanghai. 1947–
中華教育界（月刊） 上海

Chung-hua hsüeh-shu-yüan T'ien-chu-chiao hsüeh-shu yen-chiu-so hsüeh-pao. Taipei. 1969–
Bulletin of Catholic Research Institute, China Academy.
中華學術院天主教學術研究所學報 臺北

Chung-kuo hsin-shu yüeh-pao. Shanghai. 1930–1933.
中國新書月報 上海

Chung-kuo i-chou. Taipei. 1950–
中國一周 臺北

Chung-kuo kung-lun. Peiping. 1939–
中國公論（月刊） 北平

Chung-kuo kuo-hsüeh. Tainan. 1981–
中國國學 臺南

Chung-kuo min-tsu-hsüeh t'ung-hsün. Taipei. 1965–
Newsletter of Chinese Ethnology.
中國民族學通訊 臺北

Chung-kuo tung-ya hsüeh-shu nien-pao. Taipei. 1962–
中國東亞學術年報 臺北

Chung-kuo wen-hsüeh. Chungking. 1944–
中國文學（月刊） 重慶

Chung-kuo wen-i. Peiping. 1939–
中國文藝（月刊） 北平

Chung-kuo wen-tzu. Taipei. 1960–1974.
中國文字 臺北

Chung-mei chou-k'an. Shanghai. 1939–
中美週刊 上海

Chung-shan wen-hua chiao-yü-kuan chi-k'an. Nanking. 1934–1937.
中山文化教育館季刊 南京

Chung-ta chi-k'an. Peiping. 1926.
中大季刊 北平

Chung-wen hsüeh-hui hsüeh-pao. Singapore. 1966–
中文學會學報 新加坡

Chung-yang ta-hsüeh wen-i ts'ung-k'an. Nanking. 1933–1936.
中央大學文藝叢刊（半年刊） 南京

Chungguk hakpo. Seoul. 1963–
Journal of Chinese Studies.
中國學報 漢城

Chūtetsubun Gakkaihō. Tokyo. 1974–
Bulletin of the Sinological Society. University of Tokyo.
中哲文學會報 東京

CHWI Chung-hua wen-i. Taipei. 1971–
中華文藝 臺北

CHYC Chiao-hsüeh yü chin-hsiu. Wuhsi. 1979–
教學與進修 無錫

CHYY Chiao-hsüeh yü yen-chiu. Peking. 1953–
教學與研究（月刊） 北京

CJ China Journal of Science and Art. Shanghai. 1923–1941.

CJL Canadian Journal of Linguistics. Toronto. 1962–

CKDG Chūkyō Daigaku Kyōyōbu Ronsō. Nagoya. 1975–
中京大學教養部論叢 名古屋

CKTH Ch'eng-kung ta-hsüeh hsüeh-pao. Tainan. 1961–
Cheng Kung University Journal.
成功大學學報 臺南

CKYT Chung-kuo yü-wen. Taipei. 1952–
中國語文 臺北

CKYW Chung-kuo yü-wen. Peking. 1952–1966; 1978–
中國語文 北京

CKYWY Chung-kuo yü-wen yen-chiu. Hong Kong. 1980–
中國語文研究 香港

CLAO Cahiers de Linguistique Asie Orientale. Paris. 1977–

CLHP Chin-ling hsüeh-pao. Nanking. 1931–
Nanking Journal.
金陵學報 南京

CLOS Cahiers de Linguistique d'Orientalisme et de Slavistique. Aix-Marseille. 1973–

CLTH Chi-lin ta-hsüeh hsüeh-pao. Changchun. 1959–
吉林大學學報　長春

CNC Ch'ing-nien chieh. Shanghai. 1931–1947.
青年界　上海

CNMT Chung-nan min-tsu hsüeh-yüan hsüeh-pao. Hankow. 1981–
中南民族學院學報　漢口

CNWH Ch'ing-nien wen-hua. Chinan. 1934–
青年文化　濟南

Contemporary China.　Hong Kong. 1955–

Correo Sino-Annamita.　Manila. 1866–

CR China Review. Hong Kong. 1872–1901.

CSCY Chiang-su chiao-yü. Nanking. 1957–
江蘇教育　南京

CSHS Chung-hsan hsüeh-shu wen-hua chi-k'an. Taipei. 1968–
Bulletin of the Sun Yat-sen Cultural Foundation.
中山學術文化集刊　臺北

CSSY Chiang-su shih-yüan hsüeh-pao. Soochow. 1962–
江蘇師院學報　蘇州

CSTH Chung-shan ta-hsüeh hsüeh-pao. Canton. 1955–1960; 1973–
中山大學學報　廣州

CSTY Chung-shan ta-hsüeh Yü-yen li-shih yen-chiu-so chou-k'an. Canton. 1927–1930.
中山大學語言歷史研究所週刊　廣州

CSWS Chung-shan ta-hsüeh wen shih yen-chiu-so chi-k'an. Canton. 1931–1932.
中山大學文史研究所輯刊　廣州

CT Chiao-yü t'ung-hsün. Shanghai. 1938–; Taipei. 1950–
教育通訊　上海；臺北

CTHP Cheng-chou ta-hsüen hsüeh-pao. Chengchow. 1962–
鄭州大學學報　鄭州

CTKK (Kuo-li) Chung-yang t'u-shu-kuan kuan-k'an. Nanking. 1947–

（國立）中央圖書館館刊　南京

CWCC Chung-shan wen-hua chiao-yü-kuan chi-k'an. Nanking. 1934–
中山文化教育館季刊　南京

CWFY Chung-hua wen-hua fu-hsing yüeh-k'an. Taipei. 1968–
Chinese Cultural Renaissance Monthly.
中華文化復興月刊　臺北

CWY Chung-kuo wen-hua yüeh-k'an. Taipei. 1953–
中國文化月刊　臺北

CWYH Chung-kuo wen-hua yen-chiu hui-k'an. Chengtu. 1940–1948.
Bulletin of Chinese Studies.
中國文化研究彙刊（年刊）　成都

CYHC Chiao-hsüeh yen-chiu hui-chi. Chengchow. 1953–1955.
教學研究滙輯　鄭州

CYHY Chiao-yü hsüeh-yüan hsüeh-pao. Chang-hua. 1976–
Journal of the Taiwan Provincial College of Education.
教育學院學報　彰化

CYS Chiao-yü yü she-hui. Pishan (Szechwan). 1942–
教育與社會　璧山（四川）

CYTC Chiao-yü tsa-chih. Shanghai. 1909–1947.
教育雜誌（月刊）　上海

CYTH Chung-kuo yü-wen t'ung-hsün. Peking. 1978–
中國語文通訊（雙月刊）　北京

CYTK Chung-kuo yü-wen-hsüeh ts'ung-k'an. Shanghai. 1933–
中國語文學叢刊　上海

CYTS (Kuo-li) Chung-yang t'u-shu-kuan kuan-k'an. Taipei. 1967–
Bulletin, National Central Library.
（國立）中央圖書館館刊（季刊）　臺北

CYY Chung-kuo yü-wen yen-chiu. Hong Kong. 1980–
中國語文研究　香港

CYYC Chiao-yü yen-chiu. Canton. 1931–1935.
教育研究　廣州

CYYK Chung-yang yen-chiu yüan yüan-k'an. Taipei. 1954—
Annals of Academia Sinica.
中央研究院院刊　臺北

CYYMC Chiao-yü yü min-chung. Wuhsi. 1929—
教育與民眾　無錫

DA Dissertation Abstracts. Ann Arbor. 1938—

DAI Dissertation Abstracts International. Ann Arbor. 1969—

Daigaku Kokubun. Osaka. 1968—
大學國文　大阪

Daitō Bunka. Tokyo. 1927—
大東文化　東京

Daitō Bunka Daigaku Kangakkaishi. Tokyo. 1973—
大東文化大學漢學會誌　東京

Daitō Bunka Gakuin Dōsōkaihō. Tokyo. 1943—
大東文化學院同窓會報　東京

DBDK Daitō Bunka Daigaku Kiyō (Bungakuhen). Tokyo. 1964—
Daito Bunka University Literature Department Bulletin.
大東文化大學紀要（文學編）　東京

Denshō Bunka. Tokyo. 1960—
傳承文化　東京

Deutsche Literaturzeitung. Leipzig. 1880—

East and West. Rome. 1950—

Exeter Linguistic Studies. Exeter. 1979.

Fan-kung. Taipei. 1949—
The Counter-Attack Magazine.
反攻（月刊）　臺北

FCCY Fu-chien chiao-yü. Foochow. 1959—
福建教育（半月刊）　福州

FCWH Fu-chien wen-hsien. Taipei. 1968—
福建文獻　臺北

FDKH Fukuoka Daigaku Kenkyūjohō. Fukuoka. 1970—
福岡大學研究所報　福岡

Feng-t'u tsa-chih. Chengtu. 1943—
風土雜誌　成都

FEQ Far Eastern Quarterly. Ithaca. 1941—1955. Succeeded by *JAS.*

FITP Fan-i t'ung-pao. Peking. 1950—
翻譯通報（月刊）　北京

FIYK Fan-i yüeh-k'an. Peking. 1950—
翻譯月刊　北京

FJHC Fu-jen hsüeh-chih. Peiping. 1928—1947; Hsinchuang (Taipei). 1968—
Fu Jen Studies.
輔仁學誌　北平；新莊（臺北）

Folklore Studies. Peiping. 1942—

FTHP Fu-tan hsüeh-pao. Shanghai. 1955—
復旦學報　上海

Fu-hsing-kang hsüeh-pao. Fu-hsing-kang (Taipei). 1961—
復興崗學報　復興崗（臺北）

Fu Jen Studies. Hsinchuang. 1968—

Fu-nü tsa-chih. Shanghai. 1915—1931.
婦女雜誌　上海

Fu-tan. Shanghai. 1959—
復旦（月刊）　上海

FW Fu-chien wen-hua. Foochow. 1932—1936.
福建文化　福州

Gakudai Kokubun. Osaka. 1958—
學大國文　大阪

Gakutō. Tokyo. 1970—
學燈　東京

GBR Gengo Bunka Ronshū. Sakuramura. 1977—
言語文化論集　櫻村

Gekkan Manshū. Fushun. 1943.
月刊滿州　撫順

Gengo. Tokyo. 1972—
言語（月刊）　東京

Gengo Bunka. Tokyo. 1977—
言語文化　東京

Gengogaku Zasshi. Tokyo. 1900—
言語學雜誌　東京

Gengo Kagaku. Fukuoka. 1965—
Linguistic Science.
言語科學　福岡

Geographical Journal. London. 1893—

GGSK Gengo Seikatsu. Tokyo. 1959—
言語生活　東京

GK Gengo Kenkyū. Tokyo. 1939–
Journal of the Linguistic Society of Japan.
言語研究 東京

Han-hiue. Bulletin du Centre d'Études Sinologiques de Pékin. Peiping-Paris. 1944–1948.
漢學

HCN Hsin ch'ing-nien. Canton. 1915–1922.
新青年 廣州

HCS Hsin chien-she. Peking. 1950–1963.
新建設 北京

HCSY Hua-chung shih-yüan hsüeh-pao. Wuchang.
1959–
華中師院學報 武昌

HCTH Hang-chou ta-hsüeh hsüeh-pao. Hangchow. 1959–
杭州大學學報 杭州

HCYY Han-yü chiao-hsüeh yü yen-chiu. Yenchi.
1980–
漢語教學與研究 延吉

HDGG Hokkaidō Daigaku Gaigokugo Gaigoku
Bungaku Kenkyū. Sapporo. 1953–
The Hokkaido University Essays in Foreign
Languages and Literatures.
北海道大學外國語外國文學研究 札晃

HFSY Ho-fei shih-fan hsüeh-yüan hsüeh-pao.
Hofei. 1959–
合肥師範學院學報 合肥

HHYK Hua-hsüeh yüeh-k'an. Taipei. 1972–
Sinological Monthly.
華學月刊 臺北

HJAS Harvard Journal of Asiatic Studies. Cambridge, Mass. 1936–

HKCH Hsiang-kang Ch'in-hui hsüeh-yüan hsüeh-
pao. Kowloon. 1962–
The Hong Kong Baptist College Journal.
香港浸會學院學報 九龍

HKCTH Hsiang-kang Chung-wen ta-hsüeh hsüeh-
pao. Hong Kong. 1973–1979.
Journal of The Chinese University of Hong
Kong.
香港中文大學學報 香港

HKCW Hsiang-kang Chung-wen ta-hsüeh Chung-
kuo wen-hua yen-chiu-so hsüeh-pao. Hong

Kong. 1968–
Journal of the Institute of Chinese Studies of
The Chinese University of Hong Kong.
香港中文大學中國文化研究所學報 香港

HKDKZ Hokkaidō Komazawa Daigaku Kenkyū
Kiyō. Iwamizawa. 1968–
北海道駒澤大學研究紀要 岩見澤

HKYK Hua-kuo yüeh-k'an. Shanghai. 1923–
1926.
華國月刊 上海

HMTH Hsia-men ta-hsüeh hsüeh-pao. Amoy.
1954–
Universitas Amoiensis Acta Sicnetiarum
Socialium.
厦門大學學報 厦門

HNCY Ho-nan chiao-yü yüeh-k'an. Kaifeng.
1935–
河南教育月刊 開封

HNSC Hai-nan shih-chuan hsüeh-pao. Haikow.
1981–
海南師專學報 海口

HNSY Hsi-nan shih-fan hsüeh-yüan hsüeh-pao.
Chungking. 1959–
西南師範學院學報 重慶

HNTH Ho-nan ta-hsüeh hsüeh-pao. Kaifeng.
1934.
河南大學學報 開封

Ho-nan ta-hsüeh chou-k'an. Kaifeng. 1932–
河南大學週刊 開封

Hon-nan t'u-shu-kuan kuan-k'an. Kaifeng. 1933–
河南圖書館館刊 (雙月刊) 開封

HPPI Hua-pei pien-i-kuan kuan-k'an. Peiping.
1943.
華北編譯館館刊 北平

HPSY Ho-pei shih-fan hsüeh-yüan hsüeh-pao.
Tientsin. 1957–
河北師範學院學報 天津

HPTH Ho-pei ta-hsüeh hsüeh-pao. Tientsin.
1961–
河北大學學報 天津

HPWH Ho-pei wen-hsüeh. Tientsin. 1963–
河北文學 天津

HRBK Hiroshima Daigaku Bungakuku Kiyō. Hiroshima.
廣島大學文學部紀要　廣島

HRPS Ha-erh-pin shih-fan hsüeh-yüan hsüeh-pao. Harbin. 1963–
哈爾濱師範學院學報　哈爾濱

HSCK Hsüeh-shu chi-k'an. Taipei. 1952–1958. Academic Review.
學術季刊　臺北

HSDK Hirosaki Daigaku Kyōyōbu Bunka Kiyō. Hirosaki. 1980–
弘前大學教養部文化紀要　弘前

Hsi-fang yü-wen. Peking. 1957–1958.
西方語文（季刊）　北京

Hsi-pei kung-lun. Tatung. 1941–
西北公論（月刊）　大同

Hsi-pei shih-fan hsüeh-yüan hsüeh-shu chi-k'an. Lanchow. 1942–
西北師範學院學術季刊　蘭州

Hsi-pei ta-hsüeh hsüeh-pao. Sian. 1957–
西北大學學報　西安

Hsiang-t'an ta-hsüeh she-hui k'o-hsüeh hsüeh-pao. Hsiangtan. 1979–
湘潭大學社會科學學報　湘潭

Hsiao-shuo yüeh-pao. Shanghai. 1910–1932.
小說月報　上海

Hsien-tai hsüeh-pao. Nanking. 1947–1948.
現代學報　南京

Hsien-tai shih-hsüeh. Canton. 1933–
現代史學　廣州

Hsin-chu shih-chuan hsüeh-pao. Hsinchu. 1977–
新竹師專學報　新竹

Hsin Chung-hua. Shanghai. 1933–1937, 1946–
新中華（半月刊）　上海

Hsin Chung-kuo. Peking. 1919–1920.
新中國（月刊）　北京

Hsin nung-ts'un. Taiyüan. 1933–
新農村（月刊）　太原

Hsin-wen chan-hsien. Peking. 1958–1960.
新聞戰線　北京

Hsin wen-i. Taipei. 1950–
New Literature and Arts.

新文藝　臺北

HSSC Hsüeh-shu shih-chieh. Shanghai. 1935–1937.
學術世界　上海

Hsü-chou shih-fan hsüeh-yüan hsüeh-pao. Hsü-chow. 1981–
徐州師範學院學報　徐州

Hsüeh feng. Anking. 1944–1945.
學風（月刊）　安慶

Hsüeh-hsi yü szu-k'ao. Peking. 1981–
學習與思考（雙月刊）　北京

Hsüeh-hsi yü t'an-so. Harbin. 1979–
學習與探索（雙月刊）　哈爾濱

Hsüeh-i. Shanghai. 1917–1943.
學藝（月刊）　上海

Hsüeh-pao. Shanghai. 1907–1908.
學報（月刊）　上海

Hsüeh-sheng tsa-chih. Shanghai. 1914–1941.
學生雜誌　上海

Hsüeh-shih. Nanking. 1947–1948.
學識（半月刊）　南京

Hsüeh-shu. Shanghai. 1940–
學術（月刊）　上海

Hsüeh-shu lun-t'an. Amoy. 1957–
學術論壇（季刊）　廈門

Hsüeh-shu lun-wen chi-k'an. Taichung. 1973–
學術論文集刊　臺中

Hsüeh-shu p'ing-lun yüeh-pao. Loyang. 1940–1941.
學術評論月報　洛陽

Hsüeh-ts'ui. Taipei. 1948–
Sinological Studies.
學粹　臺北

HSYK Hsüeh-shu yüeh-k'an. Shanghai. 1957–
學術月刊　上海

HTCK Hsia-men ta-hsüeh chi-k'an. Amoy. 1927.
廈門大學季刊　廈門

HTST Hua-tung shih-(fan) ta-(hsüeh) hsüeh-pao. Shanghai. 1956–
華東師（範）大（學）學報　上海

Hu-nan shih-yüan hsüeh-pao. Changsha. 1956–
湖南師院學報　長沙

Hu-nan ta-hsüeh chi-k'an. Changsha. 1935.
湖南大學季刊 長沙

Hu-nan ta-hsüeh ch'i-k'an. Changsha. 1932–1933.
湖南大學期刊 長沙

Hu-nan wen-hsien. Taipei. 1970–
湖南文獻（季刊） 臺北

Hu-ta chiao-yü. Shanghai. 1933–1934.
滬大教育（年刊） 上海

Hua-chung shih-(fan hsüeh)-yüan hsüeh-pao. Wu-han. 1955–
華中師（範學）院學報 武漢

Hua-kang hsüeh-pao. Yangmingshan. 1965–
Hwa Kang Journal.
華岡學報 陽明山

Hua-kuo. Hong Kong. 1957–
華國 香港

Hua-kuo yüeh-k'an. Shanghai. 1923–1926.
華國月刊 上海

Hua-wen yüeh-k'an. Chengtu. 1942–1943.
華文月刊 成都

HWPY Hsin wen-tzu pan-yüeh-k'an. Nanning. 1936; Shanghai. 1950–1952.
新文字半月刊 南寧；上海

HWSC Hua-wen shih-chieh. Taipei. 1974–
The World of Chinese Language.
華文世界 臺北

HWTC Hsin wen-tzu chou-k'an. Shanghai. 1950–1952.
新文字週刊 上海

HYHH Han-yü hsüeh-hsi. Yenchi. 1981–
漢語學習 延吉

HYSY Hsin-ya shu-yüan hsüeh-shu nien-k'an. Hong Kong. 1959–
New Asia College Academic Annual.
新亞書院學術年刊 香港

HYT Han-hsüeh yen-chiu t'ung-hsün. Taipei. 1982–
Newsletter for Research in Chinese Studies.
漢學研究通訊 臺北

HYW Hsüeh yü-wen. Hofei. 1960–
學語文（月刊） 合肥

I-a. Takatsuki. 1971–
咿啞 高槻

I feng. Hangchow. 1933–1936.
藝風（月刊） 杭州

I-wen chih. Taipei. 1965–
Art and Literature Journal.
藝文誌（月刊） 臺北

Indexer. London. 1958–

Insha Ronsō. Kyoto. 1974–
均社論叢 京都

JA Journal Asiatique. Paris. 1822–

JAH Journal of Asian History. Wiesbaden. 1967–

JAOS Journal of American Oriental Society. 1851–

JAS Journal of Asian Studies. Ann Arbor. 1957–

JazA Jazykovědně Aktuality. Prague. 1975–

JBG Jinbungaku. Kyoto. 1948–
人文學 京都

JBGH Jinbun Gakuhō. Tokyo. 1952–
人文學報 東京

JBK Jinbun Kenkyū. Osaka. 1949–
Studies in the Humanities, Journal of the Literary Association of Osaka City University.
人文研究 大阪

JBRS Jinbun Ronshū. Tokyo. 1963–
Humanitas.
人文論集 東京

JCL Journal of Chinese Linguistics. Berkeley. 1973–
中國語言學報

JCLTA Journal of the Chinese Language Teachers Association. South Orange. 1966–

Jen-wen k'o-hsüeh-lun-ts'ung. Taipei. 1948.
人文科學論叢 臺北

Jen yü she-hui. Taipei. 1973–
Man and Society.
人與社會 臺北

JMCY Jen-min chiao-yü. Peking. 1950–1958.
人民教育（月刊） 北京

JMWH Jen-min wen-hsüeh. Peking. 1950–
人民文學 北京

JOS Journal of Oriental Studies. Hong Kong. 1954–
東方文化 香港

Journal de Psychologie Normale et Pathologique. Paris. 1904–

Journal of Chemical Education. Easton. 1924–

Journal of Chinese Teaching and Studies. Australia. 1977–

Journal of University of Bombay. Bombay. 1950–

JRAS Journal of the Royal Asiatic Society of Great Britain and Ireland. London. 1826–

JRASMB Journal of Royal Asiatic Society, Malayan Branch. Singapore. 1920–

JRASNCB Journal of the Royal Asiatic Society of Great Britain and Ireland. North China Branch. Shanghai. 1859–

JRASSB Journal of the Royal Asiatic Society, Straits Branch. Singapore. 1878–

JWHP Jen-wen hsüeh-pao. Hsinchuang (Taipei). 1970–
人文學報 新莊（臺北）

JWTC Jen-wen tsa-chih. Sian. 1957–
人文雜誌 西安

K'a-shih shih-yüan hsüeh-pao. Kashih. 1980–
喀什師院學報 喀什

K'ai-ming. Shanghai. 1928–1947.
開明（月刊） 上海

Kan-nan shih-chuan hsüeh-pao. Kanchow. 1981–
贛南師專學報 贛州

Kanbungaku. Fukui. 1952–
漢文學 福井

Kanji no Jōshiki. Tokyo. 1981–
漢字の常識 東京

K'ao-ku hsüeh-she she-k'an. Peiping. 1934–1937.
考古學社社刊（半年刊） 北平

KBJGD Kōbe Jogakuin Daigaku Ronshū. Kobe. 1970–
神戶女學院大學論集 神戶

KBKS Kanbun Kyōshitsu. Tokyo. 1957–
漢文教室 東京

KCSY Kuang-chou shih-yüan hsüeh-pao. Canton. 1981–
廣州師院學報 廣州

KDBR Kōnan Daigaku Bungakkai Ronshū. Kobe. 1954–
甲南大學文學會論集 神戶

KDKK Kumamoto Daigaku Kyōiku Gakubu Kiyo. Kumamoto. 1970–
熊本大學教育學部紀要 熊本

KG Kokugogaku. Tokyo. 1948–
國語學 東京

KGC Kikan Gendai Chūgoku. Osaka. 1974–
季刊現代中國 大阪

KGDKR Kyōto Gaikokugo Daigaku Kenkyū Ronsō. Kyoto. 1958–
京都外國大學研究論叢 京都

KGIZ Kokugakuin Zasshi. Tokyo. 1893–
國學院雜誌 東京

KGK Kangaku Kenkyū. Tokyo. 1963–
漢學研究 東京

KGKB Kokugo Kokubun. Kyoto. 1931–
國語國文 京都

KGKK Kago Kenkyū. Tenri. 1946–
華語研究 天理

KGKZ Kangakkai Zasshi. Tokyo. 1933–1944.
漢學會雜誌 東京

KGR Kōbe Gaidai Ronsō. Kobe. 1949–
Kobe City University Journal.
神戶外大論叢 神戶

KHCK Kuo-hsüeh chi-k'an. Peking. 1923–1946; 1950–1952.
Journal of Sinological Studies.
國學季刊 北京

KHHP K'o-hsüeh hui-pao. Taipei. 1953–
科學彙報 臺北

KHLH Kuo-hsüeh lun-heng. Soochow. 1933–1937.
國學論衡（半年刊） 蘇州

HKMC Kuo-hsüeh-men chou-k'an. Peking. 1925–1926.

（北京大學研究所）國學門週刊　北京

KHTP K'o-hsüeh t'ung-pao. Peking. 1950–
科學通報　北京

KHYP Kuo-hsüeh yüeh-pao. Peking. 1927–
國學月報　北京

Kindai. Kobe. 1952–
近代　神戶

KKDGK Kita Kyūshū Daigaku Gaikokugo Gakubu Kiyō. Kita Kyushu. 1958–
Bulletin, Faculty of Foreign Languages.
北九州大學外國語學部紀要　北九州

KKNP (Tōyō Daigaku Ajia-Afurika Bunka Kenkyūjo) Kenkyū Nenpō. Tokyo. 1981–
（東洋大學アジア・アフリカ文化研究所）研究年報　東京

KKR Kokubungaku Kanbungaku Ronsō. Tokyo. 1968–
國文學漢文學論叢　東京

KMCY Kuo-min chiao-yü chih-tao yüeh-k'an. Lanchow. 1941–
國民教育指導月刊　蘭州

KMHP K'ung-Meng hsüeh-pao. Taipei. 1961–
Journal of Confucius and Mencius Society of the Republic of China.
孔孟學報（半年刊）　臺北

KMSY K'un-ming shih-yüan hsüeh-pao. Kunming. 1981–
昆明師院學報（季刊）　昆明

KMWH Kuo-min wen-hsüeh. Shanghai. 1934–1935.
國民文學（月刊）　上海

KMYK K'ung Meng yüeh-k'an. Taipei. 1962–
孔孟月刊　臺北

KNKB Kōnan Kokubun. Kobe. 1960–
甲南國文　神戶

K'o-hsüeh. Shanghai. 1915–1929.
科學（月刊）　上海

K'o-hsüeh te Chung-kuo. Nanking. 1933–1935.
科學的中國（半月刊）　南京

KRMR Kurume Daigaku Ronsō. Kurume. 1958–
Kurume University Journal.
久留米大學論叢　久留米

KSBR Kansai Daigaku Bungaku Ronshū. Osaka. 1951–
關西大學文學論集　大阪

KSCGH Kyūshū Chūgoku Gakkaihō. Fukuoka. 1955–
九州中國學會報　福岡

KSGT Kansai Gaigukugo Tanki Daigaku Kenkyū Ronshū. Osaka. 1959–
關西外國語短期大學研究論集　大阪

KSIV Kratie Soobshcheniia Instituta Vostokovedeniia. Moscow. 1951–
Short Report of the Institute of Oriental Studies.

KSTZ Kansai Daigaku Tōzai Gakujutsu Kenkyūjo Kiyō. Suita. 1952–
關西大學東西學術研究所紀要　吹田

Ku-kung po-wu-yüan yüan-k'an. Peking. 1958–
故宮博物院院刊（季刊）　北京

Kuan-tung wen-hua yüeh-pao. 1926.
關東文化月報

Kuang-po chou-pao. Nanking. 1934–1936.
廣播週報　南京

Kuang-tung chien-she yen-chiu. Canton. 1946–1947.
廣東建設研究　廣州

Kuang-tung min-chiao. Canton. 1937.
廣東民教　廣州

Kung hsin. Shanghai. 1937.
共信（週刊）　上海

Kuo-hsüeh tsa-chih. Foochow. 1933.
國學雜誌　福州

Kuo-hsüeh ts'ung-k'an. Nanking. 1923–1926.
國學叢刊（季刊）　南京

Kuo hun. Taipei. 1950–
國魂　臺北

Kuo-li Pei-p'ing shih-fan ta-hsüeh yüeh-k'an. Peiping. 1932–
國立北平師範大學月刊　北平

Kuo-li pien-i-kuan kuan-k'an. Taipei. 1971–
國立編譯館館刊（季刊）　臺北

Kuo-ts'ui hsüeh-pao. Shanghai. 1905–1911.
國粹學報（月刊）　上海

Kuo-wen hsüeh-hui ts'ung-k'an. Peking. 1922–1924.
國文學會叢刊　北京

KWHP Kuo-wen hsüeh-pao. Taipei. 1972–
Bulletin of Chinese of National Taiwan Normal University.
國文學報　臺北

KWTCK Kuo-wen tsa-chih (Kweilin). Kweilin. 1942–1946.
國文雜誌（桂林）（雙月刊）　桂林

KWYK Kuo-wen yüeh-k'an. Kunming. 1940–1949.
國文月刊　昆明

KYAO Ko-yao chou-k'an. Peiping. 1922–1937.
歌謠週刊　北平

KYCK Kuo-yü chou-k'an. Peiping. 1931–1937.
（北平）世界日報：國語週刊　北平

KYCKL Kuo-yü chou-k'an (Lan-chou). Lanchow. 1944–1946.
國語週刊（蘭州）　蘭州

KYCKN Kuo-yü chou-k'an (Nan-cheng). Nan-cheng. 1941–1943.
國語週刊（南鄭）　南鄭

KYHK Kuo-yü hsün-k'an. Peiping. 1929.
國語旬刊　北平

Kyōgaku. Tokyo. 1978–
教學　東京

KYYK Kuo-yü yüeh-k'an. Shanghai. 1922–1925.
國語月刊　上海

KZDG Komazawa Daigaku Gaikokugobu Ron-shū. Tokyo. 1972–
駒澤大學外國語部論集　東京

LCTH Lan-chou ta-hsüeh hsüeh-pao. Lanchow. 1957–
蘭州大學學報　蘭州

Lg Language. Journal of the Linguistic Society of America. Baltimore. 1925–

Li hsing. Chinan. 1938–
力行（月刊）　濟南

Li-lun hsüeh-hsi (CLTH). Changchun. 1975–1978.
理論學習（吉林大學學報）　長春

Li-shih chiao-hsüeh wen-t'i. Shanghai. 1957–
歷史教學問題（月刊）　上海

Li su. Peiping. 1931–
禮俗（半月刊）　北平

Liao-ning shih-yüan hsüeh-pao. Talien (Dairen). 1978–
遼寧師院學報　大連

Library Journal. New York. 1924–

Library Quarterly. Chicago. 1931–

Lingua. International Review of General Linguistics. Amsterdam. 1947–

LNHP Ling-nan hsüeh-pao. Canton. 1929–1949.
嶺南學報（季刊）　廣州

LNTH Liao-ning ta-hsüeh hsüeh-pao. Shenyang. 1960–
遼寧大學學報　瀋陽

LSCH Li-shih chiao-hsüeh. Tientsin. 1953–
歷史教學　天津

LSYC Li-shih yen-chiu. Peking. 1956–
歷史研究（月刊）　北京

Man-Mō. Dairen. 1930–
滿蒙　大連

MCWH Min-chien wen-hsüeh. Peking. 1960–
民間文學（月刊）　北京

MCWI Min-chien wen-i. Canton. 1927–1928.
民間文藝　廣州

Meiji Daigaku Kyōiku Gakubu Kenkyū Kiyō. Tokyo.
明治大學教育學部研究紀要　東京

MGRS Meiji Gakuin Ronsō. Tokyo. 1933–
明治學院論叢　東京

MIHEC Mélanges Publiés par l'Institut des Hautes Études Chinoises. Paris. 1957–

Min-chien. Hangchow. 1931–1937.
民間（月刊）　杭州

Min-chien chih-shih. Taipei. 1950–
民間知識（半月刊）　臺北

Min-chung chiao-yü. Chinan. 1930–1937.
民衆教育（月刊）　濟南

Min-chung chiao-yü chi-k'an. Hangchow. 1933–1937.
民衆教育季刊　杭州

Min-su. Canton. 1928–1933.
民俗（週刊） 廣州

Min-su ch'ü-i. Taipei. 1980–
民俗曲藝（月刊） 臺北

MIO Mitteilungen des Instituts für Orientforschung. Berlin. 1921–

Mission Bulletin. Shanghai; Hong Kong. 1948–

MN Monumenta Nipponica. Tokyo. 1938–
日本文化誌叢

MS Monumenta Serica. Peking, Nagoya, Los Angeles, St. Augustin. 1938–
華裔學志

MSBGK Min-Shin Bungaku Gengo Kenkyūkai Kaihō. Osaka. 1962–
明清文學言語研究會會報 大阪

MSBGKT Min-Shin Bungaku Gengo Kenkyūkai Kaihō Tankan. Osaka.
明清文學言語研究會會報單刊 大阪

MSL Mémoires de la Société Linguistique de Paris. Paris. 1920–1935.

MSOS Mitteilungen des Seminars für Orientalische Sprachen. Berlin. 1920–1937.

MT Min-tsu t'uan-chieh. Peking. 1957–
民族團結 北京

MTTC Min-to tsa-chih. Shanghai. 1916–1929.
民鐸雜誌（月刊） 上海

Mu-to. Yangmingshan. 1975–
木鐸 陽明山

MZTW Minzoku Taiwan. Taipei. 1941–1944.
民俗臺灣 臺北

NAA Narody Azii i Afriki. Moscow. 1961–

NCGH Nippon Chūgoku Gakkaihō. Tokyo. 1950–
Bulletin of the Sinological Society of Japan.
日本中國學會報 東京

NCR New China Review. Shanghai. 1919–

NCTH Nan-ching ta-hsüeh hsüeh-pao. Nanking. 1955–
南京大學學報 南京

New Indian Antiquary. Bombay. 1938–

Newsletter of the American Oriental Society. New Haven. 1979.

NHDJ Nihon Daigaku Jinbun Kagaku Kenkyūjo Kenkyū Kiyō. Tokyo. 1979.
日本大學人文科學研究所研究紀要 東京

NHTH Ning-hsia ta-hsüeh hsüeh-pao. Yinchwan. 1981–
寧夏大學學報 銀川

Nihon Minzokugaku. Tokyo. 1954–
日本民俗學 東京

NKHP Nan-k'ai hsüeh-pao. Tientsin. 1975–
南開學報（雙月刊） 天津

NLHP Nung-lin hsin-pao. Nanking. 1924–1946.
農林新報 南京

NMSY Nei Meng-ku shih-yüan hsüeh-pao. Huhehot. 1958–
內蒙古師院學報 呼和浩特

NMTH Nei Meng-ku ta-hsüeh hsüeh-pao. Huhehot. 1959–
內蒙古大學學報（社會科學） 呼和浩特

Notes and Queries on China and Japan. Hong Kong. 1867–

NSGS Nishō Gakusha Daigaku Ronshū. Tokyo. 1965–
二松學社大學論集 東京

NSHP Nan-shih hsüeh-pao. Nanking. 1959–
南師學報 南京

NSTH Nü-shih-ta hsüeh-shu chi-k'an. Peiping. 1930–1931.
女師大學術季刊 北平

NYWH Nan-ying wen-hsien. Tainan. 1949–
南瀛文獻 臺南

O-wen chiao-hsüeh. Peking. 1951–1960.
俄文教學 北京

OBRD Ōbirin Daigaku Chūgoku Bungaku Ronsō. Machida. 1968–
櫻美林大學中國文學論叢 町田

Ōbun Ronsō. Tokyo. 1970–
櫻文論叢 東京

OE Oriens Extremus. Hamburg. 1954–

OGDG Ōsaka Gaikokugo Daigaku Gakuhō. Osaka. 1952–
大阪外國語大學學報 大阪

OKBK Okayama Daigaku Bungakubu Kiyō. Okayama. 1980–
岡山大學文學部紀要　岡山

OKHB Okayama Daigaku Hōbun Gakubu Gakujutsu Kiyō. Okayama. 1952–
岡山大學法文學部學術紀要　岡山

OLZ Orientalische Literaturzeitung. Berlin. 1898–

Orbis Bulletin International de Docuementation Linguistique. Louvain. 1952–

Oriens. Leiden. 1948–

Ōtani Joshidai Kokubun. Osaka. 1971–
大谷女子大國文　大阪

Ōtani Joshi Kokubun. Kyoto. 1979–
大谷女子國文　京都

OYCH O-yü chiao-hsüeh yü yen-chiu. Harbin. 1955–1960.
俄語教學與研究　哈爾濱

Pacific Affairs. Richmond; Honolulu; Camden. 1928–

Pai-k'o chih-shih. Peking. 1979–
百科知識　北京

Pakistan Journal of Science. Lahore. 1949–

P'an-ku. Hong Kong. 1967–
盤古（月刊）　香港

P'an-shih tsa-chih. Peiping. 1932–1936.
盤石雜誌　北平

PCIC Papers of the CIC Far Eastern Language Institute. Ann Arbor. 1963–

PCST Pei-ching shih-fan ta-hsüeh hsüeh-pao. Peking. 1959–
北京師範大學學報　北京

PCTH Pei-ching ta-hsüeh hsüeh-pao. Peking. 1961–
北京大學學報　北京

Pei-ch'iang yüeh-k'an. Peiping. 1934–1935.
北强月刊　北平

Pei-ching ta-hsüeh yüeh-k'an. Peking. 1919–1922.
北京大學月刊　北京

PICO Proceedings of the International Congress of Orientalists. 1873–

Pien-ts'e chou-k'an. Peiping. 1932.
鞭策週刊　北平

POLA Project on Linguistic Analysis. Columbus. 1962–; Berkeley. 196 –

PPTS Pei-p'ing t'u-shu-kuan kuan-k'an. Peiping. 1929–1937.
北平圖書館館刊（雙月刊）　北平

Proverbium. Bulletin d'Informations sur les Recherches Parémiologiques. Helsinki. 1965–

PY P'in-yin. Peking. 1956–1957. Succeeded by *WTKK*. 拼音　北京

QBCB Quarterly Bulletin of Chinese Bibliography (English Language ed.). Shanghai. 1943–

RBS Revue Bibliographique de Sinologie. The Hague and Paris. 1955–

RDR Ryūkoku Daigaku Ronshū. Kyoto. Journal of Ryukoku University.
龍谷大學論集　京都

Relations de Chine. Paris. 1903–

Revue Britannique. Paris. 1825–

Revue Critique. Paris. 1901–1906.

Revue Indo-chinoise. Hanoi. 1904–

Revue Internationale d'Onomastique. Paris. 1949–

RMBG Ritsumeikan Bungaku. Kyoto. 1934– The Ritsumeikan Litarature Review.
立命館文學　京都

RO Rocznik Orientalistyczny. Warsaw. 1920–

RSO Rivista degli Studi Orientali. Rome. 1951–

San-min chu-i pan-yüeh-k'an. Taipei. 1953–
三民主義半月刊　臺北

SCCY Szu-ch'uan chiao-yü t'ung-hsün. Chengtu. 1948–
四川教育通訊（月刊）　成都

SCTH Szu-ch'uan ta-hsüeh hsüeh-pao. Chengtu. 1955–1963.
四川大學學報　成都

Seinan Gakuin Daigaku Ronshū. Fukuoka. 1959–
西南學院大學論集　福岡

Senshū Jinbun Ronshū. Tokyo. 1982–
專修人文論集　東京

SGK Shinago Kenkyū. Tenri. 1938–1942.
支那語研究　天理

SGKK Shinagaku Kenkyū. Hiroshima. 1950–
支那學研究　廣島

Shakai Chiri. Tokyo. 1949.
社會地理　東京

Shan-hsi chiao-yü. Taiyüan. 1956–
山西教育（月刊）　太原

Shan-hsi shih-yüan hsüeh-pao. Linfen. 1973–
山西師院學報　臨汾

Shan-hsi wen-hsien. Taipei. 1970–
陝西文獻（季刊）　臺北

Shan-tung sheng-li t'u-shu-kuan chi-k'an. Chinan. 1931–1936.
山東省立圖書館季刊　濟南

Shan-tung wai-yü chiao-hsüeh. Chinan. 1981–
山東外語教學　濟南

Shan-tung wen-hsien. Taipei. 1974–
山東文獻　臺北

Shang-hai chiao-yü. Shanghai. 1959–1963.
上海教育（半月刊）　上海

Shao-hsing shih-chuan hsüeh-pao. Shaohsing. 1981–
紹興師專學報　紹興

She-hui k'o-hsüeh chi-k'an. Shenyang. 1981–
社會科學輯刊（雙月刊）　瀋陽

Shibun. Tokyo. 1919–
斯文　東京

Shih hsüeh. Peking. 1926–
實學（月刊）　北京

Shih-huo yüeh-k'an (fu-k'an). Taipei. 1971–
食貨月刊（復刊）　臺北

Shin Chūgoku. Osaka. 1946–
新中國　大阪

Shin Chūka. Tokyo. 1946–
新中華　東京

Shina Mondai. Peiping. 1931–1932.
支那問題　北平

Shinagaku. Kyoto. 1920–
支那學　京都

Shinago. Tokyo. 1932–1940.
支那語（月刊）　東京

Shinago to Jibun. Tokyo. 1943.
支那語と時文　東京

Shinshū Daigaku Kyōyōbū Kiyō. Nagano. 1977–
Journal of Faculty of Liberal Arts, Shinshū University.
信州大學教養部紀要　長野

SHJ Shu ho jen. Taipei. 1969–
書和人　臺北

SHST Shang-hai shih-fan ta-hsüeh hsüeh-pao. Shanghai. 1979–
上海師範大學學報　上海

SHSY Shan-hsi shih-fan hsüeh-yüan hsüeh-pao. Taiyüan. 1957–
山西師範學院學報　太原

SHTH Shan-hsi ta-hsüeh hsüeh-pao. Taiyüan. 1978–
山西大學學報　太原

Shu-lin. Canton. 1937.
書林　廣州

Shuo-wang pan-yüeh-k'an. Shanghai. 1933.
朔望半月刊　上海

SHWY Shang-hai wai-kuo-yü hsüeh-yüan chi-k'an. Shanghai. 1958–
上海外國語學院季刊　上海

Sinica. Frankfurt. 1926–1939.

Sinica-Sonderausgabe. Frankfurt. 1934–1942.

Sinologica. Basel. 1948–

SK Shina Kenkyū. Shanghai. 1918–
支那研究　上海

SKCH She-hui k'o-hsüeh chan-hsien. Changchun. 1979–
社會科學戰線　長春

SKY She-hui k'o-hsüeh yen-chiu. Peking. 1979–
社會科學研究　北京

SL Shu lin. Shanghai. 1979–
書林　上海

SMBG Shinmatsu Bungaku Gengo Kenkyūkai Kaihō. Osaka. 1961–
清末文學言語研究會會報　大阪

SMCK (Chung-kuo) *Shu-mu chi-k'an*. Taipei. 1966–
（中國）書目季刊　臺北

SOS Shina oyobi Shinago. Osaka. 1940–
支那及支那語　大阪

Southwestern Journal of Anthropology. Santa Fe. 1945–

SPSM Shu-p'ing shu-mu. Taipei. 1972–
Book Review and Bibliography.
書評書目（月刊）　臺北

SSTH Shang-hai shih-fan hsüeh-yüan hsüeh-pao. Shanghai. 1959–1960.
上海師範學院學報　上海

STHK Shih-ta hsüeh-k'an. Peiping. 1942–1943.
師大學刊　北平

STHL Shan-tung ta-hsüeh hsüeh-sheng k'o-hsüeh lun-wen chi-k'an. Chinan. 1956.
山東大學學生科學論文集刊　濟南

STHP Shih-ta hsüeh-pao. Taipei. 1956–
Bulletin of Taiwan Normal University.
師大學報　臺北

STMC Shan-tung min-chung chiao-yü yüeh-k'an. Chinan. 1933–1937.
山東民衆教育月刊　濟南

STKT Shih-ta kuo-hsüeh ts'ung-k'an. Peiping. 1930–1932.
師大學叢刊　北平

STSY Shan-tung shih-fan hsüeh-yüan hsüeh-pao. Chinan. 1959–1962.
山東師範學院學報　濟南

STTH Shan-tung ta-hsüeh hsüeh-pao. Chinan. 1963–
山東大學學報　濟南

STYK Shih-ta yüeh-k'an. Peiping. 1932–1934.
師大月刊　北平

Su-chung hsiao-k'an. Soochow. 1930–1935.
蘇中校刊（半月刊）　蘇州

SV Sovetskoe Vostokovedenie. Moscow. 1940–

SWYK Shuo-wen yüeh-k'an. Shanghai; Chungking. 1939–1947.
說文月刊　上海；重慶

Szu-wen. Nanking. 1940–1943.
斯文（半月刊）　南京

Szu yü yen. Taipei. 1963–
思與言（雙月刊）　臺北

Ta-chung. Shanghai. 1945.
大衆（月刊）　上海

Ta-chung yü-wen lun chan (hsü erh). Shanghai. 1935.
大衆語文論戰（續二）　上海

Ta-hsüeh. Chengtu. 1942–1947.
大學（月刊）　成都

Ta-hsüeh tsa-chih. Shanghai. 1933–1934; Taipei. 1955–
大學雜誌　上海；臺北

Ta-tao. Taipei. 1963.
大道（月刊）　臺北

Tabi to Densetsu. Tokyo. 1928–1939.
旅と傳說　東京

T'ai-chung shih-chuan hsüeh-pao. Taichung. 1970–
Journal of Taichung Junior Teachers' College.
臺中師專學報　臺中

T'ai-wan sheng-li T'ai-pei t'u-shu-kuan kuan-k'an. Taipei. 1964–
臺灣省立臺北圖書館館刊　臺北

Taiwan Bunka Ronsō. Taipei. 1943–
臺灣文化論集　臺北

Taiwan Kanshū Kiji. Taipei. 1901–1907.
臺灣慣習記事（月刊）　臺北

Takushoku Daigaku Ronshū. Tokyo. 1951–
拓殖大學論集　東京

Tan-tung shih-chuan hsüeh-pao. Tantung. 1981–
丹東師專學報　丹東

TCH Ta Chung-hua. Shanghai. 1915–1916.
大中華（月刊）　上海

TCHP Tan-chiang hsüeh-pao. Taipei. 1958–
Tamkang Journal.
淡江學報（年刊）　臺北

TCFY T'ai-wan chiao-yü fu-tao yüeh-k'an. Taipei. 1950–
臺灣教育輔導月刊　臺北

TCSC T'ien-chin shih-chuan hsüeh-pao. Tientsin. 1974—
天津師專學報　天津

TCSY T'ein-chin shih-fan hsüeh-yüan hsüeh-pao. Tientsin. 1957—
天津師範學院學報　天津

TFTC Tung-fang tsa-chih. Shanghai. 1904—1948; Taipei. 1967—
The Eastern Miscellany.
東方雜誌　上海；臺北

THG Tōhōgaku. Tokyo. 1951—
Eastern Studies.
東方學　東京

THGHK Tōhō Gakuhō (Kyotō). Kyoto. 1931—
Journal of Oriental Studies.
東方學報（京都）　京都

THGRS Tōhōgaku Ronshū. Tokyo. 1954—1955.
東方學論集　東京

THHP Tung-hai hsüeh-pao. Taichung. 1959—
Tunghai Journal.
東海學報　臺中

Ti-li chih-shih. Peking. 1950—
地理知識　北京

Ti-ming chih-shih. Peking. 1979—
地名知識　北京

T'ien-chin wen-hua. Tientsin. 1948.
天津文化（半月刊）　天津

T'ien-wen t'ai. Shanghai. 1947.
天文臺（月刊）　上海

TLTC Ta-lu tsa-chih. Taipei. 1950—
The Continent Magazine.
大陸雜誌　臺北

TNWH T'ai-nan wen-hua. Tainan. 1951—
臺南文化　臺南

Tōhō. Tokyo. 1980—
Eastern Book Review.
東方　東京

Tōhōgakushi. Nagoya. 1968—
東邦學誌　名古屋

Tōkai Daigaku Kiyō. Hiratsuka. 1958—
Proceedings of Faculty of Letters, Tokai University.
東海大學紀要　平塚

Tōyō Bunka. Tokyo. 1950—
Oriental Culture.
東洋文化　東京

Tōyō Testugaku. Tokyo. 1919—
東洋哲學　東京

TP T'oung Pao. Leiden. 1890—
〔通報〕

TPPYK T'ai-pai pan-yüeh k'an. Shanghai. 1934—1935.
太白半月刊　上海

TPS Transactions of the Philological Society. Oxford. 1854—

TPTHCK Tung-pei ta-hsüeh chou-k'an. Shenyang. 1926—1930.
東北大學週刊　瀋陽

TPWH T'ai-pei wen-hsien. Taipei. 1949—
臺北文獻　臺北

TPWW T'ai-pei wen-wu. Taipei. 1952—
臺北文物　臺北

TRGH Tenri Daigaku Gakuhō. Tenri. 1949—
天理大學學報　天理

TS Tu shu. Peking. 1979—
讀書　北京

TSCK T'u-shu chi-k'an. Peiping. 1934—1947.
Quarterly Bulletin of Chinese Bibliography.
圖書季刊　北平

TSCW T'u-shu chan-wang. Hangchow. 1935—1949.
圖書展望（月刊）　杭州

Tse-shan pan-yüeh-k'an. Chengtu. 1940—1941.
責善半月刊　成都

TSGH Tōkyō Shina Gakuhō. Tokyo. 1955—
東京支那學報　東京

TSKC T'u-shu-kuan-hsüeh chi-k'an. Peiping. 1926—1937.
圖書館學季刊　北平

TSKHK T'u-shu-kuan hsüeh-k'an. Taipei. 1967—
Bulletin of Department of Library Science, National Taiwan University.
圖書館學刊　臺北

TSKHP T'u-shu-kuan hsüeh-pao. Taichung. 1959—
圖書館學報（年刊）　臺中

TSKZ Toshokan Zasshi. Tokyo. 1970–
圖書館雜誌 東京

Tso-p'in. Taipei. 1960–
The Writing Monthly.
作品（月刊） 臺北

TSPL T'u-shu p'ing-lun. Nanking. 1932–1934.
圖書評論 南京

TSST T'ai-wan Sheng-li Shih-fan ta-hsüeh Kuo-
wen yen-chiu-so chi-k'an. Taipei. 1957–
Journal of Research Institute of Chinese
Literature of Taiwan Normal University.
臺灣省立師範大學國文研究所集刊 臺北

TSTH Tu-shu t'ung-hsün. Chungking. 1940–;
Shanghai. 1946–
讀書通訊（半月刊） 重慶；上海

Tsu-kuo i-chou. Taipei. 1965–
祖國一週 臺北

TSYC Tz'u-shu yen-chiu. Shanghai. 1979–
Lexicographical Studies.
辭書研究 上海

TSYK T'u-shu yüeh-k'an. Chungking. 1941–
1945; Taipei. 1946–
圖書月刊 重慶；臺北

TTHP Ta-t'ung hsüeh-pao. Taipei. 1970–
Tatung Journal.
大同學報（年刊） 臺北

T'u-shu-kuan-hsüeh yü tzu-hsün k'o-hsüeh. Taipei. 1974–
Journal of Library and Information Science.
圖書館學與資訊科學 臺北

Tung-hsi wen-hua. Yangmingshan. 1967–
Eastern and Western Culture.
東西文化 陽明山

Tung-nan. Hangchow. 1943.
東南 杭州

Tung-pei wen-hsien. Taipei. 1970–
東北文獻 臺北

TW T'ai-wan wen-hua. Taipei. 1946–1950.
臺灣文化 臺北

TWFW T'ai-wan feng-wu. Taipei. 1951–
The Taiwan Falkways.
臺灣風物 臺北

TWWH T'ai-wan wen-hsien. Taipei. 1949–

臺灣文獻 臺北

TWWH (chuan-k'an). T'ai-wan wen-hsien (chuan-
k'an).
Report of Historico-geographical Studies of
Taiwan.
臺灣文獻（專刊） 臺北

TYDB Tōyō Daigaku Kiyō, Bungakuhen. Tokyo.
1940–
東洋大學紀要，文學篇 東京

TYDD Tōyō Daigaku Daigakuin Kiyō. Tokyo.
1968–
東洋大學大學院紀要 東京

TYGH Tōyō Gakuhō. Tokyo. 1911–
Reports of the Oriental Society.
東洋學報 東京

TYSK Tōyōshi Kenkyū. Kyoto. 1935–
Journal of Oriental Researches.
東洋史研究 京都

TYT Tz'u-tien yen-chiu ts'ung-k'an. Chengtu.
1960–
辭典研究叢刊 成都

Tzu-yu T'ai-p'ing-yang. Cholon. 1957–1966.
Free Pacific Magazine.
自由太平洋 堤岸

VIa Voprosy Iazykoznaniia. Moscow. 1952–

Wang ch'ü. 1940–
王曲

WCCK Wu-han ta-hsüeh wen-che chi-k'an. Wuchang. 1930–1942.
武漢大學文哲季刊 武昌

WCI Wai-yü chiao-hsüeh i-ts'ung. Harbin. 1954–
1955.
外語教學譯叢 哈爾濱

WCYF Wai-yü chiao-hsüeh yü fan-i. Shanghai.
1959–
外語教學與翻譯（月刊） 上海

WCYY Wai-yü chiao-hsüeh yü yen-chiu. Peking.
1959–
外語教學與研究（雙月刊） 北京

Wei-hsing. Soochow. 1937.
衛星（月刊） 蘇州

Wei-yin yüeh-k'an. Shanghai. 1931–1933.
微音月刊 上海

Wen-che yüeh-k'an. Peiping. 1935–1936.
文哲月刊　北平

Wen-chou shih-chuan hsüeh-pao. Wenchow. 1981–
溫州師專學報　溫州

Wen-feng hsüeh-pao. Canton. 1947–1948.
文風學報　廣州

Wen hsing. Taipei. 1957–1965.
文星（月刊）　臺北

Wen-hsüeh. Canton. 1947–1948.
文學（月刊）　廣州

Wen-hsüeh chi-k'an. Peiping. 1934–1935.
文學季刊　北平

Wen-hsüeh ts'ung-k'an. Chengtu. 1929.
文學叢刊　成都

Wen-hsüeh yen-chiu. Shanghai. 1939.
文學研究（月刊）　上海

Wen-hua chien-she yüeh-k'an. Shanghai. 1934–1937.
文化建設月刊　上海

Wen-hua yüeh-k'an. Shanghai. 1942.
文化月刊　上海

Wen-i ch'uang-tso. Taipei. 1951–
文藝創作　臺北

Wen-i yüeh-k'an. Nanking. 1935.
文藝月刊　南京

Wen-shih hsüeh-pao. Taichung. 1971–
Journal of Art and History.
文史學報　臺中

Wen-shih hui-k'an. Tainan. 1959–
文史薈刊（年刊）　臺南

Wen t'an. Taipei. 1952–
文壇（月刊）　臺北

Wennti Wennti Papers. New Haven. 1952–
問題

WHNP Wen-hsüeh nien-pao. Peiping. 1932–1941.
文學年報　北平

WHTH Wu-han ta-hsüeh jen-wen k'o-hsüeh hsüeh-pao. Wuhan. 1956–
From 1962 title changed to Wu-han ta-hsüeh hsüeh-pao.
武漢大學人文科學學報　武漢
自1962年改爲武漢大學學報

WHTS Wen-hua t'u-shu-kuan-hsüeh chuan-k'o hsüeh-hsiao chi-k'an. Wuchang. 1929–1937.
文華圖書館學專科學校季刊　武昌

WHYC Wen-hua yü chiao-yü. Peiping. 1933–1936.
文化與教育（旬刊）　北平

WJGKK Waseda Jitsugyō Gakkō Kenkyū Kiyō. Tokyo. 1979–
早稻田實業學校研究紀要　東京

WSC Wen shih che. Chinan. 1951–1958; 1961–1963.
文史哲（月刊）　濟南

WSCCK Wen shih che chi-k'an. Nanking. 1943–
（中央大學）文史哲季刊　南京

WSCH Wen shih che hsüeh-pao. Taipei. 1950–
Bulletin of the College of Arts, National Taiwan University.
文史哲學報　臺北

WSCS Wen shih chih-shih. Peking. 1981–
文史知識　北京

WSHK Wen-shih hui-k'an. Canton. 1935.
文史滙刊（季刊）　廣州

WSHP Wen shih hsüeh-pao. Kowloon. 1964–
Chinese Literature and History Journal.
文史學報　九龍

WTKC Wen-hua t'u-shu-k'o chi-k'an. Wuchang. 1929–1937.
文化圖書科季刊　武昌

WTKK Wen-tzu kai-ko. Peking. 1957–
文字改革　北京

WZKM Wiener Zeitschrift für de Kunde des Morgenlandes. Viena. 1887–

YATH Yen-an ta-hsüeh hsüeh-pao. Yen'an. 1981–
延安大學學報　延安

YC Yü-wen chan-hsien. Hangchow. 1976–
語文戰線　杭州

YCHP Yen-ching hsüeh-pao. Peiping. 1927–1949.

Yenching Journal of Chinese Studies.
燕京學報　北平

YCT Yü-wen chih-shih ts'ung-k'an. Peking. 1981–
語文知識叢刊　北京

YCYY Yü-yen chiao-hsüeh yü yen-chiu. Peking. 1977–
語言教學與研究　北京

Yen-ching she-hui k'o-hsüeh. Peiping. 1948–1949.
燕京社會科學　北平

YHH Yü-wen hsien-tai-hua. Shanghai. 1980–
語文現代化　上海

YIT Yü-yen-hsüeh i-ts'ung. Peking. 1979–
語言學譯叢　北京

YLT Yü-yen-hsüeh lun-ts'ung. Shanghai; Peking. 1957–
語言學論叢　上海；北京

YNLH Yün-nan lü-Hu hsüeh-hui hui-k'an. Shanghai. 1935.
雲南旅滬學會會刊（半年刊）　上海

YPTH Yen-pien ta-hsüeh hsüeh-pao. Yenchi. 1977–
延邊大學學報　延吉

YSDR Yokohama Shiritsu Daigaku Ronsō. Yokohama.
Bulletin of Yokohama City University.
橫濱市立大學論叢（人文學科系列）　橫濱

YSHC Yu-shih hsüeh-chih. Tapei. 1962–
Youth Quarterly.
幼獅學誌（季刊）　臺北

YSHP Yu-shih hsüeh-pao. Taipei. 1958–1961.
Youth Journal. Succeded by *YSHC.*
幼獅學報（見：幼獅學誌）　臺北

YSYK Yu-shih yüeh-k'an. Taipei. 1953–
Youth Monthly.
幼獅月刊　臺北

Yü-wen. Shanghai. 1937; Chungking. 1959–
語文（月刊）　上海；重慶

Yü-wen chiao-hsüeh yü yen-chiu. Chinchow. 1978–
語文教學與研究　錦州

Yung yen. Tientsin. 1912–1914.
庸言（半月刊）　天津

YWCH Yü-wen chiao-hsüeh. Shanghai; Nanchang. 1956–
語文教學　上海；南昌

YWCS Yü-wen chih-shih. Peking. 1952–1960.
語文知識　北京

YWHH Yü-wen hsüeh-hsi. Peking. 1951–1960.
語文學習（月刊）　北京

YWHT Yü-wen hsüeh-hsi ts'ung-k'an. Shanghai. 1977–
語文學習叢刊　上海

YWLT Yü-wen lun-ts'ung. Shanghai. 1981–
語文論叢　上海

YWTC Yü-wen tsa-chih. Hong Kong. 1979–
Language Forum.
語文雜誌　香港

YWYC Yü-wen yen-chiu. Taiyüan. 1981–
語文研究　太原

YWYT Yü-wen yüan-ti. Nanning. 1981–
語文園地　南寧

YYHT Yü-yen-hsüeh tung-t'ai. Peking. 1978–
語言學動態　北京

YYWH Yü-yen wen-hsüeh. Hohehot. 1958–
語言文學（月刊）　呼和浩特

YYYC Yü-yen yen-chiu. Wuhan. 1981–
語言研究　武漢

ZDMG Zeitschrift der Deutschen Morgenländischen Gesellschaft. Leipzing. 1847–

Zeirin. Kyoto. 1949–
說林　京都

Zenrin. Dairen. 1930–
善隣　大連

ZMRW Zeitschrift für Missionkunde und Religionswissenschaft. Berlin. 1886–

Zphon Zeitschrift für Phonetik, Sprachwissenschaft und Kommunikationsforschung. Berlin. 1947–

List of Abbreviations

annot.	annotation, annotator	n. p.	no pagination
C. S.	Chinese summary	no., nos.	number, numbers
Chap.	Chapter	p.	page(s)
col.	column	pl.	plate(s)
comm.	commentary, commentator	portr.	portrait
comp.	compiler, compiled (by)	print.	printed (by), printing
d. p.	double pages	pt.	part
E. S.	English summary	publ.	published (by)
ed.	editor, edited (by), edition	repr.	reprint, reprinted
enl.	enlarged	rev.	revised
et al.	et alii (and others)	s. p.	separate pagination
F. S.	French summary	tab.	table(s)
fasc.	fasciculus (fascicle)	transl.	translated (by)
fl.	flourished	U.	University
illus.	illustrated	UM	University Microfilm International order number
M. A.	Master of Arts		
mimeogr.	mimeographed	unpl. doc. diss.	unpublished doctoral dissertation
monogr.	monograph		
n. d.	no date	v. p.	various pagination
N. p.	no place of publication	vol., vols.	volume, volumes

Part I
Chinese Lexicology

(0001−2870)

1. REFERENCE, HISTORY, AND METHODOLOGY (0001—0139)
1.1. Reference (0001—0092)
1.1.1. Bibliographies (0001—0036)

0001 Association for Asian Studies (ed.): *Bibliography of Asian studies.*—Ann Arbor: Ditto, 1965—./ An annual bibliography. Section on China: Language, including lexicography and linguistics.

0002 Chu, Chieh-fan: Chung-kuo yen-yü shu-mu t'i-yao.—*TSKHP* 6, 1964, 85—123; also repr. in *Chung-kuo yen-yü lun* (2178), 533—588. [A briefly annotated bibliography on Chinese proverbs.]
朱介凡：中國諺語書目提要

0003 Chūgoku Gogaku Kenkyūkai: *Chūgoku gogaku bunken mokuroku 1945.8—1957.7.*—Tokyo: Kōnan shoin, 1957, iii, 61 p./ 26—31: Lexicology; 49—51: Lexicography. [Bibliography on Chinese linguistics—August 1945—July 1957.]/ Restricted to to Japanese sources.
中國語學研究會：中國語學文獻目錄
1945. 8—1957. 7

0004 Chūgoku Gogaku Kenkyūkai: *Chūgoku gogaku bunken mokuroku. II hen. 1957.8—1961.12.*—Tokyo: Kōseikan, 1963, iii, 61 p./ 22—29: Lexicology; 45—49: Lexicography. [Bibliography on Chinese linguistics II — August 1957 — December 1961.]/ Restricted to Japanese sources.
中國語學研究會：中國語學文獻目錄・II篇
1957. 8—1961. 12

0005 Chung-kuo k'o-hsüeh-yüan Li-shih yen-chiu-so Ti-i ti-erh-so, Pei-ching ta-hsüeh Li-shih-hsi: *Chung-kuo shih-hsüeh lun-wen so-yin.*— Peking: K'o-hsüeh, 2 vols., 1957, iv, 421; viii, 676, 116 p./ Vol. II, 341—354: Lexicography & Chinese traditional semantics. [An index to periodical articles on Chinese history.]
中國科學院歷史研究所第一、二所，北京大學
歷史系：中國史學論文索引

0006 Chung-kuo she-hui k'o-hsüeh yüan Li-shih yen-chiu-so: *Chung-kuo shih-hsüeh lun-wen so-yin. Ti-erh pien* (hsia ts'e).—Hong Kong: San-lien, 1980, 753 p./ 452—458: Chinese traditional semantics; 469: Dictionaries. [An index to periodical articles on Chinese history. 2nd series, Vol. II.]
中國社會科學院歷史研究所：中國史學論文索
引第二編（下冊）

0007 Chung-kuo k'o-hsüeh-yüan Yü-yen yen-chiu-so: *Chung-kuo yü-yen-hsüeh lun-wen so-yin. Chia pien.*—Peking: Shang-wu, 1978, viii, 210 p./ Covers pre-1949 publications. [An index to periodical articles on Chinese linguistics. Vol. I.]
中國科學院語言研究所：中國語言學論文索引
甲編

0008 Chung-kuo k'o-hsüeh-yüan Yü-yen yen-chiu-so: *Chung-kuo yü-yen-shüeh lun-wen so-yin. I pien* (Tseng-ting pen).— Peking: Shang-wu, 1978, rev. & enl. ed., vi, 326 p.; *YWTC* 3, 1980, 73, Liu An-li./ Covers 1950—1963. [An index to periodical articles on Chinese linguistics. Vol. II.]
中國科學院語言研究所：中國語言學論文索引
乙編（增訂本）／劉安立評

0009 Cordier, Henri: *Bibliotheca Sinica: Dictionnaire bibliographique des ouvrages relatifs à l'Empire Chinois.*—Paris: Librairie Orientale & Américaine, 5 vols., 1922—1924, 4439 col.; Taipei: Ch'eng-wen, 1966, repr./ XIII: Language and literature.

0010 Feng, Cheng: *Chin san-shih nien kuo-wai Chung-kuo-hsüeh kung-chü shu chien chieh.*—Peking: Chung-hua, 1981, [8], 4, 358 p. [A short introduction to Sinological reference works published abroad during the past thirty years.]
馮蒸：近三十年國外中國學工具書簡介

0011 Fukuda, Naomi: *Bibliography of reference works on Japanese studies.* — Ann Arbor: Center for Japanese Studies, U. of Michigan, 1979, ix, 210 p.

0012   Gordon, Leonard H. D. & Shulman,
Frank J.: *Doctoral dissertations on China:
A bibliography of studies in Western
languages, 1945–1970.* —Seattle & London:
U. of Washington Press, 1972, xviii, 317
p./ *AM* 18, 1973, 127, George Weys; *JAOS*
95, 1975, 128, David R. Knechtges; *JCLTA*
11:3, 1976, 222–223, Teresa S. Yang.
/ See below (0025).
〔關於中國之博士論文西方語言之參考書錄〕

0013   Gotō, Kimpei: Postwar Japanese studies
on the Chinese language.—*MS* 20, 1961,
368–393./ An annotated bibliography;
387–391: Grammar and vocabulary.
〔後藤均平〕

0014   Kokuritsu Kokkai Toshokan: *Zasshi kiji
sakuyin——Jinbun, shakai kagaku hen.*
—Tokyo: Kinokuniya, 1948–./ Monthly,
quarterly, semi-annually. [A Japanese
periodicals index — Humanities and social
science.]
國立國會圖書館：雜誌記事索引──人文，社會
科學編

0015   Kuo-li Chung-yang t'u-shu-kuan: *Chung-
hua min-kuo ch'i-k'an lun-wen so-yin.*—
Taipei: Ditto, 1970–./ Monthly. [An
index to periodical articles of the Republic
of China.]
國立中央圖書館：中華民國期刊論文索引

0016   Kuo-li Chung-yang t'u-shu-kuan: *Chung-
hua min-kuo ch'u-pan t'u-shu mu-lu.*—
Taipei: Ditto, 1960–. [A catalogue of
publications of the Republic of China.]
國立中央圖書館：中華民國出版圖書目錄

0017   Kuo-li Chung-yang t'u-shu-kuan: *Chung-
kuo chin erh-shih nien wen shih che lun-wen
fen-lei so-yin.*——Taipei: Ditto & Cheng-
chung shu-chü, 1970, xl, 852 p./ Covers
1948–1968; 132–135: Ancient and modern
dictionaries; 136–139: Chinese traditional
semantics. [A classified index to periodical
articles during the past 20 years on Chinese
literature, history and philosophy.]
國立中央圖書館：中國近二十年文史哲論文分

類索引

0018   Kuo-li T'ai-wan ta-hsüeh t'u-shu-kuan:
Chung-wen ch'i-k'an lun-wen fen-lei so-yin.
—Taipei: Ditto, 1960–1982. [A classified
index to Chinese periodical articles.]
國立台灣大學圖書館：中文期刊論文分類索引

0019   Kyōto Daigaku Jinbun Kagaku Kenkyūjo: *Tōyōshi kenkyū bunken ruimoku.*
—Kyoto: Ditto, 1934– (publ. in 1935–).
/ From 1963 publ. under the title *Tōyōgaku
bunken ruimoku;* Section XV: Philology.
[Annual bibliography of Oriental studies,
1934–.]
京都大學人文科學研究所：東洋史研究文獻類
目（自1963年改爲：東洋學文獻類目）

0020   Loon, Piet van der (ed.): *Revue bibliographique de Sinologie* (Année 1955–.)—
The Hague and Paris: Mouton, 1957./
Annually. Section XV: Language; *TP* 45,
1957, 219–220, P. Demiéville; *JAOS* 61,
1961, 446–448, C.S. Goodrich.

0021   Lust, John: *Index Sinicus: A catalogue
of articles relating to China in periodicals
and other collective publications 1920–
1955.*——Cambridge: W. Heffer & Sons,
1962, xxx, 663 p./ 327–328: Semantics
& lexicography; *AM* 11, 1965, 251–252,
George Weys.

0022   Ōkōchi, Yasunori: Kaihōgo Chūgoku
happyō no *tz'u* oyobi *tz'u-hui* kankei
bunken mokuroku.—*CGGG* 1968:7, 1–
18. [A catalogue of books and articles
on Chinese "words" and "lexicon"
published in China after the liberation
(1949).]
大河內康憲：解放後中國發表の『詞』および
『詞彙』關係文獻目錄

0023   Permanent International Committee of
Linguists: *Linguistic Bibliography for the
Year 1939–.*—Utrecht and Antwerp:
Spectrum, 1949–./ Section on languages
of Southeast Asia, Sino-Tibetan languages,
Sinitic group, 5: Vocabulary.

0024 Shafer, Robert (ed.): *Bibliography of Sino-Tibetan languages.* —— Wiesbaden: Harrassowitz, 2 vols. Vol. I, 1957, xi, 211 p.; Vol. II, 1963, ix, 141 p./ I, 31–38, II, 23–67: Dictionaries and vocabularies; *BSL* 60, 1965, fasc. 2, 248, A.G. Haudricourt.

0025 Shulman, Frank Joseph: *Doctoral dissertations on China, 1971–1975: A bibliography of studies in Western languages.* — Seattle & London: U. of Washington Press, 1978, xx, 329 p./ See above (0012). 〔關於中國之博士論文西方語言之參考書錄〕

0026 Skachkov, P. E.: *Bibliografiia Kitaiia.* — Moscow: Izdatel'stvo Vostochnoi Literatury, 1960, 691 p./ 476–491: Language and writing; *RBS* 6, 1960, 3, M. Doleželova-Velingerová. [Chinese bibliography.]

0027 Ting, Stella: American doctoral dissertations in Chinese linguistics: A bibliography. — *JCL* 1:1, 1973, 170–182; 9:1, 1981, 140–141; 10:1, 1982, 173–177.

0028 Torii, Hisayasu: *Chūgoku gengo kenkyū shomoku (kō).* — Tenri: The Author, 1961, 33 p. [A catalogue of studies on Chinese proverbs (draft).]/ A classified bibliography. 鳥居久靖：中國諺語研究書目（稿）

0029 Torii, Hisayasu: Chūgoku gengo kenkyū shomoku (kō) — Wa-Kanbun hen [shiryō]. —*TRGH* 13:2, 1961, 46–68; 13:3, 1962, 61–70./ *RBS* 7, 1961, 4, M. Soymié; 8, 1962, 20, Anonymous. [A catalogue of studies on Chinese proverbs (draft) — Japanese-Chinese section (materials).] 鳥居久靖：中國諺語研究書目（稿）—和漢文篇〔資料〕

0030 Wang, William S-Y. & Liu, Lillian: *Bibliography and glossary for Chinese grammar.* —— Columbus: Ohio State U., Project on Linguistic Analysis Report No. 5, 1963, viii, 131 p.

0031 Wang, William S-Y. & Lyovin, Anatole:

CLIBOC: Chinese linguistics bibliography on computer.—Cambridge: Cambridge U. Press, 1970, 513 p., 3 maps in pocket./ 332–489: Abstracts; *JCLTA* 8:2, 1973, 111–114, Carl Leban.

0032 Yamagiwa, Joseph K.: *Bibliography of Japanese encyclopedias and dictionaries.* — Ann Arbor: The Panel on Far Eastern Language Institutes of The Committee on Institutional Cooperation, 1968, ix, 139 p.

0033 Yang, Paul Fu-mien: *Chinese linguistics: A selected and classified bibliography.* — Hong Kong: The Chinese U. of Hong Kong, 1974, xxvi, 292 p./ *JCL* 3:2–3, 1975, 259–265, Timothy Light; *JAOS* 96, 1976, 479–480, Teng Shou-hsin; *JCLTA* 11:3, 1976, 216–217, G.W. Roy; *JAS* 36:2, 1977, 349–350, Jerry Norman. 〔楊福綿：中國語言學分類參考書目〕

0034 Yang, Paul Fu-mien: *Chinese dialectology: A selected and classified bibliography.* — Hong Kong: The Chinese U. Press, 1981, xxxvi, [i], 189 p./ *JAS* 42:1, 1982, 158–159, William H. Baxter III; *HYT* 2:2, 1983, 120–121, Yao Jung-sung. 〔楊福綿：中國方言學分類參考書目〕／姚榮松評

0035 Yang, Winston L.Y. & Yang, Teresa S.: *A bibliography of the Chinese language.* — New York: Paragon Book Gallery (distributor), 1966, xiv, 171 p./ III: Language dictionaries & vocabularies; IV: Subject dictionaries & glossaries; V: Lexicography & indexing; VI: Terms, names, phrases; *JAS* 26:3, 1967, 488–489, Henry H. Tai; *East and West* 17:1–2, 135, Lanciotti Lionello. 〔中國語文論著目錄〕

0036 Yuan, Tung-li: *China in Western literature.* A continuation of Cordier's *Bibliotheca Sinica* (0009). — New Haven: Far Eastern Publications, Yale U., 1958, xix, 802 p./ 397–402: Dictionaries, lexicography &

indexing.
〔袁同禮〕

1.1.2. Encyclopedias and Collected Essays (0037–0092)

1.1.2.1. Encyclopedias (0037–0046)

0037   Chūgoku Gogaku Kenkyūkai: *Chūgoku gogaku jiten.* —— Tokyo: Kōnan shoin, 1958, xxiii, 1129 p./ *RBS* 4, 1958, 531, W. Simon; *Orbis* 15, 1966, 95–96, Paul Fu-mien Yang; *Sekai meicho daijiten* (0041), 4:254, Hirayama Hisao. [An encyclopedia of Chinese linguistics.]
中國語學研究會：中國語學事典／平山久雄評

0038   Chūgoku Gogaku Kenkyūkai: *Chūgoku gogaku shinjiten.* —— Tokyo: Kōseikan, 1969, 12, 339 p.; 1970, 2nd ed., with minor corrections./ *Chin san-shih nien . . . chien chieh* (0010), 94. [A new dictionary of Chinese linguisitcs.]
中國語學研究會：中國語學新辭典

0039   Fu-tan ta-hsüeh Chung-wen-hsi, et al.: *Yü-yen wen-tzu-hsüeh tz'u-tien.*——Hong Kong: Erh-ya, 1979, 10, 92, 10 p. [A dictionary of (Chinese) linguistics and logography.]/ A reprint of (0046).
復旦大學中文系等：語言文字學詞典

0040   Heibonsha: *Ajia rekishi jiten.* — Tokyo: Ditto, 1959–1962, 10 vols. [An encyclopedia of Asian history.]
平凡社：アジア歴史事典

0041   Heibonsha: *Sekai meicho daijiten.* — Tokyo: Ditto, 1960–1962, 8 vols. [A comprehensive encyclopedia of world famous books.]
平凡社：世界名著大事典

0042   Heibonsha: *Sekai dai hyakka jiten.* —Tokyo: Ditto, 1981, 34 vols. [A comprehensive world encyclopedia.]
平凡社：世界大百科事典

0043   Kondō, Haruo: *Chūgoku gakugei dai jiten.* — Tokyo: Taishūkan, 1978, 5, 1000 p. / A continuation of the author's father's work (0044). [A comprehensive encyclopedia of Chinese literary sciences.]
近藤春雄：中國學藝大事典

0044   Kondō, Moku: *Chūgoku gakugei daijiten.* — Tokyo: Gengensha, 1959, rev. ed., 4, 8, 4, 110, 1446, (appendices:) 168, 82 p./ *Chin san-shih nien . . . chien chieh* (0010), 93–94; cf. (0043). [A comprehensive dictionary of Chinese literary sciences.]
近藤杢：中國學藝大辭典

0045   Shōgakkan: *Dai Nihon hyakka jiten.* — Tokyo: Ditto, 1968–1971, 18 vols. [Encyclopaedia Japponica.]
小學館：大日本百科事典

0046   Tz'u-hai pien-chi wei-yüan-hui: *Tz'u-hai. Yü-yen wen-tzu fen-ts'e.* —— Shanghai: Shang-hai tz'u-shu, 1978, [2], 10, 92, 10 p. [The sea of words and phrases. Fascicle on language and writing.]/ Reprinted in Hong Kong (0039).
辭海編輯委員會：辭海・語言文字分冊

1.1.2.2. Collected Essays (0047–0092)

0047   Chang, Shuang-ch'ing (ed.): *Chung-kuo yü-wen yen-chiu hsüan-chi.*—— Hong Kong: Wen-hsin shu-wu, 1976 (preface), 2, 174 p. [Selected studies on the Chinese language and writing.]
張雙慶編：中國語文研究選集

0048   Chao, Yuen Ren. Ed. by Dil, Anwar L.: *Aspects of Chinese sociolinguistics.*—— Stanford: Stanford U. Press, 1976, xiv, 415 p., maps; 402–415: Bibliography of Yuen Ren Chao's works./ *JAOS* 97, 1977, 410, Alvin P. Cohen; *JCLTA* 12:1, 1978, 88–91, Chauncey C. Chu.

0049   Ch'en, Wang-tao, et al.: *Chung-kuo wen-fa ko-hsin lun-ts'ung.*—Peking: Chung-hua, 1958, ii, iii, 327 p. [Collected essays on the renovation of Chinese grammar.]

陳望道等：中國文法革新論叢

0050 Ch'eng, Fa-jen (ed.): *Liu-shih nien lai chih Kuo-hsüeh.* Ti erh ts'e: *Yü-yen wen-tzu chih pu.*——Taipei: Cheng-chung, 1972, 654 p. [Sinology during the past sixty years. Vol. II: Section on language and writing.]

程發軔主編：六十年來之國學，第二冊：語言文字之部

0051 Chou, Fa-kao: *Chung-kuo yü-wen yen-chiu.*——Taipei: Chung-hua wen-hua, 1955, ii, 168 p., maps./ *RBS* 2, 1957, 544, C.Y. Wu; *KHHP* 5:3, 1956, 6–8, Chang Hsi-chen; *HSCK* 5:2, 1956, 146–147, Hsü Shih-ying. [Studies on the Chinese language and writing.]

周法高：中國語文研究／張席珍評；許世英評

0052 Chou, Fa-kao: *Chung-kyo yü-wen lun-ts'ung.*——Taipei: Cheng-chung, 1963, vi, 451 p. [Collected essays on the Chinese language and writing.]

周法高：中國語文論叢

0053 Chou, Fa-kao: *Chung-kuo yü-yen-hsüeh lun-wen-chi.* —— Hong Kong: Ch'ung-chi shu-tien, 1968, i, 484 p. [Collected essays on Chinese linguistics.]

周法高：中國語言學論文集

0054 Chou, Tsu-mo: *Wen-hsüeh chi.*——Peking: Chung-hua, 1966, 2 vols., iv, 930 p. [Collected essays on asking and learning.]/ Chinese language and writing.

周祖謨：問學集

0055 Chung-hua han-shou hsüeh-hsiao: *Yü-wen hsüeh-hsi te chi-ch'u.* —— Hong Kong: Shang-wu, 1980, 6, 325 p. [The basis of learning language and writing.]

中華函授學校：語文學習的基礎

0056 Chung-kuo yü-yen-hsüeh-hui: *Pa wo kuo yü-yen k'o-hsüeh t'ui hsiang ch'ien chin.* — Wuhan: Hu-pei jen-min, 1981, [ii], 215 p. [To push forward the linguistic science of our nation.]/ Collected essays.

中國語言學會：把我國語言科學推向前進

0057 Chung-kuo yü-wen hsüeh-she: *Chung-kuo yü-yen-hsüeh shih-hua.*——Hong Kong: Lung-men, 1969, 61 p. [Lectures on the history of Chinese linguistics.]/ 10 articles by different authors.

中國語文學社：中國語言學史話

0058 Chung-kuo yü-wen hsüeh-she: *Yü-wen hui-pien.*——Hong Kong: Ditto, 1970–. [A collection of publications on (the Chinese) language and writing.]/ Photo-offset reprint of books.

中國語文學社：語文彙編

0059 Chung-kuo yü-wen tsa-chih-she: *Yü-fa lun-chi* (Ti-i chi).——Peking, Chung-hua, 1957, 235 p./ *RBS* 3, 1957, 567, A. Rygaloff. [Collected essays on Chinese grammar (Vol. I).]

中國語文雜誌社：語法論集（第一集）

0060 Chung-yang yen-chiu-yüan: *Chung-yang yen-chiu-yüan Kuo-chi Han-hsüeh hui-i lun-wen-chi. Yü-yen wen-tzu tsu.*——Taipei: Academia Sinica, 1981, 2, 586 p. [Collected essays delivered at the Academia Sinica International Conference on Sinology. Section on language and writing.]

中央研究院：中央研究院國際漢學會議論文集語言文字組

0061 Egerod, Søren & Glahn, Else (eds.): *Studia Serica Bernhard Karlgren dedicata.* — Copenhagen: Ejnar Munksgaard, 1959, ix, 282 p., 13 pl./ *Lg* 37, 1961, 180–186, H.M. Stimson.

0062 Hong, Beverly (ed.): *Chinese language in use.* —— Canberra: Contemporary China Centre, Australian National U., 1978, xx, 138 p./ Contemporary China papers, 13.

0063 Hsien-tai Han-yü kuei-fan wen-t'i hsüeh-shu hui-i mi-shu-ch'u: *Hsien-tai Han-yü kuei-fan wen-t'i hsüeh-shu hui-i wen-chien hui-pien.* ——Peking: K'o-hsüeh, 1956, 334 p., 5 pl./ *RBS* 2, 1956, 405, M.A.K.

Halliday. [Proceedings of the Academic Committee for the Problems of Standardization of Modern Chinese.]

現代漢語規範問題學術會議秘書處：現代漢語規範問題學術會議文件滙編

0064　Hu, Yü-shu (ed. in chief): *Hsien-tai Han-yü ts'an-k'ao tzu-liao* (chung-ts'e).— Shanghai: Shang-hai chiao-yü, 1981, 3, 631 p. [Reference materials for (the study of) Modern Chinese (Vol. II).]

胡裕樹主編：現代漢語參考資料（中册）

0065　Huang, Hsüan-fan: *Yü-yen-hsüeh yen-chiu lun-ts'ung.* — Taipei: Li-ming, 1974, 6, 2, 350 p. [Collected essays on the study of linguistics.]

黃宣範：語言學研究論叢

0066　Huang, K'an. Ed. by Chung-hua shu-chü Shang-hai pien-chi-so: *Huang K'an lun-hsüeh tsa-chu.* — Shanghai: Chung-hua, 1964, 14, 4, 2, 488 p.; Taipei: Chung-hua, 1969, repr./ With an introduction by Chang Shih-lu; *RBS* 10, 1964, 442, M. J. Künstler. [Miscellaneous writings of Huang K'an on Sinology.]

黃侃著，中華書局上海編輯所：黃侃論學雜著

0067　Kao, Ming: *Kao Ming hsiao-hsüeh lun-ts'ung.*—Taipei: Li-ming, 1978, 4, 2, 516 p. [Kao Ming's collected essays on (Chinese) philology.]

高明：高明小學論叢

0068　Kao, Ming-k'ai. Ed. by Chou, K'ang-hsieh: *Han-yü yü-fa lun-chi.*—Hong Kong: Ch'ung-wen, 1971, 188 p. [Collected essays on Chinese grammar.]/ Articles published in *YCHP* 1946.

高名凱著，周康燮編：漢語語法論集

0069　Li, Chung-hao (ed.): *Wen-tzu li-shih-kuan yü ko-ming lun.* — Peiping: Pei-p'ing wen-hua-she, 1931, iv, 620 p. [Essays on the historical aspect of writing and the theory of revolution.]

李中昊編：文字歷史觀與革命論

0070　Li, Tien-yi: *Selected works of George A. Kennedy.*— New Haven: Far Eastern Publications, Yale U., 1964, viii, 544 p./ *AM* 12:1, 1966, 127–130, E.G. Pulleyblank.

〔李田意〕

0071　Lin, Han-ta, et al.: *Han-yü te tz'u-erh ho p'in-hsieh-fa* (Ti-i chi).—Peking: Chung-hua, 1955, 1st ed.; 1956, 2nd print., 152 p.; *Yü-wen hui-pien* (0058), 6:26. [Chinese words and methods of spelling them (Vol. I).]

林漢達等：漢語的詞兒和拼寫法（第一集）

0072　Lin, Yü-t'ang: *Yü-yen-hsüeh lun-ts'ung.* — Shanghai: K'ai-ming, 1933, iii, 376 p.; Taipei: Wen-hsing, 1967, repr./ *WCCK* 6:3, 1937, 671–684, Li Hsiao-t'ung. [Collected essays on linguistics.]

林語堂：語言學論叢／厲嘯桐評

0073　Liu, P'an-sui: *Wen-tzu yin-yün-hsüeh lun-ts'ung.* — Peiping: Jen-wen shu-tien, 1935, 2, 4, 324 p. [Collected essays on Chinese writing and phonology.]

劉盼遂：文字音韻學論叢

0074　Nan-k'ai ta-hsüeh Chung-wen-hsi yü-yen-hsüeh chiao-yen-shih: *Yü-yen yen-chiu lun-ts'ung.*—Tientsin: T'ien-chin jen-min, 1980, [2], 288 p. [Collected essays on linguistic studies.]

南開大學中文系語言學教研室：語言研究論叢

0075　Ogawa, Tamaki: *Chūgoku gogaku kenkyū.* — Tokyo: Sōbunsha, 1977, 361, 13 p./ English table of contents. [Studies in Chinese linguistics.]

小川環樹：中國語學研究

0076　Pei-ching-shih Kung-nung chiao-yü yen-chiu-shih & Pei-ching jen-min kuang-po tien-t'ai: *Yü-wen chi-ch'u chih-shih* (60 chiang). — Peking: Pei-ching, 1981, 4, 721 p. [Fundamental knowledge of language and writing (60 lectures).]

北京市工農教育研究室、北京人民廣播電臺：語文基礎知識（六十講）

0077 Ratchnevsky, Paul (ed.): *Beiträge zum problem des wortes im Chinesischen.*—Berlin: Akademie-Verlag, 1960, vi, 110 p./ Ostasiatische Forschungen 1; *AO* 38:3, 1970, 381–384, O. Švarný.

0078 Sebeok, Thomas A. (ed.): *Current trends in linguistics, II. Linguistics in East Asia and South East Asia.*—The Hague & Paris: Mouton, 1967, xix, 979 p.

0079 Shu, Chung (ed.): *Chung-kuo yü-wen yen-chiu ts'an-k'ao tzu-liao hsüan-chi.*—Peking: Chung-hua, 1957, 269 p./ *RBS* 1, 1955, 266, M.A.K. Halliday. [Selected reference materials on the study of the Chinese language and writing.]
叔重編：中國語文研究參考資料選輯

0080 Ta-lu tsa-chih-she: *Yü-yen wen-tzu-hsüeh.*—Taipei: Ditto, 1963, iv, 261 p./ *Ta-lu tsa-chih yü-wen ts'ung-shu.* Ti-i chi, Ti-san ts'e. [Language and writing.]/ Articles published in *TLTC* 1–24, 1950–1962.
大陸雜誌社：語言文字學 「大陸雜誌語文叢書」第一輯，第三冊

0081 Ta-lu tsa-chih-she: *Yü-fa sheng-yün wen-tzu.* — Taipei: Ditto, 1970, 3, 452 p./ *Ta-lu tsa-chih yü-wen ts'ung-shu.* Ti-erh chi, Ti-szu ts'e. [Grammar, phonology, and writing.]/ Articles published in *TLTC* 25–38, 1963–1969.
大陸雜誌社：語法聲韻文字 「大陸雜誌語文叢書」第二輯，第四冊

0082 T'ang, T'ing-ch'ih: *Kuo-yü yü-fa yen-chiu lun-chi.*—Taipei: T'ai-wan hsüeh-sheng shu-chü, 1979, xii, 430 p. [Collected essays on the study of the grammar of the National Language.]
湯廷池：國語語法研究論集

0083 Tung, T'ung-ho. Ed. by Ting, Pang-hsin: *Tung T'ung-ho hsien-sheng yü-yen-hsüeh lun-wen hsüan-chi.* — Taipei: Shih-huo, 1974, i, 434 p. [Selected essays on linguistics by Prof. Tung T'ung-ho.]
董同龢著，丁邦新編：董同龢先生語言學論文選集

0084 Tung-pei shih-ta hsüeh-pao pien-chi-pu: *Yü-yen-hsüeh lun-chi.*—Changchun: Tung-pei shih-ta, 1980, 290 p. [Collected essays on (Chinese) linguistics.]
東北師大學報編輯部：語言學論集

0085 Ushijima, Tokuji; Kōsaka, Jun'ichi & Tōdō, Akiyasu (eds.): *Gengo.* — Tokyo: Taishūkan, 1967, 472 p., maps./ *Chūgoku bunka sōsho*, 1. *CGGG* 1968:4, 9–17, Suzuki Naoji; *GGSK* 198, 1968, 70–71, Matsumoto Akira. [(Chinese) language.]
牛島德次、香坂順一、藤堂明保編集：言語／「中國文化叢書」1／鈴本直治評，松本昭評

0086 Wang, Li: *Lung-ch'ung ping-tiao-chai wen-chi.* —— Peking: Chung-hua, 1980, Vols. I & II, 1, 818 p.; 1982, Vol. III, 2, 2, 502 p. [Collected essays from the Dragon and Worm Carving Studio.]
王力：龍蟲並雕齋文集

0087 Wen shih che tsa-chih pien-chi wei-yüan-hui: *Han-yü lun-ts'ung.*—— Peking: Chung-hua, 1958, 277 p. [Collected essays on the Chinese language.]
文史哲雜誌編輯委員會：漢語論叢

0088 Wen-tzu kai-ko ch'u-pan-she: *P'u-t'ung-hua lun-chi.* —— Peking: Ditto, 1956, 3, 191 p. [Collected essays on the Common Language.]
文字改革出版社：普通話論集

0089 Wu, Wen-ch'i (ed. in chief): *Yü-yen wen-tzu yen-chiu chuan-chi* (shang). — Shanghai: Shang-hai ku-chi, 1982, 8, 539 p. [A special issue of studies on (the Chinese) language and writing (Vol. I).]/ Collected essays.
吳文祺主編：語言文字研究專輯（上）

0090 Ya, Hsüan (ed.): *Chung-kuo yü-yen-hsüeh lun-chi.* —Taipei: Yu-shih wen-hua shih-yeh kung-szu, 1977, iii, 470 p. [Collected essays on Chinese linguistics.]
瘂弦編：中國語言學論集

0091 Yang, Shu-ta: *Chi-wei-chü hsiao-hsüeh shu-lin.*—— Peking: Chung-kuo k'o-hsüeh-yüan, 1954, 9, 12, 322 p. [Collected essays on philology from the Chi-wei-chü.]

楊樹達：積微居小學述林

0092 Yang, Shu-ta: *Chi-wei-chü hsiao-hsüeh chin-shih lun-ts'ung.*——Peking: K'o-hsüeh, 1955, rev. & enl. ed., 10, 14, 308 p. [Collected essays on philology and bronze-stone inscriptions from the Chi-wei-chü.]

楊樹達：積微居小學金石論叢

1.2. History (0093–0107)

0093 Chou, Fa-kao: *Chung-kuo yü-yen-hsüeh te kuo-ch'ü hsien-tsai ho wei-lai.* — Hong Kong: Hsiang-kang Chung-wen ta-hsüeh, 1966, 21 p., E.S. [The past, present, and future of Chinese linguistics.]

周法高：中國語言學的過去現在和未來

0094 Chou, Fa-kao. Transl. by Liu, San-fu: Chūgoku gengogaku no kakyo genzai to mirai. — *Seinan Gakuin Daigaku Bunri Ronsnū* 17:1, 1976, 33–51. [The past, present, and future of Chinese linguistics.] (0093).

周法高著，劉三富譯：中國言語學の過去現在と未來

0095 Chou, Fa-kao: Erh-shih shih-chi te Chung-kuo yü-yen-hsüeh. —— *HKCW* 1, 1973, 297–322; *YSYK* 40:6, 1974, 9–21; *Chung-kuo yü-yen-hsüeh lun-wen-chi* (0053), 1–35; also repr. in Paul Fu-mien Yang's *Chinese linguistics . . . bibliography* (0033), 268–292. [Chinese linguistics in the 20th century.]

周法高：二十世紀的中國語言學

0096 Chūgoku Gogaku Kenkyūkai: *Chūgoku gogaku jiten* (0037), 5: Section on research history./ See (0106). [An encyclopedia of Chinese linguistics.]

中國語學研究會：中國語學事典／5:研究史篇

0097 Chung-kuo yü-wen pien-chi-pu: Shih

nien-lai wo-kuo yü-yen-hsüeh-chieh chi-shih. — *CKYW* 1959:10, 501–506; (Addenda) 11, 556–557. [A record of events of linguistic circles of China in the past ten years (1949–1959).]

中國語文編輯部：十年來我國語言學界記事

0098 Chung-kuo yü-yen-hsüeh-chia pien-hsieh-tsu: *Chung-kuo hsien-tai yü-yen-hsüeh-chia* (Ti-i fen-ts'e, Ti-erh fen-ts'e). —— Shih-chiachuang: Ho-pei jen-min, 1981, Vol. I, 2, 3, 2, 302 p., portr.; 1982, Vol. II, 2, 2, 322 p., portr. [Contemporary linguists of China (Fascic. I, II).]/ Biographies and bibliographies of 30 & 45 Chinese linguists.

中國語言學家編寫組：中國現代語言學家
（第一分冊，第二分冊）

0099 Ijichi, Yoshitsugu: Goi. —— *CGGG* 1960:12, 11–12. [(Chinese) vocabulary.]/ Japanese studies on Chinese lexicon.

伊地智善繼：語彙

0100 Li, Ch'i-fa: T'an Chung-kuo ta-lu tui hsien-tai yü tz'u-hui te yen-chiu.—*P'an-ku* 39, 1971, 34–39; 40, 19–23. [On researches of the modern (Chinese) vocabulary in mainland China.]

李啓發：談中國大陸對現代語詞滙的研究

0101 Tai, Lien-chang: Liu-shih nien-lai chih wen-fa-hsüeh.—*Liu-shih nien-lai chih Kuo-hsüeh* 2 (0050), 417–460. [Grammatical studies in the past sixty years.]

戴璉璋：六十年來之文法學

0102 Ts'en, Ch'i-hsiang: *Yü-yen-hsüeh shih kai-yao.*—— Peking: K'o-hsüeh, 1958, xvi, 332 p./ Including Chinese lexicology and lexicography. [An outline of the history of linguistics.]

岑麒祥：語言學史概要

0103 Wang, Li: *Han-yü shih lun-wen-chi.*— Peking: K'o-hsüeh, 1958, [ii], 411 p., map./ *RBS* 4, 1958, 538, J. Chmielewski. [Collected essays on the hisotry of the Chinese language.]

王力：漢語史論文集

0104 Wang, Li: Chung-kuo yü-yen-hsüeh shih.
—*CKYW* 1963:3, 232–245, 265; 4, 309–
326, 347; 5, 411–427, 431; 6, 496–510,
474; 1964:1, 62–75; 2, 103–105; Hong
Kong: Lung Men, 1967, repr., 99 p./ *RBS*
9, 1963, 476, A. Rygaloff. [A history of
Chinese linguistics.]
王力：中國語言學史

0105 Wang, Li: *Chung-kuo yü-yen-hsüeh shih.*
—Taiyüan: Shan-hsi jen-min, 1981, 2,
214 p. [A history of Chinese linguistics.]
王力：中國語言學史

0106 Wang, Li-ta (transl.): *Han-yü yen-chiu
hsiao-shih.* —— Peking: Shang-wu, 1959,
viii, 162 p./ An adapted translation of
chapter 5 of *Chūgoku gogaku jiten* (0037).
[A short history of the study of the
Chinese language.]
王立達編譯：漢語研究小史

0107 Yin, Meng-lun: T'an-t'an Han-yü tz'u-hui
yen-chiu te tuan-tai wen-t'i. —— *WSC*
1981:2, 49–52. [A discussion on the
problem of periodization in the study
of Chinese vocabulary.]
殷孟倫：談談漢語詞彙研究的斷代問題

1.3. Methodology (0108–0139)
1.3.1. Linguistic Terminology (0108–0115)

0108 Chung-kuo she-hui k'o-hsüeh-yüan Min-
tsu yen-chiu-so Yü-yen yen-chiu-shih:
Ying-Han tui-chao yü-wen-hsüeh yung-yü
(ch'u kao). —— Peking: Chung-kuo she-hui
k'o-hsüeh-yüan Min-tsu yen-chiu-so Yü-yen
yen-chiu-shih, 1979, 5, 436 p. [A glossary
of English-Chinese linguistic and literary
terminology (A first draft).]
中國社會科學院民族研究所語言研究室：英漢
對照語文學用語（初稿）

0109 Donner, Frederick W., Jr.: *A preliminary
glossary of Chinese linguistic terminology.*
—San Francisco: Chinese Materials Center,
1977, x, 117 p.; 115–117: Bibliography./

English-Chinese & Chinese-English.

0110 Hartmann, R.R.K. & Stork, F.C. Transl.
by Huang, Ch'ang-chu, et al.: *Yü-yen yü
yü-yen-hsüeh tz'u-tien.*—— Shanghai: Shanghai tz'u-shu, 1981, iii, 18, 460, 50 p./
TSYC 1981:1, 214–221, Huang Ch'ang-
chu, et al.; *TSYC* 1982:4, 121–126, 133,
Hsü Kuo-chang. [A dictionary of language
and linguistics.]
哈特曼、斯托克著，黃長著等譯：語言與語言
學詞典／黃長著等評，許國璋評

0111 Lee, Daniel T.Y.: *Chinese-English glossary
of linguistic terms.* ——Washington, D.C.:
Center for Chinese Research Materials,
Association of Research Libraries, 1971,
x, 165 p.

0112 Liu, Yung-ch'üan & Chao, Shih-k'ai:
Ying-Han yü-yen-hsüeh tz'u-hui. ——Peking:
Chung-kuo she-hui k'o-hsüeh, 1979, [iv],
345 p. [A glossary of English-Chinese
linguistic terminology.]
劉涌泉、趙世開：英漢語言學詞滙

0113 Pei-ching ta-hsüeh yü-yen-hsüeh chiao-
yen-shih: *Yü-yen-hsüeh ming-tz'u chieh-shih.*
—Peking: Shang-wu, 1962, ii, 156 p.
[Linguistic terminology explained.]
北京大學語言學教研室：語言學名詞解釋

0114 Wang, William S-Y. & Liu, Lillian:
*Bibliography and glossary for Chinese
grammar* (0030).

0115 Yeh, Ch'ang-ch'ing: *Wen-tzu-hsüeh ming-
tz'u ch'üan-shih.* —— Shanghai: Ch'ün-chung
t'u-shu, 1927, viii, 224 p.; Hong Kong:
Shen-chou, 197?, repr. [Logographic
terminology explained.]
葉長青：文字學名詞詮釋

**1.3.2. Lexicon and Lexical Problems
(0116–0129)**

0116 Budagov, R.A. Transl. by Lü, T'ung-lun,
et al.: *Yü-yen-hsüeh kai-lun.* ——Peking:
Shih-tai, 1956, 321 p./ Chap. 1: Basic

vocabulary and lexicon. [Ocherki po iazykoznaniiu (An introduction to linguistics).]
布達哥夫著，呂同崙等譯：語言學概論／第一
章：語言的基本詞彙和詞彙

0117   Chao, Yüan-jen: Kuo-yü te yü-fa ho
tz'u-hui wen-ti.—*CKYT* 5:3, 1959, 4–11.
[Grammar of the National Language and
lexical problems.]
趙元任：國語的語法和詞彙問題

0118   Chao, Yüan-jen: *Yü-yen wen-t'i.* —
Taipei: Shang-wu, 1968, [4], 223 p.;
Peking: Shang-wu, 1980, 5, 232 p./ Lecture
4: Lexicon & grammar. [Problems in
language.]
趙元任：語言問題／第四講：詞彙跟語法

0119   Chao, Yuen Ren: *Language and symbolic
systems.* —— Cambridge: Cambridge U.
Press, 1968, xv, 240 p./ 51–65: Vocabulary
and grammar.

0120   Chin, Hsiang-tse: Tz'u-hui shih shen-ma?
—*CKYW* 1955:6, 34. [What is a lexicon?]
金湘澤：詞滙是甚麼？

0121   Fang, Shih-to: Chien-li tz'u-hui te t'i-hsi.
—*CKYT* 17:1, 1965, 31–34. [Establish-
ment of a lexical system.]
方師鐸：建立詞彙的體系

0122   Kao, Ming-k'ai: *Yü-yen lun.*—— Peking:
K'o-hsüeh, 1965, vii, 525 p./ Pt. 2, Chap.
4: The structure of lexical systems in
languages and its development. [On
language.]
高名凱：語言論／第二部分，第四章：語言中
詞滙系統的結構及其演變

0123   Kao, Ming-k'ai & Shih, An-shih: *Yü-
yen-hsüeh kai-lun.*——Peking: Chung-hua,
1963; 1982, 7th repr., 6, 262 p., map./
Chap. 4: Lexicon. [An introduction to
linguistics.]
高名凱、石安石：語言學概論／第四章：詞滙

0124   Li, Jung: Tzu-hui ho tz'u-hui (Ta Li
Hsiang-chen hsien-sheng).——*CKYW* 1953:

5, 17–21. [Glossary and lexicon (A reply
to Mr. Li Hsiang-chen (1389).]
李榮：字彙和詞彙（答李向眞先生）

0125   Matsumoto, Akira: Goi ni tsuite.——
Chūgokugo 97, 1968, 30–33; 98, 27–29.
[On vocabulary.]
松本昭：語彙について

0126   Sun, Liang-ming: *Han-yü tz'u-hui* chung
chi-ko wen-t'i te shang-ch'üeh.——*CKYW*
1958:8, 396–399. [Deliberations on several
problems in *Han-yü tz'u-hui* (0165).]
孫良明：『漢語詞滙』中幾個問題的商榷

0127   Ueno, Keiji: Gendai Chūgokugo goi
kenkyū no mondaiten.——*GBR* 1, 1977,
149–173. [The central problem of the
studies on Modern Chinese vocabulary.]
上野惠司：現代中國語彙研究の問題點

0128   Wang, Fu-ch'üan: Yü-hui shih lun. —
Chung-kuo wen-fa ko-hsin lun-ts'ung
(0049), 175–181. [A preliminary discussion
on vocabulary.]
汪馥泉：語彙試論

0129   Wu, Chan-k'un: *Tz'u-hui.*—Shanghai:
Shang-hai chiao-yü, 1983, 2, 180 p. [A
lexicon.]/ A general study.
武占坤：詞滙

1.3.3. Lexicology and Lexicological Problems (0130–0139)

0130   Akhmanova, O. S., et al.: Lun miao-
hsieh tz'u-hui-hsüeh, li-shih tz'u-hui-hsüeh
chi li-shih pi-chiao tz'u-hui-hsüeh te jen-wu
ho chi-ko wen-t'i. —— *YIT* 1958:1, 2–15.
[On the tasks and some problems of
descriptive lexicology, historical lexicology,
and comparative historical lexicology.]
阿赫曼諾娃等：論描寫詞滙學、歷史詞滙學及
歷史比較詞滙學的任務和幾個問題

0131   Chang, Yung-yen: *Tz'u-hui-hsüeh chien-
lun.*—Wuhan: Hua-chung kung-hsüeh-yüan,
1982, [ii], 2, 131 p. [A simple discussion
on lexicology.]

張永言：詞滙學簡論

0132 Chou, Tsu-mo: Tz'u-hui ho tz'u-hui-hsüeh.—*YWHH* 1958:9, 23–25; 11, 9–12. [Lexicon and lexicology.]
周祖謨：詞彙和詞彙學

0133 Chu, Hsing: *Yü-yen-hsüeh kai-lun.* — Tientsin: T'ien-chin jen-min, 1957, iii, 200 p./ 133–140: Fundamental concepts of lexicology; *CKYW* 1958:11, 543–545, Chao Chen-to. [An introduction to linguistics.]
朱星：語言學概論／133-140：詞彙學的基本概念；趙振鐸評

0134 Fang, Shih-to: Tz'u-hui-hsüeh shih kan-shen-ma te? — *CKYT* 17:12, 1965, 22–27. [What are the tasks of lexicology?]
方師鐸：詞彙學是幹甚麼的？

0135 Huang, Ching-hsin: Shih lun tz'u-hui-hsüeh chung te chi-ko wen-t'i.——*CKYW* 1961:3, 18–22./ See (0136). [A preliminary discussion on several problems in lexicology.]
黃景欣：試論詞滙學中的幾個問題

0136 Liu, Shu-hsin: Lun tz'u-hui t'i-hsi wen-t'i — yü Huang Ching-hsin t'ung-chih

shang-ch'üeh. — *CKYW* 1964:3, 203–213./ *RBS* 10, 1964, 507, V. Alleton. [On problems in lexical systems — deliberations with colleague Huang Ching-hsin (0135).]
劉叔新：論詞滙體系問題——與黃景欣同志商榷

0137 Shang-hai wai-kuo-yü hsüeh-yüan & Ha-erh-pin wai-kuo-yü hsüeh-yüan: *Yü-yen-hsüeh yin-lun.*—— Peking: Shih-tai, 1958, 318 p./ Chap. 5: Lexicology. [An introduction to linguistics.]
上海外國語學院、哈爾濱外國語學院：語言學引論／第五章：詞彙學

0138 Sung, Chen-hua & Wang, Chin-cheng: *Yü-yen-hsüeh kai-lun.*—Changchun: Chi-lin jen-min, 1957, v, 306 p./ 28–73: Lexicology and lexical meanings. [An introduction to linguistics.]
宋振華、王今錚：語言學概論／28-73：詞滙學和詞義學

0139 Yang, Tsu-yü: Tz'u-hui-hsüeh san-lun. — *Hsüeh-shu lun-wen chi-k'an* 2, 1973, 183–196. [A random discussion on lexicology.]
楊祖聿：詞彙學散論

2.   LEXICAL UNITS: WORD AND WORD FORMATION (0140–0414)

2.1.   Definition, Differentiation, and Classification of Word (0140–0253)

2.1.1.   Definition of Word (0140–0168)

0140   Chang, Kun: Descriptive linguistics. — *Current trends in linguistics* (0078), 59–90./ 71–73: The definition of a word.

0141   Chang, Shih-lu: Chien-li tz'u te kuan-nien. —*YWCH* 1958:9, 25–29. [To establish the concept of a word.]
張世祿：建立詞的觀念

0142   Chao, Yuen Ren: *A grammar of spoken Chinese.*—Berkeley & Los Angeles: U. of California Press, 1968, xxxi, 847 p./ Chap. 3: Word and morpheme; Chap. 4: Morphological types; Chap. 5: Syntactical types; Chap. 6: Compounds; *Lg* 46, 1970, 513–524, Paul Kratochvíl; *JCL* 1:1, 1973, 126–149, Li Ying-che; *YCYY* 3, 1980, 84–92, Chin Feng.
〔趙元任：中國話的文法〕／李英哲評，金風評

0143   Chao, Yuen Ren. Transl. by Ting, Pang-hsin: *Chung-kuo-hua te wen-fa.* — Hong Kong: Chinese U. Press, 1980, [i], 2, 3, [i], 458 p.; 1982, 2nd print. [A grammar of spoken Chinese.] (0142)
趙元任著，丁邦新譯：中國話的文法／第三章：詞跟語位；第四章：構詞類型；第五章：造句類型；第六章：複合詞

0144   Cheng, Li: Kuan-yü shen-ma shih tz'u-erh te wen-t'i.—*Yü-fa lun-chi* 1 (0059), 52–62. [Concerning the problem of what is a word.]
鄭力：關於甚麼是詞兒的問題

0145   Chou, Pien-ming: Tz'u te chieh-shuo.—*KYYK* 1:11, 1922, 1–3; *K'o-hsüeh* 8:4, 1933, 446–455. [The definition of a word.]
周辨明：詞的界說

0146   Ch'ü, Pei-wei: *T'an-t'an tz'u-erh.*——Chinan: Shan-tung jen-min, 1956, [ii], 18 p. [A discussion on words.]
曲北韋：談談詞兒

0147   Fu, Tung-hua: Chuan-chu-chia ho tz'u te kuan-nien.——*YWCS* 1958:2, 25–27. [Commentators (on the Classics) and the concept of a word.]
傅東華：傳注家和詞的觀念

0148   Fu, Tzu-tung: Tz'u te chih-wu ho wei-tz'u.—— *CKYW* 1953:9, 13–18. [The functions and positions of words.]
傅子東：詞的職務和位次

0149   Hsiang, Jo, et al.: Kuan-yü *Shen-ma shih tz'u-erh* i wen te t'ao-lun.—*CKYW* 1956:5, 43–47. [A discussion concerning the article *Shen-ma shih tz'u-erh* (0163).]
向若等：關於『甚麼是詞兒』一文的討論

0150   Hu, Fu & Wen, Lien: Tz'u te fan-wei, hsing-t'ai, kung-neng.—— *CKYW* 1954:8, 3–7. [The scope, form, and function of words.]
胡附、文鍊：詞的範圍、形態、功能

0151   Hung, Tu-jen: *Tz'u shih shen-ma?*——Shanghai: Hsin chih-shih, 1957, 56 p; *Yü-wen hui-pien* (0058), 64:212. [What is a word?]
洪篤仁：詞是甚麼？

0152   Ijichi, Yoshitsugu: Chūgokugo no gengo tan'i——Chō Genjinshi no syntactic word ni tsuite.——*OGDG* 1, 1952, 135–160. [Linguistic units of the Chinese language —on Chao Yuen Ren's "syntactic word".]/ See (0142), 182–187.
伊地智善繼：中國語の言語單位——趙元任氏の"syntactic word"について

0153   Jen, Ming-shan: Yü-yen te ts'ai-liao.—*YWHH* 1957:3, 22–23. [The materials of language.]/ Words.
任銘善：語言的材料

0154   Kalousková, Jarmila: Le problème du mot dans les traveaux du Lu Chih-wei.—*AO* 27:3, 1960, 488–493./ *RBS* 6, 1960, 398, A. Rygaloff.

0155 Kuo, Hou-chüeh: Chung-kuo hsin yü-wen te tz'u te wen-t'i.——*Yü-wen* 1:3, 1937, 17–19. [The problem of (what are) words in the new language and writing of China.]
郭後覺：中國新語文的詞的問題

0156 Lin, Han-ta: Shen-ma pu-shih tz'u-erh—hsiao yü tz'u-erh te pu-shih tz'u-erh.—*CKYW* 1955:4, 6–10. [What is not a word——the one which is smaller than a word is not a word.]
林漢達：甚麼不是詞兒——小於詞兒的不是詞兒

0157 Lin, Han-ta: Shen-ma pu-shih tz'u-erh——ta yü tz'u-erh te pu-shih tz'u-erh.—*CKYW* 1955:5, 6–8. [What is not a word——the one which is bigger than a word is not a word.]
林漢達：甚麼不是詞兒——大於詞兒的不是詞兒

0158 Lu, Chih-wei: The status of the word in Chinese linguistics.——*Beiträge zum . . . im Chinesischen* (0077), 34–47.

0159 Meng, Ch'i: Tz'u te hsing-chih.——*Yü-wen* 1:4, 1937, 54–55. [The nature of a word.]
孟起：詞的性質

0160 Miyata, Ichirō: Tango no genkai ni tsuite.—*CGGG* 1958:9, 5–9; *Kanbungaku* 7, 1958, 9–21. [On the boundaries of words.]
宮田一郎：單語の限界について

0161 Mochizuki, Yasokichi: Shi.——*JBK* 7:6, 1956, 10–21./ *RBS* 2, 1956, 392, M.C. van der Loon. [(Chinese) words.]/ Discusses the delineation of word classes.
望月八十吉：詞

0162 Po, Han: Ying-tang chien-li tz'u te kuan-nien.——*CKYW* 1952:5, 4–5. [The concept of word should be established.]
伯韓：應當建立詞的觀念

0163 Shih, Ts'un-chih: Shen-ma shih tz'u-erh?—*CKYW* 1956:3, 20–22. [What is a word?]
史存直：甚麼是詞兒？

0164 Shih, Ts'un-chih: Tsai lun shen-ma shih tz'u-erh.——*CKYW* 1956:9, 3–11. [Another discussion on what is a word.]
史存直：再論甚麼是詞兒

0165 Sun, Ch'ang-hsü: *Han-yü tz'u-hui.*——Changchun: Chi-lin jen-min, 1956, 6, 26, 493 p.; *Yü-wen hui-pien* (0058), 52:171./ Pt. I, Chap. 1: The nature and structure of words; *RBS* 3, 1957, 591, J. Chmielewski; *CKYW* 1957:8, 43, Lao Chün-fang; *YWCS* 1957:4, 47–49, Hu Ko-fei; *YWHH* 1957:7, 36, Lin Yün-lai & Lin Chin. [Chinese lexicons.]
孫常叙：漢語詞彙／第一部分，第一篇：詞的性質和結構；勞君方評，胡格非評，林運來、林瑾評

0166 T'an Yung-hsiang: Tz'u te ting-i.——*Yü-fa lun-chi* 1 (0059), 47–51. [The definition of a word.]
譚永祥：詞的定義

0167 Torii, Katsuyuki: Chūgokugo no tango ni tsuite.——*JBK* 17:4, 1966, 34–49./ *RBS* 12–13, 1980, 636, Kawaguchi Junji. [On Chinese words.]
鳥居克之：中國語の單語について

0168 Yü, Min: Shen-ma shih i-ko tz'u?—*YCHP* 40, 1951, 131–150. [What is a word?]
俞敏：甚麼是一個詞？

2.1.2. Differentiation of Word (0169–0199)
2.1.2.1. General Studies (0169–0178)

0169 Chung, Ch'in: T'an tsen-yang fen-pieh tz'u ho yü.——*CKYW* 1954:12, 12–14. [A discussion on how to distinguish words and phrases.]
鍾梫：談怎樣分別詞和語

0170 Chung, Ch'in: Tz'u yü fei tz'u te ch'ü-fen wen-t'i.——*YWTC* 6, 1981, 28–31. [The problem of distinguishing 'words' and 'non-words'.]
鍾梫：詞與非詞的區分問題

0171 Ho, Jung: Tz'u yü chü.—— *Wen t'an*

54, 1964, 14—16. [Words and sentences.]
何容：詞與句

0172 Hung, Tu-jen: Tz'u ho tz'u-tsu te ch'ü-pieh.——*Hsüeh-shu lun-t'an* 2, 1957, 1—7./ *CKYW* 1957:9, 46, Li Yüan. [The distinctions between words and phrases.]
洪篤仁：詞和詞組的區別／黎原評

0173 I, San-k'o [Isaenko, B.S.]: Lun Han-yü chung tz'u te chieh-hsien wen-t'i.——*CKYW* 1958:5, 233; 6, 283—287; 7, 330; 8, 392; 9, 439—441. [On the problem of word boundaries in Chinese.]
伊三克：論漢語中詞的界限問題

0174 Kung, Hsiu-shih: Ch'üeh-ting tz'u-erh yung yü-fa piao-chun hai-shih yung yü-i piao-chun?——*Yü-fa lun-chi* 1 (0059), 63—66. [Should one determine (water) a word (is) using grammatical criteria or using semantic criteria?]
龔秀石：確定詞兒用語法標準還是用語義標準?

0175 Lin, Han-ta: Kuan-yü fen-hsi tz'u-erh te chi-tien chieh-shih.——*CKYW* 1953:9, 34—35. [Several explanations concerning the analysis of words.]
林漢達：關於分析詞兒的幾點解釋

0176 Shih, Ts'un-chin: Lun tz'u-erh ho p'an-ting tz'u-erh te fang-fa.——*Yü-fa lun-chi* 1 (0059), 1—46. [On words and methods of determining words.]
史存直：論詞兒和判定詞兒的方法

0177 Wang, Li: Tz'u ho le-yü te chieh-hsien wen-t'i.——*CKYW* 1953:9, 3—8. [Problems in the boundaries of words and phrases.]
王力：詞和仂語的界限問題

0178 Yang, Yung-ch'üan: Yü-fa chieh-kou shih p'an-ting tz'u-erh te piao-chun.——*Yü-fa lun-chi* 1 (0059), 67—70. [Grammatical structure is the criterion of determining words.]
楊永泉：語法結構是判定詞兒的標準

2.1.2.2. Word and Morpheme (0179—0184)

0179 Chao, Yuen Ren: *A grammar of spoken Chinese* (0142), Chap. 3: Word and morpheme.
趙元任：中國話的文法／第三章：詞跟語位

0180 Henne, Henry, et al.: *A handbook on Chinese language structure.* ——— Oslo: Universitetsforlaget, 1977, [ix], 293 p./ 14—21: The word; 103—115: The word and the morpheme.

0181 Li, Chao-t'ung & Hsü, Szu-i (eds. in chief): *Yü-yen-hsüeh tao-lun.* — Urumchi: Hsin-chiang jen-min, 1981, [2], 3, 326 p./ Chap. 4: Morpheme and word. [An introduction to linguistics.]
李兆同、徐思益主編：語言學導論／第四章：語素和詞

0182 Solncev, V. M.: Morpheme and word in Chinese.——*Studies in general and Oriental linguistics, presented to Shirō Hattori on the occasion of his sixtieth birthday* (Ed. by Jakobson, Roman & Kawamoto, Shigeo.——Tokyo: TEC Co., 1970), 545—551.

0183 Švarný, Oldřich: *K otázce morfému a slova v monerní hovorové čínštině.* —— Prague: Orientální ústavu Čekoslovenské akademie věd, 1963, iv, 198 p./ Unpubl. doc. diss. [The problem of morpheme and word in modern colloquial Chinese.]

0184 Tu, Hsüeh-chih: Yü-ken yü yü-tz'u.——*Chien-she* 2:12, 1954, 12—14. [Word-roots and words.]
杜學知：語根與語詞

2.1.2.3. Word and Character (0185—0199)

0185 Chang, Ch'ing-ch'ang: Tzu yü tz'u.——*KWYK* 1:7, 1941, 28—30. [Characters and words.]
張清常：字與詞

0186 Chang, Wen-cheng: Lüeh lun tzu ho tz'u.——*TPPYK* 1:6, 1934, 289—291. [A short discussion on characters and words.]

張文正：略論字和詞

0187 Chao, Yu-p'ei: Tzu ho tz'u. — *Chu-i yü kuo-ts'e* 62, 1955, 11–16. [Characters and words.]
趙友培：字和詞

0188 Ch'i, T'ieh-hen: Tzu ho tz'u te yen-chiu. —*CKYT* 1:1, 1952, 4–6; 2, 4–7; 3, 16–19; 4, 24–25; 5, 6–8; 6, 4–6; 2:1, 1953, 11–12; 2, 18–19. [A study of characters and words.]
齊鐵恨：字和詞的研究

0189 Hou, Jo-nung: *Tzu tz'u yü wen-t'i.*— Taipei: The Author, 1974, [3], 11, 222 p. [Characters, words, and stylistics.]
侯若農：字詞與文體

0190 Hsiang, Jo: P'ing *Tzu ho tz'u.*—*YWHH* 1954:11, 75–77. [A critique of *Tzu ho tz'u* (0192).]
向若：評『字和詞』

0191 Hsü, Shih-ying: *Chung-kuo wen-fa chiang-hua.*—— Taipei: K'ai-ming, 1966; 1976, 12th rev. ed., 3, 6, 6, 420 p./ Chap. 2: Characters, words, and compounds. [Lectures on Chinese grammar.]
許世瑛：中國文法講話／第二章：字、詞、複詞

0192 I, Hsi-wu: Tzu ho tz'u.——*YWCS* 1953: 10, 20–23. [Characters and words.]/ See (0190)
易熙吾：字和詞

0193 Li, Pao-jui: I-t'i tzu ho tz'u te fen-hua.——*Yü-yen-hsüeh lun-chi* (0084), 25–41. [Variant characters and differentiation of words.]
李葆瑞：異體字和詞的分化

0194 Lin, Yü-wen: Tz'u ho tzu.——*YWCS* 1954:12, 9–12. [Words and characters.]
林裕文：詞和字

0195 Lü, Shu-hsiang: *Chung-kuo wen-fa yao-lüeh.*——Shanghai: Shang-wu, 1942–1944, 3 vols., v, 206; 2, iv, 310; iii, 214, 16 p.;

Peking: Shang-wu, 1956, 2nd rev. ed., 4, 4, 469 p./ Chap. 1: Characters and words; *CKYW* 1956:12, 48, Liang Yin. [Essentials of Chinese grammar.]
呂叔湘：中國文法要略／第一章：字和詞；梁吟評

0196 Ts'ao, Po-han: Tzu ho tz'u te mao-tun pi-hsü chieh-chüeh. —— *CKYW* 1952:2, 14–15. [The contradictions between characters and words must be resolved.]
曹伯韓：字和詞的矛盾必須解決

0197 Ts'ao, Po-han: Tzu, tz'u, tuan-yü.— *YWHH* 35, 1954, 40–45. [Characters, words, and phrases.]
曹伯韓：字、詞、短語

0198 Wang, Liao-i: Tzu ho tz'u. —*KWYK* 31–32, 1944, 13–15. [Characters and words.]
王了一：字和詞

0199 Yang, Liu-ch'iao: Han-yü yü-fa chung tzu ho tz'u te wen-t'i.— *CKYW* 1957:1, 6–8. [The problems of *tzu* ('character') and *tz'u* ('word') in Chinese grammar.]
楊柳橋：漢語語法中『字』和『詞』的問題

2.1.3. Classification of Word (0200–0253)
2.1.3.1. General Studies (0200–0209)

0200 Chan, Ch'eng: Shih-tz'u ho hsü-tz'u.— *YWCS* 1953:8, 18–19. [Plerematic words and cenematic words.]/ See (0207).
展成：實詞和虛詞

0201 Chang, Chih-kung: T'an hsü-tz'u.— *YWHH* 1953:8, 11–15. [A discussion on cenematic words.]
張志公：談虛詞

0202 Feng, Ch'eng-lin: Tan-ch'un tz'u yü ho-ch'eng tz'u te chieh-hsien wen-t'i.—*JWTC* 1957:4, 67–71. [Problems in the boundaries of simple words and compound words.]
馮成麟：單純詞與合成詞的界限問題

0203 Ho, Jung: Tz'u te lei-pieh ho p'ei-ho

fang-shih.——*CKYT* 4:3, 1959, 55—57.
[The classifications and coordination
patterns of words.]
何容：詞的類別和配合方式

0204   Hu, J.P.: A new attempt to classify
Chinese words. —— *Journal of Chinese
Teaching and Studies* 1:1, 1977, 28—38.

0205   Kalousková, Jarmila: Des catégories de
mots dans la langue chinoise.——*AO* 25,
1957, 287—294./ *RBS* 3, 1957, 581, U.
Unger.

0206   Kao, Kung-yi: *The classification of
Chinese words.*—— Stanford: Stanford U.,
1970, 274 p./ Unpubl. doc. diss.; *DA*
31:4749-A; UM 71—2783.
〔高恭億〕

0207   Liu, Chung-wu: Tu-le *Shih-tz'u ho
hsü-tz'u* i-hou.——*YWCS* 1953:10, 18—19.
[After reading *Shih-tz'u ho hsü-tz'u*
(0200).]/ See (0209)
劉鍾武：讀了『實詞和虛詞』以後

0208   Shih, An-shih: Shen-ma shih Han-yü
hsü-tz'u?—*YWHH* 1957:3, 32—33. [What
is a cenematic word in Chinese?]
石安石：甚麼是漢語虛詞？

0209   Yao, Hsüan-chao: Wo-te i-chien.——
YWCS 1954:1, 17—18. [My opinion
(concerning plerematic and cenematic
words).]/ A review of Liu Chung-wu's
article (0207).
姚選釗：我的意見

2.1.3.2. Monosyllabic Word (0210—0215)

0210   Cheng, Lin-hsi: Kuan-yü Han-yü te
tz'u ho Han-yü tan-yin-chieh shuo.—*CKYW*
1955:5, 14—18. [Concerning Chinese
words and the theory of the monosyllabicity
of Chinese.]
鄭林義：關於漢語的詞和漢語單音節說

0211   Ch'i, Ch'ung-t'ien: Han-yü tan-yin-chieh-
tz'u te kou-ch'eng wen-t'i.——*YLT* 8, 1981,

118—141. [The problems in the formation
of Chinese monosyllabic words.]
齊冲天：漢語單音節詞的構成問題

0212   Lu, Chih-wei: Tui-yü tan-yin-tz'u te
i-chung ts'o-wu te chien-chieh.——*CKYW*
1955:4, 11—12. [An incorrect view
concerning monosyllabic words.]
陸志韋：對於單音詞的一種錯誤的見解

0213   Lü, Shu-hsiang: Hsien-tai Han-yü tan
shuang yin-chieh wen-t'i ch'u-t'an.——
CKYW 1963:1, 10—22; *Hsien-tai Han-yü
. . . tzu-liao* (0064), 284—310. [A preliminary investigation into the problems
of monosyllabicity and polysyllabicity in
Modern Chinese.]
呂叔湘：現代漢語單雙音節問題初探

0214   P'eng, Ch'u-nan: Tan-yin-chieh-yü wen-
t'i te shih-chih.——*CKYW* 1955:4, 13—17.
[The essence of the problem in a monosyllabic language.]
彭楚南：單音節語問題的實質

0215   Wei, Chü-hsien: Yu fu-yin-yü pien-wei
tan-yin-yü te chu-li.—— *Jen-wen hsüeh-pao*
6, 1976, 225—286. [Examples of disyllabic
words changed to monosyllabic words.]
衛聚賢：由複音語變爲單音語的舉例

2.1.3.3. Polysyllabic Word (0216—0236)

0216   Chang, Ch'i-ch'un & Hsin, Ting-ming:
Shuang-yin-tz'u te tzu-hsü.——*YWHH* 1953:
2, 54—55. [The character order of
disyllabic words.]
張其春、忻鼎明：雙音詞的字序

0217   Chang, Hsün-ju: Kuo-yü chung chih
fu-yin-tz'u.—— *KWYK* 63, 1948, 12—16.
[Disyllabic words in the National Language.]
張洵如：國語中之複音詞

0218   Chang, Yung-mien: Chin-tai Han-yü
chung tzu-hsü tui-huan te shuang-yin-tz'u.
—*CKYW* 1980:3, 177. [Disyllabic words
with interchangeable word orders in Modern
Chinese.]

張永綿：近代漢語中字序對換的雙音詞

0219 Ch'en, Ai-wen & Yü, P'ing: Ping-lieh shuang-yin-tz'u te tzu-hsü. —— *CKYW* 1979:2, 101–105. [The character order of coordinate disyllabic words.]

陳愛文、于平：並列雙音詞的字序

0220 Ch'i, T'ieh-hen: Fu-yin-tz'u te chan-k'ai ying-yung. ——*Chu-i yü kuo-ts'e* 46, 1955, 26–28. [The development and usage of disyllabic words.]

齊鐵恨：複音詞的展開應用

0221 Ching, Eugene: Four-syllable expressions in Chinese. ——*POLA* 7, 1964, 1–62.

〔荆允敬〕

0222 Ching, Eugene: Dissyllabicity of Modern Mandarin.—— *Chinese Culture* 10:4, 1969, 88–104.

〔荆允敬〕

0223 Ching, Yün-ching: Hsien-tai Han-yü te shuang-yin-chieh-hsing.——*Hua-kang hsüeh-pao* 6, 1970, 21–43. [The disyllabicity of the modern Chinese language.]

荆允敬：現代漢語的雙音節性

0224 Hsia, Mien-tsun: Shuang tzu tz'u-yü te kou-ch'eng fang-shih.—— *KWYK* 41, 1946, 19–21. [The formation patterns of words and phrases with paired characters.]

夏丏尊：雙字詞語的構成方式

0225 Hsü, Shih-jung: Shuang-yin-chui-tz'u te chung-yin kuei-lü.—*CKYW* 1956:2, 35–37. [Accent (stress) rules of disyllabic words.]

徐世榮：雙音綴詞的重音規律

0226 Hsü, Shih-jung: Shuang-yin-chieh-tz'u te yin-liang fen-hsi.——*YCYY* 1982:2, 4–19. [An analysis of the sound volume of disyllabic words.]

徐世榮：雙音節詞的音量分析

0227 Huang, Ch'i: Shuang-yin-chieh tz'u-hsü te tien-tao chi ch'i i-i te ts'e-chung.—*WSC* 1954:5, 46–50. [The reversal of word order in disyllabic words and its emphasis on meaning.]

黃綺：雙音節詞序的顛倒及其意義的側重

0228 I, Hsi-wu: Han-yü chung te shuang-yin-tz'u.—*CKYW* 1954:10, 28–32; 11, 9–12. [Disyllabic words in the Chinese language.]

易熙吾：漢語中的雙音詞

0229 Liu, Ta-wei: Shih lun shuang-yin-tz'u te ch'ung-tieh. —— *SHST* 1979:1, 96–100. [A preliminary discussion on the reduplication of disyllabic words.]

劉大為：試論雙音詞的重疊

0230 Shen, Shih-ying: Tzu-hsü tui-huan te shuang-yin-tz'u hsin t'an.—*AHST* 1979:3, 40–45. [A new investigation into disyllabic words with interchangeable character order.]

沈士英：字序對換的雙音詞新探

0231 Sheng, Yü-tung & Chang, Hung-hung: Kuan-yü Han-yü tz'u-hui shuang-yin-chieh-hua.—*K'a-shih shih-yüan hsüeh-pao* 1980:1, (not seen). [Concerning the disyllabization of Chinese vocabulary.]

盛育冬、張宏洪：關於漢語詞滙雙音節化

0232 Ting, Pang-hsin: Kuo-yü chung shuang-yin-chieh ping-lieh yü liang ch'eng-fen-chien te sheng-tiao kuan-hsi.—*BIHP* 39, 1969, 155–174; E.S. [Tonal relationships between the two constituents of disyllabic coordinate constructions in the National Language.]

丁邦新：國語中雙音節並列語兩成分間的聲調關係

0233 Torii, Hisayasu: San'onsetsu meishi no yomikata.—*CGZS* 4:3, 1944, 15–21. [The method of reading trisyllabic nouns.]

鳥居久靖：三音節名詞の讀み方

0234 T'ung, Hui-chün: Ju-ho pien-hsi t'ung su fan hsü tz'u.—— *YCYY* 1982:2, 82–93, 154. [How to differentiate and analyze words with identical morphemes in reversed order.]

佟慧君：如何辨析同素反序詞

0235   Wang, Li: Fu-yin-tz'u te ch'uang-tsao.
—*KWYK* 40, 1946, 5–9. [The creation
of disyllabic words.]

王力：複音詞的創造

0236   Yin, Meng-lun: Kuan-yü Han-yü fu-
yin-tz'u kou-tz'u hsing-shih erh san li te
shih chieh.—*WSC* 1958:4, 15–19. [A
tentative explanation concerning two or
three examples of word-formation patterns
in Chinese disyllabic words.]

殷孟倫：關於漢語複音詞構詞形式二三例的試
解

2.1.3.4.   Trochaic Word (0237–0253)

0237   Chang, Hsün-ju: *Pei-ching-hua ch'ing-
sheng tz'u-hui.* — Peking: Chung-hua, 1957,
154 p.; *Yü-wen hui-pien* (0058),
14:56./ *CKYW* 1957:12, 47, Ni Chi-yü;
RBS 3, 1957, 590, Paul Kratochvíl;
Orbis 15, 1966, 113, Paul Yang. [A
glossary of neutral-tone words in the
Peking dialect.]

張洵如：北京話輕聲詞滙／倪寄予評

0238   Ch'eng, Jung: Nien ch'ing-sheng te
kuei-lü.—*WTKK* 1951:2, 11–12. [Rules
of reading neutral-tone words.]

承融：念輕聲的規律

0239   Dow, Francis D.M.: *The analysis of
trochaic words of Mandarin Chinese.*—
Canberra: Committee of the Faculty
of Asian Studies, Australian National
University of Canberra, 1971, vi, 58 p.;
Edinburgh: The Author, 1972, 2nd ed.,
[vi], 104 p.

〔竇道明〕

0240   Feng, Ch'uan-huang: *Hua-yü ch'ing-
sheng tz'u-hui.*—Singapore: Nan-yang
ta-hsüeh Hua-yü yen-chiu chung-hsin, 1975,
viii, 38 p. [A glossary of Chinese neutral-
tone words.]

馮傳璜：華語輕聲詞滙

0241   Hayashi, Takuji: Lao She *Lung-hsü kou
chung te san-pai-ko ch'ing-sheng-tz'u.*—
NHDJ 25, 1981, 1–33. [Three hundred
neutral-tone words in Lao She's *Lung-hsü
kou.*]

林卓治：老舍『龍鬚溝』中的三百個輕聲詞

0242   Kao, Ching-ch'eng: Lüeh t'an ju-ho
chang-wo ch'ing-sheng-tz'u.—*WTKK* 1958:
4, 18. [A short discussion on how to
master neutral-tone words.]

高景成：略談如何掌握輕聲詞

0243   Ling, Hsiao-kuang: Ch'ing-sheng-tzu
chü-li.—*CKYT* 44:6, 1979, 29–41; to
be continued. [Examples of neutral-tone
characters.]

靈小光：輕聲字舉例

0244   P'u-t'ung-hua yü-yin yen-chiu pan: *P'u-
t'ung-hua ch'ing-sheng-tz'u hui-pien.*—
Peking: Shang-wu, 1964, 2, 89 p. [A
collection of neutral-tone words in the
Common Language.]

普通話語音研究班：普通話輕聲詞滙編

0245   Torii, Hisayasu & Hiraiwa, Fusajirō:
Jōhō keiseishi ichiranhyō.— *SGK* 8, 1943,
79–115. [A list of commonly used
neutral-tone words.]

鳥居久靖、平巖房次郎：常用輕聲詞一覽表

0246   Torii, Hisayasu: Dō-shokubutsu seiri
keiseishi ichiranhyō.—*SGK* 8, 1943,
116–120. [A list of neutral-tone words
concerning the physiology of fauna and
flora.]

鳥居久靖：動植物生理輕聲詞一覽表

0247   Torii, Hisayasu: *Kokugo jiten* keiseishi
ichiranhyō. — *SGK* 8, 1943, 129–144.
[A list of neutral-tone words (found) in
Kuo-yü tz'u-tien (1357).]

鳥居久靖：『國語辭典』輕聲詞一覽表

0248   Torii, Hisayasu: Keisei no hanashi.—
Zenrin 15:1, 1944, 31–34; 2, 6–10. [A
discussion of the neutral tone.]

鳥居久靖：輕聲の話

0249 Torii, Hisayasu & Chin, Hung-shou: Jōyō keiseishi reikai.—*Zenrin* 16:4, 1945, 53–55; 5, 15–29. [Explanations of commonly used neutral-tone words with examples.]
鳥居久靖、金鴻壽：常用輕聲詞例解

0250 Torii, Hisayasu: Jōyō keisei shii.— *KGKK* 9, 1946, 16–30. [Commonly used neutral-tone vocabulary.]
鳥居久靖：常用輕聲詞彙

0251 Torii, Hisayasu: Keisei yori mitaru genkō jiten.—*CGZS* 3:1, 1948, 23–24; 4:1, 1949, 27–28; 4:4, 12–14. [Current (Chinese) dictionaries as seen from the neutral tone.]
鳥居久靖：輕聲より見たる現行詞典

0252 Torii, Hisayasu: *Kokugo jiten* keisei kankō oboegaki——shohyō ni kaete.— *TRGH* 3:3, 1952, 45–68. [A memorandum on the corrigenda of the neutral-tone (words) in *Kuo-yü tz'u-tien*—instead of a book review.]
鳥居久靖：『國語辭典』輕聲勘校覺え書——書評にかえて

0253 Yeh, Te-ming: *Kuo-yü ch'ing-sheng-tzu tsai yü-fa shang te tso-yung yen-chiu.*— Taipei: K'o-wen, 1973, 201 p. [A study on the grammatical functions of neutral-tone characters in the National Language.]
葉德明：國語輕聲字在語法上的作用研究

2.2. Word Formation in General (0254–0301)
2.2.1. Word Structure (0254–0263)

0254 Chao, Yuen Ren: Rhythm and structure of Chinese words.—*Lg* 22, 1946, 4–13; *Aspects of Chinese sociolinguistics* (0048), 260–274.

0255 Chao, Yuen Ren: Rhythm and structure in Chinese word conceptions.—*Aspects of Chinese sociolinguistics* (0048), 275–292.

0256 Hsü, Pin-pin: *Chung-wen tz'u-hui chieh-kou chung te pa-nan-chu-i.*—Hsinchuang: Fu Jen U., 1976, 5, 131 p./ Unpubl. M.A. thesis. [Male chauvinism in the lexical structure of Chinese.]
許彬彬：中文詞彙結構中的霸男主義

0257 Kao, Pao-t'ai: *Yü-fa hsiu-tz'u liu chiang.* ——Yinchuan: Ning-hsia jen-min, 1981, 5, [ii], 286 p./ Lecture 1: The nature and structure of words. [Six lectures on grammar and rhetoric.]
高葆泰：語法修辭六講／第一講：詞的性質和構造

0258 Li, Charles N. & Thompson, Sandra A.: *Mandarin Chinese: A functional reference grammar.*—— Berkeley, Los Angeles, London: U. of California Press, 1981, xviii, 691 p./ 3: Word structure.

0259 Liu, Eric S.: Mandarin word structure. —*JAOS* 89, 1969, 410–412.

0260 Milsky, Constantin: La structure du mot en chinois.—*CLOS* 11, 1978, 91–115.

0261 Shi, Seikō: Chūgokugo no tango kozō. —*CGGG* 225, 1978, 30–36. [The structure of Chinese words.]
施清香：中國語の單語構造

0262 Ting, Mien-tsai: T'ung-su tz'u te chieh-kou hsing-shih ho i-i te kuan-hsi.—*HSYK* 1957:2, 48–54. [The relationships of the structural patterns and meanings of homomorphemic words.]
丁勉哉：同素詞的結構形式和意義的關係

0263 ·Weingartner, Friedrich F.: *Die Struktur des chinesischen Wortes.*—Hamburg: Meggenhofen, 1965, v, 202 p.

2.2.2. Morpheme and Morphology (0264–0275)

0264 Chmielewski, Janusz. Transl. by Ning, Ch'ü: Han-yü te chü-fa ho hsing-t'ai wen-t'i. —*CKYW* 1954:12, 7–11. [The problem of syntax and morphology in Chinese.]/ Later published as (0265).

赫邁萊夫斯基著，寗架譯：漢語的句法和形態問題

0265 Chmielewski, Janusz: The problem of syntax and morphology in Chinese. — *RO* 21, 1959, 71–84./ *RBS* 3, 1957, 584, A. Rygaloff.

0266 Kratochvíl, Paul: *The Chinese language today.* ——London: Hutchinson U. Library, 1968, 199 p., map./ III. Morphology; 89–99: Words; *Lg* 45, 1969, 423–439, Sandra A. Thompson.
〔現代漢語〕

0267 Liu, Han-ch'eng: Tan-yin-tz'u — tzu-yu shih ho nien-cho-shih.——*LCTH* 1982:3, 145– (not seen). [Monosyllabic words — free forms and bound forms.]
劉漢城：單音詞：自由式和黏着式

0268 Lü, Shu-hsiang: Shuo tzu-yu ho nien-cho. —*CKYW* 1962:1, 1–6./ *RBS* 8, 1962, 489, S.N. Cartier. [On 'free' and 'bound' (morphemes).]
呂叔湘：說『自由』和『黏着』

0269 Matsumoto, Akira: Gendai Chūgokugo ni sonzaisuru replacive morpheme no ichirei. —*CGGG* 1955:10, 3–16. [An example of the existence of the replacive morpheme in Modern Chinese.]
松本昭：現代中國語に存在する replacive morphemeの一例

0270 Mastumoto, Akira: Chūgokugo keitaiso no katachi oyobi imi ni kansuru kōsatsu. —*KKR* 13, 1968, 1–13. [An inquiry concerning the forms and meanings of Chinese morphemes.]
松本昭：中國語形態素の形及び意味に關する考察

0271 Mochizuki, Yasokichi: Chūgokugo no gokei henka.——*JBK* 12:9, 1961, 23–33./ *RBS* 7, 1961, 450, S.N. Cartier. [Morphological changes of the Chinese language.]
望月八十吉：中國語の語形變化

0272 Mochizuki, Yasokichi: Chūgokugo no keitaiso.——*JBK* 17:4, 1966, 21–33./ *RBS* 12–13, 1980, 637, Kawaguchi Junji. [Chinese morphemes.]
望月八十吉：中國語の形態素

0273 Ōkōchi, Yasunori: Morpheme ni tsuite. —*CGGG* 1964:2, 1–17. [On the morpheme (in Chinese).]/ A problem in structuralism.
大河內康憲：Morpheme について

0274 Solnceva, Nina V.: Gendai Chūgokugo no keitairon no mondai.——*CAAAL* 10, 1979, 11–13. [Problems of the morphology in Modern Chinese.]
Solnceva, Nina V.：現代中國語の形態論の問題

0275 Yamagishi, Tomoni: Keitai o shutoshite mita Chūgokugo bunpō. — *CGKR* 1, 1953, 95–106. [Chinese grammar as seen mainly from (its) morphology.]
山岸共：形態を主として見た中國語文法

2.2.3. Problems of Word Formation (0276–0301)

0276 Chang, Chih-kung (ed. in chief): *Yü-fa ho yü-fa chiao-hsüeh.* —— Peking: Jen-min chiao-yü, 1956, 324 p. [Grammar and the teaching of grammar.]/ Collected essays by different authors.
張志公主編：語法和語法教學

0277 Chang, Shou-k'ang: Kuan-yü Han-yü kou-tz'u-fa.——*Yü-fa ho yü-fa chiao-hsüeh* (0276), 90–113. [Concerning the methods of Chinese word formation.]/ See (0295)
張壽康：關於漢語構詞法

0278 Chang, Shou-k'ang: Lüeh lun Han-yü kou-tz'u-fa.——*CKYW* 1957:6, 1–8; *Hsien-tai Han-yü . . . tzu-liao* (0064), 241–256. [A brief discussion on the methods of Chinese word formation.]
張壽康：略論漢語構詞法

0279 Chang, Shou-k'ang: *Kou-tz'u-fa ho kou-hsing-fa.*——Wuhan: Hu-pei jen-min, 1981, 96 p. [Methods of word formation and

'form formation'.]
張壽康：構詞法和構形法

0280 Chmielewski, Janusz: Syntactic relations and word-formation in Chinese. — *PICO* 25, 1960, vol. 5, 124–127.

0281 Chmielewski, Janusz: Syntax and word-formation in Chinese.——*RO* 28, 1964, 107–125./ A reply to Lu Chih-wei's criticism (0290); *RBS* 10, 1964, 504, S.N. Cartier.

0282 Hsüeh, Hsiao-hsiang: Kuan-yü Han-yü tz'u-fa.——*WSC* 1955:1, 37–41. [Concerning Chinese word formation.]
薛曉蕱：關於漢語詞法

0283 Hung, Yüan: Tz'u ho tz'u te kou-ch'eng pien-hua.——*CSCY* 1959:20, 16–18. [Words and the formation and development of words.]
洪元：詞和詞的構成變化

0284 Kao, Ming-k'ai: *P'u-t'ung yü-yen-hsüeh* (0421), Pt. 4, Chap. 6: Methods of word formation. [General linguistics.]
高名凱：普通語言學／第四編，第六章：構詞法

0285 Ko, Hsin-i: Han-yü kou-tz'u te t'e-tien ho fang-fa.—— *YCYY* 1979:2, 30–40. [Special features and methods of word formation in Chinese.]
葛信益：漢語構詞的特點和方法

0286 Li, Chin-hsi: Chung-kuo yü-fa chung te tz'u-fa yen-t'ao.——*CKYW* 1953:9, 8–13. [A discussion on the methods of word formation in Chinese grammar.]
黎錦熙：中國語法中的詞法研討

0287 Li, Hsing-chien: Han-yü kou-tz'u-fa yen-chiu chung te i-ko wen-t'i.——*YWYC* 1982:2, 61–68. [A problem in the study of the methods of Chinese word formation.]
李行健：漢語構詞法研究中的一個問題

0288 Lien, Chin-fa: T'an yü-tz'u te kou-ch'eng.——*Szu yü yen* 13:6, 1976, 40–44. [A discussion on the formation of phrases and words.]
連金發：談語詞的構成

0289 Lin, Yü-wen: Kou-tz'u-fa.——*YWCS* 1955:1, 9–12; 2, 26–29. [Methods of word formation.]
林裕文：構詞法

0290 Lu, Chih-wei: Kuan-yü Ho-mai-lai-fu-szu-chi hsien-sheng te "Han-yü te chü-fa ho hsing-t'ai wen-t'i".——*CKYW* 1955:3, 22–24. [Concerning Mr. Chmielewski's "The problem of syntax and morphology in Chinese" (0265).]
陸志韋：關於赫邁萊夫斯基先生的『漢語的句法和形態問題』

0291 Lu, Chih-wei: Kou-tz'u-hsüeh te tui-hsiang ho shou-hsü.——*CKYW* 1956:12, 3–11; *Hsien-tai Han-yü . . . tzu-liao* (0064), 223–240. [The objectives and procedures for the study of word formation.]
陸志韋：構詞學的對象和手續

0292 Mo, Ju-pan & Chang, Shih-lu: Tz'u te kou-ch'eng ho tz'u-hui te kou-ch'eng. — *YWCS* 1957:3, 49–51. [The formation of words and the formation of lexicon.]
莫如邦、張世祿：詞的構成和詞滙的構成

0293 Sun, Liang-ming: Han-yü kou-tz'u-fa chung te chi-ko li-lun wen-t'i.——*STSY* 1959:1, 54–66. [Several theoretical problems in the methods of word formation of the Chinese language.]
孫良明：漢語構詞法中的幾個理論問題

0294 Sun, Liang-ming: Han-yü tz'u-fa yen-chiu te chi-ko wen-t'i.——*JWTC* 1959:5, 44–51. [Several problems of the study of Chinese morphology.]
孫良明：漢語詞法研究的幾個問題

0295 T'ang, Chün-li & Miao, Shu-ch'eng: Tui *Kuan-yü Han-yü kou-tz'u-fa* te chi-tien i-chien.——*CKYW* 1957:6, 13. [Several opinions concerning *Kuan-yü Han-yü kou-tz'u-fa.*] / A deliberation with Chang Shou-k'ang (0277).

唐君勵、繆樹晟：對『關於漢語構詞法』的幾點意見

0296 T'ang, T'ing-ch'ih: Hua-yü te tz'u-hui chieh-kou yü kou-tz'u kuei-lü.——*HWSC* 25, 1981, 42–47; 26, 1982, 19–28; 27, 1982, 69–71. [The lexical structure and rules for word formation in Chinese.]

湯廷池：華語的詞彙結構與構詞規律

0297 T'ang, T'ing-ch'ih: Kuo-yü tz'u-hui-hsüeh tao-lun——Tz'u-hui chieh-kou yü kou-tz'u kuei-lü.—— *Chiao-hsüeh yü yen-chiu* 4, 1982, 39–57. [An introduction to Chinese lexicology——Lexical structure and rules for word formation.]

湯廷池：國語詞彙學導論——詞彙結構與構詞規律

0298 Ts'en, Ch'i-hsiang: Kuan-yü Han-yü kou-tz'u-fa te chi-ko wen-t'i.——*CKYW* 1956:12, 12–14. [Several problems concerning methods of word formation in Chinese.]

岑麒祥：關於漢語構詞法的幾個問題

0299 Ts'en, Ch'i-hsiang: Kuan-yü kou-tz'u-fa wen-t'i te i-hsieh i-chien.——*CKYW* 1964:4, 176–177. [Some opinions concerning the problems in the methods of word formation.]

岑麒祥：關於構詞法問題的一些意見

0300 Ts'ui, Po-fu: Kuan-yü Han-yü kou-tz'u-fa.——*WSC* 1958:5, 62–64. [Concerning the methods of word formation in Chinese.]

崔伯阜：關於漢語構詞法

0301 Wang, Fu-ch'üan: Tz'u-erh kou-ch'eng ti fen-hsi. —— *Chung-shan wen-hua chiao-yü-kuan chi-k'an* 3:4, 1936, 1419–1436. [An analysis of the formation of words.]

汪馥泉：詞兒構成底分析

2.3. Methods of Word Formation (0302–0414)

2.3.1. General Studies (0302–0315)

0302 Fang, Shih-to: *Kuo-yü tz'u-hui-hsüeh: Kou-tz'u p'ien.*——Taipei: I-chih shu-chü, 1970, 8, 223 p. [Lexicology of the National Language: Section on word formation.]

方師鐸：國語詞彙學：構詞篇

0303 Feng, Ch'ang-ch'ing: *Kuo-yü kou-tz'u.*——Taipei: Kuo-yü jih-pao-she, 1962, 2, 2, 123 p. [Word formation in the National Language.]

馮常青：國語構詞

0304 Fu, Hsing-ling & Ch'en, Chang-huan (eds. in chief): *Ch'ang-yung kou-tz'u tzu-tien.*—Peking: Chung-kuo jen-min ta-hsüeh, 1982, 42, 531 p. [A dictionary of commonly used word formations.]

傅興嶺、陳章煥主編：常用構詞字典

0305 Hsu, Po-wen: Mo-chuang te hsing-jung-tz'u ho ming-tz'u—Han-yü te i-chung kou-tz'u fang-shih.—*YWHH* 1954:10, 73–75. [Adjectives and nouns depicting state—A pattern of word formation in Chinese.]

許博文：摹狀的形容詞和名詞——漢語的一種構詞方式

0306 Huang, Yüeh-chou: Hsien-tai Han-yü hsü-tz'u te kou-ch'eng fang-shih.——*YWCS* 1957:6, 16–20. [The word formation patterns of Modern Chinese cenematic words.]

黃岳洲：現代漢語虛詞的構成方式

0307 Jen, Hsüeh-liang: *Han-yü tsao-tz'u-fa.*——Peking: Chung-kuo she-hui k'o-hsüeh, 1981, [3], 2, 289 p. [Methods of word formation in Chinese.]

任學良：漢語造詞法

0308 Karlgren, B.: *Sound and symbol in Chinese.* —— London: Oxford U. Press, 1923, 112 p.; Hong Kong: Hong Kong U. Press, rev. ed., 1962, 99 p./ 3: Methods of word formation; *Lg* 40, 1964, 102–108, Roy A. Miller.

0309 Karlgren, B. Transl. by Chang, Shih-lu: *Chung-kuo-yü yü Chung-kuo-wen.*—Shanghai: Shang-wu, 1931, 150 p.; Taipei: Wen-hsing, 1965, repr., 2 vols./ 3: Methods of word formation. [Sound and symbol in Chinese.] (0308)

高本漢著，張世祿譯：中國語與中國文／第三章：構詞法

0310 Liu, Ling: Hsien-tai Han-yü kou-tz'u-fa. —*Han-yü lun-ts'ung* (0087), 106–131. [Methods of word formation in Modern Chinese.]

劉伶：現代漢語構詞法

0311 Lu, Chih-wei: *Han-yü te kou-tz'u-fa.*—Peking: K'o-hsüeh, 1957, 4, 2, 155 p.; 1964, rev. ed., vi, 148 p.; Hong Kong: Chung-hua, 1975, repr., vi, 133 p./ *RBS* 3, 1957, 589, I.M. Oshanin. [Methods of word formation in Chinese.]

陸志韋：漢語的構詞法

0312 Ma, Sung-t'ing: *Han-yü yü-fa hsiu-tz'u.*—Chinan: Shan-tung jen-min, 1981, 2, 6, 305 p./ (Section on) Chinese grammar, 3: Methods of word formation; 4: Methods of form formation. [Chinese grammar and rhetoric.]

馬松亭：漢語語法修辭／漢語語法第三節：構詞法；第四節：構形法

0313 Sun, Ch'ang-hsu: *Han-yü tz'u-hui* (0165), Pt. I, Chap. 3: Methods of word formation. [Chinese lexicon.]

孫常叙：漢語詞彙／第一部分，第三篇：造詞法

0314 Ting, Sheng-shu, et al.: *Hsien-tai Han-yu yü-fa chiang-hua.*—Peking: Shang-wu, 1963, x, 228, p.; *Yü-wen hui-pien* (0058), 12:48; Chap. 20: Methods of word formation./ *CKYW* 1962:6, 279–284, Lü Chi-p'ing; *CGGG* 1963:9–10, 2–3, Torii Katsuyuki; *RBS* 9, 1963, 506, S.N. Cartier. [Lectures on the grammar of Modern Chinese.]

丁聲樹等：現代漢語語法講話／第二十章：構詞法；呂冀平評，鳥居克之評

0315 Ts'ui, Fu-yüan: *Hsien-tai Han-yü kou-tz'u-fa li-chieh.*—Chinan: Shan-tung jen-min, 1957, [vi], 74 p.; *Yü-wen hui-pien* (0058), 42:137./ *CKYW* 1958:3, 144, Liu K'ai-ming. [Modern Chinese methods of word formation explained with examples.]

崔復爰：現代漢語構詞法例解／劉凱鳴評

2.3.2. Affixation (0316–0346)
2.3.2.1. Affixation in General (0316–0319)

0316 Chang, Ching: Hsien-tai Han-yü te tz'u-ken ho fu-chia ch'eng-fen.—*YLT* 4, 1960, 211–224. [Word roots and affixes in Modern Chinese.]

張靜：現代漢語的詞根和附加成分

0317 Heřmanová-Novotná, Zdeňka: *Affix-like word-formation patterns in Modern Chinese.*—Prague: Academia Publishing House, Czechoslovak Academy of Sciences, 1969, 225, 3 p./ *AM* 17, 1971, 99–101, Paul Kratochvíl.

0318 Peng, Fred C.C.: On the concept of affixes in Standard Chinese.——*AO* 34, 1966, 73–79.

0319 Sun, Ch'ang-hsü: *Han-yü tz'u-hui* (0165), Chap. 11.2: Word formation by affixation. [Chinese lexicon.]

孫常叙：漢語詞彙／第十一章，第二節：附綴造詞

2.3.2.2. Prefixation (0320–0321)

0320 Chao, Yuen Ren: *A grammar of spoken Chinese* (0142), 4.3: Prefixes.

趙元任：中國話的文法／4.3: 詞頭

0321 Jen, Hsüeh-liang: *Han-yü tsao tz'u-fa* (0307), 31–51: Prefixes. [Methods of word formation in Chinese.]

任學良：漢語造詞法／31—51：加詞頭

2.3.2.3. Suffixation (0322–0338)

0322 Chang, Hsün-ju: Yü-wei tzu tzu yung-fa

tiao-ch'a.——*KWYK* 65, 1948, 11–14, 17; *Chung-kuo yü-wen . . . hsüan-chi* (0079), 132–147. [A survey of the methods of using the character -*tzu* as a suffix.]

張洵如：語尾『子』字用法調查

0323　Chao, Yuen Ren: *A grammar of spoken Chinese* (0142), 4.4: Suffixes.

趙元任：中國話的文法／4. 4: 詞尾

0324　Fang, Shih-to: Hou-chui ch'ing-sheng tzu-wei te ho-ch'eng-tz'u.——*CKYT* 20:2, 1967, 41–45; 3, 42–43. [Compound words with the neutral tone -*tzu* suffix.]

方師鐸：後綴輕聲『子』尾的合成詞

0325　Fang, Shih-to: Hou-chui t'ou tz'u-wei huo t'ou-erh tz'u-wei te ho-ch'eng-tz'u.—— *CKYT* 20:5, 1967, 54–59. [Compound words with the suffix -*t'ou* or the suffix -*t'ou-erh.*]

方師鐸：後綴『頭』詞尾或『頭兒』詞尾的合成詞

0326　Fang, Shih-to: Chen tz'u-wei ho chia tz'u-wei te fen-chieh hsien.—— *CKYT* 20:6, 1967, 54–58; 21:1, 1967, 64–70; 2, 40–44. [The line of demarcation between 'real' suffixes and 'false' suffixes.]

方師鐸：眞詞尾和假詞尾的分界線

0327　Hsing, Kung-wan: Hsien-tai Han-yü hsing-jung-tz'u hou-fu tzu t'an yüan.—— *NKHP* 1981:1, 36–43. [Tracing the origins of adjectival suffixes in Modern Chinese.]

邢公畹：現代漢語形容詞後附字探源

0328　Jen, Hsüeh-liang: *Han-yü tsao-tz'u-fa* (0307), 51–102: Suffixes. [Methods of word formation in Chinese.]

任學良：漢語造詞法／51–102：加詞尾

0329　Lu, Chih-wei: *Han-yü te kou-tz'u fa* (0311), Chap. 20: Suffixes. [Methods of word formation in Chinese.]

陸志韋：漢語的構詞法／第二十章：後置成分

0330　Lu, Tzu-jan: Fu-chia tzu te yen-chiu.

——*KYYK* 1:11, 1922, 1–8. [A study of appended characters.]/ i.e. suffixes, etc.

盧自然：附加字的研究

0331　Ma, K'o-ch'ien: Tieh-tzu tz'u-wei ch'u-pu yen-chiu. —— *CKYW* 1957:10, 44–46, 43. [A preliminary study of suffixes in reduplicatives.]

馬克前：疊字詞尾初步研究

0332　Mochizuki, Yasokichi: Gendai Kango no keitaiteki kōsatsu.——*JBK* 11:10, 1960, 21–36./ *RBS* 6, 1960, 400, S.N. Cartier. [An inquiry of Modern Chinese morphology.]/ Suffixes.

望月八十吉：現代漢語の態的考察

0333　Mou, Kou-yüan: Tzu tzu tz'u-wei t'an yüan.——*CWY* 8, 1980, 94–104. [Tracing the origins of the character *tzu* as a suffix.]

牟枸垣：『子』字詞尾探源

0334　Mu, Tun-mo: T'ou tzu tz'u-ch'ün te yü-i fen-hsi.——*CWY* 8, 1980, 53–75. [Semantic analysis of word groups with the character *t'ou* as a suffix.]

穆敦謨：『頭』字詞羣的語義分析

0335　Nai, Fan: Yü ho yü-wei te kou-ch'eng. —*CKYW* 4, 1940, 85–88. [The formation of words and suffixes.]

耐煩：語和語尾的構成

0336　Rygaloff, A.: Note sur le suffixe *zi* 子 en Chinois moderne.——*MS* 26, 1967, 97–102.

0337　Torii, Hisayasu: Chūgokugo goshi no kōsei — *shou* no yōhō ni tsuite.——*Shin Chūka* 1:5, 1946, 18–19; *CGZS* 2:1, 1947, 22–23. [The formation of words in the Chinese language—on the uses of *shou.*]

鳥居久靖：中國語語詞の構成——『手』の用法について

0338　Torii, Hisayasu: T'ou no yōhō — Chūgokugo goshi no kōsei.—— *CGZS* 2:2, 1947, 19–21; 3, 21–23; 4, 20–21. [The uses of *t'ou* —— the formation of words in the Chinese language.]

鳥居久靖：『頭』の用法——中國語語詞の構成

2.3.2.4. Erization (0339–0346)

0339   Chang, Hsün-ju: Kuo-yü li chüan-she-yün chih kung-yung.——*KWYK* 54, 1947, 12–16, 30; *Chung-kuo yü-wen . . . hsüan chi* (0079), 7–20. [Functions of the retroflex final (*-erh*) in the National Language.]

張洵如：國語裏捲舌韻之功用

0340   Chao, Yuen Ren: *A grammar of spoken Chinese* (0142), 4.4.4: Noun suffixes *-l, -tz*, etc.

趙元任：中國話的文法／4. 4. 4: 名詞詞尾兒、子等

0341   Dragunov, A.A.: The categories of dependent and independent subject in contemporary spoken Chinese (the suffixes *-er* and *-dz*).——*SV* 6, 1949, 102–109.

0342   Fang, Shih-to: Ch'ing-sheng tzu-wei yü erh-hua tz'u-wei te ts'o-tsung kuan-hsi.——*CKYT* 20:4, 1967, 51–54. [The complex relationship between the neutral-tone *-tzu* suffix and the *-erh* suffix.]

方師鐸：輕聲『子』尾與『兒化』詞尾的錯綜關係

0343   Hsü, Shih-jung: Erh-hua yün te chi-pen pien-hua kuei-lü.——*YWHH* 1960:1, 18, 12. [Rules for the basic changes in erization.]

徐世榮：兒化韻的基本變化規律

0344   Sun, Ch'ang-hsü: *Han-yü tz'u-hui* (0165), Chap. 11.2.4.: A short history of suffix *-erh* and its functions. [Chinese lexicon.]

孫常叙：漢語詞彙／第十一章，第二節，肆：後綴『兒』的略史跟它的作用

0345   T'ao, Yin-p'ei and Yin, Jun-hsiang: Lüeh t'an erh-hua.——*YWHH* 1957:10, 31–32. [A short dicussion of erization.]

陶蔭培、尹潤蘚：略談兒化

0346   Tiee, Henry Hung-yeh: *The function of the retroflex suffix -r in the morphological process of Mandarin Chinese.*—— Washington, D.C.: U.S. Department of Health, Education and Welfare, 1970, 9 p.

2.3.3.   Compounding (0347–0380)

0347   Chang, Kung-kuei: Liang-chung hsin chieh-kou te fu-ho-tz'u.——*YWHH* 1954:6, 58–60, 80. [Two types of compound words with new constructions.]

張拱貴：兩種新結構的複合詞

0348   Chao, Yuen Ren: *A grammar of spoken Chinese* (0142), Chap. 6: Compounds.

趙元任：中國話的文法／第六章：複合詞

0349   Fang, Shih-to: Ho-ch'eng-tz'u ho tz'u-tsu te fen-pieh.——*CKYT* 17:4, 1965, 94–98. [The differences between compound words and phrases.]

方師鐸：合成詞和詞組的分別

0350   Fang, Shih-to: Cheng-ch'ang chieh-kou te fu-ho-shih ho-ch'eng-tz'u.——*CKYT* 17:6, 1965, 52–56; 18:1, 1966, 47–52; 2, 51–57. [Disyllabic pattern compound words with normal constructions.]

方師鐸：正常結構的複合式合成詞

0351   Fang, Shih-to: Fei cheng-ch'ang chieh-kou te fu-ho-shih ho-ch'eng-tz'u.—— *CKYT* 18:3, 1966, 43–49. [Disyllabic pattern compound words with abnormal constructions.]

方師鐸：非正常結構的複合式合成詞

0352   Fang, Shih-to: To-yin-chieh te fu-ho-shih ho-ch'eng-tz'u.——*CKYT* 18:4, 1966, 49–56. [Polysyllabic pattern compound words.]

方師鐸：多音節的複合式合成詞

0353   Fang, Shih-to: Ho-ch'eng-tz'u te fu-chia-shih. ——*CKYT* 19:5, 1966, 60–65. [The affixational patterns of compound words.]

方師鐸：合成詞的附加式

0354 Fang, Shih-to: Tsen-yang pien-pieh tz'u-tsu ho ho-ch'eng-tz'u.—*CKYT* 21:4, 1967, 9–14. [How to differentiate between phrases and compound words.]
方師鐸：怎樣辨別詞組和合成詞

0355 Fang, Shih-to: P'ien-cheng tsu-ho te tz'u-tsu.——*CKYT* 21:6, 1967, 52–60. [Phrases (made) of subordinate compounding.]
方師鐸：偏正組合的詞組

0356 Fang, Shih-to: Chu-shu tsu-ho te tz'u-tsu. —*CKYT* 22:3, 1968, 25–28. [Phrases (made) of subject-predicate compounding.]
方師鐸：主述組合的詞組

0357 Fang, Shih-to: Tung-pin tsu-ho te tz'u-tsu.——*CKYT* 22:4, 1968, 10–12; 5, 15–18. [Phrases (made) of verb-object compounding.]
方師鐸：動賓組合的詞組

0358 Heřmanová-Novotná, Zdeňka: Morphemic reproductions of foreign lexical models in Modern Chinese.——*AO* 43:2, 1975, 146–171.

0359 Ho, Chung-chieh: Tui-ch'en tz'u—Fu-ho-tz'u te i-chung kou-ch'eng fang-shih.——*YWHH* 1954:5, 61–64. [Symmetric words—A formation pattern of compound words.]
何鍾杰：對襯詞——複合詞的一種構成方式

0360 Hu, Che-ch'i: Lüeh t'an fu-tz'u.—*CKYT* 47:1, 1980, 29–34. [A short discussion on compound words.]
胡哲齊：略談複詞

0361 Huang, Yüeh-chou: Lun lien-ho-shih ho-ch'eng-tz'u kou-ch'eng te chung-chung fang-shih.——*YWCS* 1957:11, 21–25. [On various patterns for the formation of coordinate pattern compound words.]
黃岳洲：論聯合式合成詞構成的種種方式

0362 Kennedy, George A.: The butterfly case (Part I). —— *Wennti* 8, 1955, 1–47; *Selected works of George A. Kennedy* (0070), 274–322./ Synonym compounds, fragmentation, noun-suffixes, philosophic viscounts.

0363 Kuo, Jung-i: *Verb-object compounds in Spoken II Chinese.*——Taipei: Shih-fan ta-hsüeh, 1977, 3, 83 p./ Unpubl. M.A. thesis.
〔郭榮一〕

0364 Li, Chin-hsi: Fu-ho-tz'u kou-ch'eng fang-shih chien p'u.——*Kuo-yü hsün-k'an* 1:12, 1929, 147–150; *Hsi-pei shih-fan hsüeh-yüan hsüeh-shu chi-k'an* 2, 1946, 5–9. [A simplified chart of the formation patterns for compound words.]
黎錦熙：複合詞構成方式簡譜

0365 Li, Chin-hsi: Han-yü fu-ho-tz'u kou-ch'eng fang-shih chien p'u.——*PCST* 1962:3, 49–56. [A simplified chart of the formation patterns for compound words in Chinese.]
黎錦熙：漢語複合詞構成方式簡譜

0366 Li, Meng-chen: *Compound verbs in spoken Chinese.*——Taipei: Shih-fan ta-hsüeh, 1977, 3, 102 p./ Unpubl. M.A. thesis.
〔李孟珍〕

0367 Li-Reichardt, Shuxin: *Zweisilbige "Adjektiv-Verb"-Kombinationen im modernen Chinesischen. Ein Beitrag zum Wort-problem.*——Leipzig: Leipzig U., 1971, iii, 200 p./ Unpubl. doc. diss.

0368 Liang, Ming: P'ai-sheng-tz'u, fu-ho-tz'u ho ho-ch'eng-tz'u.—*YYWH* 1960:3, 25–26. [Derivative words, compound words, and combined words.]
艮明：派生詞、複合詞和合成詞

0369 Lu, Chih-wei: Han-yü te ping-li szu-tzu ko.—*YYYC* 1, 1956, 45–82./ *RBS* 2, 1956, 382, A. Rygaloff. [Four-syllable

coordinate patterns of Chinese.]
陸志韋：漢語的並立四字格

0370   Mao, Hsi-p'ang: Kuan-yü tzu-hsü k'o-i tien-tao te tz'u.——*YWCS* 1956:7, 28–29. [Concerning words of which the order of characters may be reversible.]
毛西旁：關於字序可以顛倒的詞

0371   Meng, Hsiang: Tz'u te ping-lieh chieh-kou yü ku-i.——*CKYW* 1966:2, 150–151. [The coordinate structures of words and (their) ancient meanings.]
夢湘：詞的並列結構與古義

0372   Nakagawa, Tōshi: Atarashii rengo ni tsuite.——*CGGG* 1959:11, 5–20. [On new compound words (in Chinese).]
中川登史：新しい連語について

0373   Ni, Chih-hsien: Fu-tz'u kou-ch'eng te chi-chung hsing-shih.——*T'ai-wan chiao-yü fu-tao yüeh-k'an* 6:1, 1956, 15–19. [Several formation patterns of disyllabic word structures.]
倪志僴：複詞構成的幾種形式

0374   Rogachev, A.P.: Idiomatika kitaiskogo yazyka, otobrazhennaya v ustoichivykh slovosochetapiyakh (chen-yui.).——*KSIV* 2, 1952, 52–56. [Notes on the *ch'eng-yü* 〔成語〕 type of compound.]

0375   Shen, Chün: Shuo ho-ch'eng yü.——*CKYW* 8, 1940, 120. [On compound words.]
沈浚：說合成語

0376   Spies, Gottfried: Semantische Aspekte der Kombination synonymer Morpheme in der Wortbildung der chinesischen Gegenwartsprache.——*Zphon* 32:6, 1979, 710–715.

0377   Sui, Shu-hua, et al: Tz'u-su hsiang-t'ung, tz'u-hsü pu-t'ung te ho-ch'eng-tz'u.——*YWHH* 1956:5, 31–33. [Compound words with identical morphemes but different word order.]

隋樹華等：詞素相同，詞序不同的合成詞

0378   Sun, Ch'ang-hsü: *Han-yü tz'u-hui* (0165), Chap. 10: Methods of structural word formation. [Chinese lexicon.]
孫常叙：漢語詞彙／第十章：結構造詞方法

0379   Wen, Chin: Chu-wei shih ho-ch'eng-tz'u ho chu-wei chien-kou te ch'ü-pieh.——*YWCS* 1958:5, 22–25. [The differences between subject-predicate pattern compound words and subject-predicate constructions.]
文金：主謂式合成詞和主謂結構的區別

0380   Wu, Ching-ts'un: Lun hsiang-hsin shih ——Hsien-tai Han-yü kou-tz'u-fa yen-chiu. ——*YLT* 1, 1957, 130–148.[On endocentric forms——A study on the methods of word formation in Modern Chinese.]
吳競存：論向心式——現代漢語構詞法研究

2.3.4. Reduplication (0381–0399)

0381   Chang, Hsün-ju: Kuo-yü ch'ung-tieh-tz'u chih tiao-ch'a.——*KWYK* 67, 1948, 11–19, 4; *Chung-kuo yü-wen . . . hsüan-chi* (0079), 105–113. [A survey of reduplicatives in the National Language.]
張洵如：國語重疊詞之調查

0382   Chao, Yuen Ren: *A grammar of spoken Chinese* (0142), 4.2: Reduplication.
趙元任：中國話的文法／4.2: 重疊

0383   Chen, Fu: Tzu te fu-tieh ho lien-mien. ——*CHS* 185, 1947, 36–37. [The reduplication and correlation of words.]
振甫：詞的複疊和聯綿

0384   Ching, Eugene: Reduplication in Chinese. ——*PCIC* 1964, 91–100.

0385   Fang, Shih-to: Ho-ch'eng-tz'u te ch'ung-tieh shih.——*CKYT* 18:5, 1966, 53–58. [The reduplicative patterns of compound words.]
方師鐸：合成詞的重疊式

0386   Fang, Shih-to: Tung-tz'u te ch'ung-tieh shih.——*CKYT* 19:1, 1966, 53–59. [The reduplicative patterns of verbs.]

方師鐸：動詞的重疊式

0387　Fang, Shih-to: Hsing-jung-hsing yü-tz'u te ch'ung-tieh shih.——*CKYT* 19:2, 1966, 36–39; 3, 53–57; 4, 60–64. [The reduplicative patterns of adjectival words and phrases.]

方師鐸：形容性語詞的重疊式

0388　Heroldová, Dana: *Lexikální jednotky typu ABB v moderní čínštině.* —— Prague: Orientální ústavu Čekoslovenské akademie věd, 1969, 296 p./ Unpubl. doc. diss. [Lexical units of the type ABB in Modern Chinese.]

0389　Hsü, Jen-fu: Han-yü ch'ung-tieh-tz'u te hsing-shih. —— *CKYW* 1954:8, 10. [The forms of Chinese reduplicatives.]

徐仁甫：漢語重疊詞的形式

0390　Hu, Hsing-chih: Tieh-tzu te tsung-ho yen-chiu.——*CKYW* 1957:11, 26–28, 32. [A general study of reduplicated characters.]

胡行之：疊字的綜合研究

0391　Jen, Hsüeh-liang: *Han-yü tsao-tz'u-fa* (0307), 105–122: Reduplicative patterns. [Methods of word formation in Chinese.]

任學良：漢語造詞法／105－122：重疊式

0392　Kōsaka, Jun'ichi: Shi no kasane-kata. —*CGKS* 3, 1960, 54–68. [The reduplicative patterns of words (in Chinese).]

香坂順一：詞のかさね型

0393　Kuo, Nai-ts'en: Jen-min huo yü-yen chung te ch'ung-tieh-tz'u.—*CKYW* 1953:12, 34. [Reduplicatives in the living language of the people.]

郭乃岑：人民活語言中的重疊詞

0394　Liu, Ta-wei: Shih lun shuang-yin-tz'u te ch'ung-tieh (0229). [A preliminary discussion on the reduplication of disyllabic words.]

劉大爲：試論雙音詞的重疊

0395　Lu, Chih-wei: *Han-yü te kou-tz'u-fa* (0311), Chap. 18: Reduplicative patterns; Chap. 19: Coordinate and reduplicative patterns.

陸志韋：漢語的構詞法／第十八章：重疊格；
第十九章：並列又重疊的格式

0396　Morikawa, Kyūjirō: Chūgokugo no chōjō keishiki ni tsuite.——*TYDB* 5, 1966, 19–50. [On the reduplicative patterns of Chinese.]

森川久次郎：中國語の重疊形式について

0397　Ōkōchi, Yasunori: Chōjō keishiki to hikyōsei rengō kōzō. —— *OGDG* 21, 1969, 41–58. [Reduplicative patterns and coordinative constructions of a comparative nature.]

大河內康憲：重疊形式と比況性連合構造

0398　Sun, Ch'ang-hsü: *Han-yü tz'u-hui* (0165), Chap. 10.2.3: Word formation by reduplication. [Chinese lexicon.]

孫常叙：漢語詞彙／第十章，第二節，叁：重疊造詞

0399　T'ang, T'ing-ch'ih: Kuo-yü hsing-jung-tz'u te ch'ung-tieh kuei-lü.——*STHP* 27, 1982, 279–294, E.S. [Rules for the reduplication of Chinese adjectives.]

湯廷池：國語形容詞的重疊規律

2.3.5. Abbreviation (0400–0406)

0400　Ch'en, Chien-min: Hsien-tai Han-yü li te chien-ch'eng (Fu lun t'ung-ch'eng ho tz'u-yü te chien-so). ——*CKYW* 1963:4, 291–298./ *RBS* 9, 1963, 538, Cheng Chi-hsien. [Abbreviations in the modern Chinese language (With an additional discussion on generalized terms and the contraction of words and phrases).]

陳建民：現代漢語裏的簡稱（附論統稱和詞語的減縮）

0401　Ch'eng, Tseng-hou: Lueh t'an Han-yü p'in-yin chien-ch'eng. —— *NCTH* 1982:2, 39–40. [A short discusssion on Chinese Pinyin abbreviations.]

程曾厚：略談漢語拼音簡稱

0402   Huang, Shan: Yü-tz'u te chien-so.—
CKYT 33:6, 1973, 83—85. [The contraction
of words and phrases.]
黃山：語詞的簡縮

0403   P'u, K'an & Wei, Ch'un: T'an tz'u-yü
te chien-so.——*CCTH* 1979:2, 65—67.
[A discussion on the contraction of words
and phrases.]
濮侃、蔚羣：談詞語的簡縮

0404   Tsou, Kuo-t'ung & Lü, Shu-hsiang:
Lüeh-yü shih-pu-shih tz'u-erh?—*CKYW*
1955:8, 43. [Are abbreviations words
or not?]
鄒國統、呂叔湘：略語是不是詞兒？

0405   Tu, Tzu-chin: Chien-so-yü lun lüeh.—
KWYK 49, 1946, 24—27. [A short
discussion on contracted words.]
杜子勁：簡縮語論略

0406   Yang, Kuei-min: Han-yü chien-ch'eng
te hsing-ch'eng chi ch'i ying-yung.——*HYHH*
1982:1, 42—46. [The formations of
Chinese abbreviations and their usages.]
楊桂敏：漢語簡稱的形成及其應用

2.3.6. Fusion (0407—0410)

0407   Chao, Yüan-jen: Lia, sa, szu-e, pa-a.—
TFTC 24:12, 1927, 85—88. [On (the
numerals) two, three, four, and eight.]/
Fusion words.
趙元任：倆、仨、四呃、八阿

0408   Chao, Yuen Ren: A note on lea^3, sa^1,
etc.—*HJAS* 1:1, 1936, 33—38.

0409   Jen, Hsüeh-liang: *Han-yü tsao-tz'u-fa*
(0307), 257—258: Sound fusion patterns.
[Methods of word formation in Chinese.]
任學良：漢語造詞法／257—258：合音式

0410   Novotná, Zdeňka: Some remarks on
the analysis of compound types of Chinese
characters. — *AO* 30, 1962, 597—623./
Dealing with fusion characters and fusion
words in Ancient and Modern Chinese.

2.3.7. Contrastive Analysis of Word Formation in Chinese and Other Languages (0411—0414)

0411   Fung, Mary M.Y.: A contrastive analysis
of word-formation of nouns in English
and Chinese.—*Babel* 25:3, 1979, 131—145.

0412   Han, Ching-ch'ing: Hsien-tai Tsang-yü
ho Han-yü tsai kou-tz'u fang-mien te
kung-t'ung tien.—*CKYW* 1959:5, 211—215.
[Common points on the aspects of word
formation in Modern Tibetan and Chinese.]
韓鏡清：現代藏語和漢語在構詞方面的共同點

0413   Juan, Shan-chih: Yüeh-nan-yü ho Han-yü
kou-tz'u-fa pi-chiao yen-chiu ch'u t'an.—
CKYW 1962:7, 325—333. [A preliminary
investigation into the comparative study
of Vietnamese and Chinese methods of
word formation.]
阮善志：越南語和漢語構詞法比較研究初探

0414   Wan, Hui-chou: Han Ying hou-chia-fa
kou-tz'u pi-chiao.——*YCYY* 1979:1, 84—
101. [A comparison of Chinese and
English word formation by suffixation.]
萬惠洲：漢英後加法構詞比較

3. SEMANTIC RELATIONS BETWEEN WORDS (0415–0773)

3.1. General Studies (0415–0430)

0415   Chao, Ya-po: Chin-tai yü-i-hsüeh ching wei.—*CSHS* 6, 1970, 531–548. [An overall view of modern semantics.]
趙雅博：近代語意學經緯

0416   Chao, Yuen Ren: *Language and symbolic systems* (0119), 66–74: Meaning.

0417   Chao, Yüan-jen: Yü-yen ch'eng-su li i-i yu wu te ch'eng-tu wen-t'i.—*CGGG* 1959:10, 11 (Summary); *CHHP* 2, 1961, 1–17. [The problems in the degrees of meaningfulness in language constituents.]
趙元任：語言成素裡意義有無的程度問題

0418   Chu, Hsing: Shih t'an Han-yü yü-i-hsüeh.—*WSC* 1980:4, 11–18. [A preliminary discussion on Chinese semantics.]
朱星：試談漢語語義學

0419   Huang, Hsüan-fan: Yü-i-hsüeh yen-chiu te chi-ko wen-t'i.—*Chung-kuo yü-yen-hsüeh lun-chi* (0090), 383–397; *Yü-yen-hsüeh yen-chiu lun-ts'ung* (0065), 7–23. [Several problems in the study of semantics.]
黃宣範：語義學研究的幾個問題

0420   Huang, Hsüan-fan: *Fan-i yü yü-i chih chien.*—Taipei: Lien-ching, 1976; 1982 3rd print., 4, 2, 304 p. [Between translation and semantics.]/Collected essays.
黃宣範：翻譯與語意之間

0421   Kao, Ming-k'ai: *P'u-t'ung yü-yen-hsüeh.*—Shanghai: Tung-fang, 1954, 2 vols., ii, 305; 2, 274 p.; Shanghai: Hsin chih-shih, 1957, rev. & enl. ed., vii, 503 p./Pt. 3: Semantics and lexicon. [General linguistics.]
高名凱：普通語言學／第三編：語義和詞彙

0422   Kao, Ming-k'ai: *Yü-yen lun* (0122), Pt. 2, Chap. 3: The structure of semantic systems in languages and its development. [On language.]
高名凱：語言論／第二部分，第三章：語言中

語義系統的結構及其演變

0423   Kao, Ming-k'ai: Lun yü-yen hsi-t'ung chung te i-wei.—*CKYW* 1961:10–11, 8–17. [On the sememes in a linguistic system.]
高名凱：論語言系統中的義位

0424   Kuo, Liang-fu: T'an i-i.—*YWYC* 1983:2, 13–19. [On meaning.]
郭艮夫：論意義

0425   Kuo, Shao-yü: Yü-i-hsüeh yü wen-hsüeh.—*HSYK* 1981:2, 88–91. [Semantics and literature.]
郭紹虞：語義學與文學

0426   Li, Chao-t'ung & Hsü, Szu-i (eds. in chief): *Yü-yen-hsüeh tao-lun* (0181), Chap. 3: Semantics.
李兆同、徐思益主編：語言學導論／第三章：語意

0427   Matsumoto, Akira: Imi kenkyū no hōhō to histuyō.—*CGGG* 1957:12, 8–12. [Methodology and necessity of the study of meaning.]
松本昭：意味研究の方法と必要

0428   Wu, Fu-heng: Yü-i-hsüeh p'i-p'an.—*WSC* 1955:5, 57–62. [A critique of semantics.]
吳富恒：語義學批判

0429   Zvegintsev, V.A.: Yü-i-hsüeh tsai yü-yen-hsüeh ko hsüeh-k'o chung te ti-wei—*WCI* 1955:9, 73–81. [The position of semantics among each of the branches of linguistics.]
茲魏庚采夫：語義學在語言學各學科中的地位

0430   Zvegintsev, V.A.: Yü-i-hsüeh yen-chiu chung te chu-yao hsüeh-p'ai.—*YIT* 1959:4, 1–16./ Partial transl. from Zvegintsev's *Semasiologiia* (Moscow: Izd. Moskovskogo Univ., 1957). [The main schools in the study of semantics.]
茲魏庚采夫：語義學研究中的主要學派

3.2. Lexical Meanings (0431–0535)

3.2.1. Differentiation of Lexical Meanings (0431–0483)

3.2.1.1. Lexical Meanings and Character Meanings (0431–0461)

0431 Chan, I: Ying-kai fen-ch'ing tz'u te i-i ho tz'u-su te i-i.—*YWCS* 1958:7, 49–50. [One should draw a clear distinction between the meaning of a word and the meaning of a morpheme.]

占宜：應該分清詞的意義和詞素的意義

0432 Chang, Shih-lu: Tzu-i lüeh shuo.— *Chung-kuo wen-hsüeh* 1:4, 1944, 35–36. [A short discussion on the meanings of characters.]

張世祿：字義略說

0433 Chang, Shih-lu: Tz'u-i ho tz'u-hsing te kuan-hsi.—*YWHH* 1956:7, 32–33; *Hsien-tai Han-yü . . . tzu-liao* (0064), 311–315. [The relationship of lexical meaning and lexical nature.]

張世祿：詞義和詞性的關係

0434 Chang, Shih-lu: Tz'u-i ho tzu-i.—*YWCS* 1957:6, 1–3. [The meaning of a word and the meaning of a character.]

張世祿：詞義和字義

0435 Chang, Ts'an-hsiung: Lüeh t'an tz'u te i-i yü tz'u te shih-yung.—*Yü-wen chi-ch'u chih-shih* (0076), 40–52. [A short discussion on the meanings of words and the usages of words.]

張粲雄：略談詞的意義與詞的使用

0436 Chen, Fu: Tz'u-i te ts'eng-tz'u ho fan-wei. —*CHS* 184, 1947, 28–31. [The level and scope of lexical meaning.]

振甫：詞義的層次和範圍

0437 Ch'en, Yu-ch'in: Tz'u-erh te ch'i i chi ch'i wu-yung.—*KWYK* 15, 1942, 32–34. [The divergent meanings of words and their misusages.]

陳友琴：詞兒的歧義及其誤用

0438 Fan, Ch'ang-shih: Chung-kuo yü-yen chung te yü-i.—*CWY* 8, 1980, 4–38. [Meanings of words in the Chinese language.]

范昌詩：中國語言中的語義

0439 Fu, Huai-ch'ing: Tz'u-i ho kou-ch'eng-tz'u te yü-su-i te kuan-hsi.—*TSYC* 1981:1, 98–110. [The relationships between lexical meanings and morphemic meanings in word formation.]

符淮青：詞義和構成詞的語素義的關係

440 Hirayama, Hisao: Tango no imi.— *Chūgokugo* 19, 1957:1, 31–33. [The meanings of words.]

平山久雄：單語の意味

0441 Ho, Ai-jen: *P'u-t'ung-hua tz'u-i.*— Shanghai: Shang-hai chiao-yü, 1958, 50 p.; Shanghai: Hsin chih-shih, 1959, 2nd print.; *Yü-wen hui-pien* (0058), 3:12./ *CKYW* 1957:4, 40–41, Hsü Ling-fang; *Yü-wen* 1959:8, 27–29, Liang Ming. [Lexical meanings in the Common Language.]

何靄人：普通話詞義／許令芳評，艮明評

0442 Ho, Jung: Tz'u-lei yü tz'ü-i.—*CKYT* 18:1, 1966, 5–8. [Word classes and lexical meanings.]

何容：詞類與詞義

0443 Hsü, Mo: I-i ti ts'o-tsung.—*Yü wen* 1:3, 1937, 49–51. [The complexity of (lexical) meanings.]

徐沫：意義底錯綜

0444 Hsüan, Ch'ang: Chiu tz'u-i.—*YWHH* 1964:7, 57–64. [Old lexical meanings.]

玄常：舊詞義

0445 Kurylowicz, J.R.: Kuan-yü tz'u-i te chi-tien i-chien.—*YIT* 1958:1, 29–33. [Several opinions concerning lexical meanings.]

庫里洛維契：關於詞義的幾點意見

0446 Li, Yu-hung: Tz'u-i yen-chiu te i-hsieh wen-t'i.—*Hsi-fang yü-wen* 2:1, 1958, 15–26. [Several problems of studies on lexical meanings.]

李友鴻：詞義研究的一些問題

0447   Lu, Tsun-wu: Yü-i ch'ang ch'ien t'an.—
Hsüeh-hsi yü szu-k'ao 1981:5, 74—76.
[A brief discussion on semantic field.]

陸尊梧：語義場淺談

0448   Lü, Shu-hsiang & Chu, Te-hsi: Tz'u-i.
—*YWHH* 1953:10, 15—23. [Lexical
meanings.]

呂叔湘、朱德熙：詞義

0449   Lü, T'ao: Kuan-yü tz'u ho tz'u-i wen-
t'i.—*O-wen chiao-hsüeh* 1957:5, 3—6.
[Concerning the problems in words and
lexical meanings.]

呂濤：關於詞和詞義問題

0450   Meng, Ch'uan-ming: Lüeh lun Han-yü
te tz'u-i chi ch'i yen-pien.—*HHYK* 114,
1981, 29—40. [A short discussion on
Chinese lexical meanings and their development.]

蒙傳銘：略論漢語的詞義及其演變

0451   Rokkaku, Tsunehiro: Igi no magirawashii
tango.—*Chūgoku gogaku jiten* (0037),
941—943. [Words with equivocal meanings.]

六角恒廣：意義 の まぎらわしい 單語

0452   Smirnitskii, A.I.: Tz'u-i.—*YIT* 1958:1,
15—20. [Lexical meanings.]

斯密爾尼茨基：詞義

0453   Sun, Ch'ang-hsü: *Han-yü tz'u-hui* (0165),
Pt. I, Chap. 2: Lexical meanings. [Chinese
lexicon.]

孫常叙：漢語詞彙／第一部分，第二篇：詞義

0454   Sun, Te-hsüan: T'an tz'u-i.—*YCT* 8,
1982, 22—31, 46. [A discussion on lexical
meanings.]

孫德宣：談詞義

0455   Ting, Mien-tsai: T'ung-su-tz'u te chieh-
kou hsing-shih ho i-i te kuan-hsi (0262).
[The relationship of the structural patterns
and meanings of homomorphemic words.]

丁勉哉：同素詞的結構形式和意義的關係

0456   Togawa, Yoshio: Jimen to gogi.—*Gengo*
3:8, 1974, 24—31. [Literal meaning and
lexical meaning.]

戶川芳郎：字面と語義

0457   Ts'ui, Fu-yüan: *Hsien-tai Han-yü tz'u-i
chiang-hua.*—Chinan: Shan-tung jen-min,
1957, 158 p./ *CKYW* 1958:6, 291—292,
Liu K'ai-ming. [Lectures on lexical meanings
in the modern Chinese language.]

崔復爰：現代漢語詞義講話／劉凱鳴評

0458   Vochala, Jaromir: A contribution to
the problem of delimiting grammatical
and lexical meanings of elementary linguistic
units in Chinese.—*AO* 32:3, 1964, 403—
427./ *RBS* 10, 1964, 490, K. Kaden.

0459   Wang, Hsi-chieh: Pu-shih tz'u-i te i-i.—
YYWH 1981:2, 33—35. [The meanings
of non-lexical meanings.]

王希傑：不是詞義的意義

0460   Wang, Lun: T'an-t'an shang-hsia wen
tui-yü ch'üeh-ting tz'u-i te tso-yung.—
YWCS 1958:2, 28—30. [A discussion of
the effect of context in determining lexical
meaning.]

王綸：談談上下文對於確定詞義的作用

0461   Wang, Tso-liang: Tz'u-i, wen-t'i, fan-i.
—*TS* 1979:5, 127—134. [Lexical meaning,
style, and translation.]

王佐良：詞義、文體、翻譯

3.2.1.2. Categories of Lexical Meanings
(0462—0465)

0462   Chang, I-jen: Lun tz'u-i te chung-lei.
—*YSHC* 16:4, 1981, 79—91. [On the
categories of lexical meanings.]

張以仁：論詞義的種類

0463   Kan, Min-chung: Lüeh t'an tz'u te p'u-
t'ung tz'u-i ho chuan-k'o tz'u-i.—*HMTH*
1979:1, 112—119. [A short discussion
on the ordinary meanings and technical

meanings of words.]
甘民重：略談詞的普通詞義和專科詞義

0464 Tu, Hsüeh-chih: Tzu-i chih lei-hsing.—
CKTH 1, 1961, 71–80. [Semantic categories
of characters.]
杜學知：字義之類型

0465 Vinogradov, V.V.: Tz'u te tz'u-hui i-i
te chu-yao lei-hsing.—*OYCH* 1958:2,
1–9; 3, 1–10. [The main categories of
lexical meanings of words.]
維諾格拉多夫：詞的詞滙意義的主要類型

3.2.1.3. Lexical Meanings and Concepts (0466–0474)

0466 Chu, Lin-ch'ing: Kuan-yü tz'u-i ho
kai-nien te chi-ko wen-t'i.—*CKYW* 1962:6,
265–271. [Several problems concerning
lexical meanings and concepts.]
朱林清：關於詞義和概念的幾個問題

0467 Hsia, Yen-chang: Lun tz'u-i, kai-nien,
shih-wu chih-chien te kuan-hsi.—*Chiang-hsi
ta-hsüeh hsüeh-pao* 1963:1, 133–141. [On
the relationships between lexical meanings,
concepts, and objects.]
夏延章：論詞義、概念、事物之間的關係

0468 Li, Chün-feng: Lüeh lun tz'u-i yü kai-
nien te liang-ko wen-t'i.—*Ho-fei shih-fan
hsüeh-yüan hsüeh-pao* 1963:2, 44–53. [A
short discussion on the two problems of
lexical meanings and concepts.]
李峻峯：略論詞義與概念的兩個問題

0469 Po, Ming: T'an tz'u-i ho kai-nien te
kuan-hsi wen-t'i.—*CKYW* 1961:8, 39–42.
[On the problems concerning the relationships between lexical meanings and
concepts.]
薄鳴：談詞義和概念的關係問題

0470 Po, Ming: Tz'u i ho kai-nien.—*PCTH*
1963:2, 67–76. [Lexical meanings and
concepts.]
薄鳴：詞義和概念

0471 Shih, An-shih: Kuan-yü tz'u-i yü kai-
nien.—*CKYW* 1961:8, 35–38. [Concerning
lexical meanings and concepts.]
石安石：關於詞義與概念

0472 Ts'en, Ch'i-hsiang: Lun tz'u-i te hsing-
chih chi ch'i yü kai-nien te kuan-hsi.—
CKYW 1961:5, 8–10. [A discussion on
the nature of lexical meanings and its
relationship with regard to concepts.]
岑麒祥：論詞義的性質及其與概念的關係

0473 Wang, Wei-hsien: Yeh t'an tz'u-i ho
kai-nien te kuan-hsi.—*Che-chiang hsüeh-
k'an* 1963:4, 35–40. [A discussion also
on the relationships of lexical meanings
and concepts.]
王維賢：也談詞義和概念的關係

0474 Zvegintsev, V.A. Transl. by Wu, T'ieh-
p'ing, et al.: *P'u-t'ung yü-yen-hsüeh
kang-yao.*—Peking: Shang-wu, 1981, 414
p./ 5.3: Concepts and lexical meanings.
[Ocherki po obshchemu iazykoznaniiu (An
outline of general linguistics).]
茲維金采夫著，伍鐵平等譯：普通語言學綱要
／5.3：概念和詞滙意義

3.2.1.4. Lexical Meanings and Emotive Meanings (0475–0483)

0475 Hsü, Chih-min: Kuan-yü tz'u te kan-
ch'ing se-ts'ai te chi-ko wen-t'i.—*YCYY*
1980:3, 51–62. [Several problems
concerning the emotive coloring of
words.]
徐志民：關於詞的感情色彩的幾個問題

0476 Huang, Hsüan-fan: Ch'ing-hsü i-i te
chieh-hsi.—*Yü-yen-hsüeh yen-chiu lun-
ts'ung* (0065), 25–39. [An analysis of
emotive meanings.]
黃宣範：情緒意義的解析

0477 Lan, Chung-wen: Tz'u te kan-ch'ing
se-ts'ai.—*YWHH* 1959:2, 32. [The emotive
coloring of words.]
藍仲文：詞的感情色彩

0478 Liu, Shu-hsin: Yü-tz'u te hsing-hsiang se-ts'ai chi ch'i kung-neng.—*CKYW* 1980:2, 150—154. [The image colors of words and their functions.]
劉叔新：語詞的形象色彩及其功能

0479 Po, T'e: T'an-t'an tz'u te kan-ch'ing se-ts'ai.—*YWCS* 1958:12, 32—34. [A discussion on the emotive coloring of words.]
伯特：談談詞的感情色彩

0480 Sun, Wei-chang: Lüeh lun tz'u-i te hsing-hsiang se-ts'ai.—*CLTH* 1981:5, 87—94. [A short discussion on the image coloring of lexical meanings.]
孫維張：略論詞義的形象色彩

0481 Tou, Kuang-yü: Shih lun tz'u te kan-ch'ing se-ts'ai.—*HYW* 1960:7, 27—30. [A preliminary discussion on the emotive coloring of words.]
竇光宇：試論詞的感情色彩

0482 Wang, Chien-hsün: T'an-t'an tz'u-i pao-pien.—*YWHH* 1955:3, 60—63. [A discussion on meliorative and pejorative meanings of words.]
汪見薰：談談詞義襃貶

0483 Yüan, Hui: Ch'ien lun tz'u te kan-ch'ing se-ts'ai.—*HYW* 1960:6, 30—32. [A simple discussion on the emotive coloring of words.]
袁暉：淺論詞的感情色彩

3.2.2. Changes in Lexical Meanings (0484—0516)

3.2.2.1. Origin and Development of Lexical Meanings (0484—0499)

0484 Chang, Ch'ing-ch'ang: Tz'u-i yen-pien yü wen-yen wen.—*Chou lun* 1:18, 1948, 9—10. [The changes of lexical meanings and the literary language.]
張清常：辭義演變與文言文

0485 Chen, Yuvoon: Über den Bedeutungswandel im Chinesischen der Gegenwart.—

OE 11, 1964, 9—20./ Dealing with the changes of meanings in Chinese words; *RBS* 10, 1964, 505, K. Kaden.

0486 Fu, Tung-hua: *Tzu-i te yen-pien.*—Peking: Pei-ching, 1964, 49 p.; *Yü-wen hui-pien* (0058), 1:4. [The changes of character meanings.]
傅東華：字義的演變

0487 Hsüan, Ch'ang: Tz'u-i te pien-ch'ien.—*YWHH* 1953:10, 23—25. [The changes of lexical meanings.]
玄常：詞義的變遷

0488 Kao, Ming-k'ai: Chung-kuo yü te yü-i pien-hua.—*T'ien-wen-t'ai* 2, 1947, 57—61. [The changes in lexical meanings of the Chinese language.]
高名凱：中國語的語義變化

0489 Liu, Pan-nung: Yü-i te pien-ch'ien.—*KYCK* 177, 1935, February 16. [The changes of lexical meanings.]
劉半農：語義的變遷

0490 Meng, Ch'uan-ming: Lüeh lun Han-yü te tz'u-i chi ch'i yen-pien (0450). [A short discussion on Chinese lexical meanings and their development.]
蒙傳銘：略論漢語的詞義及其演變

0491 Ogawa, Tamaki: Fūryū no goi no henka. —*KGKB* 20:8, 1951, (not seen); *Chūgoku gogaku kenkyū* (0075), 200—214. [The changes of meanings of the word *feng-liu.*]
小川環樹：『風流』の語義の變化

0492 Shōmura, Tadayoshi: Imi no hensan ni tsuite.—*CGKS* 4, 1961, (not seen). [On the changes of meanings.]
莊村忠艮：意味の變遷について

0493 Stroeva, T.V.: Tz'u-i pien-hua te yüan-yin.—*YIT* 1959:1, 24—30. [The causes of the changes in lexical meanings.]
斯特洛也娃：詞義變化的原因

0494 Sun, Liang-ming: Tz'u te tuo-i-hsing

ken tz'u-i yen-pien te kuan-hsi ho ch'ü-pieh.—*CKYW* 1958:5, 241–242. [The relationships and differences of polysemy and the changes of lexical meanings.]
孫良明：詞的多義性跟詞義演變的關係和區別

0495 Sun, Liang-ming: Tz'u-i yen-pien te yüan-yin.—*YYWH* 1959:3, 28–29. [The causes of changes in lexical meanings.]
孫良明：詞義演變的原因

0496 Sun, Liang-ming: Kuan-yü tz'u-i yen-pien te liang-ko wen-t'i.—*CKYW* 1961:3, 23–25. [Two problems concerning the changes of lexical meanings.]
孫良明：關於詞義演變的兩個問題

0497 Tu, Hsüeh-chih: Tzu-i te fa-sheng.—*TLTC* 27:6, 1963, 8–11; *Yü-fa sheng-yün wen-tzu* (0081), 355–358. [The rise of the meanings of characters.]
杜學知：字義的發生

0498 Wang, Liao-i: Hsin tzu-i te ch'an-sheng.—*KWTCK* 1:2, 1942, 6–7; *Lung ch'ung ping-tiao chai wen-chi* 3 (0086), 6–10. [The rise of new meanings of characters.]
王了一：新字義的產生

0499 Yü, Kao: Ts'ung tz'u-i pien-hua shuo-ch'i.—*TSYC* 1982:3, 119–120. [A discussion starting from the changes of lexical meanings.]
于皋：從詞義變化說起

3.2.2.2. Original Lexical Meanings and Extended Lexical Meanings (0500–0516)

0500 Han, Ch'en-ch'i: Tz'u te chieh-tai i.—*Hsü-chou shih-fan hsüeh-yüan hsüeh-pao* 1981:2, 75–80. [The borrowed meanings of words.]
韓陳其：詞的借代義

0501 Hsiang, Ying: Tz'u te ch'ang-yung i ho pen i.—*YWCS* 1957:4, 54–55. [Commonly used meanings and original meanings of words.]
向穎：詞的常用義和本義

0502 Hsiao, Wen: Tz'u te yin-shen i ho pi-yü i.—*YWHH* 1959:2, 21. [Extended meanings and metaphorical meanings of words.]
肖文：詞的引伸義和比喻義

0503 Kao, Shou-kang: Tz'u-i yin-shen te ken-chü ho fang-shih.—*TCSY* 1981:2, 64–69. [The basis and pattern of the extension of lexical meaning.]
高守綱：詞義引伸的根據和方式

0504 Kao, Shou-kang: Han-yü chung tz'u-i chuan-hua chien-lei tz'u.—*YLT* 7, 1981, 169–186. [Concurrence of word classes in words arising from the shifts of meanings in Chinese.]
高守綱：漢語中詞義轉化兼類詞

0505 Liu, Ch'ien-hsien: Tz'u-i te p'ai-sheng t'u-ching ch'u t'an.—*Yü-yen-hsüeh lun-chi* (0084), 181–199. [A preliminary inquiry into the processes for derivation of lexical meanings.]
劉乾先：詞義的派生途徑初探

0506 Liu, Yu-hsin: T'an-t'an tzu te pen i ho yin-shen i.—*TYT* 2, 1981, 1–8. [A discussion on the original and extended meanings of characters.]
劉又辛：談談字的本義和引伸義

0507 Pai, Wen: Yin-shen ho pi-yü yu shen-ma ch'ü-pieh?—*YWCS* 1960:4, 54–55. [What is the difference between 'extended (meaning)' and 'metaphorical (meaning)'?]
白文：『引伸』和『比喻』有甚麼區別？

0508 P'u, Hua: Tz'u-i yin-shen yü tz'u-lei huo-yung te kuan-hsi.—*YYWH* 1981:3, 29–31. [The relationship between the extension of lexical meaning and the alternative use of word classes.]
浦華：詞義引伸與詞類活用的關係

0509 Shibata, Minoru: Han-yü tz'u-hui te yin-shen.—*CGGG* 1966:8, 1–5. [The extension of the vocabulary of the Chinese language.]

芝田稔：漢語詞彙的引伸

0510   Tsou, Feng: Lun yü i p'ai-sheng te
        i-pan kuei-lü.—*TSYC* 1982:6, 83–89. [On
        the general rules of the derivations of
        linguistic meanings.]

鄒酆：論語義派生的一般規律

0511   Ts'ui, Ch'ung-ch'ing: Shih lun tz'u-lei
        huo-yung tui tz'u-i yin-shen te ying-hsiang.
        —*Hsüeh-hsi yü t'an-so* 1981:2, (not seen).
        [A preliminary discussion on the influence
        of flexible uses of word classes upon the
        extension of lexical meanings.]

崔重慶：試論詞類活用對詞義引伸的影響

0512   Tu, Hsüeh-chih: I-i yin-shen yü lien-
        hsiang fa-tse.—*TLTC* 20:12, 1960, 1–4;
        Yü-yen wen-tzu-hsüeh (0080), 229–232.
        [Extensions of meanings and rules for
        associations.]

杜學知：意義引伸與聯想法則

0513   Tu, Hsüeh-chih: Tzu-i yin-shen shuo.—
        TLTC 26:9, 1963, 3–5; *Yü-fa sheng-yün
        wen-tzu* (0081), 351–354. [A discussion
        on the extended meanings of characters.]

杜學知：字義引伸說

0514   Tung, Kuo-tung: Shih t'an tz'u te yin-
        shen i ho pi-yü i.—*YYWH* 1960:5–6,
        54–55. [A preliminary discussion on ex-
        tended meaning and metaphorical meaning.]

董國棟：試談詞的引伸義和比喻義

0515   Wang, Kuei-hua: Shih lun tz'u te
        chieh-tai i.—*TCSY* 1981:4, 82–85. [A
        preliminary discussion on the borrowed
        meanings of words.]

王桂華：試論詞的借代義

0516   Yüan, Shih-ch'üan: Pen i, chi-pen i
        chi ch'i-t'a.—*YWHH* 1981:5, 42. [Original
        meaning, basic meaning, etc.]

袁世全：本義、基本義及其他

3.2.3. Explanation and Analysis of Lexical Meanings (0517–0535)

3.2.3.1. Explanation of Lexical Meanings (0517–0521)

0517   Liu, Shu-hsin: Tz'u-hsing ho tz'u te
        shih-i.—*TCSY* 1979:2, 73–77. [The
        nature of words and explanations of the
        meanings of words.]

劉叔新：詞性和詞的釋義

0518   Liu, Shu-hsin: Tz'u-yü te i-i ho shih-i.
        —*TSYC* 1980:4, 172–181. [The meanings
        and the explanations for the meanings
        of words and phrases.]

劉叔新：詞語的意義和釋義

0519   Liu, Yung-jang: T'an tz'u-yü te chieh-
        shih.—*CKYT* 5:6, 1959, 41–44. [A
        discussion on the explanations of words
        and phrases.]

劉永讓：談詞語的解釋

0520   Shih, An-shih: Tz'u-i ho shih-i chung te
        chieh-chi-hsing wen-t'i.—*PCTH* 3, 1978,
        94–99. [The problem of class nature in
        lexical meanings and explanations of
        meanings.]

石安石：詞義和釋義中的階級性問題

0521   Sun, Liang-ming: *Tz'u-i ho shih-i.*—
        Wuhan: Hu-pei jen-min, 1982, [ii], iv,
        153 p. [Lexical meanings and explanations
        of lexical meanings.]

孫良明：詞義和釋義

3.2.3.2. Analysis of Lexical Meanings (0522–0535)

0522   Chan, Jen-feng & Liu, Hsiao-nan:
        Tz'u-i pien-hsi.—Harbin: Hei-lung chiang
        jen-min, 1978, 2 vols., 79; 126 p.
        [Differentiation and analysis of lexical
        meanings.]

詹人鳳、劉小南：詞義辨析

0523   Ch'en, Ping-chao: *Tz'u-i pien-hsi.*—Foo-
        chow: Fu-chien jen-min, 1980–1982, 2
        Vols., 9, 198; 18, 308 p. [Differentiation
        and analysis of lexical meanings.]

陳炳昭：詞義辨析

0524   Ch'en, Tu-hsiu: *Tzu-i lei li.*—Shanghai: Tung-ya t'u-shu-kuan, 1925, 2, 115 d.p.; Kowloon: Shih-yung, 1969, repr. [Classified explanations with examples of the meanings of characters.]
陳獨秀：字義類例

0525   Chu, Hsing: *Han-yü tz'u-i chien hsi.*—Wuhan: Hu-pei jen-min, 1981, [v], 95 p. [A simple analysis of Chinese lexical meanings.]
朱星：漢語詞義簡析

0526   Chung-kuo yü-wen tsa-chih-she: *Tz'u-i pien-hsi.*—Peking: Jen-min chiao-yü, 1958–1962, 3 vols., 4, 70; 2, 3, 84; 2, 3, 65 p. [Differentiation and analysis of lexical meanings.]
中國語文雜誌社：詞義辨析

0527   Ho, Chiu-ying: Tz'u-i pien-huo.—*CKYW* 1965:1, 49–50, 64. [Clarification of doubtful meanings of words.]
何九盈：詞義辨惑

0528   Ho, Chiu-ying: Tz'u-i so t'an.—*YLT* 7, 1981, 49–58. [Miscellaneous remarks on (ancient) lexical meanings.]
何九盈：詞義瑣談

0529   Huang, Yüeh: Tz'u-i cha-chi.—*CKYW* 1964:4, 319–320. [Notes on lexical meanings.]
黃鉞：詞義札記

0530   Kao, Ch'ing-szu: *Hsien-tai Han-yü tz'u-i pien-hsi.*—Wuhan: Hu-pei jen-min, 1980, (not seen). [Differentiation and analysis of lexical meanings in Modern Chinese.]
高慶賜：現代漢語詞義辨析

0531   Kuo, Hsi-liang, et al.: Tz'u-i fen-hsi chü-li.—*YWYC* 1, 1981, 111–127. [Examples for analysis of lexical meanings.]
郭錫良等：詞義分析舉例

0532   Liu, Yu-hsin: Tz'u-i t'an yüan hsiao chien.—*HNSY* 1981:1, (not seen). [Brief notes on the investigation of the origins of lexical meanings.]
劉又辛：詞義探源小箋

0533   Su, Jui-chang: To-yin-chieh te ch'i-yin tz'u tz'u-i pi-chiao yung-li.—*CKYT* 30:12, 1971–32:1, 1973. [A comparison with examples of the lexical meanings of (identical) polysyllabic words with variant readings.]
蘇瑞章：多音節的歧音詞詞義比較用例

0534   Wu, Yung-te: *Hsien-tai Han-yü tz'u-i pien-hsi* (hsü pien).—Wuhan: Hu-pei jen-min, 1981, [i], vi, 313 p. [Differentiation and analysis of the lexical meanings of Modern Chinese (a continuation).]
吳永德：現代漢語詞義辨析（續編）

0535   Yang, Kuo-an: *Tz'u-i pien-hsi.*—Kwei-yang: Kuei-chou jen-min, 1981, rev. & enl. ed., 2, 9, 203 p. [Differentiation and analysis of lexical meanings.]
楊國安：詞義辨析

3.3.   Relationships between Forms, Sounds, and Meanings (0536–0561)

3.3.1.   Forms, Sounds, and Meanings in General (0536–0548)

0536   Chou, Tsu-mo: Han-tzu yü Han-yü te kuan-hsi.—*Wen-hsüeh chi* (0054), 13–23; *Chung-kuo yü-wen yen-chiu hsüan-chi* (0047), 58–70./ 17–23: The phenomenon of contradictions between the forms, sounds and meanings of Chinese characters. [The relationship of Chinese writing and the Chinese language.]
周祖謨：漢字與漢語的關係

0537   Fang, Shih-to: Hsing yin i te ts'o-tsung kuan-hsi.—*CKYT* 17:3, 1965, 27–30. [The complex relationship between forms, sounds, and meanings.]
方師鐸：形音義的錯綜關係

0538   Hsiang, Yen: Hsing yin i te chiu-ko.—*CKYW* 1981:6, 423. [The entanglement of forms, sounds, and meanings.]
向巖：形音義的糾葛

0539   Kao, Heng: *Wen-tzu hsing-i-hsüeh kai-lun.*—Chinan: Shan-tung jen-min, 1963; Kowloon: Shao-hua wen-hua fu-wu-she, n.d., repr., iii, 330 p.; Chinan: Ch'i-lu shu-she, 1981, repr., 10, 3, 330 p. [An introduction to the study of the forms and meanings of (Chinese) writing.]

高亨：文字形義學概論

0540   Kao, Shu-fan & Wang, Hsiu-ming: *Cheng-chung hsing yin i tsung-ho ta tzu-tien.*—Taipei: Cheng-chung, 1971, [10], 6, 34, 2250, 28, 30 p., illus, tables; 1974, rev. ed., [10], 6, 35, 2284, 28, 28 p. [Cheng-chung's integrated comprehensive dictionary of forms, sounds, and meanings (of Chinese characters).]

高樹藩、王修明：正中形音義綜合大字典

0541   Ku, Yüeh: Han tzu hsing, yin, i kuan-hsi chung-chung.—*YCYY* 1981:2, 128–132, 61. [Various relationships of the forms, sounds, and meanings of Chinese characters.]

顧越：漢字形、音、義關係種種

0542   Li, Hsing-chien: Han tzu te hsing, yin, i pien.—*Hsien-tai Han-yü . . . tzu-liao* (0064), 44–51. [Differentiation of the forms, sounds, and meanings of Chinese characters.]

李行健：漢字的形、音、義辨

0543   Lü, Shu-hsiang: T'an hsing, yin, i.—*WTKK* 1964:3, 10–12; 4, 9–10. *Hsien-tai Han-yü . . . tzu-liao* (0064), 34–43. [A discussion on forms, sounds, and meanings (of Chinese characters).]

呂叔湘：談形、音、義

0544   Shen, Chien-shih: Yen-chiu wen-tzu-hsüeh hsing ho i te chi-ko fang-fa.—*Pei-ching ta-hsüeh yüeh-k'an* 1:8, 1921, 47–50. [Several methods for the study of forms and meanings in (Chinese) logography.]

沈兼士：研究文字學形和義的幾個方法

0545   Wang, Liao-i: *Wen-tzu te hsing, yin, i.*—Peking: Chung-kuo ch'ing-nien, 1953, vi, 65 p./ See (0546). [The forms, sounds,

and meanings of Chinese characters.]

王了一：文字的形、音、義

0546   Wang, Liao-i: *Tzu te hsieh-fa, tu-yin ho i-i.*—Shanghai: Hsin chih-shih, 1957, vi, 63 p./ A rev. ed. of (0545). [The orthography, pronunciation, and meaning of (Chinese) characters.]

王了一：字的寫法、讀音和意義

0547   Wang, Lun: Yü-yin, tz'u-i ho tzu-hsing.—*YWHH* 1957:11, 13–15. [Sounds, lexical meanings, and character forms.]

王綸：語音、詞義和字形

0548   Wang, Yü-ch'ün: *Han-tzu hsing, yin, i pien-hsi.*—Changsha: Hu-nan jen-min, 1975, 211 p. [Differentiation and analysis of the forms, sounds, and meanings of Chinese characters.]

王與輦：漢字形、音、義辨析

3.3.2.   Sounds and Meanings (0549–0561)

0549   Ch'en, Chu-tsun: Wen-tzu sheng i hsiang yin k'ao.—*Chen-chih hsüeh-pao* 1:4, 1942, 19–23; 3:2, 1943, 14–19. [A study on the interdependency of the sounds and meanings of (Chinese) writing.]

陳柱尊：文字聲誼相因考

0550   Chiang, Liang-fu: Chung-kuo wen-tzu te sheng-yin yü i te kuan-hsi.—*CNC* 7:5, 1935, 28–36. [The relationships between the sounds and meanings of Chinese writing.]

姜亮夫：中國文字的聲音與義的關係

0551   Chiang, Shui: Chung-kuo wen-tzu yin i te kuan-hsi.—*Hsi-pei kung-lun* 2:3, 1941, 41–43. [The relationships of sounds and meanings of Chinese writing.]

江水：中國文字音義的關係

0552   Chou, Fa-kao: Yü-yin ch'ü-pieh tz'u-lei shuo.—*BIHP* 24, 1953, 197–212; *Chung-kuo yü-yen-hsüeh lun-wen-chi* (0053), 349–364. [The theory of distinction of word-classes by sound (tone) changes.]

周法高：語音區別詞類說

0553   Chou, Tsu-mo: Szu-sheng pieh i shih li.—*Wen-hsüeh chi* (0054), 81–119. [Explanations with examples of differentiating meanings by (the change of) the four tones.]
周祖謨：四聲別義釋例

0554   Downer, G.B.: Derivation by tone-change in Classical Chinese.—*BSOAS* 22, 1959, 258–290./ *RBS* 5, 1959, 484, J. Chmielewski.

0555   Ishida, Takeo: Seichō ni yotte kotonaru kotoba.—*Chūgoku gogaku jiten* (0037), 945–948. [Words that are different according to their tones.]
石田武夫：聲調によって異ることば

0556   Liu, Ho & Ma, Chen-ya: Yin t'ung i chin shuo chih i.—*Yü-yen-hsüeh lun-chi* (0084), 139–155. [An inquiry into the theory that 'identical sounds indicate similar meanings'.]
劉禾、馬振亞：『音同義近』說質疑

0557   Lu, Tsung-ta & Wang, Ning: Yin sheng ch'iu i lun.—*Liao-ning shih-yüan hsüeh-pao* 1980:6, 1–10. [On 'finding meaning via sound'.]
陸宗達、王寧：『因聲求義』論

0558   Mochizuki, Shinchō: Chūgoku koten bungo ni okeru shisei ni yoru imi kubetsu ni tsuite.—*CGGG* 1955:10, 16–20. [The distinction of meaning by means of the four tones in Classical Chinese.]
望月眞澄：中國古典文語における四聲による意味區別について

0559   Sakamoto, Ichirō: Chūgokugo on-gi no kankei.—*CGGG* 1947:6, (not seen). [The relationships between sounds and meanings in Chinese.]
坂本一郎：中國語音義關係

0560   Tu, Hsüeh-chih: Wen-tzu te i hsing chien i yü yüan sheng chih i.—*TLTC* 8:10, 1954, 152–154. [The meanings of characters as seen from their forms and as known from their sounds.]
杜學知：文字的依形見義與緣聲知義

0561   Tu, Hsüeh-chih: Shu sheng chien i shuo —I-i fen-shu chih i li.—*TLTC* 25:7, 1962, 9–11. [A theory of 'the meanings (of characters) are indicated by (their) tones' —An example of semantic category.]
杜學知：殊聲見義說——意義分屬之一例

3.4.   Synonymous, Antonymous, and One-sided Meaning Words (0562–0658)
3.4.1.   Synonymous Words (0562–0622)
3.4.1.1.   Definition (0562–0578)

0562   Chang, Shih-lu: Yü-yen pien-hua yü t'ung-i i-tz'u te hsien-hsiang.—*Hsüeh-shih* 2:1, 1947, 12; 2:2–3, 23–25. [Linguistic change and the phenomenon of 'identical meanings but different words'.]
張世祿：語言變化與『同義異詞』的現象

0563   Ch'ang, Ching-yü: Ch'ien t'an hsien-tai Han-yu t'ung-i-tz'u te hsing-chih ho fan-wei.—*YCYY* 1979, Feb., 26–33. [A brief discussion of the nature and scope of modern Chinese synonyms.]
常敬宇：淺談現代漢語同義詞的性質和範圍

0564   Ch'en, Ping-t'iao: Han-yü te t'ung-i-tz'u shih pu shih i-ting yao tz'u-hsing hsiang-t'ung.—*YWCS* 1958:6, 41–43. [Do Chinese synonyms necessarily have the same lexical nature?]
陳炳迢：漢語的同義詞是不是一定要詞性相同

0565   Hsieh, Wen-ch'ing: T'ung-i-tz'u te fa-chan.—*NMSY* 1981:1, (not seen). [The development of synonyms.]
謝文慶：同義詞的發展

0566   Hsieh, Wen-ch'ing: Hsien-tai Han-yü t'ung-i-tz'u te lei-hsing.—*YCYY* 1982:2, 72–81. [The typology of synonyms in Modern Chinese.]
謝文慶：現代漢語同義詞的類型

0567   Ishiyama, Akeo: Chūgokugo ni okeru

dōgishi no mondai.—*HKDKZ* 3, 1968, 49–70. [The problem of synonyms in Chinese.]

石山曙生：中國語における同義詞の問題

0568   Jen, Ming-shan: T'ung-i-tz'u ho tz'u te to-i-hsing.—*YWHH* 1957:4, 22–23. [Synonyms and the polysemy of words.]

任銘善：同義詞和詞的多義性

0569   Kao, Ch'ing-szu: T'ung-i-tz'u yen-chiu te chu-yao tui-hsiang.—*YWCS* 1956:12, 1–3. [The primary objectives of the study of synonyms.]

高慶賜：同義詞研究的主要對象

0570   Kao, Ch'ing-szu: T'ung-i-tz'u shih tsen-yang ch'an-sheng te? —*YWCS* 1957:2, 4–11. [How are synonyms produced?]

高慶賜：同義詞是怎樣產生的？

0571   Kuei, I: T'an t'ung-i-tz'u.—*YWHH* 1953: 8, 26–30. [A discussion on synonyms.]

壞一：談同義詞

0572   Kung, Jen-nien: Kuan-yü Han-yü t'ung-i-tz'u te tz'u-hsing wen-t'i.—*HRPS* 1963:4, 522–529. [Concerning the problem of the lexical nature of Chinese synonyms.]

貢仁年：關於漢語同義詞的詞性問題

0573   Liu, Kuan-ch'ün: Kuan-yü t'ung-i-tz'u te liang-ko wen-t'i.—*YWHH* 1957:7, 26–28. [Concerning two problems of synonyms (1. The boundaries between polysemous words, synonyms, and homonyms, 2. The relationships between word classes and synonyms).]

劉冠羣：關於同義詞的兩個問題

0574   Ōmura, Masuo: Chūgokugo ruigigo kenkyū shiron.—*JBRS* 8, 1970, 21–40. [A preliminary discussion on the study of synonyms in Chinese.]

大村益夫：中國語類義語研究試論

0575   Sun, Liang-ming: T'ung-i-tz'u tsai yü-yen chung te tso-yung.—*YWCS* 1957:12, 16–18. [The functions of synonyms in

language.]

孫良明：同義詞在語言中的作用

0576   Sun, Liang-ming: T'ung-i-tz'u te hsing-chih ho fan-wei.—*YWHH* 1958:3, 11–12. [The nature and scope of synonyms.]

孫良明：同義詞的性質和範圍

0577   Wu, Chan-k'un: Chiao-ch'a t'ung-i-tz'u chi ch'i t'e-tien.—*YWCS* 1956:12, 3–7. [Synonyms which overlap and their special features.]

伍占昆：交叉同義詞及其特點

0578   Wu, Chan-k'un: Lüeh t'an t'ung-i-tz'u te fa-chan pien-hua.—*YWHH* 1957:12, 34. [A brief discussion on the development and changes of synonyms.]

武占坤：略談同義詞的發展變化

3.4.1.2. Differentiation (0579–0591)

0579   Anonymous: Kuan-yü ch'ü-pieh t'ung-i-tz'u.—*YWCS* 1956:11, 46–48. [Concerning the differentiation of synonyms.]

無名氏：關於區別同義詞

0580   Chang, Ch'eng-chu: T'ung-i-tz'u te pien-hsi.—*CSCY* 1962:9, 19. [Differentiation and analysis of synonyms.]

張成珠：同義詞的辨析

0581   Chang, Chih-i: T'ung-i-tz'u tsai yü-fa shang te i-hsieh ch'ü-pieh.—*YWHH* 1958: 12, 36. [Some differences of synonyms in grammar.]

張志毅：同義詞在語法上的一些區別

0582   Hai, Liu: Tsen-yang pien-hsi t'ung-i-tz'u? —*FCCY* 1961:10, 19–21. [How to differentiate and analyze synonyms?]

海流：怎樣辨析同義詞？

0583   Hung, Meng-hsiang: T'ung-i-tz'u te ch'a-pieh.—*YWHH* 1957:7, 28–29. [The differences of synonyms.]

洪夢湘：同義詞的差別

0584   Sun, Hsüan-ch'ang: *Tsen-yang pien-pieh*

t'ung-tz'u?—Peking: T'ung-su tu-wu, 1956. 56 p. [How to differentiate synonyms?]
孫玄常：怎樣辨別同義詞？

0585　Tzu, Lang: Chieh-shao i-chung pien-hsi t'ung-i-tz'u te fang-fa.—*YWCS* 1959:10, 38. [Introducing a method of differentiating and analyzing synonyms.]
子朗：介紹一種辨析同義詞的方法

0586　W. L.: I-hsieh t'ung-i-tz'u te ch'ü-pieh. —*YWCS* 1958:2, 49—50. [The differences of some synonyms.]
W. L.：一些同義詞的區別

0587　Wang, Chien-hsün: Pien-pieh t'ung-i-tz'u ying chu-i te chi tien.—*YWHH* 1956:4, 31—32. [Several points that should be emphasized in differentiating synonyms.]
王見熏：辨別同義詞應注意的幾點

0588　Wang, Li-chia & Hou, Hsüeh-ch'ao: Tsen-yang ch'üeh-ting t'ung-i-tz'u?—*YLT* 5, 1963, 232—249./ *RBS* 9, 1963, 537, M. Désirat. [How to define synonyms?]
王理嘉、侯學超：怎樣確定同義詞？

0589　Wei, Chien-kung: T'ung-i-tz'u ho fan-i-tz'u.—*YWHH* 1956:9, 17—19; 10, 39—41; 11, 36—38. [Synonyms and antonyms.]
魏建功：同義詞和反義詞

0590　Wei, Ch'ün & P'u, K'an: T'ung-i-tz'u chi ch'i pien-hsi fa.—*Shan-hsi shih-yüan hsüeh-pao* 1979:3, 85—89. [Synonyms and their methods of differentiation and analysis.]
蔚羣、濮侃：同義詞及其辨析法

0591　Wei, Li-hsiang: T'ung-i-tz'u, fan-i-tz'u chi ch'i-t'a.—*CSCY* 1959:21, 23—27. [Synonyms, antonyms, etc.]
魏立湘：同義詞、反義詞及其它

3.4.1.3. Collection and Analysis (0592—0617)

0592　Ai, Ch'ü: T'ung-i-tz'u.—*YWCS* 1955:7, 25; 8, 31; 9, 34—35; 10, 42—43; 12, 44—55. [Synonyms.]
靄區：同義詞

0593　Alekseev, V.M.: O novykh sinonimi-cheskikh slovariakh kitaiskoi pis'mennosti. —*Bibliografiia Vostoka* 5—6, 1934, 4—9. [New synonym dictionaries of Chinese writing.]

0594　Anonymous: *Hsiang-fan-tz'u ho t'ung-i-tz'u.*—Hong Kong: Feng-hsing, 1966, 4th ed., [i], 40 p. [Antonyms and synonyms.]
無名氏：相反詞和同義詞

0595　Chang, Chih-i: *Chien-ming t'ung-i tz'u-tien.*—Shanghai: Shang-hai tz'u-shu, 1981, 4, 2, 14, 248, 12 p./ *CKYW* 1982:3, 237—239, Lu Jun-hsiang. [A concise dictionary of synonyms.]
張志毅：簡明同義詞典／盧潤祥評

0596　Chao, T'ien-li: T'ung-i-tz'u piao-chieh.— *CYHC* 1953:2, 26—33; 1954:7, 37—43. [Diagrammatic explanations on synonyms.]
趙天吏：同義詞表解

0597　Ch'i, T'ieh-hen: T'ung-i i-tu ko tan-tzu te yen-chiu ts'ao-an.—*CKYT* 3:4, 1958, 38—45; 5, 37—46; 6, 43—51; 4:1, 1959, 60—67; 3, 46—54; 4, 45—50; 5, 40—51; 6, 35—41; 5:1, 43—48; 2, 50—57; 3, 45—49; 4, 53—57; 5, 53—59; 6, 55—57. [A draft of a study on single characters having identical meanings but different readings.]
齊鐵恨：同義異讀各單字的研究草案

0598　Ch'i, T'ieh-hen: *T'ung-i i-tu tan-tzu yen-chiu.*—Taipei: Fu-hsing shu-chü, 1963, 4, 127 p. [A study on single characters having identical meanings but different readings.]
齊鐵恨：同義異讀單字研究

0599　Fang, Wen-i: *T'ung-i-tz'u pien-hsi.*— Hangchow: Che-chiang jen-min, 1980, 6, 12, 346 p.; 1982, 2nd repr. [Differentiation and analysis of synonyms.]
方文一：同義詞辨析

0600　Feng, Shih: *T'ung-i-yü tz'u-tien.*—Hong

Kong: Ch'ung-ming, 1963, 289 p. [A dictionary of synonyms.]

馮式：同義語辭典

0601   Ho, Ch'ung-wen & Liu, Ch'i-fen: *Ch'ang-yung t'ung-i-tz'u pien-hsi.*—Hsining: Ch'ing-hai jen-min, 1980, 211 p. [Differentiation and analysis of commonly used synonyms.]

何崇文、劉啓芬：常用同義詞辨析

0602   Hsieh, Wen-ch'ing: *T'ung-i-tz'u.*—Wuhan: Hu-pei jen-min, 1982, [iv], 126 p. [Synonyms.]

謝文慶：同義詞

0603   Hsü, Ming: *T'ung-yin-tz'u, t'ung-hsing-tz'u, t'ung-i-tz'u.*—Hong Kong: Chin-hsiu, 1975, 3rd ed., 92 p. [Homophones, homographs, and synonyms.]

徐明：同音詞、同形詞、同義詞

0604   Kao, Ch'ing-szu: *T'ung-i-tz'u ho fan-i-tz'u.*—Shanghai: Hsin chih-shih, 1957, [iii], 57 p; *Yü-wen hui-pien* (0058), 3:14. [Synonyms and antonyms.]

高慶賜：同義詞和反義詞

0605   Kao, Wei-hsien: I-hsieh ch'ang-yung t'ung-i-tz'u.—*TRGH* 78, 1972, 354–373; 85, 1973, 288–305. [Several commonly used synonyms.]

高維先：一些常用同義詞

0606   Kuo, Kuo-ying: T'an k'an te t'ung-i-tz'u. —*YCT* 1, 1981, 52–56. [A discussion on the synonyms of (the word) *k'an* ('to see').]

郭國英：談『看』的同義詞

0607   Lei, T'ien-i: *Ts'o pieh tzu chi t'ung-i-tz'u li shih.*—Peking: Wu-shih nien-tai, 1954, 132, 6 p. [Explanations of incorrect and variant characters and synonyms with examples.]

雷天奕：錯別字及同義詞例釋

0608   Li, Wen-chien, et al.: *Ch'ang-yung t'ung-i-tz'u pien-hsi.*—Changsha: Hu-nan jen-min,

1982, 2, 35, 583 p. [Differentiation and analysis of commonly used synonyms.]

李文健等：常用同義詞辨析

0609   Liu, Hsi-chung: *Hsien-tai Han-yü t'ung-i-tz'u pien-hsi.*—Huhehot: Nei Meng-ku jen-min, 1981, [ii], 11, 289 p. [Differentiation and analysis of Modern Chinese synonyms.]

劉希忠：現代漢語同義詞辨析

0610   Nara, Kazuo: Dōgigo sakuin.— *CGGG* 1955:8, 18–21. [An index to 'synonyms'.]

奈良和男：『同義語』索引

0611   Ni, Li-min: Lüeh shuo ping-lieh-shih t'ung-su i-hsü t'ung-i-tz'u.—*YC* 1981:4–5, 89–91. [A short discussion on coordinate pattern synonyms with identical morphemes but different word order.]

倪立民：略說並列式同素異序同義詞

0612   Ōuchida, Saburō: *Suikoden* no gengo —dōgigo ni okeru ichi kōsatsu.—*CBKK* 13, 1972, 1–10. [The language of *Shui-hu chuan*—A study on the synonyms.]

大內田三郎：『水滸傳』の言語――同義語 における一考察

0613   Ōuchida, Saburō: *Suikoden* no gengo —tan'onsetsugo to taonsetsugo no dōgigo ni tsuite.—*TRGH* 92, 1974, 12–26. [The language of *Shui-hu chuan*—On the monosyllabic and polysyllabic synonyms.]

大內田三郎：『水滸傳』の言語――單音節語 と多音節語の同義語について

0614   Torii, Hisayasu & Hiraiwa, Fusajirō: Ruigo yōhō no kaisetsu.—*Zenrin* 14:5, 1943, 16–23; 6, 7–10; 8, 38–41; 10, 23–27; 11, 42–47; 12, 13–19. [Explanations of the usages of synonyms.]

鳥居久靖、平巖房次郎：類語用法の解說

0615   Tung, Kuei-hsien: *T'ung-i-yü tz'u-tien.* —Taipei: P'ing-p'ing, 1964, [ii], 2, 228 p.; Taipei: Wu-chou, 1976, repr. [A dictionary of synonyms.]

董桂先：同義語辭典

0616 Viscarra, Huafang: *Synonymes en chinois moderne: Étude de contraintes en lexicologie.*—Paris: Editions Langages Croisés, 1983, 277 p.

0617 Wu, Hua: *T'ung-i-yü fan-i-tz'u tz'u-tien.* —Taipei: Wen-t'ung, n.d., 16, 289, 131 p. [A dictionary of synonyms and antonyms.]
吳華：同義語反義詞辭典

3.4.1.4. Near-synonymous Words (0618–0622)

0618 Li, Szu-ming: *Chūgokugo no nyuansu—Machigae-yasui ruigigo dōgigo.*—Tokyo: Tōhō shoten, 1981, vi, 320 p. [Nuances of the Chinese language—Near-synonyms and synonyms easily mistaken.]
李嗣明：中國語のニュアンス—まちがえやすい類義語，同義語

0619 Liu, Shu-hsin: *T'ung-i-tz'u ho chin-i tz'u te hua-fen.*—*Yü-yen yen-chiu lun-ts'ung* (0074), 58–84. [The division between synonyms and near-synonyms.]
劉叔新：同義詞和近義詞的劃分

0620 Sheng, Shou-mou: Yu-kuan i-i hsiang-chin te tz'u te chi-ko wen-t'i.—*YYWH* 1958:2, 23–24. [Several problems concerning words having mutually close meanings.]
盛守謀：有關意義相近的詞的幾個問題

0621 Shih, Yun-feng: Chin-i-tz'u li shih.— *Chung-hsüeh yü-wen chiao-hsüeh* 1981:3, 41–44. [Explanations of near-synonymous words with examples.]
石雲風：近義詞例釋

0622 Sun, Yün-ho & Kao, Ming-fen: *Chin-i-tzu pien-hsi.*—Chengtu: Szu-ch'uan jen-min, 1981, 2, 2, 12, 352, 11, 27 p. [Differentiation and analysis of near-synonymous characters.]
孫雲鶴、高明芬：近義字辨析

3.4.2. Antonymous Words (0623–0653)
3.4.2.1. Definition and Differentiation (0623–0636)

0623 Chang, Kung: Hsien-tai Han-yü fan-i-tz'u t'an-t'ao.—*HPTH* 1979:4, 36–52. [An investigation into Modern Chinese antonyms.]
張弓：現代漢語反義詞探討

0624 Ch'en, Yung-yü: Fan-i-tz'u te wen-t'i. —*Kuo-yü yü-fa yen-chiu lun-chi* (0082), 417–419. [The problem of antonyms.]
陳永禹：反義詞的問題

0625 Fu, Huai-ch'ing: Yen-yü fan-i-tz'u.— *YCT* 2, 1981, 40–44. [Contextual antonyms.]
符淮青：言語反義詞

0626 Hai, Liu: Tsen-yang fen-pien fan-i-tz'u? —*FCCY* 1960:21–22, 25. [How to differentiate antonyms?]
海流：怎樣分辨反義詞？

0627 Kung, Ta-ch'ing: Fan-i-tzu te tu-yin ho shih-i wen-t'i.—*Han-yü lun-ts'ung* (0087), 78–105. [The problems of readings and explanations of meanings of antonymous characters.]/ In Classical Chinese.
龔達清：反義字的讀音和釋義問題

0628 Rygaloff, A.: A propos de l'antonymie: l'exemple du chinois.—*Journal de Psychologie Normale et Pathologique* 1958, 358–376./ *RBS* 5, 1959, 515, W. Simon.

0629 Sheng, Shou-mou: Yu-kuan i-i hsiang-fan te tz'u te chi-ko wen-t'i.—*YYWH* 1958:3, 24. [Several problems concerning words having mutually contrary meanings.]
盛守謀：有關意義相反的詞的幾個問題

0630 Sun, Liang-ming: Fan-i-tz'u.—*YWHH* 1958:1, 30–31. [Antonyms.]
孫艮明：反義詞

0631 T'ang, T'ing-ch'ih: Tsai t'an fan-i-tz'u

te wen-t'i.—*Kuo-yü yü-fa yen-chiu lun-chi* (0082), 45–47. [Another discussion on the problems of antonyms.]

湯廷池：再談反義詞的問題

0632   Wang, Chen-k'un & Hsieh, Wen-ch'ing: Fan-i-tz'u te i-su fen-hsi.—*TCSY* 1982:3, 75–76. [An analysis of the sememes in antonyms.]

王振昆、謝文慶：反義詞的義素分析

0633   Wang, Ch'ung-te: Kuang-yü fan-i-tz'u.— *CKYW* 1960:3, 336. [Concerning antonyms.]

王崇德：關於反義詞

0634   Wei, Li-hsiang: T'ung-i-tz'u, fan-i-tz'u chi ch'i-t'a (0591). [Synonyms, antonyms, etc.]

魏立湘：同義詞反義詞及其它

0635   Wu, Chan-k'un: Lüeh t'an to-i-tz'u ho fan-i-tz'u te kuan-hsi.—*YWHH* 1958:1, 32. [A brief discussion on the relationships of polysemous words and antonyms.]

武占坤：略談多義詞和反義詞的關係

0636   Yen, Szu: Mei-ko tz'u shih pu shih i-ting yu i-ko fan-i-tz'u?—*YWHH* 1960:2, 32. [Does necessarily each word have an antonym?]

言寺：每個詞是不是一定有一個反義詞？

3.4.2.2. Functions and Uses (0637–0641)

0637   Chang, Kung-kuei: Fan-i-tz'u chi ch'i tsai kou-tz'u shang ho hsiu-tz'u shang te tso-yung.—*CKYW* 1957:8, 32–36; *Hsientai Han-yü . . . tzu-liao* (0064), 541–554. [Antonyms and their functions in word formation and in rhetoric.]

張拱貴：反義詞及其在構詞上和修辭上的作用

0638   Chang, Kung-yen: Lun fan-i-tz'u te tso-yung.—*HYW* 1960:4, 32–33. [On the functions of antonyms.]

張公言：論反義詞的作用

0639   Lu, Chia-wen: Tan-yin-chieh fan-i-tz'u

te fen-lei chi yün-yung.—*YLT* 8, 1981, 34–49. [The classifications and applications of monosyllabic antonyms.]

盧甲文：單音節反義詞的分類及運用

0640   Ni, Pao-yüan: Fan-i-tz'u te hsiu-tz'u tso-yung.—*YWCS* 1957:9, 19–21. [Rhetorical functions of antonyms.]

倪寶元：反義詞的修辭作用

0641   Tseng, Ti: *Hsiang-fan tz'u-yü yung-fa chih-tao.*—Hong Kong: Chiao-yü shu-tien, n.d., [i], 133 p. [A guide to the usage of antonymous words and phrases.]

曾蒂：相反詞語用法指導

3.4.2.3. Collection and Analysis (0642–0653)

0642   Anonymous: *Hsiang-fan-tz'u ho t'ung-i-tz'u* (0594). [Antonyms and synonyms.]

無名氏：相反詞和同義詞

0643   Feng, Shih: *Fan-i-yü tz'u-tien.*—Hong Kong: Ch'ung-ming, 1963, 123 p. [A dictionary of antonymous words.]

馮式：反義語辭典

0644   Hsü, Ming: *To-i-tz'u, fan-i-tz'u, p'ien-i-tz'u* (0674). [Polysemous words, antonyms, and one-sided meaning (compound) words.]

徐明：多義詞、同義詞、偏義詞

0645   Kao, Ch'ing-szu: *T'ung-i-tz'u ho fan-i-tz'u* (0604). [Synonyms and antonyms.]

高慶賜：同義詞和反義詞

0646   Keng, Fei: Fan-i hsing-jung-tz'u.— *CKYW* 1981:5, 362. [Antonymous adjectives.]

耿非：反義形容詞

0647   Keng, Fei: Fan-i tung-tz'u.—*CKYW* 1981:6, 415. [Antonymous verbs.]

耿非：反義動詞

0648   T'ang, T'ing-ch'ih: Yü i hsiang-fan te hsing-jung-tz'u.—*Kuo-yü yü-fa yen-chiu lun-chi* (0082), 23–29. [Antonymous adjectives.]

湯廷池：語義相反的形容詞

0649 T'ang, T'ing-ch'ih: Tsai t'an yü i hsiang-fan te hsing-jung-tz'u.—*Kuo-yü yü-fa yen-chiu lun-chi* (0082), 31—36. [Another discussion on antonymous adjectives.]
湯廷池：再談語義相反的形容詞

0650 T'ang, T'ing-ch'ih: San-t'an yü i hsiang-fan te hsing-jung-tz'u.—*Kuo-yü yü-fa yen-chiu lun-chi* (0082), 37—43. [A third discussion on antonymous adjectives.]
湯廷池：三談語義相反的形容詞

0651 Tung, Kuei-hsien: *Fan-i-yü tz'u-tien.*—Taipei: P'ing-p'ing, 1965, 3, 123 p. [A dictionary of antonyms.]
董桂先：反義語辭典

0652 Wu, Hua: *T'ung-i-yü fan-i-tz'u tz'u-tien* (0617). [A dictionary of synonyms and antonyms.]
吳華：同義語反義詞辭典

0653 Yang, Chih-chou: Fou-ting-tz'u te fan-i-tz'u.—*CKYW* 1981:2, 143. [The antonyms of negatives.]
楊之舟：否定詞的反義詞

3.4.3. One-sided Meaning Words (0654—0658)

0654 Hsü, Ming: *To-i-tz'u, fan-i-tz'u, p'ien-i-tz'u* (0674). [Polysemous words, antonyms, and one-sided meaning (compound) words.]
徐明：多義詞、反義詞、偏義詞

0655 Li, Chin-hsi: Kuo-yü chung fu-ho-tz'u te ch'i-i ho p'ien-i.—*NSTH* 1:1, 1930, 1—14. [Divergent meanings and one-sided meanings of compound words in the National Language.]
黎錦熙：國語中複合詞的歧義和偏義

0656 Liu, P'an-sui: Chung-kuo wen-fa fu-tz'u p'ien-i li.—*Wen-tzu yin-yün-hsüeh lun-ts'ung* (0073), 127—137. [Examples of one-sided meanings for compound words in Chinese grammar.]
劉盼遂：中國文法複詞偏義例

0657 Liu, P'an-sui: Chung-kuo wen-fa fu-tz'u chung p'ien-i li hsü chü.—*YCHP* 12, 1932, 2589—2594. [A continuation of the examples of one-sided meanings for compound words in Chinese grammar.]
劉盼遂：中國文法複詞中偏義例緒舉

0658 Wang, Chien-fan: P'ien-i fu-tz'u chü yü.—*YCT* 2, 1981, 36—39. [Examples of compound words with one-sided meanings.]
王建凡：偏義複詞舉隅

3.5. Polysemous, Homophonous, Polyphonous, and Onomatopoeic Words (0659—0773)
3.5.1. Polysemous Words (0659—0676)
3.5.1.1. Definition and Differentiation (0659—0668)

0659 Chao, Yuen Ren: Ambiguity in Chinese.—*Studia Serica Bernhard Karlgren dedicata* (0061), 1—13; *Aspects of Chinese sociolinguistics* (0048), 293—308./ *RBS* 5, 1959, 481, W.A.C.H. Dobson.

0660 Chou, Sheng-ya: Lun i-tz'u to lei.—*CLTH* 1979:1, 67—75. [On one word which belongs to multiple word classes.]
周生亞：論一詞多類

0661 Ishida, Takeo: Dō-ji i-gi no kotoba.—*Chūgoku gogaku jiten* (0037), 943—945. [Words with the same characters but different meanings.]
石田武夫：同字異義のことば

0662 Ishiyama, Akeo: Chūgokugo ni okeru *tagishi* to *dōonshi* no mondai.—*HKDKZ* 6, 1971, 1—17. [The problems concerning the polysemous words and homophones in the Chinese language.]
石山曙生：中國語における『多義詞』と『同音詞』の問題

0663 Kao, Ch'ing-szu: Shih lun Han-yü i-tz'u to-i te nei-pu lien-hsi.—*CKYW* 1978:3, 184—188, 205. [A preliminary discussion on the internal relationships of one word having multiple meanings.]
高慶賜：試論漢語一詞多義的內部聯系

0664   Lin, Hsing-kuang: I-tz'u to-i ch'ien shuo.—*YCT* 1, 1981, 62–67. [A brief discussion on one word having multiple meanings.]
林杏光：一詞多義淺說

0665   Liu, Ching-fu: Tui hsien-tai Han-yü tz'u te to-i hsien-hsiang te kuan-ch'a.—*YLT* 2, 1958, 120–132. [An observation on the phenomenon of the multiple meanings of words in Modern Chinese.]
劉鏡芙：對現代漢語詞的多義現象的觀察

0666   Sun, Ch'ang-hsu: *Han-yü tz'u-hui* (0165), Chap. 15: Polysemous words. [Chinese lexicon.]
孫常叙：漢語詞彙／第十五章：多義詞

0667   Wu, Chan-k'un: Kuan-yü to-i-tz'u te chi-ko wen-t'i.—*YWHH* 1957:5, 32–34. [Several problems concerning polysemous words.]
武占坤：關於多義詞的幾個問題

0668   Yü, Chia-chi: To-i-tz'u, t'ung-hsing-tz'u, t'ung-yin-tz'u.—*YYWH* 1981:2, 36–37. [Polysemous words, homographs, and homophones.]
餘家驥：多義詞、同形詞、同音詞

3.5.1.2. Collection and Analysis (0669–0676)

0669   Anonymous: *Ch'ang-yung to-yin to-i tzu shou-ts'e* (0711). [A handbook of commonly used polyphonous and polysemous characters.]
無名氏：常用多音多義字手冊

0670   Ch'i, Hsüeh-ch'u: *To-yin to-i tzu yung-fa chü-li* (0715). [Examples of the uses of polyphonous and polysemous characters.]
齊學初：多音多義字用法舉例

0671   Chou, Cheng-kuei: *I-tzu to-i hsi.*—Hofei: An-hui jen-min, 1981, 235 p. [An analysis of polysemous characters.]
周正貴：一字多義析

0672   Chu, Sheng-k'o: *Ch'ang-yung to-yin to-i tzu* (0720). [Commonly used polyphonous and polysemous characters.]
朱盛科：常用多音多義字

0673   Hou, Chia-hsü: *To-yin to-i-tzu hui shih* (0724). [A collection with explanations of polyphonous and polysemous characters.]
侯家序：多音多義字滙釋

0674   Hsü, Ming: *To-i-tz'u, fan-i-tz'u, p'ien-i-tz'u.*—Hong Kong: Chin-hsiu, 1974, 3rd ed., 2, 86 p. [Polysemous words, antonyms, and one-sided meaning (compound) words.]
徐明：多義詞、反義詞、偏義詞

0675   Huai, K'u: Ch'ang-yung te t'ung-tzu i-i tz'u.—*YWCS* 1952:6, 21–22. [Commonly used homographic polysemous words.]
懷庫：常用的同字異義詞

0676   Takahashi, Kunpei: Dō shi i gi.—*CGKK* 32, 1954, 174–177; *Kindai* 25, 1959, 1–27. [Identical words with different meanings.]
高橋君平：同詞異義

3.5.2. Homophonous Words (0677–0699)
3.5.2.1. Definition and Differentiation (0677–0684)

0677   Chou, Yao-wen: Kuan-yü ch'ü-pieh t'ung-yin-tz'u ho tz'u te piao-chun wen-t'i.—*CKYW* 1955:6, 13–14. [Problems concerning the distinction of homophones and the standardization of words.]
周耀文：關於區別同音詞和詞的標準問題

0678   Liu, Kuan-ch'un: Lun t'ung-yin-tz'u.—*CKYW* 1956:11, 20–22. [On homophones.]
劉冠羣：論同音詞

0679   Liu, Tse-hsien: T'ung-yin-tz'u te wen-t'i pu ta.—*CKYW* 1956:11, 18–20. [The problem of homophones is not great.]
劉澤先：同音詞的問題不大

0680   Sun, Ch'ang-hsü: *Han-yü tz'u-hui* (0165), Chap. 14: Homophones. [Chinese lexicon.]
孫常敘：漢語詞彙／第十四章：同音詞

0681   Sun, Liang-ming: Han-yü t'ung-yin-tz'u to-i-tz'u yen-chiu chung te chi-ko wen-t'i. —*STSY* 1962:1, 50—63. [Several problems in the study. of Chinese homophones and polysemous words.]
孫良明：漢語同音詞多義詞研究中的幾個問題

0682   Ts'ao, Hsien-cho: Kuan-yü t'ung-yin t'i-tai.—*YWYC* 1, 1981, 101—105. [Concerning substitution (of words) by homophones.]
曹先擢：關於同音替代

0683   T'sou, Benjamin K.: Homophony and internal change in Chinese.—*CAAAL* 3, 1976, 67—86. J.S./ English, Mandarin, and Cantonese examples.

0684   Yü, Chia-chi: To-i-tz'u, t'ung-hsing-tz'u, t'ung-yin-tz'u (0668). [Polysemous words, homographs, and homophones.]
餘家驥：多義詞、同形詞、同音詞

3.5.2.2. Collection and Analysis (0685—0699)

0685   Ai, Hung-i: *T'ung-yin tzu-tien.*—Ching-shuichen (Taichung-hsien): 1953; 1974, 14th ed., 2 [2], 2, 12, 76, 417, 15 p., 2 tab. [A dictionary of homophonous characters.]
艾弘毅：同音字典

0686   Chang, Shih-ying: *T'ung-yin chin-yin tz'u yung-fa li chieh.*—Chengchow: Ho-nan jen-min, 1982, 2, 6, 98 p. [Explanations with examples of methods of using homophones and near-homophones.]
張世英：同音近音詞用法例解

0687   Che-chiang-sheng chiao-yü-t'ing: *T'ung-yin ch'ang-yung tzu-tien.*—Hangchow: Che-chiang jen-min, 1959, [i], 45, 233 p., illus. [A dictionary of commonly used homophonous characters.]
浙江省教育廳：同音常用字典

0688   Chung-kuo ta tz'u-tien pien-tsuan-ch'u: *T'ung-yin tzu-tien.*—Peking: Shang-wu, 1956, 12, 4, 209, 3, 4, 759 p. [A dictionary of homophonous characters.]
中國大辭典編纂處：同音字典

0689   Fang, Shih-to: *Tseng pu Kuo-yin tzu-hui* —Taipei: K'ai-ming, 1968; 1974, 3rd ed., [1], 171 p. [An augmented edition of a glossary of (homophonous) characters in the National Pronunciation.]
方師鐸：增補國音字彙

0690   Hsü, Ming: *T'ung-yin-tz'u, t'ung-hsing-tz'u, t'ung-i-tz'u* (0603). [Homophones, homographs, and synonyms.]
徐明：同音詞、同形詞、同義詞

0691   Hu-nan jen-min ch'u-pan-she: *Ch'ang-yung t'ung-yin tzu-hui.*—Changsha: Hu-nan jen-min, 1958, 16, 306 p. [A glossary of commonly used homophonous characters.]
湖南人民出版社：常用同音字滙

0692   Ku, Yüeh: *Han-yü p'in-yin tz'u-hui* t'ung-yin-tz'u tsai t'ung-chi.—*YWYC* 1, 1981, 99—100. [Another statistic on the homophones in *Han-yü p'in-yin tz'u-hui.*]/ Referring to Mochizuki's statistics (0695).
顧越：『漢語拼音詞滙』同音詞再統計

0693   Liu, Tsai-fu: *Piao-chun Kuo-yin t'ung-yin tzu-hui.*—Taichung: Lan teng wen-hua shih-yeh, 1977, [i], 3, 157 p. [A glossary of homophonous characters in the standard National Pronunciation.]
劉載福：標準國音同音字彙

0694   Ma, Hsüeh-liang: *Chung-wen t'ung-yin tzu-tien.*—*CYTS* 2, 1947, 33—35. [(A review of) *Chung-wen t'ung-yin tzu-tien* (by Tu Sung-shou).]
馬學良：『中文同音字典』（杜松壽編）

0695   Mochizuki, Yasokichi. Transl. by Sung, Hsüeh: Jih-yü ho Han-yü te t'ung-yin-tz'u t'ung-chi pi-chiao.—*YHH* 1980:1, 216—217. [A statistical comparison of the homophones in Japanese and Chinese.]/

See Ku Yüeh (0692).

望月八十吉著，宋學譯：日語和漢語的同音詞統計比較

0696   T'ai-wan-sheng Kuo-yü t'ui-hsing wei-yüan-hui: *Kuo-yin piao-chun hui-pien.*— Taipei: T'ai-wan k'ai-ming shu-tien, 1952; 1968, 18th print., 6, 80, 49 p. [Collection of (homophonous) characters in the standard National Pronunciation.]

臺灣省國語推行委員會：國音標準彙編

0697   Wang, Chih-jung & Chao, Ching-yün: *T'ung-yin-tzu yung-fa.*—Shenyang: Liaoning jen-min, 1954, [i], 4, 184, 20 p. [Methods of using homophonous characters.]

王志榮、趙景雲：同音字用法

0698   Wang, Hsing-hua: *Kuo-yin tzu-tien.*— Taipei: Cheng-chung, 1955; 1966, 6th ed., 5, 105, 565 p. [A (character) dictionary in the National Pronunciation.]/ Arranged by homophones.

王星華：國音字典

0699   Yü, Ping-chao: *T'ung-yin tzu-hui.*— Hong Kong: Hsin Ya-chou, 1979, [8], 64, 230 p. [A glossary of homophonous characters.]

余秉昭：同音字彙

3.5.3. Polyphonous Words (0700–0744)
3.5.3.1. Definition and Differentiation (0700–0710)

0700   Chang, Yao-hsiung: Chūgokugo no taonji ni tsuite.—*Senshū jinbun ronshū* 28, 1982, 67–104. [On polyphonous characters in Chinese.]

張耀雄：中國語の多音字について

0701   Ch'i, T'ieh-hen: To-yin-tzu te lai-li.— *CKYT* 3:2, 1958, 30–37. [The origin of polyphonous characters.]

齊鐵恨：多音字的來歷

0702   Ch'i, T'ieh-hen: To-yin-tzu li te yü-tz'u pien-yin.—*CKYT* 3:3, 1958, 39–42.

[Lexico-phonetic changes of polyphonous characters.]

齊鐵恨：多音字裏的語詞變音

0703   Chou, Yu-kuang: Hsien-tai Han-tzu chung te to-yin-tzu wen-t'i.—*CKYW* 1979:6, 401. [Problems of polyphonous characters in Modern Chinese writing.]

周有光：現代漢字中的多音字問題

0704   Hung, Hsin-heng: Kuan-yü tu-p'o te wen-t'i.—*CKYW* 1965:1, 37–43./ *RBS* 11, 1965, 394, N.G.D. Malmqvist. [Concerning the problem of 'different readings' (of characters in ancient Chinese).]

洪心衡：關於『讀破』的問題

0705   Jen, Ming-shan: Ku-chi chung te p'o-yin i-tu wen-t'i pu-i.—*CKYW* 1965:1, 44–48./ *RBS* 11, 1965, 395, N.G.D. Malmqvist. [Additional meanings to the problems of 'polyphonous and different readings' in ancient texts.]/ Addenda to Lü Chi-p'ing & Ch'en Hsin-hsiang's article (0706).

任銘善：古籍中的『破音異讀』問題補義

0706   Lü, Chi-p'ing & Ch'en, Hsin-hsiang: Ku-chi chung te p'o-yin i-tu wen-t'i.— *CKYW* 1964:5, 368–375./ *RBS* 10, 1964, 508, M.J. Künstler. [The problems of polyphonous and different readings in ancient texts.]

呂冀平、陳欣向：古籍中的破音異讀問題

0707   Wang, K'o-chung: Kuan-yü i-tu ho tz'u-hsing chuan-hua te yung-tzu wen-t'i.— *SHST* 1979:2, 81–86. [Concerning the problems in using characters with different readings and with changes in lexical features.]

王克仲：關於異讀和詞性轉化的用字問題

0708   Wu, Hai-jan: Ch'ien t'an t'ung-tzu i-tu. —*YCT* 1, 1981, 36–40. [A brief discussion on identical characters with different readings.]

吳海然：淺談同字異讀

0709   Yang, Po-chün: P'o-yin lüeh k'ao.—

KWYK 74, 1948, 22–24. [A brief study of polyphonous characters.]

楊伯峻：破音略考

0710   Yoshino, Mineō: *Chūgokugo no haon no kenkyū.*—*OGDG* 7, 1959, 147–169. [A study of Chinese polyphonous characters.]

吉野美彌雄：中國語の破音の研究

3.5.3.2. Collection and Analysis (0711–0744)

0711   Anonymous: *Ch'ang-yung to-yin to-i tzu shou-ts'e.*—Hong Kong: Shang-hai shu-chü, 1978, 5, 120 p. [A handbook of commonly used polyphonous and polysemous characters.]

無名氏：常用多音多義字手册

0712   Chang, Cheng-nan: *Lien-kuan Kuo-yü p'o-yin tz'u-tien.*—Taipei: Lien-kuan, 1972, [xi], 493, 18, [ii] p. [The Lien-kuan dictionary of polyphonous characters in the National Language.]

張正男：聯貫國語破音辭典

0713   Ch'en, Hsüan: *Han-tzu i-i i-tu chü-li.*—Peking: Shang-wu, 1964, vi, 42 p. [Examples of Chinese characters having different meanings and readings.]

陳玄：漢字異義異讀舉例

0714   Ch'eng, Yang-chih: *P'u-t'ung-hua i-tu tz'u shen-yin chien-tzu.*—Peking: Wen-tzu kai-ko, 1965, 23, 92 p./ Arranged according to the Four-corner System. [Pronunciations and index to words with different readings in the Common Language.]

程養之：普通話異讀詞審音檢字

0715   Ch'i, Hsüeh-ch'u: *To-yin to-i tzu yung-fa chü-li.*—Shanghai: Shang-hai chiao-yü, 1964, 1st ed.; 1965, 2nd print., 96 p.; *Yü-wen hui-pien* (0058), 35:119. [Examples of the uses of polyphonous and polysemous characters.]

齊學初：多音多義字用法舉例

0716   Ch'i, Su-chen: *Ch'ang-yung te p'o-yin*

tzu.—*HWSC* 12, 1978, 43–49; 13, 32–36. [Commonly used polyphonous characters.]

齊素貞：常用的破音字

0717   Ch'i, T'ieh-hen: *Ch'ang-yung to-yin tzu lien-hsi k'o-pen.*—Taipei: Shang-wu, 1962, 6, 200 p. [An exercise book for commonly used polyphonous characters.]

齊鐵恨：常用多音字練習課本

0718   Ch'i, T'ieh-hen: *P'o-yin tzu chiang-i.*—Taipei: Ch'iao-liang, 1963; 1969, 2nd ed., 2, 104 p. [Lectures on polyphonous characters.]

齊鐵恨：破音字講義

0719   Chou, Chieh-ch'en: *Wo yao cheng-fu p'o-yin tzu.*—Taipei: Ming-jen, 1978, 244 p. [I want to conquer polyphonous characters.]

周介塵：我要征服破音字

0720   Chu, Sheng-k'o: *Ch'ang-yung to-yin to-i tzu.*—Chengtu: Szu-ch'uan jen-min, 1979, 2, 14, 194 p. [Commonly used polyphonous and polysemous characters.]

朱盛科：常用多音多義字

0721   Chü, Ch'un-hsin: *Ch'ieh-yün chih to-yin tzu yen-chiu.*—Hong Kong: Chu-hai College, 1976, 9, 3, 12, 598 p./ Unpubl. M.A. thesis. [A study of the polyphonous characters (found) in *Ch'ieh-yün.*]

橘純信：『切韻』之多音字研究

0722   Fu, Tung-hua: *Pei-ching-yin i-tu tzu te ch'u-pu t'an-t'ao.*—Peking: Wen-tzu kai-ko, 1958, 2, 44 p. [A preliminary inquiry of characters with different readings in Peking pronunciation.]

傅東華：北京音異讀字的初步探討

0723   Han-lin ch'u-pan-she pien-chi wei-yüan-hui: *Tsui hsin shih-yung p'o-yin tz'u-tien.*—Tainan: Ditto, 1964, 2nd ed., 6, 238 p. [A new practical dictionary of polyphonous characters.]

翰林出版社編輯委員會：最新實用破音辭典

0724 Hou, Chia-hsü: *To-yin to-i tzu hui shih.*
—Kunming: Yün-nan jen-min, 1979, [ii],
2, 8, 162 p. [A collection with explanations of polyphonous and polysemous
characters.]
侯家序：多音多義字滙釋

0725 Hsieh, Te-shui: *P'o-yin tzu-tien.*—Kaohsiung: Te-hsing-shih, 1979, [iv], 146 p.
[A dictionary of polyphonous characters.]
謝德水：破音字典

0726 Hsü, Hsüeh-wen: *To-yin to-i tzu hui-
pien.*—Huhehot: Nei Meng-ku chiao-yü,
1981, 140 p. [A collection of polyphonous
and polysemous characters.]
徐學文：多音多義字滙編

0727 Hsü, Yü-yen: *Hsin-pien p'o-yin tzu-tien.*
—Tainan: Kuang-t'ien, 1975, 13, 65, 17
p. [A newly compiled dictionary of
polyphonous characters.]
徐毓晏：新編破音字典

0728 Hsüeh-yu t'u-shu ch'u-pan-she pien-chi-
pu: *Ching-pien p'o-yin tzu-tien.* Fu *Kuo-yü
fen-lei hui-pien.*—Taipei: Ditto, 1963, 35,
315 p. [A carefully compiled dictionary
of polyphonous characters. With a collection
of classified vocabulary in the National
Language.]
學友圖書出版社編輯部：精編破音字典
附國語分類彙編

0729 Jui, Chia-chih: *Tsui-hsin shih-yung p'o-
yin tzu-tien.*—Taipei: T'ai-wan hsüeh-
sheng, 1971, 4, 80 p. [A new practical
dictionary of polyphonous characters.]
芮家智：最新實用破音字典

0730 Jui, Chia-chih: *P'o-yin tzu-tien.*—Chiayi:
Wen-yu shu-chü, 1975, 4, 160 p. [A
dictionary of polyphonous characters.]
芮家智：破音字典

0731 K'o, Sun-t'ien: *Ch'ang-yung p'o-yin tzu-
tien.*—Taipei: Hsin-sheng, 1957, 7, 103 p.;
1962, rev. ed., 7, 125 p. [A dictionary of
commonly used polyphonous characters.]
柯遜添：常用破音字典

0732 Lin, Sung-p'ei: *Shih-yung p'o-yin tzu-
tien.*—Taipei: Kuo-yü jih-pao-she, 1979,
2, [i], 29, 324 p. [A practical dictionary
of polyphonous characters.]
林松培：實用破音字典

0733 Liu, Ping-nan: *Tz'u-hsing piao-chu
p'o-yin tzu chi chieh.*—Taipei: I-chih
shu-chu, 1960; 1973, 8th ed., 2, 5, 183,
7 p. [A collection with explanations of
polyphonous characters and indications
of their word classes.]
劉秉南：詞性標註破音字集解

0734 Lu, Shih-ch'eng: *Piao-chun p'o-yin
tz'u-tien.*—Taipei: Wen-hua t'u-shu, 1967,
11, 450 p. [A standard dictionary of
polyphonous characters.]
陸師成：標準破音辭典

0735 P'u-t'ung-hua shen-yin wei-yüan-hui: *P'u-
t'ung-hua i-tu tz'u san-tz'u shen-yin tsung-
piao ch'u-kao.*—Peking: Wen-tzu kai-ko,
1963, 4, 247 p. [A first draft of the third
revised list of characters with variant
readings in the Common Language.]
普通話審音委員會：普通話異讀詞三次審音總
表初稿

0736 P'u-t'ung-hua yu-yin yen-chiu-pan: *To-
yin to-i tzu hui-pien.*—Peking: Shang-wu,
1963, 14, 86 p. [A collection of
polyphonous and polysemous characters.]
普通話語音研究班：多音多義字滙編

0737 Su, Jui-chang: *Ch'ang-yung p'o-yin
tz'u-tien.*—Taipei: Kuo-yü jih-pao-she,
1978, 19, 171 p. [A dictionary of
commonly used polyphonous words.]
蘇瑞章：常用破音詞典

0738 Sun, Yü-yen: *P'o-yin chih-nan.*—Tainan:
(？), 1975, 17, 75 p. [A guide to polyphonous characters.]
孫毓晏：破音指南

0739 Tanaka, Shū & Torii, Tsurumi: *Chūgoku*

haonji reikai.—Tokyo: Eiwa Gogakusha, 1956; 1981, rev. ed., 359. [Explanations with examples of polyphonous characters in Chinese.]
田中秀、鳥居鶴美：中國破音字例解

0740 Torii, Hisayasu & Tanaka, Tatsusaburō: *Jōyō haonji reikai.*—*Shinago to jibun* 5:10, 1943, 11–15; 11, 14–18; 12, 13–19. [Explanations of commonly used polyphonous characters with examples.]
鳥居久靖、田中辰佐武郎：常用破音字例解

0741 Tseng, Kuo-t'ai: *P'o-yin tzu ta-ch'üan.*—Taipei: Ming-jen, 1978; 1980, 4th ed., 405 p. [A compendium of polyphonous characters.]
曾國泰：破音字大全

0742 Tsuchiya, Meiji & Miyahara, Minpei: *Shina haon jiten.*—Tokyo: Bunkyūdō, 1932, 2, 28, 358, 12, 20 p.; Tokyo: Ryū-mon shokyoku, 1944, repr. [A dictionary of Chinese polyphonous characters.]
土屋明治、宮原民平：支那破音字典

0743 Tung, Kuei-hsien: *T'ung-tzu i-yin t'zu-tien.*—Taipei: P'ing-p'ing, 1964, 228 p. [A dictionary of identical characters with different sounds.]
董桂先：同字異音辭典

0744 Yü, Yin: *To-yin to-i tzu hui-pien.*—Peking: Shang-wu, 1973, (not seen). [A collection of polyphonous and polysemous characters.]
于殷：多音多義字滙編

3.5.4. Onomatopoeic Words (0745–0773)
3.5.4.1. Definition and General Studies (0745–0768)

0745 Chang, Ching: T'an hsiang-sheng tz'u.—*HYHH* 1982:4, 3–8. [A discussion of onomatopoeic words.]
張靜：談象聲詞

0746 Chang, Yen: *Yü-wen ts'ung-hua.*—Taipei: Hua-ming shu-chü, 1955, 2, 4, 68 p./

43–52: Onomatopoeic words, alliterative and rhyming binomes, tongue twisters, 'cut-foot phrases', *hsieh-hou-yü*, proverbs. [Collected talks on (Chinese) language and writing.]
張嚴：語文叢話／43–52：擬聲詞、雙聲疊韻吃口令、切腳語、歇後語、諺語

0747 Chao, Chin-ming: Yüan-jen tsa-chü chung te hsiang-sheng tz'u.—*CKYW* 1981:2, 144–146. [Onomatopoeic words (found) in Yüan dramas.]
趙金銘：元人雜劇中的象聲詞

0748 Ch'en, Yüeh: Hsiang-sheng tzu ho i-yin tzu te chien-hua wen-t'i.—*CKYW* 1961:3, 34–37. [The problems in simplification of onomatopoeic characters and trans-literation characters.]
陳越：象聲字和譯音字的簡化問題

0749 Chiao, J.W.: Zur Onomatopöie in der chinesischen Sprache: Synchrone und diachrone Analyse der verschiedenen Strukturtypen.—*OE* 16, 1969, 209–258.

0750 Chih, Han: Yen-chiu mo-sheng tzu.—*CKYT* 35:1, 1974, 36–37. [A study on onomatopoeic words.]
稚翰：研究摹聲字

0751 Ch'u, Szu-ching: Hsiang-sheng tzu.—*YWHH* 1953:9, 57–60. [Onomatopoeic words.]
褚四荆：象聲字

0752 Fang, I-ch'ün: Ni-sheng tz'u kai yung p'in-yin.—*WTKK* 1962:6, 18. [Changing onomatopoeic words into Pinyin spellings.]
方軼羣：擬聲詞改用拼音

0753 Hoa, M.: *Les onomatopées en chinois commun—putonghua.*—Paris: l'École des Hautes Études en Sciences Sociales, 1976, 180 p./ Unpubl. doc. diss.

0754 Keng, Erh-ling: Hsien-tai Han-yü chung te ku hsiang-sheng tz'u.—*YCT* 1, 1981, 58–61. [Ancient onomatopoeic words

found in Modern Chinese.]
耿二嶺：現代漢語中的古象聲詞

0755   Liao, Hua-chin: Shuo hsiang-sheng tz'u.
—*CKYW* 1956:9, 17–18. [On onomatopoeic words.]
廖化津：説象聲詞

0756   Lin, Wen-chin: Mo-sheng yu t'ung-kan.
—*YWHT* 4, 1978, 95–100. [Onomatopoea and synesthesia.]
林文金：摹聲與通感

0757   Liu, Hui-kuang: *Ni-sheng tzu yen-chiu.*
—Taichung: The Author, 1974, 250 p.
[A study on onomatopoeic words.]
劉惠光：擬聲字研究

0758   Liu, Ping-wen, et al.: Tsai t'an hsiang-sheng tz'u.—*YWHH* 1957:7, 32–33. [Once more on onomatopoeic words.]
劉秉文等：再談象聲詞

0759   Nishikawa, Kazuo: Gendai Chūgokugo no giseigo, gitaigo no hyōki hōhō ni tsuite.
—*I-a* 5, 1975, (left) 15–34. [On the methods for transcription of Modern Chinese onomatopoeic words and mimetic words.]
西川和男：現代中國語の擬聲語、擬態語の表記方法について

0760   Noguchi, Munechika: Chūgokugo giseigo no tokushitsu ni tsuite.—*KDKK* 26, 1977, 15–24. [On the characteristics of Chinese onomatopoeic words.]
野口宗親：中國語擬聲語の特質について

0761   Noguchi, Munechika & Wang, Ch'ang-chiang: Chūgokugo ni okeru giseigo goi no kenkyū.—*KDKK* 28, 1979, 11–19; 29, 1980, 9–15. [A study of onomatopoeic vocabulary in the Chinese language.]
野口宗親、王長江：中國語における擬聲語語彙の研究

0762   Rai, Tsutomu: Kango no onomatopea.
—*GGSK* 151, 1964, 26–31. [The onomatopoea of the Chinese language.]

賴惟勤：漢語のオノマトパア

0763   Sakamoto, Ichirō: Giseigo gitaigo ni yūrai-suru Chūgokugo goi.—*KSTZ* 4, 1971, 21–28. [Vocabulary of the Chinese language originated from onomatopoeic and mimetic words.]
坂本一郎：擬聲語擬態語に由來する中國語語彙

0764   Satō, Haruhiko: Gendai Kango ni okeru shōseishi.—*I-a* 6, 1976, 63–68. [Onomatopoeic words in Modern Chinese.]
佐藤晴彦：現代漢語における象聲詞

0765   Shao, Ching-min: Ni-sheng tz'u ch'u t'an.—*YCYY* 1981:4, 57–66. [A preliminary investigation into onomatopoeic words.]
邵敬敏：擬聲詞初探

0766   Tamamura, Fumio: Nihongo to Chūgokugo ni okeru onshōchōgo.—*Ōtani Joshidai Kokubun* 9, 1979, 208–216. [Sound symbolism in Japanese and Chinese.]
玉村文郎：日本語と中國語における音象徵語

0767   Tsuchiya, Shin'ichi: Chūgokugo no giseigo ni tsuite.—*Takushoku Daigaku Ronshū* 22, 1959, 1–16. [Onomatopoeic words of Chinese.]
土屋申一：中國語の擬聲語について

0768   Wanaka, Masayuki & Okamoto, Yasushi: Giseigo, gitaigo.—*Chūgoku gogaku jiten* (0037), 951–955. [Onomatopoeic words and mimetic words.]
和中昌之、岡本靖：擬聲語、擬態語

3.5.4.2. Functions and Uses (0769–0773)

0769   Chang, Hsing-hua: Hsiang-sheng tz'u te yü-fa ti-wei.—*YWYT* 1981:4, 25. [The grammatical status of onomatopoeic words.]
張興華：象聲詞的語法地位

0770   Chung, Lung-lin: Hsien-tai Han-yü chung te hsiang-sheng tz'u shih hsu-tz'u ma?—

Chiang-han hsüeh-pao 1962:3, 43–45. [Are onomatopoeic words in Modern Chinese cenematic words?]

鍾隆林：現代漢語中的象聲詞是虛詞嗎？

0771 Hua, Hung-i: Shih lun hsiang-sheng tz'u te hsiu-tz'u tso-yung.—*YCT* 2, 1981, 129–134. [A preliminary discussion on the rhetorical functions of onomatopoeic words.]

華宏義：試論象聲詞的修辭作用

0772 Huang, P'ei-wen: Hsiang-sheng tz'u te yü-fa kung-neng ho piao-tien fu-hao.—

YCT 3, 1982, 136–141. [The grammatical functions and punctuation marks of onomatopoeic words.]

黃佩文：象聲詞的語法功能和標點符號

0773 Ōkōchi, Yasunori: Onomatopea—Nichi-Chū giseigo yōrei shū.—*Chūgokugo* 229, 1979, 2–16. [Onomatopoea—A collection with examples of usages of onomatopoeic words in Japanese and Chinese.]

大河內康憲：オノマトペア―日中擬聲語用例集

4. CHINESE TRADITIONAL SEMANTICS
(0774–0952)

4.1. Definition (0774–0789)

0774   Chang, I-jen: *Chung-kuo yü-wen-hsüeh lun-chi.*—Taipei: Tung-sheng, 1981, 2, 2, 248 p. [Collected essays on Chinese language and writing.]/ Includes articles on Chinese traditional semantics.
張以仁：中國語文學論集

0775   Chang, I-jen: *Shuo-wen* hsün ku chieh. —*Chung-kuo . . . lun-chi* (0774), 21–33. [Explanations of (the meanings of) *hsün* and *ku* in *Shuo-wen.*]
張以仁：『說文』『訓』『詁』解

0776   Chang, I-jen: Ts'ung jo-kan yu-kuan tzu-liao k'an hsün-ku i tz'u tsao ch'i te han-i.—*BIHP* 44:1, 1972, 83–88; *Chung-kuo . . . lun-chi* (0774), 35–52. [The meanings of the term *hsün-ku* in an earlier period as seen from several related materials.]
張以仁：從若干有關資料看『訓詁』一詞早期的涵義

0777   Chang, Shih-lu: Hsün-ku-hsüeh yu wen-fa-hsueh.—*Hsüeh-shu* 3, 1940, 117–122; *Chung-kuo wen-fa ko-hsin lun-ts'ung* (0049), 167–174. [Chinese traditional semantics and the study of grammar.]
張世祿：訓詁學與文法學

0778   Ch'eng, Kuan-lin: Hsün-ku-hsüeh ch'ang-yung te shu-yü.—*YWHH* 1985:5, 51–52. [Commonly used terms in Chinese traditional semantics.]
程觀林：訓詁學常用的術語

0779   Chou, Fa-kao: Chung-kuo hsün-ku-hsüeh fa-fan.—*TLTC* 10:11, 1955, 11–14; *Chung-kuo yü-wen yen-chiu* (0051), 58–81. [An introduction to Chinese traditional semantics.]
周法高：中國訓詁學發凡

0780   Huang, Chi-kang: Hsün-ku shu lüeh.— *Chih-yen* 7, 1935, 1–9. [A brief account of Chinese traditional semantics.]
黃季剛：訓詁述略

0781   Huang, Chien-p'ing: Hsün-ku shih i.— *HCSY* 1981:3, 111–117. [Explanation of the meaning of Chinese traditional semantics.]
黃建平：訓詁釋義

0782   Jo, Shih: Hsüeh tien hsün-ku-hsüeh.— *PCST* 1982:2, 90–95, 54; 3, 88–95. [Learn a little bit of Chinese traditional semantics.]
若石：學點訓詁學

0783   Kanda, Kiichirō: Kunkogaku.—*Sekai dai hyakka jiten* (0042) 8, 591. [Chinese traditional semantics.]
神田喜一郎：訓詁學

0784   Kuraishi, Takeshirō: Kunkogaku.—*Ajia rekishi jiten* (0040) 3, 81–82. [Chinese traditional semantics.]
倉石武四郎：訓詁學

0785   Lin, Yin: Hsün-ku shu yao.—*Mu-to* 3–4, 1975, 1–10. [A brief account of the essentials in Chinese traditional semantics.]
林尹：訓詁述要

0786   Lin, Yin: Hsün-ku te yung-t'u yü t'iao-li.—*KMYK* 19:11, 1981, 23–28. [The usages and rules of Chinese traditional semantics.]
林尹：訓詁的用途與條例

0787   Lu, Tsung-ta: T'an-i-t'an hsün-ku-hsüeh. —*CKYW* 1957:4, 24–26. [A discussion on Chinese traditional semantics.]
陸宗達：談一談訓詁學

0788   Ma, Tsung-hsiang: Hsün-ku lüeh shuo. —*STHK* 1, 1942, 1–4. [A short discussion on Chinese traditional semantics.]
馬宗薌：訓詁略說

0789   Yin, Meng-lun: Lüeh t'an hsün-ku-hsüeh che men k'o-hsüeh te tui-hsiang ho jen-wu.—*WSC* 1957:6, 20–26. [A short discussion on the objectives and tasks of the scientific branch of Chinese traditional semantics.]

殷孟倫：略談訓詁學這門科學的對象和任務

4.2. History (0790–0802)

0790 Chang, I-jen: Hsün-ku-hsüeh te fa-chan yü ju-chia te kuan-hsi.—*Chung-kuo . . . lun-chi* (0774), 53–83. [The relationship between the development of Chinese traditional semantics and Confucianism.]

張以仁：訓詁學的發展與儒家的關係

0791 Chang, Shun-hui: Cheng Hsüan hsün-ku-hsüeh fa-wei.—*HCSY* 1981:3, 102–108. [The quintessence of Cheng Hsüan's Chinese traditional semantics.]

張舜徽：鄭玄訓詁學發微

0792 Chang, Wen-pin: Kao-yu Wang shih fu tzu hsün-ku-hsüeh chih ch'eng-chiu.—*CHN* 2, 1978, 113–135. [The achievements of Wang Nien-sun, the father, and Wang Yin-chih, the son, from Kaoyu, in Chinese traditional semantics.]

張文彬：高郵王氏父子訓詁學之成就

0793 Ch'en, Hui-chih: Kao-yu Wang shih fu tzu chih hsün-ku-hsüeh lüeh-lun.—*HHYK* 99, 1980, 43–47. [A short discussion on the Chinese traditional semantics of Wang Nien-sun, the father, and Wang Yin-chih, the son, from Kaoyu.]

陳徽治：高郵王氏父子之訓詁學略論

0794 Hamaguchi, Fujio: Ō Nenson ni okeru kunko no igi.—*THG* 65, 1983, 89–103; E.S. [The significance of Wang Nien-sun's Chinese traditional semantics.]

濱口富士雄：王念孫における訓詁の意義

0795 Hu, P'u-an: *Chung-kuo hsün-ku-hsüeh shih.*—Shanghai: Shang-wu, 1939, 5, 18, 359 p.; Taipei: Hua-lien, 1969, repr. [A history of Chinese traditional semantics.]

胡樸安：中國訓詁學史

0796 Huang, Yung-wu: Liu-shih nien lai chih

hsün-ku-hsüeh.—*Liu-shih nien lai chih Kuo-hsüeh* 2 (0050), 375–416. [Chinese traditional semantics in the past sixty years.]

黃永武：六十年來之訓詁學

0797 Li, Chin-hsi: Chin-tai Kuo-yü wen-hsüeh chih hsün-ku yen-chiu shih li.—*Wen-hsüeh chi-k'an* 1:1, 1934, 14–44. [Examples of studies of Chinese traditional semantics found in recent National Language literature.]

黎錦熙：近代國語文學之訓詁研究示例

0798 Lin, Chiung-yang: Liu-shih nien lai chih hsün-ku-hsüeh.—*HHYK* 27, 1974, 20–22. [Chinese traditional semantics in the past sixty years.]

林炯陽：六十年來之訓詁學

0799 Liu, Shih-chün: Shih lun *Ch'un-ch'iu san-chuan* chung te hsün-ku.—*NHTH* 1981:2, 16– (not seen). [A preliminary discussion on the semantic interpretations in the three commentaries of *Ch'un-ch'iu*.]

劉世俊：試論『春秋三傳』中的訓詁

0800 T'ang, Wen, et al.: Shih lun *Chi-yün* tsai hsün-ku-hsüeh shang te ti-wei.—*TYT* 2, 1981, 19–34. [A preliminary discussion on the position of *Chi-yün* in Chinese traditional semantics.]

唐文等：試論『集韻』在訓詁學上的地位

0801 Yin, Meng-lun: Hsün-ku-hsüeh te hui-ku yü ch'ien-chan.—*WSC* 1982:3, 51–62. [The past and future of Chinese traditional semantics.]

殷孟倫：訓詁學的回顧與前瞻

0802 Yü, Nai-yung: Hsün-ku chih hui-su yü ch'ien-chan.—*HKCH* 7, 1980, 57–61. [The past and future of Chinese traditional semantics.]

余廼永：訓詁之回溯與前瞻

4.3. Methodology (0803–0823)

0803 Chang, I-jen: Hsün-ku-hsüeh te chiu

yeh yü hsin yu.—*TFTC* 4:4, 1970, 41–46; *Chung-kuo . . . lun-chi* (0774), 1–20. [The old profession and new approach to Chinese traditional semantics.]
張以仁：訓詁學的舊業與新猷

0804 Ch'en, Chao-jung: Hsün-ku-hsüeh te hsin kou-hsiang te li cheng.—*THHP* 21, 1980, 227–240; E.S. [Evidence with examples for a new concept of Chinese traditional semantics.]
陳昭容：訓詁學的新構想的例證？

0805 Ch'en, Ch'eng-tse: Tzu i yen-chiu fa chi tzu chih hsün-ku fa.—*Hsüeh-i* 3:4, 1921, 1–7; 5, 1–11. [Methods of studying the meanings of characters and methods of interpreting the meanings of characters.]
陳承澤：字義研究法及字之訓詁法

0806 Chu, Hsing: Shih t'an hsin hsün-ku-hsüeh.—*HPSY* 1981:1, 15–24. [A preliminary discussion on the new Chinese traditional semantics.]
朱星：試談新訓詁學

0807 Fang, Shih-to: Hsün-ku-hsüeh te hsin kou-hsiang.—*THHP* 21, 1980, 25–43; E.S. [A new conception of Chinese traditional semantics.]
方師鐸：訓詁學的新構想

0808 Fu, Mao-chi: Chung-kuo hsün-ku te k'o-hsüeh-hua.—*Ta-hsüeh* 1:7, 1942, 18–29. [The scientification of Chinese traditional semantics.]
傅懋勣：中國訓詁的科學化

0809 Hatano, Tarō: Ō Riki no shin kunkogaku, sono ta.—*CGZS* 4:1, 1949, 23–25. [Wang Li's new Chinese traditional semantics, etc.]/ See (0822).
波多野太郎：王力の新訓詁學，其他

0810 Hung, Ch'eng: Hsün-ku tsa i.—*CKYW* 1979:5, 363–370. [Miscellaneous discussions on Chinese traditional semantics.]
洪誠：訓詁雜議

0811 Hung, Ch'eng-yü: Tz'u-i fen-hsi ho yü-fa fen-hsi—Hsün-ku-hsüeh hsin t'an.—*TCSY* 1982:2, 88–93. [An analysis of lexical meaning and an analysis of grammar—A new discussion on Chinese traditional semantics.]
洪成玉：詞義分析和語法分析——訓詁學新談

0812 Jen, Ming-shan: Wo ju-ho chiang hsün-ku-hsüeh?—*KWYK* 49, 1946, 1–3. [How do I teach the (a course on) Chinese traditional semantics?]
任銘善：我如何講訓詁學？

0813 Liu, Tsung-te: Jen ming ho hsün-ku.—*CCSY* 1981:2, 53–55. [Personal names and Chinese traditional semantics.]
劉宗德：人名和訓詁

0814 Lung, Yü-ch'un: Cheng-ming-chui-i chih yü-yen yü hsün-ku.—*BIHP* 45:4, 1974, 585–598./ 599–603: Supplementary notes by Ch'en P'an. [The language and the semantic interpretations of the (Confucian) doctrine of rectification of names.]
龍宇純：正名主義之語言與訓詁／陳槃：附記

0815 Nan, Hai: Hsün-ku-hsüeh yen-chiu te hsin t'u-ching.—*YSYK* 34:1, 1971, 7–9. [New ways for the study of Chinese traditional semantics.]/ A deliberation with Mr. Chang I-jen (0803).
南海：訓詁學研究的新途徑

0816 Takahashi, Kunpei: Kunko kenkyūhō to jisho.—*CGGG* 1964:7, 10–16. [Methods of studying Chinese traditional semantics and dictionaries.]
高橋君平：訓詁研究法と辭書

0817 Ts'ai, Mou-fang: *Hsün-ku t'iao-li chih chien-li chi yün-yung.*—Taipei: Wen-shih-che, 1975, 118 p. [The establishment of the rules and uses of Chinese traditional semantics.]
蔡謀芳：訓詁條例之建立及運用

0818 Tung, T'ung-ho: Ku-chi hsün-chieh ho ku-yü tzu-i te yen-chiu.—*BIHP* 36, 1965,

1–9; *Tung T'ung-ho . . . hsüan-chi* (0083), 313–321./ A posthumous article; *RBS* 11, 1965, 386, M.J. Künstler. [The semantic interpretation of ancient texts and the study of the meanings of characters in ancient Chinese.]
董同龢：古籍訓解和古語字義的研究

0819   Wang, Jen-lu: *Shuo-wen* hsün-ku shih li. —*WSHP* 11, 1982, 11–20. [Explanations with examples of Chinese traditional semantic interpretations (found) in *Shuo-wen.*]
王仁祿：『說文』訓詁釋例

0820   Wang, Li: Wen-hua chien-she yü hsin hsün-ku-hsüeh.—*Kuang-tung chien-she yen-chiu* 1:2, 1946, 10–12. [Cultural reconstruction and new Chinese traditional semantics.]
王力：文化建設與新訓詁學

0821   Wang, Li: Hsün-ku-hsüeh shang te i-hsieh wen-t'i.—*CKYW* 1962:1, 7–14; *Lung-ch'ung ping-tiao-chai wen-chi* (0086), 328–344./ *RBS* 8, 1962, 437, A. Rygaloff. [A few problems in Chinese traditional semantics.]
王力：訓詁學上的一些問題

0822   Wang, Liao-i [Wang, Li]: Hsin hsün-ku-hsüeh.—*K'ai-ming shu-tien erh-shih chou-nien chi-nien wen-chi* (Shanghai: K'ai-ming, 1947), 173–188; *Chung-kuo yü-wen yen-chiu hsüan-chi* (0047), 114–130; *Han-yü-shih lun-wen-chi* (0103), 277–289; *Lung-ch'ung ping-tiao-chai wen-chi* (0086), 315–327. [New Chinese traditional semantics.]
王了一〔王力〕：新訓詁學——『開明書店二十周年紀念文集』

0823   Wang, Lun: Yen-chiu hsün-ku chih hsin t'u-ching.—*KWYK* 75, 1949; 1–5. [New ways of studying Chinese traditional semantics.]
王綸：研究訓詁之新途徑

4.4.   General Studies (0824–0835)

0824   Chang, Shih-lu: *Chung-kuo hsün-ku-*
hsüeh kai-yao.—Kweiyang: Wen-t'ung, 1942, ii, 128 p. [An outline of Chinese traditional semantics.]
張世祿：中國訓詁學概要

0825   Chao, Chung-i: Hsün-ku-hsüeh kai-lun. —*CYY* 3, 1981, (not seen). [An introduction to Chinese traditional semantics.]
趙仲邑：訓詁學概論

0826   Ch'i, P'ei-jung: *Hsün-ku-hsüeh kai-lun.* —Peking: Kuo-li Hua-pei pien-i-kuan, 1943, 376 p.; Taipei: Kuang-wen, 1963, repr., author's name omitted./ *CFHY* 2, 1946, 161, Anonymous. [An introduction to Chinese traditional semantics.]
齊佩瑢：訓詁學概論

0827   Chou, Ta-p'u: *Hsün-ku-hsüeh yao lüeh.* —Wuhan: Hu-pei jen-min, 1980, [2], 152 p. [An outline of Chinese traditional semantics.]
周大璞：訓詁學要略

0828   Ho, Chung-ying: *Hsün-ku-hsüeh yin-lun.* —Shanghai: Shang-wu, 1934, ii, 108 p. [An introduction to Chinese traditional semantics.]
何仲英：訓詁學引論

0829   Ho, Tsung-chou: *Hsün-ku-hsüeh tao-lun.* —Taipei: Hsiang-ts'ao shan, 1981, 10, 190 p. [An introduction to Chinese traditional semantics.]
何宗周：訓詁學導論

0830   Hsü, Shan-t'ung: *Hsün-ku-hsüeh.*—Hong Kong: Kuan-yüan shan-fang, n.d., 173 p. [Chinese traditional semantics.]
徐善同：訓詁學

0831   Hu, Ch'u-sheng: *Hsün-ku-hsüeh ta-kang.* —Taipei: Lan-t'ai shu-chü, 1975, [21], 414 p. [A general outline of Chinese traditional semantics.]
胡楚生：訓詁學大綱

0832   Lin, Yin: *Hsün-ku-hsüeh kai-yao.*— Taipei: Cheng-chung, 1972; 1974, 3rd ed., 8, 340 p. [Essentials of Chinese traditional semantics.]

林尹：訓詁學概要

0833 Lu, Tsung-ta: *Hsün-ku chien lun.*—Peking: Pei-ching, 1980, 2, 172 p. [A simple discussion on Chinese traditional semantics.]

陸宗達：訓詁簡論

0834 Tu, Hsüeh-chih: *Hsün-ku-hsüeh kang-mu.*—Taipei: Shang-wu, 1970; 1974, 2nd ed., 2, 12, 135 p. [A general outline of Chinese traditional semantics.]

杜學知：訓詁學綱目

0835 Yang, Shu-ta: Wen-tzu hsün-ku-hsüeh lun-wen shih p'ien.—*CHHP* 10:4, 1935, 941—950. [Ten essays on logography and Chinese traditional semantics.]

楊樹達：文字訓詁學論文十篇

4.5. Sound Glosses (0836—0856)
4.5.1. General Studies (0836—0844)

0836 Bodman, Nicholas C.: *A linguistic study of the Shih-ming.*—Cambridge, Mass.: Harvard U. Press, 1954, xi, 146 p./ 6—11: Sound glosses in historical perspective; *TP* 44, 1956, 266—287, Roy A. Miller; *AM* 6, 1958, 137—199, Paul L-M. Serruys.

0837 Chang, Shih-lu: *Chung-kuo yin-yün-hsüeh shih* (2909), Chap. 3.1: The origin and principles of sound glosses. [A history of Chinese phonological studies.]

張世祿：中國音韻學史／第三章，第一節：聲訓的淵源和體例

0838 Chang, Wei-szu: Sheng-yin yü hsün-ku chih kuan-hsi.—*Tse-shan pan-yüeh-k'an* 1:17, 1940, 21—23. [The relationship between the sounds and interpretations (of ancient words).]

張維思：聲音與訓詁之關係

0839 Ch'i, P'ei-jung: *Hsün-ku-hsüeh kai-lun* (0826), Chap. 3.9—10: Sound glosses. [An introduction to Chinese traditional semantics.]

齊佩瑢：訓詁學概論／第三章，第九、十節：音訓

0840 Fang, Chün-chi: *Shih-ming k'ao shih.*—Taipei: Wen-shih-che, 1978, 2, 1, 159 p./ Chap. 1: The origin of sound glosses. [A study and explanation of *Shih-ming.*]

方俊吉：釋名考釋／第一章：音訓之起源

0841 Hsü, Te-an: T'an-t'an yin-hsün.—*KWYK* 20, 1943, 12—14. [A discussion on sound glosses.]

徐德庵：談談音訓

0842 Hu, Ch'u-sheng: *Hsün-ku-hsüeh ta-kang* (0831), Chap. 5.2: Sound glosses. [A general outline of Chinese traditional semantics.]

胡楚生：訓詁學大綱／第五章，第二節：音訓

0843 Lin, Yin: *Hsün-ku-hsüeh kai-yao* (0832), Chap. 6.1: Rules of sound glosses. [Essentials of Chinese traditional semantics.]

林尹：訓詁學概要／第六章，第一節：聲訓條例

0844 Lung, Yü-ch'un: Lun sheng-hsün.—*CHHP* 9:1—2, 1971, 86—95; E.S. [On sound glosses.]

龍宇純：論聲訓

4.5.2. Sound Glosses in *Shih-ming, Shuo-wen,* and Textual Commentaries (0845—0856)

0845 Chang, Chien-pao: *Shuo-wen* sheng-hsün k'ao.—*TSST* 8, 1964, 1—137. [A study of the sound glosses in *Shuo-wen.*]

張建葆：『說文』聲訓考

0846 Chang, Chien-pao: *Shuo-wen sheng-hsün k'ao.*—Taipei: Hung-tao wen-hua shih-yeh, 1974, 77, 8, 664 p. [A study of the sound glosses in *Shuo-wen.*]

張建葆：說文聲訓考

0847 Chang, I-jen: *Ching-chuan shih-tz'u pu, Ching-chuan shih-tz'u tsai pu i-chi Ching-tz'u yen-shih* te yin-hsün wen-t'i.—*BIHP* 39, 1969, 45—49; *Chung-kuo . . . lun-chi*

(0774), 97–103. [Problems of sound glosses (found) in *Ching-chuan shih-tz'u pu*, *Ching-chuan shih-tz'u tsai pu* and *Ching-tz'u yen-shih*.]

張以仁：『經傳釋詞補』、『經傳釋詞再補』以及『經詞衍釋』的音訓問題

0848　Chang, I-jen: *Ching-chuan shih-tz'u* te yin-hsün wen-t'i.—*Chung-kuo . . . lun-chi* (0774), 85–95. [Problems of 'sound glosses' in *Ching-chuan shih-tz'u*.]

張以仁：『經傳釋詞』的『音訓』問題

0849　Ch'i, P'ei-jung: *Shih-ming* yin-hsün chü-li chi ch'i tsai yü-yen-hsüeh shang chih kung-hsien.—*Chih-chen chou-k'an* March 28, 1941; see also *Hsün-ku-hsüeh kai-lun* (0826), 137–191. [Examples of sound glosses in *Shih-ming* and their contributions to linguistics.]

齊佩瑢：『釋名』音訓舉例及其在語言學上之貢獻

0850　Hsü, Te-an: *Chuang-tzu Nei-p'ien* [*Wai-p'ien*, *Tsa-p'ien*] lien-yü yin-hsün.—*KWYK* 66, 1948, 35–38; 67, 35–38; 70, 26–29; 71, 28–32; 74, 28–31. [Sound glosses of sound-correlated words in *Nei-p'ien* (*Wai-p'ien* and *Tsa-p'ien*) of *Chuang-tzu*.]

徐德庵：『莊子』　『內篇』〔『外篇』、『雜篇』〕連語音訓

0851　Li, Wei-fen: *Shih-ming yen-chiu*. Fu *Yüan-wen ping so-yin*.—Taipei: Ta-hua shu-chü, 1979, 4, 10, 197, (original text:) 36 p./ Chap. 3: An analysis of sound glosses. [A study of *Shih-ming*. With the original text and an index.]

李維棻：釋名研究　附原文並索引／第三章：聲訓之分析

0852　Lin, Yin: *Shuo-wen* yü *Shih-ming* sheng-hsün pi-chiao yen-chiu.—*Chung-yang . . . lun-wen chi* (0060), 469–482. [A comparative study of the sound glosses (found) in *Shuo-wen* and *Shih-ming*.]

林尹：『說文』與『釋名』聲訓比較研究

0853　Lo, Pang-chu: Mao chuan sheng-hsün

chü-li.—*WHTH* 1980:3, 73–76. [Examples of the sound glosses in Mao's commentary (on *Shih-ching*).]

羅邦柱：毛傳聲訓舉例

0854　Sato, Susumu: *Shakumei* seikun kō.—*JBGH* 112, 1976, 63–80. [A study on the sound glosses in *Shih-ming*.]

佐藤進：『釋名』聲訓考

0855　Shih, Ch'i: Chin pen *Chuang-tzu Chih-lo p'ien* chih yin-hsün k'ao pien.—*HTST* 1957:3, 12–22. [A study on the sound glosses in the chapter *Chih-lo p'ien* of the current edition of *Chuang-tzu*.]

施畸：今本『莊子』『至樂篇』之音訓考辨

0856　Shih, Ling-ling: *Shih-ching Mao chuan yin-hsün pien-cheng*.—Taipei: Li-ming, n.d., 2, 1, 198 p. [Discernible evidence of sound glosses in Mao's commentary on *Shih-ching*.]

史玲玲：詩經毛傳音訓辨證

4.6.　Form Glosses (0857–0861)

0857　Chang, I-jen: Hsing-hsün te li-shih yüan-yüan chi ch'i tsai hsün-ku fang-fa shang te ti-wei.—*CWFY* 3:6, 1970, 28–29; *Chung-kuo . . . lun-chi* (0774), 45–52. [The historical origin of 'form glosses' and their positions in the methods of Chinese traditional semantics.]

張以仁：『形訓』的歷史淵源及其在訓詁方法上的地位

0858　Ch'en, Ying-t'ang: *Mao-shih* hsün-ku shih li—tzu-hsing chih hsün.—*TLTC* 32:11, 1966, 12–16; 12, 27–32; *Yü-fa sheng-yün wen-tzu* (0083), 420–430. [Explanations with examples of Chinese traditional semantics in Mao's commentary on *Shih-ching*—character-form glosses.]

陳應棠：『毛詩』訓詁釋例——字形之訓

0859　Ch'en, Ying-t'ang: *Mao-shih hsün-ku hsin ch'üan*.—Taipei: Chung-hua, 1969, 6, 466 p. [New interpretations of the Chinese traditional semantics of Mao's commentary on *Shih-ching.*] / Form glosses, sound glosses and semantic glosses.

陳應棠：毛詩訓詁新銓

0860 Li, Yün-i: Lun hsing-hsün.—*HNSY* 1982:4, 75–89. [On form glosses.]

李運益：論形訓

0861 Lin, Yin: *Hsün-ku-hsüeh kai-yao* (0832), Chap. 6.3: Rules of form glosses. [Essentials of Chinese traditional semantics.]

林尹：訓詁學概要／第六章，第三節：形訓條例

4.7. Semantic Glosses (0862–0866)

0862 Ch'i, P'ei-jung: *Hsün-ku-hsüeh kai-lun* (0826), Chap. 3.11: Semantic glosses. [An introduction to Chinese traditional semantics.]

齊佩瑢：訓詁學概論／第三章，第十一節：義訓

0863 Chou, Pien-ming: Lun i-hsün chi i-hsün te pien-ch'ien.—*HMTH* 3, 1944, 65–82. [On semantic glosses and the development of semantic glosses.]

周辨明：論義訓及義訓的變遷

0864 Hsieh, Yün-fei: *Erh-ya i-hsün shih li.* —Taipei: Hua-kang, 1969, 10, 170 p. [Explanations with examples of the semantic glosses in *Erh-ya.*]

謝雲飛：爾雅義訓釋例

0865 Hu, Ch'u-sheng: *Hsün-ku-hsüeh ta-kang* (0831), Chap. 5.3: Semantic domain. [A general outline of Chinese traditional semantics.]

胡楚生：訓詁學大綱／第五章，第三節：義界

0866 Lin, Yin: *Hsün-ku-hsüeh kai-yao* (0832), Chap. 6.2: Rules of semantic glosses. [Essentials of Chinese traditional semantics.]

林尹：訓詁學概要／第六章，第二節：義訓條例

4.8. Contradictory Glosses (0867–0874)

0867 Chang, Yung-mien: Lüeh t'an ku Han-yü li te fan-hsün.—*YYWH* 1960:1, 31. [A short discussion on contradictory glosses in ancient Chinese.]

張永綿：略談古漢語裏的反訓

0868 Higuchi, Yasushi: Iwayuru *fan-hsün* ni tsuite.—*KZDG* 5, 1976, 17–31. [On the so-called 'contradictory glosses'.]

樋口靖：いわゆる『反訓』について

0869 Hsü, Chao-hua: Fan-hsün ch'eng-yin ch'u t'an.—*NKHP* 1981:2, 41–46. [A preliminary investigation into the causes of the formation of contradictory glosses.]

徐朝華：反訓成因初探

0870 Hsü, Shih-jung: Fan-hsün t'an yüan.— *CKYW* 1980:4, 272–277. [Tracing the origin of contradictory glosses.]

徐世榮：反訓探原

0871 Hu, Ch'u-sheng: *Hsün-ku-hsüeh ta-kang* (0831), Chap. 5.5: Contradictory glosses. [A general outline of Chinese traditional semantics.]

胡楚生：訓詁學大綱／第五章，第五節：反訓

0872 Lung, Yü-ch'un: Lun fan-hsün.—*Hua kuo* 4, 1963, 32–42. [On contradictory glosses.]

龍宇純：論反訓

0873 Tung, Chi-yeh: T'an ku Han-yü chung te fan-hsün tz'u.—*Yü-wen chiao-hsüeh yü yen-chiu* 1982:3, 30–32. [A discussion on words with contradictory glosses in ancient Chinese.]

董繼業：談古漢語中的反訓詞

0874 Tung, Fan: Fan-hsün tsuan li.—*YCHP* 22, 1937, 119–174. [Collected examples of contradictory glosses.]

董璠：反訓纂例

4.9. Loan Characters (0875–0890)

0875 Chang, I-jen: *Ku-shu hsü-tzu chi shih te chia-chieh li-lun te fen-hsi yü p'i-p'ing.*

—*BIHP* 38, 1968, 233–245; *Chung-kuo . . . lun-chi* (0774), 105–124. [An analysis and critique of the loan-character theory in *Ku-shu hsü-tzu chi shih.*]
張以仁：『古書虛字集釋』的假借理論的分析與批評

0876 Chang, Shuang-ti: Lun chia-chieh.— *TSYC* 1980:2, 181–192. [On phonetic loans.]
張雙棣：論假借

0877 Chen, Shang-ling: Han tzu chia-chieh i shih t'an.—*TYT* 1, 1980, 2–20. [A preliminary investigation into the borrowed meanings of Chinese characters.]/ for dictionary entries.
甄尚靈：漢字假借義試探

0878 Chou, Fu-mei: *Shang-shu* chia-chieh tzu chi cheng.—*TLTC* 36:6–7, 1968, 18–74. [A collection with evidence of loan characters in *Shang-shu.*]
周富美：『尚書』假借字集證

0879 Chu, Ts'un: *Shuo-wen chia-chieh i cheng.*—N.p.: Chia-shu shan-fang, 1895, 28 *chüan;* Chung-kuo t'u-shu k'an-ch'uan hui, 1926, repr. [Evidence of borrowed meanings in *Shuo-wen.*]
朱珔：說文假借義證

0880 Hu, Ch'u-sheng: *Hsün-ku-hsüeh ta-kang* (0831), Chap. 7: The problem of interchangeable loan characters. [A general outline of Chinese traditional semantics.]
胡楚生：訓詁學大綱／第七章：通假字的問題

0881 Hung, Tu-jen: T'ung-chia i shih i wen-t'i te jen-shih.—*TSYC* 1982:5, 124–130. [Understanding the problem of explanation of meanings in the case of interchangeable loan characters.]
洪篤仁：通假義釋義問題的認識

0882 Karlgren, Bernhard: Loan characters in pre-Han texts.—*BMFEA* 35, 1963, 1–128; 36, 1964, 1–105; 37, 1965, 1–136; 38, 1966, 1–82; 39, 1967, 1–39; 39, 1967, 41–51 (Index to texts I–V); Stockholm: MFEA, 1968, repr.

0883 Li, Hsien: *Chao-ming wen-hsüan* t'ung-chia wen-tzu k'ao.—*TSST* 7, 1963, 1–382. [A study of interchangeable loan characters in *Chao-ming wen-hsüan.*]
李鋈：『昭明文選』通假文字考

0884 Lu, Chih-wei: Chieh tzu ch'ien shuo.— *Yen-ching she-hui k'o-hsüeh* 1, 1948, 1–5. [A brief discussion on loan characters.]
陸志韋：借字淺說

0885 Lu, Hsi-hsing: T'ung-chia tzu kuan-chien.—*TSYC* 1981:3, 120–125, 139. [My opinion concerning interchangeable loan characters.]
陸錫興：通假字管見

0886 Sheng, Chiu-ch'ou: T'ung-chia tzu hsiao i.—*TSYC* 1980:1, 53–59. [A short discussion on interchangeable loan characters.]
盛九疇：通假字小議

0887 Sheng, Chiu-ch'ou: T'ung-chia tzu tsai i.—*TSYC* 1982:5, 141–145. [Another discussion on interchangeable loan characters.]
盛九疇：通假字再議

0888 Tu, Fang-ch'in, et al.: Chia-chieh tzu, t'ung-chia tzu, ku-chin tzu hsin pien — chien yü Sheng Chiu-ch'ou, Chu Min-ch'e t'ung-chih shang-ch'üeh.—*YWYC* 1982:2, 40–44. [New distinctions between loan characters, interchangeable loan characters, and ancient/modern characters—a deliberation with colleagues Sheng Chiu-ch'ou (0886) and Chu Min-ch'e (3226).]
杜芳琴等：假借字、通假字、古今字新辨——兼與盛九疇、祝敏徹同志商榷

0889 Wang, Chung-lin: *Shuo-wen* yin ching t'ung-chia tzu k'ao.—*Ch'ing-chu Kao-yu Kao Chung-hua hsien-sheng liu-chih tan-ch'en lun-wen chi* (Taipei: Kuo-li shih-fan ta-hsüeh Kuo-wen yen-chiu-so, 1968), 215–400. [A study of interchangeable loan characters in Chinese Classics as cited in *Shuo-wen.*]

王忠林：『說文』引經通假字考——『慶祝高郵高仲華先生六秩誕辰論文集』

0890   Yang, Shu-ta: Tsao-tzu shih yu t'ung-chieh cheng.—*Chi-wei-chü hsiao-hsüeh shu-lin* (0091), 97–109. [Evidence for the existence of interchangeable loan characters when new characters were coined.]

楊樹達：造字時有通借證

4.10 Etymology (0891–0952)
4.10.1 Methodology (0891–0898)

0891   Chang, Shih-lu: Han-yü tz'u-yüan-hsüeh te p'ing-chia chi ch'i-t'a—Yü Ts'en Ch'i-hsiang hsien-sheng shang-ch'üeh.—*CHHK* 1963:7, 47–52. [An evaluation of Chinese etymology, etc.—a deliberation with Mr. Ts'en Ch'i-hsiang (0898).]

張世祿：漢語詞源學的評價及其他——與岑麒祥先生商榷

0892   Chou, Liao-yin: Pa kua wei yüan-shih yü-ken fu-hao k'ao.—*Shuo-wang pan-yüeh k'an* 5, 1933, 7–11; 6, 12–14; 8, 12–13; 9, 19–21. [A study on the Eight Trigrams as primitive word root symbols.]

周了因：八卦爲原始語根符號考

0893   Hsü, F. C.: *Analysis of the Chinese language: An etymological approach.*—New York: Mt. Tremper, 1976, 310 p., illus.

0894   Liang, Ch'i-ch'ao: Ts'ung fa-yin shang yen-chiu Chung-kuo wen-tzu chih yüan. —*TFTC* 18:21, 1921, 111–117; *Wen-tzu li-shih kuan yü ko-ming lun* (0069), 63–79. [The etymologies of Chinese characters as studied from their pronunciations.]

梁啟超：從發音上研究中國文字之源

0895   Liu, Tse: Ku sheng t'ung-niu chih tzu i to hsiang-chin shuo.—*WCCK* 2:2, 1932, 369–378; *Chih-yen* 9, 1936, 1–11. [A theory that many of the meanings for characters with the same initials in ancient

Chinese were relatively close.]

劉賾：古聲同紐之字義多相近說

0896   Shen, Chien-shih: Yu-wen-shuo tsai hsün-ku-hsüeh shang chih yen-ko chi ch'i t'ui-ch'an.—*BIHPEV* 1, 1933, 777–854./ *P'an-shih tsa-chih* 1:4, 1933, 33–34, Shih and Lin Yü-t'ang. [The vicissitudes of the *yu-wen* ('right graph') theory in Chinese traditional semantics and its extended propagation.]

沈兼士：右文說在訓詁學上之沿革及其推闡／詩評，附林語堂致沈兼士書

0897   Takahata, Hikojirō: Shina gogen kenkyūhō no ichi shitan.—*Fujioka hakushi kōseki kinen gengogaku ronbunshū* (Tokyo: Iwanami, 1935), 355–373. [A preliminary investigation of the methodology of Chinese etymology.]

高畑彥次郎：支那語源研究法の一試探——『藤岡博士功績記念言語學論文集』

0898   Ts'en, Ch'i-hsiang: Tz'u-yüan yen-chiu te i-i ho chi-pen yüan-tse.—*HCS* 1962:8, 1–7. [The significance and the fundamental principles of studies on etymology.]/ See (0891)

岑麒祥：詞源研究的意義和基本原則

4.10.2. General Studies (0899–0909)

0899   Chang, Ping-lin: *Wen shih.*—Hangchow: Che-chiang t'u-shu-kuan, 1917–1919, 9 *chüan.*/ Chang shih ts'ung-shu ed. [The beginnings of Chinese writing.]/ Etymological studies.

章炳麟：文始——「章氏叢書」本

0900   Chang, Wei-szu: Yü-yüan li ts'e.— *CWYH* 5:2, 1945, 1–18; E.S. [A superficial estimation of etymologies.]

張維思：語源蠡測

0901   Hsieh, Pi-hsien: *Wen shih yen-chiu.*— Taipei: Wen-chin, 1973, [ii], 290, (bibliography) 4 p. [A study of *Wen shih* (0899).]

謝碧賢：文始研究

0902　Liang, Ch'i-ch'ao: Kuo-wen yü-yüan chieh.—*TCH* 2:1, 1916, 1–7; 2:2, 1–6; 2:3, 1–8; 2:4, 1–6; 2:5, 1–7. [Explanations on the etymologies of the National Language.]
梁啓超：國文語源解

0903　Liu, Shih-p'ei: Wu ming su yüan.— *Kuo-ts'ui hsüeh-pao* 3rd year, 6th *ts'e*, 26, 1907, 1–5; 28, 1–8. [Tracing the origins of the names for objects.]
劉師培：物名溯源

0904　Pao, Yün: Kuo-wen yü-yüan chieh.— *Hsüeh-pao* 1:3, 1907, 1–50. [Explanations on the etymologies of the National Language.]
寶雲：國文語源解

0905　Teng, Chia-yen: *Min-tsu yü-yüan.*— Taipei: Chung-yang wen-wu, 1954, 11, 36 p. [Folk etymology.]
鄧家彦：民族語原

0906　Tōdō, Akiyasu: *Chūgokugo gogen manpitsu.*—Tokyo: Daigaku shorin, 1955, 148 p., illus. [Random notes on Chinese etymology.]
藤堂明保：中國語語源漫筆

0907　Tōdō, Akiyasu: *Kotoba no keifu.*— Tokyo: Shinchōsha, 1964, 266 p. [The genealogy of language.]/ Classified etymology of Chinese characters.]
藤堂明保：言葉の系譜

0908　Yü, Min: Ku Han-yü li te li-su yü-yüan. —*YCHP* 36, 1949, 47–70. [Folk etymology in ancient Chinese.]
俞敏：古漢語裏的俚俗語源

0909　Yüeh, Chai: Yü-yüan lüeh li.—*Tung-nan* 1:7, 1943, 10–14. [Simple examples of etymology.]
約齋：語源略例

4.10.3. Studies on Individual Words (0910–0931)

0910　Chiang, Liang-fu: Chih-ch'u ch'ih-ch'ü

chuan-yü k'ao.—*HNTH* 1:1, 1934, 1–5. [A study of the derivation of the words *chih-ch'u* and *ch'ih-ch'ü.*]
姜亮夫：『踟躕』『馳驅』轉語考

0911　Chou, Fa-kao: Chi-ko ch'ang-yüng tz'u te lai-yüan.—*TLTC* 4:7, 1952, 6–9; *Chung-kuo yü-wen lun-ts'ung* (0052), 150– 160; *Yü-yen wen-tzu-hsüeh* (0080), 48– 51. [The origins of several commonly used words.]/ *t'a, ni, shih, tzu, erh.*
周法高：幾個常用詞的來源／『他』、『你』、『是』、『子』、『兒』

0912　Hsiao, Chang: Lu, li, ch'ih, li, li, lieh, li, li yü-yüan chih yen-chiu.—*Che-chiang ta-hsüeh wen-hsüeh-yüan chi-k'an* 1, 1941, 77–96. [An etymological study of (the words) *lu, li, ch'ih, li, li, lieh, li,* and *li.*]
蕭璋：『鹿』、『麗』、『离』、『秝』、『豐』、『劦』、『豎』、『蠡』語原之研究

0913　Li, Chin-hsi: *Han-yü shih tz'u lun-wen chi.*—Peking: K'o-hsüeh, 1957, 148 p.; Hong Kong: Po wen, n.d., repr./ *RBS* 3, 1957, 592, G.B. Downer. [Collected essays on the explanations of Chinese words.]/ Nine essays on the origins and meanings of Chinese words.
黎錦熙：漢語釋詞論文集

0914　Lü, Shu-hsiang: Che na k'ao yüan.— *KWYK* 61, 1947, 3–4. [A study on the origins of *che* and *na.*]
呂叔湘：『這』、『那』考源

0915　Miller, Roy A.: The etymology of Chinese *liu* 〔榴〕 (pomegranate).—*Lg* 27, 1951, 154–158.

0916　Shen, Chien-shih: Kuei tzu yüan-shih i-i chih shih-t'an.—*KHCK* 5:3, 1935, 45–59. [A preliminary investigation into the primitive meaning of the character *kuei.*]
沈兼士：『鬼』字原始意義之試探

0917　Shen, Chien-shih. Transl. by Ying, Ts'ien-li: An essay on the primitive meaning of the character *kuei.—MS* 2, 1936–1937, 1–20.

〔沈兼士著，英千里譯：『鬼字原始之意義試探』（ 0916 ）

0918 Shen, Chien-shih: I, sha, chi ku yü t'ung yüan k'ao.—*FJHC* 8:2, 1939, 1–13. [A study on *i, sha,* and *chi* as from the same etymon in ancient vocabulary.]

沈兼士：『希』、『殺』、『祭』古語同源考

0919 Sun, Tso-yün: Fei-lien k'ao.—*HPPI* 2:3, 1943, 29 s.p.; 2:4, 1943, 22 s.p. [An etymological study of (the word) *fei-lien.*]

孫作雲：『飛廉』考

0920 T'ang, Yüeh: *Kuo ku hsin t'an.—* Shanghai: Shang-wu, 1926, 3 *chüan,* 2, 2, 3, 100; 104; 100, [2] p.; Taipei: Shang-wu, 1966, repr. [New investigations into national literary heritage.] / Collected essays.

唐鉞：國故新探

0921 T'ang, Yüeh: Pai-hua tzu yin k'ao yüan ch'i tse.—*Kuo ku hsin t'an* (0920), *chüan* 2, 79–104. [An etymological study of seven colloquial words.]

唐鉞：白話字音考原七則

0922 Tōdō, Akiyasu: So to sha no gogen ni tsuite—mojigaku no shinten no tameni. —*TSGH* 3, 1957, 20–30. [Etymologies of (the words) *tsu* and *she*—in the advancement of Chinese logography.]

藤堂明保：『祖』と『社』の 語源について―文字學の進展のために

0923 Tōdō, Akiyasu: Setsu no keifu.—*TSGH* 4, 1958, 74–81./ *RBS* 4, 1958, 558, M.J. Künstler. [The genealogy of (the word) *shuo.*]

藤堂明保：『說』の 系譜

0924 Tōdō, Akiyasu: Hōō to hiren ni tsuite —Kan-Tai kyōtsū kigo no ichimen.— *THG* 18, 1959, 104–114; E.S./ *RBS* 5, 1959, 541, Kawakatsu Yoshio. [*Feng-huang* and *fei-lien*—an aspect of the Proto-Sino-Tai.]

藤堂明保：『鳳凰』と『飛廉』について―漢タイ共通基語の一面

0925 Tōdō, Akiyasu: Futatsu o imi suru kotoba.—*NCGH* 19, 1967, 218–223./ *RBS* 12–13, 1966–1967, 643, Kawaguchi Junji. [Words with the meaning 'two' (in Chinese).]

藤堂明保：『ふたつ』を 意味 するコトバ

0926 Ts'ai, Feng-ch'i: Hun-tun (Yü-yüan ch'u-kao chih i-chieh).—*SWYK* 2:11, 1941, 39–48. [(On the word) *hun-tun* (a paragraph for the first draft of etymology).]

蔡鳳圻：『混沌』（ 語源初稿之一節 ）

0927 Yang, Shu-ta: Yü-yüan-hsüeh lun-wen ch'i p'ien.—*Kuo-li Pei-p'ing shih-fan ta-hsüeh yüeh-k'an* 14, 1934, 26–32. [Seven essays on etymology.]/ Seven words.

楊樹達：語源學論文七篇

0928 Yang, Shu-ta: Yü-yüan-hsüeh lun-wen shih-erh p'ien.—*CHHP* 9:4, 1934, 897–911. [Twelve essays on etymology.]/ Twelve words.

楊樹達：語源學論文十二篇

0929 Yang, Shu-ta: Yü-yüan-hsüeh lun-wen shih-pa p'ien.—*CHHP* 12:3, 1937, 541–560. [Eighteen essays on etymology.]/ Twenty-five words.

楊樹達：語源學論文十八篇

0930 Yang, Shu-ta: Yü-yüan-hsüeh lun-wen shih p'ien.—*WSCCK* 1:2, 1943, 49–56. [Ten essays on etymology.]/ Ten words.

楊樹達：語源學論文十篇

0931 Yang, Shu-ta: *Chi-wei-chü hsiao-hsüeh shu-lin* (0091). [Collected studies on logography from the Chi-wei-chü Studio.]/ Including 45 etymological studies on individual words.

楊樹達：積微居小學述林

4.10.4. Cognate Words (0932–0952)

0932 Boltz, William George: *Studies in Old*

Chinese word families.—Berkeley: U. of California, 1974, iv, 166 p./ Unpubl. doc. diss.

0933 Ching, Pen-chih: Yu-kuan Han-yü t'ung-yüan tz'u te chi-ko wen-t'i.—*SCTH* 1981:3, 41–45. [Several problems concerning cognate words in Chinese.]
經本植：有關漢語同源詞的幾個問題

0934 Fang, Chien-ch'ang: T'ung hsieh-sheng te t'ung-yüan tzu tsu yü tz'u-shu chung te t'ung-chia tzu.—*TSYC* 1982:5, 151–155. [Cognate characters from the same phonetic series and interchangeable loan characters in a dictionary.]
房建昌：同諧聲的同源字族與辭書中的通假字

0935 Hu, Ch'u-sheng: *Hsün-ku-hsüeh ta-kang* (0831), Chap. 9: The study of cognate words. [A general outline of Chinese traditional semantics.]
胡楚生：訓詁學大綱／第九章：同源詞研究

0936 Karlgren, Bernhard: Word families in Chinese.—*BMFEA* 5, 1933, 1–120./ *BSOAS* 7, 1933–1935, 931–941, Yoshitake S.; *TSCK* 2:4, 1935, 217–221, Wang Liao-i.
王了一評

0937 Karlgren, Bernhard. Transl. by Chang, Shih-lu: *Han-yü tz'u-lei.*—Shanghai: Shang-wu, 1939, xv, 259 p., 1 portr. [Word families in Chinese.] (0936)
高本漢著，張世祿譯：漢語詞類

0938 Karlgren, Bernhard: Cognate words in the Chinese phonetic series.—*BMFEA* 28, 1956, 1–18./ *RBS* 2, 1956, 364, W. Simon.

0939 Maspero, Henri: Préfixes et dérivation en chinois archaïque.—*MSL* 23, 1930, 313–327.

0940 Pulleyblank, Edwin G.: Word families —A reconsideration.—*Chi-Lin*, 9, 1972, 1–19.

0941 Takashima, Ken: The Early Archaic Chinese word *yu*〔有〕in the Shang oracle-bone inscriptions: Word-family, etymology, semantics and sacrifice.—*CLAO* 8, 1980, 81–112.

0942 Tōdō, Akiyasu: *Kanji no gogen kenkyū.* —Tokyo: Gakutōsha, 1963, 794 p., 1 pl./ *RBS* 9, 1963, 540, L. Vandermeetsch; *CGGG* 1963:11, 7–13, Suzuki Naoji. [An etymological study of Chinese characters.]/ The first ed. of (0943).
藤堂明保：漢字の語源研究／鈴木直治評

0943 Tōdō, Akiyasu: *Kanji gogen jiten.*—Tokyo: Gakutōsha, 1965; 1983, 23rd ed., 914 p.; E.S./ *KG* 67, 1966, 74–81, Togawa Yoshio; *AM* 14, 1968, 110–111, E.G. Pulleyblank; *CTKK* 1:3, 1968, 66–71, Liu Wen-hsien. [Etymological dictionary of Chinese characters.]/ Arranged according to word families.
藤堂明保：漢字語源辭典／戶川芳郎評，劉文獻評

0944 Tōdō, Akiyasu: Mu to iu shisō no honshitsu (sono kotoba no haseihō kara).—*TSGH* 12, 1966, 44–54./ *RBS* 12–13, 1966–1967, 642, Kawaguchi Junji. [The essence of the concept *wu* (a discussion from the derivational methods of this word).]/ A study of word families.
藤堂明保：『無』という 思想の本質（そのコトバの 派生法 から ）

0945 Wang, Li: *Han-yü shih kao.*—Peking: K'o-hsüeh, 1957–1958, 3 vols., xiv, 613 p./ Chap. 4.57: Words of the same class, and words of the same etymon; *RBS* 4, 1958, 537, U. Unger. [A draft of a history of the Chinese language.]
王力：漢語史稿／第四章，第五十七節：同類詞和同源詞

0946 Wang, Li: T'ung-yüan tzu lun.—*CKYW* 1978:1, 28–33; *Lung-ch'ung ping-tiao-chai wen-chi* 3 (0086), 30–44. [On cognate words.]
王力：同源字論

0947   Wang, Li: Analyse grammaticale des mots dérivés de la langue chinoise.—*CLAO* 7, 1980, 5–14./ Cognate words in Archaic Chinese.

0948   Wang, Li: Han-yü tzu-sheng-tz'u te yü-fa fen-hsi.—*YLT* 6, 1980, 3–15; *Lung-ch'ung ping-tiao-chai wen-chi* 3 (0086), 45–55. [A grammatical analysis of Chinese derivative words.]
王力：漢語滋生詞的語法分析

0949   Wang, Li: *T'ung-yüan tzu-tien.*—Peking: Shang-wu, 1982, 695 p. [A dictionary of cognate words.]
王力：同源字典

0950   Yang, Shu-ta: Tzu-i t'ung yüan-yü yü-yüan t'ung li cheng.—*Chi-wei-chü hsiao-hsüeh chin-shih lun-ts'ung* (0092), 52–74 [Pt. 1]; *Chi-wei-chü hsiao-hsüeh shu-lin* (0091), 171–181 [Pt. 2]. [Evidence with examples of characters with identical meanings being derived from identical etymologies.]
楊樹達：字義同緣於語源同例證

0951   Yao, Jung-sung: Kao Pen-han Han-yü t'ung-yüan tz'u shuo p'ing hsi.—*KWHP* 9, 1980, 211–229. [A critical analysis of B. Karlgren's theory on cognate words in the Chinese language.]/ See (0936) & (0938).
姚榮松：高本漢漢語同源詞說評析

0952   Yao, Jung-sung: *Shang-ku Han-yü t'ung-yüan tz'u yen-chiu.*—Taipei: Kuo-li T'ai-wan shih-fan ta-hsüeh Kuo-wen yen-chiu so, 1982, iii, 456 p./ Unpubl. doc. diss. [A study on the cognate words in Archaic Chinese.]
姚榮松：上古漢語同源詞研究

5. LEXICAL STRATA IN MODERN CHINESE (0953–1279)

5.1. Words in Archaic and Literary Chinese (0953–1011)

5.1.1. Word Formation (0953–0961)

0953   Chou, Fa-kao: *Chung-kuo ku-tai yü-fa. Kou-tz'u pien.*—Taipei: Academia Sinica, 1962, 40, 446 p. [Ancient Chinese grammar. Part II: Word formation.]
周法高：中國古代語法：構詞編

0954   Chu, Min-ch'e: Ts'ung *Shih-chi Han-shu Lun-heng* k'an Han-tai fu-yin tz'u te kou-tz'u-fa.—*YLT* 8, 1981, 142–156. [The methods of word formation of disyllabic words in Han times as seen from *Shih-chi, Han-shu,* and *Lun-heng.*]
祝敏徹：從『史記』、『漢書』、『論衡』看漢代複音詞的構詞法

0955   Kennedy, George A.: Word-classes in Classical Chinese.—*Selected works . . . Kennedy* (0070), 323–433./ Originally written to serve as an introduction to *A grammar of Mencius;* includes word formation.

0956   Ku, Yüeh: Wen-yen tz'u-fa ch'ang-shih.—Peking: Pei-ching, 1964, 3, 2, 50 p. [Common knowledge on word formation in the literary language.]
顧越：文言詞法常識

0957   Kuan, Hsieh-ch'u: *Hsi Chou chin wen yü-fa yen-chiu.*—Peking: Shang-wu, 1981, 5, 212 p./ 12: Methods of word formation; *CKYW* 1982:6, 469–471, Wang Hai-fen. [A study on the grammar of the bronze inscriptions from the Western Chou.]
管燮初：西周金文語法研究／12：構詞法；王海棻評

0958   P'an, Tsu-yen: Lüeh t'an *Shih-ching* fu-yin tz'u te kou-tz'u hsing-shih.—*Shao-hsing shih-chuan hsüeh-pao* 1981:1, 76. [A short discussion on the patterns of word formation of disyllabic words in *Shih-ching.*]
潘祖炎：略談『詩經』複音詞的構詞形式

0959   Shadick, Harold & Ch'iao, Chien: *A first course in literary Chinese.*—Ithaca: Cornell U. Press, 1968, 3 vols., xv, xi, xi, 888 p., 2 maps./ Vol. III, Chap. 6: The formal structure of words; *JCLTA* 5:2, 1970, 74–75, Charles K.H. Chen; 75–80, John S. Tong.
〔謝迪克、喬健編著：文言文入門〕

0960   Wang, Li-hua: *Fan-yen* kou-tz'u-fa yü tsao-chü-fa yen-chiu.—*TCHP* 18, 1981, 51–75. [A study on the methods of word formation and sentence structure in (Yang Hsiung's) *Fa-yen.*]
王麗華：『法言』構詞法與造句法研究

0961   Yang, Po-chün: *Wen-yen yü-fa.*—Peking: Pei-ching, 1956, 7, 247 p.; Hong Kong: Shao-hua wen-hua, n.d., repr., ix, 337 p./ Chap. 2: Word formation; *RBS* 4, 1958, 567, W.A.C.H. Dobson. [A grammar of literary Chinese.]
楊伯峻：文言語法／第二章：詞法概述

5.1.2. Compound Words (0962–0987)
5.1.2.1. Compound Words in General (0962–0972)

0962   Chang, Chün & Chang, Chia-t'ai: Ku Han-yü p'ien-i fu-tz'u shuo lüeh.—*LNTH* 1982:5, 92–96. [A brief discussion on ancient Chinese compound words with one-sided meanings.]
張軍、張家太：古漢語偏義複詞說略

0963   Cheng, Tien: Ku Han-yü chung tzu-hsü tui-huan te shuang-yin tz'u.—*CKYW* 1964:6, 445–453. [Disyllabic words of which the word order was interchangeable in ancient Chinese.]
鄭奠：古漢語中字序對換的雙音詞

0964   Chmielewski, Janusz: Sur la dissyllabisation des mots en chinois ancien d'après les glosses de Kouo P'o dans le *Eul-ya* et le *Fang-yen.*—*PICO* 21, 1948, publ. in 1949, 270–271 (summary).

0965 Chmielewski, Janusz: Shang-ku Han-yü li te shuang-yin tz'u wen-t'i.—*CKYW* 1956:10, 23–25. [The problem of disyllabic words in Archaic Chinese.]
赫邁萊夫斯基：上古漢語裏的雙音詞問題

0966 Chmielewski, Janusz: Remarques sur le problème des mots dissyllabiques en chinois archaïque.—*MIHEC* 1, 1957, 423–445./ *RBS* 3, 1957, 585, P[iet] v[an] d[er] L[oon].

0967 Hsiang, Hsi: *Shih-ching* li te fu-yin tz'u.—*YLT* 6, 1980, 27–54. [Disyllabic words in *Shih-ching.*]
向熹：『詩經』裏的複音詞

0968 Hu, Ch'u-sheng: Ku Han-yü chung tan-yin tz'u yü fu-yin tz'u chih kuan-hsi.—*Chung-yang . . . lun-wen-chi* (0060), 431–443. [The relationships between monosyllabic and disyllabic words in ancient Chinese.]
胡楚生：古漢語中單音詞與複音詞之關係

0969 Lu, Te-nan: Ku-tai Han-yü te shuang-yin tz'u.—*KCSY* 1981:1, 18– (not seen). [Disyllabic words in ancient Chinese.]
陸德南：古代漢語的雙音詞

0970 Ma, Chen: Hsien Ch'in fu-ho tz'u ch'u t'an.—*PCTH* 1980:5, 54–63; 1981:1, 76–84. [A preliminary investigation into pre-Ch'in compound words.]
馬眞：先秦複合詞初探

0971 Ting, Pang-hsin: *Lun-yü Meng-tzu* chi *Shih-ching* chung ping-lieh-yü ch'eng-fen chih-chien te sheng-tiao kuan-hsi.—*BIHP* 47:1, 1975, 17–25. [Tonal relationships between the constituents of coordinate constructions in *Lun-yü, Meng-tzu,* and *Shih-ching.*]
丁邦新：『論語』『孟子』及『詩經』中並列語成份之間的聲調關係

0972 Wu, Fu-hsi: *Ku-tai Han-yü.*—Lanchow: Kan-su jen-min, 1980, 3, 320 p./ Pt. 2,

Chap. 3: Compound words. [Ancient Chinese.]
吳福熙：古代漢語／第二編，第三章：合成詞

5.1.2.2. Sound-correlated Disyllabic Words (0973–0987)

0973 Chang, Shou-lin: San-pai p'ien lien-mien tzu yen-chiu.—*YCHP* 13, 1933, 171–196. [A study on sound-correlated disyllabic words in the three hundred poems of *Shih-ching.*]
張壽林：三百篇聯綿字研究

0974 Chou, Fa-kao: Lien-mien tzu t'ung-shuo.—*WSCH* 6, 1954, 75–90; *Chung-kuo yü-wen lun-ts'ung* (0052), 132–149. [A general discussion on sound-correlated disyllabic words.]
周法高：聯綿字通說

0975 Chu, Fang-p'u: Lien-mien tzu kai shuo. —*MTTC* 9:5, 1928, 1–29. [A general discussion on sound-correlated disyllabic words.]
朱芳圃：聯綿字概說

0976 Chuang, Ya-chou: *Erh-ya* lien-mien tzu ch'ien t'an.—*Hsin-chu shih-chuan hsüeh-pao* 5, 1979, 97–102. [A simple investigation into sound-correlated disyllabic words in *Erh-ya.*]
莊雅州：『爾雅』聯綿字淺探

0977 Fu, Ting-i: *Lien-mien tzu-tien.*—Shanghai: Shang-wu, 1943, 36 *chüan,* 10 vols., v.p.; Shanghai: Chung-hua, 1954, repr.; Taipei: Chung-hua, 1964, repr., 3 vols., 117, 4775, 4, 12 p.; Peking: Chung-hua, 1982, repr./ *Han-hiue* 1, 1944, 231–241, Tun Weng; *SCCY* 23, 1947, 2–6, Sun Fu-yüan. [A dictionary of sound-correlated disyllabic words.]
符定一：聯綿字典／鈍翁評，孫伏園評

0978 Hsü, Chia-ch'ang & Tai, Hung-sen: Kuan-yü lien-mien tz'u te liang-feng hsin.—*PCST* 1981:4, 38. [Two letters concerning sound-correlated disyllabic

words.]
徐家昌、戴鴻森：關於聯綿詞的兩封信

0979 Hu, Ch'u-sheng: *Hsün-ku-hsüeh ta-kang* (0831), Chap. 4: A brief discussion on sound-correlated disyllabic words. [A general outline of Chinese traditional semantics.]
胡楚生：訓詁學大綱／第四章：聯綿字略論

0980 Kao, Heng: Lien-mien yü ken shu lüeh. —*Shih-hsüeh* 2, 1926, 36–45. [A brief account of the word roots of sound-correlated disyllabic words.]
高亨：連綿語根述略

0981 Shih, Ping-hua: T'an lien-mien tzu.— *CKYT* 47:3, 1980, 67–71. [A discussion on sound-correlated disyllabic words.]
施炳華：談聯綿字

0982 Shih, Tsung-chou: *Chung-kuo wen-tzu lun-ts'ung.*—Taipei: Chung-hua ts'ung-shu, 1978, 2, 2, 14, 498 p./ 65–79: Sound-correlated disyllabic words. [Collected essays on Chinese writing.]
史宗周：中國文字論叢／65－79：聯綿字

0983 Sun, Te-hsüan: Lien-mien tzu ch'ien shuo.—*FJHC* 11:1–2, 1942, 159–186; E.S. [A simple discussion on sound-correlated disyllabic words.]
孫德宣：聯綿字淺說

0984 Tu, Ch'i-jung: *Mao-shih* lien-mien tz'u p'u.—*WSCH* 9, 1960, 129–292./ *RBS* 6, 1960, 375, R.A. Miller, [An annotated list of sound-correlated disyllabic words in Mao's commentary on *Shih-ching.*]
杜其容：『毛詩』連綿詞譜

0985 Wang, Kuang-ch'ing: Fu-yin yü-tz'u fa-wei.—*Hsüeh-ts'ui* 1:1, 1958, 25–26; 4:2, 1962, 25–26. Publ. in 17 issues./ See (0986). [Discoveries of the quintessence of (sound-correlated) disyllabic words and phrases.]
王廣慶：複音語詞發微

0986 Wang, Kuang-ch'ing: *Fu-yin hu-yung*

fa-wei.—Taipei: Chung-hua ts'ung-shu, 1963, 7, 151, 3 p. [Discoveries of the quintessence of the interchangeable usages of (sound-correlated) disyllabic words.]
王廣慶：複音互用發微

0987 Wang, Kuang-ch'ing: *Fu-yin tz'u sheng i ch'an-wei.*—Taipei: Shang-wu, 1973, 4, 13, 20, 420 p. [Discoveries of the quintessence of the sounds and meanings of (sound-correlated) disyllabic words.]
王廣慶：複音詞聲義闡微

5.1.3. Reduplicatives (0988–1007)
5.1.3.1. Total Reduplication (0988–0998)

0988 Chou, Fa-kao: Reduplicatives in the *Book of Odes.*—*BIHP* 34, 1963, 661–698./ *RBS* 9, 1963, 526, H.M. Stimson.
〔周法高〕

0989 Fujita, Hideo: *Shikyō* no jōjigo no taisuru ichi kōsatsu.—*KSCGH* 3, 1957, 36–48. [A study of reduplicatives in *Shih-ching.*]
藤田秀雄：『詩經』の疊字語の對する一考察

0990 Ho, K'ai: *Shih-ching* chung te ch'ung-yen tz'u ho lien-mien tz'u te fen ho yün-yung.—*SHSY* 1959:3, 43–51. [The separate and uniform usages of reduplicated words and rhyming binomes found in *Shih-ching.*]
賀凱：『詩經』中的重言詞和聯綿詞的分合運用

0991 Huang, T'ieh-cheng: *Shih-ching* tieh-tzu chih yen-chiu.—*Hua-kuo* 2, 1958, 108–135. [A study of reduplicatives in *Shih-ching.*]
黃鐵錚：『詩經』疊字之研究

0992 Lin, Chih-t'ang: *Shih-ching* ch'ung-yen tzu shih-li.—*KHYP* 2:12, 1927, 639–675. [Examples with explanations of reduplicated characters in *Shih-ching.*]
林之棠：『詩經』重言字釋例

0993 Lo, Pang-chu: *Mao shih* tieh-yin tz'u

ch'ien shuo.—*Hsüeh-shu lun-t'an* 1981:3, 88–91. [A simple discussion of reduplicatives in *Shih-ching.*]

羅邦柱：『毛詩』疊音詞淺說

0994 T'ang, Yüeh: Tieh-tzu.—*Kuo ku hsin t'an* (0920), 63–72. [Reduplicatives.]

唐鉞：疊字

0995 Ts'ao, Hsien-cho: *Shih-ching* tieh-tzu.—*YLT* 6, 1980, 16–26. [Reduplicatives in *Shih-ching.*]

曹先擢：『詩經』疊字

0996 Wei, P'ei-ch'üan: *Chuang-tzu yü-fa yen-chiu.*—Taipei: Kuo-li T'ai-wan shih-fan ta-hsüeh Kuo-wen yen-chiu so, 1982, 7, 432 p./ Unpubl. M.A. thesis; Chap. 2: Adverbs, including reduplicated nouns. [A study of the grammar in *Chuang-tzu.*]

魏培泉：莊子語法研究／第二章：狀詞，附相關疊音名詞

0997 Yang, Chi-mo: *Shih* san-pai p'ien tieh-tzu lei chi.—*Chen-chih hsüeh-pao* 3:1, 1943, 30–47. [Collected and classified reduplicatives from the 300 poems of *Shih-ching.*]

楊即墨：『詩』三百篇疊字類輯

0998 Yüan, Hsiang-huai: Tieh-tzu yü *Shih-ching.*—*Ch'u-pan chou-k'an (hsin)* 89, 1934, 6–11. [Reduplicatives and *Shih-ching.*]

袁湘槐：疊字與『詩經』

5.1.3.2. Partial Reduplication: Alliteratives and Rhyming Binomes (0999–1007)

0999 Fang, Te-ch'ien: Shuang-sheng tieh-yün yü ku Han-yü yü-yin tz'u-hui.—*AHST* 1983:1, 114–119. [Alliteratives and rhyming binomes and the phonetics and vocabulary in ancient Chinese.]

方德乾：雙聲疊韻與古漢語語音詞滙

1000 Kan, Ta-hsin: Shuang-sheng tieh-yün lien-mien tzu yen-chiu.—*KWYK* 50, 1946, 1–11. [A study on alliterative and rhyming sound-correlated disyllabic words.]

甘大昕：雙聲疊韻聯綿字研究

1001 Lo, Ch'ang-p'ei: Shuang-sheng tieh-yün shuo.—*CSTY* 4:41, 1928, 1–11. [On alliteratives and rhyming binomes.]

羅常培：雙聲疊韻說

1002 Lo, Hsin-t'ien [Lo, Ch'ang-p'ei]: Shen-ma chiao shuang-sheng tieh-yün?—*KWYK* 1:13, 1942, 11–15. [What are alliteratives and rhyming binomes?]

羅莘田〔羅常培〕：甚麼叫『雙聲』『疊韻』？

1003 Lo, Shao-pin: *Ch'u-tz'u* lien-yü shih li. Fu *Ch'u tz'u* shuang-sheng tieh-yün tzu p'u.—*Hu-nan ta-hsüeh ch'i-k'an* 8, 1933, 30–40. [Examples with explanations of binomes in *Ch'u-tz'u.* With a list of alliteratives and rhyming binomes in *Ch'u-tz'u.*]

駱紹賓：『楚辭』連語釋例　附『楚辭』雙聲疊韻詞譜

1004 Wang, Li: Shuang-sheng tieh-yün te ying-yung chi ch'i liu pi.—*WHNP* 1937:3, 21–23; *Han-yü-shih lun-wen-chi* (0103), 407–411; *Lung-ch'ung ping-tiao-chai wen-chi* 3 (0086), 1–5. [The applications of alliteratives and rhyming binomes and their abuses.]

王力：雙聲疊韻的應用及其流弊

1005 Wang, Sen-jan: Shuang-sheng yü tieh-yün.—*STHK* 2, 1943, 1–10. [Alliteratives and rhyming binomes.]

王森然：雙聲與疊韻

1006 Wang, Ti-p'ing: Ku-chi shang chih shuang-sheng tieh-yün tzu.—*SWYK* 2:2, 1940, 51–53. [Alliteratives and rhyming binomes in ancient texts.]

王砥平：古籍上之雙聲疊韻字

1007 Wu, T'ing-jang: *Shuo-wen* shuang-sheng tieh-yun lien-yü k'ao shih.—*TPTHCK* 53, 1928, 10–12; 54, 10–12; 55, 10–12; 56, 8–10; 57, 17–19; 58, 15–17; 59, 18–20; 60, 28–30; 61, (?); 62, 1929, 9–11; 63, 16–18; 64, 20–22. [A study with explanations of alliteratives and rhyming binome compound words in *Shuo-wen*.]

吳庭讓：『說文』雙聲疊韻聯語考釋

5.1.4. Fusion Words (1008–1011)

1008 Kennedy, George A.: Equation No. 5 (Chinese fusion words).—*JAOS* 67, 1947, 56–59.

1009 Leslie, D.D.: Fusion equation for *chu* 〔諸〕 in the *Analects* and *Mencius*, with an appendix on verbs and their prepositions.—*TP* 51:2–3, 1964, 140–216.

1010 Ratchnevsky, Paul: Zur frage der fusion im Archaischen Chinesisch.—*Beiträge zum problem des wortes im Chinesischen* (0077), 48–70.

1011 Yao, Lin-yüan (ed.): *Chung-hsüeh yü-wen chiao-shih shou-ts'e.*—Shanghai: Shang-hai chiao-yü, 1982, [iii], 18, 1096 p./ 247–248; Fusion words. [A handbook for middle school language teachers.]

姚麟園主編：中學語文教師手册／247－248：兼詞

5.2. Lexicon of Archaic and Literary Chinese (1012–1112)

5.2.1. Definition and Problems (1012–1022)

1012 Chang, Shih-lu: Hsien-tai yü li te ku yü-tz'u.—*YWCS* 1956:10, 31–36; *Hsien-tai Han-yü . . . tzu-liao* (0064), 349–356. [Ancient words in the modern (Chinese) language.]

張世祿：現代語裏的古語詞

1013 Chang, Shih-lu: Wen-yen tz'u shih pu-shih hsien-tai yü te tz'u?—*CKYW* 1961:10–11, 91–92. [Are or are not literary words of the present-day language?

張世祿：文言詞是不是現代語的詞？

1014 Chao, K'o-ch'in: *Ku-tai Han-yü tz'u-hui wen-t'i.*—Chengchow: Chung-chou shu-

hua-she, 1980, 2, 108 p. [The problem of an ancient Chinese lexicon.]

趙克勤：古代漢語詞滙問題

1015 Dobson, W.A.C.H.: *Late Archaic Chinese —A grammatical study.*—Toronto: U. of Toronto Press, 1959, xxviii, 254 p./ Chap. 1: The lexic & the word; *RBS* 5, 1959, 496, A. Rygaloff; *AcOr* 25, 1960, 173–178, Søren Egerod; *JAOS* 81, 1961, 299–308, Chang Kun; *AM* 12, 1966, 115–119, E.G. Pulleyblank; *AO* 34, 1966, 153–154, T. Pokora.

1016 Dobson, W.A.C.H.: *Early Archaic Chinese —A descriptive grammar.*—Toronto: U. of Toronto Press, 1962, xxxi, 288 p./ Chap. 1: The lexic & the word; *JAS* 21, 1962, 539–540, Li Fang-kuei; *Lg* 39, 1963, 567–574, H. Stimson.

1017 Dobson, W.A.C.H.: *The language of the Book of Songs.*—Toronto: U. of Toronto Press, 1968, xxix, 321 p., 2 pl./ Chap. 1: The word; *Chinese Culture* 9:2, 1968, 122–123, Hu Ping-chung.

1018 Hsü, Wei-hsien: *Ku-tai Han-yü* ch'ang-yung tz'u pu-fen te chi-ko wen-t'i.—*CKYW* 1966:1, 17–24./ *RBS* 12–13, 1966–1967, 644, S.N. Cartier. [Several problems in the section on commonly used words in (Wang Li's) *Ku-tai Han-yü* (1052).]

許惟賢：『古代漢語』常用詞部份的幾個問題

1019 Lu, Hsü-yüan: Chiu-ching shen-ma shih wen-yen tz'u?—*CKYW* 1961:3, 3. [What is a literary word after all?]

盧緒元：究竟甚麼是文言詞？

1020 Sun, Ch'ang-hsü: Ku Han-yü wen-hsüeh yü-yen tz'u-hui te hsing-chih.—*Yü-yen-hsüeh lun-chi* (0084), 117–138. [The nature of the vocabulary in the ancient Chinese literary language.]

孫常叙：古漢語文學語言詞滙的性質

1021 Wang, Liao-i: Ku yü te szu-wang ts'an-liu ho chuan-sheng.—*KWYK* 1:9, 1941,

2–4; *Chung-kuo yü-wen . . . hsüan-chi* (0079), 91–96; *Lung-ch'ung ping-tiao-chai wen-chi* (0086), 413–418. [The death, survival and revival of ancient words.]

王了一：古語的死亡殘留和轉生

1022 Yüan, Pin: Ku Han-yü tz'u-tsu ho ku-ting chieh-kou te tz'u-hua hsien-hsiang. —*YYWH* 1981:2, 38–39. [Ancient Chinese phrases and the phenomenon of lexicalization of fixed structures.]

袁賓：古漢語詞組和固定結構的詞化現象

5.2.2. Lexical Meanings (1023–1038)

1023 Chiang, Shao-yü: Kuan-yü ku Han-yü tz'u-i te i-hsieh wen-t'i.—*YLT* 7, 1981, 28–48. [A few problems concerning the lexical meanings of ancient Chinese.]

蔣紹愚：關於古漢語詞義的一些問題

1024 Chiang, Shao-yü: Tsen-yang chang-wo ku Han-yü te tz'u-i—chien t'an *i-wei* ho *i-su* tsai tz'u-i fen-hsi chung te yün-yung. —*YWYC* 1981:2, 80–86. [How to grasp the lexical meanings of ancient Chinese—with a discussion on the utilizations of *semanteme* and *sememe* in the analysis of lexical meanings.]

蔣紹愚：怎樣掌握古漢語的詞義——兼談『義位』和『義素』在詞義分析中的運用

1025 Chung-shan ta-hsüeh Chung-wen-hsi Ku-tai Han-yü chiao-hsüeh hsiao-tsu: *Ku-tai Han-yü.*—Hong Kong: Erh-ya, 1977, 2 vols., [v], 831 p./ Including analysis and differentiation of ancient lexical meanings. [Ancient Chinese.]

中山大學中文系古代漢語教學小組：古代漢語／包括詞義辨析

1026 Han, Ch'en-ch'i: Hsien-tai Han-yü tz'u-yü chung te ku i.—*Chiao-hsüeh yü chin-hsiu* 1981:4, (not seen). [Ancient meanings in Modern Chinese words and phrases.]

韓陳其：現代漢語詞語中的古義

1027 Kao, Ch'ing-szu: *Ku-tai Han-yü chih-shih liu chiang.*—Wuhan: Hu-pei jen-min, 1979,

[2], 111 p./ Lecture 1: Systems of lexical meanings. [Six lectures on common knowledge of ancient Chinese.]

高慶賜：古代漢語知識六講／第一講：詞義系統

1028 Kuo, Chao-mu: *Wen-yen-wen yüeh-tu ch'ang-shih.*—Chengtu: Szu-ch'uan jen-min, 1981, 3, 2, 127 p./ Chap. 2: Words and lexical meanings. [Common knowledge for reading literary Chinese.]

郭昭穆：文言文閱讀常識／第二章：詞和詞義

1029 Kuo, Hsi-liang, et al.: *Ku-tai Han-yü* (shang ts'e).—Peking: Pei-ching, 1981, 2, 2, 3, 377 p./ 85–123: Ancient and modern lexical meanings; 359–377: Examples of differentiation and analysis of lexical meanings. [Ancient Chinese (Vol. I).]

郭錫良等：古代漢語（上册）／85-132：古今詞義的同異；359-377：詞義分析舉例

1030 Kuo, Tsai-i: Ku Han-yü tz'u-i cha-chi. —*CKYW* 1979:2, 125–127, 139. [Notes on lexical meanings of ancient Chinese.]

郭在貽：古漢語詞義札記

1031 Li, Li: Cheng-ch'üeh jen-shih ku-tien wen te tz'u-i.—*Fu-tan* 1959:6, 29–34. [Correctly recognizing the lexical meanings of classical texts.]

李笠：正確認識古典文的詞義

1032 Liang, Tung-ch'ing: Ku-tai Han-yü tz'u-i fa-chan chü yü.—*HNSC* 1981:1, 18– (not seen). [Certain aspects of the development of lexical meanings in ancient Chinese.]

梁冬青：古代漢語詞義發展舉隅

1033 Lu, Tsung-ta & Wang, Ning: Ku Han-yü tz'u-i yen-chiu.—*TSYC* 1981:2, 31–42. [A study of lexical meanings in ancient Chinese.]

陸宗達、王寧：古漢語詞義研究

1034 T'an, Ch'üan-chi: *Ku-tai Han-yü chi-ch'u.* —Hong Kong: Chung-hua, 1978, 6, 234 p./ 1–65: Section on lexical meanings.

[The fundamentals of ancient Chinese.]
譚全基：古代漢語基礎／1-65：詞義部分

1035 Tōdō, Akiyasu: Kodaigo no imi to koten no kaidoku.—*NCGH* 13, 1961, 132–144; E.S./ *RBS* 7, 1961, 452, F. Litsch. [The meanings of ancient words and the explanations of classical texts.]
藤堂明保：古代語の意味と古典の解讀

1036 Wu, Hsiao-ju: Lüeh t'an ku-tien shih ko chung te tz'u-i.—*YWHH* 1957:1, 30–32. [A short discussion on the lexical meanings of poems and songs (found) in classical texts.]
吳小如：略談古典詩歌中的詞義

1037 Yin, Meng-lun: Yu-kuan ku Han-yü tz'u-i pien-hsi te wen-t'i.—*Yü-yen wen-tzu . . . chuan-k'an* (0089), 426–437. [Problems concerning the differentiation and analysis of lexical meanings in ancient Chinese.]
殷孟倫：有關古漢語詞義辨析的問題

1038 Yin, Meng-lun, et al.: *Ku Han-yü chien lun.*—Chinan: Shan-tung jen-min, 1979, 9, 444 p./ Introduction, Chap. 4: Changes and development of lexical meanings. [A simple discussion on ancient Chinese.]
殷孟倫等：古漢語簡論／緒論，第四章：詞義演變和發展

5.2.3. General Studies (1039–1053)

1039 Chang, Shih-lu: *Ku-tai Han-yü.*—Shanghai: Shang-hai chiao-yü, 1978, [1], 247 p./ Chap. 3: Lexicon. [Ancient Chinese.]
張世祿：古代漢語／第三章：詞滙

1040 Cheng, Tien & Mai, Mei-ch'iao: *Ku Han-yü yü-fa-hsüeh tzu-liao hui-pien.*—Peking: Chung-hua, 1964, viii, 336 p.; Hong Kong: Chung-hua, 1972, repr./ Pt. I.2: Cenematic and plerematic words. [Collected materials on ancient Chinese grammar.]
鄭奠、麥梅翹：古漢語語法學資料彙編／第一部分，二：虛字和實字

1041 Chiang, Shao-yü & Li, Hsin-chien: *Ku Han-yü chiang-hua.*—Chengchow: Chung-chou shu-hua-she, 1981, [ii], 4, 214 p./ Lecture 3: Lexicon of ancient Chinese; Lecture 5–6; Cenematic words of ancient Chinese. [Lectures on ancient Chinese.]
蔣紹愚、李新建：古漢語講話／第三講：古代漢語的詞滙；第五、六講：古代漢語的虛詞

1042 Chou, Ping-chün: *Ku Han-yü kang-yao.*—Changsha: Hu-nan jen-min, 1981, 2, 5, 560 p./ 236–330: Lexicon. [An outline of ancient Chinese.]
周秉鈞：古漢語綱要／236-330：詞滙篇

1043 Chu, Hsing: *Ku Han-yü kai-lun.*—Tientsin: T'ien-chin jen-min, 1955, 5, 6, 843 p./ Chap. 4: Vocabulary, including the origin and development of words, the analysis of words, and Chinese traditional semantics; *CKYW* 1960:6, 295–300, Shan-tung ta-hsüeh Chung-wen-hsi yü-yen chiao-yen tsu. [An introduction to ancient Chinese.]
朱星：古漢語概論／第四章：詞彙；山東大學中文系語言教研組評

1044 Chu, Hsing: *Ku-tai Han-yü.*—Tientsin: T'ien-chin jen-min, 1980, 2 vols., 3, 333 p.; 5, 248 p./ Vol. II, Chap. 3: Lexicon. [Ancient Chinese.]
朱星：古代漢語／下冊，第三章：詞滙

1045 Chung-shan ta-hsüeh Chung-wen-hsi: *Ku Han-yü chi-ch'u chih-shih.*—Canton: Kuang-tung jen-min, 1979, 4, 314 p./ Chap. 2: Lexicon. [Fundamental knowledge of ancient Chinese.]
中山大學中文系：古漢語基礎知識／第二章：詞滙

1046 Ho, Chiu-ying & Chiang, Shao-yü: *Ku Han-yü tz'u-hui chiang-hua.*—Peking: Pei-ching, 1980, 3, 148 p. [Lectures on ancient Chinese lexicon.]
何九盈、蔣紹愚：古漢語詞滙講話

1047 Hsiang, Hsia: *Han-yü wen-yen yü-fa kang-yao.*—Hong Kong: Chung-nan, 1961,

223 p./ Chap. 2: Words and phrases. [An outline of the grammar of literary Chinese.]

向夏：漢語文言語法綱要／第二章：詞和短語

1048 Sun, Chün-hsi: *Wen-yen chi-ch'u chih-shih.*—Shihchiachuang: Ho-pei jen-min, 1980, 4, 2, 277 p./ Chap. 1: Literary characters and words; Chap. 2: Literary plerematic words; Chap. 3: Literary cenematic words. [Fundamental knowledge of literary Chinese.]

孫鈞錫：文言基礎知識／第一章：文言的字和詞；第二章：文言的實詞；第三章：文言的虛詞

1049 Togawa, Yoshio: Kotengo no goi.—*Gengo* (0085), 239–254. [Vocabulary of the language of classical texts.]/ Materials taken from *Lun-yü, Meng-tzu, Shih-chi,* etc.

戶川芳郎：古典語の語彙

1050 Tsou, Lien-yen; Liu, Chien-p'ing, et al.: *Wen-yen tz'u-hui chi-ch'u chih-shih.*—Tientsin: T'ien-chin jen-min, 1982, [ii], 6, 143 p. [Fundamental knowledge of the lexicon of literary Chinese.]

鄒聯琰、劉鑒平等：文言詞滙基礎知識

1051 Wang, Cheng-pai: *Wen-yen shih-tz'u chih-shih.*—Hofei: An-hui jen-min, 1978, 2, 2, 234 p. [Knowledge of literary plerematic words.]

王政白：文言實詞知識

1052 Wang, Li: *Ku-tai Han-yü.*—Peking: Chung-hua, 1962, 4 vols., 16, 2, 8, 1718 p./ *RBS* 8, 1962, 434, W.A.C.H. Dobson./ Includes commonly used words, etc. [Ancient Chinese.]

王力：古代漢語／包括常用詞等

1053 Wang, Li: *Ku-tai Han-yü ch'ang-shih.*—Peking: Jen-min chiao-yü, 1979, [i], 78 p./ Chap. 5: Ancient Chinese lexicon. [Common knowledge of ancient Chinese.]

王力：古代漢語常識／第五章：古代漢語的詞滙

5.2.4. Collection and Analysis (1054–1112)
5.2.4.1. Plerematic Words (1054–1090)

1054 Chang, Heng: *Hsün-tzu* yü-hui yen-chiu.—*Chung-kuo tung-ya hsüeh-shu nien-pao* 1, 1962, 277–377. [A study on the vocabulary of *Hsün-tzu.*]

張亨：『荀子』語彙研究

1055 Chang, I-jen: *Kuo-yü yin-te.*—Taipei: Chung-yang yen-chiu yüan, 1976, 2, 2, 16, 18, 850 p. [An index to *Kuo-yü.*]

張以仁：國語引得

1056 Chang, T'ing-yü, et al.: *P'ien-tzu lei-pien.*—Peking: Palace block ed., 1728, 240 *chüan,* 120 *ts'e;* Shanghai: T'ung-wen shu-chü, 1887, 48 *ts'e;* Taipei: T'ai-wan hsüeh-sheng, 1963, 8 vols. [A classified collection of paired-character phrases.]

張廷玉等：駢字類編

1057 Chang, Yü-shu, et al.: *P'ei-wen yün-fu.*—Peking: Palace block ed., 1711 & 1720, 115 *ts'e;* Shanghai: T'ung-wen shu-chü, 1891, repr., 60 *ts'e;* Shanghai: Shang-wu, 1937, photocopy of the Palace ed., 6 vols, 4785 p.; Taipei: Hsin-hsing shu-chü, 1960, repr., 4 vols., 4785 p.; Taipei: Shang-wu, 1966, repr., 6 vols., 4785 p., with a four-corner numerical index. [The *P'ei-wen* thesaurus of rhyming phrases.]

張玉書等：佩文韻府

1058 Chuang, Wei-szu: *P'ien-tzu lei-pien yin-te.*—Taipei: Szu-k'u shu-chü, 1966, 24, 261 p. [An index to *P'ien-tzu lei-pien* (1056).]

莊為斯：駢字類編引得

1059 Ch'en, Chün-an: Ku chin tz'u-yü pu-t'ung erh-shih li.—*YCT* 2, 1981, 60–62. [Twenty examples showing the differences of ancient and modern words and phrases.]

陳君安：古今詞語不同二十例

1060 Ch'en, K'o-chiung: *Tso-chuan* hsing-jung-tz'u chien hsi.—*HCSY* 1979:4, 99–106. [A simple analysis of adjectives in *Tso-chuan.*] / With a list of monosyllabic and disyllabic words.

陳克炯：『左傳』形容詞簡析

1061 Ch'en, K'o-chiung: *Tso-chuan* tz'u-hui yü Ch'un-ch'iu wen-hua shuo-lüeh.—*CNMT* 1981:1, 91— (not seen). [A brief discussion on the vocabulary of *Tso-chuan* and the culture of the Spring and Autumn period.]

陳克炯：『左傳』詞彙與春秋文化說略

1062 Ch'en, K'o-chiung: *Tso-chuan* tz'u-hui chien lun.—*HCSY* 1982:1, 114–123. [A simple discussion on the vocabulary of *Tso-chuan.*]

陳克炯：『左傳』詞滙簡論

1063 Chiang, Li-hung: *I fu hsü tiao.*—Peking: Chung-hua, 1981, I, 5, 5, 153 p. [A continuation of *I fu.*] / A collection with explanations of ancient words.

蔣禮鴻：義府續貂

1064 Chu, Ch'i-feng: *Tz'u t'ung.*—Shanghai: K'ai-ming, 1934, 2 vols., 44, 2847 p.; Taipei: K'ai-ming, 1960, repr., 2 vols., 65, 2814, 340 p.; Shanghai: Shang-hai ku-chi, 1982, repr./ *TSCK* 1:2, 1934, 81–87, Tu Ming-fu; *QBCB* 1, 1934, 55–58, Hu Shih; *Sekai meicho daijiten* (0041), 6:456, Tōdō Akiyasu; *TSYC* 1980:4, 197–207, Chin Wen-ming, Wang T'ao & Szu Ying-ch'i. [A thoroughfare of words.] / Ancient and literary polysyllabic words.

朱起鳳：辭通／杜明甫評，胡適評，藤堂明保評，金文明、王濤、斯英琦評

1065 Ho, Chiu-ying: Ku Han-yü tz'u-i cha-chi.—*CKYW* 1983:1, 57–60. [Notes on the meanings of Ancient Chinese words.]

何九盈：古漢語詞義札記

1066 Hsin, Ying-chü: Ku Han-yü yü-tz'u cha-chi.—*CKYW* 1980:4, 292–294. [Notes on Ancient Chinese words and phrases.]

信應舉：古漢語語詞札記

1067 Huang, Hsün-chai: Yeh t'an ku chin t'ung hsing i i tz'u.—*Hu-nan shih-yüan hsüeh-pao* 1982:4, (not seen). [Also discussing ancient and modern words with identical forms but different meanings.]

黃巽齋：也談古今同形異義詞

1068 Karlgren, Bernhard: *Grammata Serica*—Script and phonetic in Chinese and Sino-Japanese.—*BMFEA* 12, 1940, 1–471; Taipei: Ch'eng-wen, 1966, repr. 471 p.; *Lg* 17, 1941, 60–67, Y.R. Chao.

〔高本漢：中日漢字形聲論〕

1069 Karlgren, Bernhard: Glosses on the *Book of Odes.*—*BMFEA* 14, 1942, 71–247; 16, 1944, 25–169; 18, 1946, 11–198.

1070 Karlgren, Bernhard: Glosses on the *Book of Documents.*—*BMFEA* 20, 1948, 29–315; 21, 1949, 63–206.

1071 Karlgren, Bernhard: *Grammata Serica recensa.*—*BMFEA* 29, 1957, 1–332; Stockholm: MFEA, 1957, repr./ *RBS* 3, 1957, 551, W. Simon; *JA* 246, 1958, 331–332, E. Gaspardone.

1072 Karlgren, Bernhard. Transl. by Tung T'ung-ho: *Kao Pen-han Shih-ching chu-shih.*—Taipei: Chung-hua ts'ung-shu, 1960, 2 vols., 10, 26, 1130, (index) 26 p., portr. [Karlgren's (*The Book of Odes* and) *Glosses on the Book of Odes.*] (1069)

高本漢著，董同龢譯：高本漢詩經注釋

1073 Karlgren, Bernhard: *Loan characters in pre-Han texts* (0882).

1074 Karlgren, Bernhard: Glosses on the *Tso Chuan.*—*BMFEA* 41, 1969, 1–157.

1075 Karlgren, Bernhard. Transl. by Ch'en, Shun-cheng: *Kao Pen-han Shu-ching chu-shih.*—Taipei: Chung-hua ts'ung-shu, 1970, 2 vols., 2, 5, 9, 1224 p. [Karlgren's Glosses on the *Book of Documents.*] (1070)

高本漢著，陳舜政譯：高本漢書經注釋

1076 Karlgren, Bernhard: Gleanings for a lexicon of classical Chinese.—*BMFEA* 44, 1972, 1–73; 45, 1973, 1–62; 46, 1974, 1–27.

1077 Karlgren, Bernhard: Moot words in some *Chuang-tze* chapters.—*BMFEA* 48, 1976, 145–163.

1078 *Ku Han-yü ch'ang-yung tzu tzu-tien* pien-hsieh-tsu: *Ku Han-yü ch'ang-yung tzu tzu-tien.*—Peking: Shang-wu, 1979, 56, 462 p./ *TSYC* 1981:1, 80–85, Chou Hsing-chien & Chou Li-shang; *TYT* 3, 1981, 57–61, Lo Wei-li. [A dictionary of commonly used characters in ancient Chinese.]
『古漢語常用字字典』編寫組：古漢語常用字字典／周行健、周荔裳評，駱偉里評

1079 Lan-chou ta-hsüeh Chung-wen-hsi *Meng-tzu i chu* hsiao-tsu: *Meng-tzu i chu.*—Peking: Chung-hua, 1960, 2 vols., 16, 483 p./ 346–483: A dictionary of *Meng-tzu*. [*Meng-tzu* translated and annotated.]
蘭州大學中文系『孟子譯註』小組：孟子譯註／346–483：孟子詞典

1080 Liu, Ch'i-i: Hsi Chou chin-wen chung yüeh-hsiang tz'u-yü te chieh-shih.—*LSCH* 1979:6, 21–26. [Explanations of lunar-phase words and phrases in the bronze inscriptions of the Western Chou (dynasty).]
劉啓益：西周金文中月相詞語的解釋

1081 Liu, Chien-p'ing & Tsou, Lien-yen: *Wen-yen ch'ang-yung tz'u shou-ts'e.*—Tientsin: T'ien-chin jen-min, 1980, 4, 269 p. [A handbook of commonly used literary words.]
劉監平、鄒聯琰：文言常用詞手册

1082 Lu, Erh-k'uei; et al.: *Tz'u-yüan.*—Shanghai: Shang-wu, 1915, 2 vols., 15, 2974, 98 p.; *Tz'u-yüan hsü-pien* by Fang, I, Shanghai: Shang-wu, 1931, 14, 1568, 120 p.; Taipei: Shang-wu, 1969, bound in 1 vol., vi, 1862, 216 p. [The sources of words] and [A supplement to *Tz'u-yüan*.]
陸爾奎等：辭源
方毅：辭源續編

1083 Shu, Hsin-ch'eng, et al.: *Tz'u-hai.*—Shanghai: Chung-hua, 1938, 2 vols., 12, 1903 p.; 1495, 379 p.; Taipei: Chung-hua, 1956, repr.; 1980, rev. ed., 3 vols. [A sea of words.]
舒新城等：辭海

1084 Suzuki, Ryūichi: *Kokugo sakuin.*—Kyoto: Tōhō Bunka Gakuin Kyōto Kenkyūjo, 1934, 14, 276 p. [An index to *Kuo-yü* ('Conversations from the States').]
鈴木隆一：國語索引

1085 T'ai-wan Chung-hua shu-chü *Tz'u-hai* pien-chi wei-yüan-hui: *Tsui-hsin tseng-ting pen Tz'u-hai.*—Taipei: Ditto, 1980, 3 vols., 6, 5151, 442, 139 p. [A newly revised and enlarged edition of *Tz'u-hai* (1083).]
臺灣中華書局『辭海』編輯委員會：最新增訂本辭海

1086 T'ai-wan Shang-wu yin-shu-kuan pien-shen wei-yüan-hui: *Tseng-hsiu Tz'u-yüan*. Fu *Szu-chiao hao-ma so-yin.*—Taipei: Ditto, 1978, 2 vols., 10, 6, 2464, 284, 20 p. [A revised and enlarged edition of *Tz'u-yüan* (1082). With a Four-corner numerical character index.]
臺灣商務印書館編審委員會：增修辭源 附四角號碼索引

1087 *Tz'u-hai* pien-chi wei-yüan-hui: *Tz'u-hai.*—Peking: Chung-hua, 1965, rev. ed., 2 vols., 32, 4257 p.; Hong Kong: Chung-hua, 1979, repr.; Shanghai: Shang-hai tz'u-shu, 1979, new ed., 3 vols., 40, 2214 p.; also reduced ed., 1 vol. [A sea of words.]/ See (1083).
『辭海』編輯委員會：辭海

1088 Yang, Chia-lo (ed. in chief): *Ku-tien fu-yin tz'u-hui chi lin.*—Taipei: Ting-wen shu-chu, 1978, 8 vols., v.p. [A collection of disyllabic vocabulary from classical texts.] A rearranged edition of *P'ien-tzu lei-pien* (1056) and *P'ei-wen yün-fu* (1057).

楊家駱主編：古典複音詞彙輯林／『駢字類編』及『佩文韻府』改編

1089 Yang, Po-chün: *Lun-yü i chu.*—Peking: Chung-hua, 1958; 1962, 2nd print., 13, 324 p./ 219–324: A dictionary of *Lun-yü*. [*Lun-yü* translated and annotated.]

楊伯峻：論語譯註／219-324: 論語詞典

1090 Yang, Tien-k'uei: *Wen-yen shih-tz'u li chieh.*—Hong Kong: Kang-ch'ing, 1980, 4, 144 p. [Explanations with examples of literary plerematic words.]

楊殿奎：文言實詞例解

5.2.4.2. Cenematic Words (1091–1112)

1091 Chang, I-jen: *Kuo-yü hsü-tz'u chi-shih.*—Taipei: Academia Sinica, 1968, 2, 13, 3, 254 p. [Collection and explanations of cenematic words in *Kuo-yü.*]

張以仁：國語虛詞集釋

1092 *Ch'ang-chien wen-yen hsü-tz'u li shih* pien-hsieh tsu: *Ch'ang-chien wen-yen hsü-tz'u li shih.*—Shanghai: Shang-hai chiao-yü, 1978; 1981, 3rd print., 6, 184 p./ *KKNP* 16, 1982, 5–6, Hatano Tarō. [Explanations with examples of commonly seen literary cenematic words.]

『常見文言虛詞例釋』編寫組：常見文言虛詞例釋／波多野太郎評

1093 Chu, T'ing-hsien: *Shang-shu hsü-tzu chi-shih.*—Taipei: Shang-wu, 1969, 7, 136 p. [Collection and explanations of cenematic words in *Shang-shu.*]

朱廷獻：尚書虛字集釋

1094 Dobson, W.A.C.H.: *A dictionary of the Chinese particles.*—Toronto: U. of Toronto Press, 1974, x, 907 p./ *JAS* 36:1, 1976, 137–138, Chang Kun; *Chin san-shih nien . . . chien chieh* (0010), 53–54.

〔張琨評〕

1095 Dobson, W.A.C.H. Transl. by Ho, Lo-shih: *Ku Han-yü hsü-tz'u tz'u-tien* hsü-lun.—*YIT* 1, 1979, 76–150. [A prolegomenon to *A dictionary of the Chinese particles* (1094).]

杜百勝著，何樂士譯：『古漢語虛詞詞典』緒論

1096 Ho, Lo-shih, et al.: *Wen-yen hsü-tz'u ch'ien shih.*—Peking: Pei-ching, 1979, 7, 449 p./ *KKNP* 16, 1982, 6–7, Hatano Tarō. [Simple explanations of literary cenematic words.]

何樂士等：文言虛詞淺釋／波多野太郎評

1097 Hsü, Shih-ying: *Ch'ang-yung hsü-tzu yung-fa ch'ien shih.*—Taipei: Fu-hsing, 1963; 1975, 8th print., 5, 11, 464 p. [Simple explanations of the uses of commonly used cenematic words.]

許世瑛：常用虛字用法淺釋

1098 Hsüeh, Ju-chang, et al.: *Wen-yen hsü-tz'u ch'ien shih.*—Sian: Shan-hsi jen-min, 1977; 1980, 3rd print., 4, 231 p. [Simple explanations of literary cenematic words.]

薛儒章等：文言虛詞淺釋

1099 Li, Ping-chieh: *Kuo-wen hsü-tzu shih li.*—Taipei: T'ai-wan hsüeh-sheng, 1976, 2, [4], 339 p. [Examples with explanations of cenematic words in literary Chinese.]

李炳傑：國文虛字釋例

1100 Li, Shu-chang: *Wen-yen hsü-tz'u li shih.*—Huhehot: Nei Meng-ku jen-min, 1979, [iii], 181 p. [Explanations with examples of literary cenematic words.]

李淑章：文言虛詞例釋

1101 Liu, Ch'i. Rev. & comment. by Chang, Hsi-shen: *Chu-tzu pien lüeh.*—Shanghai: K'ai-ming, 1940, repr.; Peking: Chung-hua, 1954, repr., 5 *chüan*, 8, 10, 316, 12 p.; Taipei: K'ai-ming, 1958, repr.; Hong Kong: Nan-kuo, 1960, repr./ First publ. in 1711. [Brief distinctions between (the uses of) particles.]

劉淇著，章錫琛校注：助字辨略

1102 Liu, Chien-ou: *Chan-kuo ts'e* hsü-tzu lei shih.—*Fu-hsing-kang hsüeh-pao* 21, 1979, 393–412. [Classified explanations of cenematic words in *Chan-kuo ts'e.*]
劉建鷗：『戰國策』虛字類釋

1103 Lu, Hsiao-hsien: *Chan-kuo ts'e hsü-tzu chi shih.*—Tainan: Hsing-yeh t'u-shu, 1976, 78 p. [Collection and explanations of cenematic words in *Chan-kuo ts'e.*]
盧孝賢：戰國策虛字集釋

1104 Lü, Shu-hsiang: *Wen-yen hsü-tzu.*—Peking: K'ai-ming, 1944; 1953, rev. ed., vii, 168 p.; Shanghai: Hsin chih-shih, 1957, xii, 226 p.; Shanghai: Shang-hai chiao-yü, 1979, 8, 155 p. [Cenematic words in literary Chinese.]
呂叔湘：文言虛字

1105 P'ei, Hsüeh-hai: *Ku shu hsü-tzu chi shih.*—Shanghai: Shang-wu, 1934, 19, 918, 16 p.; Taipei: Kuang-wen, 1962, repr. [Collection and explanations of cenematic words in ancient books.]
裴學海：古書虛字集釋

1106 Shih, Ming-ts'an: *Li-chi hsü-tz'u yung-fa shih li.*—Taipei: Wen-shih-che, 1974, 2, 2, 6, 384 p. [Examples with explanations of methods of using cenematic words in *Li-chi.*]
施銘燦：禮記虛詞用法釋例

1107 Sun, T'ien-chang, et al.: *Wen-yen hsü-tz'u li shih yü lien-hsi.*—Chengchow: Ho-nan jen-min, 1982, [ii], 6, 312 p. [Explanations with examples and exercises on literary cenematic words.]
孫天章等：文言虛詞例釋與練習

1108 Wang, Shu-min: *Ku shu hsü-tzu hsin i.*—Taipei: Lien-ching, 1978, 4, 7, 2, 151 p. [New (explanations of) meanings of cenematic words (found) in ancient books.]
王叔岷：古書虛字新義

1109 Wang, Yin-chih: *Ching-chuan shih-tz'u.*—Peking: Chung-hua, 1957, repr., 10 chüan, with supplements, 350 p.; Taipei: Shih-chieh, 1956, 4, 132 p.; Taipei: Shang-wu, 1968, 11, 81, 85 p. [Explanations of words (found) in the Classics and commentaries.]/ Explanations of 160 particles.
王引之：經傳釋詞

1110 Yang, Po-chün: *Wen-yen hsü-tz'u.*—Peking: Chung-hua, 1965, xvi, 238 p. [Cenematic words in literary Chinese.]
楊伯峻：文言虛詞

1111 Yang, Po-chün: *Ku Han-yü hsü-tz'u.*—Peking: Chung-hua, 1981, 2, 8, 392 p./ *KKNP* 16, 1982, 7–9, Hatano Tarō. [Cenematic words in ancient Chinese.]
楊伯峻：古漢語虛詞／波多 野太郎評

1112 Yang, Shu-ta: *Tz'u ch'üan.*—Shanghai: Shang-wu, 1928, 42, 618 p.; Peking: Chung-hua, 1957, 3, 19, 20, 626 p.; 1979, 31, 479 p. [Words explained.]/ Explanations of cenematic words.
楊樹達：詞詮

5.3. Lexicon of Han and Six Dynasties (1113–1135)
5.3.1. Han Dynasty (1113–1120)

1113 Ch'ü, Shou-yüeh: *Chung-ku tz'u-yü k'ao-shih.*—Taipei: Shang-wu, 1968, 2, 518, (Index by strokes) 30 p.; *Hsü-pien.*—Taipei: I-wen, 1972, 24, 315 p. [A study with explanations of words and phrases of Middle Chinese.] and [Supplement.]/ Late Han to early T'ang dynasty.
曲守約：中古辭語考釋 續編

1114 Ch'ü, Shou-yüeh: *Tz'u shih.*—Taipei: Lien-ching, 1979, 53, 274 p.; Hong Kong: Wan feng, n.d., repr. [Words explained.]/ From Han and later texts.
曲守約：辭釋

1115 Fujita, Shizen: *Go Kansho goi shūsei.*—Kyoto: Kyōto Daigaku Jinbun Kagaku Kenkyūjo, 1960–1962, 3 vols., 6, 3, 3336 p./ *Chin san-shih nien . . . chien chieh*

(0010), 234–235. [A compendium of the vocabulary of *Hou Han-shu.*]
藤田至善：後漢書語彙集成

1116 Hsü, Pi: *Shih-chi ch'eng-tai-tz'u yü hsü-tz'u yen-chiu.*—Taipei: The Author, 1973, 10, 928 p. [A study of the pronouns and cenematic words in *Shih-chi.*]
許璧：史記稱代詞與虛詞研究

1117 Kuo, Tsai-i: *Shuo-wen Tuan-chu yü Han-yü tz'u-hui yen-chiu.—She-hui k'o-hsüeh chan-hsien* 3, 1978, 330–345. [*Shuo-wen tuan-chu* (3546) and the study of Chinese lexicon.]
郭在貽：『說文段注』與漢語詞滙研究

1118 Kuo, Tsai-i: *Han-shu* tzu-i cha-chi.—*HCTH* 1979:1–2, 64–76, 125. [Notes on the meanings of characters in *Han-shu.*]
郭在貽：『漢書』字義札記

1119 Ushijima, Tokuji: *Kango bunpōron* (Kodai hen).—Tokyo: Taishūkan, 1967, viii, 410, 33 p./ 389–406: Bibliography; Pt. II, Chap. 2: Words; 16–27: Index to vocabulary. [On Chinese grammar (Ancient period).]/ Han dynasty.
牛島德次：漢語文法論（古代編）／第二編，第二章：詞；（卷末索引）16–27：語彙索引

1120 Yamada, Katsumi: *Entetsuron sakuin.*—Tokyo: Tōyō Daigaku Chūtetsubun Kenkyūshitsu, 1960, 5, 464 p. [An index to *Yen t'ieh lun.*]
山田勝美：鹽鐵論索引

5.3.2. Six Dynasties (1121–1135)

1121 Chou, Sheng-ya: *Shih-shuo hsin-yü* chung te fu-yin tz'u wen-t'i.—*CLTH* 1982:2, 81–88. [The problem of disyllabic words in *Shih-shuo hsin-yü.*]
周生亞：『世說新語』中的複音詞問題

1122 Fan, Wei-kang: Chin Nan-pei ch'ao yüeh-fu min-ko tz'u-yü shih.—*CKYW* 1980:6, 461–463. [Explanations of words and phrases (found) in the folk songs of

Yüeh-fu of the Chin and the Northern and Southern Dynasties.]
樊維綱：晉南北朝樂府民歌詞語釋

1123 Fujii, Mamoru: *Sankokushi* goi shū.—*HRBK* 40:2, 1980, 1–212; Hiroshima: Hiroshima Daigaku Bungakubu, 1980, 212 p.; E.S. [A collection of vocabulary from *San-kuo chih.*]
藤井守：『三國志』語彙集

1124 Fujii, Mamoru: *Sankokushi Haishi chū goi shaku.*—*HRBK* 41:3, 1981, 1–200, E.S.; Hiroshima: Chūgoku Chūse Bungaku Kenkyūkai, 1981, repr. [A collection of the vocabulary of P'ei's commentary on *San-kuo chih.*]
藤井守：三國志裴氏注語彙集

1125 Harada, Taneshige: *Sōshinki* goi sakuin (1).—*DTBK* 19, 1981, 129–161; 20, 1982, 135–178. [An index to the vocabulary of *Sou-shen chi* (1).]
原田種成：『搜神記』語彙索引（一）

1126 Harvard-Yenching Institute: *Shih-shuo hsin-yü yin-te.* Fu *Liu-chu yin-shu yin-te.*—Peking: Ditto, 1933, xvi, 56 p.; Taipei: Ch'eng-wen, 1966, repr./ Sinological Index Series, 12. [An index to *Shih-shuo hsin-yü.* With the titles cited in Liu's commentary.]
哈佛燕京社：世說新語引得　附劉注引書引得

1127 Hsü, Chen-o: *Shih-shuo hsin-yü* li te Chin Sung k'ou yü shih i.—*HTST* 1957:3, 50–61. [Semantic explanations for Chin and Sung (dynasty) colloquial words (found) in *Shih-shuo hsin-yü.*]
徐震堮：『世說新語』裏的晉宋口語釋義

1128 Itō, Tomio: Rikuchō goi no danpen.—*SGKK* 11, 1954, 1–3. [Fragments of the vocabulary of the Six Dynasties.]
伊藤富雄：六朝語彙の斷片

1129 Liang, Yung-ch'ang: *Shih-shuo hsin-yü* tzu tz'u tsa chi.—*HTST* 1981:3, 47–53. [Miscellaneous notes on characters and words in *Shih-shuo hsin-yü.*]
梁永昌

梁永昌：『世說新語』字詞雜記

1130   Morino, Shigeō: Rikuchō yakukyō no goi.—*HRBK* 36, 1976, 215–236. [The vocabulary of Six Dynasties translations of Buddhist Sutras.]
森野繁夫：六朝譯經の語彙

1131   Morino, Shigeo: *Kōsōden goi sakuin.* —Hiroshima: Chūgoku Chūse Bungaku Kenkyūkai, 1979, 6, 79, [i]p. [An index to the vocabulary of *Kao-seng chuan.*]
森野繁夫：高僧傳語彙索引

1132   Morino, Shigeo: *Rikuchō hyōgo shū— Sesetsu shingo, Sesetsu shingo chū, Kōsōden.*—Hiroshima: Chūgoku Chūse Bungaku Kenkyūkai, 1980, 7, 224 p. [A collection of *p'ing-yü* of the Six Dynasties —*Shih-shuo hsin-yü, Shih-shuo hsin-yü chu, Kao-seng chuan.*]
森野繁夫：六朝評語集──世說新語、世說新語注、高僧傳

1133   Morino, Shigeo & Fujii, Mamoru: Rikuchō ko shōsetsu goi shū.—*HRBK* 39:1, 1979, 1–134; E.S. [A collection of the vocabulary from old novels of the Six Dynasties.]
森野繁夫、藤井守：六朝古小說語彙集

1134   Takahashi, Kiyoshi: *Sesetsu shingo sakuin.*—Hiroshima: Hiroshima Daigaku Chūgoku Bungaku Kenkyūshitsu, 1959, [ii], 18, 21, 649 p. [An index to *Shih-shuo hsin-yü.*]
高橋清：世說新語索引

1135   Ushijima, Tokuji: *Kango bunpōron (Chūko hen).*—Tokyo: Taishukan, 1971, 8, 472, 31 p./ 420–465: Bibliography; Pt. II, Chap. 2: Word; 14–24: Index to vocabulary. [On Chinese grammar (Middle period)./ Six dynasties.
牛島德次：漢語文法論（中古編）／第二編，第二章：詞；14－24：語彙索引

5.4.   Lexicon of T'ang and Sung Dynasties (1136–1185)

5.4.1.   T'ang Dynasty (1136–1165)

1136   Aoyama, Hiroshi: *Kakanshū sakuin.*— Tokyo: Tōyō Bunka Kenkyūjo fuzoku Tōyō Bunken Senta, 1974, 23, xxxvi, 286 p. [An index to *Hua-chien chi.*]/ Five Dynasties.
青山宏：花間集索引

1137   Chang, Hsiang: *Shih tz'u ch'ü yü-tz'u hui shih.*—Shanghai: Chung-hua, 1953, 788 p.; 1955, 3rd ed., 26, 892 p.; Taipei: Chung-hua, 1962, repr., 4, 782 p.; Taipei: I-wen, 1957, repr., 10, 16, 730 p., with changed title: *Shih tz'u ch'ü yü tz'u-tien;* Peking: Chung-hua, 1979, repr., 26, 892 p./ *CKYW* 1953:11, 30, 35, Chung Ying; *CGGG* 29, 1954, 1–15, Iriya Toshitaka; *CBH* 1, 1954, 137–156, Iriya Yoshitaka; *CHHP* 1:2, 1957, 255–258, Yang Lien-sheng; *CKYW* 1960:4, 193–200, Chang Yung-yen. [Collection and explanations of words and phrases from *shih* poetry, *tz'u* poetry, and *ch'ü* dramas.]/ T'ang, Sung, Yüan, and Ming dynasties.
張相：詩詞曲語辭滙釋　（臺灣版：）詩詞曲語辭典／仲穎評，入矢義高評，楊聯陞評，張永言評

1138   Chiang, Li-hung: *Tun-huang pien-wen tzu-i t'ung-shih.*—Peking: Chung-hua, 1959; 1962, rev. ed., 4, 12, 239, 12 p.; Shanghai: Shang-hai ku-chi, 1981, rev. & enl. ed., 4, 8, 450, 12 p./ *TP* 47, 1959, 274–275, Chen Tsu-lung; *RBS* 6, 1960, 404, Chen Tsu-lung; *CKYW* 1964:3, 238–239, Chang Yung-yen; *CKYW* 1982:3, 233–236, Lü Shu-hsiang. [General explanations of the meanings of characters in the *pien-wen* literature from Tunhuang.]
蔣禮鴻：敦煌變文字義通釋／張永言評，呂叔湘評

1139   Chiang, Shao-yü: *T'ang shih tz'u-yü cha-chi.*—*PCTH* 1980:3, 69–86. [Notes on words and phrases in T'ang poetry.]
蔣紹愚：唐詩詞語札記

1140   Chiang, Shao-yü: Tu shih tz'u-yü

cha-chi.—*YLT* 6, 1980, 94–127. [Notes on words and phrases (found) in the poems of Tu Fu.]
蔣紹愚：杜詩詞語札記

1141 Chou, Kuang-ch'ing: Tun-huang pien-wen shih tz'u.—*CYTH* 1981:2, 15–16. [Explanations of words (found) in the *pien-wen* literature from Tunhuang.]
周光慶：敦煌變文釋詞

1142 Ch'ü, Shou-yüeh: *Pei-shih* tz'u-yü k'ao-shih.—*TLTC* 35:7, 1967, 21–25; 8, 27–34; 9, 30–34; 10, 20–24. [A study with explanations of words and phrases in *Pei-shih*.]
曲守約：『北史』辭語考釋

1143 Hsiang, Ch'u: Tun-huang pien-wen yü-tz'u cha-chi.—*SCTH* 1981:2, 52–60; *TYT* 4, 1982, 70–89. [Notes on words and phrases in the *pien-wen* literature from Tunhuang.]
項楚：敦煌變文語辭札記

1144 Hsü, Fu: Tun-huang pien-wen tz'u-yü yen-chiu.—*CKYW* 1961:8, 29–34. [A study on words and phrases found in the *pien-wen* literature from Tunhuang.]
徐復：敦煌變文詞語研究

1145 Hu, Chu-an: Tun-huang pien-wen chung te shuang-yin lien-tz'u.—*CKYW* 1961:10–11, 41–46. [Disyllabic conjunctions in the *pien-wen* literature from Tunhuang.]
胡竹安：敦煌變文中的雙音連詞

1146 Iriya, Yoshitaka: *Tonkō henbunshū kogo goi sakuin.*—Kyoto: The Author, 1961, mimeogr., 34 p./ *RBS* 7, 1961, 515, Chen Tsu-lung. [An index to the colloquial vocabulary in *Tun-huang pien-wen chi.*]
入矢義高：敦煌變文集口語語彙索引

1147 Iwamoto, Yutaka: *Nichijō Bukkyōgo.*—Tokyo: Chuō kōronsha, 1972, vi, 244, (vocabulary index:) vii p. [Everyday Buddhist vocabulary.]
巖本裕：日常佛教語

1148 Jen, Ming-shan: *Mu-lan tz'u* te tz'u-yü.—*YWCH* 1956:6, 31–33. [Words and phrases of *Mu-lan tz'u.*]
任銘善：『木蘭辭』的詞語

1149 Kao, Ming-k'ai: T'ang-tai ch'an-chia yü-lu so chien te yü-fa ch'eng-fen.—*YCHP* 34, 1948, 49–83; 316–317: E.S.; *Han-yü yü-fa lun-chi* (0068), 141–176. [Grammatical elements as seen in the transcripts of Ch'an (Zen) masters of T'ang times.]
高名凱：唐代禪家語錄所見的語法成分

1150 Kuo, Tsai-i: *Yu-hsien k'u* shih tz'u.—*HCTH* 1981:4, 36–41. [Explanations of words in *Yu-hsien k'u.*]
郭在貽：『遊仙窟』釋詞

1151 Lin, Chao-te: Shih tz'u ch'ü tz'u-yü tsa shih.—*HNSY* 1982:1, 37– (not seen). [Miscellaneous explanations of words and phrases in *shih* poetry, *tz'u* poetry, and *ch'ü* dramas.]
林昭德：詩詞曲詞語雜釋

1152 Liu, Chien: Chiao-k'an tsai su-yü tz'u yen-chiu chung te yün-yung.—*CKYW* 1981:6, 446–451. [The application of textual criticism in the study of the vocabulary of popular sayings.]/ from *pien-wen* literature.
劉堅：校勘在俗語詞研究中的運用

1153 Lu, Jun-hsiang: Kuan-yü *T'ang-Sung tz'u ch'ang-yung yü shih-li.*—*TSYC* 1981:1, 86, 79. [Concerning *T'ang-Sung tz'u ch'ang-yung yü shih-li* (1165).]
盧潤祥：關於『唐宋詞常用語釋例』

1154 Nakagawa, Jūan: *Zengo jii.*—Tokyo: Morie shoten, 1935; 1956, 2nd rev. ed., 6, 711, 134 p./ *Bibliography . . . Japanese studies* (0011), B100. [A glossary of Ch'an (Zen) terms.]
中川渉庵：禪語字彙

1155 Ogiwara, Unrai: *Bon-Kan taiyaku Bukkyō jiten: honyaku meigi taishū.*—Tokyo:

Heigo shuppansha, 1915; 1925; 1937; Tokyo: Sankibō, 1959, 11, 163, 4 p.; Taipei: Hsin wen-feng, 1976, repr., v.p. [A Sanskrit-Chinese dictionary of Buddhist technical terms: A compendium of translation of the meanings of terms.]

荻原雲來：梵漢對譯佛教辭典：翻譯名義大集

1156   Osada, Natsuki: Chū-Tō shijin no hakuwashi ni awareta goi.—*CGGG* 1956:7, 3–8. [Vocabulary appearing in colloquial poems of Middle T'ang poets.]

長田夏樹：中唐詩人の白話詩に現われた語彙

1157   Ōta, Tatsuo: *Sodōshū kogo goi sakuin.* —Kyoto: Hōyū shoten, 1962, 61 p./ *Chin san-shih nien . . . chien chieh* (0010), 235–236. [An index to the colloquial vocabulary of *Tsu-t'ang chi.*]

太田辰夫：祖堂集口語語彙索引

1158   Shinohara, Hisao: *Zengo kaisetsu jiten sakuin.*—Tokyo: Komazawa Daigaku Zenshū Jiten Hensanjo, 1959, 164, 60 p. [An index to *Zengo kaisetsu jiten* (A dictionary of explanations of Ch'an (Zen) terms).]

篠原壽雄：禪語解說辭典索引

1159   Shiomi, Kunihiko: Tōshi zokugo shinkō.—*RMBG* 430–432, 1981, 281–314; *HSDK* 17, 1982, 1–27; 18, 1983, 1–19; 19, 1984, 35–78; to be continued. [A new study on colloquial words in T'ang poetry.]

鹽見邦彥：唐詩俗語新考

1160   Shiomi, Kunihiko: Haku Kyoi shi ni okeru zokugo hyōgen.—*HSDK* 16, 1982, 31–50. [Colloquial expressions in Po Chü-i's poetry.]

鹽見邦彥：白居易詩 における俗語表現

1161   Stimson, Hugh M.: *T'ang poetic vocabulary.*—New Haven: Far Eastern Publications, Yale U., 1976, xii, 142 p.

1162   Tu, Chung-ling: T'ang shih tz'u-hui te shih-tai t'e-cheng.—*YWYT* 1982:1, 6–10. [The epochal special features of the vocabulary of T'ang poetry.]

杜仲陵：唐詩詞滙的時代特徵

1163   Wang, Ying: Shih tz'u ch'ü yü-tz'u chü li.—*CKYW* 1978:3, 193–195. [Examples of words and phrases (found) in *shih* poetry, *tz'u* poetry, and *ch'ü* dramas.]

王鍈：詩詞曲語辭舉例

1164   Wang, Ying: *Shih tz'u ch'ü yü-tz'u li shih.*—Peking: Chung-hua, 1980, 12, 185 p. [Explanations with examples of words and phrases (found) in *shih* poetry, *tz'u* poetry, and *ch'ü* dramas.]

王鍈：詩詞曲語辭例釋

1165   Wen, Kuang-i: *T'ang-Sung tz'u ch'ang-yung yü shih-li.*—Huhehot: Nei Meng-ku jen-min, 1978; 1979, 221 p./ *TSYC* 1981:1, 66, 79, Lu Jun-hsiang. [Examples with explanations of commonly used words in the *tz'u* poetry of the T'ang and Sung dynasties.]

溫廣義：唐宋詞常用語釋例／盧潤祥評

5.4.2. Sung Dynasty (1166–1185)

1166   Chang, Hsü-hou: *T'ang yü lin* chung te k'ou-yü ch'eng-fen.—*AHSY* 1959:1, 38–59. [Colloquial language elements (found) in *T'ang yü lin.*]

張煦侯：『唐語林』中的口語成分

1167   Chang, Yung-mien: Kuan-yü Sung Yüan hua-pen su-yü fang-yen te cheng-li.— *CKYW* 1957:12, 50. [Concerning the putting in order of popular idioms and dialect words (found) in the *hua-pen* of the Sung an Yüan dynasties.]

張永綿：關於宋元話本俗語方言的整理

1168   Hagio, Chōichirō: Chūgoku kyū hakuwa shōsetsu goi.—*Wahon ni tsuite* kaidai. —*FDKH* 13, 1970, 73–199; 14, 1971, 73–124; 16, 1972, 167–285; 18, 1973, 69–223; 22, 1974, 1–129; 26, 1976, 53–218; 28, 1977, 57–226; to be continued. [Vocabulary from Chinese old colloquial novels (4)—A continuation with a changed title from *Wahon ni tsuite* ('On *hua-pen* literature').]

荻尾長一郎：中國舊白話小説語彙——『話本について』改題

1169   Hatano, Tarō (ed.): *Chu lu su-yu chieh.* —Yokohama: Yokohama Shiritsu Daigaku, 1961, 28, 422, 65 p./ *Chin san-shih nien . . . chien chieh* (0010), 57–58. [Explanations of colloquial words and phrases (found) in various (Zen Buddhist) *Yü-lu* ('records of sayings').]

波多野太郎編：緒録俗語解

1170   Hayakawa, Michisuke: *Shushi gorui ni mirareru chōfuku keishiki.*—*AGDR* 16:3, 1968, 499–539. [Reduplicative patterns as seen in *Chu-tzu yü-lei.*]

早川通介：『朱子語類』に見られる重複形式

1171   Hayakawa, Michisuke: *Zenshū goroku ni awarareta chōfuku keishiki.*—*AGDR* 16:4, 1969, 770–809. [The reduplicative patterns as appearing in *yü-lu* ('records of sayings') of Zen masters.]/ Sung dynasty materials.

早川通介：禪宗語録にあらわれた重複形式

1172   Hayakawa, Michisuke: *Rinzairoku no goi gohō kenkyū* (1).—*AGDR* 17:3, 1969, 411–433. [A study on the vocabulary and grammar of *Lin-chi lu* (1).]

早川通介：『臨濟録』の 語彙，語法研究(1)

1173   Kallgren, Gerty: Study in Sung time colloquial as revealed in Chu Hi's *Ts'üan-shu.*—*BMFEA* 30, 1958, 1–67./ *RBS* 4, 1958, 577, W. Simon.

〔『朱熹全書』〕

1174   Kuo, Tsai-i: *T'ai-p'ing kuang-chi li te su yü-tz'u k'ao shih.*—*CKYW* 1980:1, 46–49. [A study with explanations of popular vocabulary (found) in *T'ai-p'ing kuang-chi.*]

郭在貽：『太平廣記』裏的俗語詞考釋

1175   Lu, Tan-an: *Hsiao-shuo tz'u-yü hui shih.*—Peking: Chung-hua, 1964, 172, 916 p./ *RBS* 10, 1964, 552, M. Doleželová-Velingerová; *Orbis* 15, 1966, 98–99, Paul Yang. [A collection with explanations of words and phrases from (Chinese) novels.]/ Based on 64 novels of Sung, Yüan, Ming and Ch'ing dynasties.

陸澹安：小説詞語滙釋

1176   Lung, Ch'ien-an: Sung Yüan yü-tz'u cha-chi.—*CKYW* 1979:5, 383–384. [Notes on words and phrases of the Sung and Yüan dynasties.]

龍潛庵：宋元語詞札記

1177   Lung, Ch'ien-an: *Sung Yüan yü-tz'u chi shih* t'i chi.—*TSYC* 1981:2, 194–203. [Topical notes on *Sung Yüan yü-tz'u chi shih*.]/ A preface to his forthcoming book.

龍潛庵：『宋元語詞集釋』題記

1178   Pai, Wei-kuo: *Hsiao-shuo tz'u-yü hui shih* wu shih chu-li.—*CKYW* 1981:6, 452–457. [Examples of incorrect explanations (found) in *Hsiao-shuo tz'u-yü hui shih* (1175).]

白維國：『小説詞語滙釋』誤釋舉例

1179   Sakai, Ken'ichi: *Kōin naka no dōon dōgi dōjigo ni tsuite.*—*KGK* 1, 1963, 17–37. [The homophonous, homosemic, and homographic words in *Kuang-yün.*]

坂井健一：『廣韻』中の同音同義同字語について

1180   Sakai, Ken'ichi: *Kōin kenkyū—Dōji igo ni tsuite.*—*NHDJ* 22, 1979, 63–72. [A study on *Kuang-yün*—On the identical characters with different meanings.]

坂井健一：『廣韻』研究——同字異語について

1181   Satō, Masashi: *Shushi gorui ji daiikkan shi daijūsankan go ku sakuin.*—Nagoya: Saika shorin, 1975, [ii], 10, 278 p. [An index to the words and phrases from *chüan* 1 to *chüan* 13 of *Chu-tzu yü-lei.*]

佐藤仁：朱子語類自第一卷至第十三卷語句索引

1182 Teramura, Masao: *Sō Gen hakuwa goi kaishaku—Shinhen godaishi heiwa* hen. —*WJGKK* 15, 1980, 89–101. [A collection with explanations of the colloquial vocabulary of the Sung and Yüan—*Hsin-pien wu-tai-shih p'ing-hua.*]
寺村政男：宋元白話語彙滙釋——『新編五代史評話』編

1183 Tōkyō Daigaku Shushigaku Kenkyūkai: *Shushi bunshū koyū meishi sakuin.*—Tokyo: Tōhō shoten, 1980, 999 p. [An index to the proper nouns in *Chu-tzu wen-chi.*]
東京大學朱子學研究會：朱子文集固有名詞索引

1184 Torii, Hisayasu: *Shōsetsu shigo kaishaku hatsuon sakuin.*—Osaka: Min Shin Bungaku Gengo Kenkyūkai, 1964, mimeogr., 54 p./ *Chin san-shih nien . . . chien chieh* (0010), 236. [A pronunciation index to *Hsiao-shuo tz'u-yü hui-shih* (1175).]
鳥居久靖：小說詞語滙釋發音索引

1185 Ueno, Keiji: *Shushi gorui* ni arawareru setsubiji shi o tomonau meishi ni tsuite. —*CGGG* 1967:1, 8–16. [On nouns combined with the suffix -*tzu* appearing in *Chu-tzu yü-lei.*]
上野惠司：『朱子語類』に現われる接尾辭『子』を伴う名詞について

5.5. Lexicon of Yüan, Ming, and Ch'ing Dynasties (1186–1279)
5.5.1. Yüan Dynasty (1186–1217)

1186 Chang, Hsin-i: T'an *Hsi hsiang chi* te tz'u-yü chieh-shih.—*CKYW* 1959:4, 185–187. [A discussion on explanations of words and phrases in *Hsi-hsiang chi.*]
張心逸：談『西廂記』的詞語解釋

1187 Chu, Chü-i: *Yüan-chü su-yü fang-yen li-shih.*—Shanghai: Shang-wu, 1956, 368 p.; Taipei: Shang-wu, 1967, repr., 368 p./ *RBS* 2, 1956, 380, M.A.K. Halliday;

Orbis 15, 1966, 98, Paul Yang. [Explanations with examples of colloquial and dialect words from Yüan dramas.]
朱居易：元劇俗語方言例譯

1188 Furuya, Tsugio: *Buō batsuchū heiwa. Shichikoku shunshū heiwa goi sakuin.* —Nagoya: Saika shorin, 1967, mimeogr., 39 p. [An index to the vocabulary of *Wu-wang fa-chou p'ing-hua* and *Ch'i-kuo ch'un-ch'iu p'ing-hua.*]
古屋二夫：武王伐紂平話、七國春秋平話語彙索引

1189 Haenisch, E.: Sinologische Früchte auf dem Felde des *Yüan-ch'ao pi-shih.*—*AM* 11:2, 1965, 153–159./ Stresses the importance of this text as a first-rate source for the lexicography and lexicology of Old Mandarin; *RBS* 11, 1965, 447, H. Franke.

1190 Halliday, M.A.K.: *The language of the Chinese Secret History of the Mongols.* —Oxford: B. Blackwell, 1959, xvi, 235 p./ Publications of the Philological Society, 17; *RBS* 5, 1959, 500, A. Rygaloff./ Includes vocabulary.
〔元朝秘史〕

1191 Hsü, Chia-jui: *Chin Yüan hsi-ch'ü fang-yen k'ao.*—Peking: Shang-wu, 1956, xvii, 53, 34 p./ *RBS* 2, 1956, 379, M.A.K. Halliday; *CKYW* 1960:5, 244–247, P'an Keng. [A study of the dialect words of the southern dramas during the Chin and Yüan dynasties.]
徐嘉瑞：金元戲曲方言考／潘庚評

1192 Huang, Li-chen: *Chin Yüan pei-ch'ü yü-hui chih yen-chiu.*—Taipei: Shang-wu, 1968, 2, 1, 1, 2, 200, 17 p. [A study of the vocabulary of the northern dramas during the Chin and Yüan dynasties.]
黃麗貞：金元北曲語彙之研究

1193 Huang, Tsu-liang: Yüan ch'ü yü-tz'u cha-chi.—*LNTH* 1982:1, 69. [Notes on words and phrases in Yüan dramas.]

黃祖貤：元曲語詞札記

1194   Iida, Kichirō: *Genkyoku jōyō goi.*
—Tokyo: Tōkyō Bunrika Daigaku
Chūgoku Bungaku Kenkyūshitsu, 1950,
mimeogr., 87 p. [Commonly used
vocabulary in Yüan dramas.]
飯田吉郎：元曲常用語彙

1195   Iida, Kichirō: *Tō-Seishō goi indoku.*—
[Tokyo]: The Author, 1951, 120 p./
Chin san-shih nien . . . chien chieh (0010),
231–232. [An index to the vocabulary
of *Tung Hsi-hsiang.*]
飯田吉郎：董西廂語彙引得

1196   Keiya, Toshinobu, et al.: *Bokutsūji
genkai sakuin.*—Nagoya: Saika shorin,
1976, mimeogr., [iv], 44, 222 p. [An
index to *Po t'ung-shih yen-chieh.*]
慶谷壽信等：朴通事諺解索引

1197   Kyōto Daigaku Jinbun Kagaku
Kenkyūjo Gen tenshō Kenkyūhan: *Gen
tenshō sakuin kō.*—Kyoto: Ditto, 1954–
1961, 4 vols., [iii], 210; [i], 71; 122;
[i], 225 p. [A draft for an index to (the
vocabulary of) *Yüan tien-chang.*]
京都大學人文科學研究所『元典章』研究班：
元典章索引稿

1198   Liao, Hsün-ying & Lan, Li-ming: *Liu
Chih-yüan Chu-kung tiao* tz'u-yü hsüan
shih.—*CKYW* 1980:1, 50–52. [Selection
and explanations of vocabulary from *Liu
Chih-yüan's Chu-kung tiao* (compiled
between Sung and Chin dynasties).]
廖珣英、藍立蕢：『劉知遠諸宮調』詞語選釋

1199   Lu, Tan-an: *Hsi-ch'ü tz'u-yü hui shih.*
—Shanghai: Shang-hai ku-chi, 1981, 4,
126, 33, 683 p./ 671–683: Set - phrases
and proverbs. [Collection and explanations
of words and phrases found in (Chinese)
dramas.]
陸澹安：戲曲詞語滙釋

1200   Ma, Szu-chou & P'an, Shen: Shih lun
Yüan tsa-chü chung szu-yin tz'u te kou-

ch'eng yüan-tse.—*YWYC* 1982:2, 69–81.
[A preliminary discussion on the structural
principles of quadrisyllabic phrases in
the dramas of the Yüan dynasty.]
馬思周、潘愼：試論元雜劇中四音詞的構成原
則

1201   Miller, Robert P.: *The particles in the
dialogue of Yüan drama—A descriptive
analysis.*—New Haven: Yale U., 1952,
ii, 88 p./ Unpubl. doc. diss.

1202   Onogawa, Hideyoshi: *Kinshi goi shūsei.*
—Kyoto: Kyōto Daigaku Jinbun Kagaku
Kenkyūjo, 1960–1962, 3 vols., 2, 2, [2],
1627, [3] p./ *Chin san-shih nien . . . chien
chieh* (0010), 235. [A compendium of
the vocabulary of *Chin-shih.*]
小野川秀美：金史語彙集成

1203,   Ōsaka Shiritsu Daigaku Bungakubu
Chūgoku Gogaku Chūgoku Bungaku
Kenkyūshitsu: *Chūgoku koden gikyoku
goshaku sakuin.*—Nagoya: Saika shorin,
1970, 4, 581, [2] p. [An index
to the explanations of words and
phrases (found) in Chinese classical
dramas.]
大阪市立大學文學部中國語學中國文學研究室
：中國古典戲曲語釋索引

1204   Ōta, Tatsuo: *Ching-pen t'ung su hsiao-
shuo, Ch'ing-p'ing shan-t'ang hua-pen goi
sakuin.*—Osaka: Min-Shin Bungaku Gengo
Kenkyūkai, 1964, 67 p./ *Chin san-shih
nien . . . chien-chieh* (0010), 236. [An
index to the vocabulary of *Ching-pen
t'ung-su hsiao-shuo,* and *Ch'ing-p'ing
shan-t'ang hua-pen.*]
太田辰夫：京本通俗小說、清平山堂話本語彙
索引

1205   Pien, Hsing-ts'an: Yüan Ming hsi ch'ü
yü-tz'u shih i shih-san tse.—*HCTH*
1981:4, 48–55. [Explanations of the
meanings of thirteen examples of words
and phrases in the dramas of the Yüan
and Ming dynasties.]
邊星燦：元明戲曲語詞釋義十三則

1206 Sawaguchi, Takeo: Chūse tsūzoku bungei no goi.—*Chūgoku gogaku jiten* (0037), 919–930. [Vocabulary from the popular literary works of the middle ages.]
澤口剛雄：中世通俗文藝の語彙

1207 Suyama, Nobuo: *Seishōki Ō Kishi chūshaku sakuin.*—Nagoya: Saika shorin, 1971, 24 p. [An index to Wang Chi-szu's commentary and notes on *Hsi-hsiang chi.*]
陶山信男：西廂記王季思注釋索引

1208 Suyama, Nobuo: *Bokutsūji genkai, Rōkitsudai genkai goi sakuin.*—Nagoya: Saika shorin, 1973, [iii], 210, 140, 33, 27 p. [An index to the vocabulary of *Po t'ung-shih yen-chieh* and *Lao-ch'i-ta yen-chieh.*]
陶山信男：朴通事諺解・老乞大諺解語彙索引

1209 Tamura, Jistuzō: *Genshi goi shūsei.*—Kyoto: Kyōto Daigaku Bungakubu Tōyōshi Kenkyūshitsu, 1961–1963, 3 vols., [iv], 3, 2825 p./ *Chin san-shih nien . . . chien chieh* (0010), 236. [A compendium of the vocabulary of *Yüan shih.*]
田村實造：元史語彙集成

1210 Teramura, Masao: Sō Gen hakuwa goi kaishaku—*Tō Seishō* hen.—*WJGKK* 14, 1979, 67–82. [Explanations of the colloquial vocabulary of the Sung and Yüan—*Tung Hsi-hsiang.*]
寺村政男：宋元白話語彙滙釋——『董西廂』編

1211 Tōkyō Bunrika Daigaku Chūbun Kokubungaku Kenkyūshitsu: *Genkyoku jōyō goi.*—Tokyo: Ditto, 1950, [ii], 87 p. [Commonly used vocabulary of Yuan dramas.]
東京文理科大學中文國文學研究室：元曲常用語彙

1212 Tsou, Chia-yen: *Lao-ch'i-ta yen-chieh tan tzu so-yin.*—Tokyo: Ajia-Afurika Gengo Bunka Kenkyūjo, 1976, 245 p. [A single character index to *Lao-ch'i-ta yen-chieh.*]
鄒嘉彥：老乞大諺解單字索引

1213 Tu, Chung-ling: Lüeh t'an T'ang Sung i-hou i-hsieh tz'u te hsin i.—*CKYW* 1980:5, 368–370. [A short discussion on the new meanings of certain words after the T'ang and Sung dynasties.]
杜仲陵：略談唐宋以後一些詞的新義

1214 Wang, Chi-szu: Yüan chü chung hsieh-yin shuang-kuan yü.—*KWYK* 67, 1948, 15–19. [Rhyming words with double meanings in Yüan dramas.]
王季思：元劇中諧音雙關語

1215 Wen, Kung-i: Yüan-jen tsa-chü yü-tz'u shih i.—*CKYW* 1980:3, 186–187. [Semantic explanations of words and phrases (found) in the dramas (composed) by the people of the Yüan (dynasty).]
溫公翊：元人雜劇語詞釋義

1216 Yang, Lien-sheng: *Lao-ch'i ta Po t'ung-shih* li te yü-fa yü-hui.—*BIHP* 29, 1957, 197–208. [The grammar and vocabulary of *Lao-ch'i ta* and *Po t'ung-shih.*]
楊聯陞：『老乞大』『朴通事』裏的語法語彙

1217 Yu, Sheng-t'ing: Yuan chu yü-tz'u cha chi.—*Hsü-chou shih-fan hsüeh-yüan hsüeh-pao* 1981:2, 74. [Notes on words and phrases in Yüan dramas.]
于盛庭：元劇語詞剳記

5.5.2. Ming Dynasty (1218–1249)

1218 Chang, Yüan-fen: *Ching-p'ing mei tz'u-hua* tz'u-yü hsüan shih.—*CYTH* 1981:2, 17–19. [Selection and explanations of words and phrases from *Ch'ing-p'ing mei tz'u-hua.*]
張遠芬：『金瓶梅詞話』詞語選釋

1219 Hatano, Tarō: *Chūgoku shōsetsu gikyoku shii kenkyū jiten, Sōgō sakuin hen.*—Yokohama: Yokohama Shiritsu Daigaku, 1956–1963, 7 vols.; I. *Hatsuon sakuin* [phonetic index], 1956, 8, 80 p.; *Hitsuga sakuin* [stroke index], 1956, 8, 91 p.; II. *Hatsuon sakuin,* 1957, 3, 107 p.; *Hitsuga sakuin,* 1958, 3, 151 p.; III.

Hatsuon hitsuga sakuin, 1958, 3, 121 p.; IV. *Hatsuon hitsuga sakuin,* 1959, 7, 129 p.; V. *Hatsuon hitsuga sakuin,* 1960, 3, 160 p.; VI. *Hatsuon sakuin,* 1961, 15, 145 p.; VII. *Hatsuon sakuin,* 1963, 11, 100 p./ *Yokohama Shiritsu Daigaku Kiyō,* Series A. 9, 10, 14, 16, 20, 23, 25, 27./ *RBS* 2, 1956, 378, G. Weys; 6, 1960, 406, A. Lévy; *Chin san-shih nien . . . chien chieh* (0010), 232–234. [A dictionary for the study of the vocabulary of Chinese novels and dramas. Combined index, phonetic index, stroke index.]/ Seven lexicographical works composed during the Tokugawa period in Japan.

波多野太郎：中國小說戲曲詞彙研究辭典，綜合索引篇，發音索引，筆劃索引──『橫濱市大學紀要』

1220 Ho, Chung-ying: *Shui-hu chuan* shih tz'u.—*CYTC* 13:6, 1921, 23 s.p.; 8, 8 s.p.; 10, 10 s.p. [Explanations of words in *Shui-hu chuan.*]

何仲英：『水滸傳』釋詞

1221 Kōsaka, Jun'ichi: Kyū hakuwa goi seirijō no mondai-ten.—*CGGG* 1965:3, 1–9. [The central problem in arranging the vocabulary of the old colloquial language.]

香坂順一：舊白話語彙整理上の問題點

1222 Kōsaka, Jun'ichi: Kinse Kindai Kango no gohō to goi.—*Gengo* (0085), 296–356. [The grammar and vocabulary of Middle and Modern Chinese.]

香坂順一：近世近代漢語の語法と語彙

1223 Kōsaka, Jun'ichi: Kinsego nōto.—*MSBGK* 7, 1966, 43–68; 8, 1967, 43–62; 9, 1967, 47–89; 10, 1968, 1–120; 11, 1968, 1–61; 12, 1970, 1–120; (Index) 23 p. [Notes on words of Middle Chinese.]

香坂順一：近世語ノート

1224 Kōsaka, Jun'ichi: *Suiko zenden goi sakuin.*—Nagoya: Saika shorin, 1973, 527 p./ *Chin san-shih nien . . . chien chieh*

(0010), 243–244. [An index to the vocabulary of *Shui-hu ch'üan-chuan.*]

香坂順一：水滸全傳語彙索引

1225 Koten Kenkyūkai (comp.) & Nagasawa, Kikuya (comment.): *Tōwa jisho ruishu.*—Tokyo: Kyūko shoin, 1969–1976, 20 vols./ *Chin san-shih nien . . . chien chieh* (0010), 41–42. [A classified collection of Chinese lexicographical works.]/ Published in Japan during the Edogawa period.

古典研究會編輯，長澤規矩也解題：唐話辭書類聚

1226 Li, Fa-pai & Liu, Ching-fu: *Shui-hu chüan* ch'üeh te tz'u-i ch'u t'an.—*CKYW* 1981:1, 66–70. [A preliminary investigation into the lexical meaning of the word *ch'üeh* in *Shui-hu chuan.*]

李法白、劉鏡芙：『水滸傳』『卻』的詞義初探

1227 Min-Shin Bungaku Gengo Kenkyūkai: *Kinpeibai shiwa goi sakuin.*—Nagoya: Saika shorin, 1972, 497 p. [An index to the vocabulary of *Chin-p'ing mei tz'u-hua.*]

明清文學言語研究會：金瓶梅詞話語彙索引

1228 Nagasawa, Kikuya (ed.): *Min-Shin zokugo jisho shūsei.*—Tokyo: Kyūko shoin, 1974, 3 vols., 604; 540; 549 p. [A compendium of colloquial language lexicographical works of the Ming and Ch'ing dynasties.]

長澤規矩也編：明清俗語辭書集成

1229 Ōsaka Shiritsu Daigaku Chūgokugaku Kenkyūshitsu: *Chūgoku hakuwa shōsetsu goshaku sakuin.*—Osaka: Ditto, 1958, [8], 171 p.; 1962, rev. ed., 317 p./ *RBS* 8, 1962, 507, S.N. Cartier; *Chin san-shih nien . . . chien chieh* (0010), 235. [An index to the vocabulary of Chinese colloquial novels.]

大阪市立大學中國學研究室：中國白話小說語釋索引

1230 Ōta, Tatsuo: *Keihon tsūzoku shōsetsu,*

Seiheisandō wahon goi sakuin.—Osaka: Min-Shin Bungaku Gengo Kenkyūkai, 1964, [7], 67 p./ *MSBGK* Monogr. 5; *RBS* 10, 1964, 513, A. Lévy. [An index to the vocabulary of *Ching-pen t'ung-su hsiao-shuo* and *Ch'ing-p'ing shan-t'ang hua-pen.*]

太田辰夫：京本通俗小説、清平山堂話本語彙索引

1231 Ōuchida, Saburō: *Suikoden* no gengo—dōgigo ni okeru ichi kōsatsu (0612). [The language of *Shui-hu chuan*—A study on the synonyms.]

大内田三郎：『水滸傳』の 言語——同義語における一考察

1232 Ōuchida, Saburō: *Suikoden* no gengo—tan'onsetsugo to taonsetsugo no dōgigo ni tsuite (0613). [The language of *Shui-hu chuan*—On the monosyllabic and poly-syllabic synonynous words.]

大内田三郎：『水滸傳』の 言語——單音節語と多音節語の同義語について

1233 Saeki, Tomi: *Fukkei zenshū goi kai.*—Kyoto: Kyōto Daigaku Tōyōshi Kenkyū-shitsu, 1952, mimeogr., 33 p.; 1958, 2nd ed., 45 p.; Kyoto: Dōhōsha, 1975, 3rd ed., 62 p. [Explanations of vocabulary in *Fu-hui ch'üan-chi.*]

佐伯富：福惠全集語彙解

1234 Shūsuien shujin: (*Gain*) *Shōsetsu jii.*—Osaka: Ōsaka shorin, 1791, v.p./ *Chin san-shih nien . . . chien chieh* (0010), 62. [(Stroke index) a vocabulary of (Chinese) novels.]

秋水園主人：（畫引）小説字滙

1235 Takashima, Toshio: *Suikoden* goi jiten kō—A oyobi B.—*CGGG* 224, 1977, 78–91. [A draft for a dictionary of the vocabulary in *Shui-hu chuan*—Section A and B.]

高島俊男：『水滸傳』語彙辭典稿—A及びB

1236 Takashima, Toshio: *Suikoden* goi jiten kō—C no bu.—*OKHB* 38, 1978, 1–23.

[A draft for a dictionary of the vocabulary in *Shui-hu chuan* —Section C.]

高島俊男：『水滸傳』語彙辭典稿——Cの部

1237 Takashima, Toshio: *Suikoden* goi jiten kō—D no bu jō.—*CGGG* 225, 1978, 63–77. [A draft for a dictionary of the vocabulary in *Shui-hu chuan*—Section D–A.]

高島俊男：『水滸傳』語彙辭典稿—Dの部上

1238 Takashima, Toshio: *Suikoden* goi jiten kō—F no bu.—*OKHB* 39, 1978, 65–81. [A draft for a dictionary of the vocabulary in *Shui-hu chuan*—Section F.]

高島俊男：『水滸傳』語彙辭典稿—Fの部

1239 Takashima, Toshio: *Suikoden* goi jiten kō—G no bu.—*CGGG* 226, 1979, 99–112. [A draft for a dictionary of the vocabulary in *Shui-hu chuan*—Section G.]

高島俊男：『水滸傳』語彙辭典稿—Gの部

1240 Takashima, Toshio: *Suikoden* goi jiten kō—H no bu.—*OKHB* 40, 1979, 83–99. [A draft for a dictionary of the vocabulary in *Shui-hu chuan*—Section H.]

高島俊男：『水滸傳』語彙辭典稿—Hの部

1241 Takashima, Toshio: *Suikoden* goi jiten kō—J no bu jō.—*CGGG* 227, 1980, 50–61. [A draft for a dictionary of the vocabulary in *Shui-hu chuan*—Section J–A.]

高島俊男：『水滸傳』語彙辭典稿—Jの部上

1242 Takashima, Toshio: *Suikoden* goi jiten kō—K no bu.—*OKBK* 2, 1981, 71–84. [A draft for a dictionary of the vocabulary in *Shui-hu chuan*—Section K.]

高島俊男：『水滸傳』語彙辭典稿—Kの部

1243 Takashima, Toshio: *Suikoden* goi jiten kō—M no bu.—*OKBK* 3, 1982, 225–243. [A draft for a dictionary of the vocabulary in *Shui-hu chuan*—Section M.]

高島俊男：『水滸傳』語彙辭典稿—Mの部

1244 Tōkyō Bunrika Daigaku Kanbungaku

Daini Kenkyūshitsu: *Kankonki goi indoku.* —Tokyo: Ditto, 1951, mimeogr., 50 p. [An index to the vocabulary in *Huan-hun chi.*]

東京文理科大學漢文學第二研究室：還魂記語彙引得

1245 Torii, Hisayasu: Nihon ni okeru Chūgokugogaku isan no seiri ni tsuite—Goi shiryō o chūshin toshite.—*CGGG* 1957:4, 8–11. [On the arrangement of the Chinese linguistic legacy in Japan—with special reference to the lexical materials.]

鳥居久靖：日本における中國語學遺産の整理について——語彙資料を中心として

1246 Torii, Hisayasu: Kinse bungaku goi kenkyū no shiryō: sono ichi.—*MSBGK* 8, 1967, 1–10. [Materials for the study of the vocabulary in modern (Chinese) literature: Part I.]/ Ming dynasty novels.

鳥居久靖：近世文學語彙研究の資料：その一

1247 Wang, Lun: Chieh-shih *Shui-hu* chung nan-tung tz'u-yu te chi-chung fang-fa. —*YWHH* 1955:2, 22–28. [Several methods of explaining the difficult words and phrases found in *Shui-hu chuan.*]

王綸：解釋『水滸』中難懂詞語的幾種方法

1248 Wang, Lun: *Shui-hu* tz'u-yü chieh-shih te hsiu-cheng.—*YWHH* 1955:9, 38. [Corrigenda of the explanations for words and phrases in *Shui-hu chuan.*]

王綸：『水滸』詞語解釋的修正

1249 Wang, Lun: *Shui-hu* nan-chieh tz'u-yü chu-shih.—*YWCS* 1957:3, 41–44; 4, 45–46; 5, 46–48; 6, 42–44; 8, 47–48. [Explanations for difficult words and phrases in *Shui-hu chuan.*]

王綸：『水滸』難解詞語注釋

5.5.3. Ch'ing Dynasty (1250–1279)

1250 Annen, Ichirō: Keigeki no kanyō goku ni tsuite.—*ADKK* 11, 1975, 41–61. [On the commonly used words and phrases in Peking operas.]

安念一郎：京劇の慣用語句について

1251 Ch'ien, Ta-chao, et al.: *Erh-yen teng wu-chung.* Fu *Tsung-ho so-yin.*—Peking: Shang-wu, 1959, 352, 40 p./ Ch'ien Ta-chao (1744–1813). [*Erh-yen* and four other works. With A combined index.]/ Five works on colloquial vocabulary and popular sayings by Ch'ing scholars:
1. Ch'ien, Ta-chao: *Erh-yen.*—6 *chüan.* [Contemporary speech.];
2. P'ing, Pu-ch'ing: *Shih-yen.*—1 *chüan.* [Proverbs explained.];
3. Hu, Shih-yü: *Yü-tou.*—1 *chüan.* [A channel of words.];
4. Cheng, Chih-hung: *Ch'ang-yü hsün yüan.* —2 *chüan.* [Tracing the origins of common words.];
5. Lo, Chen-yü: *Su-shuo.*—1 *chüan.* [Popular sayings.]

錢大昭等：迿言等五種　附綜合索引
　　1. 錢大昭：迿言
　　2. 平步靑：釋諺
　　3. 胡式鈺：語竇
　　4. 鄭志鴻：常語尋源
　　5. 羅振玉：俗說

1252 Ch'ien, Ta-hsin: *Heng yen lu* & Ch'en, Chan: *Heng yen kuang cheng,* bound in one vol.—Peking: Chung-hua, 1958, 704, (index) 19 p./ Ch'ien Ta-hsin (1728–1804); *RBS* 4, 1958, 561, M. Velingerová. [A record of common sayings.] & [Expanded corroboration of common sayings.]/Dealing with the etymology of colloquial words and phrases, etc.

錢大昕：恆言錄
陳　鱣：恆言廣證

1253 Endō, Mitsumasa: *Gyokukan hishō* goi sakuin.—*TYDD* 5, 1969, 91–107. [An index to the vocabulary of *Yü-han mich'ao.*]

遠藤光正：『玉函秘抄』語彙索引

1254 Endō, Mitsumasa: *Gyokukan hishō goi sakuin oyobi kōkan.*—Machida: Mukyūkai Tōyō Bunka Kenkyūjo, 1971, 273 p. [An index to the vocabulary of *Yü-han mi-ch'ao*

with critical comments.]
遠藤光正：玉函秘抄語彙索引並びに校勘

1255   Hatano, Tarō (ed.): *Hakuwa kyoshi kenkyū shiryō sōkan.*—Tokyo: Fuji shuppansha, 1981, 3 vols., 1180 p. [A collection of materials for the study of colloquial cenematic words.]
波多野太郎編：白話虚詞研究資料叢刊

1256   Hatano, Tarō & Kawakami, Ikuko: *Rigo chōjitsu* sakuin.—*TYDD* 17, 1981, 111–138. [An index to *Li-yü cheng-shih* (1275).]
波多野太郎、川上郁子：里語徴實索引

1257   Iriya, Yoshitaka: *T'ung-su p'ien, Chih-yü pu-cheng, Heng-yen lu, Fang-yen tsao, Erh-yen sōgō sakuin.*—Kyoto: Kyōto Daigaku Chūgoku Gobungaku Kenkyūshi-tsu, 1950, 91 p. [A combined index to *T'ung-su p'ien, Chih-yü pu-cheng, Heng-yen lu, Fang-yen tsao,* and *Erh-yen.*]
入矢義高：通俗篇，直語補正，恒言錄，方言藻，邇言綜合索引

1258   Kōsaka, Jun'ichi & Miyata, Ichirō: *Jijo eiyūden goi sakuin.*—Nagoya: Saika shorin, 1970, [iii], 580 p. [An index to the vocabulary of *Erh-nü ying-hsiung chuan.*]
香坂順一、宮田一郎：兒女英雄傳語彙索引

1259   Kōsaka, Jun'ichi: *Jurin gaishi goi sakuin.*—Osaka: Min-Shin Bungaku Gengo Kenkyūkai, 1971, 3, 231 p. [An index to the vocabulary of *Ju-lin wai-shih.*]
香坂順一：儒林外史語彙索引

1260   Mi, Sung-i: *Erh-nü ying-hsiung chuan* yü-hui shih.—*CKYW* 1981:5, 351–357, 346. [Explanations of the vocabulary in *Erh-nü ying-hsiung chuan.*]
彌松頤：『兒女英雄傳』語滙釋

1261   Miyata, Ichirō: *Nijū nen mokuto shi kaigenjō* goi chōsa.—*MSBGK* 7, 1965, 21–42./ *RBS* 11, 1965, 438, A. Lucas. [A survey of the vocabulary of *Erh-shih*

nien mu tu chih kuai hsien-chuang.]
宮田一郎：『二十年目睹之怪現狀』語彙調査

1262   Miyata, Ichirō: *Kanjō genkeiki* no hanpon. *Kanjō genkeiki* goi chūshaku sakuin.—*MSBGK* 8, 1965, 28–195./ *RBS* 11, 1965, 439, M. Cartier; *Chin san-shih nien . . . chien chieh* (0010), 236–237. [The editions of *Kuan-ch'ang hsien-shing chi.* An index to the explanations of the vocabulary of *Kuan-ch'ang hsien-hsing chi.*]
宮田一郎：『官場現形記』の版本，『官場現形記』語彙注釋索引

1263   Miyata, Ichirō: *Kōrōmu goi sakuin.*—Nagoya: Saika shorin, 1974, 5, 533 p./ *Chin san-shih nien . . . chien chieh* (0010), 244. [An index to the vocabulary of *Hung-lou meng.*]
宮田一郎：紅樓夢語彙索引

1264   Muramatsu, Kazuya: *Kyōgeki ongaku goi kai.*—*JBGH* 140, 1980, 101–116. [Explanations of the musical vocabulary of Peking opera.]
村松一彌：京劇音樂語彙解

1265   Nasu, Kiyoshi: (Kaitei) *Kanwa shinan* no goi.—*BGRS* 17, 1970, 1–11. [Vocabulary of the (Revised) *Kuan-hua chih-nan* (See 1278–1279).]
那須清：（改訂）「官話指南」の語彙

1266   Nasu, Kiyoshi: *Kyūshūhen* no goi.—*BGRS* 19, 1972, 1–29. [The vocabulary of *Chi-chiu p'ien* (comp. by Miyajima Ōya).]
那須清：『急就篇』の語彙（宮島大八編）

1267   Nasu, Kiyoshi: *Kanwa tanron shinhen* no goi.—*Bungaku Ronshū.*—20, 1973, (left) 1–15. [The vocabulary of *Kuan-hua t'an-lun hsin pien.*]
那須清：『官話談論新編』の語彙

1268   Ogata, Kazuo: Yao Mei-po hsüan *Hung-lou meng* tz'u-yü hui shih.—*OGDG* 17, 1967, 99–111. [Collection with explanations of words and phrases in the selected edition of *Hung-lou meng* by Yao Mei-po.]

緒方一男：姚梅伯選『紅樓夢』詞語滙釋

1269 Onogawa, Hideyoshi: *Minpō sakuin.*—Kyoto: Kyōto Daigaku Jinbun Kagaku Kenkyūjo, 1970–1972, 2 vols., 710, 39, 49 p./ *Chin san-shih nien . . . chien chieh* (0010), 242–243. [An index to *Min Pao*.]/ Published in Japan, 1905–1908.

小野川秀美：民報索引

1270 Ōta, Tatsuo: *Shakai shōsetsu Shōgaku goshaku oyobi sakuin.*—Kobe: The Author, 1969, 60, 65 p. [Explanations of words and an index to the social novel *Hsiao-o.*]

太田辰夫：社會小說小額語釋及索引

1271 Ōta, Tatsuo: *Shōgaku* no gohō to goi.—*KGR* 21:3, 1970, 5–18; 23:3, 1972, 47–62. [The grammar and vocabulary of *Hsiao-o.*]

太田辰夫：『小額』の語法と語彙

1272 Ozaki, Minoru: *Yü-yen tzu-erh chi* goi sakuin (shokō).—*MSBGKT* 9, 1965, 1–90./ *Chin san-shih nien . . . chien chieh* (0010), 237–238. [An index to the vocabulary of *Yü-yen tzu-erh chi* (first draft).]

尾崎實：『語言自邇集』語彙索引（初稿）

1273 Satō, Toshiyuki: *Kyūshūhen* hihan no mondai-ten to zehi—Fu goi chōsa.—*KSCGH* 8, 1962, 11–21. [The central problem and the correctness or incorrectness of the criticism of *Chi-chiu p'ien* (See 1266)—With a survey of vocabulary.]

佐藤利行：『急就篇』批判の問題點と是非—附語彙調查

1274 Suzuki, Naoji: *Rōzan yūki* goi chūshaku (sakuin).—*SMBG* 3, 1963, 1–59./ *RBS* 9, 1963, 532, S.N. Cartier. [Explanations of the vocabulary of *Lao-ts'an yu-chi* (An index).]

鈴木直治：『老殘遊記』語彙注釋（索引）

1275 T'ang, Hsün-fang: *Li-yü cheng-shih.*—Ch'ang-ning: T'ang-shih Kuei-wu lu, 1892, 3 *chüan*. [Verification of popular words.]/ See (1256).

唐訓方：里語徵實

1276 Umehara, Takashi: *Tōkyō mukaroku, Muryōroku nado goi sakuin.*—Kyoto: Dōhōsha, 1979, iv, 556 p. [An index to the vocabulary of *Tung-ching meng-hua lu, Meng-liang, lu,* etc.]/ Seven works.

梅原郁：東京夢華錄、夢粱錄等語彙索引

1277 Wei, Fu: *Hung-lou meng* p'u-tung yü-tz'u cha-chi.—*TSYC* 1980:3, 65–75. [Notes on common words and phrases in *Hung-lou meng.*]

韋甫：『紅樓夢』普通語詞札記

1278 Wu, Ch'i-t'ai & Cheng, Yung-pang. Transl. by Hopkins, Lionel Charles: *The guide to Kuan-hua. A translation of the Kuan-hua chih-nan with an essay on tone and accent in Pekinese and a glossary of phrases.*—Shanghai: Kelly & Walsh, 1889, 230 p.; 1900, 3rd & rev. ed., 193 p./ *CR* 18:2, 1890, 129, E.J. Eitel.

〔吳啓太、鄭永邦：官話指南〕

1279 Wu, Ch'i-tai & Cheng, Yung-pang. Transl. by Boucher, Henri: *Koan-hoa tche-nan. Boussole du langage Mandarin.*—Shanghai: Imprimerie de la Mission Catholique, 1893, 2nd ed., 2 vols., I. vi, 247 p.; II. ii, 232 p.; 1906, 4th ed., vi, 482 p./ 444–482: Vocabularie.

〔吳啓太、鄭永邦：官話指南〕

6. LEXICON OF MODERN CHINESE (1280–1853)
6.1. Historical Development (1280–1315)
6.1.1. General Development (1280–1301)

1280 Chang, I-jen: Lun yü-tz'u te yen-pien. —*Chung-kuo kuo-hsüeh* 10, 1982, 149–162. [On the evolutionary changes of words and phrases.]
張以仁：論語詞的演變

1281 Chang, Shih-lu: Han-yü li-shih shang te tz'u-hui pien-hua.—*YWCS* 1957:12, 12–15. [Lexical development in the history of the Chinese language.]
張世祿：漢語歷史上的詞滙變化

1282 Cheng, Tien: Han-yü tz'u-hui shih sui-pi.—*CKYW* 1959:6, 265–266; 7, 329–331; 8, 380–382; 9, 436–437; 11, 546–548; 12, 599–601; 1960:3, 135–136; 1961:3, 38–39, 33; 4, 33–35; 6, 37–38. [Jottings on the history of Chinese lexicons.] / Tracing the origins and development of words in Modern Chinese.
鄭奠：漢語詞滙史隨筆

1283 Chmielewski, Janusz: The typological evolution of the Chinese language.—*RO* 15, 1949, 371–429./ Dealing with words and word formation.

1284 Chou, Fa-kao: Chung-kuo-yü te t'e-chih chi ch'i pien-ch'ien ta-shih.—*TLTC* 9:12, 1954, 11–14; *Chung-kuo yü-wen yen-chiu* (0051), 23–26./ Including lexical development. [Special qualities of the Chinese language and general trends in its evolution.]
周法高：中國語的特質及其變遷大勢

1285 Chou, Fa-kao: Stages in the development of the Chinese language.—*Bulletin of Visiting Scholars Association, China Branch* 1, 1962, 2–5; *Chung-kuo yü-wen lun-ts'ung* (0052), 432–438./ Including lexical development; *Lg* 39, 1963, 567–574, H. Stimson.

1286 Chou, Fa-kao: Chung-kuo-yü te t'e-chih

ho fa-chan ch'ing-hsing.—*Han-hsüeh lun-chi* (Taipei: The Author, 1964), 109–133; *Chung-kuo yü-wen yen-chiu hsüan-chi* (0047), 1–32. [Special qualities of the Chinese language and conditions of its development.]
周法高：中國語的特質和發展情形——『漢學論集』

1287 Chou, Ting-i: Tz'u-hui te hsin-ch'en tai-hsieh.—*KHTP* 3:7, 1952, 446–448; *Hsien-tai Han-yü . . . tzu-liao* (0064), 316–322. [The metabolism of lexicons.]
周定一：詞滙的新陳代謝

1288 Chü, Hao-jan: Tz'u-hui te pien-ch'ien yü yü-wen te pien-ch'ien.—*Wen-hsing* 6:3, 1960, 4–5. [Lexical evolution and linguistic evolution.]
居浩然：詞彙的變遷與語文變遷

1289 Herdan, Gustav: *The structuralistic approach to Chinese grammar and vocabulary.*—The Hague: Mouton, 1964, 56 p./ Janua Linguarum, Series Practica, 6; 43–54: The development of Chinese vocabulary as a gradual approach to efficient coding; *AO* 34, 1966, 281–282, Z. Novotná.

1290 Hsiang, Kuang-chung: Lun tz'u-hui te yen-pien yü she-hui te fa-chan.—*TCSC* 1981:1, 36– (not seen). [On the evolutionary changes of lexicons and the development of society.]
向光忠：論詞彙的演變與社會的發展

1291 Katayama, Harumasa: Goi no shiteki kenkyū—Gaki no baai.—*HKDKZ* 6, 1971, 59–74. [A historical study of lexicons—the case of *o-kuei* ('hungry devil').]
片山晴賢：語彙の史的研究——餓鬼の場合

1292 Kōsaka, Jun'ichi: Futsūwa goi shōshi. —*CGGG* 1963:1–2, 1–7; 3, 9–14. [A short history of the vocabulary of the Common Language.]
香坂順一：『普通話』語彙小史

1293 Ōhara, Nobukazu: Gendai Chūgokugo no goi henka ni tsuite.—*CGGG* 1959:10, 8–9. [On the changes in the vocabulary of the modern Chinese language.]
大原信一：現代中國語の語彙變化について

1294 Ōhara, Nobukazu: Gendai Chūgokugo no goi to buntai no hensan ni kansuru ichi kōsatsu.—*JBG* 44, 1959, 1–13. [A study concerning Modern Chinese vocabulary and the changes and development of stylistics.]
大原信一：現代中國語の語彙と文體の變遷に關ける一考察

1295 Ōhara, Nobukazu: Gendai Chūgokugo no shii henka.—*JBG* 82, 1965, 108–123. [The changes in the vocabulary of the modern Chinese language.]
大原信一：現代中國語の詞彙變化

1296 Ōkōchi, Yasunori: Saikin no shomengo kara mita Go-Shi no hakuwabun—*CGGG* 1961:3, 1–6, 17. [The colloquial literature of the May Fourth Movement as seen from the current written language.]/ From the point of view of the functions of words and their changes.
大河内康憲：最近の書面語から見た五四の白話文

1297 Pei-ching shih-fan hsüeh-yüan Chung-wen-hsi Han-yü chiao-yen-tsu: *Wu-szu i-lai Han-yü shu-mien yü-yen te pien-ch'ien ho fa-chan.*—Peking: Shang-wu, 1959, 7, 180 p.; Tokyo: Daian, 1962, repr./ Pt. II: The development of Chinese vocabulary; *RBS* 5, 1959, 478, A. Rygaloff; *CKYW* 1961:2, 41–45, Chang Hsin-hua. [Changes and development of the Chinese written language since the May Fourth Movement.]
北京師範學院中文系漢語教研組：五四以來漢語書面語言的變遷和發展／章信華評

1298 Wang, Li: *Han-yü shih kao* (0945), Chap. 4: Lexical development. [A draft for a history of the Chinese language.]
王力：漢語史稿／第四章：詞彙的發展

1299 Wu, Min: Wu-szu i-lai Han-yü tz'u-hui te i-hsieh pien-hua.—*CKYW* 1959:4, 170–174. [A few changes in the Chinese lexicon since the May Fourth Movement.]
伍民：五四以來漢語詞滙的一些變化

1300 Yang, Po-chün: Ts'ung shang-ku Han-yü chi tsu t'ung-i-tz'u te k'ao-ch'a shih t'an tsai tz'u-hui fang-mien ku chin fen ho hsien-hsiang te kuei-lü.—*PCTH* 1956:2, 81–103. [A preliminary investigation into the rules for the phenomenon of lexical division and union from ancient to modern periods based on an observation of certain groups of synonymous words in Archaic Chinese.]
楊伯峻：從上古漢語幾組同義詞的考察試探在詞滙方面古今分合現象的規律

1301 Yin, Meng-lun: T'an-t'an Han-yü tz'u-hui yen-chiu te tuan-tai wen-t'i (0107). [A discussion on the problem of periodization in the study of Chinese vocabulary.]
殷孟倫：談談漢語詞彙研究的斷代問題

6.1.2. Development Since 1949 (1302–1315)

1302 Arita, Tadahiro: Jūnenrai Chūgokugo ni okeru goi no hensan.—*KSGT* 6, 1961, 28–42. [The lexical changes and development in the Chinese language during the last decade.]
有田忠弘：十年來中國語における語彙の變遷

1303 Chi, Wen-shen: Some semantic changes of the Chinese language since 1949.—*JCLTA* 16:1, 1981, 17–33./ Explanations of words and phrases.

1304 Chowdhuri, J. P. Roy: Certain terminological problems as encountered in economic and statistical documents published in China since 1949.—*Babel* 10, 1964, 66–69.

1305 Chu, Hsing-hua & Chin, Lien-ch'eng: Shih-nien lai wo-kuo nung-ts'un yü-yen te pien-hua ho fa-chan.—*CKYW* 1959:6, 251–255. [The changes and development of the Chinese rural languages during the last decade.]

朱興華、金連城：十年來我國農村語言的變化和發展

1306   Hu, Shuang-pao: Tui *Shih-nien lai Han-yü tz'u-hui te fa-chan ho yen-pien te i-chien.—CKYW* 1960:3, 150. [An opinion on *Shih-nien lai Han-yü tz'u-hui te fa-chan ho yen-pien* (1315).]

胡雙寶：對『十年來漢語詞滙的發展和演變』的意見

1307   Li, Yün-han & Ch'eng, Ta-ming: Ta yüeh-chin chung Han-yü tz'u-hui te hsin fa-chan.—*CKYW* 1958:11, 531–532. [The new developments of Chinese lexicons during (the period of) the 'Great Leap Forward.']

黎運漢、程達明：大躍進中漢語詞滙的新發展

1308   Liang, James: Lexical changes in Modern Chinese.—*JCLTA* 11:2, 1976, 88–95.

1309   Mao, Ch'eng-tung; Fang, Yü-ch'ing & Wang, Huan: Chien-kuo i-lai Han-yü tz'u-hui te fa-chan pien-hua.—*JCL* 2:3, 1974, 249–256; *YCYY* 1977:1, 98–111. [The developmental changes of Chinese lexicons since the founding of the P.R.C.]

毛成棟、房玉清、王還：建國以來漢語詞滙的發展變化

1310   Tai, James H-Y.: Vocabulary changes in the Chinese language: some observations on extent and nature.—*JCL* 3:2–3, 1975, 233–244.

〔戴浩一〕

1311   Tai, Hao-i. Transl. by P'an, Wen-kuang: Han-yü tz'u-hui te fa-chan pien-hua.— *Yü-wen* 2, 1976, 47–50, 54. [Vocabulary changes in the Chinese language.] (1310)

戴浩一著，潘文光譯：漢語詞彙的發展變化

1312   Torii, Hisayasu: Kin jūnen ni okeru bungaku goi kenkyū no shiryō.—*CGGG* 1956:5, 8–12. [Research materials on

vocabulary from literary sources published during the last decade.]

鳥居久靖：近十年における文學語彙研究の資料

1313   Wang, Huan: 1949 nien chien-kuo i-lai Han-yü te pien-hua.—*JCLTA* 17:2, 1982, 35–43. [Changes in the Chinese language since the founding of the P.R.C. in 1949.]/ Lexical changes.

王還：1949年建國以來漢語的變化

1314   Wang, Huan: Chien-kuo i-lai Han-yü tz'u-hui te pien-hua chi ch'i yüan-yin.— *YCYY* 1982:3, 70–80. [Chinese lexical changes since the founding of the P.R.C. and their causes.]

王還：建國以來漢語詞滙的變化及其原因

1315   Wu, Chan-k'un; Wang, Ch'in & Ch'eng, Ch'ui-ch'eng: Shih-nien lai Han-yü tz'u-hui te fa-chan ho yen-pien.—*CKYW* 1959:7, 301–307. [The development and changes of Chinese lexicons during the last decade.]/ See (1306).

武占坤、王勤、程垂成：十年來漢語詞滙的發展和演變

6.2.   General Vocabulary (1316–1382)
6.2.1.   General Studies (1316–1353)

1316   Chang, Chih-kung (ed. in chief): *Hsien-tai Han-yü* (shang ts'e, shih-yung pen).—Peking: Jen-min chiao-yü, 1982, [3], 6, 5, 523, 16 p./ Pt. II: Chinese vocabulary. [Modern Chinese (Vol. I, trial edition).]

張志公主編：現代漢語（上册，試用本）／第二編：漢語語滙

1317   Chang, Ching (ed. in chief): *Hsin pien hsien-tai Han-yü.*—Shanghai: Shanghai chiao-yü, 1980, 2 vols., 2, 3, 305 p.; 3, 338 p./ Vol. II, Chap. 3: Lexicon and lexical usage. [A new edition of Modern Chinese.]

張靜主編：新編現代漢語／下册，第三章：詞滙和用詞

1318 Chang, Shih-lu: Tz'u-hui chiang-hua. —*YWCS* 1956:1, 5–7; 2, 16–20; 3, 25–31; 4, 30–34; 5, 5–8; 6, 16–20. [Lectures on lexicons.]
張世祿：詞滙講話

1319 Chang, Shih-lu: *P'u-t'ung-hua tz'u-hui.* —Shanghai: Hsin chih-shih, 1957, [ii], 78 p; *Yü-wen hui-pien* (0058), 3:11./ *YWCS* 1957:9, 48, Chu Hsi-yü. [A lexicon of the Common Language.]
張世祿：普通話詞滙／朱錫裕評

1320 Chi-lin shih-fan ta-hsüeh Chung-wen-hsi: *Yü-wen chi-ch'u chih-shih.*—Changchun: Chi-lin jen-min, 1972, 1st ed.; 1980, 2nd ed.; 1980, 5th print., 10, 557 p./ 4: Modern Chinese lexicon. [Fundamental knowledge of language and writing.]
吉林師範大學中文系：語文基礎知識／四：現代漢語詞滙

1321 Chou, Tsu-mo: Han-yü tz'u-hui chiang-hua.—*YWHH* 1955:4, 33–40; 5, 9–11; 6, 58–60; 7, 16–19; 8, 36–38; 10, 29–32; 1956:1, 38–40; 2, 38–40; 4, 29–31; 5, 30–31; 8, 34–36; 9, 20–21; 11, 33–35; 1957:2, 30–33; 3, 29–30; 5, 29–31; 7, 24–25; 10, 33–34. [Lectures on Chinese lexicons.]
周祖謨：漢語詞滙講話

1322 Chou, Tsu-mo: *Han-yü tz'u-hui chiang-hua.*—Peking: Jen-min chiao-yü, 1959; 1962, 2nd ed., 2, 110 p./ *YWHH* 1959:12, 35–36, Meng Yüan. [Lectures on Chinese lexicons.]
周祖謨：漢語詞滙講話／孟原評

1323 Chou, Tsu-mo: Hsien-tai Han-yü tz'u-hui yen-chiu.—*YWYC* 1982:2, 1–4. [A study on Modern Chinese lexicons.]
周祖謨：現代漢語詞滙研究

1324 Chu, Yao-lung & Hsia, Hua: *Tz'u-hui ch'ang-shih.*—Taiyuan: Shan-hsi jen-min, 1978; 1980, 132 p. [Common knowledge of lexicons.]
朱耀龍、夏華：詞滙常識

1325 Fan, Ch'ang-shih: Chung-kuo yü-yen chung te tz'u-hui.—*CWY* 7, 1980, 57–87. [Lexicons in the Chinese language.]
范昌詩：中國語言中的詞彙

1326 Hsü, Chung-hua: Han-yü tz'u-hui te chi-ch'u chih-shih.—*Yü-wen hsüeh-hsi te chi-ch'u* (0055), 84–116. [Fundamental knowledge of Chinese lexicons.]
徐仲華：漢語詞滙的基礎知識

1327 Hsü, Wei-han & Li, Jun-sheng: *Han-yü tz'u-hui chi-ch'u chih-shih.*—Wuhan: Hu-pei jen-min, 1959, iii, 108 p. [Fundamental knowledge of Chinese lexicons.]
許威漢、李潤生：漢語詞滙基礎知識

1328 Hu, Yü-shu (ed.): *Hsien-tai Han-yü.*—Shanghai: Shang-hai chiao-yü, 1962; 1979, 2nd ed.; 1981, 3rd rev. & enl. ed.; 1982, 4th print., 2, 568 p./ Chap. 3: Lexicon. [Modern Chinese.]
胡裕樹主編：現代漢語（增訂本）／第三章：詞滙

1329 Hua-chung shih-fan hsüeh-yüan Chung-wen-hsi hsien-tai Han-yü chiao-yen-shih: *Hsien-tai Han-yü tz'u-hui chih-shih.*—Wuhan: Hu-pei jen-min, 1973, 1st ed.; 1979, 2nd ed.; 1979, 3rd print., [ii], 4, 140 p. [Knowledge of a Modern Chinese lexicon.]
華中師範學院中文系現代漢語教研室：現代漢語詞滙知識

1330 Hua-nan shih-fan hsüeh-yüan Chung-wen-hsi: *Tz'u-hui ch'ang-shih.*—Canton: Kuang-tung jen-min, 1978, 67 p. [Common knowledge of lexicons.]
華南師範學院中文系：詞滙常識

1331 Huang, Po-jung & Liao, Hsü-tung (eds.): *Hsien-tai Han-yü.*—Lanchow: Kan-su jen-min, 1979; 1981, 2nd ed., 2 vols., [ii], 4, 508 p., Appendices./ Chap. 3:

Lexicon. [Modern Chinese.]
黃伯榮、廖序東主編：現代漢語／第三章：詞
滙

1332 Jen-min chiao-yü chu-pan-she: *Han-yü chih-shih.*—Peking: Jen-min chiao-yü, 1959, 1st ed.; 1979, 2nd ed.; 1980, 6th print., 2, 8, 332 p.; 1982, 10th print.,/ Pt. II: Lexicon. [Knowledge of Chinese.]
人民教育出版社：漢語知識／第二篇：詞滙

1333 Kao, Ming-k'ai: *Han-yü yü-fa lun.*—Shanghai: K'ai-ming, 1948, 696 p.; Peking: K'o-hsüeh, 1957, rev. ed., 9, 554 p./ Introduction, Chap. 3: Words of the Chinese language; *YCHP* 34, 1948, 281–286, Lin T'ao; *FEQ* 12, 1953, 64–68, Roy A. Miller; *RBS* 3, 1957, 568, J. Chmielewski. [On Chinese grammar.]
高名凱：漢語語法論／緒論，第三章：漢語的
詞；林燾評

1334 Kao, Wen-ta & Wang, Li-t'ing: *Tz'u-hui chih-shih.*—Chinan: Shan-tung jen-min, 1980, 2, 175 p. [Knowledge of lexicon.]
高文達、王立廷：詞滙知識

1335 Ko, Pen-i: *Hsien-tai Han-yü tz'u-hui.*—Chinan: Shan-tung jen-min, 1975, 45 p. [A Modern Chinese lexicon.]
葛本儀：現代漢語詞彙

1336 Kōsaka, Jun'ichi: *Chūgoku gogaku no kiso chishiki.*—Tokyo: Kōseikan, 1971, 14, 337 p./ Chap. 5: Vocabulary. [Fundamental knowledge of Chinese linguistics.]
香坂順一：中國語學の基礎知識／第五章：語
彙

1337 Li, Keng-chün, et al.: *Tz'u-hui ch'ü t'an.*—Shanghai: Shao-nien erh-t'ung, 1981, 2, 2, 146 p., illus. [Interesting talks about lexicons.]/ Collected essays.
李賡均等：詞滙趣談

1338 Lin, Yü-wen: *Tz'u-hui, yü-fa, hsiu-tz'u.*—Shanghai: Hsin chih-shih, 1957, [ii], 92 p.; *Yü-wen hui-pien* (0058), 3:13./

CKYW 1957:7, 48–49, Hsü Ling-fang. [Lexicon, grammar, and rhetoric.]
林裕文：詞滙、語法、修辭／許令芳評

1339 Lo, Szu-ping: Kuo-yü tz'u kai-lun.—*KYYK* 1:11, 1922, 1–9. [An introduction to the words of the National Language.]
樂嗣炳：國語詞概論

1340 Lü, Shu-hsiang & Chu, Te-hsi: *Yü-fa hsiu-tz'u chiang-hua.*—Peking: Chung-kuo ch'ing-nien, 1979, 5, 2, 337 p./ Lecture 2: Lexicon. [Lectures on grammar and rhetoric.]
呂叔湘、朱德熙：語法修辭講話／第二講：詞
滙

1341 Ōkōchi, Yasunori: Gendaigo no goi.—*Gengo* (0085), 376–389. [The vocabulary of Modern Chinese.]
大河內康憲：現代語の語彙

1342 Pei-ching chiao-yü hsüeh-yüan shih-fan chiao-yen-shih: *Yü-wen chi-ch'u chih-shih.*—Peking: Pei-ching, 1975; 1982, 7th print., 3, 274 p./ 69–91: Lexicon. [Fundamental knowledge of language and writing.]
北京教育學院師範教研室：語文基礎知識／69
—91：詞滙

1343 Pei-ching-shih Kung-nung chiao-yü yen-chiu-shih: *Yü-wen chih-shih tien-shih chiang-tso.*—Peking: Kuang-po, 1981; 1982, 2nd print., 3, 234 p./ 2: Knowledge about Modern Chinese lexicons. [TV lectures on knowledge of (Chinese) language and writing.]
北京市工農教育研究室：語文知識電視講座／
貳：現代漢語詞滙知識

1344 Pei-ching ta-hsüeh Chung-kuo yü-yen-wen-hsüeh-hsi Han-yü chiao-yen-shih: *Hsien-tai Han-yü.*—Peking: Shang-wu, 1962, 289 p.; *Yü-wen hui-pien* (0058), 2:47./ Chap. 4: Lexicon; *RBS* 8, 1962, 435, S.N. Cartier. [Modern Chinese.]
北京大學中國語言文學系漢語教研室：現代漢
語／第四章：詞滙

1345 Samejima, Kunizō: *Chūgoku goi no tayōsei.—Kurume daigaku Shōgakubu sōritsu nijūgo shūnen kinen ronbunshū* (Kurume, 1977), 219–249. [The diversity of Chinese vocabulary.]
鮫島國三：中國語彙の多樣性——『久留米大學商學部創立二十五周年記紀論文集』

1346 Sun, Ch'ang-hsü: *Han-yü tz'u-hui* (0165). [Chinese lexicons.]
孫常叙：漢語詞彙

1347 T'an, Ch'üan: *Shih-yung tz'u-hui hsin chih-shih.*—Hong Kong: Shang-wu, 1978, 3, 160 p. [New knowledge for a practical lexicon.]
譚全：實用詞彙新知識

1348 Wang, Ch'in & Wu, Chan-k'un: *Hsien-tai Han-yü tz'u-hui.*—Changsha: Hu-nan jen-min, 1959, 354 p./ *JWTC* 1960:2, 74–79, Ma T'ien-hsiang; 80–82, Liu K'ai-ming. [A lexicon of Modern Chinese.]
王勤、武占坤：現代漢語詞彙／馬天祥評，劉凱鳴評

1349 Wang, Li: *Han-yü chiang-hua.*—Peking: Wen-hua chiao-yü, 1955, rev. ed., 76 p./ Chap. 4: Lexicon. [Lectures on the Chinese language.]
王力：漢語講話／第四章：詞彙

1350 Wu, Chan-k'un: *Tz'u-hui* (0129). [A lexicon.]/ A general study.
武占坤：詞滙

1351 Wu, Chi-ts'ai & Ch'eng, Chia-shu: *Hsien-tai Han-yü.*—Kunming: Yün-nan jen-min, 1981, 2, 7, 524 p./ Chap. 3: Lexicon. [Modern Chinese.]
吳積才、程家樞：現代漢語／第三章：詞滙

1352 Yang, Hsin-an: *Hsien-tai Han-yü.*—Chungking: Ch'ung-ch'ing jen-min, 1956–1958, 4 vols./ Vol. II, Pt. IV: Lexicon. [Modern Chinese.]
楊欣安：現代漢語／第二冊，第四編：詞彙

1353 Yao, Lin-yüan (ed. in chief): *Chung-*

hsüeh yü-wen chiao-shih shou-ts'e (1011), 51–72: Lexicon. [A handbook for middle school language teachers.]
姚麟園主編：中學語文教師手冊／51–72：詞滙

6.2.2. Collection and Analysis (1354–1369)

1354 Chiao-yü-pu *Ch'ung-pien Kuo-yü tz'u-tien* pien-chi wei-yüan-hui: *Ch'ung pien Kuo-yü tz'u-tien.*—Taipei: Shang-wu, 1981, 6 vols., lxvi, 5736, 39, 83, 143, 29, 83 p. [A recompiled edition of a dictionary of the National Language (1357).]
教育部『重編國語辭典』編輯委員會：重編國語辭典

1355 Ching, Shih-chün: *Hsien-tai Han-yü hsü-tz'u.*—Huhehot: Nei Meng-ku jen-min, 1980, [i], 20, 323 p./ *KKNP* 16, 1982, 4, Hatano Tarō. [Cenematic words in Modern Chinese.]
景士俊：現代漢語虛詞／波多野太郎評

1356 Chung-kuo k'o-hsüeh-yüan Yü-yen yen-chiu-so tz'u-tien pien-chi-shih: *Hsien-tai Han-yü tz'u-tien.*—Peking: Shang-wu, 1965, [v], 88, 1400 p., illus.; Hong Kong: Shang-wu, 1977, repr.; Hong Kong: I-lin, 1977, repr.; Peking: Shang-wu, 1978, rev. ed., [ii], 155, 1567 p., illus. [A dictionary of the modern Chinese language.]
中國社會科學院語言研究所詞典編輯室：現代漢語詞典

1357 Chung-kuo ta tz'u-tien pien-tsuan-ch'u: *Kuo-yü tz'u-tien.*—Shanghai: Shang-wu, 1937, 8 vols., 31, 4485, 220 p.; Taipei: Shang-wu, 1953, repr., 4 vols.; 1976, repr. [A dictionary of the National Language.]/ See (1354).
中國大辭典編纂處：國語辭典

1358 Chung-kuo ta tz'u-tien pien-tsuan-ch'u: *Han-yü tz'u-tien.*—Shanghai: Shang-wu, 1957, 8, [4], 1254, 27 p.; Hong Kong: Shang-wu, 1968, 4th print.; Taipei: Shang-wu, 1969, repr./ An abbreviated ed. of *Kuo-yü tz'u-tien* (1357). [A dictionary

of the Chinese language.]
中國大辭典編纂處：漢語辭典

1359 Chung-kuo wen-tzu kai-ko wei-yüan-hui tz'u-hui hsiao-tsu: *Han-yü p'in-yin tz'u-hui.* —Peking: Wen-tzu kai-ko, 1958, 4, 394 p.; 1963, rev. & enl. ed., [ii], 669 p. [A Chinese lexicon in the Pinyin system.]
中國文字改革委員會詞滙小組：漢語拼音詞滙

1360 Ho, Jung: *Kuo-yü jih-pao tz'u-tien.* — Taipei: Kuo-yü jih-pao-she, 1974, 2, 16, 1075 p., tabs./ *CKYT* 36:4, 1975, 70–71, Wang Meng-wu; *SHJ* 269, 1975, 1–7, Liu Ch'ung-ch'un; *SHJ* 269, 1975, 7–8, Liang Jung-jo; *SPSM* 24, 1975, 67–70, Hu Chi-chün; *JCL* 4:2–3, 1976, 307–311, Dayle Barnes. [The National Language Daily News dictionary.]
何容：國語日報辭典／王孟武評，劉崇純評，梁容若評，胡基俊評

1361 *Hsin-hua tz'u-tien* pien-tsuan-tsu: *Hsin-hua tz'u-tien.*—Peking: Shang-wu, 1981, [i], 87, 1243 p. [A new China dictionary.]
『新華辭典』編纂組：新華辭典

1362 Hsü, Shih-ying: *Ch'ang-yung hsü-tzu yung-fa ch'ien-shih.*—Taipei: Fu-hsing, 1975, 8th ed., 5, 11, 464 p. [Simple explanations of the uses of commonly used cenematic words.]
許世英：常用虛字用法淺釋

1363 Hua-nan shih-fan hsüeh-yüan Chung-wen-hsi: *Hsien-tai Han-yü hsü-tz'u.*— Canton: Kuang-tung jen-min, 1981, [i], 13, 346 p. [Cenematic words in Modern Chinese.]
華南師範學院中文系：現代漢語虛詞

1364 Li, P'u-ying: *Hsien-tai Han-yü ch'ang-yung hsü-tz'u hsüan shih.*—Nanning: Kuang-hsi jen-min, 1981, 4, 164 p. [Selection and explanations of commonly used cenematic words in Modern Chinese.]
李譜英：現代漢語常用虛詞選釋

1365 Lü, Shu-hsiang (ed. in chief): *Hsien-tai*

Han-yü pa-pai tz'u.—Peking: Shang-wu, 1980, 3, 668 p./ *CKYW* 1981:2, 154– 156, Wang Huan; *KKNP* 16, 1982, 1–4, Hatano Tarō. [Eight hundred Modern Chinese words.]/ With their grammatical usages.
呂叔湘主編：現代漢語八百詞／王還評，波多野太郎評

1366 Pei-ching ta-hsüeh Chung-wen-hsi 1955, 1957 chi yü-yen-pan: *Hsien-tai Han-yü hsü-tz'u li shih.*—Peking: Shang-wu, 1982, 575 p. [Explanations with examples of cenematic words in Modern Chinese.]
北京大學中文系1955、1957級語言班：現代漢語虛詞例釋

1367 Sawayama, Seizaburō: *Chūgokugo bunrui tangoshū.*—Tokyo: Daigaku shorin, 1980, ix, 283 p. [A classified collection of Chinese words.]
澤山晴三郎：中國語分類單語集

1368 Suzuki, Naoji; Mochizuki, Yasokichi & Yamagishi, Tomoni: *Chūgokugo jōyō kyoshi jiten.*—Tokyo: Kōnan shoin, 1956, 2, 4, 160, 6 p. [A dictionary of commonly used cenematic words in Chinese.]
鈴木直治、望月八十吉、山岸共：中國語常用虛詞辭典

1369 Suzuki, Naoji; Yamagishi, Tomoni & Mochizuki, Yasokichi: Kyoshi no mochii-kata.—*Chūgoku gogaku jiten* (0037), 551–661. [Ways to use cenematic words.]
鈴木直治、山岸共、望月八十吉：虛詞の用いかた

6.2.3. Vocabulary From Literary Sources (1370–1382)

1370 Collier, David: *Chinese-English dictionary of colloquial terms used in modern Chinese literature.*—New Haven: Far Eastern Publications, Yale U., 1979, xix, 233 p.

1371 Ho, Kwok-cheung: *A comparative study of the Chinese vocabulary in several textbooks for Westerners.*—Hong Kong:

Chinese U. Press, 1979, vii, 387 p.
〔何國祥：西文漢語教科書中詞彙之比較研究〕

1372 Kubler, Cornelius C.: *Vocabulary and notes to Ba Jin's Jia: an aid for reading the novel.*—Ithaca: China-Japan Program, 1976, xvi, 285 p.
〔巴金：家〕

1373 Lau, D.C.: *Lu Xun xiao shuo ji: Vocabulary.*—Hong Kong: Chinese U. Press, 1979, 224 p.
〔劉殿爵：魯迅小説集詞彙〕

1374 Mō Dakutō Chosaku Gengo Kenkyūkai: *Mō Dakutō senshū goi jikō sakuin.*—Ōsaka: Ōsaka Shiritsu Daigaku Bungakubu Chūgoku Gogaku Kenkyūshitsu, 1972, [ii], 506 p. [An index to lexical items of *Mao Tse-tung hsüan chi.*]
毛澤東著作言語研究會：毛澤東選集語彙事項索引

1375 Ōta, Tatsuo: Shakai shōsetu *Pekin* no gohō to goi.—*KGR* 24:3, 1973, 1–17. [The grammar and vocabulary of the social novel *Pei-ching.*]
太田辰夫：社會小説『北京』の語法と語彙

1376 Ōta, Tatsuo: *Rikon* no gohō to goi. —*KGR* 25:1, 1974, 39–62. [The grammar and vocabulary of *Li-hun.*]
太田辰夫：『離婚』の語法と語彙

1377 Samejima, Kunizō: Mō Dakutō ronbun no goi to buntai.—*KRMR* 15, 1966, 59–72. [The vocabulary and literary style of Mao Tse-tung's essays.]
鮫島國三：毛澤東論文の語彙と文體

1378 Samejima, Kunizō: Mō Dakutō chosaku no goi henka to shūji gihō.—*KRMR* 23:1, 1974, 21–31. [Lexical changes and rhetorical techniques in Mao Tse-tung's works.]
鮫島國三：毛澤東著作の語彙變化と修辭技法

1379 Shibagaki, Yoshitarō: *Mō Dakutō goroku* no goi.—*RDR* 386, 1968, 18–31.

[The vocabulary of *Mao Tse-tung yü-lu.*]
柴垣芳太郎：『毛澤東語錄』の語彙

1380 Ueno, Keiji: Ro Jin sakuhin no gohō to goi.—*GBR* 3, 1978, 93–110. [The grammar and vocabulary of Lu Hsün's works.]
上野惠司：魯迅作品の語法と語彙

1381 Ueno, Keiji: Yō Seitō sakuhin no gohō to goi.—*GBR* 5, 1978, 139–154. [The grammar and vocabulary of Yeh Sheng-t'ao's works.]
上野惠司：葉聖陶作品の語法と語彙

1382 Ueno, Keiji: *Ro Jin shōsetsu goi sakuin —Totsukan, Hōkō, Koji shinpen.*—Tokyo: Ryūkei shosha, 1979, [iii], 16, 547 p. [An index to the vocabulary in Lu Hsün's novels: *Na-han, P'ang-huang,* and *Ku-shih hsin-pien.*]
上野惠司：魯迅小説語彙索引—呐喊、彷徨、故事新編

6.3. Basic Vocabulary (1383–1426)
6.3.1. Definition and Problems (1383–1396)

1383 Chang, Shih-lu: Chi-pen tz'u-hui te hsing-chih ho fan-wei.—*YWCS* 1956:8, 1–6. [The nature and scope of basic vocabulary.]
張世祿：基本詞滙的性質和範圍

1384 Chao, Chen-to: Hsü-tz'u pu-neng kuei-ju chi-pen tz'u-hui ma? —*JWTC* 1959:3, 39–40. [Are cenematic words not able to be included in basic vocabulary?]
趙振鐸：虛詞不能歸入基本詞滙嗎？

1385 Chin, Lun-hai: Tsai-shuo *Kuo-min chi-pen tzu-hui.*—*CYS* 7:1–2, 1948, 29–31. [Another discussion on *Kuo-min chi-pen tzu-hui.*]
金輪海：再說『國民基本字彙』

1386 Fang, Shih-to: Tseng-yang ts'ai suan shih chi-pen tz'u?—*CKYT* 17:5, 1965, 46–50. [What counts as basic vocabulary?]

方師鐸：怎樣才算是基本詞？

1387   Hsieh, Hsiao-an: Hsien-tai Han-yü te chi-pen tz'u-hui.—*JWTC* 1958:1, 48–52. [Basic vocabulary of Modern Chinese.]/ A discussion with Mr. Sun Ch'ang-hsü (0165) on the special features and essence of basic vocabulary.

謝曉安：現代漢語的基本詞滙

1388   Hsü, Tse-min: Min-chung chi-pen tzu-hui wen-t'i.—*STMC* 6:7, 1935, 89–106. [The problem of basic vocabulary of the masses.]

徐則敏：民眾基本字滙問題

1389   Li, Hsiang-chen: Kuan-yü Han-yü te chi-pen tz'u-hui.—*CKYW* 1953:5, 17–21. [Concerning basic vocabulary of Chinese.]/ See (0124) and (1393).

李向眞：關於漢語的基本詞滙

1390   Li, Jung: Han-yü te chi-pen tz'u-hui. —*KHTP* 3:7, 1952, 449–452. [Basic vocabulary of Chinese.]/ See (1393).

李榮：漢語的基本詞滙

1391   Li, Tso-nan: Ts'ung tzu te tsu-ho t'an chi-pen tz'u-hui.—*CKYW* 1956:12, 14, 36. [A discussion of basic vocabulary from the point of view of compounding of characters.]

李作南：從字的組合談基本詞滙

1392   Lin, T'ao: Han-yü chi-pen tz'u-hui chung te chi-ko wen-t'i.—*CKYW* 1954:7, 4–10. [Several problems in Chinese basic vocabulary.]

林燾：漢語基本詞滙中的幾個問題

1393   Po, Han: Li Jung, Li Hsiang-chen liang-wei hsien-sheng kuan-yü chi-pen tz'u-hui te lun-wen tu hou kan.—*CKYW* 1953:7, 14–15. [Impressions after reading the essays of Mr. Li Jung and Mr. Li Hsiang-chen concerning basic vocabulary.]/ See (1389) and (1390).

伯韓：李榮、李向眞兩位先生關於基本詞滙的論文讀後感

1394   Sun, Ch'ang-hsü: *Han-yü tz'u-hui* (0165), Pt. II, Chap. 4–5: Basic vocabulary. [Chinese lexicons.]

孫常叙：漢語詞彙／第二部分，第四、五篇：基本詞彙

1395   Sun, Fu-yüan: Chi-pen tz'u-hui yen-chiu shu yao.—*SCCY* 28, 1947, 2–6. [A summary account of studies on basic vocabulary.]

孫伏園：基本詞滙研究述要

1396   Wang, Wen-hsin: Ko chia chi-pen tzu-hui yen-chiu chih chieh-kuo chi ch'i te shih.—*CT* 3:6, 1947, 13–16. [Results of the studies on basic vocabulary by different scholars and their gains and losses.]

王文新：各家基本字彙研究之結果及其得失

6.3.2. Formation and Development (1397–1401)

1397   Ch'i, Ch'ung-t'ien: Han-yü chi-pen tz'u-hui te fa-chan chi yu-kuan wen-t'i.—*NMTH* 1960:1, 75–122. [The development of Chinese basic vocabulary and related problems.]

齊冲天：漢語基本詞滙的發展及有關問題

1398   Hu, An-liang & Ch'eng, Hsiang-hui: Ts'ung fa-chan chung k'an chi-pen tz'u-hui te wen-ku-hsing.—*YWCS* 1958:3, 18–20. [The stability of basic vocabulary as seen from its development.]

胡安良、程祥徽：從發展中看基本詞滙的穩固性

1399   Ozaki, Minoru: Futsūwa jōyō shi no hensen.—*CGGG* 1967:5, 1–14. [The changes and development of commonly used words in the Common Language.]/ Lexical changes from the end of the Ch'ing dynasty to the present age.

尾崎實：普通話常用詞の變遷

1400   P'an, Yün-chung: Han-yü chi-pen tz'u-hui te hsing-ch'eng chi ch'i fa-chan.— *CSTH* 1959:1–2, 98–121. [The formation of Chinese basic vocabulary and its development.]

潘允中：漢語基本詞滙的形成及其發展

1401 T'ien, So: Ts'ung kung shih t'an-ch'i —kuan-yü Han-yü chi-pen tz'u-hui fa-chan te li-shih chi-ch'eng-hsing.—*YLT* 1, 1957, 34–50. [A discussion starting from (the words) *kung* ('a bow') and *shih* ('an arrow') —Concerning the historical continuity of the development of Chinese basic vocabulary.]

天瑣：從『弓』、『矢』談起—關於漢語基本詞彙發展的歷史繼承性 ·

6.3.3. Frequency Count (1402–1412)

1402 Hashimoto, Mantarō: Gendai Chūgokugo goi no konpyūtā kaunto.—*CAAAL* 7, 1977, 29–41. [A computer count of Modern Chinese vocabulary.]

橋本萬太郎：現代中國語語彙コンピュータ ーカウント

1403 Ho, Kwok-cheung: A study of the relative frequency distribution of syllabic components in Mandarin Chinese.—*HKCW* 8:1, 1976, 275–352.

〔何國祥：漢語常用音素之研究〕

1404 Jen, Hsiao-hsien: *A frequency count of contemporary Chinese vocabulary based on seven leading newspapers.*—Columbia: U. of South Carolina, 1975, 161 p./ Unpubl. doc. diss.; *DAI* 36:11, 1976: 7258–A; UM 76–10, 462.

1405 Li, Chin-hsi: Kuo-yü chung chi-pen yü-tz'u te t'ung-chi yen-chiu.—*Kuo-wen hsüeh-hui ts'ung-k'an* 1:1, 1922, 1–4. [A statistical study of basic vocabulary in the National Language.]

黎錦熙：國語中基本語詞的統計研究

1406 Li, Min, et al.: Shuang-yin-chieh chi-pen tz'u ch'u-hsien p'in-lü t'ung-chi piao.— *WTKK* 1960:1, 18–22. [A statistical table for frequencies of appearance of disyllabic basic vocabulary.]

李敏等：雙音節基本詞出現頻率統計表

1407 Lin, Hsi: Ts'ung i-chung t'ung-chi k'an Han-yü tz'u-hui.—*CKYW* 1954:4, 15–17. [Chinese lexicons from a statistical point of view.]

林曦：從一種統計看漢語詞滙

1408 Liu, Eric Shen: *Frequency dictionary of Chinese words.*—Stanford: Stanford U., 1965, 487 p./ Unpubl. doc. diss.; *DA* 26, 1966, 3940.

1409 Liu, Eric Shen: *Frequency dictionary of Chinese words.*—The Hague & Paris: Mouton, 1973, xliv, 236 p.

1410 Liu, Tse-hsien: Tz'u-erh te shu-mu. —*CKYW* 1954:5, 9. [The (total) number of words.]

劉澤先：詞兒的數目

1411 Liu, Ying-mao; Chuang, Chung-jen & Wang, Shou-chen: *Ch'ang-yung Chung-wen tz'u te ch'u-hsien tz'u-shu.*—Taipei: Liu-kuo, 1975, [v], 377 p. [Frequency count of commonly used Chinese words.]

劉英茂、莊仲仁、王守珍：常用中文詞的出現次數

1412 Ma, Szu-chou: Tan-tzu tsai tz'u-li ch'u-hsien te p'in-lü.—*CKYW* 1956:12, 15–26, 44. [The frequency of appearance of single characters in (Chinese) words.]

馬思周：單字在詞裏出現的頻率

6.3.4. Collection and Analysis (1413–1426)

1413 André, Yvonne: *Vocabulaire de base du chinois modern (Chinois-Français).*— Paris: Éditions Klincksieck, 1965, 155 p./ *AO* 37, 1969, 130, O. Švarný.

1414 Chiao-yü ch'u-pan-she pien-chi-pu: *Hsiao-hsüeh chi-pen tz'u-yü ching chieh.*—Hong Kong: Chiao-yü, n.d., 2, 2, 170 p. [Explanations for the basic vocabulary of elementary schools.]

教育出版社編輯部：小學基本詞語精解

1415   Chin, Lun-hai: Chieh-shao i-t'ao chu yin te kuo-min chi-pen hsin tzu-hui.—*CYTC* 32:5, 1947, 16–26. [Introducing a set of new phonetically orientated citizens' basic vocabulary.]

金輪海：介紹一套主音的國民基本新字滙

1416   Chuang, Tse-hsüan: *Chi-pen tzu-hui.*— Canton: Chung-hua, 1930, 292 p./ *CYYMC* 2:3, 1930, 1–8, Fu Pao-shen. [A (dictionary of) basic vocabulary.]

莊澤宣：基本字彙／傅葆琛評

1417   Chuang, Tse-hsüan: Chi-pen tzu-hui pien-tsuan te ching-kuo.—*CYYC* 17, 1930, 987–991. [The experience of compiling (a dictionary of) basic vocabulary.]

莊澤宣：基本字彙編纂的經過

1418   Kennedy, George A.: *Minimum vocabularies of written Chinese.*—New Haven: Far Eastern Publications, Yale U., 1954, 40 p.

1419   Koshimizu, Masaru: *Chūgokugo kihongo nōto.*—Tokyo: Taishūkan, 1980; 1982, 4th ed., viii, 318 p. [Notes on Chinese basic vocabulary.]

輿水優：中國語基本語ノート

1420   Koshimizu, Masaru: Kihongo nōto.— *Chūgokugo* 1980:4, 26; 5, 16; 6, 16; 7, 16; 8, 16; 9, 26; 10, 20; 11, 16; 12, 28; 1981:1, 16; 2, 16; 3, 21; 4, 21; 5, 19; 6, 19; 7, 13; 8, 13; 9, 23; 10, 21; 11, 13; 12, 25; 1982:1, 11; 2, 13; 3, 18; 4, 23; 5, 17; 6, 13; 7, 13; 8, 13; 9, 23; 10, 13; 11, 14; 12, 26; 1983:1, 13; 2, 13; 3, 23; 4, 24; to be continued. [Notes on (Chinese) basic vocabulary.]

輿水優：基本語ノート

1421   Miyakoshi, Kentarō: *Shinago kiso tango 4000.*—Tokyo: Times shuppansha, 1942, 4th ed., 210 p. [4000 basic words from the Chinese language.]

宮越健太郎：支那語基礎單語四〇〇〇

1422   Shibagaki, Yoshitarō: *Chūgokugo kihon goi.*—Tokyo: Kōnan shoin, 1956, 124 p., tab. [Basic vocabulary of the Chinese language.]

柴垣芳太郎：中國語基本語彙

1423   Suzuki, Kaijō: *Ichidoku Shina tsū: jijō, gengo.*—Tokyo: Maki shobō, 1942, in 2 pts., 16, 154; 160 p./ Pt. II, Chap. 3: Basic vocabulary. [To thoroughly understand China by one reading: affairs, language.]

鈴木快城：一讀支那通：事情・言語／言語篇，第三章：基本單語

1424   Takeda, Yasunobu & Okamoto, Yoshinosuke: *Shinago kihon goi.*—Tokyo: Shun'yōdō, 1936, 3, 10, 225, 27 p. [Basic vocabulary of the Chinese language.]

武田寧信、岡本吉之助：支那語基本語彙

1425   Ushijima, Tokuji: *Chūgokugo kihon shii 3000 go.*—Tokyo: Daigaku shorin, 1958; 1979, 19th print., 201 p. [A 3000 word Chinese basic vocabulary.]

牛島德次：中國語基本詞彙3000語

1426   Yano, Fujisuke: *Chūgokugo kiso 1500 go.*—Tokyo: Daigaku shorin, 1950, 3rd. ed., 115 p. [1500 basic words from the Chinese language.]

矢野藤助：中國語基礎1500語

6.4.   Commonly Used Vocabulary and Characters (1427–1500)

6.4.1.   Commonly Used Vocabulary (1427–1457)

6.4.1.1.   General Studies (1427–1435)

1427   Ch'en, Jen-che: Min-chung shih-yung tzu-hui te yen-chiu.—*Hu-ta chiao-yü*, 2, 1934, 32–58. [A study of the practical vocabulary of the masses.]

陳人哲：民衆實用字滙的研究

1428   Chou, Ch'i-ch'en: Min-chung tz'u-hui te yen-chiu.—*CYYMC* 6:2, 1934, 213–276; 3, 421–450. [A study of the vocabulary of the masses.]

周其辰：民衆詞滙的研究

1429 Chu, Tso-t'ing: Min-chung tzu-hui wen-t'i.—*HNCY* 5:4, 1935, 30–33. [The problem of the vocabulary of the masses.]
朱佐廷：民衆字滙問題

1430 Ho, Chih-yüan: *Kuo-yü ch'ang-yung tz'u-hui p'ei-tz'u fan-li.*—Sanchung (Taipei): P'ing-p'ing, 1968, 57 p. [Examples of the matching of words in the commonly used vocabulary of the National Language.]
何志遠：國語常用詞彙配詞範例

1431 Huang, Jo-chou: Pien-tsao kuo-min ch'ang-yung tzu-hui chih wo-chien.—*KMCY* 4:3–4, 1946, 7. [My opinion on compiling citizens' commonly used vocabulary.]
黃若舟：編造國民常用字彙之我見

1432 Satō, Toshiyuki: Jōyōgo sentei ni okeru jakkan no kijun ni tsuite.—*KSCGH* 9, 1963, 60–72. [On several standards for the selection of commonly used words.]
佐藤利行：常用語選定における若干の基準について

1433 Tu, Tso-chou & Chiang, Ch'eng-k'un: Erh-t'ung chi ch'eng-jen ch'ang-yung tzu-hui yen-chiu.—*CYYMC* 4:8, 1933, 1445–1463. [A study of the commonly used vocabulary of children and adults.]
杜佐周、蔣成坤：兒童及成人常用字滙研究

1434 Wang, Hsien-en: Min-chung shih-yung tz'u shih t'an.—*CYYMC* 4:8, 1933, 1465–1476. [A preliminary investigation into the practical vocabulary of the masses.]
王顯恩：民衆實用詞試探

1435 Wei, Ping-hsin: Pien-tsao ch'ang-yung tzu-hui te yen-chiu.—*KMCY* 4:3–4, 1946, 8–11. [A study of the compilation of commonly used vocabulary.]
魏氷心：編造常用字彙的研究

6.4.1.2. Collection and Analysis (1436–1457)

1436 Chao-ch'ing shih-fan chuan-k'o hsüeh-hsiao Chung-wen-hsi: *Ch'ang-yung tz'u pien-hsi.*—Canton: Kuang-tung jen-min, 1979, 6, 194 p. [Differentiation and analysis of commonly used words.]
肇慶師範專科學校中文系：常用詞辨析

1437 Chia, Ch'i-ming: *Ch'ang-yung tz'u pien-hsi.*—Urumchi: Hsin-chiang jen-min, 1982, [i], 8, 347 p. [Differentiation and analysis of commonly used words.]
賈啓明：常用詞辨析

1438 Ch'en, Chien-ch'iu: Ch'ang-yung miao-hsieh tz'u-hui.—*HWSC* 13, 1978, 64–73; 14, 78–83; 16, 1979, 70–74; 17, 70–73; 21, 1980, 76–83; 22, 1981, 76–81; 23, 82–84. [Commonly used descriptive vocabulary.]
陳劍秋：常用描寫詞彙

1439 Ch'en, Tung-hai & Ushijima, Tokuji: *Chūgokugo jōyō 6000 go.*—Tokyo: Dai-gaku shorin, 1960, 282 p. [6000 commonly used Chinese words.]
陳東海、牛島德次：中國語常用6000語

1440 Chung-kuo wen-tzu kai-ko wei-yüan-hui yen-chiu t'ui-kuang-ch'u: *P'u-t'ung-hua san-ch'ien ch'ang-yung tz'u piao* (ch'u kao). —Peking: Wen-tzu kai-ko, 1962, 179 p. [A list of three thousand commonly used words in the Common Language (first draft).]
中國文字改革委員會研究推廣處：普通話三千常用詞表（初稿）

1441 Hall, Ronald Acott & Whymant, Neville: *The 3000 commonest Chinese terms.*— London: Luzac, 1948, viii, 213 p.

1442 Hu-ho-hao-t'e-shih ti-erh chung-hsüeh yü-wen chiao-yen-tsu: *Hsien-tai Han-yü ch'ang-yung tz'u-hui.*—Huhehot: Nei Meng-ku jen-min, 1979, [i], 250 p. [Commonly used vocabulary of the modern Chinese language.]
呼和浩特市第二中學語文教研組：現代漢語常用詞彙

1443 Hu-nan shih-fan hsüeh-yüan Chung-wen-

hsi: *Ch'ang-yung tz'u-yü hui shih.*—Changsha: Hu-nan chiao-yü, 1982, 65, 494 p. [Collection and explanations of commonly used words and phrases.]
湖南師範學院中文系：常用詞語滙釋

1444   Huo, Li (comp. & transl.): *Han-Ying-O-Te-Fa-Hsi-Jih fen-lei ch'ang-yung tz'u-hui hsüan pien.*—Peking: Shang-wu, 1981, 301 p. [Classification of selected commonly used vocabulary in Chinese, English, Russian, German, French, Spanish, and Japanese.]
霍力編譯：漢英俄德法西日分類常用詞滙選編

1445   Kōsaka, Jun'ichi: *Chūgokugo jōyōgo jiten.*—Tokyo: Kōseikan, 1968; 1982, 15th ed., 9, 307 p. [A dictionary of commonly used words in the Chinese language.]
香坂順一：中國語常用語辭典

1446   Kuang-hsi shih-fan hsüeh-yüan Chung-wen-hsi: *Ch'ang-yung tz'u pien-hsi hsüan pien.*—Nanning: Kuang-hsi jen-min, 1977; 1978, 2nd ed., 10, 278 p. [Differentiation and analysis of selected commonly used words.]
廣西師範學院中文系：常用詞辨析選編

1447   Li, Ch'ih: *Ch'ang-yung tz'u shih-yung fa.*—Hong Kong: Shang-hai shu-chü, 1956, 92 p. [Methods of using commonly used words.]
李池：常用詞使用法

1448   Li, P'u-ying: *Hsien-tai Han-yü ch'ang-yung hsü-tz'u hsüan shih* (1364). [Selection and explanations of commonly used cenematic words in Modern Chinese.]
李譜英：現代漢語常用虛詞選釋

1449   Liu, Hua; *Gendai Chūgoku jōyōgo jiten.*—Tokyo: Kashiwa shobō, 1980, 263 p. [A dictionary of commonly used words in modern China.]
劉華：現代中國常用語辭典

1450   Pei-ching wai-yü hsüeh-yüan: *Wai-kuo-jen shih-yung Han-yü ch'ang-yung tz'u piao.*—Peking: Ditto, 1981, 2, 130 p. [A practical table of Chinese words commonly used by foreigners.]
北京外語學院：外國人實用漢語常用詞表

1451   Shibagaki, Yoshitarō, et al.: Chūgoku jōyō goi.—*Chūgoku gogaku jiten* (0037), 817–853./ CGGG 1957:1, 19–20, Satō Toshiyuki. [Chinese commonly used vocabulary.]
柴垣芳太郎等：中國常用語彙／佐藤利行評

1452   Suzuki, Naoji, et al.: *Chūgokugo jōyō kyoshi jiten.*—Tokyo: Kōnan shoin, 1956, 2, 4, 160, 6 p./ *Chin san-shih nien . . . chien chieh* (0010), 54–55. [A dictionary of Chinese commonly used cenematic words.]
鈴木直治等：中國語常用虛詞辭典

1453   Ts'ao, Chien-ch'en & Ting, Wei-t'ang: *Ch'ang-yung tz'u-yü san-yung tz'u-tien.*—Shanghai: Shao-nien erh-t'ung, 1981, (not seen). [A three-purpose dictionary of commonly used words and phrases.]
曹劍塵、丁慰堂：常用詞語三用詞典

1454   Wang, Kuo-chang & An, Ju-p'an: *Ch'ang-yang tz'u yung-fa li shih.*—Peking: Chung-kuo jen-min ta-hsüeh, 1981, [2], 12, 459 p. [Examples with explanations of usages of commonly used words.]
王國璋、安汝磐：常用詞用法例釋

1455   Wang, Tzu-ch'iang: *Ch'ang-yung hsin tz'u li shih.*—Hangchow: Che-chiang jen-min, 1981, [ii], 83 p.; 1982, repr. [Examples with explanations of commonly used new words.]
王自强：常用新詞例釋

1456   Waseda Daigaku Gogaku Kyōiku Kenkyūshitsu: *Han-yü san-ch'ien ch'ang-yung tz'u piao.*—Tokyo: Ditto, 1962, 7, 240 p. [A list of three thousand commonly used Chinese words.]
早稻田大學語學教育研究室：漢語三千常用詞表

1457 Yen, T'ien-chan: *Ch'ang-yung tz'u-yü li chieh.*—Peking: Shang-wu, 1959, 1st ed.; 1960, new ed.; 1960, 1st repr., 13, 176 p./ *CKYW* 1959:6, 287–288, Lao Ning; *YWHH* 1959:7, 35–36, Hsiang Jo. [Examples with explanations of commonly used words and phrases.]
燕天展：常用詞語例解／勞寧評，向若評

6.4.2. Commonly Used Characters (1458–1500)
6.4.2.1. General Studies (1458–1463)

1458 Fu, Pao-chen: Han-tzu chi-pen tzu yen-chiu te ch'u-pu.—*CYYMC* 2:2, 1930, 1–4. [The first step of the study on Chinese basic characters.]
傅葆臻：漢字基本字研究的初步

1459 Huang, Chüeh-min: Ch'ang-yung tzu yen-chiu te tsung chien-t'ao.—*CT* 3:8, 1947, 19–25. [A general review and discussion of the study on commonly used characters.]
黃覺民：常用字研究的總檢討

1460 Pai, Han: T'an chi-pen Han-tzu.—*KWTCK* 3:1, 1944, 19–21. [A discussion of basic Chinese characters.]
柏寒：談基本漢字

1461 Ta, Fang: Ch'ang-yung tzu yü ch'ang-yung tz'u shu-liang te t'ui-ts'e.—*TLTC* 6:2, 1953, 1–6; *Yü-yen wen-tzu-hsüeh* (0080), 13–18. [An estimation of the quantity of commonly used characters and commonly used words.]
大方：常用字與常用詞數量的推測

1462 Yang, Hung-ch'ang: Kuan-yü ch'ang-yung tzu.—*SCCY* 25, 1947, 9–11. [Concerning commonly used characters.]
楊鴻昌：關於常用字

1463 Yano, Harutaka: *Jōyō Chūgokugo ji ni tsuite.*—*OBRD* 2, 1970, 118–141. [On commonly used characters in the Chinese language.]
矢野春隆：常用中國語字に就て

6.4.2.2. Collection and Analysis (1464–1500)

1464 Anonymous: *Chung-kuo ch'ang-yung tzu piao.*—N.p., 194?, 37 p. [A table of commonly used Chinese characters.]/ 1400 characters.
無名氏：中國常用字表

1465 Anonymous: *Ch'ang-yung Han-tzu p'in-yin piao.*—Hong Kong: Chung-hua, 1976, [ii], 60 p. [A table in the Pinyin system of commonly used Chinese characters.]
無名氏：常用漢字拼音表

1466 Chang, Chih-kung (ed. in chief): *Hsien-tai Han-yü* (1316), 392–422: A table of commonly used Modern Chinese characters. [Modern Chinese.]
張志公主編：現代漢語／392-422: 現代常用漢字表

1467 Chang, Hsiao-yü: *Ch'ang-yung tzu pien.*—Taipei: Kuo-yü jih-pao-she, 1958, 153 p. [Differentiation of commonly used characters.]
張孝裕：常用字辨

1468 Chang, Hsüan: *The etymologies of 3000 Chinese characters in common usage.*—Hong Kong: Hong Kong U. Press; London: Oxford U. Press, 1968, xii, 960 p./ *HKCW* 3:2, 1970, 575–577, Ch'ang Tsung-hao; *JAS* 29:4, 1970, 911–912, Wang Fang-yu; *AM* 15:2, 1970, 246–247, H.C. Chang; *JCL* 1:3, 1973, 479–492, Paul L–M. Serruys; *JCLTA* 8:1, 1973, 38–41, James R. Landers.
張瑄：中文常用三千字形義釋／常宗豪評

1469 Chang, Po-yü: Chiao pu *Chu-yin kuo tzu ch'ang-yung tzu-mo piao.*—*SHJ* 229, 1974, 1–8. [Corrigenda and addenda to *Chu-yin kuo tzu ch'ang-yung tzu-mo piao.*]
張博宇：校補『注音國字常用字模表』

1470   Ch'en, T'ao & Tung, Chih-kuo: *Hsüeh-sheng ch'ang-yung Han-tzu ch'ien shih.* —Tientsin: T'ien-chin jen-min, 1981, [ii], 340 p. [Simple explanations of students' commonly used Chinese characters.]
陳濤、董治國：學生常用漢字淺釋

1471   Ch'i, T'ieh-hen, et al.: *Kuo-yin ch'ang-yung tzu-tien.*—Taipei: Fu-hsing shu-chü, 1961, 2, 2, 43, 324, 14, 9 p., illus. [A commonly used character dictionary in the National Language pronunciation.]
齊鐵恨等：國音常用字典

1472   Chiao-yü-pu Kuo-yü t'ung-i ch'ou-pei wei-yüan-hui: *Kuo-yin ch'ang-yung tzu-hui.* —Shanghai: Shang-wu, 1932; 1939, 6th ed., iv, 8, xx, 286, 4, 76 p. [A glossary of commonly used characters in the National Language pronunciation.]
教育部國語統一籌備委員會：國音常用字彙

1473   Chiao-yü-pu: *Ch'ang-yung kuo-tzu piao-chun tzu-t'i piao.*—Taipei: Cheng-chung, 1979; 1982, rev. ed., 6, 3, 250 p. [A table of standard character forms for commonly used Chinese characters.]
教育部：常用國字標準字體表

1474   Chiao-yü-pu She-hui chiao-yu-szu: *Kuo-min ch'ang-yung tzu piao ch'u kao.* —Taipei: Ditto, 1975, 3, 337 p. [A preliminary draft for a table of citizens' commonly used characters.]
教育部社會教育司：國民常用字表初稿

1475   Chiao-yü-pu She-hui chiao-yü-szu: *Tz'u-yung kuo-tzu piao-chun tzu-t'i piao (I piao).* Fu *I-t'i tzu piao kao (Ping piao).* —Taipei: Ditto, 1981, 5, 395, 143 p. [A table of standard character forms for less commonly used Chinese characters (Table B). With a draft for a table of variant characters (Table C).]
教育部社會教育司：次用國字標準字體表（乙表） 附異體字表稿（丙表）

1476   Chung-kuo ta tz'u-tien pien-tsuan-ch'u:

Ch'ang-yung Han-tzu san-ch'ien wu-pai tzu piao.—Peking: Pei-ching shih-fan ta-hsüeh, 1952, [i], 50 p. [A table of thirty-five thousand commonly used Chinese characters.]
中國大辭典編纂處：常用漢字三千五百字表

1477   Hsiao-hsüeh chiao-yü yen-chiu-she: *Hsiang-kang chung-hsüeh ju-hsüeh shih san-ch'ien Chung-wen tzu-hui.*—Hong Kong: Min-sheng, 1962, 3, 20, 205 p. [A glossary of three thousand Chinese characters for the entry examinations of middle schools in Hong Kong.]
小學教育研究社：香港中學入學試三千中文字彙

1478   Hsin-hua tz'u-shu-she: *Ch'ang-yung tzu yung-fa chü-li.*—Peking: Jen-min chiao-yü, 1953, 12, 304 p., illus./ Later rev. as (1479). [Examples with the uses of commonly used characters.]
新華辭書社：常用字用法舉例

1479   Hsin-hua tz'u-shu-she: *Ch'ang-yung tzu-hui.*—Peking: Shang-wu, 1959, 3rd ed., xiv, 309, 35 p./ A rev. ed. of (1478). [A glossary of commonly used characters.]
新華辭書社：常用字滙

1480   Hsü, Lo-szu, et al.: *Hsin-chia-po Hua-yü ch'ang-yung tzu yen-chiu.*—Singapore: Nan-yang ta-hsüeh Hua-yü yen-chiu chung-hsin, 1976, 113 p. [A study on the commonly used characters in the Chinese language spoken in Singapore.]/ 2000 characters used in local newspapers.
許樂斯等：新加坡華語常用字研究

1481   Huang, Chih-shang: *Kuo-yin ch'ang-yung tzu-hui.*—*TSPL* 1:5, 1932, 83–88. [(A review of) *Kuo-yin ch'ang-yung tzu-hui* (1472).]
黃志尚：國音常用字彙

1482   Huang, Po-jung & Liao, Hsü-tung (eds. in chief): *Hsien-tai Han-yü* (1331), Vol. I, 123–152: A table of commonly used characters belonging to the same rhymes.

[Modern Chinese.]
黄伯榮、廖序東主編：現代漢語／上册，123–152：常用同韻字表

1483 Hung, Shen: I-ch'ien i-pai-ko chi-pen Han-tzu shih-yung fa.—*TFTC* 32:14, 1935, 5–19. [Practical uses of one thousand one hundred basic Chinese characters.]
洪深：一千一百個基本漢字實用法

1484 Hung, Shen: I-ch'ien i-pai-ko chi-pen Han-tzu.—*CNWH* 3:3, 1936, 7–12. [One thousand one hundred basic Chinese characters.]
洪深：一千一百個基本漢字

1485 Ku, Hsing-hua: *Ch'ang-yung Han-tzu yin hsing pien-hsi shou-ts'e.*—Fukien: Fu-chien chiao-yü, 1981, 47, 348 p. [A handbook for differentiating and analyzing the sounds and forms of commonly used Chinese characters.]
顧星華：常用漢字音形辨析手册

1486 Kuo-li pien-i-kuan: *Kuo-min hsüeh-hsiao ch'ang-yung tzu-hui yen-chiu.*—Taipei: Chung-hua, 1967, 2 pts., 2, [i], 50; 244, 38, 36 p. [A study on the commonly used vocabulary in (Chinese) national schools.]
國立編譯館：國民學校常用字彙研究

1487 Li, Chin-hsi: *Kuo-yin ch'ang-yung tzu-hui.*—Shanghai: Shang-wu, 1949, rev. & enl. ed., 565 p. [A glossary of commonly used characters in National Language pronunciation.]
黎錦熙：國音常用字彙

1488 Mao, Sung-nien: *Hai-wai Hua-wen ch'ang-yung tzu tzu-tien.*—Taipei: Ch'iao-wu wei-yüan-hui Chung-hua han-shou hsüeh-hsiao, 1977, 6, 342 p. [A dictionary of commonly used characters for overseas Chinese.]
毛松年：海外華文常用字字典

1489 Nei Meng-ku shih-yüan fu-chung Yü-wen chiao-yen-tsu: *Ch'ang-yung Han-tzu tzu-hui.*—Huhehot: Nei Meng-ku jen-min, 1973, 157 p. [A glossary of commonly used Chinese characters.]
內蒙古師院附中語文教研組：常用漢字字滙

1490 Ōsaka Gaigokugo Daigaku Chūgoku Gogaku Kenkyūshitsu: *Chūgoku jōyō jiten.*—Tokyo: Kōnan shoin, 1953, 141 p./ *Chin san-shih nien . . . chien chieh* (0010), 36. [A dictionary of commonly used characters in China.]
大阪外國語大學中國語學研究室：中國常用字典

1491 Pei-ching chiao-yü hsüeh-yüan chiao-ts'ai chiao-yen pu: *Ch'ang-yung Han-tzu piao.*—Peking: Jen-min, 1978, 116 p. [A table of commonly used Chinese characters.]
北京教育學院教材教研部：常用漢字表

1492 Po, Yü: *Kuo-min ch'ang-yung tzu piao ch'u-kao tu hou.*—*CKYT* 38:6, 1976, 25–26. [After reading *Kuo-min ch'ang-yung tzu piao ch'u-kao* (1474).] / A review.
伯禹：『國民常用字表初稿』讀後

1493 Ts'ai, Ch'ang-chin: *Tang-tai ch'ang-yung tzu yen-chiu.*—Taichung: Tung-hai U., 1978, 3, 545, 7 p./ Unpubl. M.A. thesis. [A study of contemporary commonly used characters.]
蔡常錦：當代常用字研究

1494 Ts'ai, Lo-sheng: *Ch'ang-yung tzu hsüan.*—Chengtu: Szu-ch'uan-sheng chiao-yü k'o-hsüeh-kuan, 1961, 72 p. [A selection of commonly used characters.]
蔡樂生：常用字選

1495 Tsujimoto, Haruhiko: Chūgoku jōyōji hyō.—*Chūgoku gogaku jiten* (0037), 1082–1084. [A table of commonly used Chinese characters.]
辻本春彦：中國常用字表

1496 Tung-pei jen-min ch'u-pan-she: *Ch'ang-yung tzu piao.*—Shenyang: Ditto, 1952, [i], 41 p. [A table of commonly used

characters.]
東北人民出版社：常用字表

1497   Tung, Po-fang: Chi-ko lai-li pu-ming
te ch'ang-yung tzu.—*CWY* 7, 1980, 88–
96. [Several commonly used characters
of unclear origins.]
董伯枋：幾個來歷不明的常用字

1498   Wang, T'ien-ch'ang: Pu pan *Ch'ang-
yung kuo-tzu piao-chun tzu-t'i piao*
p'ing chieh.—*SHJ* 389, 1980, 1–6. [A
critical   introduction   to   *Ch'ang-yung
kuo-tzu piao-chun tzu-t'i piao* (1473)
published by the Ministry of Education.]
王天昌：部頒『常用國字標準字體表』評介

1499   Wen-hua hsüeh-hsi-she: *Wen-hua hsüeh-
hsi ch'ang-yung tzu piao.*—Shanghai:
Hua-tung jen-min, 1951, 1st ed.; 1952,
8th ed., [iv], 60 p. [A table of commonly
used characters for learning (Chinese)
culture.]
文化學習社：文化學習常用字表

1500   Wu, I-keng & Wu, Yang: *San-ch'ien
ch'ang-yung   tzu   yung-fa.*—Foochow:
Fu-chien jen-min, 1958, 20, 109 p.;
Hong Kong: Lo-t'o, 1977, 21, 138 p.
[Methods of usages for three thousand
commonly used characters.]
吳怡耕、吳揚：三千常用字用法

6.5.   Dialect Vocabulary (1501–1515)
6.5.1.   General Problems and Studies
(1501–1511)

1501   Astrakhan, R.B.: *Formivoranie leksiki
putunkhua—Problemy   dialektnykh   isto-
chnikov leksiki natsional'nogo iazyka.*—
Moscow: Moskovskii   Gosudarstvenyi
Universitet, Institut Stran Azii i Afriki,
1980, (not seen)./ Unpubl. doc. diss.
[The creation of a P'u-t'ung-hua vocabulary
—Problems of dialectal sources in a
National Language vocabulary.]

1502   Ch'ang, Chün-feng, et al.: Kuan-yü
wen-i tso-p'in shih-yung fang-yen t'u-yü

te   wen-t'i.—*CKYW*   1959:7,   326–328.
[Concerning the problem of using dialect
words and patois in literary works.]
常峻峯等：關於文藝作品使用方言土語的問題

1503   Chou, Ting-i: Lun wen-i tso-p'in chung
te   fang-yen   t'u-yü.—*CKYW*   1959:5,
222–225. [On dialect words and patois
(found) in literary works.]
周定一：論文藝作品中的方言土語

1504   Lao, She: T'u-hua yü P'u-t'ung-hua.
—*CKYW* 1959:9, 421. [Patois and the
Common Language.]
老舍：土話與普通話

1505   Li,   Ch'en-tung: Lun   fang-yen   yü
wen-hsüeh te kuan-hsi.—*CKYT* 6:6, 1960,
7–15.   [On   the   relationship   between
dialects and literature.]
李辰冬：論方言與文學的關係

1506   Li, Hsing-chien: Fang-yen tz'u-yü tsai
hsün-ku   chung   te   tso-yung.—*NKHP*
1981:5.   [The   functions   of   dialect
words and phrases in Chinese traditional
semantics.]
李行健：方言詞語在訓詁中的作用

1507   Li,   Hsing-wen: Kuan-yü   yün-yung
fang-yen.—*JMWH* 1951:3, 56. [Concerning
the uses of dialect words.]
李興文：關於運用方言

1508   Liu, Chung-ho: Fang-yen yü hsieh-tso.
—*CKYT* 7:4, 1960, 9–11. [Dialects and
creative writing.]
劉中和：方言與寫作

1509   Liu,   Hou-ch'un: Fang-yen,   shu-yü,
su-yü.—*CKYT*   10:2,   1962,   14–18.
[Dialects, technical terms, and popular
sayings.]
劉厚醇：方言、術語、俗語

1510   Sun, Ch'ang-hsü: *Han-yü tz'u-hui* (0165),
Chap. 19: Dialect vocabulary. [Chinese
lexicons.]
孫常敘：漢語詞彙／第十九章：方言詞彙

1511   T'ien, Shui: Kuan-yü fang-yen tz'u
te wen-t'i.—*YWCS* 1958:5, 33—36; *Hsien-
tai Han-yü . . . tzu-liao* (0064), 323—327.
[Problems concerning dialect words.]
天水：關於方言詞的問題

6.5.2. Collection and Analysis (1512–1515)

1512   Fu, Ch'ao-yang: *Fang-yen tz'u li-shih.*
—Peking: T'ung-su tu-wu, 1957, [i],
348 p.; *Yü-wen hui-pien* (0058), 38:124./
CKYW 1957:11, 47—48, Hui, Mao Hsi-
p'ang, I Ting; *YSDR* 9:2, 1958, 26—31,
Hatano Tarō. [Examples with explanations
of dialect words.]
傅朝陽：方言詞例釋／灰、毛西旁、一丁評，
波多野太郎評

1513   Fu, Ch'ao-yang: *Fang-yen hsiao tz'u-
tien.*—Chinan: Shan-tung jen-min, 1982,
(not seen). [A small dialect dictionary.]
傅朝陽：方言小詞典

1514   Pei-ching ta-hsüeh Chung-kuo yü-yen
wen-hsüeh-hsi Yü-yen-hsüeh chiao-yen-shih:
Han-yü fang-yin tzu-hui.—Peking: Wen-tzu
kai-ko, 1962, xiii, 272 p./ *CKYW* 1963:2,
176—182, Shih Wen-t'ao; *Orbis* 15, 1966,
110, Paul Yang; *Lg* 45, 1969, 687—697,
Anatole Lyovin. [A glossary of characters
with Chinese dialect pronunciations.]/ 17
localities: Peking, Chinan, Sian, Taiyuan,
Hankow, Chengtu, Yangchow, Soochow,
Wenchow, Changsha, Shuangfeng, Nanchang,
Meihsien, Canton, Amoy, Chaochow, Foochow. The phonology of each locality
is given at the beginning of the book.
北京大學中國語言文學系語言學教研室：漢語
方音字滙／施文濤評

1515   Pei-ching ta-hsüeh Chung-kuo yü-yen
wen-hsüeh-hsi Yü-yen-hsüeh chiao-yen-shih:
Han-yü fang-yen tz'u-hui.—Peking: Wen-
tzu kai-ko, 1964, xxvi, 460 p./ *CKYW*
1965:1, 60—64, Hsü Pao-hua; *TYGH*
48:1, 1965, 144—146, Tōdō Akiyasu;
Orbis 15, 1966, 110, Paul Yang. [A
lexicon of Chinese dialects.]/ 18 localities:
Peking, Chinan, Shenyang, Sian, Chengtu,

Kunming, Hofei, Yangchow, Soochow,
Wenchow, Changsha, Nanchang, Meihsien,
Canton, Yangchiang, Amoy, Chaochow,
Foochow. The phonology of each locality
is given at the beginning of the book.
北京大學中國語言文學系語言學教研室：漢語
方言詞滙／許寶華評，藤堂明保評

6.6. Loan-words (1516–1575)
6.6.1. Definition and Problems (1516–1529)

1516   Chang, Ch'ing-yüan: Ts'ung hsien-tai
Han-yü wai-lai-yü ch'u-pu fen-hsi chung
te-tao te chi-tien jen-shih.—*YLT* 1, 1957,
149—169. [Several points of knowledge
obtained from a preliminary analysis of
foreign loan-words in Modern Chinese.]
張清源：從現代漢語外來語初步分析中得到的
幾點認識

1517   Chao, I-po: Kuan-yü Han-yü wai-lai
tz'u te chi-ko wen-t'i.—*YWHH* 1958:3,
8—10. [Several problems concerning
foreign loan-words in Chinese.]
趙懌伯：關於漢語外來詞的幾個問題

1518   Chao, Yuen Ren: Interlingual and
interdialectal borrowings in Chinese.—
*Studies in general and Oriental linguistics:
Presented to Shirō Hattori on the occasion
of his sixtieth birthday* (Ed. by Jakobson,
Roman & Kawamoto, Shigeo, Tokyo: TEC
Company, 1970), 39—51; *Aspects of
Chinese sociolinguistics* (0048), 184—200.
〔趙元任：中外借詞跟中國方言之間的借詞〕

1519   Ch'en, Chung: Han-yü chieh-tz'u yen-
chiu chung te chi-ko wen-t'i.—*CHHK*
1963:1, 42—46. [Several problems in
studying Chinese loan-words.]
陳忠：漢語借詞研究中的幾個問題

1520   Ch'en, Fa-wei: Han-yü chieh-tz'u t'an-
t'ao.—*HPTS* 1958:3, 65—72. [An
exploratory discussion of Chinese loan-
words.]
陳法衞：漢語借詞探討

1521   Ch'en, Yüan: *Yü-yen yü she-hui sheng-*

huo.—Hong Kong: San-lien, 1979, [i], 2, 120 p./ 62–71: Loan-words. [Language and social life.]

陳原：語言與社會生活／62-71：借詞—外來詞

1522   Hu, Shuang-pao: Tui *Hsien-tai Han-yü wai-lai tz'u yen-chiu* te chi-tien pu-ch'ung i-chien.—*CKYW* 1958:7, 348–349. [Several additional opinions on *Hsien-tai Han-yü wai-lai tz'u yen-chiu* (1547).]

胡雙寶：對『現代漢語外來詞研究』的幾點補充意見

1523   Kao, Kuang-yü: T'an wai-lai-yü ming-tz'u te lai-yüan ho ch'u-li.—*PY* 1957:4, 3–4. [A discussion on the origin and handling of foreign loan-words.]

高光宇：談外來語名詞的來源和處理

1524   Kao, Tzu-jung & Chang, Ying-te: I-i tz'u shih wai-lai tz'u ma?—*YWHH* 1958:3, 10. [Are freely translated words foreign loan-words?]

高子榮、張應德：意譯詞是外來詞嗎？

1525   Liu, Hsi-yin: I-i pu-shih wai-lai-yü.—*CKYW* 1958:6, 295. [Free translations are not foreign loan-words.]

劉喜印：意譯不是外來語

1526   Liu, Tse-hsien: Han-yü pu-neng jung-na wai-lai-yü ma? —1957:5, 40–41. [Is Chinese unable to tolerate foreign loan-words?]

劉澤先：漢語不能容納外來語嗎？

1527   Nakazawa, Shinzō: Gendai Chūgokugo ni okeru gairaigo no kihan mondai.—*NSGS* 1965:3, 1–20. [The problem of standardization of foreign loan-words in Modern Chinese.]

中澤信三：現代中國語における外來語の規範問題

1528   Novotná, Zdeňka: Linguistic factors of the low adaptability of loan-words to the lexical system of Modern Chinese. —*MS* 26, 1967, 103–118.

1529   Torii, Katsuyuki: Kyōtsūgo hattatsu shijō no ichi sokumen—Gairaigo no mondai ni tsuite—*Chūken nōto* 9, 1962, 1–10. [A sideview of the history of the development of the Common Language —concerning the problem of foreign loan-words (in Chinese).]

鳥居克之：共通語發達史上の一側面——外來語の問題について

6.6.2.   Methods of Transcription (1530–1534)

1530   Chou, Yu-kuang: Wai-lai tz'u p'in-hsieh-fa wen-t'i.—*CKYW* 1959:3, 106–113, 139. [The problems in the orthography for foreign loan-words.]

周有光：外來詞拼寫法問題

1531   Ishiyama, Akeo: Chūgokugo ni okeru shakushi no hyōkihō ni tsuite—Eigo.—*HKDKZ* 8, 1974, 1–17. [On methods of (phonetic) notation for loan-words in Chinese—English (loan-words).]

石山曙生：中國語における借詞の表記法について——英語

1532   Liang, Jung-jo: Ju-ho kai-shan wai-lai-yü te fan-i.—*San-min chu-i pan-yüeh k'an* 36, 1954, 9–15. [How to improve the translation of foreign loan-words?]

梁容若：如何改善外來語的翻譯？

1533   Liang, Jung-jo: Ju-ho kai-shan Chung-wen li wai-lai-yü te fan-i.—*THHP* 1:1, 1959, 165–184. [How to improve the Chinese translation of foreign loan-words?]

梁容若：如何改善中文裡外來語的翻譯？

1534   Yi, Won-shik: Hyŏndae Chunggukŏ ŭi waeraeŏ pyoki.—*Chungguk hakpo* 8, 1968, 83–92. [The transcription of foreign loan-words in Modern Chinese.]

李元植：現代中國語의外來語表記

6.6.3.   General Studies (1535–1566)

1535   Brough, John: Buddhist Chinese etymological notes.—*BSOAS* 38:3, 1975, 581–585.

1536　Chang, Ch'ing-ch'ang: Man t'an Han-yü chung te Meng-yü chieh-tz'u.—*CKYW* 1978:3, 196–198. [A random discussion on Mongolian loan-words in Chinese.]
張清常：漫談漢語中的蒙語借詞

1537　Chang, Ying-te: Hsien-tai Han-yü chung neng yu che-ma to Jih-yu chieh-tz'u ma? —*CKYW* 1958:6, 299. [Is Modern Chinese able to have so many Japanese loan-words?]
張應德：現代漢語中能有這麼多日語借詞嗎？

1538　Cheng, Tien: T'an hsien-tai Han-yü chung te Jih-yü tz'u-hui.—*CKYW* 1958:2, 95, 94. [A discussion on Japanese vocabulary in Modern Chinese.]
鄭奠：談現代漢語中的日語詞彙

1539　Ch'ih, P'ing: Han-yü chung te wai-lai-yü.—*PY* 1957:4, 4–6; *Hsien-tai Han-yü . . . tzu-liao* (0064), 357–360. [Loan-words in the Chinese language.]
持平：漢語中的外來語

1540　Chou, Fa-kao: Chung-kuo-yü te chieh-tzu.—*Chung-kuo yü-wen yen-chiu* (0051), 99–110. [Loan-words of the Chinese language.]
周法高：中國語的借字

1541　Fang, Chuang-yu: Hsiung-nu yü-yen k'ao.—*KHCK* 2:4, 1930, 693–740. [A study on the Hsiung-nu language.]/ Hsiung-nu words in Chinese.
方壯猷：匈奴語言考

1542　Heřmanová, Zdeňka: *Příspěvky ke studiu výpůjček a hybridních slov v moderní čínštině.*—Prague: Orientální ústavu Československé akademie věd, 1966, iv, 258, vii p./ Unpubl. doc. diss. [Contributions to the study of loan-words and hybrid words in Modern Chinese.]

1543　Hu, Hsing-chih: *Wai-lai-yü tz'u-tien.*—Shanghai: T'ien-ma shu-tien, 1936, 412 p. [A dictionary of foreign loan-words.]
胡行之：外來語辭典

1544　Huang, Hsüan-fan: T'an Chung-kuo yü-wen chung te wai-lai-yü.—*Yü-yen-hsüeh yen-chiu lun-ts'ung* (0065), 191–200. [A discussion on foreign loan-words in the language and writing of China.]
黃宣範：談中國語文中的外來語

1545　Iida, Kōji: Chūgokugo ni shakuyōsareta Nihon no kindai yakugo.—*Gengo Kagaku* 3, 1967, 25–40. [Borrowings in the Chinese language of Modern Japanese translations of words.]
井田好治：中國語に借用された日本の近代譯語

1546　Kan, Ch'i-t'ing: Shih t'an Han-yü chung te shao-shu min-tsu yü-yen chieh-tz'u.—*HCYY* 1980, 116–119. [A preliminary discussion of minority language loan-words in the Chinese language.]
甘祺庭：試談漢語中的少數民族語言借詞

1547　Kao, Ming-k'ai & Liu, Cheng-t'an: *Hsien-tai Han-yü wai-lai tz'u yen-chiu.* —Peking: Wen-tzu kai-ko, 1958, v, 189 p./ *RBS* 4, 1958, 562, J. Chmielewski; *CKYW* 1958:7, 347–349, Shao Jung-fen, Hu Shuang-pao. [A study of foreign loan-words in Modern Chinese.]
高名凱、劉正琰：現代漢語外來詞研究／邵榮芬評，胡雙寶評

1548　Kao, Tseng-liang: Jo-kan chieh-tz'u t'an yüan.—*YCYY* 1979, Feb., 117–122. [Tracing the origins of certain loan-words.]
高增良：若干借詞探源

1549　Kuo-yü jih-pao ch'u-pan-pu pien-i-tsu: *Kuo-yü jih-pao wai-lai-yü tz'u-tien.*—Taipei: Ditto, 1981, 16, 42, 532 p. [The National Language Daily News dictionary of foreign loan-words.]
國語日報出版部編譯組：國語日報外來語詞典

1550　Ladstätter, Otto: Zur Integration abendländischen Begriffs-und Wortgutes ins Chinesische, Pt. 1: Versuch einer typologischen Klassifikation.—*OE* 14:1,

1967, 1–26./ *RBS* 12–13, 1966–1967, 650, K. Kaden.

1551   Liu, Cheng-t'an: *Han-yü wai-lai tz'u tz'u-tien* hsü-yen.—*TSYC* 1981:3, 135–139. [A preface to *Han-yü wai-lai tz'u tz'u-tien* (A dictionary of Chinese loan-words).] / See (1562).
劉正琰：『漢語外來詞辭典』序言

1552   Lo, Ch'ang-p'ei: Chung-kuo-yü li te chieh-tzu.—*Chung-kuo-jen yü Chung-kuo-wen* (Shanghai: K'ai-ming, 1945), 85–92. [Loan-words in the Chinese language.]
羅常培：中國語裏的借字—『中國人與中國文』

1553   Novotná, Zdeňka: Contributions to the study of loan-words and hybrid words in Modern Chinese.—*AO* 36, 1968, 295–325; 37, 1969, 48–75./ *RBS* 12–13, 1966–1967, 651, V. Alleton.

1554   P'an, Yün-chung: Ya-p'ien chan-cheng i-ch'ien Han-yü chung te chieh-tz'u.—*CSTH* 1957:3, 98–113. [Loan-words in the Chinese language before the Opium War.]
潘允中：鴉片戰爭以前漢語中的借詞

1555   Shao, Jung-fen: P'ing *Hsien-tai Han-yü wai-lai tz'u yen-chiu.*—*CKYW* 1958:7, 347–348. [A review of *Hsien-tai Han-yü wai-lai tz'u yen-chiu* (1547).]
邵榮芬：評『現代漢語外來詞研究』

1556   Sun, Ch'ang-hsü: *Han-yü tz'u-hui* (0165), Chap. 21: Foreign loan-words. [Chinese lexicons.]
孫常叙：漢語詞彙／第二十一章：外來語詞彙

1557   Tai, I-hsüan: A-la-po ming-ch'eng tsai Chung-kuo ku chi chung te chuan-pien.—*Hsien-tai shih-hsüeh* 1:1, 1933, 203–216. [The transformation of Arabic names (as found) in ancient texts of China.]
戴裔煊：阿拉伯名稱在中國古籍中的轉變

1558   Takahashi, Moritaka: Chūgokugo ni

haitta Yōroppago.—*Chūgoku gogaku jiten* (0037), 1043–1045. [European loan-words in the Chinese language.]
高橋盛孝：中國語に入ったヨーロッパ語

1559   Takahashi, Moritaka: Genkyoku ni arawareta kogo to shinji.—*CGGG* 1961:8, 1–2. [Tartar words and inserted characters appearing in Yüan dramas.] / Mongolian and Sanskrit words.
高橋盛孝：元曲に現れた胡語と襯字

1560   Tchen, Ting-ming [Ch'en, Ting-min]: L'emprunt des mots étrangers dans la langue chinoise.—*Proceedings of the Third International Congress of Phonetic Sciences* (Gant, 1938), 392–395.
〔陳定民〕

1561   Ts'ai, Mei-piao: Yüan-tai tsa-chü chung te jo-kan i-yü.—*CKYW* 1957:1, 34–36, 33. [Certain translated words found in dramas of Yüan times.]
蔡美彪：元代雜劇中的若干譯語

1562   Ts'en, Ch'i-hsiang: *Han-yü wai-lai tz'u tz'u-tien* hsü-yen.—*CYY* 2, 1981, 125–127. [A preface to *Han-yü wai-lai tz'u tz'u-tien.*] / See (1551).
岑麒祥：『漢語外來詞辭典』序言

1563   Wang, Chia-chün: T'ien-chin liu-hsing yü chung chih wai-lai-yü shih i.—*T'ien-chin wen-hua* 2, 1948, 9; 3, 9. [Explanation of the meanings of foreign loan-words (found) in the contemporary speech of Tientsin.]
王家俊：天津流行語中之外來語釋義

1564   Wang, Li-ta: Hsien-tai Han-yü chung ts'ung Jih-yü chieh-lai te tz'u-hui.—*CKYW* 1958:2, 90–94. [Japanese loan-words in Modern Chinese.]
王立達：現代漢語中從日語借來的詞彙

1565   Wang, Li-ta: Ts'ung kou-tz'u-fa shang pien-pieh pu-liao Jih-yü chieh-tz'u (ho Chang Ying-te t'ung-chih shang-t'ao Han-yü li Jih-yü chieh-tz'u wen-t'i).—

CKYW 1958:9, 442–443. [One can not recognize Japanese loan-words from identification of the methods of word formation (a discussion with colleague Chan Ying-te (1537) on the problem of Japanese loan-words in Chinese).]
王立達：從構詞法上辨別不了日語借詞（和張應德同志商討漢語裏日語借詞問題）

1566 Yang, Yün-yüan: Chung-kuo yü-wen chung te Yin-tu tz'u-yü shih li.—*TFTC* 13:7, 1980, 35–41. [Examples with explanations of words and phrases from India in the Chinese language.]
楊允元：中國語文中的印度詞語釋例

6.6.4. Studies on Individual Loan-words (1567–1575)

1567 Chi, Hsien-lin: Fu-t'u yü fo.—*BIHP* 20, 1948, 93–105. [*Fu-t'u* and *fo.*] / Tracing the Chinese transliterations for the word 'Buddha'.] / See (1571)
季羨林：浮屠與佛

1568 Chmielewski, Janusz: The problem of early loan-words in Chinese as illustrated by the word *p'u-t'ao.*—*RO* 22:2, 1958, 7–45./ *RBS* 4, 1958, 563, U. Unger.

1569 Chmielewski, Janusz. Transl. by Kao, Ming-k'ai: I p'u-t'ao i-tz'u wei li lun ku-tai Han-yü te chieh-tz'u wen-t'i.— *PCTH* 1957:1, 71–81. [The problem of early loan-words in Chinese as illustrated by the word *p'u-t'ao*.] (1568)
赫邁萊夫斯基著，高名凱譯：以『葡萄』一詞爲例論古代漢語的借詞問題

1570 Chmielewski, Janusz: Two early loan-words in Chinese.—*RO* 24:2, 1960, 65–86./ *RBS* 6, 1960, 413, W. Simon; The two words are *mu-su* 'lucerne' and *shan-hu* 'coral'.
〔苜蓿、珊瑚〕

1571 Chou, Fa-kao: Lun fu-t'u yü fo.— *BIHP* 27, 1956, 197–203; *Chung-kuo yü-yen-hsüeh lun-wen-chi* (0053), 283–

289./ *RBS* 2, 1956, 376, C.Y. Wu. [On *Fu-t'u yü fo* (1567).]
周法高：論『浮屠與佛』

1572 Franke, Herbert: Das chinesische Wort 'mummy'.—*Oriens* 10, 1957, 253–257./ *RBS* 3, 1957, 594, P. van der Loon.
〔木乃伊〕

1573 Maenchen-Helfin, Otto: Are Chinese *hsi-p'i* and *kuo-lo* IE loan-words? —*Lg* 21, 1945, 256–260.
〔犀毗、廓落〕

1574 Sedláček, Kamil: The Chinese term *ch'ai-fa* 差發 a Tibetan loan-word? —*MS* 28, 1969, 215–229.

1575 Serruys, Henry: Two loan-words in fifteenth century Chinese.—*MS* 26, 1967, 89–96./ The two words are *ta-hu* 'fur coat with the fur outside' and *i-sa* 'a kind of robe'.
〔裕護、一撒〕

6.7. New Terms (Neologisms) (1576–1638)
6.7.1. New Terms Before 1949 (1576–1586)

1576 Committee of the Educational Association of China: *Technical terms: English and Chinese.*—Shanghai: Methodist Publishing House, 1910, 5, [ii], 352 p.
〔教育會：術語辭彙〕

1577 Hsing, Mo-ch'ing: *Hsin ming-tz'u tz'u-tien.*—Shanghai: Hsin sheng-ming shu-chü, 1934, 24, 176 p. [A dictionary of new terms.]
邢墨卿：新名詞辭典

1578 Ku, Chih-chien: *Hsin chih-shih tz'u-tien.*—Shanghai: Pei-hsin, 1935, 364 p.; 1948, rev. & enl. ed., 629 p. [A dictionary of new knowledge.] / Chinese-English.
顧志堅：新知識辭典

1579 Li, Ting-sheng: *Hsien-tai yü tz'u-tien.*—Shanghai: Kuang-ming shu-chü, 1933, 71, 722 p.; 1941, 8th ed., [77], 722 p.

[A modern language dictionary.] / New terms.

李鼎聲：現代語辭典

1580   Mateer, Ada Haven: *New terms for new ideas, a study of the Chinese newspaper.*—Shanghai: Presbyterian Mission Press, 1913, 2, 1, 10, 189 p.

1581   Mateer, Ada Haven: *Handbook of new terms and newspaper Chinese.*—Shanghai: Presbyterian Mission Press, 1917, [ii], 309, iv p./ Chinese-English & English-Chinese.

1582   Morgan, Evan: *Chinese new new terms.* —Shanghai: Kelly & Walsh, 1926, xiii, 525, (supplementary terms) 1 p./ With English translations, classifications, introduction, and indexes.

1583   Schlegel, Gustaf: Coining of new Chinese terms.—*TP* 2, 1892, 183—184.

1584   T'ang, Ching-kao: *Hsin wen-hua tz'u-shu.*—Shanghai: Shang-wu, 1923, 1107, 69, 88 p. [A dictionary of new culture.]

唐敬杲：新文化辭書

1585   Wieger, Léon, S.J.: *Locutions modernes: Néologie.*—Sien-hsien: Imprimerie de 獻縣 Sien-hsien, 1935, 3rd ed., 288 p.; 1939, 4th ed., [ii], 436 p.

1586   Wu, Nien-tz'u, et al.: *Hsin shu-yü tz'u-tien.*—Shanghai: Nan-ch'iang shu-chü, 1932—1933, 2 vols., 69, 1028 p.; 1936, 8th ed., 40, 4, 1078, 43 p. [A dictionary of new technical terms.]

吳念慈等：新術語辭典

6.7.2.   New Terms Since 1949 (1587—1638)
6.7.2.1.   General Studies (1587—1606)

1587   Chang, A.S.: Communist influence on the Chinese language. New economic, sociological and technical terms.—*Contemporary China* 1, 1955, 139—150.

1588   Chuang, H.C.: *The Great Proletarian Cultural Revolution: a terminological study.* —Berkeley: Center for Chinese Studies, Institute of International Studies, U. of California, 1967, vii, 72 p./ Studies in Chinese Communist Terminology, 12; *RBS* 12—13, 1966—1967, 653, V. Alleton.

1589   Finkelstein, David: The language of Communist China's criminal law.—*JAS* 27:3, 1968, 503—521.

1590   Hsia, T. A.: *Metaphor, myth, ritual and the people's commune.*—Berkeley: Center for Chinese Studies, Institute of International Studies, U. of California, 1961, vi, 60 p./ Studies in Chinese Communist Terminology, 7.

1591   Hsia, T. A.: *A terminological study of the Hsia-fang Movement.*—Berkeley: Center for Chinese Studies, Institute of International Studies, U. of California, 1963, vi, 68 p./ Studies in Chinese Communist Terminology, 10.

1592   Hsia, T. A.: *The commune in retreat as evidenced in terminology and semantics.* —Berkeley: Center for Chinese Studies, Institute of International Studies, U. of California, 1964, ii, 91 p./ Studies in Chinese Communist Terminology, 11.

1593   Hsiang, Ch'ao: Kuan-yü hsin tz'u ho hsin i.—*YWHH* 1952:1, 3—7. [Concerning new words and new meanings.]

向超：關於新詞和新義

1594   Li, Chi: *General trends of Chinese linguistic changes under Communist rule.* —Berkeley: East Asia Studies, Institute of International Studies, U. of California, 1956, iii, 42 p./ Studies in Chinese Communist Terminology, 1.

1595   Li, Chi: *Preliminary study of selected terms.*—Berkeley: East Asia Studies, Institute of International Studies, U. of California, 1956, 23 p./ Studies in Chinese

Communist Terminology, 2.

1596 Li, Chi: *Part I, Literary and colloquial terms in new usage. Part II, Terms topped by numerals.*—Berkeley: East Asia Studies, Institute of International Studies, U. of California, 1957, 51 p./ Studies in Chinese Communist Terminology, 3.

1597 Li, Chi: *Part I, The Communist term 'the Common Language' and related terms. Part II, Dialectal terms in common usage, literary and colloquial terms in new usage* (continued).—Berkeley: East Asia Studies, Institute of International Studies, U. of California, 1957, iv, 88 p./ Studies in Chinese Communist Terminology, 4.

1598 Li, Chi: *The use of figurative language in Communist China.*—Berkeley: East Asia Studies, Institute of International Studies, U. of California, 1958, ii, 85 p./ Studies in Chinese Communist Terminology, 5.

1599 Li, Chi: *New features in Chinese grammatical usage.*—Berkeley: Center for Chinese Studies, Institute of International Studies, U. of California, 1962, v, 76 p./ Studies in Chinese Communist Terminology, 9.

1600 Maekawa, Akira: Gendai Chūgokugo to sono shakaiteki haikei ni tsuite—toku ni shingo shinyaku ni tsuite.—*Tōkai Daigaku Kiyō* 29, 1978, 88–91. [On the modern Chinese language and its social background—with special reference to the new words and the new interpretations.]
前川晃：現代中國語とその社會的背景について——特に新語新釋について

1601 Ōshiba, Takashi: Chūgokugo shingo no seikaku.—*CGGG* 1957:2, 8–11. [The characteristics of new words in Chinese.]/ Concerning cinematographic terms.
大芝孝：中國語新語の性格

1602 P'an, P'ei-fan: Ch'uang-tsao hsin yü-tz'u.

—*CKYT* 1:2, 1952, 10–12. [The creation of new words and phrases.]
潘培藩：創造新語詞

1603 Serruys, Paul L–M.: *Survey of the Chinese language reform and the anti-illiteracy movement in Communist China.*—Berkeley: Center for Chinese Studies, Institute of International Studies, U. of California, 1962, 208 p./ Studies in Chinese Communist Terminology, 8.

1604 Shibata, Minoru: Chūgoku ni okeru shingo no yakutei zokusei.—*KDBR* 13:3, 1963, 1–14. [The establishment of new words by usage in China.]
芝田稔：中國における新語の約定俗成

1605 Shōmura, Tadayoshi: Shingo ni okeru imi henka ni tsuite.—*CGGG* 1959:10, 21–22. [On the changes of meanings in new words.]/ Chinese neologism.
莊村忠㺃：新語における意味變化について

1606 Wu, Caroline Hsiao: Changing speech patterns in the People's Republic of China.—*JCLTA* 8:2, 1973, 70–74.

6.7.2.2. Collection and Analysis (1607–1638)

1607 Chang, I-ch'ü: *Hsien-tai yung-yü ta tz'u-tien.*—Hong Kong: Chung-kuo, 1956, 714 p. [A comprehensive dictionary of modern terms.]/ See (1608) & (1609).
張一渠：現代用語大辭典

1608 Chang, I-ch'ü: *Hsin ming-tz'u tz'u-tien.*—Hong Kong: Chung-kuo, 1970, [ii], 714 p. [A dictionary of new terms.]/ A repr. of (1607).
張一渠：新名詞辭典

1609 Chang, I-ch'ü: *Tsui-hsin hsin ming-tz'u tz'u-tien.*—Hong Kong: Shang-hai yin-shu kuan, 1970, 714 p. [A new dictionary of new terms.]/ A repr. of (1607).
張一渠：最新新名詞辭典

1610 Chi, Wen-shun: *Chinese-English dictionary*

of contemporary usage.—Berkeley, Los Angeles & London: U. of California Press, 1977, xix, 484 p./ *BSOAS* 41, 1978, 617–618, H.D.R. Baker, *JAS* 37:4, 1978, 751–753, Jerry Norman; *JCL* 6:1, 1978, 169–170, Yuen Ren Chao; *Chin san-shih nien . . . chien chieh* (0010), 26–27.

1611 Ching, Eugene: From 'lover' to 'spouse' —a glossary of neologisms of the P.R.C. —*JCLTA* 17:1, 1982, 35–65.

1612 Chou, Ch'i-yü: *Hsin ming-tz'u hsün-tsuan.*—Taipei: Kuang-wen shu-chü, 1979, 89 p. [Explanations of new terms.]
周起予：新名詞訓纂

1613 Ch'un-ming shu-tien pien-chi-pu: *Hsin ming-tz'u tz'u-tien.*—Shanghai: Ditto, 1949; 1950, rev. ed.; 1951, 2nd rev. ed., [vi], 56, 9130, 4 p.; 1952, 60, 9134, 28 p. [A dictionary of new terms.]
春明書店編輯部：新名詞辭典

1614 *Chung Kung shu-yü hui chieh* pien-chi wei-yüan-hui: *Chung Kung shu-yü hui chieh.*—Taipei: Chung-kuo ch'u-pan, 1971, 3, 2, 42, 455 p. [Collection and explanations of Chinese Communist terminology.]
『中共術語彙解』編輯委員會：中共術語彙解

1615 Dien, Albert E.: *Dictionary of Chinese current terminology.*—Honolulu: U. of Hawaii, Center for Cultural and Technical Interchange Between East and West, Institute of Advanced Projects, Research Translations, 1962, 331 p.

1616 Doolin, Dennis J. & Ridley, Charles P.: *A Chinese-English dictionary of Communist Chinese terminology.*—Stanford: Hoover Institution Press, 1973, xiii, 569 p./ *JAS* 33:3, 1974, 468–469, James J. Wrenn; *AcOr* 39, 1978, 304–306, P. Mohr.

1617 Hoshi, Ayao: *Chūgoku shakai keizaishi goi.*—Tokyo: Tōyō Bunko Kindai Chūgoku Kenkyū Sentā, 1966, 425 p.; *Zokuhen.*

—Yamagata: Kōbundō shoten, 1975, 168 p. [The vocabulary of China's social and economic history.] and [A continuation.]
星斌夫：中國社會經濟史語彙・續編

1618 Hsiao, Tsan-yü & Teng, Kung-hsüan: *Hsien-tai chih-shih hsin tz'u-tien.*—Taipei: Pa-t'i shu-chü, 1953, v.p., illus., maps. [A new dictionary of modern knowledge.]
蕭贊育、鄧公玄：現代知識新辭典

1619 Hsin Chung-kuo tz'u-shu pien-i-she: *Hsin ming-tz'u tsung-ho ta tz'u-tien.*—Shanghai: Ta-ti shu-tien, 1950; 1951, 4th rev. ed., 6 pts., 20, 106, 99 p.; A. 300 p.; B. 447 p.; C. 156 p.; D. 202 p.; E. 148 p.; F. 286 p. [A general comprehensive dictionary of new terms.]
新中國辭書編譯社：新名詞綜合大辭典

1620 Hsin-hua t'ung-hsün-she Wai-wen kan-pu hsüeh-hsiao: *Han-Ying shih shih yung yü tz'u-hui.*—Peking: Hsin-hua shu-tien, 1964, iv, ii, 599 p.; Hong Kong: Shang-wu, 1972, repr., iv, 594 p. [A Chinese-English current political phrases and terms dictionary.]/ See (4058)
新華通訊社外文幹部學校：漢英時事用語詞滙

1621 Hsin tz'u-shu pien-i-she: *Chung-kuo jen-min shu-yü tz'u-tien.*—Shanghai: T'ai-p'ing-yang, 1950, 3, 3, 21, 431 p. [A dictionary of technical terms of the Chinese people.]
新辭書編譯社：中國人民術語辭典

1622 Kōsaka, Jun'ichi: *Gendai Chūgokugo —Shingo shinshaku.*—Tokyo: Kōseikan, 1972, 231 p. [The modern Chinese language —New explanations for new words.]
香坂順一：現代中國語——新語新釋

1623 Kuo, Warren [Kuo, Hua-lun]: *A comprehensive glossary of Chinese Communist terminology.*—Taipei: Institute of International Relations, National Chengchi U., 1978, [v], 907 p., tab., map.
〔郭華倫：中共名詞術語辭典〕

1624 Lau, Yee-fui, et al.: *Glossary of Chinese political phrases.*—Hong Kong: Union Research Institute, 1977, [6], 590, [11] p./ *JAS* 37:4, 1978, 752–753, Jerry Norman.

1625 Li, Chin, et al.: *Hsin pien Hsin chih-shih tz'u-tien.*—Shanghai: Pei-hsin, 1948, rev. ed.; 1951, repr., 4, 11, 726 p.; 1971, repr., 11, 4, 726 p. [A new edition of *Hsin chih-shih tz'u-tien* (1578).]
李進等：新編新知識辭典

1626 Li, Chin, et al.: *Hsü pien Hsin chih-shih tz'u-tien.*—Shanghai: Pei-hsin, 1951, 2, 2, 11, 568, 4, 96, 33 p.; 1952, 2, 2, 11, 568, 4, 147, 33 p. [A supplementary edition of *Hsin chih-shih tz'u-tien* (1625).]
李進等：續編新知識辭典

1627 Nishikubo, Ryōji: Saikin no goi sanshaku. —*CGGG* 1961:12, 11–12. [Fragmentary explanations of the most recent (Chinese) vocabulary.]
西窪了慈：最近の語彙散釋

1628 Sung, Yüan-fang (ed. in chief): *Chien-ming she-hui k'o-hsüeh tz'u-tien.*—Shanghai: Shang-hai tz'u-shu, 1982, 1110 p. [A concise dictionary of the social sciences.]
宋原放主編：簡明社會科學辭典

1629 Ts'ang, Nien: *Hsin ming-tz'u shou-ts'e.*—Shanghai: T'ang-ti, 1949, 137 p. [A handbook of new terms.]
倉年：新名詞手册

1630 U.S. Department of State, Foreign Service Institute: *A Chinese-English glossary of current reading texts.*—Taichung, 1961, 146 p.

1631 U.S. Joint Publications Research Service: *J.P.R.S. Handbook: Standard translations of Chinese Communist terms.*—Washington, D.C.: Ditto, 1963, 133 p.

1632 U.S. Joint Publications Research Service (transl.): *Chinese-English dictionary of modern Communist Chinese usage.*—Washington, D.C.: Ditto, 1966, 2nd ed., [viii], 845 p./ This is an English conversion of *Han-Te tz'u-tien* (4122); *Chin san-shih nien . . . chien chieh* (0010), 24–25; *JCLTA* 1:1, 1966, 43–44, W. Allyn Rickett.

1633 Wang, Hsien-sheng: *Ying-Han hsin tzu tz'u-tien.*—Taipei: Wu-chou, 1981, 11, 460 p. [An English-Chinese dictionary of new terms.]
王憲生：英漢新字辭典

1634 Wang, Tzu-ch'iang: *Ch'ang-yung hsin tz'u li shih* (1455). [Explanations with examples of commonly used new words.]
王自强：常用新詞例釋

1635 Wang, Yün-wu (ed. in chief): *Wang Yün-wu she-hui k'o-hsüeh ta tz'u-tien.*—Taipei: Shang-wu, 1970–1971, 12 vols., illus. [Wang Yün-wu's encyclopedia of social sciences.]
王雲五主編：王雲五社會科學大辭典

1636 Wei, Wen: *Han-Ying tz'u-hui shou-ts'e.*—Peking: Wai-wen, 1970, v, 1618 p. [A handbook of Chinese-English vocabulary.]/ Chinese Communist terminology.
蔚文：漢英詞滙手册

1637 Wu, T'ieh-p'ing: Li-mao yü-yen chung te tz'u-hui.—*YWYC* 1982:2, 5–8. [A lexicon in polite speech.]/ A typological and contrastive study.
伍鐵平：禮貌語言中的詞滙

1638 Yang, Chien-ch'ang: Hsin Chung-kuo ch'u-hsien te mou-hsieh Han-yü tz'u-yü hui-pien.—*JCLTA* 16:2, 1981, 17–25. [A collection of certain Chinese words and phrases appearing in new China.]
楊建昌：新中國出現的某些漢語詞語滙編

6.8. Scientific and Technical Terms (1639–1678)

6.8.1. General Problems (1639–1653)

1639 Hsiao, Yeh-lun: K'o-hsüeh ming-tz'u pi-hsü shih-tang hsi-shou wai-lai-yü.—*WTKK* 1958:5, 30–32. [Scientific terminology needs to appropriately absorb foreign loan-words.]
肖業倫：科學名詞必須適當吸收外來語

1640 Liu, Tse-hsien: Tui k'o-hsüeh chi-shu ming-tz'u te chi-tien i-chien.—*YWCS* 1956:8, 25–26. [Several opinions on scientific and technical terminology.]
劉澤先：對科學技術名詞的幾點意見

1641 Liu, Tse-hsien: K'o-hsüeh ming-tz'u te tu-yin wen-t'i.—*WTKK* 1957:8, 37–40. [The problems in the pronunciations of scientific terminology.]
劉澤先：科學名詞的讀音問題

1642 Liu, Tse-hsien: So-wei i-k'an chiu ming-pai te k'o-hsüeh ming-tz'u.—*YWCS* 1958:5, 11–13. [The so-called scientific terminology of "take a look and then you understand."]
劉澤先：所謂『一看就明白』的科學名詞

1643 Liu, Tse-hsien: K'o-chi shu-yü fen-ch'i ch'ing-k'uang te i-ko tiao-ch'a pao-kao.—*WTKK* 1963:1, 1–8. [A report on a survey of the situation of divergencies in scientific and technical terminology.]
劉澤先：科技術語分歧情況的一個調查報告

1644 Maomao: K'o-hsüeh ming-tz'u man-t'an.—*HWPY* 1951:75, 4–6. [A random discussion on scientific terminology.]
Maomao: 科學名詞漫談

1645 Po, Han: Hua-hsüeh ming-tz'u men-wai t'an.—*CKYW* 1953:8, 5–8. [A layman's discussion on the terminology of chemistry.]
伯韓：化學名詞門外談

1646 Suchov, N. K.: Mezhdunarodnaia rabota v oblasti nauchno-technicheskoi termino-logii.—*VIa* 1956:3, 145–152. [International work concerning scientific and technical terminology.]

1647 Suchov, N. K. Transl. by Liu Hsiung-hsiang: Kuo-chi shang kuan-yü k'o-hsüeh chi-shu shu-yü te kung-tso.—*CKYW* 1957:1, 38–42, 8. [International work concerning scientific and technical terminology.] (1646)
蘇賀夫著，劉雄翔譯：國際上關於科學技術術語的工作

1648 T'an, Ch'in-yü: Chi tai shang-ch'üeh chih hua-hsueh ming-tz'u.—*TFTC* 40:1, 1944, 30–36. [The urgently awaited discussion on the terminology of chemistry.]
譚勤余：急待商榷之化學名詞

1649 Tseng, Chao-lun: K'o-hsüeh ming-tz'u chung te tsao-tzu wen-t'i.—*CKYW* 1953:8, 3–4. [The problem of creation of characters in scientific terminology.]
曾昭倫：科學名詞中的造字問題

1650 Tu, Hou-wen: K'o-hsüeh shu-yü te kou-ch'eng fang-fa.—*YCYY* 1982:2, 58–71. [Methods of formation of scientific terminology.]
杜厚文：科學術語的構成方法

1651 Yamagata, Tadashi: Jinmin Chūgoku ni okeru senmon gakujutsu-go no seiri kōsaku.—*CGGG* 1958:5, 3–12. [Work in the putting in order of specialized and technical terminology in the People's Republic of China.]
山形直：人民中國における專門、學術語の整理工作

1652 Yang, En-fu: Wen-tzu kai-ko chung te k'o-hsüeh ming-tz'u wen-t'i.—*KHTP* 1956:3, 92–93. [The problems of scientific terminology in the reform of writing.]
楊恩孚：文字改革中的科學名詞問題

1653 Yen, Hsi-ch'un: Han-yü p'in-yin tzu-mu yü tzu-jan k'o-hsüeh ming-tz'u.—*WTKK* 1958:1, 28–29. [The Chinese Pinyin alphabet and terminology for the natural sciences.]
嚴希純：漢語拼音字母與自然科學名詞

6.8.2. Methods of Translation (1654–1660)

1654 Ch'en, P'eng-hsiang (ed. in chief): *Fan-i shih. Fan-i lun.*—Taipei: Hung-tao wen-hua shih-yeh, 1975, 3 [i], 466 p./ 356–385: A discussion on the translation of scientific and technological articles. [The history of translation. On translation.]
陳鵬翔主編：翻譯史・翻譯論／356–385: 談談科技論文的翻譯

1655 Liu, Tse-hsien: Ts'ung k'o-hsüeh hsin ming-tz'u te fan-i k'an Han-tzu te ch'üeh-tien (p'in-yin wen-tzu ho Han-tzu te pi-chiao).—*CKYW* 1953:8, 9–13. [The shortcomings of Chinese characters as seen from the translations of new scientific terms (a comparison of alphabetic writing and Chinese characters).]
劉澤先：從科學新名詞的翻譯看漢字的缺點（拼音文字和漢字的比較）

1656 Szu, Kuo: *Fan-i yen-chiu.*—Taipei: Ta-ti, 1972; 1977, 4th print., 269 p./ 65–69: Translation of new and technical terms. [A study on translation.]
思果：翻譯研究／65–69：新詞、專門名詞的翻譯

1657 T'ang, Hsin-yü: Fan-i chuan-men ming-tz'u te i-chung fang-fa.—*FITP* 1950:1–3, 20–21. [A method of translating the terminology of specialized fields.]
湯心豫：翻譯專門名詞的一種方法

1658 Wang, Kuang: Wai-chiao ming-tz'u i-ming te shang-ch'üeh.—*TFTC* 32:13, 1935, 175–181. [A discussion of the translation of diplomatic terms.]
王光：外交名詞譯名的商榷

1659 Wang, Shih-hsieh: I-hsieh ch'ang-chien tung-chih-wu te i-ming wen-t'i.—*WCYY* 1963:3, 66–67. [The problem in the translation of names of some commonly seen fauna and flora.]
王士燮：一些常見動植物的譯名問題

1660 Yü, Yu-sun: T'an Jih-i hsüeh-shu ming-tz'u.—*Wen-che yüeh-k'an* 1:7, 1936, 111–123. [A discussion on Japanese translations of scientific terms.]
余又蓀：談日譯學術名詞

6.8.3. Collection and Analysis (1661–1678)

1661 Alleton, Viviane & Alleton, Jean-Claude: *Terminologie de la chimie en chinois moderne.*—Paris & The Hague: Mouton, 1966, 61 p./ Maison des Sciences de l'Homme. Matériaux pour l'étude de l'Extrême-Orient moderne et contemporain. Études linguistiques, 1; *RBS* 12–13, 1966–1967, 654, M. Cartier.

1662 Anonymous: *K'o-hsüeh chi-shu tz'u-tien.*—Peking: Hsin-hua, 1960, 2 vols., 1207 p. [A dictionary of science and technology.]
無名氏：科學技術辭典

1663 Anonymous: *Modern Chinese-English technical and general dictionary.*—New York: McGraw-Hill, 1963, 3 vols., vii, 152; vii, 1900; vii, 1788 p./ *JCLTA* 1:1, 1966, 41–43, W. Allyn Rickett.
〔現代漢英技術及普通辭典〕

1664 Chao, Yuen Ren: Popular Chinese plant words—A descriptive lexico-grammatical study.—*Lg* 29, 1953, 379–414; *Aspects of Chinese sociolinguistics* (0048), 343–376.

1665 *Chien-ming k'o-chi tz'u-tien* pien-chi wei-yüan-hui: *Chien-ming k'o-chi tz'u-tien.*—Shanghai: K'o-hsüeh chi-shu, 1958, 2050, 57 p., tab., illus. [A concise dictionary of science and technology.]
『簡明科技辭典』編輯委員會：簡明科技辭典

1666 Ch'ing-hua ta-hsüeh *Ying-Han chi-shu tz'u-tien* pien-hsieh-tsu: *Ying-Han chi-shu tz'u-tien.*—Peking: Kuo-fang kung-yeh, 1978, xiv, 1098 p. [An English-Chinese dictionary of technology.]
清華大學『英漢技術詞典』編寫組：英漢技術詞典

1667   Chung-kuo K'o-hsüeh-yüan Tui wai lien-lo-chü fan-i-shih: *Han-Ying k'o-chi ch'ang-yung tz'u-hui.*—Peking: Shang-wu, 1962, iv, 405 p. [Chinese-English glossary of commonly used scientific and technical terms.]
中國科學院對外聯絡局翻譯室：漢英科技常用詞滙

1668   Ho, Ping-sung, et al.: *Pai-k'o ming hui.*—Shanghai: Shang-wu, 1931, 419 p. [A dictionary of encyclopedic terminology.] / English-Chinese scientific and technical terms.
何炳松等：百科名彙

1669   Hominal, François: *Terminologie mathématique en chinois moderne.*—Paris: U. of Paris, 1973, 159 p./ Unpubl. doc. diss.

1670   Hominal, François: Traits généraux de la terminologie mathématique chinoise.—*CLAO* 4, 1978, 81–88.

1671   Kuo-li pien-i-kuan: *K'o-hsüeh ming-tz'u hui-pien.*—Taipei: Cheng-chung, 1958, 7 vols./ Includes 34 branches of science. [A collection of scientific and technical terms.]
國立編譯館：科學名詞彙編

1672   Métaille, Georges: *La terminologie botanique en chinois moderne.*—Paris: U. of Paris, 1974, (not seen)./ Unpubl. doc. diss.

1673   Schramm, Gottfried: *Schriftzeichen-Analysen medizinischer termini technici in der chinesischen Sprache.*—Leipzig: Leipzig U., 1956, 80 p./ Unpubl. thesis.

1674   Suter, R.: Naming chemical elements in Chinese.—*Journal of Chemical Education* 40, 1963, 388.

1675   Taranzano, Charles, S.J.: *Vocabulaire des sciences mathématiques, physiques et naturelles.*—Sien-hsien: Imprimerie de la Mission Catholique, 1936, 3rd ed., 2 pts.,

xii, 1151, 29 pl. [i], 951 p./ French-Chinese & Chinese-French.
〔法漢科學詞典〕

1676   Torii, Katsuyuki: *Hsin ch'ing-nien* ni okeru senmon yōgo (1).—*KSTZ* 7, 1974, (left) 1–20. [Specialized terms in *Hsin ch'ing-nien* ('New Youth') (1).]
鳥居克之：『新青年』における 專門用語(1)

1677   Wong, Sybil: *Dictionary of Chinese Communist agricultural terminology.*—Hong Kong: Union Research Institute, 1968, [ii], 555, 17 p., illus./ Chinese-English.
〔中共農業用語辭典〕

1678   *Ying-Han k'o-chi ch'ang-yung tz'u-hui* pien-chi hsiao-tsu: *Ying-Han k'o-chi ch'ang-yung tz'u-hui.*—Peking: Kuo-fang kung-yeh, 1973, 469 p. [An English-Chinese glossary of commonly used scientific and technical terms.]
『英漢科技常用詞滙』編輯小組：英漢科技常用詞滙

6.9.   Kinship Terms and Terms of Address (1679–1706)

6.9.1.   Kinship Terms (1679–1690)

1679   Benedict, Paul K.: Tibetan and Chinese kinship terms.—*HJAS* 6, 1942, 313–337.

1680   Chen, T. S. & Shryock, J. K.: Chinese relationship terms.—*AA* 34, 1932, 623–669.

1681   Cheng, Elizabeth: Some features of the kinship terminology used in New York Chinatown.—*Southwestern Journal of Anthropology* 8, 1952, 97–107.

1682   Chia, Yen-te: Hsien-tai Han-yü ch'ang-yung ch'in-shu tz'u te i-su fen-hsi.—*CGGG* 228, 1981, 120–125. [An analysis of sememes of commonly used kinship terms in the modern Chinese language.]
賈彥德：現代漢語常用親屬詞的義素分析

1683 Feng, Han-yi: Teknonymy as a formative factor in the Chinese kinship system.—*AA* 38, 1936, 59–66.

1684 Feng, Han-yi: The Chinese kinship system.—*HJAS* 2, 1937, 141–275.
〔馮漢驥〕

1685 Hirayama, Hisao: Shingozku kankei. —*Chūgoku gogaku jiten* (0037), 959–962. [Kinship relations.]
平山久雄：親屬關係

1686 Hsu, Francis L.K.: The differential functions of relationship terms illustrated from a study of a North China community.—*AA* 44, 1942, 248–256.

1687 Jui, I-fu: Po shu i chiu ku k'ao.—*BIHP* 14, 1948, 151–211. [A study on (the Chinese kinship terms) *po, shu, i, chiu,* and *ku.*]
芮逸夫：伯叔姨舅姑考

1688 Jui, I-fu: Chiu-tsu-chih yü *Erh-ya shih-ch'in.*—*BIHP* 22, 1950, 209–231. [The system of nine generations and the *shih-ch'in* ('explanation of kinship terms') section of *Erh-ya.*]
芮逸夫：九族制與『爾雅』『釋親』

1689 Jui, I-fu: *Erh-ya shih-ch'in* pu cheng. —*WSCH* 1, 1950, 101–136. [Addenda and corrigenda to the *shih-ch'in* ('explanation of kinship terms') section of *Erh-ya.*]
芮逸夫：『爾雅』『釋親』補正

1690 Wu C. C.: The Chinese family: organization, names, and kinship terms. *AA* 29, 1927, 316–325.

6.9.2. Terms of Address (1691–1706)

1691 Chao, Yuen Ren: Chinese terms of address.—*Lg* 32, 1956, 217–241; *Aspects of Chinese sociolinguistics* (0048), 309–342./ *RBS* 2, 1956, 383, M.A.K. Halliday.

1692 Fukuchi, Shigeko: Pekingo ni okeru shinzoku meishō no icho yōhō— Shinzoku kankei ga nai baai no taikeiteki yōhō.—*CGGG* 1974:1, 8–19. [One of the uses of kinship terms in the Peking dialect—The systematic use of kinship terms among non-related persons.]
福地滋子：北京語における親族名稱の一用法
——親族關係がない場合の體系的用法

1693 Jui, I-fu: Lun Chung-kuo ku chin ch'in-shu ch'eng-wei te i chih.—*CYYK* 1, 1954, 53–67. [On different systems of kinship terms of address in ancient and modern China.]
芮逸夫：論中國古今親屬稱謂的異制

1694 Kuo, Ming-k'un: *Chūgoku no kazokusei oyobi gengo no kenkyū.*—Tokyo, Tōhō Gakkai, 1962, 16, 564 p./ *RBS* 8, 1962, Lü Chiung-chen. [A study of the family system and language of China.]
郭明昆：中國の家族制及び言語の研究

1695 Kuo, Ming-k'un: Fukurowa hōgen ni okeru shinzoku shōi no ni-san ni tsuite. —*Chūgoku no kazokusei oyobi gengo no kenkyū* (1694), 295–316. [Notes on the kinship terms of address in the Hoklo dialect.]
郭明昆：福老話方言に於ける親族稱謂の二三
について

1696 Li, Pei-ta: *Hsien-tai Han-yü chung fei-ch'in-tsu kuan-hsi te ch'eng-hu.*—Hong Kong: U. of Hong Kong, 1979, 102 p./ 99–102: Bibliography; Unpubl. M.A. thesis. [The analysis of vocative non-kinship terms of address in Modern Chinese.]
李北達：現代漢語中非親族關係的稱呼

1697 Lin, Mei-jung: Chung-kuo ch'in-shu ch'eng-wei te yü-hsing k'uo-chan yü yü-i yen-chan.—*BIE* 52, 1982, 33–114. [The expansion of linguistic forms and extension of linguistic meanings in Chinese kinship terms of address.]
林美容：中國親屬稱謂的語形擴展與語意延展

1698   Liu, Charles A.: Chinese kinship terms as forms of address.—*JCLTA* 16:1, 1981, 35—45.

1699   Liu, Pin-hsiung: Ch'in-shu ch'eng-wei yen-chiu te fa-chan.—*Chung-kuo min-tsu-hsüeh t'ung-hsün* 4, 1966, 1—7. [The development of studies on kinship terms of address.]
劉斌雄：親屬稱謂研究的發展

1700   Matsumoto, Kazuo: Binnango ni okeru jinmei to shinzoku no yobikake kata ni tsuite.—*CGGG* 1960:6, 8—12. [Personal names and kinship terms of address in the South Min dialect.]
松本一男：閩南語における人名と親族の呼びかけ方について

1701   Ōkōchi, Yasunori: *Chinese terms of address.*—Kyoto: Ditto, 1957, 18 p.
〔大河內康憲〕

1702   Peyraube, Alain: Les termes d'addresse dans les opéras de Yuan (XIIIe—XIVe siècles).—*CLAO* 11:2, 1982, 3—36.

1703   Takahashi, Moritaka.—Chūgokugo ni okeru kazoku shōko ni tsuite.—*THG* 33, 1967, (left) 127—131./ *RBS* 12—13, 1966—1967, 641, M. Cartier. [On kinship terms of address in the Chinese language.]
高橋盛孝：中國語に於ける家族稱呼について

1704   Takashima, Toshio: *Suikoden* no shōko —(2) Taishōgo.—*CGGK* 20, 1981, 1—20. [Terms of address in *Shui-hu chuan*—(2) On mutual address.]
高島俊男：『水滸傳』の稱呼（二）對稱語

1705   Takizawa, Toshiaki: Chūgoku no ninshō.—*TSGH* 14, 1968, 74—85. [Terms of address in China.]
瀧澤俊亮：中國の人稱

1706   Tsukamoto, Terukazu: *Jurin gaishi* koshōgo sakuin.—*TRGH* 24:5, 1973, (left) 45—118. [An index to the terms of address in *Ju-lin wai-shih.*]
塚本照和：『儒林外史』呼稱語索引

6.10. Chinese Surnames and Personal Names (1707—1750)
6.10.1 Naming (1707—1710)

1707   Hayashi, Tani: Chung-kuo-jen te ch'ü ming-erh ken i-pan te ch'eng-hu.—*CGKS* 3, 1960, 49—52. [The naming and general terms of address of the Chinese people.]
林谷：中國人的取名兒跟一般的稱呼

1708   Kehl, Frank: Chinese nicknaming behaviour: a sociolinguistic pilot study. —*JOS* 9:1, 1971, 149—172./ Examples taken mainly from Cantonese.

1709   Pei, Ming: Chung-kuo-jen ming ming ch'ü t'an.—*I-wen chih* 94, 1973, 72—73. [A discussion of interest on naming among the Chinese.]
北冥：中國人命名趣談

1710   Sung, Margaret M.Y.: Chinese personal naming.—*JCLTA* 16:2, 1981, 67—90b.
〔宋嚴棉〕

6.10.2 Ancient Chinese Surnames and Personal Names (1711—1719)

1711   Chou, Fa-kao: *Chou Ch'in ming-tzu chieh-ku hui shih* pu-i.—*TLTC* 20:8, 1960, 1—8; 9, 10—17; 10, 14—19. [Addenda to *Chou Ch'in ming-tzu chieh-ku hui shih* (1718).]
周法高：『周秦名字解詁彙釋』補遺

1712   Chu, T'an: *Chou Ch'in ming-tzu chieh-ku* pa.—*Shu lin* 1:3, 1937, 12—17. [A postscript to *Chou Ch'in ming-tzu chieh-ku* (1718).]
朱偰：『周秦名字解詁』跋

1713   Ch'u, Chuang: Chung-kuo ku-jen te hsing-shih tzu hao.—*WSCS* 1981:6, 61—66. [The surnames, courtesy names, and poetic names of ancient Chinese people.]
楚莊：中國古人的姓氏字號

1714   Dien, Albert E.: The bestowal of surnames under the Western Wei-Northern Chou; a case of counter-acculturation. —*TP* 63:2–3, 1977, 47–109.

1715   Kryukov, M.V.: *Hsing* and *shih* (on the problem of clan name and patronymic in ancient China).—*AO* 34, 1966, 535–553.
〔姓、氏〕

1716   Liu, P'an-sui: *Ch'un-ch'iu ming-tzu chieh-ku* pu cheng.—*Shih hsüeh* 1, 1926, 7–18; 3, 14–19. [Addenda and corrigenda to *Ch'un-ch'iu ming-tzu chieh-ku* ('Explanations of names during the Spring and Autumn period').]
劉盼遂：『春秋名字解詁』補正

1717   Matsumoto, Nobuhiro: Shina kosei to totemizumu.—*Shinagaku* 1921, 101–112, 245–276. [Old surnames and totemism in China.]
松本信廣：支那古姓とトテミズム

1718   Wang, Yin-chih (comp.). Ed. by Chou, Fa-kao: *Chou Ch'in ming-tzu chieh-ku hui shih.*—Taipei: Chung-hua ts'ung-shu, 1958, 2, 18, 30, 318, 8 p. [Collected explanations of personal names during the Chou and Ch'in dynasties.]/ See (1707).
王引之撰，周法高輯著：周秦名字解詁彙釋

1719   Yang, Hsi-mei: Hsing tzu ku-i hsi cheng. —*BIHP* 23, 1952, 409–442. [Analytical evidence for the ancient meanings of the character *hsing* ('surnames').]
楊希枚：『姓』字古義析證

6.10.3. Modern Chinese Surnames and Personal Names (1720–1750)
6.10.3.1. General Studies (1720–1737)

1720   Arlington, L.C.: The Chinese female names.—*CJ* 1, 1923, 316–325, 454–462, 561–571.

1721   Bauer, Wolfgang: Das P'ai-hang system in der Chinesischen Personnamengebung. —*ZDMG* 107, 1957, 595–634.

1722   Bauer, Wolfgang: *Der Chinesische Personname; die Bildungsgesetze und hauptsächlischten Bedeutungsinhalte von Ming, Tzu und Hsiao-Ming.*—Wiesbaden: Otto Harrassowitz, 1959, 406 p.
〔名、字、小名〕

1723   Bauer, Wolfgang: Der Chinesische Eigenname und seine Beziehung zu Wort und Schrift.—*Oriens* 13–14, 1961, 256–264./ A general and theoretical discussion of Chinese proper names; *RBS* 7, 1961, 463, C. S. Goodrich.

1724   Boodberg, Peter A.: The chronogrammatic use of animal cycle terms in proper names.—*HJAS* 4, 1939, 273–275.

1725   Boodberg, Peter A.: Chinese zoographic names as chronograms.—*HJAS* 5, 1940, 128–136; *Selected works of Peter A. Boodberg* (comp. by Cohen, Alvin P. —Berkeley-Los Angeles-London: U. of California Press, 1979), 442–450.

1726   Chang, Y. Z.: China's strange names. —*Fu Jen Studies* 7, 1973, 33–38.

1727   Ch'en, Ming-yüan & Wang, Tsung-hu: Chung-kuo hsing-shih yü hsien-tai tz'u-tien. —*TSYC* 1982:4, 79–86. [Chinese surnames and modern (Chinese) dictionaries.]
陳明遠、汪宗虎：中國姓氏與現代辭典

1728   Giles, Herbert A.: The family names. —*JRASNCB* 21, 1886, 255–288./ An alphabetical arrangement of *Pai-chia hsing* ('one hundred family names') with genealogical notes.

1729   Hauer, E.: Das *Po-kia-sing.*—*MSOS* 29, 1926, 115–169; 30, 1927, 19–85.
〔百家姓〕

1730   Hsiao, Yao-t'ien: *Chung-kuo jen-ming te yen-chiu.*—Penang: Educational

Publication House, 1970, 18, 3, 342, 2 p. [A study of Chinese personal names.]
蕭遙天：中國人名的研究

1731　Li, Chia-fu: Chung-kuo-jen hsing-ming te lai-li.—*Tsu-kuo i-chou* 355, 1972, 13–16. [The origins of the surnames and personal names of the Chinese people.]
李甲孚：中國人姓名的來歷

1732　Lin, I-feng; Cheng, I-mei; et al.: *Hsing-ming chang-ku.*—Kowloon: Chung-shan t'u-shu, 1974, 2, 2, 105 p. [Anecdotes on (Chinese) surnames and personal names.]
林一峰、鄭逸梅等：姓名掌故

1733　Schuler, W.: Der Chinesische Familien-name.—*Zeitschrift für Missionskunde* 23, 1908, 1–11, 33–39.

1734　Shimamura, Shūji: *Gaikokujin no seimei.*—Tokyo: Gyōsei, 1971; 1980, 3rd ed., [ii], 18, 306 p./ 17–40: China, Korea. [Surnames and personal names of foreigners.]
島村修治：外國人の姓名／17-40: 中國、朝鮮

1735　Shimamura, Shūji: *Sekai no seimei.*—Tokyo: Kōdansha, 1977, 2, 442 p./ 251–340: Confucian culture circle: China, Korea, Vietnam, Japan. [Surnames and personal names of the world.]
島村修治：世界の姓名

1736　Tsai, Frederick: On Chinese names.—*Mission Bulletin* 8, 1956, 266–268.

1737　Wojtasiewicz, Olgierd: The origin of Chinese clan names.—*RO* 19, 1954, 22–44.

6.10.3.2. Collection and Analysis (1738–1746)

1738　Fang, I, et al.: *Chung-kuo jen–ming ta tz'u-tien.*—Shanghai: Shang-wu, 1921; 1933, repr., 4, 3, 12, 1808, 25, 83, 34, 2, 3, 16, 32, 11, 66, 44, 43 p. [A comprehensive dictionary of Chinese personal names.]

方毅等：中國人名大辭典

1739　Hua, Yün & Chi, Lin: *Pai-chia hsing chieh-shih.*—Peking: Jen-min yu-tien, 1980, rev. ed., [ii], 2, 8, 122 p. [Explanations of one hundred family names.]/ In alphabetical order of Pinyin.
華雲、紀林：百家姓解釋

1740　Huang, Yu-te: *Hsing ming hui-tien.*—Tainan: Hsin shih-chi, 1977, 305 p., illus. [A glossary of surnames and personal names.]
黃有德：姓名彙典

1741　Mu, Liu-sen: *Pai-chia hsing tz'u-tien.*—Hong Kong: I-wen, 1970 (?), 7, 36, 6, 653 p. [A dictionary of one hundred family names.]
穆柳森：百家姓辭典

1742　Nichi-Chū Minzoku Kagaku Kenkyūjo: *Chūgoku seishi jiten.*—Tokyo: Kokusho Kankōkai, 1978, 19, 299 p. [A dictionary of Chinese surnames.]
日中民族科學研究所：中國姓氏事典

1743　P'eng, Tso-chen: *Ku chin t'ung hsing ming ta tz'u-tien.*—Peiping: Hao-wang shu-tien, 1936, 3, 36, 1240 p.; Taipei: T'ai-wan hsüeh-sheng, 1970, repr. [A comprehensive dictionary of ancient and modern identical surnames and personal names.]
彭作楨：古今同姓名大辭典

1744　Teng, Hsien-ching: *Chung-kuo hsing-shih chi.*—Taipei: Chih-ta t'u-shu, 1971, 2, 72, 657 p. [A collection of Chinese surnames.]
鄧獻鯨：中國姓氏集

1745　U.S. Bureau of Immigration and Naturalization: *List of Chinese family names.*—Washington, D.C.: Government Printing Office, 1909, 207 p.

1746　Wang, Su-ts'un: *Chung-hua hsing fu.*—Taipei: Chung-hua ts'ung-shu, 1969, 2 vols., 969 p. [A thesaurus of Chinese surnames.]

王素存：中華姓府

6.10.3.3. Taiwan Surnames and Personal Names (1747–1750)

1747   Ch'en, Jui-lung: *T'ai-wan hsing-shih yüan-yu.*—Fengshan: Hsing-t'ai wen-hua, 1980, 5, 185 p., map, illus. [The origins of surnames in Taiwan.]

陳瑞隆：臺灣姓氏源由

1748   P'eng, Kuei-fang: *T'ai-wan pai-chia hsing k'ao.*—Taipei: Li-ming, 1973, 2, 8, 300 p. [A study of the hundred family names in Taiwan.]

彭桂芳：臺灣百家姓考

1749   P'eng, Kuei-fang: *T'ai-wan hsing-shih chih yen-chiu.*—Hsinchu: T'ai-wan sheng-li Hsin-chu she-hui chiao-yü-kuan, 1975–1977, 4 vols., [iii], 2, 170, 3 maps; [ii], 253; [iv], 278; [ii], 104 p. [A study of surnames of Taiwan.]

彭桂芳：臺灣姓氏之研究

1750   Wu, K'un-lun & Lin, Hsien-mu: *T'ai-wan hsing-shih yüan-liu.*—Taichung: T'ai-wan sheng-cheng-fu hsin-wen-ch'u, 1969; 1974, 4th ed., 6, 4, 124 p., maps, illus. [The origin and development of surnames in Taiwan.]

吳昆倫、林獻穆：臺灣姓氏源流

6.11. Chinese Place Names (1751–1817)
6.11.1. Transcription of Chinese Place Names (1751–1756)

1751   Anonymous: The romanization of Chinese place-names.—*Geographical Journal* 102, 1943, 67–71.

1752   Geelan, P.J.M.: Chinese geographical names: the Pinyin problem.—*Asian Affairs* 10:3, 1979, 314–316.

1753   Komai, Shōichi: Chūgoku chimei no hyōonhō ni tsuite.—*Shinshū Daigaku*

Kyōyōbu Kiyō 1:11, 1977, 57–82. [On the methods of phonetic notation for Chinese place names.]

駒井正一：中國地名の表音法について

1754   Tseng, Shih-ying: *Chung-kuo ti-ming p'in-hsieh fa yen-chiu.*—Peking: Ts'e-hui, 1981, [i], 4, 184 p. [A study of methods of spelling Chinese place names.]

曾世英：中國地名拼寫法研究

1755   Wen-tzu kai-ko ch'u-pan-she: *Chung-kuo jen-ming ti-ming Han-yü p'in-yin p'in-hsieh fa.*—Peking: Wen-tzu kai-ko, 1975, 25 p. [Methods of writing Chinese personal and place names in the Chinese Pinyin system.]

文字改革出版社：中國人名地名漢語拼音拼寫法

1756   Wu, Wen-ch'ao: Han-yü p'in-yin tzu-mu shih p'in-hsieh Chung-kuo jen-ming ti-ming te shih-chieh-hsing fa-ting piao-chun.—*YWTC* 1, 1979, 32–33. [The Chinese Pinyin alphabetic system is the world-wide prescribed standard for transcribing Chinese personal names and place names.]

吳文超：漢語拼音字母是拼寫中國人名地名的世界性法定標準

6.11.2. Ancient Chinese Place Names (1757–1763)

1757   Aoyama, Sadao: *Tokushi hōyo kiyō sakuin Shina rekidai chimei yōran.*—Tokyo: Tōhō Bunka Gakuin Tōkyō Kenkyūjo, 1933, 17, 721, 12, [3], p.; Taipei: Lo-t'ien, 1973, repr. [An index to *Tu-shih fang-yü chi-yao* ('Geographical essentials for the readers of history'), a guide to Chinese place names of successive dynasties.]

青山定男：讀史方輿紀要索引支那歷代地名要覽

1758   Bretschneider, E.: Chinese ancient geographical names.—*Notes and Queries on China and Japan* 4, 1870, 49–61, 104–113.

1759 Ch'eng, Fa-jen: *Ch'un-ch'iu* ti-ming chiao chu.—*STHP* 4, 1959, 93–114. [Comments on the place names (found) in *Ch'un-ch'iu.*]
程發軔：『春秋』地名斠注

1760 Ch'eng, Fa-jen: *Ch'un-ch'iu* ti-ming t'u k'ao.—*STHP* 6, 1961, 1–158. [A study on the place names found in *Ch'un-ch'iu* on maps.]
程發軔：『春秋』地名圖考

1761 Ch'eng, Fa-jen: *Ch'un-ch'iu* ti-ming k'ao yao.—*STHP* 11, 1966, 225–298. [A summarized study on the place names (found) in *Ch'un-ch'iu.*]
程發軔：『春秋』地名考要

1762 Li, Chao-lo: *Li-tai ti-li chih yün-pien chin shih.*—Taipei: Chung-hua, 1966, repr., 2 *ts'e*, (Szu-pu pei-yao ed.); Taipei: Shang-wu, 1968, repr., 1 *ts'e.* [Modern explanations of geographic records of successive dynasties arranged in rhymes.]/ An index to ancient place names.
李兆洛：歷代地理志韻編今釋——「四部備要」本

1763 Tsang, Li-ho, et al.: *Chung-kuo ku chin ti-ming ta tz'u-tien.*—Shanghai: Shang-wu, 1931, 27, 1410, 348 p.; Taipei: Shang-wu, 1960, 27, 1410, 11, 287 p. [A comprehensive dictionary of ancient and modern Chinese place names.]
臧勵龢等：中國古今地名大辭典

6.11.3. Modern Chinese Place Names (1764–1804)
6.11.3.1. General Studies (1764–1784)

1764 Carr, William K.: Some characteristics of Chinese place-names.—*Asian Survey* 1, 1961, 25–29.

1765 Chao, Yuen Ren: The socio-political overtones of Chinese place names.—*MS* 33, 1977–1978, 136–139; *Aspects of Chinese sociolinguistics* (0048), 144–147.

1766 Ch'en, Cheng-hsiang: *Chung-kuo te ti-ming.*—Hong Kong: Shang-wu, 1978, 3, 167 p., maps. [Place names of China.]
陳正祥：中國的地名

1767 Ch'en, Chien-min: Ti-ming hsiao i. —*SKC* 1979:4, 336–337. [A short discussion on place names.]
陳建民：地名小議

1768 Cowgill, J. V.: Chinese place names in Johore.—*JRASMB* 2, 1924, 221–251.

1769 Egerod, Søren: A note on the origin of the name of Macao.—*TP* 47, 1959, 63–66./ *RBS* 5, 1959, 520, N.G.D. Malmqvist.

1770 Firmstone, H. W.: Chinese names of streets and places in Singapore and the Malay Peninsula.—*JRASSB* 42, 1905, 53–208.

1771 Giles, Lionel: *Glossary of Chinese topographical terms.*—London: Geographical Section, General Staff, War Office, 1943, 29 p.

1772 Han, Yu-shan: A historical survey of some geographical names of China.—*Sinologica* 1, 1948, 152–170.

1773 Hell, H.: Los noms propres chinois.—*Revue Indochinoise* 13, 1910, 335–342./ Place and personal names.

1774 Kao, Channing Rwen: *The derivation of Chinese place names.*—Bloomington: (?), 1952, 12 p.

1775 Kawahara, Masahiro: Chūgoku chimei no hensan—2, 3 no oboegaki chūshin ni shite. —*Shakai chiri* 11, 1949, 16–18. [Changes in Chinese place names—A memorandum focusing on two or three cases.]
河原正博：中國地名の變遷——2, 3の覺書を中心にして

1776 Kee, Briggs: *English-Chinese geographical*

terms.—Eugene: U. of Oregon, 1959, 47 p.

1777   Knight, A.: Chinese names of streets. —*JRASSB* 45, 1906, 287—288.

1778   Li, Ju-lung: Ti-ming tz'u te t'e-tien ho kuei-fan.—*CKYW* 1980:3, 206—211. [Special features and standardization of place names.]

李如龍：地名詞的特點和規範

1779   Mahdihassan, S.: The Chinese names of Ceylon and their derivatives.—*Journal of U. of Bombay* 19, Pt. 2, 1950, 80—84.

1780   Saussure, L. de: L'étymologie du noms des monts k'ouen louen.—*TP* 20, 1921, 370-371.

〔崑崙山〕

1781   Schafer, Edward H.: The camel in China down to the Mongol dynasty.— *Sinologica* 2, 1950, 165—194, 263—290./ 5. Place names and landmarks; 6. Nicknames and sobriquets.

1782   Serruys, Paul L-M.: Aspects linguistiques de l'hydronymie chinoise.—*Revue Internationale d'Onomastique* 7, 1955, 114—123, map./ *RBS* 1, 1955, 282, P. Demiéville.

1783   Tung, Tso-pin: Pei-ching ch'eng-li fang-yen-hua te ti-ming.—*KYAO* 70, 1924, 1—4. [Dialectalized place names inside the city of Peking.]

董作賓：北京城裏方言化的地名

1784   Wu, Liang-tso: Kuan-yü ti-ming yung tzu.—*Ti-ming chih-shih* 1981:1, 4—5. [Concerning the use of characters for place names.]

吳良祚：關於地名用字

6.11.3.2. Collection and Analysis (1785—1804)

1785   Ch'en, Cheng-hsiang: *T'ai-wan ti-ming shou-ts'e.*—Taipei: T'ai-wan sheng wen-

hsien wei-yüan-hui, 1959, 285 p., maps. [A handbook of Taiwan place names.]

陳正祥：臺灣地名手冊

1786   Ch'en, Cheng-hsiang: *T'ai-wan ti-ming tz'u-tien.*—Taipei: Fu-ming ch'an-yeh ti-li yen-chiu-so, 1960, xiii, 349 p. [Gazetteer of Taiwan place names.]

陳正祥：臺灣地名辭典

1787   Gaimushō Jōhōbu: *Shina chimei shūsei.* —Tokyo: Nippon Gaiji Kyōkai, 1935; 1938, rev. & enl. ed., vi, 626 p. [A compendium of Chinese place names.]

外務省情報部：支那地名集成

1788   Hoshi, Ayao: *Shina chimei jiten.*— Tokyo: Fuzanbō, 1941, 670 p. [A dictionary of Chinese place names.]

星斌夫：支那地名辭典

1789   Izumi, Shin: *Gendai Chūgoku chimei jiten.*—Tokyo: Gakushūsha, 1981, 672 p. [A dictionary of modern Chinese place names.]

和泉新：現代中國地名辭典

1790   Ko, Sui-ch'eng: *Tsui-hsin Chung-wai ti-ming tz'u-tien.*—Shanghai: Chung-hua, 1940; 1948, 2nd ed., 2, 4, 6, 2, 22, 1729, 52, 9, 39 p. [The newest dictionary of Chinese and foreign place names.]

葛綏成：最新中外地名辭典

1791   Lai, Ho-ch'u: *Chung-kuo ti-ming so-yin.*—Shanghai: Hsin chih-shih, 1955, 142 p. [An index to Chinese place names.]

來荷初：中國地名索引

1792   Lien ch'in ts'e-liang chih-t'u ch'ang: *T'ai-wan-sheng wu-wan-fen-i chi erh-shih-wu-wan-fen-i t'u ti-ming tz'u-tien.*—Taipei: T'ai-pei-shih lien-ho ch'in-wu tsung-szu-ling-pu ts'e-liang-ch'u, 1956, 132 p. [Gazetteer to CMS 1:50,000 and 1:250,000 maps of Taiwan.] / Chinese-English.

聯勤測量製圖廠：臺灣省五萬分一及二十五萬分一圖地名詞典

1793   Liu, Chün-jen: *Chung-kuo ti-ming ta tz'u-tien.*—Peiping: Kuo-li Pei-p'ing yen-chiu-yüan, 1930, 22, 1118, 232 p.; Taipei: Wen-hai, 1967, 8, 1118, 232 p. [A comprehensive dictionary of Chinese place names.]
劉鈞仁：中國地名大辭典

1794   Lu, Ching-yü: *Hsin-pien Chung-kuo ti-ming tz'u-ticn.*—Taipei: Wei-hsin shu-chü, 1977, 1, 1, 20, 935, 83 p. [A newly edited dictionary of Chinese place names.]
陸景宇：新編中國地名辭典

1795   Miao, Hsin-cheng: *Ying-Han Chung-wai ti-ming tz'u-hui.*—Hong Kong: Shang-wu, 1977, [iii], 346 p. [An English-Chinese dictionary of Chinese and foreign place names.]
繆鑫正：英漢中外地名詞滙

1796   Okano, Ichirō: *Manshū chimei jiten.*—Tokyo: Nippon Gaiji Kyōkai, 1933, 2, 24, 293, (romanized index) 30 p. [A dictionary of place names of Manchuria.]
岡野一郎：滿州地名辭典

1797   Ōmura, Kin'ichi: *Shina seiji chiri shi.*—Tokyo: Maruzen, 1913, vol. 1, 1913, 938 p.; vol. 2, 1915, 1025, 21 p.; maps./ Including geographic data on place names, etc. [Political and geographical gazetteers of China.]
大村欣一：支那政治地理誌

1798   Playfair, G.M.H.: *The cities and towns of China: A geographical dictionary.*—Hong Kong: Noronha & Co., 1879, xii, 417, 31, lviii p.; Hong Kong: Kelly & Walsh, 1910, 2nd ed., xii, 582, lxxvi p.

1799   Ti-t'u ch'u-pan-she: *The administrative divisions of the People's Republic of China.*—Peking: Ditto, 1981, [iv], 168 p.
〔地圖出版社〕

1800   Times shuppansha: *Saishin Chūka minkoku Manshū teikoku jinmei chimei benran.*—Tokyo: Ditto, 1939, 64, 3, 8, 223, 4, 2 p. [The newest handbook of personal and place names of the Republic of China and Manchuria.]
タイムス出版社：最新中華民國滿州帝國人名地名便覽

1801   Ting, Ch'a-an & Ko, Sui-ch'eng: *Chung-wai ti-ming tz'u-tien.*—Shanghai: Chung-hua, 1930, v.p. [A dictionary of Chinese and foreign place names.]
丁謷盦、葛綏成：中外地名辭典

1802   U.S. Department of Interior, Office of Geography: *Mainland China, administrative divisions and their seats.*—Washington, D.C.: Government Printing Office, 1963, 253 p./ Lists place names.

1803   U.S. Department of Interior, Office of Geography: *Hong Kong, Macao, Sinkiang, Taiwan, and Tibet: Official standard names approved by the U.S. Board on Geographic Names.*—Washington, D.C.: Government Printing Office, 1955, 390 p.

1804   Yen, Ti: *Han-yü p'in-yin Chung-kuo ch'ang-chien ti-ming piao* (Han-Ying-Fa-Hsi tui-chao).—Peking: Ts'e-hui, 1977, 34 p. [A table of commonly seen Chinese place names in Chinese Pinyin spelling (Chinese-English-French-Spanish).]
嚴地：漢語拼音中國常見地名表（漢、英、法西對照）

6.12. Foreign Personal and Place Names (1805–1853)
6.12.1 Translation of Foreign Names (1805–1832)
6.12.1.1. General Studies (1805–1822)

1805   Ch'en, Tu-hsiu: Hsi-wen i-yin szu i.—*HCN* 2:4, 1916, 1–6. [My opinion on the transliteration of Western names.]
陳獨秀：西文譯音私議

1806   Chou, Hua-sung: T'ung-i i-ming ho

La-ting-hua.—*FITP* 2:2, 1951, 29–30. [Unification of translation of names and Latinazation.]

周華松：統一譯名和拉丁化

1807 Chu, P'ei-hsüan: I-ming.—*Hsin Chung-kuo* 1:7, 1919, 95–118. [The translation of names.]

朱佩弦：譯名

1808 Godwin, Christopher D.: Writing foreign terms in Chinese.—*JCL* 7:2, 1979, 246–267.

1809 Ho, Ping-sung & Ch'eng, Ying-chang: Wai-kuo chuan-ming Han-i wen-t'i chih shang-ch'üeh.—*TFTC* 23:23, 1926, 71–85. [A discussion of the problems in translating foreign proper nouns into Chinese.]

何炳松、程瀛章：外國專名漢譯問題之商榷

1810 Hsiung, Wen-hua: Han-Ying ming-tz'u te tui-i.—*YCYY* 1979:2, 70–87. [On translations (and transliterations) of Chinese and English nouns.]

熊文華：漢英名詞的對譯

1811 Hu, I-lu: Lun i-ming.—*Yung yen* 2:1–2, 1914, 1–20. [On translating names.]

胡以魯：論譯名

1812 Lei, Hai-tsung: Wai-kuo shih i-ming t'ung-i wen-t'i.—*FITP* 3:2, 1951, 33–34. [The problem of unification of translations of names in foreign histories.]

雷海宗：外國史譯名統一問題

1813 Lin, Yü-t'ang: Kuan-yü i-ming t'ung-i te t'i-i.—*Yü-yen-hsüeh lun-ts'ung* (0072), 343–350. [Proposals concerning the unification of translation of names.]

林語堂：關於譯名統一的提議

1814 Lin, Yüeh-hua: Kuan-yü min-tsu i-tz'u te shih-yung ho i-ming wen-t'i.—*LSYC* 1963:2, 171–190. [Concerning the problem in usage and translation of the term *min-tzu* ('race').]

林躍華：關於『民族』一詞的使用和譯名問題

1815 Liu, Tse-hsien: Ming-tz'u yin-i ho ming-tz'u kuo-chi-hua te ch'ü-chieh.—*YWCS* 1953:3, 22–23. [Misinterpretations of transliterations and internationalization of terminology.]

劉澤先：名詞音譯和名詞國際化的曲解

1816 P'eng, Ch'u-nan: Chieh-k'o ho Po-lan chuan-yu ming-tz'u te i-fa.—*FITP* 3:5, 1951, 70–71. [Rules of the translations of Czechoslavakian and Polish proper nouns.]

彭楚南：捷克和波蘭專有名詞的譯法

1817 P'eng, Ch'u-nan: T'an-t'an Ch'ao-hsien chuan-ming te fan-i.—*FITP* 1952:4, 34–35. [A discussion on the translations of Korean proper nouns.]

彭楚南：談談朝鮮專名的翻譯

1818 Shih, Sheng-han: Kuan-yü piao-chun i-yin te chien-i.—*TSPL* 1:10, 1933, 1–7. [Proposals concerning standard transliteration.]

石聲漢：關於標準譯音的建議

1819 T'ien, Mu-ching: T'an i-ming.—*YWCS* 1959:4, 41–43. [A discussion on the translation of names.]

田慕荊：談譯名

1820 Wang, Kuo-tung: Chuan-yu ming-tz'u i-fa te i-hsieh wen-t'i.—*OYCH* 1959:3, 53–57. [A few problems in the methods of translation for proper nouns.]

王國棟：專有名詞譯法的一些問題

1821 Yang, Jen-p'ien: Shih-lun ku-yu ming-tz'u te yin-i chi ch'i t'ung-i.—*FITP* 2:4, 1951, 23–24. [A preliminary discussion on the transliteration of proper nouns and its unification.]

楊人楩：試論固有名詞的音譯及其統一

1822 Yu, Hsiung: I-ming shang-ch'üeh.—*K'ai ming* 30, 1931, 1–3. [A discussion on translation of names.]

幼雄：譯名商榷

6.12.1.2. Personal Names and Place Names (1823–1832)

1823   Chan, Ya-ta: Lun wai-kuo ti-ming i fa.—*Hsüeh-i* 9:6, 1929, 1–19. [On the methods for translating foreign place names.]
湛亞達：論外國地名譯法

1824   Ch'en, Yüan: Kuan-yü wai-kuo ti-ming Han-i te chi-tien i-chien.—*FIYK* 3:2, 1950, 62–65. [Several opinions concerning Chinese translations of foreign place names.]
陳原：關於外國地名漢譯的幾點意見

1825   Chin, Tsu-meng: Ti-ming chuan-i wen-t'i.—*Hsin Chung-hua* 3:1, 1945, 80–92. [The problem of transliterating place names.]
金祖孟：地名轉譯問題

1826   Chou, Yu-kuang: Yin-i ti-ming cheng-tzu-fa te chi-shu ko-hsin.—*WTKK* 1962:1, 8–10; 2, 16–18. [The renovation techniques for correct orthography in the transliterations of place names.]
周有光：音譯地名正字法的技術革新

1827   Han, Sheng: Jen ti-ming yin-i te t'ung-i.—*FITP* 2:4, 1951, 19–20. [The unification of transliterations of personal and place names.]
寒笙：人地名音譯的統一

1828   Lu, Chih-wei: Wai-kuo-yü jen ti-ming i-yin t'ung-i wen-t'i.—*CKYW* 1953:8, 14–17. [The problem of unification in transliterating foreign personal and place names.]
陸志韋：外國語人地名譯音統一問題

1829   Lu, Tien-yang: Yung Han-yü p'in-yin tzu-mu yin-i wai-kuo jen-ming ti-ming chi-shu-shang te shang-ch'üeh.—*WCYF* 1959:10, 32–39. [A discussion on the technical aspects of using the Chinese Pinyin alphabet in transliterating foreign personal and place names.]
陸殿揚：用漢語拼音字母音譯外國人名地名技術上的商榷

1830   Ti-ming i-yin wei-yüan-hui: Ti-ming fan-i yüan-tse ts'ao-an szu-chung.—*Ti-li chih-shih* 1959:11, 520–522; *WTKK* 1959:12, 2–4; *WCYF* 1960:1, 30–32. [Four draft plans for principles in translating place names.]
地名譯音委員會：地名翻譯原則草案四種

1831   Tung, T'ung-ho: Lun wai-kuo ti jen-ming te yin-i.—*Hsien-tai hsüeh-pao* 1:4–5, 1947, 1–13. [On the transliteration of foreign place names and personal names.]
董同龢：論外國地人名的音譯

1832   Wang, Liao-i: Lun Han-i ti-ming jen-ming te piao-chun.—*Chin-jih p'ing-lun* 1:11, 1939, 13–14. [On the standard for Chinese translations of place names and personal names.]
王了一：論漢譯地名人名的標準

6.12.2. Collection and Analysis (1833–1853)
6.12.2.1. Foreign Personal Names (1833–1841)

1833   Fol'kman, E.A.: *Slovar' Iaponskikh imen i familii.*—Moscow: Gosudarstvennoe Izdatel'stvo Inostrannykh i Natsional'nykh Slovarei, 1953; 1958, rev. ed., 1207, [4] p. [A dictionary of Japanese family names.]
〔日本姓名辭典〕

1834   Gillis, I.V. & Pai, Ping-ch'i: *Japanese surnames.*—Peking: Hwa Hsing Press, 1939, 2 Sections, 4, [ii], 11, 173, 4, 4; 171, 4, [18] p.; Ann Arbor: Edwards Brothers, 1942, repr.

1835   Gillis, I.V. & Pai, Ping-ch'i: *Japanese personal names.*—Peking: Hwa Hsing Press, 1940, 2 Sections, [v], 10, 70; 70 p.; Ann Arbor: Edwards Brothers, 1943, repr./ Index by strokes and romanization.

1836   Hsin, Hua: *Ying-yü hsing ming i-ming*

shou-ts'e.—Peking: Shang-wu, 1973, rev. & enl. ed., ii, 442 p./ 1st ed., 1965, under title: *Ying-yü kuo-chia hsing ming i-ming shou-ts'e.* [A handbook of translations of English surnames and personal names.]

辛華：英語姓名譯名手册（初版原名：英語國家姓名譯名手册）

1837   O'Neill, P. G.: *Japanese names: A comprehensive index by characters and readings.*—New York & Tokyo: John Weatherhill, 1972, xvi, 359 p.

〔日本人名地名辭典〕

1838   P'an, Nien-chih & Chin, Ming-jo: *Shih-chieh jen-ming ta tz'u-tien*—Shanghai: Shih-chieh, 1936, 1886, 15, 167 p. [A comprehensive dictionary of world personal names.]

潘念之、金溟若：世界人名大辭典

1839   Shih, Ch'ün: *Jih-pen hsing ming tz'u-tien* (La-ting tzu-mu hsü).—Peking: Shang-wu, 1979, [iii], 666 p. [A dictionary of Japanese surnames and personal names (in Latin alphabetical order).]

史群：日本姓名詞典（拉丁字母序）

1840   T'ang, Ching-kao: *Hsien-tai wai-kuo jen-ming ta tz'u-tien.*—Shanghai: Shang-wu, 1933, 1022, 5 p. [A comprehensive dictionary of foreign personal names.]

唐敬杲：現代外國人名大辭典

1841   Wang, Yün-wu, et al.: *Piao-chun Han-i wai-kuo jen-ming ti-ming piao.*—Shanghai: Shang-wu, 1934, 490, 157 p. [A list of standard Chinese transliterations of foreign personal and place names.]/ English-Chinese & Chinese-English.

王雲五等：標準漢譯外國人名地名表　附漢英對照表

6.12.2.2. Foreign Place Names (1842–1853)

1842   Abolmasov, A. P. & Nemzer, L. A.: *Slovar' Iaponskikh geograficheskikh nazva-*

nii.—Moscow: Gosudarstvennoe Izdatel'stvo Inostrannykh i Natsional'nykh Slovarei, 1959, 577 p. [A dictionary of Japanese geographical names.]

〔日本地名辭典〕

1843   Ajia Kenkyūjo: *Gendai sekai chimei jinmei shinbun tsūshinmei Chūgokogo Nichi Eigo jiten.*—Tokyo: Ditto, 1966, 925 p. [A Chinese-Japanese-English dictionary of modern place names, personal names, and names of world press today.]

アジア研究所：現代世界地名人名新聞通信名中國語日英語辭典

1844   Hsin, Hua: *Shih-chieh pao-k'an t'ung-hsün-she tien-t'ai i-ming shou-ts'e.*—Peking: Shang-wu, 1965, x, 258 p. [A handbook of translations of world newspapers, news agencies, and broadcasting stations.]/ English-Chinese.

辛華：世界報刊通訊社電臺譯名手册

1845   Hsin, Hua: *Shih-chieh ch'uan-po mei-chieh i-ming shou-ts'e.*—Hong Kong: Shang-wu, 1979, [i], 9, 301 p. [A handbook of world communication media.]/ English-Chinese; a rev. ed. of (1844).

辛華：世界傳播媒介譯名手册

1846   Hsin-hua shu-tien: *O-Hua shih-chieh ti-ming chien-ming shou-ts'e.*—Peking: Ditto, 1954, 236 p. [A concise Russian-Chinese handbook of world place names.]

新華書店：俄華世界地名簡明手册

1847   Hu, Tzu-tan: *Kuo-chi Han-i ti-ming tz'u-tien.*—Taipei: Kuo-chi wen-hua shih-yeh, 1980, [i], 282 p. [A dictionary of Chinese translation of international place names.]/ Including street names of Hong Kong, Japanese city and town names, Singapore place names, and Thailand place names.

胡子丹：國際漢譯地名辭典

1848   Jen-min   chiao-t'ung   ch'u-pan-she:

Chung-O-Ying shih-chieh chiao-t'ung ti-ming tz'u-tien.—Peking: Ditto, 1955, 245 p.; Hong Kong: Ta-chung shu-chü, 1958, repr., 493 p.; with an alphabetical listing from English to Chinese, under title: *Chung-Ying tui-chao shih-chieh chiao-t'ung ti-ming tz'u-tien.* [A Chinese-Russian-English dictionary of world-communications place names.]

人民交通出版社：中俄英世界交通地名辭典
（ 香港版：中英對照世界交通地名辭典 ）

1849　Kuo-li pien-i-kuan: *Wai-kuo ti-ming i-ming.*—Taipei: Cheng-chung, 1966, [ii], 153, 13 p. [Translations of foreign place names.]

國立編譯館：外國地名譯名

1850　Lu, Ching-yü: *Wai-kuo ti-ming tz'u-tien.*—Taipei: Wei-hsin, 1967, [ii], 9, 878, 30, 165 p. [A dictionary of foreign place names.]

陸景宇：外國地名辭典

1851　Maeda, Kiyoshige & Miyoshi, Seibi: *Chū-Nichi-Ō taishō sekai chimei jiten.*—Tenri: Tenri Daigaku shuppanbu, 1967, 9, 176 p. [A Chinese-Japanese-European dictionary of place names of the world.]

前田清茂、三好成美：中日歐對照世界地名辭典

1852　Takenouchi, Yasumi: *Sekai no chimei Chūgokugo jiten.*—Kagoshima: Ditto (?), 1959, 358 p. [An encyclopedia of place names of the world in Chinese.]

竹之內安巳：世界の地名中國語事典

1853　Ti-t'u ch'u-pan-she: *Han-O-Ying tui-chao ch'ang-yung wai-ko ti-ming ts'an-k'ao tzu-liao.*—Peking: Ditto, 1959, 167 p. [Chinese-Russian-English reference materials for commonly used foreign place names.]

地圖出版社：漢俄英對照常用外國地名參考資料

7. SET-PHRASES, PROVERBS, *HSIEH-HOU-YÜ* AND WITTICISMS (1854–2748)

7.1. Set-phrases (1854–2168)

7.1.1. Definition and Problems (1854–1885)

1854 Arita, Tadahiro: Chūgokugo ni okeru seigo.—*RDR* 409, 1976, 30–49. [Set-phrases in Chinese.]
有田忠弘：中國語における成語

1855 Chang, Hsü-hou: Kuan-yü ch'eng-yü.—*HYW* 1960:1, 40. [Concerning set-phrases.]
張煦侯：關於成語

1856 Chang, Hsüeh-hsien: Shih t'an ch'eng-yü te fan-hsin ho kai-tsao.—*YCT* 1, 1981, 74–77. [A preliminary discussion on the renovation and remodeling of set-phrases.]
張學賢：試談成語的翻新和改造

1857 Chang, Kuo-ch'ing: *Ch'eng-yü ch'ien shuo.*—Harbin: Hei-lung-chiang jen-min, 1974, 122 p. [A simple discussion on set-phrases.]
張國慶：成語淺說

1858 Ch'ang, Hsüan & Chüan, Chi: Lun ch'eng-yü.—*CKYW* 1958:10, 471–474. [On set-phrases.]
昌煊、全基：論成語

1859 Chih, Han: Pa ch'eng-yü hua chiu wei hsin.—*CKYT* 34:6, 1974, 24–25. [Turn old set-phrases into new ones.]
稚翰：把成語化舊為新

1860 Ch'in, Wang: Yeh lai t'an wen-yen ch'eng-yü.—*YWCS* 1955:3, 39. [Let us also discuss literary set-phrases.]
秦望：也來談文言成語

1861 Ching, Eugene: Four-syllable expressions in Chinese.—*POLA* 7, 1964, 1–62./ Including set-phrases.

1862 Chou, Tsu-mo: T'an ch'eng-yü.—*YWHH* 1955:1, 33–38. [A discussion on set-phrases.]
周祖謨：談成語

1863 Feng, Shih: *Ch'eng-yü te ch'ü-wei.*—Hong Kong: Ch'ung-ming, 1963, 167 p. [The fun of set-phrases.]
馮式：成語的趣味

1864 Ho, Ai-jen: Han-yü te ch'eng-yü.—*YWCS* 1957:7, 18–22. [Chinese set-phrases.]
何靄仁：漢語的成語

1865 Hsiang, Kuang-chung: *Ch'eng-yü kai-shuo.*—Wuhan: Hu-pei jen-min, 1982, [ii], 106 p. [A general discussion of set-phrases.]
向光忠：成語概說

1866 Hsin, Hsiang: Ch'eng-yü te t'e-hsing.—*CKYW* 1958:10, 474–476. [Characteristics of set-phrases.]
欣向：成語的特性

1867 Hsü, Chao-pen: *Ch'eng-yü chih-shih ch'ien-t'an.*—Peking: Pei-ching, 1980, [i], 199 p. [A simple discussion on knowledge of set-phrases.]
許肇本：成語知識淺談

1868 Hu, Ch'i-yün: T'an ch'eng-yü.—*CSCY* 1963:1, 18–19. [A discussion on set-phrases.]
胡啓雲：談成語

1869 Hui, Chün: *Ch'eng-yü te t'ien-ti.*—Hong Kong: Shang-wu, 1980, [ii], 108 p. [The world of set-phrases.]/ A general introduction.
卉君：成語的天地

1870 Lin, Wen-chin: Ts'ung hsing-chih ho t'e-tien k'an ch'eng-yü te fan-wei.—*CKYW* 1959:2, 76, 61. [The scope of set-phrases as seen from their characteristics and special features.]
林文金：從性質和特點看成語的範圍

1871 Liu, Chieh-hsiu: *Ch'eng-yü.*—Peking: Shang-wu, 1983, 62 p. [Set-phrases.]
劉潔修：成語

1872 Ma, Kuo-fan: Han-yü ch'eng-yü.—

NMSY, 1958:1, 25—35. [Chinese set-phrases.]
馬國凡：漢語成語

1873   Ma, Kuo-fan: *Ch'eng-yü chien-lun.*—Shenyang: Liao-ning jen-min, 1959, [ii], 51 p.; *Yü-wen hui-pien* (0058), 35:120. [A brief discussion on set-phrases.]
馬國凡：成語簡論

1874   Ma, Kuo-fan: *Ch'eng-yü.*—Huhehot: Nei Meng-ku jen-min, 1978, 2, 341 p. [Set-phrases.]
馬國凡：成語

1875   P'u, Yung-ch'uan: Ts'ung *Tzu yeh* chung yün-yung te ch'eng-yü lai t'an-t'an ch'eng-yü te chi-ko wen-t'i.—*YWCS* 1958:3, 24—29. [A discussion on several problems of set-phrases from the set-phrases used in (the novel) *Tzu yeh* (of Mao Tun).]
蒲永川：從〔茅盾〕『子夜』中運用的成語來談談成語的幾個問題

1876   Shih, Shih: *Han-yü ch'eng-yü yen-chiu.*—Chengtu: Szu-ch'uan jen-min, 1979, 2, 2, 577 p. [A study on Chinese set-phrases.]
史式：漢語成語研究

1877   Sun Liang-ming: Lun Han-yü ch'eng-yü shih i piao-hsien tz'u-hsing wen-t'i.—*STSY* 1981:2, (not seen). [On the problem of explaining the meanings of Chinese set-phrases which indicate the word classes.]
孫良明：論漢語成語釋義表現詞性問題

1878   Sun, Shen-chih: Shih t'an ch'eng-yü.—*STHL* 1956:1—2, 1—8. [A preliminary discussion on set-phrases.]
孫慎之：試談成語

1879   T'ang, Ch'i-yün: *Ch'eng-yü, yen-yü, hsieh-hou-yü, tien-ku kai-shuo.*—Canton: Kuang-tung jen-min, 1981, [2] 121 p. [A general discussion on set-phrases, proverbs, *hsieh-hou-yü,* and literary allusions.]

唐啓運：成語、諺語、歇後語、典故概說

1880   Toropov, A.A.: Chen-yui i ikh svoistva.—*Spornye voprosy stroia Kitaiskogo iazyka* (Moscow: Izd. Nauk, 1965), 110—134. [Set-phrases and their characteristics.]

1881   Toropov, A.A.. Transl. by Yü, Yün-hsia: Han-yü ch'eng-yü chi ch'i t'e-hsing.—*YCYY* 1982:1, 79—84, 148. [Chinese set-phrases and their characteristics.] (1880)
塔羅波夫著，余雲霞譯述：漢語成語及其特性

1882   Wang, Wen-yü: T'an-t'an ch'eng-yü.—*Yü-wen chi-ch'u chih-shih* (0076), 53—62. [A discussion on set-phrases.]
王問漁：談談成語

1883   Wen, Ch'i-chih: *Ch'eng-yü chiang-hua.*—Hong Kong: Shang-hai shu-chü, 1962, 69 p. [Lectures on set-phrases.]
文起之：成語講話

1884   Wu, Chan-k'un: Yu-kuan ch'eng-yü te chi-ko wen-t'i.—*HPTH* 1962:2, 99—118. [Several problems concerning set-phrases.]
武占坤：有關成語的幾個問題

1885   Wu, Mo-an: T'an-t'an ch'eng-yü.—*YWHT* 3, 1978, 125—131. [A discussion on set-phrases.]
吳默庵：談談成語

7.1.2. Differentiation (1886—1900)
7.1.2.1. General Differentiation (1886—1894)

1886   Chiang, K'un-wu: Ch'eng-yü yü ch'eng-tz'u.—*SKCH* 1979:4, 329—335. [Set-phrases and set-words.]
姜昆武：成語與成詞

1887   Chou, Hung-ming: Ch'eng-yü pien hsi.—*YWHH* 1981:4, 54—55. [Differentiation and analysis of set-phrases.]
周宏溟：成語辨析

1888   Chu, Chieh-fan: Yen-yü yü fang-yen, su-hua, ko-yen, ch'eng-yü.—*TLTC* 24:12,

1962, 13–19. [Proverbs and dialects, popular sayings, maxims, and set-phrases.]

朱介凡：諺語與方言、俗話、格言、成語

1889 Fo, Lang: Ch'eng-yü ken su-yü.— *TPPYK* 1:1, 1934, 22–23. [Set-phrases and popular sayings.]

佛郎：成語跟俗語

1890 Kuei, I: Ch'eng-yü, yen-yü, ko-yen, su-yü, li-yü te ch'ü-pieh.—*YWHH* 1958:1, 35. [The differences between set-phrases, proverbs, maxims, popular sayings, and slang.]

瓊一：成語、諺語、格言、俗語、俚語的區別

1891 Li, Tao-i: Shih lun p'i-chieh yü chi ch'i yü hsieh-hou-yü, ch'eng-yü, yen-yü te ch'ü-pieh.—*CCSY* 1981:1, 67–76. [A preliminary discussion on *p'i-chieh yü* ('metaphor-explanation phrases') and their differences from *hsieh-hou-yü,* set-phrases, and proverbs.]

李道一：試論譬解語及其與歇後語、成語、諺語的區別

1892 T'ang, Sung-po: Shu-yü ho ch'eng-yü te chung-shu kuan-hsi.—*CKYW* 1960:11, 375–376. [The relationship as to category of idioms and set-phrases.]

唐松波：熟語和成語的種屬關係

1893 T'ung, Chih-ho: Ch'eng-yü yü hsieh-hou-yü.—*YWCS* 1957:9, 14–19. [Set-phrases and *hsieh-hou-yü.*]

童致和：成語與歇後語

1894 Yang, Hsin-an: Ch'eng-yü ho yen-yü te ch'u-pieh.—*CKYW* 1961:3, 31–33. [The differences of set-phrases and proverbs.]

楊欣安：成語和諺語的區別

7.1.2.2. Set-phrases and Commonly Used Idioms (1895–1900)

1895 Lang, Chün-chang: Hsien-tai Han-yü li te kuan-yung yü.—*CLTH* 1963:1, (not seen). [Commonly used idioms in Modern Chinese.]

郎峻章：現代漢語裏的慣用語

1896 Shen, Meng-ying: Hsien-tai Han-yü kuan-yung yü ch'u t'an.—*WSC* 1982:2, 23–28. [A preliminary investigation into the commonly used idioms in Modern Chinese.]

沈孟瓔：現代漢語慣用語初探

1897 Shih, Pao-i, et al: Han-yü kuan-yung yü chien-shuo.—*YCYY* 1982:4, 87–101. [A brief discussion of commonly used idioms in the Chinese language.]

施寶義等：漢語慣用語簡說

1898 Wang, Kuei-hua: Ch'ien t'an kuan-yung yü.—*YCT* 1, 1981, 78–84. [A simple discussion on commonly used idioms.]

王桂華：淺談慣用語

1899 Yang, Hsin-an: T'an-t'an kuan-yung yü. —*HNSY* 1979:2, 90–93. [A discussion on commonly used idioms.]

楊欣安：談談慣用語

1900 Yün, Sheng: Kuan-yü *shu-yü.*—*CKYW* 1959:7, 349. [Concerning idioms.]

雲生：關於『熟語』

7.1.3. Formation and Structure (1901–1918)

1901 Chang, Kung-kuei: Shu-tz'u ch'eng-yü te kou-ch'eng fang-shih.—*YWCS* 1953:7, 18–20. [The formation patterns of set-phrases with numerals.]

張拱貴：數詞成語的構成方式

1902 Chang, Kung-kuei: Ch'eng-yü chung te ch'eng-t'ao ko-shih.—*NSHP* 1962:3, 90–109. [The complete set of patterns in set-phrases.]

張拱貴：成語中的成套格式

1903 Chu, Chien-mang: Ch'eng-yü te chi-pen hsing-shih chi ch'i tsu-chih kuei-lü te t'e-tien.—*CKYW* 1955:2, 32–34, 31; *Hsien-tai Han-yü . . . tzu-liao* (0064), 361–370. [Basic patterns of set-phrases and special features of their rules of structure.]

朱劍芒：成語的基本形式及其組織規律的特點

1904   Hayakawa, Tetsu: Seigo no kōsei.—*Chūken nōto* 6, 1959, (not seen). [The formation of (Chinese) set-phrases.]

早川徹：成語の構成

1905   Hsü, Te-nan: Shih t'an ch'eng-yü szu-yin-hua wen-t'i.—*YCYY* 1979, Feb., 19–25. [A preliminary discussion on the problem of quadrisyllabization of set-phrases.]

許德楠：試談成語四音化問題

1906   Hsueh, P'ing: *Ch'eng-yü te chieh-kou ho yün-yung.*—Hong Kong: Lo-t'o, 1977, 8, 92 p. [The structures and usages of set-phrases.]

薛平：成語的結構和運用

1907   Hu, Li-wen: T'an fan-i-tz'u tsu-ch'eng te ch'eng-yü.—*YWCH* 1958:10, 35. [A discussion on set-phrases made of antonyms.]

胡力文：談反義詞組成的成語

1908   Katō, Hideo: Sūshi to gumiawaseru shiji no seigo ni tsuite.—*KKDGK* 1:2, 1959, 41–43. [On four-character set-phrases which are combined with numerals.]

加藤秀雄：數詞と組み合せる四字の成語について

1909   Katō, Hideo: 1930-nen *Hsiao-shuo yüeh-pao* ni mirareru shiji seigo.—*KKDGK* 22, 1972, 41–52. [Four-character set-phrases as seen in the 1930 *Hsiao-shuo yüeh-pao.*]

加藤秀雄：1930年『小說月報』に見られる四字成語

1910   Lan, Chung-wen: Ch'eng-yü hai-shih pu-neng sui-pien huan tzu.—*CKYW* 1959:4, 188. [Set-phrases still do not allow optional changing of characters.]

藍仲文：成語還是不能隨便換字

1911   Lin, Hai-chen: *Chung-kuo ch'eng-yü te chieh-kou.*—Hsinchuang: Fu Jen U., 1976, 1, 2, 66 p./ Unpubl. M.A. thesis. [The structure of Chinese set-phrases.]

林海珍：中國成語的結構

1912   Ma, Kuo-fan: Ch'eng-yü te ting-hsing ho kuei-fan-hua.—*CKYW* 1958:10, 477–478. [The fixed patterns and standardization of set-phrases.]

馬國凡：成語的定型和規範化

1913   P'an, Kung: Ts'ung *Mao Tse-tung hsüan-chi* chung te lien-ho-shih ch'eng-yü t'an ch'eng-yü te ch'uang-tsao.—*YWCH* 1959:7, 32–35. [A discussion on the creation of set-phrases from the coordinate type of set-phrases in *Mao Tse-tung hsüan-chi.*]

潘汞：從『毛澤東選集』中的聯合式成語談成語的創造

1914   Rogachev, A.P.: Idiomatika kitaiskogo yazyka, otobrazhennaya v ustoichivykh slovosochetapiyakh (chen-yui.) (0374). [Notes on the *ch'eng-yü* 〔成語〕 type of compound.]

1915   Shih, K'uei: I-i hsiang-chin te szu-tzu ch'eng-yü.—*YWCS* 1958:7, 37–38. [Four-character set-phrases of which meanings are mutually close.]

師葵：意義相近的四字成語

1916   Shih, Wai-han & Kuo, Ku-hsi: Ch'eng-yü ch'ai huan kuei-lü ch'u t'an.—*YWTC* 8, 1981, 28–34; *Hu-nan shih-yüan hsüeh-pao* 1981:3, 71–76. [A preliminary investigation into the rules on the separation and change of set-phrases.]

師外漢、郭谷兮：成語拆換規律初探

1917   Ting, T'ai: Ch'eng-yü k'o-i pao-k'uo tuan chü.—*TSYC* 1982:6, 121–122. [Set-phrases may include short sentences.]

定泰：成語可以包括短句

1918   Togawa, Yoshio: Seigo no sugata.—*CGGG* 219, 1974, 30–31, 7. [The forms

of set-phrases.]
戸川芳郎：成語のすがた

7.1.4. Origin and Development (1919–1934)

1919   Ch'en, Ju-fa: Ch'eng-yü yin yüan wen-t'i lüeh shuo.—*TSYC* 1981:4, 122–124. [A brief discussion on the problem of citing the origins of set-phrases (in dictionaries).]
陳汝法：成語引源問題略說

1920   Ch'en, Kuo-hung: *Ch'eng-yü yüan.*—Tainan: Ditto, 1979, 2, 189, 911 p. [The origins of set-phrases.]
陳國弘：成語源

1921   Ch'en, Kuo-hung: *Ch'eng-yü yüan.*—Tainan: Ditto, 1981, 1, 2, 2, 2, 1648 p. [The origins of set-phrases.]
陳國弘：成語源

1922   Li, Yüan: *Ch'eng-yü t'an-yüan.*—Hong Kong: Chung-liu, n.d., 5, 85 p. [Tracing the origins of set-prhases.]
李元：成語探源

1923   Ma, Kuo-fan: Ch'eng-yü te yen-pien.—*YYWH* 1958:2, 21–22. [The evolution of set-phrases.]
馬國凡：成語的演變

1924   P'an, Yün-chung: Ch'eng-yü, tien-ku te hsing-ch'eng ho fa-chan.—*CSTH* 1980:2, 98–106. [The formation and development of set-phrases and literary allusions.]
潘允中：成語、典故的形成和發展

1925   Szu, Erh-tung: Hsien chieh-tuan ch'eng-yü yen-pien te ch'ü-shih.—*YCT* 2, 1981, 45–49. [The trend in the current stage of the development of set-phrases.]
斯爾螽：現階段成語演變的趨勢

1926   Tōdō, Akiyasu: Kango no jukugo wa dō-shite dekitaka?—*KBKS* 27, 1956, 1–7. [How were Chinese idioms formed?]
藤堂明保：漢語の熟語はどうしてできたか？

1927   Tung, Ming-chieh: T'an-t'an ku-tai ch'eng-yü te lai-yüan ho hsing-ch'eng.—*CCSY* 1981:1, 77–78. [A discussion on the origin and formation of ancient set-phrases.]
董銘傑：談談古代成語的來源和形成

1928   Wang, Li: *Han-yü shih kao* (0945), Chap. 4:61: (The development of) set-phrases and literary allusions. [A draft history of the Chinese language.]
王力：漢語史稿／第四章，第六十一節：成語和典故（的發展）

1929   Wu, Chien-yang: Shih t'an ch'eng-yü te hsin fa-chin.—*CKYW* 1959:2, 77. [A preliminary discussion on the recent developments of set-phrases.]
吳劍揚：試談成語的新發展

1930   Wu, Fa: *Ch'eng-yü chung te li-shih—ts'ung Ch'in mo tao Han ch'u.*—Hong Kong: T'ien-ti, 1977, 2, 2, 2, 206 p. [Histories (found) in set-phrases—from the end of the Ch'in to the beginning of the Han (dynasties).]
吳法：成語中的歷史──從秦末到漢初

1931   Wu, Yüeh: T'ung-i ch'eng-yü te lai-yüan.—*YWHT* 6, 1978, 103–105. [The origins of synonymous set-phrases.]
吳越：同義成語的來源

1932   Yang, Hsin-chou: *Ch'eng-yü t'an-yüan.*—Taipei: Wu-chou, 1963, 173 p. [Tracing the origins of set-phrases.]
楊新洲：成語探源

1933   Yang, T'ien-ko: Ch'eng-yü k'ao-yüan—*Tui Han-yü ch'ang-yung ch'eng-yü shou-ts'e te pu cheng.*—*YCT* 2, 1981, 50–54. [A study of the origins of set-phrases—Addenda and corrigenda to *Han-yü ch'ang-yung ch'eng-yü shou-ts'e* (2083).]
楊天戈：成語考源──對『漢語常用成語手冊』的補正

1934   Yang, T'ien-ko: *Han-yü ch'eng-yü su yüan.*—Peking: Wai-yü chiao-hsüeh yü yen-chiu, 1982, 13, 154 p. [Tracing the origins of Chinese set-phrases.]

楊天戈：漢語成語溯源

7.1.5. Explanation of Meaning (1935–1947)

1935 Araya, Susumu: Sūshi o fukumu seigo no imi ni tsuite—Ba Hō no sakuhin o megutte.—*DTBDK* 18, 1980, 169–186. [On the meanings of set-phrases containing numerals—centering around Ma Feng's works.]

荒屋勧：數詞を含む成語の意味について——馬峰の作品をめぐって

1936 Chang, Po-yüan: Kuan-yü ch'eng-yü te chiang hsi.—*YWHT* 3, 1978, 131–133. [Concerning the explanation and analysis of set-phrases.]

張伯元：關於成語的講析

1937 Harada, Minoru: Gendai Chūgoku ni okeru koji seigo no shin kaishaku. *GGSK* 144, 1963, 59–63. [New explanations of the set-phrase historical allusions in modern China.]

原田稔：現代中國における故事成語の新解釋

1938 Hattori, Masayuki: *Chūgokugo atarashii seigo no hanashi.*—Tokyo: Kōseikan, 1972, 6, 212 p. [The story of new set-phrases in the Chinese language.]

服部昌之：中國語新しい成語の話

1939 1414 Hu, Li-wen: T'ung-i ch'eng-yü chi ch'i pien-hsi.—*YWHT* 6, 1978, 105–108. [Synonymous set-phrases and their differentiation and analysis.]

胡力文：同義成語及其辨析

1940 Huang, Yüeh-chou: Ch'eng-yü chung shu-tz'u so piao-shih te ch'ou-hsiang i.—*CKYW* 1980:6, 416–419. [The abstract meanings expressed in the numerals of set-phrases.]

黃岳洲：成語中數詞所表示的抽象義

1941 Kao, Kuang-lieh: *Chung-hsüeh-sheng ch'ang-yung ch'eng-yü li shih.*—Changchun:

Chi-lin jen-min, 1980, 2, 20, 334 p. [Examples with explanations of set-phrases commonly used by middle school students.]

高光烈：中學生常用成語例釋

1942 Lin, Pao-hua: Chi-ko ch'eng-yü te chien shih.—*YWHH* 1959:3, 26–27. [Brief explanations of several set-phrases.]

林保華：幾個成語的簡釋

1943 Liu, Chieh: Ku-tai ch'eng-yü fen-hsi chü li.—*LNHP* 10:1, 1949, 83–97. [Examples of the analysis of ancient set-phrases.]

劉節：古代成語分析舉例

1944 Ni, Pao-yüan: *Ch'eng-yü pien-hsi.*—Peking: Chung-kuo she-hui k'o-hsüeh, 1979, 2, 8, 369 p. [Differentiation and analysis of set-phrases.]

倪寶元：成語辨析

1945 Szu, Erh-tung: Ch'eng-yü shih i i-te.—*YWHT* 6, 1978, 109–111. [My humble opinion on explaining the meanings of set-phrases.]

斯爾鑫：成語釋義一得

1946 Wang, Chien-hsün: T'an ch'eng-yü te pao pien.—*YWHH* 1955:9, 39–40. [A discussion on the meliorative and pejorative meanings of set-phrases.]

王見薰：談成語的褒貶

1947 Wang, Wei-yung: *Ch'ang-yung ch'eng-yü chieh-hsi.*—Taiepi: Wei-wen t'u-shu, 1978, 6, 156 p. [An explanatory analysis of commonly used set-phrases.]

王偉勇：常用成語解析

7.1.6. Scientific and Cultural Aspects (1948–1952)

1948 Fu-chien k'o-chi pao-she: *Ch'eng-yü li te k'o-hsüeh* (Ti-i chi).—Foochow: Fu-chien k'o-hsüeh chi-shu, 1981, 2, 5, 153 p., illus. [Science (found) in set-phrases (Vol. I.).]

福建科技報社：成語裏的科學　第一輯

1949 Hsiang, Kuang-chung: Ch'eng-yü yü min-tsu tzu-jan huan-ching, wen-hua ch'uan-t'ung, yü-yen t'e-tien te kuan-hsi. —*CKYW* 1979:2, 135–139; *Hsien-tai Han-yü . . . tzu-liao* (0064), 371–379. [The relationships between set-phrases, the natural environment of races, cultural traditions, and linguistic characteristics.]

向光忠：成語與民族自然環境、文化傳統、語言特點的關係

1950 Li, I-fu, et al.: *Ch'eng-yü chung te k'o-hsüeh.*—Nanking: Chiang-su jen-min, 1981, [iv], 132 p. [Science (found) in set-phrases.]

勵藝夫等：成語中的科學

1951 Liu, Kang: Mou hsieh ch'eng-yü chung te ku Han-yü chih-shih.—*YCYY* 1982:2, 99–107. [Knowledge of the ancient Chinese language from certain set-phrases.]

劉綱：某些成語中的古漢語知識

1952 Morris, Peter Thomas: *Chinese sayings —What they reveal of Chinese history and culture.*—Hong Kong: Po Wen Book Co., 1981, xii, 278 p.

〔潘敏賢：從成語看中國歷史文化〕

7.1.7. Historical Sources (1953–2008)

1953 Anonymous: *Ch'eng-yü ku-shih chi-ch'eng.*—Kaohsiung: Ta-chung shu-chü, n.d., 2 vols., in 1, [xiii], 321; [xi], 353 p. [A general compendium of set-phrase historical allusions.]

無名氏：成語故事集成

1954 Anonymous: *Ch'eng-yü ku-shih ta-ch'üan.*—Taipei: Ch'ün-feng, n.d., 509 p. [A complete collection of set-phrase historical allusions.]

無名氏：成語故事大全

1955 Anonymous: *Ch'eng-yü ku-shih.*—Tainan: Hsi-pei, 1975, 6, 319 p., illus. [Set-phrase historical allusions.]

無名氏：成語故事

1956 Anonymous: *Ch'eng-yü ku-shih ch'üan chi.*—Yunghochen: Ta-fang, 1975, 8, 312 p. [A complete collection of set-phrase historical allusions.]

無名氏：成語故事全集

1957 Anonymous: *Chung-kuo ch'eng-yü ku-shih.*—Tainan: Tsung-ho, 1977, 8, 383 p. [Chinese set-phrase historical allusions.]

無名氏：中國成語故事

1958 Anonymous: *Ch'eng-yü ku-shih.*—Tainan: Li-ta, 1978, 7 357 p., illus. [Set-phrase historical allusions.]

無名氏：成語故事

1959 Anonymous: *Chung-kuo ch'eng-yü ku-shih.*—Kowloon: Pai-ling, 1978, 163 p. [Chinese set-phrase historical allusions.]

無名氏：中國成語故事

1960 Anonymous: *Chung-kuo ch'eng-yü ku-shih.*—Hong Kong: Shang-hai shu-chü, 1980, [ii], 168 p., illus. [Chinese set-phrase historical allusions.]

無名氏：中國成語故事

1961 Anonymous: *Chung-kuo ch'eng-yü ku-shih.*—Taipei: Chiang-men, 1982, 16, 479 p. [Chinese set-phrase historical allusions.]

無名氏：中國成語故事

1962 Ashida, Takaaki: *Chūgoku no koji, kotowaza.*—Tokyo: Shakai shisōsha, 1970, 242 p. [(Set-phrase) historical allusions and proverbs of China.]

蘆田孝昭：中國の故事，ことわざ

1963 Chang, Shu-ch'eng: *Ch'eng-yü ku-shih hsin pien.*—Singapore: Hsing-chou shih-chieh, 1956, 140 p. [A new collection of set-phrase historical allusions.]

張書城：成語故事新編

1964 Ch'en, Ch'ing-ling: *Ch'eng-yü tien-ku.*—Tainan: Piao-chun, 1968, 173 p. [Set-phrase historical allusions.]

陳清凌：成語典故

1965   Cheng-yen ch'u-pan-she: *Tsui hsin ch'eng-yü ku-shih ta-ch'üan.*—Tainan: Ditto, n.d., 406 p. [The newest complete collection of set-phrase historical allusions.]

正言出版社：最新成語故事大全

1966   Chiang, Yüeh-ch'iao: *Piao-chun ch'eng-yü ku-shih.*—Taipei: Wen-hua t'u-shu, 1963–1964, 2 vols., illus., (not seen). [Standard set-phrase historical allusions.]

蔣月樵：標準成語故事

1967   Chiang-hsi Shih-yüan Chung-wen-hsi: *Ch'eng-yü ku-shih hsüan.*—Nanchang: Chiang-hsi jen-min, 1980, 282 p. [Selected set-phrase historical allusions.]

江西師院中文系：成語故事選

1968   Ch'ien, Shih-wei: *Ch'eng-yü ku-shih hsin pien.*—Tainan: Tsung-ho, 1962, 160 p. [A new edition of set-phrase historical allusions.]

錢世偉：成語故事新編

1969   Ch'ing P'ing, et al.: *Ch'eng-yü ku-shih.*—Hong Kong: Wei-ch'ing, 1958, 6, 153 p., illus. [Set-phrase historical allusions.]

清平等：成語故事

1970   Chiu-chiu ch'u-pan-she: *Chung-kuo ch'eng-yü ku-shih.*—Taipei: Ditto, 1981, 431 p. [Chinese set-phrase hsitorical allusions.]

久久出版社：中國成語故事

1971   Chou, Lo-shan: *Li-shih ch'eng-yü ku-shih.*—Kaohsiung: Ta-chung shu-chü, 1963, 224 p. [Historical allusions of set-phrases.]

周樂山：歷史成語故事

1972   Chou, Lo-shan: *Hsin pien ch'eng-yü ku-shih.*—Kaohsiung: Ta-chung shu-chü, 1063, 8, 246 p. [A new edition of set-phrase historical allusions.]

周樂山：新編成語故事

1973   Chou, Lo-shan: *Ch'eng-yü ku-shih ta-ch'üan.*—Kaohsiung: Ta-chung shu-chü, 1964, 6, 351 p. [A complete collection of set-phrase historical allusions.]

周樂山：成語故事大全

1974   Chu, Tien-hsin & Jen, Shuai-ying: *Ch'eng-yü ku-shih.*—Peking: T'ung-su tu-wu, 1955, 37 p. [Set-phrase historical allusions.]

朱典馨、任率英：成語故事

1975   Endō, Tetsuo: *Koji seigo seiku jiten.*—Tokyo: Meiji shoin, 1973, 415 p./ *Chin san-shih nien . . . chien chieh* (0010), 59. [A dictionary of set-phrase historical allusions.]

遠藤哲夫：故事成語成句辭典

1976   Feng, Tso-min & Sung, Hsiu-ling: *Chung-kuo ch'eng-yü ming yen tien yüan.*—Taipei: Hsing-kuang, 1981, 3, 12, 749 p. [Sources of Chinese set-phrases and famous literary allusions.]

馮作民、宋秀玲：中國成語名言典源

1977   Fu, Wei: *Ch'eng-yü ku-shih i-pai p'ien.*—Kaohsiung: Pai-ch'eng shu-tien, 1974, 112 p. [One hundred set-phrase historical allusions.]

傅偉：成語故事一百篇

1978   Ho, Lin: *Piao-chun ch'eng-yü ku-shih.*—Tainan: Fu-han, 1974, 465 p. [Standard set-phrase historical allusions.]

鶴麟：標準成語故事

1979   Hosoda, Mikio: *Chūgoku koji tatoe jiten.*—Tokyo: Tōkyōdō, 1972, 330 p./ *Chin san-shih nien . . . chien chieh* (0010), 58–59. [A dictionary of Chinese historical allusions and metaphors.]/ Allusions, set-phrases, proverbs, etc.

細田三喜夫：中國故事たとえ辭典

1980   Hsüan, Wen: *Ch'eng-yü ku-shih.*—Hong Kong: Kuang-ch'eng, 1972, 8, 105 p. [Set-phrase historical allusions.]

宣文：成語故事

1981 Hsüeh, P'ing: *Chung-kuo ch'eng-yü ku-shih.*—Hong Kong: Kuang-lu shu-tien, 1959, 153 p. [Chinese set-phrase historical allusions.]

雪萍：中國成語故事

1982 Iitsuka, Akira: *Koji henreki—Chūgoku seigo shū.*—Tokyo: Jiji tsūshinsha, 1982, 264 p. [A pilgrimage to historical allusions —A collection of Chinese set-phrases.]

飯塚朗：故事遍歷——中國成語集

1983 Ikeda, Shirōjirō: *Koji jukugo daijiten.* —Tokyo & Osaka: Hōbunkan, 1924; 1940, 92nd print., 4, 5, 6, 206, 4, 1750, 204, 8 p.; 1960, repr., 300, 1750, 204 p./ *Chin san-shih nien . . . chien chieh* (0010), 56–57. [A comprehensive dictionary of (Chinese) historical allusions and idiomatic expressions.]

池田四郎次郎：故事熟語大辭典

1984 Jung, Sheng: *Ch'eng-yü ku-shih hsüan tu.*—Peking: Wen-tzu kai-ko, 1982, 1, 301 p. [Selected readings on set-phrase historical allusions.]

蓉生：成語故事選讀

1985 Kanno, Dōmei: *Koji seigo daijiten.*— Tokyo: Meiji shoin, 1907; 1912, rev. ed.; 1929, repr.; 1936, repr., 1851, 134 p./ *Chin san-shih nien . . . chien chieh* (0010). 56. [A comprehensive dictionary of set-phrase historical allusions.]/ Drawn from Chinese classics.

簡野道明：故事成語大辭典

1986 Kao, Mo-yeh & Chou, Lo-shan: *Ch'eng-yü ku-shih* (ho ting pen).—Kaohsiung: Cheng-yen, 1964, 8, 509 p. [Set-phrase historical allusions (one volume edition).]

高莫野、周樂山：成語故事（合訂本）

1987 Katō, Jōken & Mizukami, Shizuo: *Chūgoku koji seigo jiten.*—Tokyo: Kadogawa shoten, 1979, 636 p. [A dictionary of Chinese set-phrase historical allusions.]

加藤常賢、水上靜夫：中國故事成語辭典

1988 Ku, Hsin-ling: *Ch'eng-yü ku-shih.*— Taipei: Kuo-hsüeh, 1973, 268 p. [Set-phrase historical allusions.]

古信凌：成語故事

1989 Li, T'ang: *Chung-kuo ch'eng-yü tien-ku.* —Hong Kong: Shang-hai shu-chü, 1980, 3, 173 p. [Chinese set-phrase literary allusions.]

李唐：中國成語典故

1990 Li, Wei-ch'ing: *Ch'eng-yü ku-shih ta tien.*—Tainan: Tahsia, 1978, 15, 761 p. [A comprehensive dictionary of set-phrase historical allusions.]

黎偉青：成語故事大典

1991 Li, Yü-fu & Wu, Tien-hsün: *Ch'eng-yü tien-ku wen-hsüan.*—Chinan: Shan-tung jen-min, 1981, 2 vols., 5, 17, 387; 26, 510 p. [An anthology of set-phrase literary allusions.]

李毓芙、武殿勛：成語典故文選

1992 Liu, Yüan-fu: *Ch'eng-yü tien-ku ku-shih hüsan.*—Harbin: Hei-lung-chiang jen-min, 1979, (not seen). [Selected set-phrase literary and historical allusions.]

劉元福：成語典故故事選

1993 Liu, Yüan-fu: *Ch'eng-yü tien-ku ku-shih hsüan* (hsü chi).—Harbin: Hei-lung-chiang jen-min, 1982, 16, 379 p. [Selected set-phrase literary and historical allusions (a continuation).]

劉元福：成語典故故事選　續集

1994 Ma, Hua: *Ch'eng-yü li-shih ku-shih.*— Sian: Shan-hsi jen-min, 1958; 1959, 3rd print., 6, [2], 118 p. [Set-phrase historical allusions.]

馬華：成語歷史故事

1995 Miwa, Noritsugu: Chūgoku minkan seigo koji (4).—*Ōbun ronsō* 7, 1977, 57–70. [Chinese popular set-phrase historical allusions (4).]

三輪典嗣：中國民間成語故事（四）

1996 Pei-ching yü-yen hsüeh-yüan: *Ch'eng-yü*

ku-shih hsüan.—Peking: Wai-wen, 1982, [iv], 178 p. [A selection of set-phrase historical allusions.]

北京語言學院：成語故事選

1997 Takahashi, Gen'ichirō: *Koji seigo gengo shūkai.*—Tokyo: Meiji shoin, 1955; 1962, repr., 699 p. [Collection and explanations of historical allusions, set-phrases, and proverbs.]

高橋源一郎：故事成語諺語集解

1998 Tseng-wen ch'u-pan-she: *Ch'eng-yü ku-shih chi-ch'eng.*—Taichung: Ditto, 1975, 5 vols., illus., (not seen). [A grand compendium of set-phrase historical allusions.]

曾文出版社：成語故事集成

1999 Tung-fang ch'u-pan-she: *Ch'eng-yü ku-shih* (Ti-i chi).—Taipei: Ditto, 1971, 8, 307 p., illus. [Set-phrase historical allusions (Vol. I).]

東方出版社：成語故事（第一輯）

2000 Weng, Ch'uan-yü: *Ch'eng-yü ku-shih.* —Kaohsiung: Pai-ch'eng shu-chü, 1973, 9, 504 p. [Set-phrase historical allusions.]

翁傳鈺：成語故事

2001 Wu, Chi-lu & Sun, Hsiao-szu: *Li-shih ch'eng-yü ku-shih hsin pien* (1).—Peking: Pei-ching, 1981, 2, 2, 152 p., illus. [A new collection of set-phrase historical allusions (1).]

吳繼路、孫孝思：歷史成語故事新編（一）

2002 Wu, P'ing-k'ang: *Ch'eng-yü te ch'u-ch'u.* —Hong Kong: Hsin shih-tai, n.d., 2 vols., 8, 293; 6, 293 p. [Sources of set-phrases.]／ Set-phrase historical allusions.

吳萍康：成語的出處

2003 Wu, Yü-ch'eng: *Ch'eng-yü ku-shih.*— Peking: Chung-kuo shao-nien erh-t'ung, 1981, 205 p. [Set-phrase historical allusions.]

伍玉成：成語故事

2004 Yamada, Katsumi: *Koji seigo jiten.*—

Tokyo: Tōkyōdō, 1981; 1982, 2nd ed., 44, 516 p. [A dictionary of set-phrase historical allusions.]

山田勝美：故事成語辭典

2005 Yang, Chen-chung & Ch'en, Jen-hsiung: *Ch'eng-yü ku-shih hsüan.*—Shanghai: Shang-hai chiao-yü, 1978, 1st ed; 1979, 2nd print., 3, 162 p., illus. [Selected set-phrase historical allusions.]

楊振中、陳人雄：成語故事選

2006 Yang, Chen-chung & Ch'en, Jen-hsiung: *Ch'eng-yü ku-shih i-pai tse.*—Shanghai: Shang-hai chiao-yü, 1981, 232 p. [One hundred set-phrase historical allusions.]

楊振中、陳人雄：成語故事一百則

2007 Yü, Szu-mu: *Ch'eng-yü ku-shih hsüan shih.*—Hong Kong: Ch'iao-kuang shu-tien, n.d., [xi], 353 p. [A selection with explanations of set-phrase historical allusions.]

余思牧：成語故事選釋

2008 Yüan, Lin & Shen, T'ung-heng: *Ch'eng-yü tien-ku.*—Shenyang: Liao-ning jen-min, 1982, 54, 776 p. [Set-phrase historical allusions]

袁林、沈同衡：成語典故

7.1.8. Collection and Analysis (2009–2152)
7.1.8.1. Chinese Works (2009–2115)

2009 Anonymous: *Hsin ch'eng-yü tz'u-tien.* —Hong Kong: Ch'iao-kuang shu-tien, 1956, 242 p. [A new dictionary of set-phrases.]

無名氏：新成語辭典

2010 Anonymous: *Hsüeh-sheng ch'eng-yü tz'u-hui.*—Hong Kong: Chung-hua wen-k'u, 1958, 954 p. [A student's glossary of set-phrases.]

無名氏：學生成語辭彙

2011 Anonymous: *Chung-kuo ch'eng-yü ta tz'u-tien.*—Hong Kong: Yüan-tung, 1960, 321 p. [A comprehensive dictionary of

Chinese set-phrases.]

無名氏：中國成語中辭典

2012   Anonymous: *Han-yü ch'eng-yü tz'u-tien.*—Hong Kong: Shang-wu, 1965, 2, 32, 292 p. [A dictionary of Chinese set-phrases.]

無名氏：漢語成語詞典

2013   Anonymous: *Shih-yung Chung-kuo ch'eng-yü ta tz'u-tien.*—Tainan: Hsin shih-chi, 1972, 19, 60, 368 p. [A practical comprehensive dictionary of Chinese set-phrases.]

無名氏：實用中國成語大辭典

2014   Anonymous: *Fen-lei ch'eng-yü ta tz'u-tien.*—Taipei: Hsin-sheng, 1973, v.p. [A classified comprehensive dictionary of set-phrases.]

無名氏：分類成語大辭典

2015   Anonymous: *Ch'eng-yü tz'u-tien.*—Tainan: Hsin shih-chi, 1974, 19, 268, 61 p. [A dictionary of set-phrases.]

無名氏：成語辭典

2016   Anonymous: *Chung-kuo ch'eng-yü ta tz'u-tien.*—Yunghochen: Ta-fang, 1975, 4, 264, 56 p. [A comprehensive dictionary of Chinese set-phrases.]

無名氏：中國成語大辭典

2017   Anonymous: *Kuo-yü chu-yin Chung-kuo ch'eng-yü ta tz'u-tien.*—Tainan: Chuang-chia, 1979, 31, 91, 552 p. [A comprehensive dictionary of Chinese set-phrases with National Language pro-nunciations.]

無名氏：國語注音中國成語大辭典

2018   Anonymous: *Shih-yung Chung-kuo ch'eng-yü ta tz'u-tien. Fu Ch'eng-yü ku-shih.*—Tainan: Chuang-chia, 1979, 20, 61, 313, 59, 7; 366 p. [A practical comprehensive dictionary of Chinese set-phrases. With set-phrase historical allusions.]

無名氏：實用中國成語大辭典　附成語故事

2019   Anonymous: *Kuo-yü chu-yin Chung-kuo ch'eng-yü ta tz'u-tien.*—Taipei: Chung-yu wen-hua shih-yeh, 1980, 3 vols., 2, 5, 229; 4, 181; 145 p. [A comprehensive dictionary of Chinese set-phrases with National Language pronunciations.]

無名氏：國語注音中國成語大辭典

2020   Chang, Kuang-i: *Chung-kuo ch'eng-yü ta tz'u-tien.*—Taipei: Yüan-tung, 1966, 16, 96, 321 p. [A comprehensive dictionary of Chinese set-phrases.]

張光義：中國成語大辭典

2021   Ch'ang-chou-shih Chiao-yü-chü: *Ch'eng-yü tz'u-tien.*—Nanking: Chiang-su jen-min, 1981, [iii], 94, 1067 p./ *TSYC* 1983:2, 138–141, 179. Chu Tsu-yü. [A dictionary of set-phrases.]

常州市教育局：成語詞典／諸祖煜評

2022   Chao, Shun: *Pa yung Chung-wen ch'eng-yü tz'u-tien.*—Yunghochen: Ditto, n.d., 24, 530 p. [An eight-usage dictionary of Chinese set-phrases.]

趙順：八用中文成語辭典

2023   Ch'ao, T'ien: *Ch'ang-yung ch'eng-yü.*—Shanghai: Shang-hai chiao-yü, 1965, 50 p. [Commonly used set-phrases.]

超天：常用成語

2024   Ch'en, Ch'eng-chih: *Chung-kuo ch'eng-yü yen-yü liu-pai chü.*—Taipei: Yüan-tung, 1974, 2, 69 p. [Six hundred Chinese set-phrases and proverbs.]

陳澄之：中國成語諺語六百句

2025   Ch'en, Chi-kang & Chou, Lo-shan: *Chung-kuo ch'eng-yü ta tz'u-tien.*—Tainan: Cheng-yen, 1980, 2 pts., 60, 188; 8, 509 p., illus. [A comprehensive dictionary of Chinese set-phrases.]

陳紀綱、周樂山：中國成語大辭典

2026   Ch'en, Chien-hsin: *Ch'eng-yü hsüan shih.*—Kunming: Yün-nan jen-min, 1981, 528 p. [A selection with explanations of set-phrases.]

陳見昕：成語選釋

2027 Ch'en, Kuo-hung: *Shih-yung ch'eng-yü tz'u-tien.*—Tainan: Ditto, 1982, [ii], 800, 97 p. [A practical dictionary of set-phrases.]

陳國弘：實用成語詞彙

2028 Ch'en, Szu-liang: *Tso-wen ch'eng-yü tz'u-tien.*—Taipei: Hsiang-sheng, 1975, [ii], 31, 28, 274 p. [A dictionary of set-phrases for composition.]

陳斯艮：作文成語辭典

2029 *Ch'eng-yü hsüan chu* tsu: *Ch'eng-yü hsüan chu.*—Canton: Kuang-tung jen-min, 1977, 82 p. [A selection with annotations of set-phrases.]

『成語選注』組：成語選注

2030 Chiang, Yin-nan: *T'ung-i ch'eng-yü li chieh.*—Chengchow: Ho-nan jen-min, 1981, 247 p. [Examples with explanations of synonymous set-phrases.]

蔣蘊楠：同義成語例解

2031 Chiang, Yüeh-ch'iao: *Chung-kuo ch'eng-yü ta tz'u-tien.*—Taipei: Hsin-lu shu-chü, 1965, 2, 2, 33, 258 p. [A comprehensive dictionary of Chinese set-phrases.]

蔣月樵：中國成語大辭典

2032 Chin, Chin: *Han-wen ch'eng-yü tz'u-tien.*—Hong Kong: Han-ying shu-chü, n.d., 44, 529 p. [A dictionary of Chinese set-phrases.]

金近：漢文成語辭典

2033 Chiu-chiu ch'u-pan-she: *Chung-kuo ch'eng-yü ta tz'u-tien.*—Taipei: Ditto, 1981, 25, 74, 399, 62 p. [A comprehensive dictionary of Chinese set-phrases.]

久久出版社：中國成語大辭典

2034 Chou, Chih-hui & Li, Tao-fan: *Chung-kuo ch'eng-yü ta tz'u-tien.*—Shanghai: Ch'ao-feng, 1948, 10th ed., 550 p. [A comprehensive dictionary of Chinese set-phrases.]

周知暉、李道藩：中國成語大辭典

2035 Chou, Ju-hui, et al.: *Hsüeh-lin ch'eng-yü ta tz'u-tien.*—Shanghai: Ch'ao-feng, 1948, 32, 520 p.; Kowloon: Hsüeh-lin shu-chü, 1957, 32, 518 p. [Hsüeh-lin's comprehensive dictionary of set-phrases.]

周如暉等：學林成語大辭典

2036 Chou, Ming: *Ch'ang-yung ch'eng-yü 1300 t'iao.*—Shanghai: Shang-hai chiao-yü, 1980, 8, 86 p.; Hong Kong: Hsiang-kang ch'ing-nien, 1980, repr. [1300 commonly used set-phrases.]

周明：常用成語1300條

2037 Chu, Hsüeh-ch'eng & Ch'en, T'ien-sung: *Chu-yin ch'eng-yü ta tz'u-tien.*—Tainan: Fu-wen, 1974, [i], 2, 109, 440 p.; 1982, 4th ed., 2, 111, [ii], 637 p. [A comprehensive dictionary of set-phrases with phonetic notation.]

朱學成、陳天送：注音成語大辭典

2038 Ch'ü, Wan-li: *Shih* san-pai p'ien ch'eng-yü ling shih.—*WSCH* 4, 1952, 1–18. [Fragmentary explanations of the set-phrases found in the three hundred poems of *Shih-ching.*]

屈萬里：『詩』三百篇成語零釋

2039 Chuang, Shih: *Kuo-wen ch'eng-yü tz'u-tien.*—Shanghai: Shang-hai t'u-shu, 1916; Shanghai: Chung-kuo t'u-shu, 1926, 7th ed., 2, 2, in 12 pts., v.p. [A dictionary of set-phrases in Chinese literary language.]

莊適：國文成語辭典

2040 Chung, Hsiang-lin: *Chung-kuo ch'eng-yü ta tz'u-tien.*—Tainan: Shih-i shu-chu, 1982, 20, 61, 313, 59 p. [A comprehensive dictionary of Chinese set-phrases.]

鍾香琳：中國成語大辭典

2041 Chung-hua shu-chü pien-chi-pu: *Ching-hua ch'eng-yü tz'u-tien.*—Taipei: Ditto, 1956, 2, 2, 17, 721 p.; 1964, repr. [A dictionary of Chinese set-phrases.]

中華書局編輯部：中華成語詞典

2042 Fan, Fang-lien, et al.: *Hsien-tai Han-yü*

ch'eng-yü tz'u-tien.—Peking: Shang-wu, 1959, 296 p./ *CKYW* 1959:2, 93–94, Cheng, Mei-chi. [A dictionary of set-phrases in modern Chinese language.]
范方蓮等：現代漢語成語詞典／鄭梅基評

2043 Feng, Jui: *Chung-wen liu yung ch'eng-yü ta tz'u-tien.*—Hong Kong: Hui-t'ung shu-tien, 1974, 26, 418, 12 p. [A six-usage comprehensive dictionary of Chinese set-phrases.]
豐瑞：中文六用成語大辭典

2044 Feng, Jui: *Pa yung Chung-wen ch'eng-yü tz'u-tien.*—Hong Kong: Hui-t'ung shu-tien, 1978, 2, 24, 532 p., illus./ *Hsi-pei ta-hsüeh hsüeh-pao* 1982:2, 67–69, 85, Ma T'ien-hsiang. [An eight-usage dictionary of Chinese set-phrases.]
豐瑞：八用中文成語辭典／馬天祥評

2045 Fu-chien jen-min ch'u-pan-she: *Ch'eng-yü hsin pien.*—Foochow: Fu-chien jen-min chiao-yü, 1961–1963, 4 vols., 73; 60; 71; 69 p. [A new collection of set-phrases.]
福建人民出版社：成語新編

2046 *Han-yü ch'eng-yü hsiao tz'u-tien* hsiu-ting hsiao-tsu: *Han-yü ch'eng-yü hsiao tz'u-tien.*—Peking: Shang-wu, 1973, 3rd rev. ed., 56, 329 p.; 1978, repr. [A small dictionary of Chinese set-phrases.]
『漢語成語小詞典』修訂小組：漢語成語小詞典

2047 Ho, Cheng-wen: *Hsin pien ch'eng-yü hsüan.*—Hong Kong: T'ien-t'ien t'u-shu, 198?, [iv], 190 p. [A newly edited selection of set-phrases.]
何正文：新編成語選

2048 Ho, Li: *Hsiao-hsüeh-sheng ch'ang-yung ch'eng-yü liu-pai chieh.*—Changchun: Chi-lin jen-min, 1981, 374 p. [Explanations of six hundred commonly used set-phrases of elementary school students.]
何荔：小學生常用成語六百解

2049 Hsieh, Min: *Szu-yung ch'eng-yü tz'u-*

tien.—Singapore: Shih-chieh, 1957 2, 12, 387 p. [A four-usage dictionary of set-phrases.]
謝敏：四用成語辭典

2050 Hsin-sheng ch'u-pan-she: *Hsin pien ch'eng-yü yen-yü tz'u-tien.*—Taipei: Ditto, 1957, 8, 546 p. [A newly edited dictionary of set-phrases and proverbs.]
新生出版社：新編成語諺語辭典

2051 Hsin-ta ch'u-pan-she: *Chu-yin pan ch'eng-yü ta tz'u-tien.*—Taipei: Ditto, 1982, [ii], 18, 78, 451 p. [A comprehensive dictionary of set-phrases with phonetic notation.]
欣大出版社：注音版成語大辭典

2052 Hsiung, Kuang-i: *Chung-kuo ch'eng-yü ta tz'u-tien.*—Taipei: Yüan-tung, 1980, 112, 321 p. [A comprehensive dictionary of Chinese set-phrases.]
熊光義：中國成語大辭典

2053 Hsü, Chih-t'ao: *Shih-yung ch'eng-yü hsin tz'u-tien.*—Hong Kong: Ming-hua shu-tien, 1957, rev. ed., 5, 44, 365 p. [A new practical dictionary of set-phrases.]
徐芝濤：實用成語新辭典

2054 Hsü, Yeh-chi: *Shih-yung ch'eng-yü tz'u-tien.*—Hong Kong: Shih-tai t'u-shu, 1978, 68, 443 p. [A practical dictionary of set-phrases.]
許業基：實用成語辭典

2055 Hsüeh-jen: *Szu-yung ch'eng-yü ta tz'u-tien.*—Taipei: Kuo-hsüeh, 1982, 2, 18, 306 p. [A four-usage comprehensive dictionary of set-phrases.]
學人：四用成語大辭典

2056 Hsüeh-sheng ch'u-pan-she: *Tsui hsin ch'eng-yü ta-ch'üan.*—Taipei: Ditto, 1971, 6, 146 p. [The newest complete collection of set-phrases.]
學生出版社：最新成語大全

2057 Hu-nan-sheng t'u-shu-kuan & Ch'ang-

sha-shih chiao-shih chin-hsiu hsüeh-yüan: *Ch'ang-yung ch'eng-yü tien-ku hsüan shih.* —Changsha: Ditto, 1978, 432 p. [A selection with explanations of commonly used set-phrase historical allusions.]
湖南省圖書館、長沙市教師進修學院：常用成語典故選釋

2058 Hua-cheng shu-chü pien-chi-pu: *Pa yung Chung-wen ch'eng-yü tz'u-tien.* —Taipei: Ditto, 1974, 530 p. [An eight-usage dictionary of Chinese set-phrases.]
華正書局編輯部：八用中文成語辭典

2059 I, Su-min: *Chien-ming ch'eng-yü.* —Hsinchuang: Ta-hsüeh wen-hsüan-she, 1971, 11, 131 p. [Concise set-phrases.]
易蘇民：簡明成語

2060 I, Su-min: *Wan-yung ch'eng-yü su-yü ta tz'u-tien.* —Hsinchuang: Ta-hsüeh wen-hsüan-she, 1971, 31, 518 p. [A multiple-usage comprehensive dictionary of set-phrases and popular proverbs.]
易蘇民：萬用成語俗諺大辭典

2061 Kan-su shih-fan ta-hsüeh Chung-wen-hsi Han-yü chiao-yen-tsu: *Han-yü ch'eng-yü hui shih.* —Kansu: Ditto, 1974, (not seen). [A collection with explanations of Chinese set-phrases.]
甘肅師範大學中文系漢語教研組：漢語成語滙釋

2062 Kan-su shih-fan ta-hsüeh Chung-wen-hsi: *Han-yü ch'eng-yü tz'u-tien.* —Shanghai: Shang-hai chiao-yü, 1978, 88, 889 p./ *CKYW* 1979:3, 232–235, 216, Wang K'o-chung; *YCT* 3, 1982, 149–154, Sun Yü-p'ing; see (2076), (2077) and (2101). [A dictionary of Chinese set-phrases.]
甘肅師範大學中文系：漢語成語詞典／王克仲評，孫毓蘋評

2063 Kao, Kuo-shu: *Chung-kuo ch'eng-yü ta tz'u-tien.* —Tainan: Hsi-pei, n.d., 19, 239, 5, 319 p. [A comprehensive dictionary of Chinese set-phrases.]
高國書：中國成語大辭典

2064 Kao, Mo-yeh: *Chung-kuo ch'eng-yü ta tz'u-tien.* —Hong Kong: Shang-hai yin-shu-kuan, 1969, 73, 298 p.; Kaohsiung: Ta-chung shu-chü, n.d., repr. [A comprehensive dictionary of Chinese set-phrases.]
高莫野：中國成語大辭典

2065 Kao, Mo-yeh: *Tsui-hsin ch'eng-yü ta tz'u-tien.* —Tainan: Cheng-yen, 1971, 2, 73, 298 p., illus./ See Kao, Mo-yeh & Chou, Lo-shan (2066). [The newest comprehensive dictionary of set-phrases.]/ Same as (2064).
高莫野：最新成語大辭典

2066 Kao, Mo-yeh & Chou, Lo-shan: *Chung-kuo ch'eng-yü ta tz'u-tien.* —Tainan: Cheng-yen, 1971, 8, 509 p./ Appended to Kao, Mo-yeh (2065). [A comprehensive dictionary of Chinese set-phrases.]
高莫野、周樂山：中國成語大辭典

2067 Kao, Te-p'ei: *Tsui-hsin ch'eng-yü ta tz'u-tien.* —Tainan: Cheng-yen, 1972; 1974, repr., 2 pts., [ii], 73, 298; 8, 509 p. [The newest comprehensive dictionary of set-phrases.]/ Pt. 2 consists of set-phrase historical allusions.
高德沛：最新成語大辭典

2068 Kao, Te-p'ei: *Chung-kuo ch'eng-yü ta tz'u-tien.* —Tainan: Cheng-yen, 1974, 44, 222, 114, 2, 8, 312 p. [A comprehensive dictionary of Chinese set-phrases.]
高德沛：中國成語大辭典

2069 K'o, Huai-ch'ing: *Fen-lei ch'eng-yü shou-ts'e.* —Shanghai: Hsin-lu shu-tien, 1948, 9th ed., *Cheng pien,* 2, 2, 4, 148 p.; *Hsü pien,* 4, 3, 125 p.; *San pien,* 2, 2, 3, 106, 64 p.; Tainan: Fu-han, 1967, repr. anonymously. [A handbook of classified set-phrases (combined ed. of vols. I, II, and III.]
柯槐青：分類成語手冊（正、續、三編合訂本）

2070 K'o, Huai-ch'ing: *Chien-ming ch'eng-yü tz'u-tien.* —Shanghai: Hsin-lu shu-tien,

1952, [ii], 96 p. [A concise dictionary of set-phrases.]
柯槐青：簡明成語辭典

2071 K'o, Huai-ch'ing: *Fen-lei ch'eng-yü ta-chüan.*—Hong Kong: Wei-ch'ing shu-tien, 1974, 422 p. [A complete collection of classified set-phrases.]
柯槐青：分類成語大全

2072 Ku, Kuang-yü: *Chung-kuo ch'eng-yü tz'u-tien.*—Taipei: Li-ming, 1983, 292 p. [A dictionary of Chinese set-phrases.]
谷光宇：中國成語辭典

2073 Kuo, Hou-chüeh: *Kuo-yü ch'eng-yü ta-ch'üan.*—Shanghai: Chung-hua, 1930, (not seen). [A complete collection of set-phrases in the National Language.]
郭後覺：國語成語大全

2074 Li, Ch'ing-jung: *Chien-ming ch'eng-yü tz'u-tien.*—Singapore: Fan T'ai-p'ing-yang shu-yeh, 1978, 16, 280 p. [A concise dictionary of set-phrases.]/ With an appendix of Chinese-English translations.
李清榮：簡明成語詞典

2075 Li, Kuo-liang: *Ch'eng-yu chi ts'ui.*—Taipei: Wen-hua t'u-shu, 1971, 2, 9, 171 p. [A selected collection of set-phrases.]
李國良：成語集粹

2076 Li, Po-ching: Yeh t'an *Han-yü ch'eng-yü tz'u-tien.*—*CHYC* 1979:4, (not seen). [A discussion also on *Han-yü ch'eng-yü tz'u-tien* (2062).]
李伯敬：也談『漢語成語詞典』

2077 Liang, Chih-i: Ch'eng-yü chih shih-i yü k'ao-ting—Tu *Han-yü ch'eng-yü tz'u-tien* hsiao i.—*CKYW* 1979:3, 236. [The explanations of meanings and researches on set-phrases—A brief discussion on reading *Han-yü ch'eng-yü tz'u-tien* (0262).]
梁之抑：成語之釋義與考訂——讀『漢語成語詞典』小議

2078 Lin, Chien-ching: *Kuo-yin ch'eng-yü tz'u-tien.*—Tainan: Hsin shih-chi, 1973, [ii], 1007, 102 p.; Kaohsiung: Ko-hsin wen-hua, n.d., repr. [A dictionary of set-phrases with National Language pronunciations.]
林建經：國音成語詞典

2079 Lin, Yü-t'ang: *Shih-yung ch'eng-yü tz'u-tien.*—Hong Kong: Hsiang-kang t'u-shu, n.d., 6, 78, 755, [2] p. [A practical dictionary of set-phrases.]
林語堂：實用成語辭典

2080 Liu, Hsing-chai: *Tsui hsin Chung-kuo ch'eng-yü ta tz'u-tien.*—Tainan: Tsung-ho, 1977, 2, 97, 421 p. [The newest comprehensive Chinese set-phrase dictionary.]
劉省齋：最新中國成語大辭典

2081 Liu, K'ai-ming: Tu shu-p'ing so hsiang-tao te.—*CKYW* 1959:5, back cover. [Thoughts on reading (several) book reviews.]/ Concerning *Hsien-tai Han-yü ch'eng-yü tz'u-tien* (2042).
劉凱鳴：讀書評所想到的

2082 Liu, Li-yeh: *Chung-kuo ch'eng-yü ta tz'u-tien.*—Tainan: Ta fu-ch'eng, 1978, 375 p. [A comprehensive dictionary of Chinese set-phrases.]
劉麗葉：中國成語大辭典

2083 Lu, Ko, et al.: *Han-yü ch'ang-yung ch'eng-yü shou-ts'e.*—Hohehot: Nei Meng-ku jen-min, 1978; 1980, repr., 64, 676 p. [A handbook of commonly used Chinese set-phrases.]
魯歌等：漢語常用成語手册

2084 Lu, Yung-ch'üan: *Chung-kuo szu-yung ch'eng-yü ta tz'u-tien.*—Taipei: Min-lo, 1973, 28, 418 p. [A Chinese four-usage comprehensive dictionary of set-phrases.]
陸湧泉：中國四用成語大辭典

2085 Ma, Hsi-chien & Ch'en, Tseng-chieh: T'ai-wan-sheng pien *Ch'eng-yü tien* so i.—*TSYC* 1981:3, 147–152. [Miscellaneous

discussions on the *Ch'eng-yü tien* compiled in Taiwan province (2086).]
馬錫鑒、陳增杰：臺灣省編『成語典』瑣議

2086   Miao, T'ien-hua: *Ch'eng-yü tien.*—Taipei: Fu-hsing hsu-chü, 1973, rev. ed., 3, 54, 886, 148 p. [A dictionary of set-phrases.]
繆天華：成語典

2087   Pei-ching ta-hsüeh Chung-kuo yü-yen wen-hsüeh-hsi 1955 chi yü-yen pan: *Han-yü ch'eng-yü hsiao tz'u-tien.*—Peking: Shang-wu, 1958, 60, 338 p.; 1972, rev. ed., 56, 329 p.; Tientsin: T'ien-chin jen-min, 1978, 2nd print./ *YWHH* 1959:1, 24, Chien Yü. [A small dictionary of Chinese set-phrases.]
北京大學中國語言文學系1955級語言班：漢語成語小詞典／見宇評

2088   P'ing-p'ing pien-chi-pu: *Hsin pien wan-yung ch'eng-yü ta tz'u-tien.*—Yung-hochen: P'ing-p'ing, 1967, 16, 710 p. [A newly edited multiple-usage comprehensive dictionary of set-phrases.]
平平編輯部：新編萬用成語大辭典

2089   Shen, I-chung: *Chung-kuo ch'eng-yü ta tz'u-tien.*—Tainan: Tsung-ho, 1975, 731 p. [A comprehensive dictionary of Chinese set-phrases.]
沈一忠：中國成語大辭典

2090   Shih, Yao: *Chung-kuo ch'eng-yü szu-yung tzu-tien.*—Kaohsiung: Pai-ch'eng shu-tien, 1965, 15, 120 p. [A four-usage dictionary of Chinese set-phrases.]
史堯：中國成語四用字典

2091   Su, Shang-yao: *Hsin-pien ch'eng-yü tz'u-tien.* Fu lu: *T'ai-wan su yen ch'eng-yü.*—Taipei: Wen-hua t'u-shu, 1977, 18, 315 p. [A newly edited dictionary of set-phrases. Wtih appendix: Popular proverbs and set-phrases of Taiwan.]
蘇尙耀：新編成語辭典、附錄：臺灣俗諺成語

2092   Sun, Hsi-chung: *Hsin pien ch'eng-yü*

shou-ts'e.—Taipei: Hsin-lu shu-chü, 1957, 2, 3, 295, 96 p. [A newly edited handbook of set-phrases.]
孫希中：新編成語手册

2093   Sung, Hsiu-ling & Feng, Tso-min: *Chung-kuo ch'eng-yü ming yen tien yüan.*—Taichung: Hsing-kuang, 1981, 749 p. [The origins of Chinese set-phrases and famous sayings.]
宋秀玲、馮作民：中國成語名言典源

2094   Szu-yung ch'eng-yü ta tz'u-tien pien-chi wen-yüan-hui: *Szu-yung ch'eng-yü ta tz'u-tien.*—Taipei: Kuo-hsüeh, 1978, 308 p. [A four-usage comprehensive dictionary of set-phrases.]
『四用成語大辭典』編輯委員會：四用成語大辭典

2095   Tanaka, Seiichirō: *Chūgokugo jukugo jiten.*—Tokyo: Hakusuisha, 1977, 31, 266 p.; 1980, 3rd print. [A dictionary of Chinese idioms.]/ Including set-phrases.
田中淸一郎：中國語熟語辭典

2096   Ting, Yeh-fu: *Chien-ming ch'eng-yü hsin pien.*—Hong Kong: Mei-mei, 1957, 11. 131 p. [A new concise collection of set-phrases.]
丁野夫：簡明成語新編

2097   Torii, Hisayasu & Shang, Li-fu: Jitsuyō seigo reikai.—*Zenrin* 14:5, 1943, 44–47; 7, 37–49; 8, 42–43; 10, 8–11; 12, 39–42. [Examples with explanations of practical set-phrases.]
鳥居久靖、尚立夫：實用成語例解

2098   Wan-yüan t'u-shu kung-szu: *Hsin pien ch'eng-yü tz'u-tien.*—Hong Kong: Ditto, 1979, 88, 889 p. [A newly edited dictionary of (Chinese) set-phrases.]
萬源圖書公司：新編成語詞典

2099   Wang, Chao & Chu, Ch'eng-chih: *Hsüeh-sheng ch'eng-yü tz'u-tien.*—Hong Kong: Hsiang-kang hung-yeh shu-chü, 1961, 5, 13, 206 p. [A student's dictionary of set-phrases.]

汪肇、諸澄之：學生成語辭典

2100 Wang, I-hsin: *Ch'eng-yü tz'u-tien.*—Tainan: Yang-yang, 1964; Taipei: I-pan, 1975, 4, [4], 514 p. [A dictionary of set-phrases.]

王一心：成語辭典

2101 Wang, K'o-chung: *Han-yü ch'eng-yü tz'u-tien* tu hou chi.—*CKYW* 1979:3, 232–235, 216. [Notes after reading *Han-yü ch'eng-yü tz'u-tien* (2062).]

王克仲：『漢語成語詞典』讀後記

2102 Wang, Shih-shih: *Shih-yung ch'eng-yü ta tz'u-tien.*—Shanghai: Ta-lu t'u-shu, 1924, (not seen). [A practical comprehensive dictionary of set-phrases.]/ Ancient Chinese set-phrases.

王士湜：實用成語大辭典

2103 Wang, Ta-ch'ang: *Chung-kuo ch'eng-yü ta tz'u-tien.*—Tainan: Ta-tung shu-chü, 1971, 2, 44, 312 p./ With an appendix of set-phrase historical allusions, proverbs, etc. [A comprehensive dictionary of Chinese set-phrases.]

王大昌：中國成語大辭典

2104 Wang, Yeh-ts'un: *Shih-yung ch'eng-yü tz'u-tien.*—Peiping: Chung-hua yin-shu-chü, 1936, (not seen). [A practical dictionary of set-phrases.]

王野村：實用成語辭典

2105 Wei, Chien-kung, et al.: *Han-yü ch'eng-yü hsiao tz'u-tien.*—Peking: Shang-wu, 1959, rev. ed., 338 p. [A small dictionary of Chinese set-phrases.]

魏建功等：漢語成語小詞典

2106 Wen, Ts'ai, et al.: *Ch'eng-yü hsüan shih.*—Taiyuan: Shan-hsi jen-min, 1978, 35, 314 p. [A selection with explanations of set-phrases.]

文才等：成語選釋

2107 Wu, Hsia-yün: *Ch'eng-yü pien cheng.*—

Taipei: Wu-ling, 1980, 382 p. [The correct differentiation of set-phrases.]

吳霞雲：成語辨正

2108 Wu, Jui-shu: *Tso-wen ch'eng-yü tz'u-tien.*—Taipei: Ta Chung-kuo t'u-shu, 1956, [ii], 4, 3, 58, 470 p. [A dictionary of set-phrases for composition.]

吳瑞書：作文成語辭典

2109 Wu, Jui-shu: *Chung-kuo ch'eng-yü ta tz'u-tien.*—Taipei: Ta Chung-kuo t'u-shu, 1975, 2, 2, 40, 323 p. [A comprehensive dictionary of Chinese set-phrases.]

吳瑞書：中國成語大辭典

2110 Wu, Jui-shu: *Tso-wen ch'eng-yü ta tz'u-tien.*—Tainan: Tung-hai, 1976, [ii], 31, 28, 2, 274 p., 86. [A comprehensive dictionary of set-phrases for composition.]

吳瑞書：作文成語大辭典

2111 Wu, Lien-ming: *Chung-hua ch'eng-yü tz'u-tien.*—Shanghai: Chung-hua, 1936; 1948, 8th ed., [23], 723 p.; Taipei: Chung-hua, 1956, repr., 21, 721 p. [A dictionary of Chinese set-phrases.]

吳廉銘：中華成語詞典

2112 Wu, P'ing-k'ang: *Ch'eng-yü tien.*—Tainan: Chin-ch'uan, 1980, 2 vols., 8, 293 p.; 6, 293 p. [A dictionary of set-phrases.]

吳萍康：成語典

2113 Wu, Shu-hui: *Shih-yung Chung-kuo ch'eng-yü ta tz'u-tien.*—Tainan: Tung-hai, 1964, 80, 362 p. [A practical comprehensive dictionary of Chinese set-phrases.]

吳淑蕙：實用中國成語大辭典

2114 Yang, Yin-shen: *Hui-t'u erh-t'ung ch'eng-yü tz'u-tien.*—Shanghai: Shang-hai tz'u-shu, 1982, [ii], 18, 146 p. [An illustrated dictionary of children's set-phrases.]

楊蔭深：繪圖兒童成語詞典

2115 Yen, K'un-yang (ed. in chief): *Shih-yung*

ch'eng-yü tz'u-tien.—Taipei: Ku-hsiang, 1980, 6, 78, 755 p. [A practical dictionary of set-phrases.]

顏崑陽主編：實用成語辭典

7.1.8.2. Western Translations (2116–2152)

2116 Anonymous: *Handbook on Chinese idioms.*—Peking: Guoji shudian, 1981, 557 p.

2117 Anonymous: *Lung-tsu te ch'eng-yü.*—Taipei: Po-wen t'ang, 1982, [vi], 250 p. [Set-phrases of the Dragon Race.]/ English transl. of Chinese set-phrase historical allusions.

無名氏：龍族的成語

2118 Bayne, Parker McEwan: *Four character Chinese expressions.*—Wolfville, Nova Scotia: Acadia U., 1958, x, 391 p./ Set-phrases.

2119 Bueler, William M. & Chang, Hou-pan: *Chinese sayings.*—Rutland, Vermont: Charles E. Tuttle, 1972, 143 p.

〔成語〕

2120 Chang, K'ai-hsin: Han-Ying ch'eng-yü, yen-yü te fan-i yü pi-chiao.—*YCYY* 1979:1, 102–108. [The translation and comparison of Chinese-English set-phrases and proverbs.]

張開信：漢英成語、諺語的翻譯與比較

2121 Ch'en, Ch'eng-chih: *Ying-Han tui-chao Chung-kuo ch'eng-yü yen-yü liu-pai chü.*—Taipei: Yüan-tung, 1959, 74 p. [Six hundred English-Chinese set-phrases and proverbs of China.]

陳登之：英漢對照中國成語、諺語六百句

2122 Ch'en, Ch'i-p'ing: *Han-Ying szu-yung Chung-kuo ch'eng-yü tz'u-tien.*—Taipei: Yung-hsin shu-chü, 1974, 74, 354 p. [A Chinese-English four-usage dictionary of Chinese set-phrases.]

陳啓平：漢英四用中國成語辭典

2123 Ch'en, Ching-jen: *Chung-wen ch'eng-yü hsüan i.*—Hong Kong: Ch'ung-ming, 1963, 45 p./ Chinese with English translations. [A selection with translations of Chinese set-phrases.]

陳靜仁：中文成語選譯

2124 Ch'en, Wen-po: *Ying-yü ch'eng-yü yü Han-yü ch'eng-yü.*—Peking: Wai-yü chiao-hsüeh yü yen-chiu, 1982, 3, 2, 2, 466 p. [English set-phrases and Chinese set-phrases.]/ A comparative study.

陳文伯：英語成語與漢語成語

2125 Chiang, Ker Chiu: *Chinese idioms.*—Singapore: Chin Fen Book Store, n.d., 273 p./ In romanized Mandarin with literal and free translations and notes in English.

〔蔣克秋：中華成語〕

2126 Daudin, Pierre: *L'Éclair des gemmes en quatre caractères.*—Saigon: S.I.L.I., 1944, xviii, 557, 55, 50 p.

〔四字瓊林〕

2127 Hsieh, Ta-jen: *Han-Ying tui-teng ch'eng-yü hsiao tz'u-tien.*—Shanghai: Shang-hai wai-yü chiao-yü, 1980, 2, 5, 114 p. [A small contrastive dictionary of Chinese-English set-phrases.]

謝大任：漢英對等成語小詞典

2128 Hu, Tzu-tan (ed.): *Kuo-chi Han-Ying ch'eng-yü tz'u-tien.*—Taipei: Kuo-chi wen-hua shih-yeh, 1979, (Index:) 48, 607 p. [An international Chinese-English dictionary of set-phrases.]

胡子丹編：國際漢英成語辭典

2129 Huang, Hsing-min: *Ying-i Han-yü ch'eng-yü tz'u-tien.*—Hong Kong: Shang-wu, 1977, [iv], 279, 31 p. [A dictionary of Chinese set-phrases with English translations.]

黃省民：英譯漢語成語詞典

2130 Huang, Yen-kai: *A dictionary of*

Chinese idiomatic phrases.—Hong Kong: Eton Press, 1964, vii, 1291 p.
〔黃元凱：中華成語辭典〕

2131 Kervyn, Louis-Marie: *Clichés usuels de la langue mandarine.*—Tientsin: Scheut Mission, 1935, vii, 387 p./ Including set-phrases; *CCS* 8, 1935, 850–852, Anonymous.

2132 Kuo, Hsiu-mei: *Han-Ying ch'eng-yü shou-ts'e.*—Nanking: Chiang-su jen-min, 1979; 1980, 2nd ed., [ii], 65, 557 p. [A handbook of Chinese-English set-phrases.]
郭秀梅：漢英成語手冊

2133 Lai, T'ien-ch'ang (transl.): *Selected Chinese sayings.*—Hong Kong: U. of Hong Kong, 1960, 191 p.; Hong Kong: Hong Kong U. Book Store, [1966], 191 p.
〔賴恬昌：成語選譯〕

2134 Lai, T'ien-ch'ang: *Chung-kuo ch'eng-yü ching-hsüan (Ying-Han tui-chao).*—Taipei: Hua-lien, 1963, viii, 191 p. [Selected Chinese set-phrases (Egnlish-Chinese).]
賴恬昌：中國成語精選（英漢對照）

2135 Lai, T'ien-ch'ang: *More Chinese sayings.*—Kowloon: Swindon Book Co., [1972], ix, 86 p.

2136 Liu, Ta-jen: *Liu-shih Han-Ying ch'eng-yü tz'u-tien.*—Taipei: Hua-ying, 1981, xx, 1448 p., illus. [Liu's Chinese-English dictionary of set-phrases.]
劉達人：劉氏漢英成語辭典

2137 Lockhart, J.H. Stewart: *A manual of Chinese quotations,* being a translation of the *Ch'eng-yü k'ao* . . . with Chinese text, notes, explanations and English and Chinese indices for easy reference.—Hong Kong: Kelly & Walsh, 1893, iv, [2], 425, lxxxiii p.; 1903, rev. ed., viii, 645, cxvii p./ English translation of Ch'iu Chün's (1419?–1495) *Ch'eng-yü k'ao* ('A study on set-phrases').

〔丘濬：成語考〕

2138 Mao, Ying-pai: *Chung-kuo ch'eng-yü hsüan i.*—Hong Kong: Ying-hua, 1975; 1979, 2nd ed., [i], 13, 180 p. [Selected translations of Chinese set-phrases.]
毛膺白：中國成語選譯

2139 Mao, Ying-pai (comp.) & P'an, Cheng-ying (transl.): *Han-Ying tui-chao Chung-kuo ch'eng-yü hsüan i.*—Taipei: Hua-lien, 1975, 13, 180 p. [A selection with Chinese-English translations of Chinese set-phrases.]/ A repr. of (2138).
毛膺白編、潘正英譯：漢英對照中國成語選譯

2140 Nan-ching ta-hsüeh wai-wen-hsi: *Chien-ming Ying-Han ch'eng-yü tz'u-tien.*—Peking: Shang-wu, 1965, 454 p. [A concise English-Chinese dictionary of set-phrases.]
南京大學外文系：簡明英漢成語詞典

2141 P'an, Cheng-ying: *Chung-kuo ch'eng-yü ching hsüan.*—Taipei: Hung-yeh shu-chü, 1967, 191 p. [Selected Chinese set-phrases.]/ English-Chinese.
潘正英：中國成語精選

2142 Pei-ching ta-hsüeh Hsi-yü-shi: *Han-Fa ch'eng-yü shou-ts'e.*—Hong Kong: San-lien, 1980, iv, 74, 565 p. [Dictionnaire chinois-français des locutions et proverbes.]
北京大學西語系：漢法成語手冊

2143 Pei-ching wai-kuo-yü hsüeh-yüan Te-yü-hsi: *Han-Te ch'eng-yü tz'u-tien.*—Peking: Shang-wu, 1981, iii, 35, 344 p. [Chinesisch-Deutsches Lexikon der sprichwörtlichen Redensarten.]
北京外國語學院德語系：漢德成語詞典

2144 P'eng, Chien-i & Wang, Ch'ing-yu: *Han-yü ch'eng-yü Ying-i shou-ts'e.*—Foochow: Fu-chien jen-min, 1981, 3, 57, 938 p. [A handbook of English translations of Chinese set-phrases.]
彭建怡、王慶酉：漢語成語英譯手冊

2145 Sabban, Françoise: "La fonction

crée-t-elle le proverbe?"—Quelques remarques sur les idiotismes du chinois moderne (2191).

2146 Sabban, Françoise: *Idiotismes quadri-syllabiques en chinois moderne.*—Hong Kong & Paris: Éditions Languages croisés, 1980, 347 p./ Four-syllable set-phrases; *CLAO* 9, 1981, 83–89, L. Polech.
〔現代漢語四字格成語〕

2147 Stuart, J.L.: *Chinese four-character phrases.*—Peiping: Faculty of Yenching U., 1946, 24 p.

2148 Sun, C.C.: *As the saying goes.*—Lawrence: U. of Queensland Press, 1982, 685 p./ Subtitle: An annotated anthology of Chinese and equivalent English sayings and expressions, and introduction to *xiehouyu* (Chinese humour).

2149 Wei, S.S.: *A practical dictionary of Chinese idioms, English idioms, English synonyms.*—Hong Kong: The Practical English Press, 1978, ix, 26, 392 p.
〔韋少成：實用中文成語、英文成語、英文同義詞辭典〕

2150 Williams, Charles A.S.: *A manual of Chinese metaphor. Being a selection of typical Chinese metaphors, with explanatory notes and indices.*—Shanghai: Statistical Dept. of Inspectorate General of the Chinese Maritime Customs, 1920, xiv, 320 p.; New York: AMS Press, 1974, repr./ *JRASNCB* 52, 1921, 195–198, F.A.; *BSOS* 2:2, 1922, 336–338, Jui; *NCR* 3, 1921, 238–239, Anonymous; *TP* 21, 1922, 426–439, Paul Pelliot.

2151 Wong, Samuel M. Season: *Chinese idioms.*—Hong Kong: Shang-wu, 1977, [4], 279, 31 p.
〔黃省民譯：英譯漢語成語詞典〕

2152 Ying, I-t'ung: *Shih-yung Chung-wen ch'eng-yü, Ying-wen ch'eng-yü, Ying-wen t'ung-i tz'u tz'u-tien.*—Taipei: Wan-jen,

1979, viii, 26, 392 p. [A practical dictionary of Chinese idioms, English idioms, English synonyms.]/ A repr. of (2149).
英伊通：實用中文成語、英文成語、英文同義詞辭典

7.1.9. Literary Allusions and Maxims (2153–2168)
7.1.9.1. Literary Allusion (2153–2158)

2153 Chang, Pao-jung: *Ch'ang-yung tien-ku hsüan shih.*—Huhehot: Nei Meng-ku jen-min, 1980, [ii], 6, 405 p. [A selection with annotations of commonly used literary allusions.]
張寶榮：常用典故選釋

2154 Liu, Hou-ch'un: Tien-ku, su-yü, k'ou-yü.—*CKYT* 34:5, 1974, 19–25. [Literary allusions, popular sayings, and colloquialisms.]
劉厚醇：典故、俗語、口語

2155 P'an, Yün-chung: Ch'eng-yü, tien-ku te hsing-ch'eng ho fa-chan (1924). [The formation and development of set-phrases and literary allusions.]
潘允中：成語、典故的形成和發展

2156 Pétillon, Corentin, S.J.: *Allusions littéraires.*—Shanghai: Imprimerie de la Mission Catholique, 1895, 1899, 2 vols., 255 p.; 561 p./ Variétiés Sinologiques, 8 & 13./ *TP* 8, 1897, 223–226, Gustaf Schlegel; *TP* 9, 1898, 235–240, Gustaf Schlegel.

2157 T'ang, Ch'i-yün: *Ch'eng-yü, yen-yü, hsieh-hou-yü, tien-ku kai-shuo* (1879). [A general discussion on set-phrases, proverbs, *hsieh-hou-yü,* and literary allusions.]
唐啓運：成語、諺語、歇後語、典故概說

2158 Zottoli, A., S.J.: *Cursus litteraturae Sinicae.*—Shanghai: T'ou-sè-wè, 1879–1882, 5 vols./ Vol. I, includes literary allusions and proverbs.

7.1.9.2. Maxims (2159–2168)

2159   Chu, Chieh-fan: Yen-yü yü fang-yen, su-hua, ko-yen, ch'eng-yü (1888). [Proverbs and dialects, popular sayings, maxims, and set-phrases.]
朱介凡：諺語與方言、俗語、格言、成語

2160   Hsiang-kang wen-hua yen-chiu-she: *Chung-kuo ko-yen ta tz'u-tien.*—Hong Kong: Ditto, 197?, [iii], 540 p. [A comprehensive dictionary of Chinese maxims.]
香港文化研究社：中國格言大辭典

2161   Kuei, I: Ch'eng-yü, yen-yü, ko-yen, su-yü, li-yü te ch'ü-pieh (1890). [The differences between set-phrases, proverbs, maxims, popular sayings, and slang.]
瓌一：成語、諺語、格言、俗語、俚語的區別

2162   Liang, Chang-chü: *Ku ko-yen.*—Taipei: Shang-wu, 1973, 12 *chüan*, v.p. [Ancient maxims.]
梁章鉅：古格言

2163   Lu, Ching-i: *Chung wai ming jen ko-yen.*—Hong Kong: Wen-yüan shu-tien, 1966, 4, 421 p. [Maxims of famous Chinese and foreigners.] / Classified.
呂敬頤：中外名人格言

2164   Ning, Chü: *Yen-yü, ko-yen, hsieh-hou-yü.*—Wuhan: Hu-pei jen-min, 1980, [i], 77 p. [Proverbs, maxims, and *hsieh-hou-yü.*]
寧集：諺語、格言、歇後語

2165   Tung, Chen-nan, et al.: *Ku chin Chung wai ko-yen chi-ch'eng.*—Shanghai: Ching-wei shu-chü, 1936, 549 p. [A grand compendium of ancient and modern Chinese and foreign maxims.]
董鎮南等：古今中外格言集成

2166   Wang, Sou-pi: *Fen-lei ko-yen chi-ch'eng.*—Panchiao: Hua-hsing, 1976, [i], 5, 430 p. [A grand compendium of classified maxims.]
汪漱碧：分類格言集成

2167   Wang, Tsung-chieh & Hung, Hui-chen: *Chung-kuo ko-yen yen-yü szu-yung ta tz'u-tien.*—Taipei: Ch'ang-ch'ing, 1979, 540 p. [A four-usage comprehensive dictionary of Chinese maxims and proverbs.]
王宗傑、洪慧貞：中國格言諺語四用大辭典

2168   Yüan-tung t'u-shu kung-szu: *Chung-kuo ko-yen ta tz'u-tien.*—Taipei: Ditto, 1972, 4, 473 p.; 1978, 7, 4, 473 p. [A comprehensive dictionary of Chinese maxims.] / Ancient and modern.
遠東圖書公司：中國格言大辭典

7.2.   Proverbs (2169–2654)
7.2.1.   Definition and General Studies (2169–2199)

2169   Baba, Haruyoshi: Shina no rigen ni tsuite.—*Tōyō Tetsugaku* 29:12, 1922, 19–29. [On proverbs of China.]
馬場春吉：支那の俚諺に就て

2170   Ch'en, Shao-hsin: Rigen ni kansuru oboegaki.—*MZTW* 2:8, 1942, 2–4. [A note concerning proverbs.]
陳紹馨：俚諺の關する覺書

2171   Ch'en, Shao-hsin: Min-chien wen-hua yü yen-yü yen-chiu.—*Chung-kuo yen-yü lun* (2178), 729–733. [Folk culture and the study of proverbs.]
陳紹馨：民間文化與諺語研究

2172   Ch'i, I: K'o-hsüeh te hsiao-shih che-li te hsiao-shih—wo tui yen-yü te jen-shih.—*MCWH* 1961:10, 62–64. [Short poems of science and short poems of philosophy—my recognition of proverbs.]
齊翼：科學的小詩哲理的小詩——我對諺語的認識

2173   Chu, Chieh-fan: Chung-kuo yen-yü te yen-chiu.—*Li hsing* 6:1, 1942, 85–92. [A study of Chinese proverbs.]

朱介凡：中國諺語的研究

2174   Chu, Chieh-fan: Ts'ung ming-ch'eng shang yen-chiu Chung-kuo te yen-yü.— *Feng-t'u tsa-chih* 1:2–3, 1943, 50–58. [A study of Chinese proverbs from names (of things or persons).]
朱介凡：從名稱上研究中國的諺語

2175   Chu, Chieh-fan: Chung-kuo yen-yü te p'in-hsing.—*Wen hsing* 10:2, 1962, 73–76. [The moral character of Chinese proverbs.]
朱介凡：中國諺語的品性

2176   Chu, Chieh-fan: Yen-yü ming-ch'eng te t'an-t'ao.—*Fan-kung* 241, 1962, 1–5. [An investigation into the (various) terms for proverbs.]
朱介凡：諺語名稱的探討

2177   Chu, Chieh-fan: Yen-yü te ting-i.— *Fan-kung* 243, 1962, 19–22. [The definition of proverb.]
朱介凡：諺語的定義

2178   Chu, Chieh-fan: *Chung-kuo yen-yü lun.*—Taipei: Hsin-hsing, 1964, 2, 25, 741 p./ *RBS* 11, 1965, 436, F. Sabban; *Chung-kuo min-tsu-hsüeh t'ung-hsiin* 1, 1965, 18–19, Tu Erh-wei. [On Chinese proverbs.]
朱介凡：中國諺語論／杜而未評

2179   Eberhard, Wolfram: *Studies in Chinese folklore and related essays.*—The Hague: Mouton & Bloomington: Indiana U. Research Center for the Language Sciences, 1970, vi, [iii], 329 p./ Pt. II: Notes on Chinese proverbs.

2180   Hsüeh, Ch'eng-chih: Yen-yü te t'an-t'ao.—*WHNP* 2, 1936, 103–131. [An investigation of proverbs.]
薛誠之：諺語的探討

2181   Hsüeh, Ch'eng-chih: Yen hua.—*WHNP* 2, 1936, 199–202. [Proverbs.]
薛誠之：諺話

2182   Huo, Hsü-tung: Lun yen-yü.—*STHK* 1956:1, 102–115. [On proverbs.]
霍旭東：論諺語

2183   Jen, Fang-ch'iu: Yen-yü chih yen-chiu. —*Li su* 6–7, 1931, 1–13. [A study of proverbs.]
任訪秋：諺語之研究

2184   Kanda, Kiichirō: Shina rigen no kenkyū ni tsuite.—*MZTW* 2:8, 1942, 6–7; 2:9, 4–5. [On the study of Chinese proverbs.]
神田喜一郎：支那俚諺の研究に就て

2185   Kōsaka, Jun'ichi: Shina no mingen. —*MZTW* 4:2, 1944, 16–21; 4:4, 28–31; 4:5, 35–39. [Popular proverbs of China.]
香坂順一：支那の民諺

2186   Kuan, Chen-hsiung: A study of the Chinese proverb—its form, function and contextual use.—*TTHP* 9, 1979, 187–197, C.S.
〔關辰雄：中諺之研究〕

2187   Kuo, Shao-yü: Yen-yü te yen-chiu. —*Hsiao-shuo yüeh-pao* 12:2, 1921, 9–15; 12:3, 25–30; 12:4, 16–23; Later repr. in *Yü-wen t'ung-lun hsü pien* (Shanghai: K'ai-ming, 1948), 155–190.; Hong Kong: T'ai-p'ing, 1963, repr. [A study of proverbs.]
郭紹虞：諺語的研究——『語文通論續編』

2188   Lou, Tzu-k'uang & Chu, Chieh-fan: *Wu-shih nien lai te Chung-kuo su wen-hsüeh.*—Taipei: Cheng-chung, 1963, [10], 8, 368 p./ 153–180: proverbs. [Chinese popular literature of the past fifty years.]
婁子匡、朱介凡：五十年來的中國俗文學／153–180：諺語

2189   Ma, Kuo-fan: Yen-yü te t'e-tien.— *CKYW* 1960:8, 377–378. [Special features of proverbs.]
馬國凡：諺語的特點

2190 Po, Han: T'an yen-yü.—*TPPYK* 1:8, 1935, 375–378. [A discussion on proverbs.]
伯韓：談諺語

2191 Sabban, Françoise: "La fonction crée-t-elle le proverbe?"—Quelques remarques sur les idiodismes du chinois moderne.—*CLAO* 6, 1979, 29–47.

2192 Sun, Wen-hui: Chung Ying yen-yü ting-i te p'i shih.—*HHYK* 118, 1981, 32–37. [Analytical explanations of the definitions of Chinese and English proverbs.]
孫文慧：中英諺語定義的闡釋

2193 Tseng, Chih: Chu Chieh-fan hsien-sheng ken t'a-te *Chung-kuo yen-yü lun.*—*CKYT* 16:4, 1965, 20–23. [Mr. Chu Chieh-fan and his *Chung-kuo yen-yü lun* (2178).]
曾知：朱介凡先生跟他的『中國諺語論』

2194 Tu, Chün-hsiao & Wang, Hsi-i: Yen-yü chien lun.—*SHSY* 1981:2, 92–94. [A simple discussion on proverbs.]
杜峻曉、王錫義：諺語簡論

2195 Tuan, Pao-lin: *Chung-kuo min-chien wen-hsüeh kai-yao.*—Peking: Pei-ching ta-hsüeh, 1981, 5, v, 327 p./ Chap. 5: Folk proverbs, riddles, *hsieh-hou-yü*; *JCLTA* 17:2, 1982, 151–152, Lo Tai-yün. [Essentials of Chinese folk literature.]
段寶林：中國民間文學概要／第五章：民間諺語、謎語、歇後語；樂黛雲評

2196 Wang, Hsiang: Shih lun yen-yü te hsing-chih yü tso-yung.—*MCWH* 1957:7, 40–50. [A preliminary discussion on the nature and functions of proverbs.]
王驤：試論諺語的性質與作用

2197 Wang, I: Lüeh lun Chung-kuo yen-yü.—*MCWH* 1961:10, 44–58. [A brief discussion on Chinese proverbs.]
王毅：略中國諺語

2198 Yamamoto, Heitarō: Chūgoku no kotowaza.—*Kanbungaku* 4, 1955, 3–13. [Chinese proverbs.]
山本平太郎：中國の諺

2199 Yashima, Genryō: Kotowaza ni tsuite.—*Daitō Bunka Gakuin Dōsōkaihō* 9, 1943, (not seen). [On proverbs.]
矢島玄亮：諺について

7.2.2. Differentiation (2200–2213)

2200 Chu, Chieh-fan: K'ou-t'ou yü-yen te lei-pieh yü hsing-shih.—*CKYT* 1:2, 1952, 16–19; 1:3, 28–34; 1:4, 19–21. [The categories and patterns of the colloquial language.]/ 16 categories, including popular sayings, proverbs, *hsieh-hou-yü*, etc.
朱介凡：口頭語言的類別與形式

2201 Chu, Chieh-fan: Yen-yü yü fang-yen, su-hua, ko-yen, ch'eng-yü (1888). [Proverbs and dialects, popular sayings, maxims, and set-phrases.]
朱介凡：諺語與方言、俗話、格言、成語

2202 Chu, Chieh-fan: Yao yen chih chien.—*Tso-p'in* 3:6, 1962, 73–76. [Folk songs versus proverbs.]
朱介凡：謠諺之間

2203 Fu, Chen-lun: Mi yen hsieh-hou-yü yen-chiu chih i-pan.—*KYAO* 68, 1924, 2–4. [A glimpse of the study on riddles, proverbs, and *hsieh-hou yü.*]
傅振倫：謎諺歇後語研究之一斑

2204 Furuya, Tsugio: Rigen seigo.—*Chūgoku gogaku jiten* (0037), 930–941. [Proverbs and set-phrases.]
古屋二夫：俚諺成語

2205 Kuei, I: Ch'eng-yü, yen-yü, ko-yen, su-yü, li-yü te ch'ü-pieh (1890). [The differences between set-phrases, proverbs, maxims, popular sayings, and slang.]
璝一：成語、諺語、格言、俗語、俚語的區別

2206 Li, Tao-i: Shih lun p'i-chieh yü chi

ch'i yü hsieh-hou-yü, ch'eng-yü, yen-yü te ch'ü-pieh (1891). [A preliminary discussion on *p'i-chieh yü* ('metaphor-explanation phrases'), and their differences from *hsieh-hou yü,* set-phrases, and proverbs.]
李道一：試論譬解語及其與歇後語、成語、諺語的區別

2207   Liu, Hou-ch'un: Tien-ku, su-yü, k'ou-yü (2154). [Literary allusions, popular sayings, and colloquialisms.]
劉厚醇：典故、俗語、口語

2208   Lü, Hung-nien: Hsieh-hou-yü chi yen-yü. —*YWCS* 1957:12, 62–63. [*Hsieh-hou-yü* and proverbs.]
呂洪年：歇後語及諺語

2209   Ma, Kuo-fan: Yen-yü yü hsieh-hou-yü. —*NMSY* 1960:2, 43–65. [Proverbs and *hsieh-hou-yü.*]
馬國凡：諺語與歇後語

2210   Ning, Chü: *Yen-yü, ko-yen, hsieh-hou-yü* (2164). [Proverbs, maxims, and *hsieh-hou-yü.*]
寧榘：諺語、格言、歇後語

2211   T'ang, Ch'i-yün: *Ch'eng-yü, yen-yü, hsieh-hou-yü, tien-ku kai-shuo* (1879). [A general discussion on set-phrases, proverbs, *hsieh-hou-yü,* and literary allusions.]
唐啓運：成語、諺語、歇後語、典故概說

2212   Wang, Ch'in: *Yen-yü hsieh-hou-yü kai-lun.*—Changsha: Hu-nan jen-min, 1980; 1981, repr., 2, 193 p. [A general discussion on proverbs and *hsieh-hou-yü.*]
王勤：諺語、歇後語概論

2213   Yang, Hsin-an: Ch'eng-yü ho yen-yü te ch'ü-pieh (1894). [The differences of set-phrases and proverbs.]
楊欣安：成語和諺語的區別

7.2.3. Structure and Style (2214–2221)

2214   Chu, Chieh-fan: Lun Chung-kuo yen-yü te ko-tiao.—*Hsin Chung-hua* 5:8, 1947, 35–36, 2. [On the styles of Chinese proverbs.]
朱介凡：論中國諺語的格調

2215   Chu, Chieh-fan: Yen-yü te chü-tzu.—*Wen-i ch'uang-tso* 39, 1954, 125–137. [The sentences of proverbs.]
朱介凡：諺語的句子

2216   Chu, Chieh-fan: Yen-yü te fu, pi, hsing.—*Fan-kung* 172, 1957, 16–19. [The *fu* ('epic narration of events'), *pi* ('direct comparison'), and *hsing* ('indirect comparison') of proverbs.]
朱介凡：諺語的賦、比、興

2217   Chu, Chieh-fan: *Wo ko ch'ieh yao (Yen-hua i pien).*—Taipei: Shih-chieh, 1959; Taipei: T'ien-i, 1975, 2nd ed., 6, [ii], 3, 167 p. [I sing songs and ballads (Proverbs, Vol. II).]/ Collected essays.
朱介凡：我歌且謠（諺話乙編）

2218   Chu, Chieh-fan: San-wen shih te yen-yü.—*CKYT* 7:1, 1960, 25–28; 7:2, 21–25. [Proverbs in prose style.]
朱介凡：散文式的諺語

2219   Chu, Chieh-fan: Yen-yü te pi hsing. —*CKYT* 13:4, 1963, 29–36. [The *pi* ('direct comparison') and *hsing* ('indirect comparison') of proverbs.]
朱介凡：諺語的比、興

2220   Chu, Chieh-fan: Yen-yü te yin-yün. —*CKYT* 14:1, 1964, 51–55; 2, 59–64. [The phonology of proverbs.]
朱介凡：諺語的音韻

2221   Juan, Hsien-chung: Yen-yü te yü-yen i-shu.—*AHTH* 1979:2, 44–51. [The linguistic art of proverbs.]
阮顯忠：諺語的語言藝術

7.2.4. Origin and Development (2222–2236)

2222   Cheng, Chih-hung: *Ch'ang yü hsün yüan.*—1877 ed., 2 *chüan.* [Tracing the origins of common words.] /See (1251).

鄭志鴻：常語尋源

2223   Chu, Chieh-fan: Yao yen pien-hua yü chien-kuo li-hsiang.—*Cheng-feng yüeh-k'an* 2, 1945, (not seen). [The changes of folk songs and proverbs and the ideal of establishing a nation.]

朱介凡：謠諺變化與建國理想

2224   Chu, Chieh-fan: Lun Chung-kuo yen-yü te yüan pien.—*Hsin Chung-hua* 5:18, 1947, 37–41. [On the origins and changes of Chinese proverbs.]

朱介凡：論中國諺語的源變

2225   Chu, Chieh-fan: Yen-yü te ch'an-sheng. —*CKYT* 11:6, 1962, 10–15. [The rise of proverbs.]

朱介凡：諺語的產生

2226   Chu, Chieh-fan: Chung-kuo ku-chi chung tsui-tsao te yen-yü.—*TLTC* 26:6, 1963, 20–24. [The earliest proverbs in Chinese ancient texts.]

朱介凡：中國古籍中最早的諺語

2227   Chu, Chieh-fan: *Shih Shu* yao su ken yen-yü te yüan-yüan.—*Wen-t'an* 32, 1963, 12–18. [Ballads in *Shih-ching* and *Shu-ching* and the origins of proverbs.]

朱介凡：『詩』、『書』謠俗跟諺語的淵源

2228   Chu, Chieh-fan: Yen-yü chih ch'uan-shu chi ch'i t'ao-t'ai yü fou.—*CKYT* 13:1, 1963, 32–33. [The transmission of proverbs and their elimination and retention.]

朱介凡：諺語之傳述及其淘汰與否

2229   Chu, Chieh-fan: Yen-yü te k'ou-t'ou ch'uan-shu.—*Wen-t'an* 38, 1963, 14–22. [The oral transmission of proverbs.]

朱介凡：諺語的口頭傳述

2230   Chu, Chieh-fan: Yen-yü te liu-pien.— *Ta-tao* 291, 1963, 16–17; 292, 15–17; 293, 22–24; 294, 20–21; 295, 22–23. [The later developments of proverbs.]

朱介凡：諺語的流變

2231   Chu, Chieh-fan: Yen-yü te wen-tzu ch'uan-shu.—*Hsin wen-i* 88, 1963, (not seen). [The written transmission of proverbs.]

朱介凡：諺語的文字傳述

2232   Chu, Chieh-fan: Chin chih yü tang-shih ch'uan-shu te yen-yü.—*Tzu-yu t'ai-p'ing yang* 8:1, 1964, 39–42. [Proverbs that have been transmitted only during a certain period.]

朱介凡：僅止於當時傳述的諺語

2233   Chu, Chieh-fan: *Yen-yu te yüan-liu kung-neng.*—Taipei: Tung-fang wen-hua kung-ying-she, 1970, 4, 144, 5 p. [The origins and functions of proverbs.]

朱介凡：諺語的源流功能

2234   Fu, Chen-lun: Ko yen te ch'i-yüan. —*KYAO* 87, 1925, 1–5. [The origins of folk songs and proverbs.]

傅振倫：歌諺的起源

2235   Li, Chien-t'ang: *Su-yü k'ao yüan.*— Shupu: Tu Yüan-ch'ing, 1937, 2, 6, 138 p.; Yunghochen: Wen-hai, 1971, repr. [A study on the origins of popular sayings.]

李鑑堂：俗語考原

2236   Torii, Hisayasu (ed.): *Zokugo kōgen goi.*—Tenri: Tenri Daigaku Chūgokugakka Kenkyūshitsu, 1954, mimeogr., 12 p. [Vocabulary of *Su-yü k'ao-yüan* (2235).]

鳥居久靖編：俗語考原語彙

7.2.5. Methods of Collecting Proverbs (2237–2249)

2237   Ch'en, I-te: Ts'ung yen-yü te sou-chi t'an tao k'ou-t'ou yü te yü-hui.—*TPPYK* 2:2, 1935, 57–59. [A discussion on colloquial vocabulary from a collection of proverbs.]

陳以德：從諺語的搜集談到口頭語的語滙

2238   Ch'en, Tzu-chan: Yen-yü te chi-lu.—

Ta-chung yü-wen lun chan (*hsü erh*) 1935, 129–135. [The recording of proverbs.]
陳子展：諺語的記錄

2239   Chu, Chieh-fan: Lun Chung-kuo yen-yü te sou-lu.—*Hsin Chung-hua* 6:8, 1948, 32–38; 9, 47–49, 46. [On the collection and recording of Chinese proverbs.]
朱介凡：論中國諺語的搜錄

2240   Chu, Chieh-fan: *Yen-hua chia-pien.*— Taipei: T'ien-i, 1957; 1974, 2nd ed., 6, 4, 236 p. [Proverbs, Vol. I.]/ Collected essays, including methods of collecting proverbs.
朱介凡：諺話甲編

2241   Chu, Chieh-fan: *T'ing jen ch'üan* (*Yen-hua ping-pien*).—Taipei: T'ien-i, 1961; 1974, 2nd ed., 6, 4, 356 p. [Listening to admonitions of the people (Proverbs, Vol. III.).]/ Collected essays, including methods of collecting proverbs.
朱介凡：聽人勸（諺話丙編）

2242   Chu, Chieh-fan: Yen-yü kung-tso chien pao.—*CKYT* 12:5, 1963, 14–16. [A short report on (my) work on proverbs.]
朱介凡：諺語工作簡報

2243   Chu, Chieh-fan: Chi-lu yen-yü te shen-ting kung-tso.—*T'ai-wan sheng-li T'ai-pei t'u-shu-kuan kuan-k'an* 1, 1964, 16–23. [The work on examination and revision of the collecting and recording of proverbs.]
朱介凡：集錄諺語的審訂工作

2244   Chu, Chieh-fan: Chung-kuo chi-lu yen-yü te li-shih.—*YSHC* 3:1, 1964, 1–23. [A history of the collecting and recording of proverbs in China.]
朱介凡：中國集錄諺語的歷史

2245   Chu, Chieh-fan: Yen-yü chi-tzu te pien-tsuan.—*CKYT* 14:6, 1964, 53–56. [The compilation of proverb anthologies.]

朱介凡：諺語集子的編纂

2246   Chu, Chieh-fan: Yen-yü san shu.— *CKYT* 17:4, 1965, 57–59; 17:5, 51–55. [Three books on proverbs.]/ An account of the author's plans of compiling three books on proverbs.
朱介凡：諺語三書

2247   Chu, Chieh-fan: Shou-t'ang yen-yü kung-tso nien-piao.—*SHJ* 459, 1983, 1–6. [A chronological table of Shou-t'ang's works on proverbs.]
朱介凡：壽堂諺語工作年表

2248   Shih, Hsiang-tsai: Wo shou-chi yen-yü te ching-kuo.—*Yen-hua chia-pien* (2240), 220–226. [My experience in collecting proverbs.]
史襄哉：我收集諺語的經過

2249   Wang, Kuo-tung: Yen-yü te sou-chi ho cheng-li.—*STYK* 22, 1935, 212–225. [The collection and arrangement of proverbs.]
王國棟：諺語的搜集和整理

7.2.6.   Ancient Proverbs and Proverbs from Literary Sources (2250–2280)

7.2.6.1.   Ancient Proverbs (2250–2262)

2250   Chai, Hao: *T'ung-su pien*. Fu Liang, T'ung-shu: *Chih-yü pu-cheng*.—Peking: Shang-wu, 1958, repr., 25 *chüan*, 11, 920, 67 p.; 1959, 2nd print.; Taipei: Shih-chieh, 1963, repr., 25 *chüan*; Taipei: Ta-hua shu-chü, 1977, repr./ Chai Hao (？–1788); Liang T'ung-shu (1723–1815). [A collection of popular sayings. With Addenda and corrigenda by Liang T'ung-shu.]/ A classified collection with explanations of popular proverbs, set-phrases, dialect words, etc.
翟灝：通俗編　附梁同書：直語補證

2251   Chu, An-ch'ün: *Ku chin yen-yü.*— Nanchang: Chiang-hsi jen-min, 1981, [i], 9, 42, 274 p. [Ancient and modern proverbs.]

朱安群：古今諺語

2252 Ho, Hsin: *Shui-hu chuan* chung te t'u-hua yen-yü.—*Shui-hu yen-chiu* (Shanghai: Wen-i lien-ho, 1954), Chap. 18, 301–337. [Patois and proverbs found in *Shui-hu chuan.*]
何心：『水滸傳』中的土話諺語——『水滸研究』

2253 Huang, Ch'i: Ku yen-yü chien-lun chi ch'i shih-i.—*TCSY* 1957:1, 45–63. [A brief discussion on ancient proverbs and their tentative modern translations.]
黃綺：古諺語簡論及其試譯

2254 Liu, Ming-shu: T'ang Sung shih yü yen-yü chih chiao-hu kuan-hsi.—*Hsüeh-shu p'ing-lun yüeh-pao* 1, 1940, 11–16. [The mutual relationship between T'ang and Sung poetry and proverbs.]
劉銘恕：唐宋詩與諺語之交互關係

2255 Ogura, Yoshihiko: Kotowaza no in'yō—*Saden* to *Shiki* no baai.—*TYSK* 37:4, 1979, 1–26. [Citation of proverbs—the cases of *Tso-chuan* and *Shih-chi.*]
小倉芳彥：諺の引用——『左傳』と『史記』の場合

2256 Ōkubo, Toku & Torii Hisayasu: *Ko yōgen gengo kensaku.*—Tenri: Ditto, 1961, 54 p. [An index to the proverbs in *Ku yao yen* (2259).]
大久保恵、鳥居久靖：古謠諺諺語檢索

2257 Sawada, Fusakiyo: *Kokugo, Kokusaku ni arawaretaru yōgen.*—*Daitō bunka* 4:8, 1927, (not seen). [Folk songs and proverbs appearing in *Kuo-yü* and *Kuo-ts'e.*]
澤田總清：『國語』、『國策』に現はれたる謠諺

2258 Sawada, Fusakiyo: *Saden* ni arawaretaru yōgen.—*KGIZ* 33:8, 1927, 53–59. [Folk songs and proverbs appearing in *Tso-chuan.*]
澤田總清：『左傳』に現はれたる謠諺

2259 Tu, Wen-lan: *Ku yao yen.*—Peking: Chung-hua, 1958, repr., 100 *chüan,* 1974 p.; Taipei: Shih-chieh, 1960, 1148 p. [Ancient folk songs and proverbs.]
杜文瀾：古謠諺

2260 Wang, Hsiang: Lun wo-kuo ku-tai te yen-yü.—*WSC* 1958:11, 47–51. [On ancient Chinese proverbs.]
王驤：論我國古代的諺語

2261 Yang, Shen: *Feng ya i p'ien. Ku chin feng yao. Ku chin yen.*—Shanghai: Ku-tien wen-hsüeh, 1958, repr., 178 p./ Yang Shen (1488–1559). [A collection of popular and elegant language. Ancient and modern folk songs. Ancient and modern proverbs.]/ Three books bound in one volume.
楊愼：風雅逸篇・古今風謠・古今諺

2262 Yang, Shen (comp.) & Shih, Meng-lan (ed.): *Ku chin yao yen pu chu szu chung.*—Taipei: Shang-wu, 1973, repr. from a 1873 ed., 6 *chüan,* v.p./ Shih Meng-lan (1813–1898). [Four supplements with commentary to Yang Shen's works on ancient and modern folk songs and proverbs (2261).]
楊愼輯，史夢蘭補註：古今謠諺補註四種

7.2.6.2. Proverbs from Literary Sources (2263–2280)

2263 Chang, Nan-chuang (comp.); Liu, Pan-nung (ed.); Chu, Chieh-fan (essay); Lou, Tzu-k'uang (comment.): *Ho tien—Chung-kuo yen-yü ch'ang-p'ien ch'i-ch'ing hsiao-shuo.*—Taipei: Tung-fang wen-hua, 1954, repr., 94 p. [*Ho-tien*—A marvelous Chinese love novel with the citing of proverbs.]
張南莊撰，劉半農校，朱介凡文，婁子匡增註：何典——中國諺語長篇奇情小說

2264 Ch'en, Chien: *Hsi-yu chi* chung yen-yü te yin-yung.—*Yü-yen yen-chiu lun-ts'ung* (0074), 273–286. [The citation of proverbs in *Hsi-yu chi.*]

陳堅：『西遊記』中諺語的引用

2265 Eberhard, Wolfram: Some notes on the uses of proverbs in Chinese novels.—*Proverbium* 9, 1967, 201–208.

2266 Furuya, Tsugio: *Sangen* shūgen—Chūgoku gengo shiryō (1).—*THGS* 3, 1970, 15–32. [Collected proverbs from *San yen*—Chinese proverbs materials (1).]
古屋二夫：『三言』集諺——中國諺語資料(1)

2267 Furuya, Tsuigo: *Nihaku* shūgen—Chūgoku gengo shiryō (2).—*THGS* 4, 1971, 1–9. [Collected proverbs from *Erh pai*—Chinese proverb materials (2).]
古屋二夫：『二拍』集諺——中國諺語資料(2)

2268 Furuya, Tsugio: *Suikoden, Suikogoden* shūgen—Chūgoku gengo shiryō (3).—*THGS* 5, 1973, 25–35. [Collected proverbs from *Shui-hu chuan* and *Shui-hu hou-chuan*—Chinese proverb materials (3).]
古屋二夫：『水滸傳』、『水滸後傳』集諺——中國諺語資料(3)

2269 Furuya, Tsugio: *Genkyokusen* shūgen—Chūgoku gengo shiryō (4).—*THGS* 6, 1974, 1–32. [Collected proverbs from *Yüan ch'ü hsiian*—Chinese proverb materials (4).]
古屋二夫：『元曲選』集諺——中國諺語資料(4)

2270 Furuya, Tsugio: *Kōrōmu* shūgen—Chūgoku gengo shiryō (5).—*CKDG* 15:4, 1975, 215–229. [Collected proverbs from *Hung-lou meng*—Chinese proverb materials (5).]
古屋二夫：『紅樓夢』集諺——中國諺語資料(5)

2271 Furuya, Tsugio: *Jijo eiyūden* (sei, zoku) shūgen—Chūgoku gengo shiryō (6).—*THGS* 7, 1975, 95–112. [Collected proverbs from *Erh-nü ying-hsiung chuan* (Vol. I and II.)—Chinese proverb materials (6).]
古屋二夫：『兒女英雄傳』(正、續) 集諺——中國諺語資料(6)

2272 Furuya, Tsugio: *Jurin gaishi, Rōsan yūki* shūgen—Chūgoku gengo shiryō (7).—*CKDG* 17:2, 1976, 173–183. [Collected proverbs from *Ju-lin wai-shih* and *Lao-ts'an yu-chi*—Chinese proverb materials (7).
古屋二夫：『儒林外史』、『老殘遊記』集諺——中國諺語資料(7)

2273 Furuya, Tsugio: *Nijū nen mokuto kaijō* shūgen—Chūgoku gengo shiryō (8).—*CKDG* 18:3, 1977, 247–256. [Collected proverbs from *Erh-shih nien mu to kuai chuang*—Chinese proverb materials (8).]
古屋二夫：『二十年目睹怪狀』集諺——中國諺語資料(8)

2274 Furuya, Tsugio: *Kanjō genkeiki* shūgen —Chūgoku gengo shiryō (9).—*CKDG* 19:3, 1978, 139–152. [Collected proverbs from *Kuan-ch'ang hsien-hsing chi* —Chinese proverb materials (9).]
古屋二夫：『官場現形記』集諺——中國諺語資料(9)

2275 Furuya, Tsugio: *Ban Shin bungaku sōshō* (shōsetsu san kan) shūgen—Chūgoku gengo shiryo (10).—*CKDG* 20:2, 1979, 85–96. [Collected proverbs from *Wan Ch'ing wen-hsüeh ts'ung ch'ao* (three novels)—Chinese proverb materials (10).]
古屋二夫：『晚清文學叢抄』(小說三卷) 集諺——中國諺語資料(10)

2276 Nagasawa, Kikuya (ed.): *Min Shin zokugo jisho shūsei.*—Tokyo: Kyūko shoin, 1974–1977, 5 vols., [vi], 604; 540; 549; 412; 390 p./ *Chin san-shih nien . . . chien chieh* (0010), 59–61. [A grand compendium of lexicographical works on the popular sayings of the Ming and Ch'ing dynasties.]
長澤規矩也編：明清俗語辭書集成

2277 Ōsaka Shiritsu Daigaku Chūgoku Gakka Daigakuin Gakusei: *Kinpeibai shūgen sakuin.*—Osaka: Ditto, 1959, (not seen). [An index to *Chin-p'ing mei chi yen* (2280).]

大阪市立大學中國學科大學院學生：金瓶梅集
諺索引

2278 Torii, Hisayasu: Shihen *Kinpeibai*
shūgen shokō.—*CBKK* 1, 1961, 22–30;
3, 1963, 11–19. [A preliminary draft
of a privately compiled collection of
proverbs from *Ching-p'ing mei.*]
鳥居久靖：私編『金瓶梅』集諺初稿

2279 Torii, Hisayasu: *Jijo eiyūden* shūgen
shokō.—*SMBG* 1, 1962, 13–25. [A
preliminary draft for a collection
of proverbs from *Erh-nü ying-hsiung
chuan.*]
鳥居久靖：『兒女英雄傳』集諺初稿

2280 Yao, Ling-hsi: *P'ing wai chih yen.*—
Nagoya: Saika shorin, 1962, repr., [ii],
4, 262, 38 p./ 241–250: *Chin-p'ing
mei chi yen* ('Collected proverbs from
Chin-p'ing mei'). [An endless flow of
words from *Chin-p'ing mei.*]
姚靈犀：瓶外巵言／241-250: 金瓶梅集諺

7.2.7. Collection and Analysis (2281–2366)
7.2.7.1. Chinese Works (2281–2316)

2281 Anonymous: *Ming hsien chi.*—Taichung: Jui-ch'eng shu-chü, 1960, 12 p.,
illus. [A collection of proverbs and
maxims from famous sages of the past.]/
See (2342).
無名氏：名賢集

2282 Anonymous: Yen-yü i shu.—*MCWH*
1960:12, 79–80. [A bundle of proverbs.]
無名氏：諺語一束

2283 Anonymous: *Fan-tung yen-yü hsüan
p'i.*—Wuhan: Hu-pei jen-min, 1975, 37
p. [A selection with critique of
reactionary proverbs.]
無名氏：反動諺語選批

2284 Ch'en, Ch'eng-chih: *Chung-kuo ch'eng-
yü yen-yü liu-pai chü* (2024). [Six
hundred Chinese set-phrases and proverbs.]
陳澄之：中國成語諺語六百句

2285 Ch'en, Chung-fang: Yen-yü chi lien.
—*CKYT* 13:1, 1963, 34–40. [A collection
of proverbs in couplets.]
陳中方：諺語集聯

2286 Ch'en, P'eng-shou: *Min-chien yen-yü.*
—Canton: Wen-hua shu-chü, 1934, (not
seen); Hong Kong: Liang-yu, (not seen).
[Folk proverbs.]
陳彭壽：民間諺語

2287 Ch'eng, Chih-wei: *Yen-yü shih.*—
Changsha: Hu-nan jen-min, 1979, 50 p.
[Proverbial poems.]
成志偉：諺語詩

2288 Chi, Ch'eng-chia, et al.: *Chung-kuo
yen-yü hsüan.*—Lanchow: Kan-su jen-min,
1981, 2 vols., [ii], 374 p; 5, 469 p.
[A (classified) collection of Chinese
proverbs.]
季成家等：中國諺語選

2289 Chu, Chieh-fan: Yen-yü lei shou.—
CKYT 3:2, 1958, 38–47; 3, 43–53;
6, 25–31; 4:1, 1959, 33–37; 5:2,
22–26; 6:4, 1960, 28–30. [A discussion
of proverbs according to categories.]
朱介凡：諺語類說

2290 Chu, Yü-tsun: *Min-chien yen-yü
ch'uan chi.*—Shanghai: Shih-chieh, 1933;
1935, 2nd ed., 4, 271 p. [A complete
collection of folk proverbs.]
朱雨尊：民間諺語全集

2291 Lan-chou i-shu hsüeh-yüan Wen-hsüen-
hsi wu-wu-chi Min-chien wen-hsüeh
hsiao-tsu: *Chung-kuo yen-yü tzu-liao.*—
Shanghai: Shang-hai wen-i, 1961, 3
vols., 384; 204; 428 p. [Chinese proverb
materials.]/ Proverbs, *hsieh-hou-yü*, etc.
蘭州藝術學院文學系五五級民間文學小組：中
國諺語資料

2292 Chung-shan ta-hsüeh Chung-wen-hsi:
Han-yü yen-yü hsiao tz'u-tien.—Canton:
Kuang-tung jen-min, 1982, 162, 435 p.
[A small dictionary of Chinese proverbs.]

中山大學中文系：漢語諺語小辭典

2293 Fan, Tzu: Yen-yü.—*MCWH* 1959:3, 99. [Proverbs.]
凡子：諺語

2294 Feng, P'eng-nien: *Mei jih i yen* (Ti-i chi).—Taipei: Min-sheng pao-she, 1982, 5, 182 p. [One proverb each day (Vol. I).]
馮鵬年：每日一諺（第一輯）

2295 Fu-chien jen-min ch'u-pan-she: *Yen-yü hsüan chi.*—Foochow: Ditto, 1982, 2, 140 p. [A selected collection of proverbs.]
福建人民出版社：諺語選輯

2296 Hsiao, Hsü, et al.: Yen-yü.—*MCWH* 1955:8, 20. [Proverbs.]
筱叙等：諺語

2297 Hsin-sheng ch'u-pan-she: *Hsin pien ch'eng-yü yen-yü tz'u-tien* (2050). [A newly edited dictionary of set-phrases and proverbs.]
新生出版社：新編成語諺語辭典

2298 Hsü, Tzu-ch'ang & Liang, Ta-shan: *Min yen.*—Shanghai: Shang-wu, 1933; 1934, 2nd ed., 128 p. [Folk proverbs.]
徐子長、梁達善：民諺

2299 Hu, P'u-an: *Su-yü tien.*—Shanghai: Kuang-i, 1929, 2 vols., v.p.; Tokyo: Kyūko shoin, 1970, repr. with Yen Fu-sun's *Shang-hai su-yü ta tz'u-tien*, 356 p. [A dictionary of popular sayings.]/ With Yen Fu-sun's *A comprehensive dictionary of Shanghai popular sayings* (2578).
胡樸安：俗語典／附嚴芙孫：上海俗語大辭典

2300 Huang, Chao-nien: Yen-yü i shu.—*Min-su* 46, 1929, 42–52. [A bundle of proverbs.]
黃詔年：諺語一束

2301 I, Su-min: *Wan-yung ch'eng-yü su-yü ta tz'u-tien* (2060). [A multiple-usage comprehensive dictionary of set-phrases and popular proverbs.]
易蘇民：萬用成語俗諺大辭典

2302 Li, Meng-pei: *Yen-yü, hsieh-hou-yü ch'ien chu.*—Kunming: Yün-nan jen-min, 1980, 123, 677 p. [Simple annotations on proverbs and *hsieh-hou-yü.*]
李孟北：諺語、歇後語淺註

2303 Li, Fang: *Min-chien su-hua.*—Taiyuan: Shan-hsi jen-min, 1952; 1957, 2nd repr., 2, 4, 61 p. [Folk popular sayings.]
立方：民間俗話

2304 Liao, Yung-min; Ts'ao I-fan & Chung, I: *Yen-yü hsüan.*—Chengchow: Ho-nan jen-min, 1981, 2, [i], 246 p. [A selection of proverbs.]
廖永民、曹一凡、鍾毅：諺語選

2305 Lin, Hsün: *I jih i yen.*—Taipei: Chin-wen, 1982, [i], 266 p. [One proverb a day.]
林洵：一日一諺

2306 Lü, Chien-shan: *Mei jih i yen* (Ti-i chi).—Taipei: Ming-yüan, 1982, 241 p., illus. [One proverb each day (Vol. I).]
呂健山：每日一諺（第一輯）

2307 P'an, Li-wen: *Chung wai su-yü tien.*—Hong Kong: Chung-hsi wen-hua, 1975, [ii], 4, 653 p. [A dictionary of Chinese and foreign popular sayings.]/ Classified, including *hsieh-hou-yü* of different localities.
潘禮文：中外俗語典／包括各地歇後語

2308 P'ing, Pu-ch'ing: *Shih-yen.*—In (1251). [Proverbs explained.]
平步青：釋諺

2309 Shao, Chih-chung, et al.: *Yen-yü shih ch'ao.*—Peking: Chung-kuo shao-nien erh-t'ung, 1980, 83 p. [A collection of proverbial poems.]
邵知中等：諺語詩抄

2310 Shih, Hsiang-tsai: *Chung-hua yen-hai.*

—Shanghai: Chung-hua, 1927; 1940, 4th ed., v.p. [A sea of Chinese proverbs.]
史襄哉：中華諺海

2311   Shih, Hsiang-tsai (comp.), Chu, Chieh-fan (ed.): *Tseng-pu Chung-hua yen-hai.* —Taipei: T'ien-i, 1975, 10, 5, 30, 477 p. [A revised and augmented edition of *Chung-hua yen-hai* (2310).]
史襄哉編，朱介凡校：增補中華諺海

2312   Wang, Ta-ch'ang: *Chung-kuo ch'eng-yü ta tz'u-tien* (2103)./ With an appendix of set-phrase historical allusions, proverbs, etc. [A comprehensive dictionary of Chinese set-phrases.]
王大昌：中國成語大辭典／附成語故事、諺語等

2313   Wang, Tsung-chieh & Hung, Hui-chen: *Chung-kuo ko-yen yen-yü szu-yung ta tz'u-tien* (2167). [A four-usage comprehensive dictionary of Chinese maxims and proverbs.]
王宗傑、洪慧貞：中國格言諺語四用大辭典

2314   Wang, Yü-kang: *Su-yü tien.* —Taipei: Wu-chou, 1976, [i], [xiii], 510 p. [A dictionary of popular sayings.]
王宇綱：俗語典

2315   Wu, Chan-k'un & Ma, Kuo-fan: *Yen-yü.* —Huhehot: Nei Meng-ku jen-min, 1980, 474 p. [Proverbs.]
武占坤、馬國凡：諺語

2316   Wu-hsi shih-fan hsüeh-hsiao: *Han-yü yen-yü tz'u-tien.* —Nanking: Chiang-su jen-min, 1981, [ii], 103, 615 p. [A dictionary of Chinese proverbs.]
無錫師範學校：漢語諺語詞典

7.2.7.2. Sino-Japanese Works (2317–2331)

2317   Fujii, Otoo: *Gengo daijiten.* —Tokyo: Yūhōdō, 1910; 1911; 1926, 1953, 1159, 13, 254 p. [A comprehensive dictionary of proverbs.]
藤井乙男：諺語大辭典

2318   Haga, Yaichi: *Kakugen daijiten.* —Tokyo: Bunshōkaku, 1920, 797 p. [A comprehensive dictionary of proverbs.]/ Japanese, Chinese, Western, classified.
芳賀矢一：格言大辭典

2319   Juken: Shina no rigen.—*Shina mondai* 1931:108, 39–42, 109, 49–50; 110, 51–54; 111, 47–50; 113, 35–38; 114, 77–78; 1932:117, 50–52; 118, 59–61; 119, 46–48; 120, 58–60; 121, 44–46; 122, 61–63; 123, 46–48; 124, 49–51; 125, 33–36; 126, 30–32; 127, 39–41; 128, 30–32. [Proverbs of China.]/ See (2321)
壽軒：支那の俚諺

2320   Kōsaka, Jun'ichi: *Shinago nangoku shūkai.*—Tokyo: Gaikokugo Gakuin Shuppansha, 1941, 2, 1, 213 p./ 67–193: Proverbs and *hsieh-hou-yü.* [A collection and explanations of difficult Chinese phrases and sentences.]
香坂順一：支那語難語句集解

2321   Matsumura, Juken: Shina no rigen. —*Man-Mō* 16:6, 1935, 16:8, (not seen); 16:11, (not seen); 16:12, (not seen). [Proverbs of China.]/ See (2319).
松村壽軒：支那の俚諺

2322   Murata, Ryōa, et al.: *Sōho rigen shūran.*—Tokyo: Meicho Kankōkai, 1965, repr., 3 vols., 8, 866; 879; 790 p. [An enlarged collection of proverbs.]
村田了阿等：增補俚言集覽

2323   Nakanishi, Jirō: *Shimin jitsuyō Shingo shū.* Fu *Gengo yōhō.*—Lüshun: Ōsakayago shiten, 1910, 2, 1, 166 p. [A collection from the Chinese language of the Ch'ing (dynasty) for the practical usage of the four classes of people. With the ways of using proverbs.]
中西次郎：四民實用清語集　附諺語用法

2324   Nakano, Yoshihei: *Rigen daijiten.*— Tokyo: Tōhō shoin, 1933, 6th print., 6, 1083, 424 p. [A comprehensive dictionary of proverbs.] / Japanese & Chinese, classified.

中野吉平：俚諺大辭典

2325 Ono, Shinobu: *Sekai no kotowaza jiten.*—Tokyo: Fukuinkan, 1964, 537 p. [A dictionary of proverbs of the world.]

小野忍：世界のことわざ辞典

2326 Suzuki, Tōzō & Hirota, Eitarō: *Koji kotowaza jiten.*—Tokyo: Tōkyōdō, 1957, 2, 983, 4 p. [A dictionary of historical allusions and proverbs.]

鈴木棠三、廣田榮太郎：故事ことわざ辞典

2327 Suzuki, Tōzō: *Zoku Koji kotowaza jiten.*—Tokyo: Tōkyōdō, 1959, 4, 456 p. [A continuation of *Koji kotowaza jiten* (2326).]

鈴木棠三：續故事ことわざ辞典

2328 Tajima, Taihei & Wang Shih-tzu: *Shina jōyō zokugen shū.*—Tokyo: Bunkyūdō, 1941, 3, 2, 224 p. [A collection of commonly used Chinese popular proverbs.]

田島泰平、王石子：支那常用俗諺集

2329 Takahashi, Gen'ichirō: *Koji seigo gengo shūkai* (1997). [Collection and explanations of historical allusions, set-phrases, and proverbs.]

高橋源一郎：故事成語諺語集解

2330 Tanaka, Seiichirō: *Chūgoku no zokugen.*—Tokyo: Hakusuisha, 1979, 349 p. [Chinese popular proverbs.]

田中清一郎：中國の俗諺

2331 Torii, Hisayasu: *Kaihen Chūgoku zokugen 4000 shu.*—[Tenri]: Ditto, 1962, [ii], 114 p./ *RBS* 8, 1962, 508, S.N. Cartier. [A rearranged edition of (Wilfrid Allan's) *A treasury of 4000 Chinese proverbs* (publ. in 1942).]

鳥居久靖：改編中國俗諺4000首

7.2.7.3. Western Translations (2332–2366)

2332 Anonymous: Proverbs and metaphors drawn from nature in use among the Chinese.—*Chinese Repository* 7, 1838, 321–327.

2333 Beilenson, Peter: *Chinese proverbs from olden times.*—Mount Vernon: Petey Pauper Press, 1956, 62 p., illus.

2334 Char, Tin-yuke: *Chinese proverbs.*—San Francisco: Jade Mountain Press, 1970, iv, 43 p.; Taipei: Ch'eng-wen, 1970, repr.

〔謝廷玉〕

2335 Ch'en, Ch'eng-chih: *Ying-Han tui-chao Chung-kuo ch'eng-yü yen-yü liu-pai chü* (2121). [Six hundred English-Chinese set-phrases and proverbs of China.]

陳澄之：英漢對照中國成語諺語六百句

2336 Ch'en, Tso-shun (comp. & transl.): *Chung-kuo yen-yü hsüan chi.*—Hong Kong: Hsiang-kang Chung-wen ta-hsüeh Ch'ung-chi hsüeh-yüan, 1973, 8, 327 p. [A selected collection of Chinese proverbs.]

陳佐舜編譯：中國諺語選集

2337 Cheng, Ying: *Sprichwörterliche Redensarten im modernen Chinesisch.*—Hamburg: Helmut Buske Verlag, 1978, 109 p.

2338 Chou, P'an-lin: *Chung-hsi yen-yü pi-chiao yen-chiu.*—Taipei: Wen-shih-che, 1975, 2, [i], 3, 138 p. [A comparative study on Chinese and Western proverbs.]

周盤林：中西諺語比較研究

2339 Colomer, Ramón: Algunos proverbios y apotegmas chinos.—*Correo Sino-Annamita* 28, 1894, 134–152.

2340 Couvreur, Séraphin, S.J.: *Guide to conversation in French, English and Chinese.*—Ho Kien Fou: Catholic Mission Press, 1899, 4th ed., viii, 222 p./ Appendix (211–214): Proverbs.

2341   Davis, Sir John Francis: *Hien Wun Shoo: Chinese moral maxims, with a free and verbal translation.*—London: John Murray & Macao: Honorable Company's Press, 1823, vii, 199 p.
〔賢文書〕

2342   Dawson-Gröne, H.: *Ming Hsien Chi, being a collection of proverbs and maxims in the Chinese language.*—Shanghai: Kelly & Walsh, 1911, 43 p./ Translated into English with a few explanatory notes; *JRASNCB* 44, 1913, 181–182, M.; See (2281).
〔名賢集〕

2343   Devloo, Edmond: *An anthology of 3600 classified Chinese proverbs and wise sayings.*—Taipei: Hua-ming, 1970, ii, 563 p.
〔羅秉鐸：分類格言選集〕

2344   Edwards, Evangeline Dora: *A collection of Chinese proverbs* (in Mandarin).—Shanghai: Kwang-hsüeh Publishing House, (Preface:) 1926, 70 p.

2345   Fabre, Alfred: *Film de la vie chinoise: proverbes et locutions.*—Hong Kong: Nazareth, 1937, xviii, 694 p./ 6305 proverbs and sayings classified under ten categories.

2346   Hart, Henry Hersch: *Seven hundred Chinese proverbs.*—Stanford: Stanford U. Press, 1937, xxvii, 83 p., illus.
〔俗諺七百首〕

2347   Hart, Henry Hersch. Transl. by Wyss-Vögtlin, Margarit von: *Siebenhundert chinesische Sprichwörter.*—Zürich: Rascher, 1945, iv, 112 p. [Seven hundred Chinese proverbs.] (2346)

2348   Hsi, Shih-chih: *Han-Ying tui-chao ching-hsüan Chung-kuo liu-pai yen-yü.*—Shanghai: Fu-tan, 1946, 104 p. [600 Chinese-English carefully selected proverbs of China.]

奚識之：漢英對照精選中國六百諺語

2349   Lai, T'ien-ch'ang & Kwong, Y.T.: *Chinese proverbs.*—Hong Kong: Kelly & Walsh, 1970, 55 p., illus.

2350   Li, Keng-hsin: *Ku yen tien Ying i.*—Taichung: Kuang-ch'i, 1973–1974, 2 vols., 2, 192; 4, 177 p. [An English translation of ancient proverbs and literary allusions.]
李更新：古諺典英譯

2351   Li, Keng-hsin: *Chung-kuo min-su yen-yü.*—Taichung: Ditto, 1982, 2 vols., 13, 3, 167; 3, 175, 3 p. [(Chinese-English) Chinese folk proverbs.]
李更新：中國民俗諺語

2352   Lum, Chung Park: *Words of wisdom from Chinese sages.*—New York: Walters & Mahon, 1933 (?), 58 p.
〔林松柏〕

2353   Mateos, Fernando, S.J.: *Florilegio de refranes Chinos.*—Madrid & Barcelona: Asociación Española de Orietalistas, 1972, 311 p.

2354   Morgan, Harry Titterton: *Chinese proverbs.*—Los Angeles: (?), 1944 (?), 20 p., illus.

2355   Motte, Joseph, S.J.: *Proverbes et dictons chinois traduits et commentés en français.*—Taichung: Kuang-ch'i, 1981, vi, 172 p.
〔穆啓蒙：法譯中國諺語〕

2356   Navarra, Bruno: *Chinesische Sinnsprüche.*—Heidelberg: Carl Winter, 1903, vii, 79 p.
〔諺語甚話〕

2357   Perny, Paul: *Proverbes chinois.*—Paris: Firmin Didot frères, fils & Cie, 1869, 135 p.
〔中國俗語〕

2358   Ricketts, Catherine Maria & Wong,

Fan: Chinese proverbial sayings.—*CR* 20:6, 1893, 381–391.

2359   Scarborough, William: *A collection of Chinese proverbs.*—Shanghai: American Presbyterian Mission Press, 1875, xxvi, 478 p.; London: Probsthain, 1926, rev. ed., vi, 381, [2], xiv p.

2360   Schaub, M.: Chinese proverbs.—*CR* 20:3, 1893, 156–166.

2361   Shepherd, Charles Reginald: *One hundred and one Chinese proverbs.*—Berkeley: Ditto, n.d., 2nd ed., 23 p. 23 p.

2362   Smith, Arthur H.: *Proverbs and common sayings from the Chinese.*—Shanghai: American Presbyterian Mission Press, 1888, ii, vii, 374 p.; 1902, xxxvi, 374 p.; New York: Paragon Book Reprint Corp., 1965, repr., vii, 374, xxix p.; Taipei: Wen-chih, 1979, repr., [i], vii, 374 p./ Subtitle: Together with much related and unrelated matter, interspersed with observations on Chinese things in general./ From material published in the *Chinese Recorder* from 1882 to 1885.

〔中國格言與俗語〕

2363   Wang, Kuo-chung, et al.: *Han-Ying-Fa-Te yü tui-chao ch'ang-yung yen-yü 600 t'iao.*—Peking: Shang-wu, 1981, [2], 194 p. [600 commonly used Chinese proverbs with English, French, and German equivalents.]

王國忠等：漢英法德語對照常用諺語600條

2364   Werner, E.T.C.: Chinese ditties.—*NCR* 3, 1921, 259–272, 368–375, 442–450; 4, 1922, 23–31, 106–113.

2365   Wu, Chih-kang & Wu, Huang Ch'i-hsiu: *Han-Ying liang ch'ien Chung-kuo su-yü hsüan.*—Hong Kong: Chung-kuo yü-wen yen-chiu hsüeh-hui, 1968, xii, 184 p. [A Chinese-English selection of two thousand Chinese popular sayings.]

吳志鋼、吳黃縈琇：漢英兩千中國俗語選

2366   Yoo, Young H.: *Wisdom of the Far East: A dictionary of proverbs, maxims, and famous classical phrases of the Chinese, Japanese, and Korean.*—Washington, D.C.: Far Eastern Research & Publications Center, 1972, 449 p.

7.2.8. Socio-cultural Aspects (2367–2513)
7.2.8.1. Sociological Aspects in General (2367–2374)

2367   Ch'en, Shao-hsin: Yen-yü chih she-hui-hsüeh te yen-chiu.—*Jen-wen k'o-hsüeh lun-ts'ung* 1, 1949, 271–282. [A study of the sociology of proverbs.]

陳紹馨：諺語之社會學的研究

2368   Ch'en, Ting-hung: Chung-kuo yen-yü chung te she-hui kuan-hsi lun.—*Ching shih* 1:11, 1937, 21–28 8. [On social relations (as reflected) in Chinese proverbs.]

陳定閎：中國諺語中的社會關係論

2369   Ch'i, Ju-shan: Yen-yü tsai she-hui chung te chung-yao-hsing.—*Ch'ang liu* 5:6, 1952, 13–14; 7, 27–28. [The importance of proverbs in society.]

齊如山：諺語在社會中的重要性

2370   Chu, Chieh-fan: Yen-yü te she-hui kung-neng.—*Ch'ang liu* 26:1, 1962, 13–14; 2, 17–18; 3, 17. [The social functions of proverbs.]

朱介凡：諺語的社會功能

2371   Chu, Chieh-fan: Chung-kuo yen-yü te she-hui-kuan.—*Ch'ang liu* 28:5, 1963, 15–16; 6, 19–21. [Sociological aspects of Chinese proverbs.]

朱介凡：中國諺語的社會觀

2372   Chu, Chieh-fan: Yen-yü chih she-hui-hsüeh te yen-chiu.—*TWFW* 16:6, 1966, 12–16. [A study of the sociology of proverbs.]

朱介凡：諺語之社會學的研究

2373   Lee, Davis Lin-chuan: *Chinese proverbs: a pragmatic and sociolinguistic approach.* —Washington, D.C.: Georgetown U., 1979, 218 p./ Unpubl. doc. diss.; *DAI* 40:3–4, 1979, 2039A; UM 7923549.

〔李林傳〕

2374   Shen, T'ien-ho: Chung-kuo yen-yü ho she-hui kuan-hsi te p'ou shih.—*Chung-mei chou-k'an* 2:12, 1940, 6–9. [An open view of Chinese proverbs and social relations.]

沈天鶴：中國諺語和社會關係的剖視

7.2.8.2. Human Livelihood (2375–2382)

2375   Ch'en, Shao-hsin: Taiwan rigen ni arawareta hito no issei.—*MZTW* 3:3, 1943, 11–13. [A man's life as reflected in the proverbs of Taiwan.]

陳紹馨：臺灣俚諺に現れた人の一生

2376   Ch'en, Shao-hsin Ts'ung yen-yü k'an jen te i-sheng.—*TW* 5:2, 1949, 35–49. [A person's whole life as seen from proverbs.]

陳紹馨：從諺語看人的一生

2377   Ch'en, Shao-hsin: Ts'ung-yen-yü k'an Chung-kuo-jen te t'ien ming szu-hsiang.—*TW* 6:2, 1950, 21–45. [The concept of destiny of the Chinese people as seen from proverbs.]

陳紹馨：從諺語看中國人的天命思想

2378   Chu, Chieh-fan: Chung-kuo yen-yü chih/ Yü-yen sheng-huo p'ien.—*CKYT* 30:5, 1972, 24–27; 30:6, 41–43; 31:1, 58–63; 31:2, 36–43. [A record of Chinese proverbs—Section on linguistic life.]

朱介凡：中國諺語志　語言生活篇

2379   Chu, Chieh-fan: Chung-kuo yen-yü chih. Wei-sheng p'ien.—*BIE* 30, 1970, 165–237. [A record of Chinese proverbs. Section on hygiene.]

朱介凡：中國諺語志　衛生篇

2380   Chu, Chieh-fan: Chung-kuo yen-yü chih. Sheng-huo p'ien hsüan.—*SHJ* 253, 1975, 1–8. [A record of Chinese proverbs. A selected section on livelihood.]

朱介凡：中國諺語志　生活篇選

2381   Takeuchi, Akio: Shina no kotowaza —Toku-ni ryokō ni kansuru.—*Tabi to densetsu* 1941:4, (not seen). [Proverbs of China—With special reference to travel.]

竹內照夫：支那の諺――特に旅行に關する

2382   Ts'ao, Chia-i: Jen sheng li-yen i-pai erh-shih tse.—*TWFW* 15:3, 1965, 44–51. [One hundred and twenty proverbs from (everyday) life.]

曹甲乙：人生俚諺一百二十則

7.2.8.3. Family and Marriage (2383–2392)

2383   A.P.: Yu-kuan nü-hsing li-yen.—*TWFW* 2:8–9, 1952, 11. [Proverbs concerning females.]

A.P.：有關女性俚諺

2384   Hung, Niang: Yu-kuan chia-ch'ü li-yen. —*TWFW* 4:1, 1954, 10. [Proverbs concerning marriage.]

紅娘：有關嫁娶俚諺

2385   Liu, I-ch'ing: *Erh-t'ung yen-yü.*— Hong Kong: T'ung-nien shu-tien, 1951, [i], 4, 72 p. [Children's proverbs.]

柳一青：兒童諺語

2386   Murakami, Futeki: Peipin katei no rigen.—*Man-Mō* 123, 1930, (not seen). [Household proverbs of Peiping.]

村上不適：北平家庭の俚諺

2387   Su, Wei-hsiung: Rigen ni arawareta Taiwan no dan jo.—*MZTW* 2:12, 1942, 18–24. [Men and women of Taiwan as appearing in proverbs.]

蘇維熊：俚諺に現れた臺灣の男女

2388   Tajima, Taihei: Shina no ie ni kansuru

zokugen shū.—*SOS* 2:10, 1940, (not seen). [A collection of Chinese proverbs concerning the family.]

田島泰平：支那の『家』に關する俗言集

2389   Ts'ao, Chia-i: T'ai-pei yu-kuan tzu-nü te li-yen.—*TPWW* 7:3, 1958, 30–35. [Proverbs of Taipei concerning sons and daughters.]

曹甲乙：臺北有關子女的俚諺

2390   Ts'ao, Chia-i: T'ai-pei yu-kuan nan nü te li-yen.—*TPWW* 8:4, 1960, 95–102. [Proverbs of Taipei concerning men and women.]

曹甲乙：臺北有關男女的俚諺

2391   Ts'ao, Chia-i: Yu-kuan hun-yin, fu-fu erh-nü te li-yen.—*TWFW* 18:2, 1968, 36–45. [Proverbs concerning matrimony, husbands and wives, and children.]

曹甲乙：有關婚姻、夫婦兒女的俚諺

2392   Yamanaka, Shōji, [Ch'en, Shao-hsin]: Rigen ni arawareta Taiwan oyobi Shina no kazoku seikatsu.—*Taiwan bunka ronsō* 2, 1945, 1–107. [Family life of Taiwan and China as appearing in proverbs.]

山中彰二〔陳紹馨〕：俚諺に現れた臺灣及び支那の家族生活

7.2.8.4. Social Contacts (2393–2396)

2393   Katō, Yoshio: Ningen ni kansuru Chūgoku no zokugen ni tsuite.—*KKDGK* 25, 1974, 52–58. [On Chinese proverbs concerning human beings.]

加藤秀雄：人間に關する中國の俗諺 について

2394   Plopper, Clifford Henry: *Chinese proverbs: the relationship of friends as brought out by the proverbs; economics as seen through the proverbs.*—Peiping: North China Union Language School, [1932], 47 p.

2395   Takeuchi, Akio: Shina no kotowaza —Toku-ni kinrin seikatsu ni kansuru.

—*Tabi to densetsu* 1941:10, (not seen). [Proverbs of China—With special reference to the lives of neighbors.]

竹內照夫：支那の諺──特に近隣生活に關する

2396   Takeuchi, Akio: Shina no kotowaza —Toku-ni kōsai ni kansuru.—*Tabi to densetsu* 1942:3, (not seen). [Proverbs of China—With special reference to social intercourse.]

竹內照夫：支那の諺──特に交際に關する

7.2.8.5. Philosophy (2397–2404)

2397   Anonymous: Chinese proverbial philosophy.—*Chinese and Japanese Repository* 1865, August, 395–398; September, 444–446; October, 488–490; November, 539–540.

2398   Brown, Brian: *The wisdom of the Chinese, their philosophy in sayings and proverbs.*—New York: Brentano's, 1920; 1921, 2nd print., 208 p., 1 portr.

2399   Chu, Chieh-fan: Yen-yü tsai szu-hsiang yü shih-wu shang te chieh-shih.—*Pan-yüeh lun-t'an* 8:21, 1963, 1–10. [Knowledge and experience in proverbs on thoughts and affairs.]

朱介凡：諺語在思想事物上的見識

2400   Chu, Chieh-fan: Chung-kuo yen-yü chih. Lun-li p'ien.—*CSHS* 9, 1972, 291–402; 10, 469–579. [A record of Chinese proverbs. Section on theory.]

朱介凡：中國諺語志　論理篇

2401   Chu, Chieh-fan: Chung-kuo yen-yü chih. Che li p'ien hsüan.—*SHJ* 222, 1973, 1–8. [A record of Chinese proverbs. A selected section on philosophical principles.]

朱介凡：中國諺語志　哲理篇選

2402   Chu, Chieh-fan: Chung-kuo yen-yü chih. Hsin-li p'ien.—*CSHS* 15, 1975, 277–371. [A record of Chinese proverbs.

Section on psychology.]

朱介凡：中國諺語志　心理篇

2403 Chu, Tse-chi: Lun yen-yü te szu-hsiang ho i-shu.—*HPSY* 1956:1, 102–115. [On the thought and art of proverbs.]

朱澤吉：論諺語的思想和藝術

2404 Moule, A.E.: Chinese proverbial philosophy.—*ChinRec* 5, 1874, 72–77.

7.2.8.6. Morality, Religion, and Education (2405–2415)

2405 Chu, Chieh-fan: Chung-kuo yen-yü te p'in-hsing.—*Wen hsing* 10:2, 1962, 73–76. [The moral character of Chinese proverbs.]

朱介凡：中國諺語的品性

2406 Chu, Chieh-fan: Yen-yü tsai chiao-yü shang te ch'ü-cheng.—*Fan-kung* 247, 1962, 12–15. [The evidence of proverbs on education.]

朱介凡：諺語在教育上的取證

2407 Chu, Chieh-fan: Chung-kuo yen-yü. Chiao-yü p'ien.—*Chin-jih Chung-kuo* 13, 1972, 25–52; 14, 84–116. [Chinese proverbs. Section on education.]

朱介凡：中國諺語　教育篇

2408 Chu, Chieh-fan: Chung-kuo yen-yü chih. Te-hsing p'ien hsüan.—*CKYT* 33:5, 1973, 109–114. [A record of Chinese proverbs. Selected section on morality and conduct.]

朱介凡：中國諺語志　德行篇選

2409 Chu, Chieh-fan: *P'i-yü yen-yü chi.*—Taipei: T'ien-i, 1974, 6, [iii], 237 p. [A collection of metaphorical proverbs.]

朱介凡：譬喻諺語集

2410 Chu, Chieh-fan: Ma-tsu hsin-yang te li-shih pei-ching—Chung-kuo yen-yü chih. Hsüan-li p'ien.—*CHWH* 10:5, 1977, 49–54. [The historical background of Ma-tsu worship —A record of Chinese

proverbs. Section on mysticism.]

朱介凡：媽祖信仰的歷史背景——中國諺語志 玄理篇

2411 Lister, Alfred: Chinese proverbs and their lessons.—*CR* 3, 1874, 129–138.

2412 Plopper, Clifford Henry: *Chinese religion seen through the proverb.*—Shanghai: China Press, 1926, xi, 381 p., illus., pl.

2413 T'ien-chin jen-min ch'u-pan-she: *Lao su-hua li te shih ho fei.*—Tientsin: Ditto, 1979, 6, 94 p. [Right and wrong concepts found in old popular sayings.]

天津人民出版社：老俗話裏的是和非

2414 Ts'ai, Yü: Ching su li-yen.—*TPWW* 6:1, 1957, 43–50. [Proverbs warning the world.]

蔡煜：警俗俚諺

2415 Ts'ao, Chia-i: Yu, wu, hao, huai te li-yen.—*TWWH* 19:2, 1968, 149–158. [Proverbs related to 'to have', 'not have', 'good' and 'bad'.]

曹甲乙：有、無、好、壞的俚諺

7.2.8.7. Politics, Economy, and Military Affairs (2416–2425)

2416 Chu, Chieh-fan: Chung-kuo ping yen yen-chiu yin li.—*Wang-ch'ü* 5:3, 1940, (not seen). [Introductory examples for the study of Chinese military proverbs.]

朱介凡：中國兵諺研究引例

2417 Chu, Chieh-fan: Ping yen tsai pu-tui chiao-yü shang te chia-chih.—*Wang-ch'ü* 9:1, 1943, (not seen). [The value of military proverbs in the education of the armed services.]

朱介凡：兵諺在部隊教育上的價值

2418 Chu, Chieh-fan: Shuo ping yen.—*Wo ko ch'ieh yao* (2217), 87–90. [A discussion on military proverbs.]

朱介凡：說兵諺

2419 Chu, Chieh-fan: Yen-yü tsai cheng-chih shang chih chien-tao.—*Kuo hun* 209, 1962, 46–50. [The 'come to know the truth' of proverbs on politics.]
朱介凡：諺語在政治上之見道

2420 Chu, Chieh-fan: Chung-kuo yen-yü. Cheng-chih p'ien.—*YSHC* 14:3–4, 1977, 104–152. [Chinese proverbs. Section on politics.]
朱介凡：中國諺語　政治篇

2421 Chu, Chieh-fan: Fa-lü yen-yü te shih-shih ku-shih ch'uan-shuo.—*CHWH* 11:4–5, 1978, 51–58. [Legends on factual historical allusions in proverbs about law.]
朱介凡：法律諺語的史實故事傳說

2422 Chu, Chieh-fan: Chung-kuo yen-yü. Ching-chi p'ien.—*Shih-huo yüeh-k'an* 8:11, 1979, 475–508; 8:12, 1–12; 9:1–2, 1979, 34–75. [Chinese proverbs. Section on economics.]
朱介凡：中國諺語　經濟篇

2423 Katō, Yoshio: Kinsen ni kansuru Chūgoku no zokugen ni tsuite.—*Kita Kyūshū daigaku kaigaku nijū shūnen kinen ronbunshū* 1966, 311–322. [On Chinese popular proverbs concerning money.]
加藤秀雄：金錢に關する中國の俗諺について ——『北九州大學開學二十周年紀念論文集』

2424 Kung, Hsiang-p'ing: Chün-chung li-su-yü.—*CKYT* 8:6, 1961, (not seen). [Popular sayings (used) among soldiers.]
龔湘萍：軍中俚俗語

2425 Li, Hsün-ch'ao: Ning-po shang yen.—*Min-chung chiao-yü* 5:4, 1937, (not seen); 5:5, 1937, (not seen). [Commercial proverbs of Ningpo.]
勵勳朝：寧波商諺

7.2.9. Scientific Aspects (2426–2513)

7.2.9.1. Mathematics (2426–2430)

2426 Katō, Yoshio: Chūgoku zokugen ni fukumareta sūshi ni tsuite.—*Kita Kyūshū daigaku kaigaku 25 shūnen kinen ronbunshū*, 1972, 643–651. [On numerals contained in Chinese popular proverbs.]
加藤秀雄：中國の俗諺に含まれた數詞について ——『北九州大學開學25周年紀念論文集』

2427 Tanaka, Katsumi: Chūgoku no koto-waza—ichi o tōji to suru.—*Seijō daigaku bungei gakubu tanki daigaku sōritsu nijūshūnen kinen ronbunshū—Bunkashi* (Tokyo, 1974), 145–182. [Proverbs of China—those beginning with the character *i* ('one').]
田中克己：中國の諺——一を頭字とする—— 『西城大學文藝學部短期大學創立二十周年紀念論文集——文化史』

2428 Ts'ao, Chia-i: Shih-erh sheng hsiao te su-yen.—*TWFW* 17:4, 1967, 22–26. [Popular proverbs concerning the relation of one's year of birth and one of twelve animals (in the Chinese zodiacal system).]
曹甲乙：十二生肖的俗諺

2429 Ts'ao, Chia-i: Yu-kuan shu-tzu te li-yen.—*TWFW* 18:1, 1968, 89–105. [Proverbs related to numerals.]
曹甲乙：有關數字的俚諺

2430 Yü, I-jen: Shu-tzu yen-yü.—*I feng* 4:1, 1936, 80–81. [Proverbs with numerals.]
余逸人：數字諺語

7.2.9.2. Zoology (2431–2433)

2431 Katō, Hideo: Chūgoku zokugen ni fukumareta dōbutsu ni tsuite.—*KKDGK* 1:2, 1959, 21–24. [On the animals contained in Chinese popular proverbs.]
加藤秀雄：中國俗諺に含まれた動物について

2432 Liao, Han-ch'en: Uma ni kansuru rigen.—*MZTW* 2:2, 1942, 36–37.

[Proverbs concerning the horse.]

廖漢臣：馬に關する俚諺

2433 Wu, Ying-t'ao: Tung-wu li-yen chi. —*TWFW* 17:6, 1967, 95–104. [A collection of proverbs concerning animals.]

吳瀛濤：動物俚諺集

7.2.9.3. Meteorology (2434–2448)

2434 Anonymous: Proverbes chinois—dictons populaires sur la pluie et le beau temps recueillis au Kiang-nan.—*Relations de Chine* 1905, July, 580–584, to be continued.

〔江南〕

2435 Ch'en, Cho-min: *Chung-kuo ch'i-hsiang yen-yü chi.*—Canton: Chung-shan ta-hsüeh, 1933, 66 p. [A collection of Chinese meteorological proverbs.]

陳卓民：中國氣象諺語集

2436 Ch'en, I-te: Yün-nan ch'i-hsiang yen-yü chi.—*Chiao-yü yü k'o-hsüeh* 1:5, 1939, 119–146. [A collection of meteorological proverbs of Yünnan.]

陳一得：雲南氣象諺語集

2437 Ch'iao, Ch'i-ming: Shan-hsi chih ch'i-hsiang yen.—*NLHP* 2, 1924, 3, 1924, (not seen); 4, 1924, (not seen); 5, 1924, (not seen). [Meteorological proverbs of Shansi.]

喬啓明：山西之氣象諺

2438 Chin, Nan: Kuan-yü t'ien-ch'i te su-yü.—*Fu-nü tsa-chih* 11:11, 1925, 1774–1775. [Popular sayings concerning the weather.]

金南：關於天氣的俗語

2439 Chu, Ping-hai: *Chung-kuo t'ien-ch'i li-yen hui chieh.*—Shanghai (?): K'o-hsüeh shu-tien, 1943, (not seen). [A collection with explanations of Chinese proverbs concerning the weather.]

朱炳海：中國天氣俚諺彙解

2440 Chu, Ping-hai: *T'ien-ch'i yen-yü.*—Peking: K'ai-ming, 1952, 114 p.; Peking: Chung-kuo ch'ing-nien, 1953, repr. [Proverbs concerning the weather.]

朱炳海：天氣諺語

2441 Hsia, Wen-t'ung: Che-chiang chih ch'i-hsiang yen-yü.—*NLHP* 1, 1924, (not seen). [Meteorological proverbs of Chekiang.]

夏文通：浙江之氣象諺語

2442 Huang, Chao-nien: Yen-yü i-shu—T'ien-ch'i, chieh-ling.—*Min-su* 46, 1929, 51–52. [A bundle of proverbs—Weather, seasons.]

黃詔年：諺語一束——天氣、節令

2443 Kamiya, Kōhei: Tenkō ni kansuru Peipin no zokugen.—*CGZS* 22, 1947, (not seen). [Peiping popular proverbs concerning the weather.]

神谷衡平：天候に關する北平の俗諺

2444 Katō, Yoshio: Jibutsu to tennen genzō ni kansuru Chūgoku no zokegen ni tsuite.—*KKDGK* 20, 1970, 39–46. [On Chinese popular proverbs concerning the affairs and natural phenomena.]

加藤秀雄：事物と天然現象に關する中國の俗諺について

2445 Ming: Ch'ang-sha nung-chia chih t'ien-ch'i chan yen.—*NLHP* 79, 1926, (not seen); 81, 1926, (not seen). [Proverbs of the farmers in Changsha forecasting the weather.]

明：長沙農家之天氣占諺

2446 Tung, Hua: T'ai-pei sui-shih te li-yen. —*TPWW* 5:2–3, 1957, 102–103. [Proverbs of Taipei on the time of the year.]

東華：臺北歲時的俚諺

2447 Wu, T'ien-fu: *Ts'e t'ien yen-yü chi.*—Changsha: Hu-nan jen-min, 1979, 103 p. [A collection of proverbs forecasting the weather.]

吳天福：測天諺語集

2448   Yü,   Fei: Nung-yen—Ch'ung-ch'ing chan-yen ch'i-hou te ko-yao.—*Min-su* 82, 1929, 4–6. [Agricultural proverbs —Folk songs for forecasting the weather in Chungking.]

于飛：農諺——重慶占驗氣候的歌謠

7.2.9.4. Agriculture (2449–2513)

2449   Anonymous: Shan-tung   nung-yen.— *NLHP* 19, 1924, (not seen). [Agricultural proverbs of Shantung.]

無名氏：山東農諺

2450   Anonymous: *Nung-yen ho nung-ko.*— Peiping: P'ei-p'ing ta-hsüeh Nung-hsüeh yüan, 1932, (not seen). [Agricultural proverbs and agricultural songs.]/ See (2507).

無名氏：農諺和農歌

2451   Anonymous: *Pai-ch'üan nung-yen chi.* —Paichuan: Pai-ch'üan   hsiang-shih shih-yen yen-chiu-so, 1934, (not seen). [A collection of agricultural proverbs of Paichüan.]/ Shansi.

無名氏：百泉農諺集

2452   Anonymous: *Che-chiang   nung-yen chi.*—Che-chiang-sheng Min-chung chiao-yü shih-yen hsüeh-hsiao, 1936, (not seen). [A collection of agricultural proverbs of Chekiang province.]

無名氏：浙江省農諺集

2453   Anonymous: Chuang-chia hua (nung- yen hsüan).—*MCWH* 1956:9, 82–96. [The sayings of farmers (selected agricultural proverbs).]

無名氏：莊稼話（農諺選）

2454   Anonymous: Ho-pei nung-yen.—*MCWH* 1959:2, 17, 19. [Agricultural proverbs of Hopei.]

無名氏：河北農諺

2455   Anonymous: Nung-yen.—*MCWH* 1961: 1, 81; 2, 80; 3, 94–96; 10, 38–42. [Agricultural proverbs.]

無名氏：農諺

2456   Chang,   Ch'ung-te: Shan-hsi   te nung-yen.—*NLHP* 25, 1925, (not seen). [Agricultural proverbs of Shansi.]

張崇德：山西的農諺

2457   Chang, Fo: *Nung-yen.*—Shanghai: Shang-wu, 1934, 2nd ed., 54 p.; 1947, repr. [Agricultural proverbs.]

張佛：農諺

2458   Chang, Pu-chou: Hai-ning nung-chia yen.—*Min-chien* 1:8, 1932, (not seen); 1:11, (not seen). [Proverbs of farmers in Haining.]/ Chekiang.

張步洲：海寧農家諺

2459   Chao, Feng-lai: Chih-li Wan-p'ing-hsien chih nung-chia yen-yü.—*NLHP* 14, 1924, (not seen). [Proverbs of farmers in Wanping-hsien, Chihli.]/ Hopei.

趙鳳來：直隸宛平縣之農家諺語

2460   Ch'en, K'ang-ch'i & Chang, Shou-yung: Hsiang yen cheng ku.—*Ta-chung* 1:1, 1945, 73–74; 2, 74–75; 3–4, 80–81; 5, 84–85. [Proving the antiquity of rural proverbs.]

陳康祺、張壽鏞：鄉諺證古

2461   Chi, Ch'eng-chia, et al.: *Chung-kuo yen-yü hsüan* (2288), Vol. II: Agricultural proverbs. [A (classified) collection of Chinese proverbs.]

季成家等：中國諺語選（下）農事篇

2462   Ch'iao, Ch'i-ming: Shan-hsi nung-yen. —*NLHP* 17, 1924, (not seen); 18, (not seen). [Agricultural proverbs of Shansi.]

喬啓明：山西農諺

2463   Ch'ien, Yeh-yün: T'ung-ch'eng-hsien nung-yen.—*NLHP* 86, 1927, (not seen). [Agricultural proverbs of Tungcheng-hsien.]/ Anhwei.

錢葉雲：桐城縣農諺

2464 Chin, Feng-ch'en: Wu-chin te nung-shih yen.—*NLHP* 8, 1924, (not seen); 41, 1925, (not seen). [Agricultural proverbs of Wuchin.] / Kiangsu.

金逢辰：武進的農事諺

2465 Chu, Hsien-li, et al.: *Nung-yen chu-chieh.*—Peking: T'ung-su tu-wu, 1957, 96 p. [Agricultural proverbs annotated.]

朱先立等：農諺注解

2466 Chün, Mien: Ju-kao nung-yen i-luan.—*NLHP* 250, 1931, (not seen); 261, 1931, (not seen); 262, 1931, (not seen). [A slice of the agricultural proverbs of Jukao.] / Kiangsu.

君勉：如皋農諺一鬱

2467 Ch'un, Hsüeh: Fu-chien nung-chia yen.—*FW* 3:23, 1936, 21–30. [Proverbs of farmers of Fukien.]

春雪：福建農家諺

2468 Endō, Jirō: Chūgoku no nōgen.—*Nihon Minzokugaku* 82, 1972, 76–77. [Chinese agricultural proverbs.]

遠藤二郎：中國の農諺

2469 Fan, Tzu: Nung-yen.—*MCWH* 1959:3, 55–58. [Agricultural proverbs.]

凡子：農諺

2470 Fan, Yen: Nung-yen yü sheng-chi chiao-yü.—*Min-chung chiao-yü chi-k'an* 2:1, 1933, (not seen). [Agricultural proverbs and the education of living.]

樊績：農諺與生計教育

2471 Fei, Chieh-hsin: *Chung-hua nung-yen.*—Shanghai: Chung-hua, 1936; Taipei: T'ien-i, 1974, 2nd ed., 6, 2, 4, 8, 2, 8, 2, 262 p. [Chinese agricultural proverbs.]

費潔心：中華農諺

2472 Fujita, Ryōka: Manshū nōka zokugen shū.—*Gekkan Manshū* 16:3, 1943, (not seen). [A collection of proverbs of farmers in Manchuria.]

藤田菱花：滿州農家俗諺集

2473 Han, Ch'ing: Ho-pei Tsun-hua-hsien nung-chia yen.—*NLHP* 249, 1931, (not seen). [Proverbs of farmers of Tsunhua-hsien, Hopei.]

漢清：河北遵化縣農家諺

2474 Hsia, Ta-shan: *Chung-hua nung-yen.*—Nanking: Chin-ling ta-hsüeh nung-lin hsin-pao-she, 1933, 203 p. [Chinese agricultural proverbs.]

夏大山：中華農諺

2475 Hsin, K'o: Hsin-chu K'o-chia nung-yen.—*TWFW* 9:3, 1959, 14–20. [Agricultural proverbs of the Hakkas in Hsinchu.] / Taiwan.

新客：新竹客家農諺

2476 Hsü, T'ing-shun: Shao-hsing nung-yen.—*Min-chien* 1:10, 1932, (not seen); 1:12, (not seen). [Agricultural proverbs of Shaohsing.] / Chekiang.

徐廷舜：紹興農諺

2477 Hu, Chin-t'ai: An-hui Feng-yang nung-yen.—*NLHP* 16, 1924, (not seen). [Agricultural proverbs of Fengyang, Anhwei.]

胡金台：安徽鳳陽農諺

2478 Hua, Po-hsiung: Che-chiang T'ang-hsi Yin-ling nung-yen.—*NLHP* 38, 1925, (not seen). [Agricultural proverbs of Yinling, Tanghsi, Chekiang.]

華伯熊：浙江湯溪銀嶺農諺

2479 Huang, Yün-sheng: Chiang-nan nung-yen.—*NLHP* 32, 1925, (not seen). [Agricultural proverbs from the regions south of the Yangtze.]

黃雲生：江南農諺

2480 Li, Hung-chien: *Nung-yen hsin chieh.*—Chungking (?): Chiao-yü-pu min-chung tu-wu pien shen wei-yüan-hui, 1943, 3 vols., 204 p. [New explanations of agricultural proverbs.]

李鴻漸：農諺新解

2481   Li, Lo-p'ing & Ch'i, Nai-ch'eng: *Ho-pei nung-yen chi chieh.*—Paoting: Ho-pei jen-min, 1957, [i], 6, 150 p. [Collection and explanation of agricultural proverbs in Hopei.]

李樂平、祁乃成：河北農諺集解

2482   Liang, Kuan & Lien, T'an: *Liang Kuang nung-yen.*—Hsichüan: Hsi-ch'üan Nung-k'o chih-yeh hsüeh-hsiao, 1933, (not seen). [Agricultural proverbs of Kwangtung and Kwangsi.]

梁冠、連灘：兩廣農諺

2483   Lin, P'ei-lu: Han-tai Ts'ui Shih te *Nung-chia yen.*—*KYAO* 2:14, 1936, 3–4. [The *Nung-chia yen* (2502) by Ts'ui Shih of the Han dynasty.]

林培廬：漢代崔寔的『農家諺』

2484   Lin, Yung-liang; Wu, Hsin-jung, et al.: Nan-pu nung-ts'un li-yen chi.—*NYWH* 2:3–4, 1955, 86–91; 3:1–2, 31–53; 3:3–4, 1956, 34–46; 4:1, 1958, 29–31./ See (2485). [A collection of proverbs of the southern villages.]/ Taiwan.

林永梁、吳新榮等：南部農村俚諺集

2485   Lin, Yung-liang & Lin, Ying-liang: *Nan-pu nung-ts'un li-yen chi* pu-i.— *NYWH* 4:1, 1958, 5; 4:2, 5; 5, 1959, 79; 6, 150; 7, 1961, 110; 8, 1962, 53. [Addenda to *Nan-pu nung-ts'un li-yen chi* (2484).]

林永梁、林英艮：『南部農村俚諺集』補遺

2486   Liu, I-ch'üan: Lu-tung nung-yen.— *NLHP* 237, 1931, (not seen). [Agricultural proverbs of eastern Shantung.]

劉一泉：魯東農諺

2487   Liu, K'uei-chiu: *Shan-hsi nung-chia li-yen ch'ien chieh.*—Taiyüan (?): Ta min-kuo yin-shua ch'ang, 1921, 46 p. [Simple explanations of the proverbs of farmers in Shansi.]

劉逵九：山西農家俚諺淺解

2488   Ma, Chüeh-weng & T'ien, Huo-nung: *Hua-pei nung-yen.*—Peking: Ts'ai-cheng ching-chi, 1957, 64 p. [Agricultural proverbs of North China.]

馬覺翁、田活農：華北農諺

2489   Meng, Keng-yeh: Szu-ch'uan te nung-yen.—*NLHP* 23, 1924, (not seen). [Agricultural proverbs of Szechwan.]

蒙耕野：四川的農諺

2490   Niu, Pa-chuang: Yü ts'un li-yen shih chin.—*TWFW* 16:1, 1966, 46. [A choice collection of fishing village proverbs.]

牛八莊：漁村俚諺拾錦

2491   Nung-yeh ch'u-pan-she: *Chung-kuo nung-yen* (Shang ts'e).—Peking: Nung-yeh, 1980, 5, 2, 2, 4, 731 p. [Chinese agricultural proverbs (Vol. I).]

農業出版社：中國農諺（上冊）

2492   Ōishi, Shinkai: Chūgoku no nōgen. —*Shin Chūgoku* 1, 1956, 28–33. [Agricultural proverbs of China.]

大石進海：中國の農諺

2493   P'eng, Chün-hsiang: Nung-yen.—*MCWH* 1960:1, 98. [Agricultural proverbs.]

彭俊祥：農諺

2494   Shih, Jung-ch'eng: Yü-nan nung-yen.—*NLHP* 26, 1925, (not seen). [Agricultural proverbs of southern Honan.]

時鎔成：豫南農諺

2495   Shou, Hsiao-ho: *Chu-yin nung-yen.* —Peking: Wen-tzu kai-ko, 1958, (not seen). [Agricultural proverbs with phonetic notation.]

壽孝鶴：注音農諺

2496   Sun, Ch'in-liang: Hang-chou nung-yen. —*Min-chien* 1:12, 1932, (not seen). [Agricultural proverbs of Hangchow.]/ Chekiang.

孫欽艮：杭州農諺

2497   Tai, Ching-k'uan: Ch'ang-chou nung-yen.—*NLHP* 40, 1925, (not seen). [Agricultural proverbs of Changchow.]

戴景寬：常州農諺

2498 Tanaka, Katsumi: Chūgoku no nōgen ni tsuite no shiron.—*Denshō Bunka* 4, 1964, 10–28. [A preliminary discussion on the agricultural proverbs of China.]

田中克己：中國の農諺についての試論

2499 Ts'ai, Chiu-kao: Tung-yang nung-yen.—*Min-chien* 1:12, 1932, (not seen). [Agricultural proverbs of Tungyang.]/ Chekiang.

蔡九臯：東陽農諺

2500 Ts'ai, Yü: Tao-chiang sui-shih yen.—*TPWW* 2:3, 1953, 113–119. [Taochiang proverbs concerning the time of the year.]/ Taiwan.

蔡煜：稻江歲時諺

2501 Ts'ao, Chia-i: Nung-yen tien-ti.—*TWWH* 19:2, 1968, 170–175; 19:4, 170–175. [A sprinkling of agricultural proverbs.]

曹甲乙：農諺點滴

2502 Ts'ui, Shih: *Nung-chia yen.*—Repr. in *Ch'ung-chiao Shuo-fu* ed. by T'ao, Tsung-i of the Yüan dynasty./ Ts'ui Shih (Han dynasty). [Proverbs of farmers.]/ See (2483).

崔寔：農家諺——元陶宗儀輯『重較說郛』

2503 Ts'un, Fu: Nung-ts'un te yen-yü.—*Hsin nung-ts'un* 7, 1933, 1–23. [Proverbs of rural villages.]

村夫：農村的諺語

2504 Tu, Ho-ch'ing: An-hui T'ai-p'ing te nung-yen.—*NLHP* 32, 1925, (not seen). [Agricultural proverbs of Taiping, Anhwei.]

杜穌清：安徽太平的農諺

2505 Tung, Tso-pin: Chi-shou nung-yen—chiu-chiu—te pi-chiao yen-chiu.—*MCWI* 4, 1927, 1–12. [Several agricultural proverbs—9 × 9—a comparative study.]/ The period of 81 (9 × 9) days counting from the winter solstice.

董作賓：幾首農諺一九九一的比較研究

2506 Wang, Meng-hsiung: Man-t'an nung-yen te yü-yen t'e-tien ho piao-hsien shou-fa.—*MCWH* 1961:1, 59–61. [A random discussion on the special linguistic features and the skills of expression of agricultural proverbs.]

王夢熊：漫談農諺的語言特點和表現手法

2507 Wang, Tien-chieh: *Nung-yen ho nung-ko chih chieh-shao.*—*Chung-kuo hsin-shu yüeh-pao* 2:9–10, 1932, (not seen). [An introduction to *Nung-yen ho nung-ko* (2450).]

王點潔：『農諺和農歌』之介紹

2508 Wang, Wo-sheng: Kuang-tung Ch'ao-chou te nung-yen.—*Min-chien* 1:9, 1932, (not seen). [Agricultural proverbs of Chaochow, Kwangtung.]

王卧生：廣東潮州的農諺

2509 Weng, Tsui-t'ing: Chiang-su Sung-chiang-hsien te nung-yen.—*NLHP* 263, 1931, (not seen); 264, 1931, (not seen). [Agricultural proverbs of Sungkiang-hsien, Kiangsu.]

翁醉亭：江蘇松江縣的農諺

2510 Yeh, Ching-ming: Shao-hsing nung-yen i-shu.—*Min-chien* 1:8, 1932, (not seen). [A bundle of agricultural proverbs of Shaohsing.]/ Chekiang.

葉鏡銘：紹興農諺一束

2511 Yeh, Te-chün: Huai-an nung-yen.—*Min-su* 83, 1929, 47–50. [Agricultural proverbs of Hwaian.]/ Kiangsu.

葉德均：淮安農諺

2512 Yen, Shen-mu: Szu-ch'uan Chü-hsien nung-yen.—*NLHP* 30, 1925, (not seen). [Agricultural proverbs of Chü-hsien, Szechwan.]

嚴參木：四川渠縣農諺

2513   Yin, Ming-huai: Chih-li Po-yeh-hsien chih nung-chia yen-yü.—*NLHP* 12, 1924, (not seen). [Proverbs of farmers in Poyeh-hsien, Chihli.] / Hopei.

尹銘槐：直隷博野縣之農家諺語

7.2.10. Regional Proverbs (2514–2654)
7.2.10.1. General and North China (2514–2535)

2514   Chao, Shih-ch'en: *Ho-nan yen-yü chi.* —Peiping: Chu-che shu-tien, 1933, 4, 2, 2, 274 p. [A collection of proverbs of Honan.]

趙實宸：河南諺語集

2515   Ch'en, Ching-t'ang: Shan-tung-sheng Lu hsi-nan t'u yen.—*Shan-tung wen-hsien* 6:1, 1980, 88–89. [Local proverbs of southwestern Shantung.]

陳鏡堂：山東省魯西南土諺

2516   Chu, Chieh-fan: *Chung-kuo feng-t'u yen-yü shih shuo.*—Taipei: Hsin-hsing, 1962; Taipei: T'ien-i, 1974, 2nd ed., 4, [17], 6, 2, 166 p. [A discussion with explanations of Chinese provincial and local proverbs.] / Classified.

朱介凡：中國風土諺語釋說

2517   Chu, Chieh-fan: Shuo Pei-p'ing feng-t'u yen-yü.—*CSHS* 6, 1970, 799–857. [A discussion on local proverbs of Peiping.]

朱介凡：說北平風土諺語

2518   Chu, Chieh-fan: Shuo Shan-tung feng-t'u yen.—*Ch'ang liu* 62:1, 1980, 25–29; 62:2, 31–34. [A discussion on local proverbs of Shantung.]

朱介凡：說山東風土諺

2519   Chu, Chieh-fan: Shuo Tung-pei feng-t'u yen.—*Tung-pei wen-hsien* 11:1, 1980, 60–63; 2, 56–59; 12:2, 1981, 57–58; 3, 1982, 44–46; 4, 51–56; 13:2, 61–64. [A discussion on local proverbs of the Northeast.]

朱介凡：說東北風土諺

2520   Eberhard, Wolfram: Pekinger Sprich-wörter, gesammelt von Ho Feng-ju.— *Baessler-Archiv* 24, 1941, 1–42.

2521   Hatano, Tarō: *Pekin Kanwa jōgen yōrei* kaidai sakuin.—*YSDR* 27:3, 1977, 159–169. [A bibliographical introduction and index to *Pekin Kanwa jogen yōrei* (2523).]

波多野大郎：『北京官話常言用例』解題索引

2522   K'ang, Chen-fan: Tung-pei yen-yü pai tse.—*Tung-pei wen-hsien* 3:2, 1972, 91–94; 3:3, 1973, 94–96; 3:4, 93–95; 4:1, 85–87; 4:2, 83–85; 4:3, 1974, 67–69; 4:4, 72–74; 5:1, 72–74; 5:2, 70–72. [One hundred Northeastern proverbs.]

康鎮藩：東北諺語百則

2523   Koji, Shinpei & Mogi, Ichirō: *Pekin Kanwa jōgen yōrei.*—Tokyo: Bunkyūdō, 1905, 4, 2, 84, 71 p. [Examples with uses of common words and phrases in the Peking Mandarin dialect.] / Including proverbs; see (2521).

小路眞平、茂木一郎：北京官話常言用例

2524   Li, Kuang-t'ing: *Hsiang-yen chieh-i* & Wang, Yu-kuang: *Wu-hsia yen-lien.*— Peking: Chung-hua, 1982, repr., 2 works bound in one vol., 7, 5, 109; 14, 134 p./ First publ. in 1850 & 1841. [Humorous explanations of rural sayings.] / Paoti, Hopei, & [Proverbs in couplets from the Wu (dialect) areas.] / See (2571).

李光庭：鄉言解頤；王有光：吳下諺聯

2525   Li, Shou-p'eng: *Hua-pei yen-yü chi.* —Yentai: T'ai-tung yin-shua-chü, 1933, (not seen). [A collection of proverbs of North China.]

李壽彭：華北諺語集

2526   Ma, Tung-ch'üan (comp.) & Liang Jung-jo (ed.): *Shan-tung yen-yü chi.*— Taipei: T'ien-i, 1974, 2nd ed., 6, 10, 196 p. [A collection of proverbs from Shantung.]

馬東泉著，梁容若編：山東諺語集

2527 Pai, Shou-i: K'ai-feng yen-yü.—*Min-su* 75, 1929, 51–54. [Proverbs of Kaifeng.]/ Honan.

白壽彝：開封諺語

2528 Shang, Ying-shih: *Chung-kuo-jen te su-hua.*—Taipei: Ch'ang-ch'un-shu shu-fang, 1979, 225 p.; Hong Kong: Hsin-feng wen-hua, n.d., repr. [Popular sayings of the Chinese people.]/ From 17 provinces.

尚英時：中國人的俗話

2529 Shimomizu, Kenji: *Pei-ching su-yü-erh tien.*—Tokyo: Kaikōsha, 1928, 1, 1, 9, 343 p. [A dictionary of popular sayings in Peking.]

下水憲次：北京俗語兒典

2530 Suzue, Mantarō & Shimomizu, Kenji: *Pekin Kanwa zokugen shūkai.*—Tokyo: Ōsakayago shoten, 1925, vi, 149 p. [A collection with explanations of popular proverbs in the Peking Mandarin dialect.]

鈴江萬太郎、下水憲次：北京官話俗諺集解

2531 Teboul, M.: Sur une famille d'expressions proverbiales du dialecte de Pékin.—*BEFEO* 62, 1975, 487–503.

2532 Ts'ao, Ching-yün: Shan-tung su-yu.—*CHWI* 22:6, 1982, 174–175. [Popular sayings of Shantung.]

曹景雲：山東俗語

2533 Wang, Kuo-tung: Ho-pei-sheng yen-yü lei chi.—*KYAO* 2:15, 1936, 4–8; 2:16, 7–8; 2:18, 6–8; 2:22, 8; 2:25, 8; (to be continued). [A classified collection of proverbs of Hopei province.]

王國棟：河北省諺語類輯

2534 Woitsch, L.: *Zum Pekinger Su Hua. I Teil.*—Peking: (?), 1908, 56 p./ *BEFEO* 9, 1909, 593, H. Maspero.

2535 Yen, Kung-shang: *Shuo-hua liu-k'ou che (Pei-p'ing k'ou-yü lien-hsi fa).*—Peiping: Shih-chieh, 1945, 104 p./ *Yen-hua chia-pien* (2240), 206–208. [Rhymes for fluent oral speech (Methods of practicing the Peiping colloquial language.]/ Including proverbs.

嚴工上：說話流口轍（北平口語練習法）

7.2.10.2. Northwest China (2536–2546)

2536 Belle, Cyr. van: Proverbes et dictons populaires du Kan-su.—*Bulletin Société Belgique Études Coloniales* 19:5, 1912, 442–453.

〔甘肅〕

2537 Chu, Chieh-fan: Shuo Shan-hsi feng-t'u yen.—*Shan-hsi wen-hsien* 40, 1980, 29–30; 41, 38–40; 42, 46–50; 44, 1981, 51–54. [A discussion on local proverbs of Shensi.]

朱介凡：說陝西風土諺

2538 Li, Chi: Kuan-tung yen-yü san lu.—*Kuan-tung wen-hua yüeh-pao* 4:12 & 5:1 (combined), 1926, 136–137. [Three records of proverbs of Honan and Shantung.]

李季：關東諺語三錄

2539 Li, Chin-hsi: Fang-yen yao yen chih.—*Lo-ch'uan hsien chih* (Sian: T'ai-hua yin-shua ch'ang, 1944), chüan 24. [A record of dialects, folk songs, and proverbs.]/ Lochwan, Shensi.

黎錦熙：方言謠諺志——『洛川縣志』卷 24

2540 Li, Chin-hsi: Fang-yen yao yen chih.—*T'ung-kuan hsien chih* (Sian: T'ai-hua yin-shua ch'ang, 1944), *chüan* 27. [A record of dialects, folk songs, and proverbs.]/ Tungkwan, Shensi.

黎錦熙：方言謠諺志——『同官縣志』卷 27

2541 Liu, Chung-ch'ien: Shan-hsi Kuan-chung i-tai te yen-yü.—*Min-chien* 2:6, 1933, (not seen). [Proverbs of the Kuanchung area of Shensi.]

劉中謙：陝西關中一帶的諺語

2542   Oost, Joseph van: *Dictions et proverbes des chinois habitant la Mongolie Sud-Ouest.*—Shanghai: Imprimerie de l'Orphelinat de T'ou-sè-wè, 1918, [iii], 356 p./ Variétés Sinologiques, 50; *JRASNCB* 50, 1919, 221–223, Anonymous.

2543   Serruys, Paul L-M.: Folklore contributions in Sino-Mongolia. Notes on customs, legends, proverbs, and riddles of the province of Jehol. Introduction and translations.—*Folklore Studies* 6:2, 1947, 1–129.

2544   Shan-hsi-sheng chiao-yü-t'ing (comp.) & Wang, Hsiao-yü (rearranged): *Shan-hsi yao yen ch'u chi.*—Sian: Ditto, 1935; Taipei: T'ien-i, 1974, 6, 4, 21, 235 p. [A preliminary collection of folk songs and proverbs of Shensi.]

陝西省教育廳編，王霄羽改編：陝西謠諺初集

2545   Sun, Chin-piao: *T'ung-su ch'ang yen shu-cheng.*—Nantung: Han-mo lin, 1934, 460 p./ Including a collection of Chingchow proverbs of Kansu. [Exegetical evidence for commonly used words and phrases.]

孫錦標：通俗常言疏證／包括涇諺彙錄

2546   Wang, Yün-hung: Kuan-chung yen-yü.—*CKYT* 14:1, 1964, 56–60. [Proverbs of Kuanchung.]/ Shensi.

王雲鴻：關中諺語

7.2.10.3. Southwest China (2547–2551)

2547   Brace, A. J., Captain: *Five hundred proverbs commonly used in West China.*—Chengtu: Chengtu Young Men's Christian Association, 1919, [2], iv, 83 p.

2548   Ch'eng-tu shih ch'ün-chung i-shu-kuan: *Szu-ch'uan ch'eng-yü, yen-yü, hsieh-hou-yü yün pen.*—Chengtu: Szu-ch'uan jen-min, 1980, 4, 248 p. [A handbook of set-phrases, proverbs, *hsieh-hou-yü* of Szechwan arranged according to rhymes.]

成都市群衆藝術館：四川成語、諺語、歇後語韵本

2549   Chu, Chieh-fan: Shuo Hu-pei feng-t'u yen.—*SHJ* 392, 1980, 1–8; 393, 1–8; 394, 1–4. [A discussion on local proverbs of Hupeh.]

朱介凡：說湖北風土諺

2550   Huang, Chao-nien: Yen-yü i-shu (Yün-nan).—*Min-su* 46, 1929, (not seen). [A bundle of proverbs (Yünnan).]

黃詔年：諺語一束（雲南）

2551   Wang, Yüan-ts'ai: Yen-yü (Hu-pei).—*MCWH* 1958:2, 49. [Proverbs (Hupeh).]

王遠才：諺語（湖北）

7.2.10.4. East China (2552–2579)

2552   Chang, Shang-an: Shao-hsing su yen.—*Min-chien* 1:8, 1932, (not seen). [Popular proverbs of Shaohsing.]/ Chekiang.

章尚盦：紹興俗諺

2553   Chu, Chieh-fan: I-hsing-jen te hsiang pang li-shih ching-shen—*I-hsing feng-t'u yen-yü* hsü shuo.—*CSHS* 1, 1968, 679–706. [The local historical spirit of the Ihsing people—An introduction to *I-hsing feng-t'u yen-yü.*]

朱介凡：宜興人的鄉邦歷史精神──『宜興風土諺語』序說

2554   Chu, Chieh-fan: Shuo An-hui feng-t'u yen.—*SHJ* 360, 1979, 1–8. [A discussion on local proverbs of Anhwei.]

朱介凡：說安徽風土諺

2555   Fan, Yin: *Yüeh yen.*—Shaohsing: Ku ying shan fang, 1882, 3 vols., 2, 2, 1, 52; 1, 65; 1, 34, 13, 2 d.p.; Peiping: Lai-hsün ko, 1932, repr./ *YSDR* 17:1, 1966, 44, Hatano Tarō. [Proverbs from (the ancient state of) Yüeh.]/ Kiangsu and Chekiang areas.

范寅：越諺／波多野太郎評

2556   Hsia, T'ing-yü: Fu-ch'un min yen.—

MCWI 6, 1927, 26–27; 11–12, 1928, 48–49. [Folk proverbs of Fuchun.]/ Chekiang.

夏廷棫：富春民諺

2557 Hsüeh, Chien-wu: *Chiang Huai min-chien wen-i chi.*—Taipei: Mao-yü, 1949, 68 p. [A collection of folk literature from the Yangtze and Huai Rivers areas.]/ Folk songs, proverbs, riddles.

薛建吾：江淮民間文藝集

2558 Hu, Tsu-te: *Hu yen.*—Shanghai: Chu-i t'ang shu-fang, 1922, 2 *chüan*, v.p./ The author is also known as He Te and Hu Yün-ch'iao. [Proverbs of Shanghai.]

胡祖德：滬諺／著者又名胡德及胡雲翹

2559 Hu, Tsu-te: *Hu yen wai pien.*— Shanghai: Chu-i-t'ang shu-fang, 1923, 2 *chüan;* Shanghai: Kuo-kuang shu-chü, 1936, 2 vols., 2, 158; 164, 2 p.; Taipei: T'ien-i, 1974, repr. of 1923 ed., 2 vols., 6, 5, 2, 94; 96 d.p./ *Yen-hua chia-pien* (2240), 192–198. [An extra volume to *Hu yen* (2558).]

胡祖德：滬諺外編

2560 Huang, Chao-nien: Yen-yü i-shu (Hang-chou).—*Min-su* 46, 1929, (not seen). [A bundle of proverbs (Hangchow).]

黃詔年：諺語一束（杭州）

2561 Hung, Wei-p'u: *Chiang-tu fang-yen chi yao.*—Taipei: Shih-chieh, 1980, 12, 279 p./ Includes proverbs and *hsieh-hou-yü*. [A selection from the Kiangtu dialect.]/ Kiangsu.

洪爲溥：江都方言輯要

2562 Juan, Huai-shan: Shao-hsing su-yen. —*Min-chien* 1:12, 1932, (not seen). [Popular proverbs of Shaohsing.]/ Chekiang.

阮懷善：紹興俗諺

2563 Kageyama, Takashi: *Gendai Shanhaigo.* —Tokyo: Bunkyūdō, 1936; 1944, 11th ed., 4, 2, 2, 6, 26, 143, 36 p., map.

[Modern Shanghai dialect.]/ Appendix: A grove of popular sayings from Shanghai.

影山巍：現代上海語／附錄：上海俗語林

2564 Kuo, Ch'eng-mou: Tung-yang yen-yü. —*Min-chien* 1:9, 1932, (not seen). [Proverbs of Tungyang.]/ Chekiang.

郭成謀：東陽諺語

2565 Shao, Ho-sheng: Shao-hsing yen-yü.— *Min-chien* 1:11, 1932, (not seen); 1:12, 1932, (not seen). [Proverbs of Shaohsing.]/ Chekiang.

邵和笙：紹興諺語

2566 Sun, Ch'in-liang: Hang-chou te yen-yü. —*Min-chien* 1:11, 1932, (not seen). [Proverbs of Hangchow.]/ Chekiang.

孫欽良：杭州的諺語

2567 T'ang, Ch'iang: *Ning-po hsiang yen ch'ien chieh.*—Taipei: Min-chu, 1972, 262 p. [Simple explanations of rural proverbs from Ningpo.]/ Chekiang.

湯強：寧波鄉諺淺解

2568 Ts'ai, Lu-fu: Tung-yang su-yen.— *Min-chien* 1:8, 1932, (not seen); 1:10, 1932, (not seen). [Popular proverbs of Tungyang.]/ Chekiang.

蔡魯馥：東陽俗諺

2569 Wang, Hung-chi: Wen-hsüeh-hua te Wu-chiang su-yen.—*Su-chung hsiao k'an* 43–44, 1930, 17–21. [Literalization of popular proverbs from Wukiang.]/ Kiangsu.

王鴻基：文學化的吳江俗諺

2570 Wang, P'ei-chien: *Sui-ch'ang yen-yü yü ko-yao.*—Suichang: Sui-ch'ang chien-i shih-fan, 1948, (not seen). [Proverbs and folk songs of Suichang.]/ Chekiang.

王佩劍：遂昌諺語與歌謠

2571 Wang, Yu-kuang: *Wu-hsia yen-lien.*— N.p.: Jui-ch'ang ko, 1841, 4 *chüan;* Peking: Chung-hua, 1982, repr. with (2524), 14, 134 p. [Proverbs in couplets from the Wu (dialect) areas.] / See (2524).

王有光：吳下諺聯

2572 Wo, Lo: Che-chiang Shao-hsing te min-yen.—*Min-su* 3, 1928, (not seen). [Folk proverbs of Shaohsing, Chekiang.]

我樂：浙江紹興的民諺

2573 Wu, Ai-chen: *Wu-chin yao yen chi.*—Shanghai: T'ai-tung t'u-shu chü, 1929, 75 p. [A collection of folk songs and proverbs of Wuchin.] / Kiangsu.

伍愛眞：武進謠諺集

2574 Wu, Chia-ch'ing: *Wu-chin li-su yao yen chi.*—Taipei: Hsin-hsing shu-chü, 1963, 189 p. [A collection of manners and customs, folk songs, and proverbs of Wuchin.]

伍稼青：吳進禮俗謠諺集

2575 Yang, Su: Shang-hai te yen-yü.—*Kung hsin* 1:2, 1931, (not seen). [Proverbs of Shanghai.]

楊肅：上海的諺語

2576 Yeh, Ching-ming: Shao-hsing te yen-yü.—*Min-su* 107, 1930, 13–15, to be continued. [Proverbs of Shaohsing.] / Chekiang.

葉鏡銘：紹興的諺語

2577 Yeh, Te-chün: *Huai-an yen-yü chi.*—Shaohsing: Min-chien ch'u-pan-pu, 193?, (not seen). [A collection of proverbs from Hwaian.] / Kiangsu.

葉德均：淮安諺語集

2578 Yen, Fu-sun: *Shang-hai su-yü ta tz'u-tien.*—Shanghai: Yün-hsüan ch'u-pan-she, 1924, 2, 3, 3, 166 p. / also appended in (2299). [A comprehensive dictionary of Shanghai popular sayings.]

嚴芙孫：上海俗語大辭典

2579 Yün, Ch'iao-man: *Hu yen.*—Shanghai: Ditto, n.d., 2 vols., 56; 63 d.p., maps. [Proverbs of Shanghai.]

筼橋漫：滬諺

7.2.10.5. Kwangtung (2580–2593)

2580 Aubazac, Louis, M.E.P.: *Proverbes de la langue Cantonnaise recueillis çà et là.*—Hong Kong: Imprimerie de Nazareth, 1918, iv, 176 p. / *Orbis* 9:1, 1960, 178, Paul Yang.

2581 Chang, Chung-chieh: P'ing-yüan yen-yü.—*Min-su* 67, 1929, 44. [Proverbs of Pingyuan.]

張仲傑：平遠諺語

2582 Chao, Jung-kuang: *Hsien-tai Yüeh-yü.*—Hong Kong: Kuang-wen t'u-shu kung-szu, 1972, 10, 40, 38, 267 p. [Modern (colloquial) Cantonese.] / Spoken in Hong Kong; Chinese character text only; including proverbs and *hsieh-hou-yü.*

趙榮光：現代粵語

2583 Ch'en, Ch'üan-wang: *Sui-ch'eng min-yen.*—Canton: Wu-kuei-t'ang, 1936, (not seen). [Folk proverbs of Canton.]

陳泉汪：穗城民諺

2584 Ch'iao, Yen-nung: *Kuang-chou-hua k'ou-yü tz'u te yen-chiu.*—Hong Kong: Hua-ch'iao yü-wen, 1966, xvii, 322 p. / Chap. 29 & 30: Popular sayings, set-phrases. [A study of Cantonese colloquial words and phrases.]

喬硯農：廣州話口語詞的研究／第二十九篇，第三十篇：俗語成語

2585 Chien, Hsiang-jung: *Hyōjun Kantongo ten.*—Taipei: Taiwan Keisatsu Kyōkai, 1935, 2, 8, 380 p. [A handbook for the standard Hakka dialect.] / Szuhsien dialect; Chap. 4, 24: Proverbs.

菅向榮：標準廣東語典／第四章，第二十四節：俚諺

2586 Chuang, Shih-kuang: *Kuang-tung-hua chih-nan.*—Taipei: Wen-shih-che, 1977, vii, 208 p. / Chap. 3: Secret language and proverbs. [A guide to the Cantonese dialect.]

莊世光：廣東話指南／第三章：隱語、諺語

2587   Hayashi, Morimichi: Hakka no chiiku shakai to sono rigen.—*KKDGK* 18, 1969, 1–18. [The society of Hakka regions and its proverbs.]

林盛道：客家の地域社會とその俚諺

2588   Schaub, M.: Proverbs in daily use among the Hakkas of the Canton province.—*CR* 21, 1893, 73–79.

〔客家〕

2589   Stevens, H.J.: Cantonese apothegms. —*CR* 25:6, 1901, 290–293.

2590   Stevens, H.J.: *Cantonese apothegms, classified, translated, and commented upon.*—Canton: Printed by E-Shing, 1902, 155 p.

2591   Tseng, Tzu-fan: *Kuang-chou-hua P'u-t'ung-hua tui-chao ch'ang-yung tz'u shou-ts'e.*—Hong Kong: Hsiang-kang P'u-t'ung-hua yen-hsi-she, 1978, 40 p./ 317–342: Idioms, (proverbs, and) *hsieh-hou-yü.* [A Cantonese-Common Language handbook of commonly used words (and phrases).]

曾子凡：廣州話普通話對照常用詞手册／317-342：熟語、歇後語

2592   Wu, Yü-ch'eng & T'an, Hsia-ts'un: Yen-yü.—*Kuang-tung min-chiao* 2:2, 1937, (not seen). [Proverbs (of Kwangtung).]

吳玉成、譚霞村：諺語

2593   Yüan, Hung-ming: Tung-kuan mi-yü yü yen-yü.—*Min-su* 123, 1933, 31–34. [Riddles and proverbs of Tungkuan.]

袁洪銘：東莞謎語與諺語

7.2.10.6. Fukien (2594–2612)

2594   Anonymous: Chinese proverbs in the Amoy vernacular, romanized.—*CR* 15, 1887, 298–300.

〔厦門〕

2595   Chao, Meng-mei: Ch'ao-chou yen-yü. —*Min-su* 34, 1928, 26. [Proverbs of Chaochow.]

趙夢梅：潮州諺語

2596   Ch'en, K'o-hua: Ch'ao-chou yen-yü chi ch'eng-yü.—*CCWH* 1:2, 1975, 37–38; 1:3, 32–34. [Proverbs and set-phrases of Chaochow.]

陳克華：潮州諺語及成語

2597   Ch'en, Yang-ch'ing: Fu-chou yen-yü chi chieh.—*FCWH* 8, 1969, 30–34; 4:1, 1971, 48–59. [A collection with explanations of proverbs from Foochow.]

陳仰青：福州諺語集解

2598   Ch'iu, Ch'ing-lien: Min pei yen-yü. —*FW* 3:23, 1936, 31–38. [Proverbs of northern Fukien.]

邱清濂：閩北諺語

2599   Chu, Chieh-fan: *P'u-t'ien yen-yü hsü-shuo.*—*TLTC* 20:11, 1960, 7–9. [An introduction to *P'u-t'ien yen-yü.*]

朱介凡：『莆田諺語』序說

2600   Chu, Chieh-fan: Shuo Fu-chien feng-t'u yen.—*SHJ* 429, 1981, 1–8; 430, 1–8; 431, 1–8; 432, 1982, 1–8. [A discussion on local proverbs of Fukien.]

朱介凡：說福建風土諺

2601   Huang, Chao-nien: Yen-yü i-shu (Min-nan).—*Min-su* 46, 1929, 45–46. [A bundle of proverbs (southern Fukien).]

黃詔年：諺語一束（閩南）

2602   Huang, Liu-p'o: Fu-chou yen-yü i-p'ieh.—*FW* 3:23, 1936, 39–44. [A glance at the proverbs of Foochow.]

黃榴坡：福州諺語一瞥

2603   Kao, Ch'iung-chen: Ch'uan-chou min-yen.—*FW* 3:23, 1936, 106–113. [Folk proverbs of Chüanchow.]

高瓊珍：泉州民諺

2604   Kao, Shih-liang & Chang, Tseng-ling: Fu-chou yen-yü.—*FW* 3:23, 1936, 45–92.

[Proverbs of Foochow.]

高時良、張增齡：福州諺語

2605   Li, Chao-min: Ts'ung wo-kuo ku yen i yen teng shuo-tao Min yen.—*FW* 3:23, 1936, 1–5. [A discussion on (the relationships between) our nation's ancient proverbs, obsolete proverbs, etc., and (modern) proverbs from Fukien.]

李兆民：從我國古諺遺諺等說到閩諺

2606   Lin, Hui-hsiang: Yen-yü chieh-lun.—*FW* 3:23, 1936, 117–118. [Concluding remarks on (the study of) proverbs from Fukien.]

林惠祥：諺語結論

2607   Liu, Ch'iang: Yü lin hung chao chih Min yen.—*FW* 3:23, 1936, 6–20. [Tidbits from proverbs of Fukien.]

劉強：魚鱗鴻爪之閩諺

2608   Ma, Yün-chang: T'ing-chou yen-yü i-luan.—*Min-su* 67, 1929, 43–44. [A slice of Tingchow proverbs.]

馬雲章：汀州諺語一臠

2609   Ohlinger, F.: Hsing-hua (Fuh-kien, China) proverbs and sayings.—*TP* 2:4, 1901, 269–273.

〔興化〕

2610   Pi, Hsi-jen: T'ung-an yen-yü.—*FW* 3:23, 1936, 114–116. [Proverbs of Tungan.]

碧溪人：同安諺語

2611   Wang, T'ien-ch'ang: Fu-chou su-yen chieh-shuo chih i.—*SHJ* 394, 1, 1980, 5–8. [An explanation of popular proverbs from Foochow.]

王天昌：福州俗諺解說之一

2612   Yang, Shu-fang: P'u-t'ien te yen-yü. —*FW* 3:23, 1936, 93–105. [The proverbs of Putien.]

楊樹芳：莆田的諺語

7.2.10.7. Taiwan (2613–2654)

2613   Chin, Chuan: Pei-t'ou li-yen shih-ling. *TWFW* 4:2, 1954, 7. [Picking up some tidbits from the proverbs of Peitou.]

金撰：北投俚諺拾零

2614   Chou, Jung-chieh: *T'ai-yü yen-yü ch'üan pien* (1).—Kaohsiung: Ta wu-t'ai shu-yüan, 1978, 4, 27, 501 p. [A collection and explanations of Taiwanese proverbs (1).]

周榮杰：臺語諺語詮編（一）

2615   Chu, Chieh-fan: T'ai-wan yen-yü ts'ai-fang.—*Wen-shih hui-k'an* 1, 1959, 26–33. [The gathering of proverbs from Taiwan.]

朱介凡：臺灣諺語探訪

2616   Chu, Chieh-fan: Shuo T'ai-wan feng-t'u yen.—*TWWH* 31:2, 1980, 1–30. [A discussion on local proverbs of Taiwan.]

朱介凡：說臺灣風土諺

2617   Chung, Hua: Kuang-fu hou T'ai-wan hsin su-yü.—*TWFW* 8:1–2, 1958, 6; 8:3, 1958, (not seen). [New popular sayings of Taiwan after the Restitution.]

忠華：光復後臺灣新俗語

2618   Hidemine: Taiwan rigen.—*Gengogaku zasshi* 1:4, 1900, 298–300. [Proverbs of Taiwan.]

秀峰：臺灣俚諺

2619   Hsü, Ch'ing-chi: T'ai-wan su-yen hsin chu.—*NYWH* 12, 1967, 37–61.; *TWWH* 18:4, 1967, 83–93; 19:1–2, 1969, 87–99; 19:3–4, 83–99. [New notes on proverbs of Taiwan.]

徐清吉：臺灣俗諺新註

2620   Huang, Chi-t'ang: T'ai-wan yen-yü hsüan chieh.—*CKYT* 10:1, 1962, 82–84. [A selection with explanations of proverbs from Taiwan.]

黃季棠：臺灣諺語選介

2621   Hung, Shun-t'ing: T'ai yen sheng-lü ch'i-meng.—*NYWH* 3:1–2, 1955, 54–63.

[Poetic rules for beginners of Taiwanese proverbs.]

洪舜廷：臺諺聲律啓蒙

2622   Jung, Feng: T'ai-pei te li-yen.—*TPWW* 9:2–3, 1960, 12. [Proverbs of Taipei.]

榮峯：臺北的俚諺

2623   Kataoka, Iwao: *Nichi-Tai rigen shōkai.* —Tainan: Taiwango Kenkyūkai, 1913, 276 p. [Detailed explanations of Japanese-Taiwanese proverbs.]

片岡巖：日臺俚諺詳解

2624   Kataoka, Iwao: Taiwan no rigen.— *Taiwan fūzoku shi* (Taipei, 1921), 529–722. [Proverbs of Taiwan.]

片岡巖：臺灣の俚諺——『臺灣風俗誌』

2625   Kumagai, Yoshimasa: *Nichi-Tai rigen nichinichi no shūyō.*—Taipei: Nichinichi no shūyōsha, 1936, 330 p. [Daily exercises on Japanese-Taiwanese proverbs.]

熊谷辰正：日臺俚諺日日の修養

2626   Li, Chi-hsien: Ch'ien shih T'ai-wan hsi-ch'ü shang te yen-yü.—*Min-su ch'ü-i* 11, 1981, 85–93. [Simple explanations of proverbs in dramas of Taiwan.]

李繼賢：淺釋臺灣戲曲上的諺語

2627   Li, Keng-hsin: *T'ai yen chi chin.*— Taichung: The Author, 1979, 206 p. [A choice collection of proverbs from Taiwan.] / Chinese-English.

李更新：臺諺集錦

2628   Liao, Han-ch'en: Tainan no rigen.— *MZTW* 2:8, 1942, 8–11; 2:10, 16–19. [Proverbs of Tainan.]

廖漢臣：臺南の俚諺

2629   Liao, Han-ch'en: T'ai-wan li-shih yü yen-yü.—*TWWH (chuan k'an)* 3:1, 1952, 18–23. [The history and proverbs of Taiwan.]

廖漢臣：臺灣歷史與諺語

2630   Liao, Han-ch'en: T'ai-nan te yen-yü.

—*TNWH* 2:4, 1953, 34–39. [Proverbs of Tainan.]

廖漢臣：臺南的諺語

2631   Liao, Han-ch'en: T'ai-wan yen-yü te hsing-shih ho nei-jung.—*TWWH* 6:3, 1955, 37–42. [The forms and contents of the proverbs from Taiwan.]

廖漢臣：臺灣諺語的形式和內容

2632   Liao, Han-ch'en: T'an T'ai-wan yen-yü.—*Min-chien chih-shih* 100, 1956, 65–74. [A discussion on proverbs of Taiwan.]

廖漢臣：談臺灣諺語

2633   Liao, Han-ch'en: T'ai-pei-shih chih t'e-shu yen-yü.—*TPWW* 5:1, 1956, 67–81. [Special proverbs of the city of Taipei.]

廖漢臣：臺北市之特殊諺語

2634   Lien, Heng: *T'ai-wan-yü tien.*—Taipei: Chung-hua, 1957, ii, iv, 152 p./ Appendix I: Commonly used speech (including proverbs). [A dictionary of the Taiwanese dialect.]

連橫：臺灣語典／附錄一：稚言

2635   Lin, Pen-yüan: T'ai-wan ch'eng-yü chieh-shuo.—*TWFW* 4:10, 1954, 17–31. [A discussion with explanations of set-phrases from Taiwan.]/ Including proverbs.

林本元：臺灣成語解說

2636   Lin, Pen-yüan: T'ai-wan jih-yung ch'eng-yü keng-kai.—*TWFW* 11:2, 1962, 2–4. [An outline of daily used set-phrases in Taiwan.]

林本元：臺灣日用成語梗概

2637   Liu, Chi-yüan: T'ai-wan su-yü k'ao. —*TPWW* 8:4, 1960, 49–51. [A study of popular sayings from Taiwan.]

劉寄園：臺灣俗語考

2638   Liu, K'o-ming: T'ai yen lei chi.—

NYWH 7, 1961, 12–35. [A classified collection of proverbs from Taiwan.]

劉克明：臺諺類集

2639 Liu, Lung-kang: T'ai yen lei chi.—*TPWW* 7:4, 1958, 85–86; 8:1, 1959, 57–61; 8:2, 125–128. [A classified collection of proverbs from Taiwan.]

劉龍岡：臺諺類集

2640 Nanmon, Kanjin: Taiwan no rigen.—*Taiwan kanshū kiji* 2:8, 1901, 67–74. [Proverbs of Taiwan.]

南門閒人：臺灣の俚諺

2641 Niu, Pa-chuang: T'ai-nan li-yen.—*TNWH* 3:1, 1953, 49. [Proverbs of Tainan.]

牛八莊：臺南俚諺

2642 Niu, Pa-chuang: T'ai-nan li-yen i-tse.—*TNWH* 3:2, 1953, 43. [A proverb of Tainan.]

牛八莊：臺南俚諺一則

2643 Su, Shang-yao: *Hsin-pien ch'eng-yü tz'u-tien* (2091). [A newly edited dictionary of set-phrases. With appendix: Popular proverbs and set-phrases of Taiwan.]

蘇尚耀：新編成語辭典　附錄：臺灣俗諺成語

2644 Taiwan Sōtokufu Gakumubu: *Taiwan rigan shūran.*—Taipei: Ditto, 1914, 4, 6, 620, (Index) 213, 5 p. [A handbook of collected proverbs of Taiwan.]

臺灣總督府學務部：臺灣俚諺集覽

2645 Wang, Chin-lien: T'ai-wan K'o-chia su-yen tzu-liao.—*TWFW* 14:3, 1964, 26–34; 14:4, 16–28. [The materials of popular proverbs of the Hakkas in Taiwan.]

王金連：臺灣客家俗諺資料

2646 Wu, Huai-yü: Meng-chia su-yü chang-ku.—*TPWW* 9:2–3, 1960, 100–103. [Popular sayings and historical anecdotes of Mengchia.]

吳懷宇：艋舺俗語掌故

2647 Wu, Wan-shui: Yang-ming-shan li-yen shih-ling:—*TWFW* 4:3, 17. [Picking up some tidbits from the proverbs of Yangmingshan.]

吳萬水：陽明山俚諺拾零

2648 Wu, Ying-t'ao: T'ai-yü ch'ang-yung su-yü chi chieh.—*TPWW* 9:1, 1960, 112–119; 9:2, 1960, 87–93. [A collection with explanations of commonly used Taiwanese popular sayings.]

吳瀛濤：臺語常用俗語集解

2649 Wu, Ying-t'ao: T'ai-yü han-yung su-yü chi chieh.—*TPWW* 10:1, 1961, 110–116. [A collection with explanations of rarely used Taiwanese popular sayings.]

吳瀛濤：臺語罕用俗語集解

2650 Wu, Ying-t'ao: T'ai-yü t'e-shu su-yü lei chi.—*TPWW* 10:2, 1961, 94–102. [A classified collection of special popular sayings of Taiwanese.]

吳瀛濤：臺語特殊俗語類集

2651 Wu, Ying-t'ao: T'ai-wan li-yen chi.—*TPWH* 13, 1966, 152–193; *NYWH* 11, 1966, 1–39. [A collection of proverbs of Taiwan.]

吳瀛濤：臺灣俚諺集

2652 Wu, Ying-t'ao: *T'ai-wan yen-yü.*—Taipei: T'ai-wan Ying-wen, 1975, 12, 747 p./ *YSDR* 27:1–2, 1975, 166–167, Hatano Tarō. [Proverbs of Taiwan.]/ Proverbs, popular sayings, folk songs, puns, etc.

吳瀛濤：臺灣諺語／波多野太郎評

2653 Yao, Han-ch'iu: Min-nan-yü yü T'ai-wan te li-yen.—*TWWH* 28, 1977, 133–143. [The South Min dialect and proverbs of Taiwan.]

姚漢秋：閩南語與臺灣的俚諺

2654 Yao, Han-ch'iu: T'ai-wan su-yen ts'ai-che lu.—*TWWH* 31:1, 1980, 219–

234; 31:2, 156–171; 31:3, 182–197. [A selected record of popular proverbs of Taiwan.]

姚漢秋：臺灣俗諺採擷錄

7.3. *Hsieh-hou-yü* and Witticisms (2655–2748)
7.3.1. *Hsieh-hou-yü* (2655–2734)
7.3.1.1. Definition and Differentiation (2655–2682)

2655 Chang, Shou-k'ang: Hsieh-hou-yü shih-pu-shih wen-hsüeh yü-yen?.—*CKYW* 1954:5, 8–9; *Hsien-tai Han-yü . . . tzu-liao* (0064), 380–383. [Is or is not *hsieh-hou-yü* a literary language?]

張壽康：歇後語是不是文學語言？

2656 Ch'eng, Ta-ming & Li, Yüan-han: Shih t'an hsieh-hou-yü.—*CSTH* 1963:1–2, 34–35. [A preliminary discussion on *hsieh-hou-yü.*]

程達明、黎遠漢：試談歇後語

2657 Ch'iao, Sui-ken: Ch'ien t'an hsieh-hou-yü.—*YCT* 3, 1982, 39–42. [A simple discussion on *hsieh-hou-yü.*]

喬隨根：淺談歇後語

2658 Chu, Chien-sung & Liu, Hsing-ts'e: Kuan-yü hsieh-hou-yü te chi-ko wen-t'i.—*HCSY* 1981:2, 117–123. [Several problems concerning *hsieh-hou-yü.*]

朱建頌、劉興策：關於歇後語的幾個問題

2659 Chu, Po-shih: Hsieh-hou-yü shih yü-yen yu-hsi ma?.—*CKYW* 1945:5, 7. [Is the *hsieh-hou-yü* a "play on words"?]

朱伯石：歇後語是『語言遊戲』嗎？

2660 Fan, Yen: Wo yeh lai t'an-t'an hsieh-hou-yü.—*TPPYK* 2:10, 1935, 435–437. [Let me also discuss *hsieh-hou-yü.*]

樊績：我也來談談歇後語

2661 Ho, Ming-yen: T'an hsieh-hou-yü.—*YWCS* 1957:6, 28–31. [A discussion on *hsieh-hou-yü.*]

何明延：談歇後語

2662 Hsia, Kuang-tsu: Kuan-yü hsieh-hou-yü.—*YWHT* 2, 1978, 122–125. [Concerning *hsieh-hou-yü.*]

夏光祖：關於歇後語

2663 Huang, Hua-chieh: Hsieh-hou-yü.—*TPPYK* 2:6, 1935, 255–260. [*Hsieh-hou-yü.*]

黃華節：歇後語

2664 Huang, Hua-chieh: Lüeh t'an so-chiao-yü.—*TPPYK* 2:9, 1935, 398–403. [A brief discussion of 'shrunken-feet phrases'.] / i.e. *hsieh-hou-yü.*

黃華節：略談『縮腳語』

2665 Kuwahara, Jihei: Gendai Kango ni okeru ketsugogo no tokushitsu to sono shiyō ni tsuite.—*CGGG* 1963:12, 1–9. [On the characteristics of *hsieh-hou-yü* and their usages in the modern Chinese language.]

桑原治平：現代漢語における歇後語の特質とその使用について

2666 Li, Tao-i: Shih lun p'i-chieh yü chi ch'i yü hsieh-hou-yü, ch'eng-yü, yen-yü te ch'ü-pieh (1891). [A preliminary discussion on *p'i-chieh yü* ('metaphor-explanation phrases'), and their differences from *hsieh-hou-yü,* set-phrases, and proverbs.]

李道一：試論譬解語及其與歇後語、成語、諺語的區別

2667 Liang, Jung-jo: Kuan-yü hsieh-hou-yü.—*T'an-pai yü shuo-huang* (Taipei: K'ai-ming, 1957, 2nd ed.), 92–94. [Concerning *hsieh-hou-yü.*]

梁容若：關於歇後語──『坦白與說謊』

2668 Lü, Hung-nien: Hsieh-hou-yü chi yen-yü (2208). [*Hsieh-hou-yü* and proverbs.]

呂洪年：歇後語及諺語

2669 Ma, Kuo-fan: Yen-yü yü hsieh-hou-yü (2209). [Proverbs and *hsieh-hou-yü.*]

馬國凡：諺語與歇後語

2670 Mao, Tun: Kuan-yü hsieh-hou-yü.—
JMWH 1954:6, 94–96; also repr.
in his *Ku ch'ui chi* (Peking:
Tso-chia, 1959), 71–76. [Concerning
hsieh-hou-yü.]

茅盾：關於歇後語——『鼓吹集』

2671 Ning, Chü: *Yen-yü, ko-yen, hsieh-
hou-yü* (2164). [Proverbs, maxims, and
hsieh-hou-yü.]

寧榘：諺語、格言、歇後語

2672 Ogata, Kazuo: *Kestugogo ni tsuite.*
—Osaka: Ditto, 1960, 23 p. [On
hsieh-hou-yü.]

緒方一男：歇後語について

2673 Ogata, Kazuo: Ketsugogo ni tsuite.
—*CGGG* 1961:2, 1–4. [On *hsieh-hou-yü.*]/
A clue to its understanding.

緒方一男：歇後語について

2674 Pai, Ch'i-ming: Ts'ai-chi ko-yao so
i chien shou te—hsieh-hou-yü.—*KYAO*
44, 1924, 1–5. [What should also be
included in the collection of folk
songs—*Hsieh-hou-yü.*]

白啓明：採輯歌謠所宜兼收的——歇後語

2675 Shen, Hui-yün: Hsieh-hou-yü ying-kai
kuei-ju ch'eng-yü ho yen-yü chih
chung ma?—*YWYC* 2, 1981, 157–158.
[Should *hsieh-hou-yü* be classified under
set-phrases and proverbs?]

沈慧雲：歇後語應該歸入成語和諺語之中
嗎？

2676 Sun, C.C.: *As the saying goes* (2148)./
Including an introduction to *hsieh-hou-yü.*

2677 T'an, Yung-hsiang: Hsieh-hou-yü ho
ts'ang tz'u.—*YCT* 2, 1981, 57–59.
[*Hsieh-hou-yü* and hidden words.]

譚永祥：歇後語和藏詞

2678 T'ung, Chih-ho: Ch'eng-yü yü
hsieh-hou-yü (1893). [Set-phrases and
hsieh-hou-yü.]

童致和：成語與歇後語

2679 Wang, T'ien-shih & Chang, Ming-ch'un:
Kuan-yü hsieh-hou-yü wen-t'i te chi-
tien i-chien.—*CKYW* 1955:1, 41–42.
[Several opinions concerning the problem
of *hsieh-hou-yü.*]

王天石、張鳴春：關於歇後語問題的幾點意見

2680 Wen, Tuan-cheng: Yin-chu yü (hsieh-
hou-yü) t'an-t'ao.—*Chin-yang hsüeh
k'an* 1980:1, 150–; 3, 150– (not seen).
[An investigation into citation-comment
phrases (*hsieh-hou-yü*).]

溫端政：引注語（歇後語）探討

2681 Wen, Tuan-cheng: Hsieh-hou-yü te
yü-i.—*CKYW* 1981:6, 424–431. [The
meanings of *hsieh-hou-yü.*]

溫端政：歇後語的語義

2682 Wen, Tuan-cheng: Shih t'an yin-chu
chieh-kou.—*YWYC* 1981:2, 145–156.
[A preliminary discussion on citation-
comment structures.]

溫端政：試談引註結構

7.3.1.2. General Studies (2683–2699)

2683 Chiang, Yü: *Hsieh-hou-yü ch'ang-shih.*
—Taiyüan: Shan-hsi jen-min, 1978, 44
p. [Common knowledge of *hsieh-hou-yü.*]

江羽：歇後語常識

2684 Fu, Chen-lun: Mi yen hsieh-hou-yü
yen-chiu chih i-pan.—*KYAO* 1:68,
1924, 2–4. [A general study on riddles,
proverbs, and *hsieh-hou-yü.*]

傅振倫：謎諺歇後語研究之一般

2685 Hattori, Ryūzō: Ketsugogo ˋno
hanashi (1).—*Chūgoku gogaku jiten*
(0037), 1070–1073. [On *hsieh-hou-yü*
(1).]

服部隆造：歇後語のはなし(1)

2686 Itō, Hitoshi: Chūgoku kaigogo no
hiyu keishiki.—*HDGG* 1, 1953, 73–80.
[The metaphorical patterns of Chinese
hsieh-hou-yü.]

伊藤整：中國諧後語の比喩形式

2687 Kōno, Tsūichi: *Shina kaigyakugo kenkyū (Kaigogo).*—Peiping: Yen-ch'en-she, 1939, 11, 7, 318 p./ *YSDR* 13:1, 1962, 52–63, Hatano Tarō. [A study on the jest language of China (*hsieh-hou-yü*).]

河野通一：支那諧謔語研究（諧後語）／波多野太郎評

2688 Ku, Mu: *Hsieh-hou-yü yen-chiu.*—Taipei: Jui-te, 1982, 4, 353 p. [A study of *hsieh-hou-yü.*]/ Based on (2690).

古牧：歇後語研究

2689 Li, Chi-sheng: Min-chung chieh-hou-yü yen-chiu.—*Chung-hua chiao-yü chieh* 1:9, 1947, 35–38. [A study on the *chieh-hou-yü* of the masses.]

李紀生：民眾『解後語』研究

2690 Ma, Kuo-fan & Kao, Ko-tung: *Hsieh-hou-yü.*—Huhehot: Nei Meng-ku jen-min, 1979, [ii], 299 p. [*Hsieh-hou-yü.*]/ See (2688).

馬國凡、高歌東：歇後語

2691 Ning, Chü: *Ku chin hsieh-hou-yü hsüan shih.*—Wuhan: Hu-pei jen-min, 1982, iv, 242 p. [A selection with explanations of ancient and modern *hsieh-hou-yü.*]

寧渠：古今歇後語選釋

2692 Tanaka, Kiyoshi: Ketsugogo no hanashi (2).—*Chūgoku gogaku jiten* (0037), 1073–1076. [On *hsieh-hou-yü* (2).]

田中潔：歇後語のはなし(2)

2693 T'ang, Ch'i-yün: *Ch'eng-yü, yen-yü, hsieh-hou-yü, tien-ku kai-shuo* (1879). [A general discussion on set-phrases, proverbs, *hsieh-hou-yü,* and literary allusions.]

唐啟運：成語、諺語、歇後語、典故概說

2694 Torii, Hisayasu: Ketsugogo kenkyū josetsu.—*TRGH* 23:1, 1971, 1–17. [An introduction to the study of *hsieh-hou-yü.*]

鳥居久靖：歇後語研究序說

2695 Ueda, Kinjirō: Ketsugogo.—*Chūgokugo* 5:9, 1963, 18–19; 10, 33–35; 11, 31–32; 12, 12–14. [*Hsieh-hou-yü.*]/ Explanations of several *hsieh-hou-yü.*

上田金次郎：歇後語

2696 Wang, Ch'in: *Yen-yü hsieh-hou-yü kai-lun* (2212). [A general discussion on proverbs and *hsieh-hou-yü.*]

王勤：諺語、歇後語概論

2697 Wang, Hsi-p'eng: Hsieh-hou-yü te yen-chiu.—*Wen-i yüeh-k'an* 7:2, 1935, 1–11. [A study of *hsieh-hou-yü.*]

汪錫鵬：歇後語的研究

2698 Wang, Te-hsin: Chung-wen hui-hua li te hsieh-hou-yü.—*KKDGK* 15, 1968, 1–15. [*Hsieh-hou yü* (used) in Chinese conversation.]

王德新：中文會話裏的歇後語

2699 Yü, Fei: Kuan-yü hsieh-hou-yü yü ko-yao te yen-chiu.—*Min-su* 84, 1929, 49–50. [A study concerning *hsieh-hou-yü* and folk songs.]

于飛：關於歇後語與歌謠的研究

7.3.1.3. Collection and Analysis (2700–2724)

2700 Ch'en, Kuang-yao: *Hsieh-hou-yü hsüan lu.*—Shanghai: Ch'i-ming hsüeh-she, 1933, (not seen). [A selected record of *hsieh-hou-yü.*]

陳光堯：歇後語選錄

2701 Ch'en, Tzu-shih: *Pei-p'ing hsieh-hou-yü tz'u-tien.*—Taipei: Ta Chung-kuo t'u-shu kung-szu, 1969, 342 p. [A dictionary of *hsieh-hou-yü* of Peiping.]/ With explanatory notes on Pekinese colloquial vocabulary.

陳子實：北平諧後語辭典／兼北平口語註釋

2702 Ch'eng-tu-shih ch'ün-chung i-shu kuan: *Szu-ch'uan ch'eng-yü, yen-yü, hsieh-hou-yü yün pen* (2548). [A handbook of set-phrases, proverbs, *hsieh-hou-yü* of Szechwan arranged according to rhymes.]

成都市群眾藝術館：四川成語、諺語、歇後語韵本

2703   Chien-hu hsien Wen-chiao-chü: *Hsieh-hou-yü hsüan pien.*—Nanking: Chiang-su jen-min, 1979, [4], 62 p. [A selected collection of *hsieh-hou-yü.*]

建湖縣文教局：歇後語選編

2704   Hattori, Ryūzō & Kanegae, Nobumitsu: *Chūgoku ketsugogo no kenkyū.*—Tokyo: Kazama shobō, 1975, 18, 330 p. [A study of Chinese *hsieh-hou-yü.*]

服部隆造、鐘个信光：中國歇後語の研究

2705   Ho, Chung-ying: *Hung-lou meng* te hsieh-hou-yü.—*SHWY* 1958:1, 44–47. [*Hsieh-hou-yü* in *Hung-lou meng.*]

何仲英：『紅樓夢』的歇後語

2706   Hsia, Kuang-fen: Shih t'an *Hsieh-hou-yü tz'u-tien* te pien-tsuan yao tien.—*TSYC* 1980:2, 261–267. [A preliminary discussion on the main points in the compilation of *Hsieh-hou-yü tz'u-tien* (A dictionary of hsieh-hou-yü).]/ Forthcoming.

夏光芬：試談『歇後語詞典』的編纂要點

2707   Huang, Min-yü, et al.: *Hsieh-hou-yü hsüan pien.*—Nanchang: Chiang-hsi jen-min, 1980, (not seen). [A selected collection of *hsieh-hou-yü.*]

黃民裕等：歇後語選編

2708   Kawase, Shōzō: *Kestugogo ihen—Chūgoku no kaigyakugo.*—Tokyo: Meizendō shoten, 1969, 5, 358, 40, 2 p. [A collection of *hsieh-hou-yü*—China's jest language.]

川瀨正三：歇後語彙編——中國の諧謔語

2709   Kōno, Tsūichi: *Shina kaigyakugoi.*—Manshū: Nichinichi shinbunsha & Dairen: Nichinichi shinbunsha, 1941; 1943, 2nd ed., 4, 2, 222, 4 p./ *YSDR* 8:3, 1957, 16–17, Hatano Tarō. [A collection from the jest language of China.]

河野通一：支那諧謔語彙／波多野太郎評

2710   Kuang-hsi jen-min ch'u-pan-she: *Chih-*

hui te hua-to (*Hsieh-hou-yü hsüan chi*).—Nanning: Kuang-hsi jen-min, 1980, 157 p. [Flowers of wisdom (A selected collection of *hsieh-hou-yü*).]

廣西人民出版社：智慧的花朵（歇後語選輯）

2711   Li, Meng-pei: *Yen-yü, hsieh-hou-yü ch'ien chu* (2302). [Simple annotations on proverbs and *hsieh-hou-yü.*]

李孟北：諺語、歇後語淺註

2712   Li, Shou-p'eng: *Hsieh-hou-yü lun-chi.*—Peiping: Ching-shan shu-she, 1936, [iii], 2, 97 d.p. [Collected essays on *hsieh-hou-yü.*]

李壽彭：歇後語論集

2713   Nien, T'ang: Min chien hsieh-hou-yü chi ts'ui.—*I-wen chih* 90, 1973, 82–83. [A choice collection of folk *hsieh-hou-yü.*]

念棠：民間歇後語集粹

2714   Ou-yang, Jo-hsiu: *Hsieh-hou-yü hsiao tz'u-tien.*—Sian: Shan-hsi jen-min, 1982, 30, 364 p. [A small dictionary of *hsieh-hou-yü.*]

歐陽若修：歇後語小詞典

2715   P'an, Li-wen: *Chung wai su-yü tien* (2307). [A dictionary of Chinese and foreign popular sayings.]/ Classified, including *hsieh-hou-yü* of different localities.

潘禮文：中外俗語典／包括各地歇後語

2716   Shih, Pao-i: *Chih-hui te hua-tuo—Hsieh-hou-yü hsüan tu chi.*—Nanning: Kuan-hsi jen-min, 1982, [iv], 219 p. [Flowers of wisdom—A selected reading collection of *hsieh-hou-yü.*]

施寶義：智慧的花朵——歇後語選讀輯

2717   Shu, Hung: *Chung-kuo hsieh-hou-yü ta-kuan.*—Taipei: Ch'ing liu, 1980, 7 vols., 192; 192; 191; 192; 192; 190; 189 p., illus. [A grand array of Chinese *hsieh-hou-yü.*]

蜀洪：中國歇後語大觀

2718   Sun, Chih-p'ing & Wang, Shih-chün: *Hsieh-hou-yü szu-ch'ien t'iao.*—Shanghai: Shang-hai wen-i, 1982, 8, 222 p. [Four thousand *hsieh-hou-yü.*]

孫治平、王士均：歇後語四千條

2719   Tiao, Yü-weng: *Miao yü ju chu.*—Taipei: Nan-ching, 1978, 7th repr., 142 p. [Clever remarks like pearls.]/ *Hsieh-hou-yü,* proverbs, popular sayings.

釣魚翁：妙語如珠

2720   Torii, Hisayasu: *Kinpeibai* ketsugogo shi shaku.—*TRGH* 18:2, 1966, 57–71; 19:1, 1967, 33–57; 19:2, 35–56; *CBKK* 7, 1967, 9–17; *MSBGK* 9, 1967, 27–46; *TRGH* 21:2, 1969, 71–84; 21:4, 1970, 48–64, 22:1, 1970, 34–51; *CBKK* 12, 1972, 15–23 (addenda). [My personal explanations of the *hsieh-hou-yü* in *Ching-p'ing mei.*]

鳥居久靖：『金瓶梅』歇後語私釋

2721   Torii, Hisayasu: Mindai getsugogo no seikaku.—*CBKK* 11, 1970, 1–7. [The characteristics of *hsieh-hou-yü* during the Ming dynasty.]/ from *Chin-p'ing mei tz'u-hua.*

鳥居久靖：明代歇後語の性格／採自『金瓶梅詞話』

2722   Torii, Hisayasu: *Saiyūki* shoken ketsugogo kōshaku.—*TRGH* 85, 1973, 306–331. [A study and explanation of the *hsieh-hou-yü* as seen in *Hsi-yu chi.*]

鳥居久靖：『西遊記』所見歇後語考釋

2723   T'ung, Sou: *Man-hua hsieh-hou-yü.*—Taipei: Hsing-kuan, 1976, 196 p., illus. [*Hsieh-hou-yü* in cartoons.]

童叟：漫畫歇後語

2724   Woitsch, L.: *Einige Hsieh-hou-yü.*—Peking: (?), 1908, 14 p.

7.3.1.4. Regional *Hsieh-hou-yü* (2725–2734)

2725   Chang, Hung-nien: Yüeh-yü chung te

hsieh-hou-yü hsien-hsiang.—*CHHP* 14:1–2, 1982, 51–103. [The *hsieh-hou-yü* phenomena in Cantonese.]

張洪年：粵語中的歇後語現象

2726   Huang, Chao-nien: Huai-an hsieh-hou-yü.—*Min-su* 19–20, 1928, 57–60. [*Hsieh-hou-yü* of Hwaian.]

黃詔年：淮安歇後語

2727   Kōsaka, Jun'ichi: *Pekingo taishō Kantongo kenkyū.*—Taiepi: Tōto shoseki, 1943, 4, 8, 686 p./ 115–128: *hsieh-hou-yü.* [A study on the Cantonese dialect as compared with the Peking dialect.]

香坂順一：北京語對照廣東語研究／115-128：歇後語

2728   Kroll, J.L.: A tentative classification and description of the structure of Peking common sayings (*Hsieh-hou-yü*).—*JAOS* 86, 1966, 267–276./ *RBS* 12–13, 1966–1967, 647, Ta Trong Hiep.

2729   P'ei, Shih: Ch'a-ho-erh-sheng te hsieh-hou-yü.—*Ch'a-ho-erh-sheng wen-hsien* 7, 1980, 90. [The *hsieh-hou-yü* of the Chahar province.]

培適：察合爾省的歇後語

2730   P'eng, A-mu: Hakka ketsugogo ni tsuite.—*SK* 30, 1933, 213–273. [On the *hsieh-hou-yü* of the Hakkas.]

彭阿木：客家歇後語に就いて

2731   Schmitt, Erich: Füngrig *hsieh-hou-yü.* aus T'ai-yüan-fu.—*AM* 9, 1939, 568–579.

〔太原府〕

2732   Schmitt, Erich: Pekinger *hsieh-hou-yü.*—*Archiv für Ostasien* 1948:1, 13–19.

2733   Yao, Chung-chü: Ch'ao-chou fang-yen hsieh-hou-yü.—*CCWH* 3:5–6, 1977, 31–35. [*Hsieh-hou-yü* of the Chaochow dialect.]

姚鍾居：潮州方言歇後語

2734   Yeh, Ching-ming: Shao-hsing te hsieh-hou-yü.—*Min-su* 73, 1929, 49–52. [*Hsieh-hou-yü* of Shaohsing.]

葉鏡銘：紹興的歇後語

7.3.2. Witticisms (2735–2748)
7.3.2.1. Definition and Problems (2735–2740)

2735   Chu, Chieh-fan: Ch'iao-p'i-hua te wen-t'i.—*Wen-t'an* 24, 1962, 31–36. [The problem of witticisms.]

朱介凡：俏皮話的問題

2736   Chu, Chieh-fan: *Chung-kuo yen-yü lun* (2178), 101–119: The problem of *ch'iao-p'i-hua* and *hsieh-hou-yü.* [On Chinese proverbs.]

朱介凡：中國諺語論／101-119：俏皮話跟歇後語的問題

2737   Hsiu, Ch'uan: Yeh t'an ch'iao-p'i-hua.—*CHWI* 135, 1982, 157–161. [Also discussing witticisms.]

修川：也談俏皮話

2738   Wang, Chu-hsüan: T'an-i-t'an wo kuo te ch'iao-p'i-hua.—*CHWI* 132, 1982, 126–129. [A brief discussion on Chinese witticisms.]

王竹軒：談一談我國的俏皮話

2739   Wen, Hsi-t'ien: Lun ch'iao-p'i-hua.—*KYCK* 91, 1933, June 24. [On witticisms.]

溫錫田：論俏皮話

2740   Wen, Hsi-t'ien: Tsai lun ch'iao-p'i-hua.—*KCYK* 92, 1933, July 1. [Once more on witticisms.]

溫錫田：再論俏皮話

7.3.2.2. Collection and Analysis (2741–2748)

2741   Anonymous: *Ch'iao-p'i-hua.* Peiping: Pao-wen t'ang T'ung-chi shu-p'u, 1935, 3 vols., 7; 7; 7 d.p. [Witticisms.]

無名氏：俏皮話

2742   Anonymous: *Ma jen te i-shu.*—Tainan: Li-ta, 197?, [i], 186 p. [The art of name calling.]/ *Hsieh-hou-yü,* witticisms, riddles, proverbs.

無名氏：罵人的藝術

2743   Ch'i, T'ieh-hen: Pei-ching te ch'iao-p'i-hua-erh.—*KYHK* 1:7, 1929, 73–74; 1:8, 96; 1:12, 157–162. [Witticisms of Peking.]

齊鐵恨：北京的俏皮話兒

2744   Ch'i, T'ieh-hen: Pei-p'ing te ch'iao-p'i-hua-erh.—*CKYT* from 11:2, 1962, 48–51, until 23:6, 1968, 58–61, publ. in 71 issues./ See (2745). [Witticisms of Peiping.]

齊鐵恨：北平的俏皮話兒

2745   Ch'i, T'ieh-hen: *Pei-p'ing te ch'iao-p'i-hua-erh* (1).—Taipei: Chung-kuo yü-wen yüeh-k'an-she, 1973, 2, 186 p. [Witticisms of Peiping (Vol. I).]

齊鐵恨：北平的俏皮話兒（一）

2746   Hsü, Huai-shih: *Ch'iao-p'i-hua.*—Tainan: Shih-i shu-chü, 1979, [i], 181 p. [Witticisms.]/ Same as (2747).

許懷石：俏皮話

2747   Shang, Ying-shih: *Ch'iao-p'i-hua.*—Taipei: Ch'ang-ch'un shu shu-fang, 1973, 181 p. [Witticisms.]/ and proverbs, slang, popular sayings, folk songs.

尚英時：俏皮話

2748   Yü, Ch'üan: Lu tung te yen-yü chi ch'iao-p'i-hua.—*CKYT* 13:3, 1963, 55–56. [Proverbs and witticisms of eastern Shantung.]

宇權：魯東的諺語及俏皮話

8. TEACHING, LEARNING, AND STANDARDIZATION OF CHINESE LEXICONS (2749–2870)

8.1. Teaching of Chinese Lexicons (2749–2784)

2749 Chang, Ching: *Tz'u-hui chiao-hsüeh chiang-hua.*—Wuhan: Hu-pei jen-min, 1957, [ii], 159 p; *Yü-wen hui-pien* (0058), 10:44. [Lectures on the teaching of lexicons.]/ See (2784).

張靜：詞滙教學講話

2750 Chang, Ch'üan-ts'ung: Yü-wen chiao-hsüeh chung te shih tz'u wen-t'i.—*YWCS* 1956:6, 39–40. [The problems in explaining words in the teaching of language and writings.]

張全聰：語文教學中的釋詞問題

2751 Chang, Shih-lu: *Hsiao-hsüeh tz'u-hui chiao-hsüeh chi-pen chih-shih chiang-hua.*—Hangchow: Che-chiang jen-min, 1956, 2, 2, 82 p.; *Yü-wen hui-pien* (0058), 34:116. [Lectures on basic knowledge for the teaching of lexicons in elementary schools.]/ See (2773).

張世祿：小學詞彙教學基本知識講話

2752 Chang, Wei: Han-yü tz'u-hui chiao-hsüeh so t'an.—*YCYY* 1979:1, 128–136. [A petty discussion on the teaching of Chinese lexicons.]

張維：漢語詞滙教學瑣談

2753 Chiang-su chiao-yü-she: *Chung-hsüeh tz'u-yü chiao-hsüeh ching-yen.*—Shanghai: Shang-hai chiao-yü, 1960, 1st ed.; 1961, 1st repr., 4, 82 p.; *Yü-wen hui-pien* (0058), 34:113. [Experiences from the teaching of words and phrases in middle schools.]

江蘇教育社：中學詞語教學經驗

2754 Chin, I: T'an tz'u-yü chiao-hsüeh.—*Shang-hai chiao-yü* 1959:9, 15–16. [A discussion on teaching words and phrases.]

金易：談詞語教學

2755 Chou, Chü-cheng: *Tzu, tz'u, chü chiao-hsüeh wen-t'i.*—Wuhan: Hu-pei jen-min, 1956, [iii], 47 p; *Yü-wen hui-pien* (0058), 50:162. [The problems in the teaching of characters, words, and sentences.]

周居正：字、詞、句教學問題

2756 Chu, Ch'uan-wei: Shih t'an t'ung-i-tz'u chiao-hsüeh te chi-ko wen-t'i.—*YWHH* 1958:2, 32–33. [A preliminary discussion on several problems in the teaching of synonyms.]

朱傳煒：試談同義詞教學的幾個問題

2757 Chu, Hsing: Tsen-yang chu-chieh k'o-wen chung te yü-tz'u.—*YWCH* 1951:1, 12–14. [How to annotate the words and phrases in textbooks.]

朱星：怎樣注解課文中的語詞

2758 Ch'üan-kuo min-tsu yüan hsiao Han-yü chiao-hsüeh yen-chiu-hui: *Han-yü chiao-hsüeh yü yen-chiu.*—Yenchi: Yen-pien chiao-yü, 1980, 2, 205 p. [Chinese language teaching and research.]/ Collected essays.

全國民族院校漢語教學研究會：漢語教學與研究

2759 Chung-hsüeh yü-wen chiao-hsüeh yen-chiu-hui hui-k'an pien-wei-hui: *Yü-wen chiao-hsüeh yen-chiu* (Ti-i chi).—Shanghai: Shang-hai chiao-yü, 1979, 3. 199 p. [Studies on the teaching of language and writing (Vol. I.).]/ Collected essays.

中學語文教學研究會會刊編委會：語文教學研究（第一集）

2760 Hsia, Hsiu-jung: T'an tz'u-hui chiao-hsüeh.—*YWHH* 1953:10, 30–33. [A discussion on the teaching of lexicons.]

夏秀容：談詞滙教學

2761 Hsiang, Ch'ao: Chung-shih yü-hui wen-t'i.—*YWHH* 1952:11, 42–45. [Pay much attention to the problem of lexicons (in teaching).]

向超：重視語滙問題

2762   Hsü, Shou-chung: Chiang-chieh tz'u-yü te chi-ko wen-t'i.—*YWHH* 1954:11, 40–42. [Several problems of explaining words and phrases.]

徐守中：講解詞語的幾個問題

2763   Huang, Chin-hung: T'an tan-tz'u chiao-hsüeh.—*Hsüeh-ts'ui* 14:4, 1972, 19–23. [A discussion on the teaching of simple words.]

黃錦鈜：談單詞教學

2764   Kung, Chao-p'ing: Ku Han-yü tz'u-i chiao-hsüeh ch'u t'an.—*YCYY* 1982:4, 138–146. [A preliminary investigation into the teaching of lexical meanings of the ancient Chinese language.]

宮兆平：古漢語詞義教學初探

2765   Kung, Ju-hsü: Wo chiang-chieh tz'u-hui te chi-ko fang-fa.—*YWCS* 1955:3, 32–34. [Several methods of which I explain lexicons.]

龔汝緒：我講解詞滙的幾個方法

2766   Kuo, Chien-chang: Kuan-yü ch'u chung yü-wen k'o te tz'u-hui chiao-hsüeh.—*YWHH* 1958:9, 32–34. [Concerning the teaching of lexicons in language and writing courses in junior middle schools.]

郭建章：關於初中語文課的詞滙教學

2767   Lei, Ching-yü & Ma, Shih-i: Tui tz'u-hui chiao-hsüeh k'o-hsüeh-hua te chien-i.—*Yü-wen chiao-hsüeh yen-chiu* (2759), 182–187. [Suggestions for the scientific teaching of lexicons.]

類警予、馬世一：對詞滙教學科學化的建議

2768   Li, Hsing-chien: Yü-wen chiao-hsüeh chung te tz'u-yü chieh-shih kung-tso.—*KMSY* 1981:2, 68–73, 82. [The work of explaining words and phrases in the teaching of language and writing.]

李行健：語文教學中的詞語解釋工作

2769   Liu, Chih-yü: Chieh-ho shang-hsia wen chiang-chieh tz'u-yü.—*YWHH* 1959:6, 21–22. [The teaching of words and phrases by associating context.]

劉之堉：結合上下文講解詞語

2770   Liu, Yung-jang: T'an tz'u-yü te chieh-shih (0519). [A discussion on the explanations of words and phrases.]

劉永讓：談詞語的解釋

2771   Lo, Wei: Tsen-yang chiao tz'u-erh.—*CKYW* 1953:5, 25–27. [How to teach words.]

羅委：怎樣教詞兒

2772   Lu, Chien-ming: Kuan-yü Han-yü hsü-tz'u chiao-hsüeh.—*YCYY* 1980:4, 69–83. [Concerning the teaching of Chinese cenematic words.]

陸劍明：關於漢語虛詞教學

2773   Lu, Yang: *Hsiao-hsüeh tz'u-hui chiao-hsüeh chi-pen chih-shih chiang-hua.*—*CKYW* 1957:1, 45. [(A review of) *Hsiao-hsüeh tz'u-hui chiao-hsüeh chi-pen chih-shih chiang-hua* (2751).]

魯揚：『小學詞滙教學基本知識講話』

2774   Lü, Tu-li: Tz'u-yü chiao-hsüeh te chi-chung tso-fa.—*Shan-hsi chiao-yü* 1959:23, 34–35. [Several methods of teaching words and phrases.]

呂篤理：詞語教學的幾種做法

2775   Su, Ling-hsien: Wo tsen-yang chiang-chieh sheng tz'u.—*YWHH* 1954:1, 64–66. [How I explain new words.]

蘇令嫻：我怎樣講解生詞

2776   Sui, Shu-hua: Yu kuan tz'u-hui chiao-hsüeh te i-hsieh t'i-hui.—*YYWH* 1959:5, 4–7. [Some personal experiences related to the teaching of lexicons.]

隋樹華：有關詞滙教學的一些體會

2777   Sun, Ch'ien: Chung-hsüeh yü-wen-k'o chung te tz'u-hui chiao-hsüeh wen-t'i.—*CKYW* 1954:12, 27–28. [The problem of teaching lexicons in language and writing courses in middle schools.]

孫潛：中國語文課中的詞滙教學問題

2778   Sung, Shu-jo: Wo tsai tz'u-hui chiao-hsueh chung te i-tien ching-yen.— *YWHH* 1954:11, 36–40. [Some experiences in my teachings on lexicons.]

宋舒若：我在詞滙教學中的一點經驗

2779   Sung, Yü-t'ung: Tz'u-hui chiao-hsüeh chung te wen-t'i chi kai-chin i-chien.— *JMCY* 1954:2, 27–30. [Problems in the teaching of lexicons and opinions for improvement.]

宋育瞳：詞滙教學中的問題及改進意見

2780   T'an, Li-tu: Wo-men tui ch'u chung yü-wen k'o tz'ui-hui chiao-hsüeh te t'i-hui.— *JMCY* 1954:12, 37–41. [Our personal experience from the teaching of lexicons in language and writing courses in the junior middle schools.]

譚麗都：我們對初中語文課詞滙教學的體會

2781   Ti, Ch'ang-lien: T'an-t'an chi-ch'u Han-yü te tz'u-hui chiao-hsüeh.— *YCYY* 1981:1, 80–87, 145. [A discussion on the teaching of lexicons in basic Chinese courses.]

狄昌蓮：談談基礎漢語的詞彙教學

2782   Wang, Kuang-ch'ing: Wen-tzu hsün-shih yü yü-wen chiao-hsüeh.— *CYYW* 9:5, 1955, 14–18. [Semantic explanation of writing and the teaching of language and writing.]

王廣慶：文字訓釋與語文教學

2783   Yen, Liang-chieh: Ju-ho chin-hsing tz'u ho yü te chiao-hsüeh.— *CKYW* 1953:10, 28. [How to carry out the teaching of words and phrases.]

燕艮杰：如何進行詞和語的教學

2784   Yung, Yung & Shu, Shih-ping: *Tz'i-hui chiao-hsüeh chiang-hua.—CKYW* 1957:11, 46–47. [(A review of *Tz'u-hui chiao-hsüeh chiang-hua* (2749).]

雍庸、舒市丙：『詞滙教學講話』

8.2. Learning of Chinese Lexicons (2785–2852)

8.2.1. Learning of Chinese Lexicons in General (2785–2792)

2785   Chao, Chih-ch'ao, et al.: How many words do Chinese know.— *JCLTA* 2:2, 1967, 44–58.

2786   Chesterman, A.P.C.: *A lexical approach to the learning of elementary Chinese.* —Edinburgh: U. of Edinburgh, 1975, (not seen).

2787   Chiang, Shao-yü: Tsen-yang chang-wo ku Han-yü te tz'u-i.— *YWYC* 2, 1981, 80–86. [How to grasp the lexical meanings of the ancient Chinese language.] / Also discusses the application of sememes and semantemes in the analysis of lexical meanings.

蔣紹愚：怎樣掌握古漢語的詞義

2788   Chu, Po-shih: Hsüeh-hsi t'ung-i-tz'u ying-kai chu-i te chi tien.— *YWHH* 1955:2, 65–68. [Several points that should be emphasized in learning synonymous words.]

朱伯石：學習同義詞應該注意的幾點

2789   Chu, Wen-shu: Hsüeh-hsi tz'u-hui te i li—*shen* ho *ch'ien*.—*Yü-wen . . . chi-ch'u* (0055), 117–122. [An example of learning vocabulary—(the words) *shen* ('deep') and *ch'ien* ('shallow').]

朱文叔：學習詞滙的一例——『深』和『淺』

2790   Hsiang, Chin-chiang: Tz'u-hui te hsüeh-hsi.—*YWHH* 1953:10, 33–37. [The learning of lexicons.]

向錦江：詞滙的學習

2791   Li, Hsi-k'ang: Wo shih tsen-yang hsüeh-hsi tz'u-hui te.—*YWHH* 1953:10, 37–40. [How I learned the lexicon.]

李熙康：我是怎樣學習詞滙的

2792   Liu, Ying-mao: Sheng tz'u hsüeh-hsi fa yen-chiu.—*CSHS* 22, 1978, 159–187. [A study on the methods of learning new words.]

劉英茂：生詞學習法研究

8.2.2. Learning Usages (2793–2852)
8.2.2.1. General Studies (2793–2809)

2793   Chang, Chih-kung: *Hsiu-tz'u kai-yao.*
—Shanghai: Shang-hai chiao-yü, 1982,
[i], 4, 192 p./ Chap. 1: The use of
words. [Essentials of rhetoric.]

張志公：修辭概要／第一章：用詞

2794   Chiang, Yin-tan & Chia, Shuang-hu:
Jung-i yung hun te tz'u.—Peking: Pei-
ching, 1978, 10, 125 p. [Words easily
confused in usage.]

蔣蔭枬、賈雙虎：容易用混的詞

2795   Chu, Po-shih: *Hsieh-tso ho yü-yen.*
—Chengtu: Szu-ch'uan jen-min, 1980,
2, 157 p./ 26–28: A discussion on the
use of words, etc. [Writing and language.]

朱伯石：寫作和語言／26—82: 談用詞等

2796   Ch'üan-kuo wai-yü yüan hsi: *Yü-fa
yü hsiu-tz'u.*—Nanning: Kuang-hsi jen-min,
1981, 6, 233 p.; 1982, 2nd ed., 6,
234 p./ Pt. II, Chap. 1: Selection and
refinement of words and phrases. [Grammar
and rhetoric.]

全國外語院系：語法與修辭／第二編，第一
章：語詞的選擇和錘煉

2797   Huang, Han-sheng (ed. in chief):
Hsien-tai Han-yü. Yü-fa hsiu-tz'u.—
Peking: Shu-mu wen-hsien, 1981, iii,
378 p./ (Section on) rhetoric, Chap. I:
Selection and usage of words and
phrases. [The modern Chinese language:
grammar and rhetoric.]

黃漢生主編：現代漢語 · 語法修辭／修辭，第
一章：詞語的選用

2798   Hung, Chia-hui: *Wo pu tsai yung-ts'o
tz'u-yü.*—Hong Kong: Hsin-feng wen-hua
shih-yeh kung-szu, n.d., 242 p. [I will
no more misuse words and phrases.]

洪嘉惠：我不再用錯詞語

2799   I, Lin & Wen, Liang: *Jung-i yung-ts'o
te tz'u.*—Shanghai: Shang-hai chiao-yü,

1980; 1981, 2nd print., 5, 71 p. [Words
easily misused.]

一麟、文良：容易用錯的詞

2800   Jen, Ming-shan: *Tz'u te yün-yung.*—
YWHH 1957:6, 20–21. [The applications
of words.]

任銘善：詞的運用

2801   Li, Ch'ih: *Ch'ang-yung tz'u shih-yung
fa.*—Hong Kong: Shang-hai shu-chü,
1956, 92 p. [Methods of using commonly
used words.]

李池：常用詞使用法

2802   Li, Hsing-chien & Liu, Shu-hsin:
Tsen-yang shih yung tz'u yü.—Tientsin:
T'ien-chin jen-min, 1976, 1st ed.; 1976,
2nd repr., [i], 176 p. [How to use
words and phrases.]

李行健、劉叔新：怎樣使用詞語

2803   Li, Hsing-chien & Liu, Shu-hsin:
Tz'u-yü te chih-shih ho yün-yung.—
Tientsin: T'ien-chin jen-min, 1979, 3rd
print., [iii], 178 p./ A rev. ed. of (2802).
[Knowledge and usages of words and
phrases.]

李行健、劉叔新：詞語的知識和運用

2804   Lin, Yü-wen: *Tsen-yang yung tz'u:*
Peking: T'ung-su tu-wu, 1957, [i], 38
p; *Yü-wen hui-pien* (0058), 50:163. [How
to use words.]

林裕文：怎樣用詞

2805   Ma, Sung-t'ing: *Han-yü yü-fa hsiu-tz'u*
(0312), (Section on) Chinese rhetoric,
24: How to select words; 25: The uses
of set-phrases, proverbs, and *hsieh-hou-yü.*]
[Chinese grammar and rhetoric.]

馬松亭：漢語語法修辭／漢語修辭第二十四節
：怎樣選詞；第二十五節：成語、諺語、歇後
語的運用

2806   Ni, Pao-yüan: *Hsiu-tz'u.*—Hangchow:
Che-chiang jen-min, 1980, 2, 2, 3-5 p./
Chap. 4: The selection and uses of words
and phrases. [Rhetoric.]

倪寶元：修辭／第四章：詞語的選用

2807   Ni, Pao-yüan: *Tz'u-yü te ch'ui-lien.*
—Lanchow: Kan-su jen-min, 1981, [ii],
172 p. [The refinement of words and
phrases.]

倪寶元：詞語的錘煉

2808   Sung, Yü-chu: Yung tz'u yao chun-
ch'üeh.—*CKYW* 1978:1, 41. [The usages
of words should be correct.]

宋玉柱：用詞要準確

2809   Yang, Tso: *Tz'u-yü huo-yung fa.*—
Hong Kong: San yü, 1972, [iv], 191 p.
[Methods of alternatively using words
and phrases.]

楊佐：詞語活用法

8.2.2.2. Usages of Set-phrases (2810–2847)

2810   Chang, Ching: *Wen-hsüeh te yü-yen.*
—Chengchow: Ho-nan jen-min, 1981, 2,
242 p./ 167–176: Uses of set-phrases,
proverbs, and *hsieh-hou-yü.* [The
language of literature.]

張靜：文學的語言／167–176：運用成語、諺語
和歇後語

2811   Chang, Chung-chü: Ch'ien t'an ch'uang-
tsao-hsing ti yün-yung ch'eng-yü.—*YATH*
1981:1, 32– (not seen). [A brief
discussion on creatively using set-phrases.]

張仲舉：淺談創造性地運用成語

2812   Chang, Shih-lu: Tsen-yang yün-yung
ch'eng-yü.—*YWHH* 1959:3, 23–25. [How
to use set-phrases.]

張世祿：怎樣運用成語

2813   Chao, Sheng-ming: Ch'eng-yü-hsing wei-
yü hsin li.—*CKYW* 1959:4, 194. [New
examples of set-phrases (acting) as
predicates.]

趙生明：成語性謂語新例

2814   Ch'en, Hsiao-ying: Ch'ien t'an ch'eng-
yü huo yung.—*Shan-hsi shih-ta hsüeh-pao*
1982:1, 90–96. [A brief discussion on

the flexible uses of set-phrases.]

陳孝英：淺談成語活用

2815   Ch'ien, Hsing: Yao cheng-ch'üeh shih-
yung ch'eng-yü.—*YCT* 2, 1981, 179–181.
[Set-phrases should be used correctly.]

錢行：要正確使用成語

2816   Chou, Ta-sheng: Ch'eng-yü yün-yung
man t'an.—*YCT* 3, 1982, 32–38. [A
random discussion on the uses of set-
phrases.]

周達生：成語運用漫談

2817   Fan, Chi-yen & Cheng, Hsüan-mu:
Chi tsu ch'eng-yü te yung-fa ch'ü-pieh.—
HYHH 1982:5, 44–47. [Differences in
the uses of several groups of set-phrases.]

范繼淹、鄭宣沐：幾組成語的用法區別

2818   Fang, Hui-sheng: Ch'eng-yü ho ch'eng-
yü te yün-yung.—*KWTC* 2:3, 1943,
21–26. [Set-phrases and the uses of
set-phrases.]

方輝繩：成語和成語的運用

2819   Harada, Matsusaburō: *Fan-tui tang
pa-ku* no tsūzokusa—Shiji seigo zokugen
no takumina tsukai kata o chūshin
ni.—*KGR* 28:3, 1977 39–51. [The
popularity of (the slogan) *fan-tui tang
pa-ku* ('oppose the Party's jargon')—A
focus on the skillful ways of using
four-character set-phrases and popular
proverbs.]

原田松三郎：『反對黨八股』の 通俗さ——四
字成語，俗諺の巧みな 使い方を中心に

2820   Hsiang, Kuang-chung: Ch'eng-yü te
huo-yung.—*TCSY* 1981:4, 77–81.
[Flexible uses of set-phrases.]

向光忠：成語的活用

2821   Huang, Tsai-ch'un: Ch'eng-yü tso
wei-yü te chü-fa kung-neng.—*CKYW*
1958:10, 478–480. [The syntactical
functions of set-phrases acting as
predicates.]

黃再春：成語做謂語的句法功能

2822   Hui, Hsiu, et al.: Tui *Yin yung ch'eng-yü yao shen-chung* te i-chien.— *YWCS* 1956:12, 7–10. [Opinions on *Yin-yung ch'eng-yü yao shen-chung* (2846).]

惠修等：對『引用成語要慎重』的意見

2823   Hung, Chia-hui: *Wo pu tsai yung-ts'o ch'eng-yü.*—Hong Kong: Hsin-feng wen-hua shih-yeh kung-szu, n.d., 242 p. [I will not again misuse set-phrases.]

洪嘉惠：我不再用錯成語

2824   Li, Chen-chieh: *Pao-feng tsou-yü chung su-yü te yün-yung.*—*YCYY* 1982: 4, 102–106. [The uses of popular sayings in *Pao-feng tsou-yü* (by Chou Li-po).]

李振杰：〔周立波〕『暴風驟雨』中俗語的運用

2825   Li, Hsing-chien: Ch'eng-yü huo yung te i-chung t'e-shu hsing-shih.—*HYHH* 1982:5, 48–50. [A special pattern in the flexible uses of set-phrases.]

李行健：成語活用的一種特殊形式

2826   Li, Ts'un-fang: Ch'eng-yü tsai piao-t'i shang te miao yung.—*CLTH* 1982:1, 98–99. [The ingenious uses of set-phrases in titles and headings.]

李存方：成語在標題上的妙用

2827   Li, Wen: Shuo-ts'o-le hsien ch'eng-hua. —*YWCS* 1957:7, 24–25. [Mistakes made in saying "ready-made expressions."]/ Set-phrases.

黎文：說錯了『現成話』

2828   Liao, Chang-hui: Chung-hsüeh-sheng chang-wo Chung-kuo ch'eng-yü neng-li ch'u t'an.—*Chiao-yü chuan t'i wen-chi* (Vol. I. Singapore: Shih tzu hsün-lien hsüeh-yüan, 1976), 32–49. [A preliminary investigation into the capability of middle school students mastering Chinese set-phrases.]

廖障廻：中學生掌握中國成語能力初探——『教育專題文集』（一）

2829   Lin, Pai: *Tu hsieh pien cheng.*—

Hong Kong: Hua-an, n.d., 360 p./ 317–345: Set-phrases easily to be used incorrectly. [How to read and write correctly.]

林白：讀寫辨正／317–345: 容易錯用的成語

2830   Lin, Shao-tsu & Huang, Pa-kuang: I-hsieh jung-i tu-ts'o te ch'eng-yü.—*YWHH* 1959:3, 27–28. [Several set-phrases easily mispronounced.]

林紹祖、黃拔光：一些容易讀錯的成語

2831   Lin, Wen-chin: Ch'eng-yü te liang-chung ling-huo yung-fa.—*YWHH* 1959:2, 30–33. [Two flexible methods for using set-phrases.]

林文金：成語的兩種靈活用法

2832   Liu, Lin: Shih-yung ch'eng-yü yao ch'ia-tang.—*YWHH* 1952:2, 31. [The usages of set-phrases ought to be apposite.]

劉琳：使用成語要恰當

2833   Ma, Sung-t'ing: *Han-yü yü-fa hsiu-tz'u* (0312), Paragr. 25: The uses of set-phrases, proverbs, and *hsieh-hou-yü.*

馬松亭：漢語語法修辭／第二十五節：成語、諺語、歇後語的運用

2834   Ni, Pao-yüan: Ch'eng-yü te t'ao-yung hsien-hsiang.—*CKYW* 1960:8, 372–374. [The phenomenon of the embedding uses of set-phrases.]

倪寶元：成語的套用現象

2835   P'an, Kung: T'an lien-ho-shih ch'eng-yü te hsiu-tz'u tso-yung.—*YWCS* 1956:12, 7–10. [A discussion on the rhetorical functions of coordinate set-phrases.]

潘汞：談聯合式成語的修辭作用

2836   P'u, Yung-ch'uan: Ts'ung *Tzu-yeh* chung yün-yung te ch'eng-yü lai t'an-t'an ch'eng-yü te chi-ko wen-t'i.—*YWCS* 1958:3, 24–29. [A discussion on several problems of set-phrases from the set-phrases which are used in *Tzu-yeh* (by Mao Tun).]

蒲永川：從〔茅盾〕『子夜』中運用的成語來談談成語的幾個問題

2837   Sui, Shu-sen: Ch'eng-yü ho ch'eng-yü te shih-yung.—*Yü-wen hsüeh-hsi te chi-ch'u* (0055), 123–154. [Set-phrases and the usages of set-phrases.]
隋樹森：成語和成語的使用

2838   Teng, Chia-ch'i: *Cheng-ch'üeh shih-yung ch'eng-yü.*—Sian: Shan-hsi jen-min, 1981, rev. & enl. ed., 2, 234 p. [To correctly use set-phrases.]
鄧家琪：正確使用成語

2839   Tung, T'ien-ch'i: T'an ch'eng-yü te huo-yung.—*YWLT* 1, 1981, 123–128. [A discussion on the flexible uses of set-phrases.]
董天琦：談成語的活用

2840   Wang, Ting-chun: Ch'iao-yung ch'eng-yü.—*CKYT* 39:2, 1976, 18–20. [Skillful uses of set-phrases.]
王鼎鈞：巧用成語

2841   Wen, Ch'i-chih: *Tsen-yang ying-yung ch'eng-yü.*—Hong Kong: 1971, Shang-hai shu-chü, 69 p. [How to use set-phrases.]
文起之：怎樣應用成語

2842   Wu, Chan-k'un: Ch'eng-yü te kuei-fan ho huo-yung.—*YWHH* 1960:4, 34–35. [The standard and flexible uses of set-phrases.]
武占坤：成語的規範和活用

2843   Yang, Tsung-jen & Chou, Yüeh-sheng: *Ch'eng-yü tsao-chü shih li.*—Taichung: T'ai-chung hsüeh-sheng shu-chü, 1968, 7, 162 p. [Examples with explanations of making sentences with set-phrases.]
楊宗仁、周月笙：成語造句釋例

2844   Yang, Wei-chen, et al.: *Ku chü hsin yung.*—Changchun: Chi-lin jen-min, 1980, [i], 21, 286 p. [New uses of old sentences.] / Including set-phrases.
楊爲珍等：古句新用

2845   Yü, Kuan-ying: T'an ch'eng-yü ts'o-wu.

—*KWYK* 1:2, 1940, 23–25. [A discussion on errors (occurring) in (the uses of) set-phrases.]
余冠英：談成語錯誤

2846   Yü, K'ung-wo: Yin-yung ch'eng-yü yao shen-chung.—*YWHH* 1956:4, 40. [One should be cautious in citing set-phrases.] / See (2822).
余空我：引用成語要愼重

2847   Yü, Shui: Man-t'an ch'eng-yü te yün-yung.—*YWCS* 1957:7, 23–24. [A random discussion on the usages of set-phrases.]
雨水：漫談成語的運用

8.2.2.3. Usages of Proverbs (2848–2852)

2848   Chu, Chieh-fan: Yen-yü tsai wen-hsüeh shang te ying-yung.—*Wen t'an* 27, 1962, 18–22. [The usages of proverbs in literature.]
朱介凡：諺語在文學上的應用

2849   Chu, Chieh-fan: Hsieh-tso ken yen-yü chih chien.—*Wen t'an* 45, 1964, 23–25; 46, 51–53; 48, 23–26. [The relationship between writing and proverbs.]
朱介凡：寫作跟諺語之間

2850   Ho, Chung-chieh: Tsen-yang yung yen-yü.—*YWHH* 1953:12, 43–51. [How to use proverbs.]
何鍾杰：怎樣用諺語

2851   Hung, Chia-hui: *Wo pu tsai yung ts'o yen-yü.*—Hong Kong: Hsin-feng wen-hua shih-yeh kung-szu, n.d., 242 p. [I will not again misue proverbs.]
洪嘉惠：我不再用錯諺語

2852   Ma, Ch'iu-hua: *Yen-yü yün-yung chih-tao.*—Hong Kong: Chiao-yü shu-tien, n.d., 120 p. [A guide to the uses of proverbs.]
馬秋華：諺語運用指導

8.3. Standardization of Chinese Lexicons (2853–2870)

2853 Cheng, Tien: Hsien-tai Han-yü tz'u-hui kuei-fan wen-t'i.—*Hsien-tai Han-yü kuei-fan . . . wen-chien hui-pien* (0063), 72–80 [Problems in the standardization of Modern Chinese lexicons.]

鄭奠：現代漢語詞彙規範問題

2854 Chou, Ta-fu: Hang-yeh-yü ho wai-lai-yü te kuei-fan-hua.—*CKYW* 1956:9, 18. [The standardization of professional terms and foreign loan-words.]

周達甫：行業語和外來語的規範化

2855 Chou, Ta-fu: Han i yü-yen-hsüeh shu-yü te kuei-fan-hua.—*CKYW* 1956:12, 33. [The standardization of Chinese translations of linguistic terminology.]

周達甫：漢譯語言學術語的規範化

2856 Chu, Po-shih: Shih-fan yüan-hsiao Chung-wen-hsi t'ung-hsüeh yao chung-shih tz'u-yü te kuei-fan-hua.—*YWHH* 1958:6, 31. [Students of Chinese departments of normal institutes and colleges should emphasize the standardization of words and phrases.]

朱伯石：師範院校中文系同學要重視詞語的規範化

2857 Chung, Chao-hu: Tsai t'an kuan-yü chuan-men ming-tz'u te t'ung-i.—*HWTC* 1950:42, 3. [Another discussion concerning the unification of terminology for specialized fields.]

鍾兆琥：再談關於專門名詞的統一

2858 Fu, Tseng-hsiang: Han-yü tz'u-hui kuei-fan-hua yü chien-hua Han-tzu.—*She-hui k'o-hsüeh chi-k'an* 1, 1979, (not seen). [The standardization of Chinese lexicons and simplification of Chinese characters.]

傅贈享：漢語詞滙規範化與簡化漢字

2859 Kuo, Liang-fu: Han-yü tz'u-hui kuei-fan wen-t'i.—*YWYC* 2, 1981, 72–79.

[Problems in the standardization of Chinese lexicons.]

郭艮夫：漢語詞滙規範問題

2860 Lin, T'ao: Hsien-tai Han-yü tz'u-hui kuei-fan wen-t'i.—*YLT* 3, 1959, 48–72. [Problems in the standardization of Modern Chinese lexicons.]

林燾：現代漢語詞滙規範問題

2861 Ling, Yüan: Lüeh t'an yü-hui te kuei-fan-hua.—*YWCS* 1956:1, 19–20. [A brief discussion on the standardization of vocabulary.]

凌袞：略談語滙的規範化

2862 Miao, Mu: Ts'ung san-tsu yü-yen-hsüeh ming-tz'u t'an tao shu-yü kuei-fan-hua wen-t'i.—*WTKK* 1959:11, 16. [A discussion from three groups of linguistic terms to the problem of standardization of terminology.]

苗木：從三組語言學名詞談到術語規範化問題

2863 Ni, Pao-yüan: Ts'u-chin Han-yü tz'u-hui kuei-fan-hua.—*HCTH* 1981:2, 20–32. [To advance the standardization of Chinese lexicons.]

倪寶元：促進漢語詞彙規範化

2864 P'ing, Ch'ün: Pao k'an yao chung-shih tz'u-erh kuei-fan-hua.—*CKYW* 1956:9, 16. [Newspapers and periodicals should emphasize the standardization of words.]

平羣：報刊要重視詞兒規範化

2865 Shen, Chih-yüan: Kuan-yü ming-tz'u t'ung-i kung-tso.—*FITP* 1:3, 1950, 2–3. [Concerning the work in unification of terminology.]

沈志遠：關於名詞統一工作

2866 Shen, T'ung: Hsüeh-shu ming-tz'u te t'ung-i ho hsüeh-shu ming-tz'u te La-ting-hua.—*KHTP* 1956:3, 93–94. [The unification and Latinization of technical terminology.]

沈同：學術名詞的統一和學術名詞的拉丁化

2867 Siao, Jelun: Tui-yü k'o-hsüeh chi-shu ming-tz'u te kuei-fan-hua te chi-tien i-chien.—*YWCS* 1956:1, 21–22. [Several opinions concerning standardization of scientific and technical terminology.]

Siao, Jelun: 對於科學技術名詞的規範化的幾點意見

2868 Wang, Sung-mao: Hsien-tai Han-yü tz'u-hui kuei-fan-hua te wen-t'i.—*CHYY* 1956:11, 35–39. [The problem of standardization of Modern Chinese lexicons.]

王松茂：現代漢語詞滙規範化的問題

2869 Wang, Sung-mao: *T'an-t'an hsien-tai Han-yü tz'u-hui kuei-fan-hua.*—Peking: T'ung-su tu-wu, 1956, 2, 35 p.; *Yü-wen hui-pien* (0058), 52:172. [A discussion on the standardization of Modern Chinese lexicons.] / See (2870).

王松茂：談談現代漢語詞滙規範化

2870 Yüan, Chih: *T'an-t'an hsien-tai Han-yü tz'u-hui kuei-fan-hua.*—*CKYW* 1957:1, 47. [(A review of) *T'an-t'an hsien-tai Han-yü tz'u-hui kuei-fan-hua* (2869).]

元直：『談談現代漢語詞彙規範化』

Part II
Chinese Lexicography

(2871–4165)

1. REFERENCE AND HISTORY (2871–2957)
1.1. Reference (2871–2908)
1.1.1. Bibliographies (2871–2885)

2871 Creamer, Thomas & Hixson, Sandra (comp.), Mathias, James (ed.): *Chinese dictionaries: An extensive bibliography of dictionaries in Chinese and other languages.*—Westport & London: Greenwood Press, 1982, xvi, 446 p./ Comp. & ed. by the Chinese-English Translation Assistance Group (CETA).

2872 Dunn, Robert: *Chinese-English and English-Chinese dictionaries in the Library of Congress.*—Washington, D.C.: Library of Congress, 1977, vii, 140 p./ An annotated bibliography.

2873 Fang, Hou-shu: Chien-kuo san-shih nien lai ch'u-pan tz'u-shu pien-mu.—*TSYC* 1980:1, 201–209; 2, 280–288; 3, 273–282; 4, 283–286; 1981:1, 279–284; 2, 273–282; 3, 279–283. [A catalogue of lexicographical works published during the 30 years since the founding of the P.R.C.]
方厚樞：建國三十年來出版辭書編目

2874 Fang, Hou-shu: Chung-wai yü-wen tz'u-shu ch'u-pan chien-mu (1949–1979).—*Tz'u-tien-hsüeh kai-lun* (2962), 213–225. [A simplified catalogue of the publications of Chinese-foreign dictionaries on language and writing (1949–1979).]
方厚樞：中外語文詞書出版簡目（1949-1979）

2875 Fang, Hou-shu: 1981 nien wo kuo ch'u-pan tz'u-shu pien-mu.—*TSYC* 1982:6, 150–154; 1983:1, 181–185; 2, 180–186; 3, 178–186. [A catalogue of lexicographical works published in China during the year 1981.]
方厚樞：1981年我國出版辭書編目

2876 Hixson, Sandra & Mathias, James: *A compilation of Chinese dictionaries.*—New Haven: Far Eastern Publications, Yale U.,

1975, xi, 87, 37 p./ A preliminary classified listing of Chinese and Chinese-foreign dictionaries.

2877 Ijichi, Yoshitsugu: Eigo ni yoru Chūgokugo jiten.—*Chugoku gogaku jiten* (0037), 430–436. [English-Chinese and Chinese-English dictionaries.]/ Annotated bibliography.
伊地智繼善：英語による中國語辭典

2878 Kondō, Haruo & Murao, Tsutomu: Chū-Chū jiten.—*Chūgoku gogaku jiten* (0037), 416–423. [Chinese-Chinese dictionaries.]/ Annotated bibliography.
近藤春雄、村尾力：中中辭典

2879 Li, Ta-chung: Tz'u-tien-hsüeh lun-wen so-yin.—*TSYC* 1980:3, 285–292; 4, 287–296. [An index to periodical articles on (Chinese) lexicography.]
李大忠：詞典學論文索引

2880 Lin, Szu-te: Chung-wen tzu-tien tz'u-tien chieh-t'i.—*TSCW* 1:3, 1935, 39–42; 5, 1936, 23–28; 7, 42–47; 10, 37–45; 11, 55–58; 12, 61–63. [Explanations on Chinese character and word dictionaries.]/ Annotated bibliography.
林斯德：中文字典辭典解題

2881 Mateos, Fernando, S.J.: Bibliografía lexicografica de la lengua china.—*BAEO* 13, 1977, 71–86./ Annotated bibliography of Chinese dictionaries.

2882 Murao, Tsutomu: Chū-Nichi jiten. Nichi-Chū jiten.—*Chūgoku gogaku jiten* (0037), 424–429. [Chinese-Japanese dictionaries. Japanese-Chinese dictionaries.]/ Annotated bibliography.
村尾力：中日辭典・日中辭典

2883 P'an, Shu-kuang: *Tz'u-tien-hsüeh lun-wen so-yin* pu-pien.—*TSYC* 1981:3, 269–278. [Addenda to *Tz'u-tien-hsüeh lun-wen so-yin* (2879).]
潘樹廣：『詞典學論文索引』補編

2884   U.S. Department of State, Office of External Research: *List of Chinese dictionaries in all languages.* Washington, D.C.: Ditto, 1967, v, 45 p./ Classified.

2885   Wilhelm, Hellmut: Some dictionaries of Chinese technical terms.—*CCS* 13, 1940, 664–676./ Classified.

1.1.2. Guides to Reference Books (2886–2908)

2886   Berton, Peter & Wu, Eugene: *Contemporary China: A research guide.*—Stanford: The Hoover Institution, 1967, xxix, 695 p./ Includes encyclopedias, dictionaries on various subjects; *JCLTA* 3:2, 1968, 76–77, William S. Wong; *Library Journal* 93, 1968, 2640; *Library Quarterly* 38, 1968, 276, T. H. Tsien.

2887   Chang, Ch'i-chung & Shih, Wen-i: *Wen shih kung-chü shu ch'ien-t'an.*—Chengtu: Szu-ch'uan jen-min, 1979, 4, 106 p./ 1–32: Character dictionaries and word dictionaries. [A simple discussion of reference books on literature and history.]
張其中、施文義：文史工具書淺談／1-32：字典、詞典

2888   Chang, Chin-lang: *Chung-wen ts'an-k'ao yung shu chiang-i.*—Taipei: Wen-shih-che, 1976, 3, 717 p./ Chap. 4: Character and word dictionaries; Chap. 5: Ancient and modern encyclopedias. [Lectures notes on Chinese reference books.]
張錦郎：中文參考用書講義／第四章：字典、辭典；第五章：類書、百科全書

2889   Chang, Chin-lang: *Chung-wen ts'an-k'ao yung shu chih-yin.*—Taipei: Wen-shih-che, 1979, 34, 746 p./ Chap. 4: Character and word dictionaries; Chap. 5: Ancient and modern encyclopedias. [A guide to Chinese reference books.]
張錦郎：中文參考用書指引／第四章：字典、辭典；第五章：類書、百科全書。

2890   Chu, T'ien-chün & Ch'en, Hung-t'ien:

Wen-k'o kung-chü shu chien chieh.—Changchun: Chi-lin jen-min, 1981, 3, 4, 326 p./ 1–81: Character dictionaries and word dictionaries. [A brief introduction to reference books on the liberal arts.]
朱天俊、陳宏天：文科工具書簡介／1-81：字典、詞典

2891   Ch'üeh, Hsün-wu: *Tsen-yang shih-yung li-shih kung-chü shu.*—Shenyang: Liaoning jen-min, 1979, 2, 2, 186 p./ 82–111: Character dictionaries and word dictionaries. [How to use reference books on history.]
闕勛吾：怎樣使用歷史工具書／82-111：字典和詞典

2892   Ho, To-yüan: *Chung-wen ts'an-k'ao shu chih-nan.*—Shanghai: Shang-wu, 1938, rev. ed.; Taipei: Wen-shih-che, 1972, rev. ed., 7, 12, 3, 961 p./ Chap. 2: Character dictionaries; Chap. 3: Word dictionaries; Chap. 4: Ancient and modern encyclopedias. [A guide to Chinese reference books.]
何多源：中文參考書指南／第二章：字典；第三章：辭典；第四章：類書百科全書

2893   Li, Chao-ch'üan: T'an yü-wen hsüeh-hsi chung pi pu-k'o-shao te kung-chü shu—tzu-tien.—*Yü-wen* 1, 1976, 42–43. [A discussion on indispensable reference books in learning language and writing—dictionaries.]
李兆權：談語文學習中必不可少的工具書——字典

2894   Li, Chih-chung & Wang, Yin-lan: *Chung-wen ts'an-k'ao yung shu chih-nan.*—Taipei: Cheng-chung, 1972; 1975, 2nd ed., iii, 647 p./ 167–203: Character dictionaries and word dictionaries. [A guide to Chinese reference books.]
李志鍾、汪引蘭：中文參考用書指南／167-203：字典、辭典

2895   Nan-ching ta-hsüeh t'u-shu-kuan, Chung-wen-hsi, Li-shih-hsi (comp.): *Wen shih che kung-chü shu chien-chieh.*—Tientsin:

T'ien-chin jen-min, 1980, [2], 4, 770 p./ 24—99: Looking up characters; 100—196: Looking up words and phrases. [A brief introduction to reference books on literature, history, and philosophy.]
南京大學圖書館、中文系、歷史系：文史哲工具書簡介／24-99: 查文字；100-196: 查詞語

2896 Nunn, G. Raymond: *Asia: reference work—A select annotated guide.*—London: Mansell, 1980, xvi, 365 p./ Q28—Q39: (Chinese) dictionaries.

2897 Ōta, Tatsuo: Chūgoku gogaku annai. —*KGR* 18:3, 1967, 67—83./ 67—69: Dictionaries & encyclopedias. [A (biblio-graphical) guide to Chinese linguistics.]
太田辰夫：中國語學案內／67-69: 辭典、事典

2898 Teng, Ssu-yü & Biggerstaff, Knight: *An annotated bibliography of selected Chinese reference works.*—Cambridge, Mass.: Harvard U. Press, 1971, 3rd ed., xi, 250 p./ Including dictionaries and encyclopedias; *AM* 18, 1973, 248, George Weys; *Pacific Affairs* 45:2, 1972, 322, Edgar Wickberg.

2899 Tseng, Ying-ching: *Chung-kuo li-shih yen-chiu kung-chü shu hsü-lu.*—Hong Kong: Lung-men, 1968, 8, 325 p./ VI: Word dictionaries. [Reference books for research on Chinese history: An annotated bibliography.]
曾影靖：中國歷史研究工具書叙錄／VI: 辭典

2900 Wang, Ming-ken, et al.: *Wen shih kung-chü shu te yüan-liu ho shih-yung.*—Shanghai: Shang-hai jen-min, 1980, 5, 389 p./ Chap. 2: Reference books for finding characters and words. [The origins and uses of reference books on literature and history.]
王明根等：文史工具書的源流和使用／第二章：查考字詞的工具書

2901 Wilkinson, Endymion: *The history of imperial China: A research guide.*— Cambridge, Mass.: East Asian Research Center, Harvard U., distributed by Harvard U. Press, 1973; 1975, 3rd print., xxi, 213 p./ 5—11: Dictionaries; *JAH* 9:1, 1975, 90—91, Dennis Sinor; *JAS* 34:3, 1975, 821—824, N. Sivin.

2902 Wolff, Ernst: *Chinese studies: A bibliographical manual.*—San Francisco: Chinese Materials Center, 1981, xiv, 152 p./ 28—56: Dictionaries; 57—70: Encyclopedias.

2903 Wu, Hsiao-ju & Chuang, Ming-ch'üan: *Chung-kuo wen shih kung-chu tzu-liao shu chü-yao.*—Hong Kong: Shang-wu, 1980, 371 p./ Including dictionaries, dictionaries of set-phrases and proverbs, etc. [A summary of books on reference materials for (the study of) Chinese literature and history.]
吳小如、莊銘權：中國文史工具資料書舉要

2904 Wu, Lei: Wen shih kung-chü shu chi-ch'i yung-fa.—*TS* 1979:1, 153—157; 2, 151—154; 3, 152—157. [Literary and historical reference books and their methods of usage.]
武雷：文史工具書及其用法

2905 Wu-han ta-hsüeh t'u-shu-kuan hsüeh-hsi: *Chung-wen kung-chü shu shih-yung fa.*—Peking: Shang-wu, 1982, [i], 263 p./ Pt. I, Chap. 2: Introduction to character dictionaries and word dictionaries. [Methods of using Chinese reference books.]
武漢大學圖書館學系：中文工具書使用法／上編，第二章：字典、辭典介紹

2906 Wylie, Alexander: *Notes on Chinese literature.*—Shanghai: American Presbyterian Mission Press, 1867, xviii, 260 p.; 1901, rev. ed., xxxix, 307 p.; New York: Paragon Book Reprint Corporation, 1964, xxxx, 307 p.; Taipei: Ch'eng-wen, 1972, repr./ 9—15: Dictionaries; 181—189: Encyclopaedias; *TP* 3, 1902, 340—341, Henri Cordier.

2907   Yao, Lin-yüan (ed. in chief): *Chung-hsüeh yü-wen chiao-shih shou-ts'e* (1011), 514–525: Reference books; 526–532: Methods of consulting reference books and commonly used terminology. [A handbook for middle school language teachers.]
姚麟園主編：中學語文教師手冊／514-525：工具書；526-532：工具書的查檢方法與常用術語

2908   Ying, Yü-k'ang & Hsieh, Yün-fei: *Chung-wen kung-chü shu chih-yin.* — Taipei: Lan-t'ai shu-chü, 1975, [4], 4, 7, 2, 48, 442 p./ *SHJ* 294, 1976, 5–8, Huang Chin-hung, Wu Fu-chu. [A guide to Chinese reference books.]
應裕康、謝雲飛：中文工具書指引／黃錦鋐評，吳福助評

1.2. History (2909–2957)
1.2.1. General Studies (2909–2918)

2909   Chang, Shih-lu: *Chung-kuo yin-yün-hsüeh shih.* — Shanghai: Shang-wu, 1938, 2 vols., 4, 222; 6, 363 p. [A history of Chinese phonological studies.]/ Including rhyme books, *fan-ch'ieh, Chu-yin fu-hao, Gwoyeu Romatzyh,* etc.
張世祿：中國音韻學史

2910   Fang, Hou-shu: Chung-kuo tz'u-shu shih hua.—*TSYC* 1979:1, 217–228. [A discussion on the history of Chinese lexicographical works.]
方厚樞：中國辭書史話

2911   Fukuda, Jōnosuke: *Chūgoku jisho shi no kenkyū.*—Tokyo: Meiji shoin, 1979, 14, 423 p., pl., illus./ *Insha Ronso* 9, 1979, 105–112, Atsuji Tetsuji. [A study of the history of Chinese (character) dictionaries.]
福田襄之介：中國字書史の研究／阿辻哲次評

2912   Hu, P'u-an: *Chung-kuo hsün-ku-hsüeh shih* (0795). [A history of Chinese traditional semantics.]/ Including *Erh-ya, Shih-ming, Fang-yen,* etc.
胡樸安：中國訓詁學史

2913   Hu, P'u-an: *Chung-kuo wen-tzu-hsüeh shih.*—Shanghai: Shang-wu, 1937, 2 vols., xix, 618 p.; Taipei: Shang-wu, 1966, repr. [A history of Chinese logography.]/ Including studies on *Shuo-wen chieh-tzu,* etc.
胡樸安：中國文字學史

2914   Kuo, Wen-jui: Tz'u-shu yüan-liu ch'u t'an.—*HPTH* 1980:1–2, 123–150; 3, 109–120. [A preliminary investigation into the origins and development of (Chinese) lexicographical works.]
郭文瑞：辭書源流初探

2915   Lin, Ch'ing-chang: Chung-wen tz'u-tien te yüan-liu yü fa-chan.—*SPSM* 81, 1980, 12–13. [The origin and development of Chinese language dictionaries.]
林慶彰：中文辭典的源流與發展

2916   Liu, Yeh-ch'iu: *Chung-kuo tz'u-shu shih hua* hsü-lun.—*TSYC* 1981:2, 186–193. [A preface to *Chung-kuo tz'u-shu shih hua* ('History of Chinese lexicographical works').]
劉葉秋：『中國辭書史話』緒論

2917   Liu, Yeh-ch'iu: *Chung-kuo tzu-tien shih lüeh.*—Peking: Chung-hua, 1983, 6, 2, 259 p. [A short history of Chinese dictionaries.]
劉葉秋：中國字典史略

2918   Tōdō, Akiyasu: Chūgoku no jisho no rekishi.—*Chūgoku gogaku jiten* (0037), 410–415. [A history of Chinese lexicographical works.]
藤堂明保：中國の辭書の歷史

1.2.2. Ancient Period (2919–2941)

2919   Chao, Ch'eng: *Chung-kuo ku-tai yün-shu.* —Peking: Chung-hua, 1979, 130 p. [Ancient Chinese rhyme books.]
趙誠：中國古代韻書

2920 Ch'en, Ping-t'iao: Wo-kuo min-tsu yü-yen tui-chao tz'u-tien chien shih.—*TSYC* 1982:1, 173–177. [A simple history of (word) dictionaries on the national minority languages of China.]
陳炳迢：我國民族語言對照詞典簡史

2921 Chiang, Li-hung: Ch'ien Chien-fu hsien-sheng *Chung-kuo ku-tai tzu-tien tz'u-tien kai-lun* hsü.—*HCTH* 1982:3, 21–22. [A preface to Mr. Ch'ien Chien-fu's *Chung-kuo ku-tai tzu-tien tz'u-tien kai-lun* ('An introduction to character and word dictionaries of ancient China').]
蔣禮鴻：錢劍夫先生『中國古代字典辭典概論』序

2922 Chiang, Liang-fu: Sui T'ang Sung yün-shu t'i-shih pien-ch'ien lüeh shuo.—*KWYK* 24, 1943, 6–9. [A brief discussion on the development of the styles and forms of rhyme books during the Sui, T'ang, and Sung dynasties.]
姜亮夫：隋唐宋韻書體式變遷略說

2923 Ch'ien, Chien-fu: Wo kuo ku-tai te hsü-tzu tz'u-tien.—*TSYC* 1980:2, 233–245. [Dictionaries on cenematic words of ancient China.]
錢劍夫：我國古代的虛字辭典

2924 D'Elia, Pasquale M.: Il primo dizionario europeo-cinese e la fonetizzaione italiana del cinese.—*PICO* 19, 1935, 172–178.

2925 Fukuda, Jōnosuke: Jisho hattatsushi jō ni okeru *Goon ruishu shisei henkai* no igi.—*NCGH* 10, 1958, 150. [The significance of *Wu-yin lei-chü szu-sheng p'ien-hai* in the history of the development of character dictionaries.]
福田襄之介：字書發達史上に於ける『五音類聚四聲篇海』の意義

2926 Keiya, Toshinobu: Insho no rekishi.—*Kanji no jōshiki* 2, 1981, 53–61. [A history of rhyme books.]
慶谷壽信：韻書の歴史

2927 Liu, Yeh-ch'iu: *Chung-kuo ku-tai te tzu-tien.*—Peking: Chung-hua, 1963; 1964, 2nd ed., [iii], 149 p.; *Yü-wen hui-pien* (0058), 14:54; Taipei: Ch'i-lin shu-tien, 1970, repr. [Ancient Chinese character (and word) dictionaries.]
劉葉秋：中國古代的字典

2928 Liu, Yeh-ch'iu: Wei Chin Nan-pei ch'ao te chi-pu tz'u-shu.—*TSYC* 1982:4, 150–154. [Several lexicographical works of the Wei, Chin, and Northern and Southern dynasties.]
劉葉秋：魏晉南北朝的幾部辭書

2929 Lu, Chih-wei: T'ang Wu-tai yün-shu pa.—*YCHP* 26, 1939, 83–128, 261–282. [Postscripts to the rhyme books of the T'ang and Five Dynasties.]/ Five essays.
陸志韋：唐五代韻書跋

2930 Ogawa, Tamaki: Sō Ryō Kin jidai no jisho.—*THGRS* 1962, 39–49; *Chūgoku gogaku kenkyū* (0075), 242–253. [Lexicographical works of the Sung, Liao, and Chin dynasties.]
小川環樹：宋遼金時代の辭書

2931 P'an, Shu-kuang: Chung-kuo ku-tai chuan-k'o tz'u-shu man hua.—*TSYC* 1982:6, 124–131. [A random discussion on special-subject lexicographical works in ancient China.]
潘樹廣：中國古代專科辭書漫話

2932 Simon, Walter: The attribution to Michael Boym of two early achievements of Western sinology.—*AM* 7, 1959, 165–169./ *RBS* 5, 1959, 527, M.J. Künstler.

2933 Szczesńiak, Boleslaw: The beginnings of Chinese lexicography in Europe with particular reference to the work of Michael Boym (1612–1659).—*JAOS* 67, 1947, 160–165.

2934 Szczesńiak, Boleslaw: The writings of

Michael Boym.—*MS* 14, 1949–1955, 481–538.

2935 Theunissen, B.: Lexicographia missionaria linguae Sinensis 1550–1800.—*CCS* 16, 1943, 220–242. [Missionary lexicography of the Chinese language 1550–1800.]

2936 Torii, Hisayasu: Shūsui shujin *Shōsetsu jii* o megutte—Kinse Nihon Chūgoku-gogaku shikō no ichi.—*TRGH* 6:2, 1954, 85–104; 6:3, 1955, 334 (supplement). [Centering around Shūsui shujin's *Shōsetsu jii*—Pt. I of A draft of a history of Chinese linguistics in Japan during the 16th-17th century.]
鳥居久靖：秋水主人『小說字彙』をめぐって —— 近世日本中國語學史稿の一

2937 Torii, Hisayasu: Nichijin hensan Chūgoku zokugo jiten no jakkan ni tsuite—Kinse Nihon Chūgokugogaku shikō no yon.—*TRGH* 8:3, 1957, 99–118./ *RBS* 3, 1957, 596, G.B. Downer. [On several Chinese colloquial dictionaries compiled by Japanese—Pt. 4 of A draft of a history of Chinese linguistics in Japan during the 16th-17th century.]
鳥居久靖：日人編纂中國俗語辭典の若干につ いて——近世日本中國語學史稿の四

2938 Torii, Hisayasu: Meiji ki ni okeru Chūgoku zokugo jisho ni tsuite—Nihon Chūgokugogaku shikō no san.—*TRGH* 14:1, 1962, 65–79. [On Chinese colloquial lexicographical works (compiled) during the Meiji period—Pt. 3 of A draft of a history of Chinese linguistics in Japan.]
鳥居久靖：明治期における中國俗語辭書につ いて——日本中國語學史稿の三

2939 Wei, Chien-kung: T'ang Sung liang-hsi yün-shu t'i-chih chih yen-pien.—*KHCK* 3:1, 1932, 133–162, pl. [The development and changes of the system of rules for two types of rhyme books during the T'ang and Sung dynasties.]/ Discusses

the fragments of the printed copy of a rhyme book found in Tunhuang.
魏建功：唐宋兩系韻書體制之演變

2940 Weingartner, Friedrich F.: El primero diccionario europeo-chino.—*BAEO* 11, 1975, 223–227.

2941 Wu, Lieh: Sui T'ang yün-shu te yüan-liu.—*KMWH* 2:1, 1935, 46–51. [The origin and development of Sui and T'ang (dynasty) rhyme books.]
吳烈：隋唐韻書的源流

1.2.3. Modern Period (2942–2957)

2942 Alleton, Viviane: Pratique lexicographie en République Populaire de Chine.—*CLAO* 4, 1978, 57–70.

2943 Alleton, Viviane: Lexicography in the People's Republic of China.—*Chinese language in use* (0062), 69–102.

2944 An, Jan: Shang-wu yin-shu-kuan wai-yü tz'u-tien ch'u-pan te chin ch'i chan-wang. —*TSYC* 1981:2, 92–94. [Prospects in the near future for the publication of foreign language dictionaries by the Commercial Press.]
安然：商務印書館外語詞典出版的近期展望

2945 Biallas, Fr. X.: Recent studies in Chinese lexicography.—*BCUP* 9, 1934, 183–186.

2946 Chang, Ti-hua: Li Chin-hsi hsien-sheng yü tz'u-tien pien-hsieh kung-tso.—*TSYC* 1980:1, 189–200. [Mr. Li Chin-hsi and work in the compilation of dictionaries.]
張滌華：黎錦熙先生與詞典編寫工作

2947 Chou, Tsu-mo: Lüeh lun chin san-shih nien lai Chung-kuo yü-wen tz'u-tien pien-tsuan fa te fa-chan.—*TSYC* 1982:5, 1–6. [A brief discussion on the development of methods for compiling Chinese language dictionaries during the past thirty years.]

周祖謨：略論近三十年來中國語文詞典編纂法的發展

2948 Fang, Hou-shu: 1981 nien wo kuo tz'u-shu pien-tsuan ch'u-pan kai-k'uang.—*TSYC* 1982:6, 147–150. [A general account of the compilation and publication of lexicographical works in China during the year 1981.]
方厚樞：1981年我國辭書編纂出版概況

2949 Lehmann, Winfred (ed.): *Language and linguistics in the People's Republic of China.*—Austin & London: University of Texas Press, 1975, ix, 168 p./ 6: Lexicography; *JCL* 5, 1977, 134–144, Liao Chiu-chung; *JAOS* 98, 1978, 294, Teng Shou-hsin; *JCLTA* 12:1, 1977, Teng Shou-hsin.

2950 Li, Chin-hsi: *Chung-kuo ta tz'u-tien* pien-tsuan-ch'u kai-k'uang.—*CT* 3:10, 1947, 20–24. [A general account of the Editorial Department for *Chung-wen ta tz'u-tien*.]
黎錦熙：『中國大辭典』編纂處概況

2951 Marakuew, A. V.: Die russischen Arbeiten auf dem Gebiete der chinesischen Lexikographie.—*Sinica Sonderausgabe*, 1935, 90–101.

2952 Mathias, Jim & Kennedy, Thomas C.: *Computers, language reform, and lexicography in China.*—[Pullman]: Washington State U. Press, 1980, [iv], 76 p.

2953 Nakajima, Motoki: Bunkakugo no jiten no shūtei o mite.—*AATS* 16, 1972, 8–18. [A glance at the revision of dictionaries after the Cultural Revolution.]
中嶋幹起：文革後の辭典の修訂を見て

2954 Shu, Jen-ch'iu & Ch'ao, Feng: Shang-hai tz'u-shu ch'u-pan-she pa-shih nien-tai kung-tso chan-wang.—*TSYC* 1981:2, 85–91. [Prospects for works by the Shanghai Lexicographical Publishing House in the 1980's.]
束紉秋、巢峯：上海辭書出版社八十年代工作展望

2955 Teng, Hsiao-lin: Lu Hsün hsien-sheng ho tz'u-tien.—*TSYC* 1981:3, 251–254. [Mr. Lu Hsün and dictionaries (that he used).]
鄧嘯林：魯迅先生和詞典

2956 Ting, Chün: Shang-hai tz'u-shu hsüeh-hui ch'eng-li chi yao.—*TSYC* 1982:6, 155–156, 146. [A recording of important facts of the founding of the Shanghai Lexicographical Society.]
丁均：上海辭書學會成立紀要

2957 Tōdō, Akiyasu: Postwar studies of the Chinese language.—*Current trends in linguistics* (0080), 633–644./ 643–644: Lexicography.

2. DEFINITION AND PROBLEMS (2958–3041)

2.1. Lexicography (2958–2973)

2958 Bulakhovskii, L. A. Transl. by Chang, Tsai-te & Yang, Tsung-i: Tz'u-tien-hsüeh. —*TYT* 3, 1981, 179–205. [Lexicography.]
布拉霍夫斯基著，張在德、楊宗義譯：詞典學

2959 Chao, En-chu: Kuan-yü tz'u-tien-hsüeh te shu-yü.—*TSYC* 1981:4, 103–111. [Technical terms concerning lexicography.]
趙恩柱：關於詞典學的術語

2960 Ch'en, Yüan: Shih ta—Kuan-yü tz'u-tien-hsüeh, yu-hüi-hsüeh ho she-hui yü-yen-hsüeh jo-kan wen-t'i te sui-hsiang. —*TSYC* 1982:2, 1–17. [Explaining the meanings of *ta*—Afterthoughts concerning several problems in lexicography, lexicology, and sociolinguistics.]
陳原：釋『大』——關於詞典學、語滙學和社會語言學若干問題的隨想

2961 Ch'en, Yüan: Shih kuei—Kuan-yü yü-i-hsüeh, tz'u-tien-hsüeh ho she-hui yü-yen-hsüeh jo-kan hsien-hsiang te k'ao-ch'a.—*TSYC* 1982:6, 1–8, 169–181. [Explaining the meanings of *kuei*—An examination concerning several phenomena in semantics, lexicography, and sociolinguistics.]
陳原：釋『鬼』——關於語義學、詞典學和社會語言學若干現象的考察

2962 Hu, Ming-yang, et al.: *Tz'u-tien-hsüeh kai-lun.*—Peking: Chung-kuo jen-min ta-hsüeh 1982, 2, 3, 225 p./ *TSYC* 1983:1, 142–147, 97, Wang Yao-nan. [An introduction to lexicography.]
胡明揚等：詞典學概論／汪耀楠評

2963 Huang, Chien-hua: Tz'u-tien lun.— *TSYC* 1983:1, 85–90; 2, 87–98; 3, 51–59; 4, 62–71, 50; 5, 80–86; 6, 63–82. [On dictionaries.]/ An introduction to lexicography.
黃建華：詞典論

2964 Kan, Min-chung: Lüeh t'an Han-yü tz'u-tien-hsüeh shang i-hsieh wen-t'i.— *HMTH* 1980:2, 96–104. [A brief discussion on a few problems in Chinese lexicography.]
甘民重：略談漢語詞典學上一些問題

2965 Kanaoka, Shōkō: Chūgokugo jiten no mondai.—*KGC* 9, 1974, 98–106; 10, 60–68. [Problems of Chinese dictionaries.]
金岡照光：中國辭典の問題

2966 Liu, Dah-jen: Computer technique and Chinese lexicography.—*Chinese Culture* 19:2, 1978, 107–120.
〔劉達人〕

2967 Liu, Ta-jen: Tien-tzu chi-suan-chi yü Chung-kuo tz'u-tien-hsüeh.—*HHYK* 79, 1978, 38–52. [Computer technique and Chinese lexicography.]/ Chinese version of (2966).
劉達人：電子計算機與中國字典學

2968 Riemschneider, Kaspar (ed.): *Probleme der Lexikographie.*—Berlin: Akademie Verlag, 1970, 110 p.

2969 Rowe, A.W.: A Chinese IDS dictionary: a unique challenge?—*Exeter Linguistic Studies* 4, 1979, 104–110./ IDS = Integrated Dictionary Research.

2970 Shcherba, L.V.: Tz'u-tien-hsüeh i-pan li-lun shih lun.—*YIT* 1959:3, 40–51. [A preliminary discussion on general lexicographical theories.]
Shcherba, L.V.：辭典學一般理論試論

2971 Shih, Szu-jen (ed.): *Tz'u-tien-hsüeh lun-wen hsüan i.*—Peking: Shang-wu, 1981, 251 p. [Selected translations of lexicographical articles.]
石肆壬選編：詞典學論文選譯

2972 Wang, Li: Tzu-tien wen-t'i tsa t'an. —*TSYC* 1983:2, 1–9, 144. [Miscellaneous talks on the problems of (character) dictionaries.]/ Discusses various lexicographical problems.

王力：字典問題雜談

2973　Yang, Tsu-hsi: Tz'u-tien-hsüeh shih lun. —*TSYC* 1979:1, 30—47. [A preliminary discussion on lexicography.]

楊祖希：詞典學試論

2.2. Dictionaries (2974—3017)
2.2.1. Character Dictionaries (2974—2977)

2974　Fukuda, Jōnosuke: Jisho ni tsuite.— *Chūtetsubun Gakkaihō* 3, 1978, 16—30. [On character dictionaries.]

福田襄之介：字書について

2975　Tai, Liu-ling: Tzu-tien chien lu.—*WHTS* 7:1, 1935, 1—60; 2, 169—213. [A short discussion on (character) dictionaries.]

戴鎦齡：字典簡論

2976　Wan, Kuo-ting: Tzu-tien lun lüeh.— *TSKC* 1:1, 1926, 61—79. [A brief discussion on (character) dictionaries.]

萬國鼎：字典論略

2977　Yeh, Lai-shih: T'an tzu-tien.—*TPPYK* 1:6, 1934, 274. [A discussion on (character) dictionaries.]

葉籟士：談字典

2.2.2. Word Dictionaries (2978—2984)

2978　Hung, Yen-ch'iu: Hsien-hua tz'u-tien. —*CKYT* 19:4, 1966, 6—9. [A random discussion on word dictionaries.]

洪炎秋：閒話辭典

2979　Kuraishi, Takeshirō: Honyaku to jiten. —*Bungaku* 35:3, 1967, 31—39. [Translations and word dictionaries.]

倉石武四郎：翻譯と辭典

2980　Lin, I-chün: Tz'u-tien ho tz'u-tien.— *TSYC* 1982:6, 122—123, 117. [Dictionary and dictionary.]/ Explaining the differences between the characters 詞 *tz'u* and 辭 *tz'u*.]

林貽俊：『詞典』和『辭典』

2981　Matsumoto, Akira: Goi jiten ni tsuite. —*Chūgokugo* 102, 1968, 33—34. [On (Chinese) vocabulary and dictionaries.]

松本昭：語彙、辭典について

2982　T'ang, Lan: Hsiao-hsüeh tsa-chi (kuan-yü tz'u-tien).—*KWTCK* 3:5—6, 1946, 32—38. [Philological notes (concerning word dictionaries.]

唐蘭：小學雜記（關於詞典）

2983　Wang, Li: Tz'u-tien ho yü-yen kuei-fan-hua.—*TSYC* 1982:4, 56—57. [Word dictionaries and the standardization of language.]

王力：詞典和語言規範化

2984　Wang, Te-ch'un: Lun tz'u-tien te lei-hsing.—*TSYC* 1980:1, 94—106. [On the types of word dictionaries.]

王德春：論詞典的類型

2.2.3. Differentiation (2985—2991)

2985　Chang, Chih-kung (ed. in chief): *Hsien-tai Han-yü* (1316), 340—354: Character and word dictionaries./ Including ancient and modern dictionaries. [Modern Chinese.]

張志公主編：現代漢語／340-354:字典和詞典

2986　Hsü, Ch'ing: Kuan-yü tzu-tien ho tz'u-tien.—*CHYY* 1979:6, (not seen). [Concerning character dictionaries and word dictionaries.]

徐青：關於字典和詞典

2987　Hsü, Ch'ing: *Tzu-tien ho tz'u-tien.* —Wuhan: Hu-pei jen-min, 1981, [ii], 80 p. [Character dictionaries and word dictionaries.]

徐青：字典和詞典

2988　Hu, Yü-shu (ed.): *Hsien-tai Han-yü* (1328), 300—309: Word dictionaries, character dictionaries, and modern Chinese dictionaries. [Modern Chinese.]

胡裕樹主編：現代漢語／300-309:詞典、字典、現代漢語詞典

2989   Jen, Yüan: Lüeh lun hsien-tai tzu-tien yü tz'u-tien te ch'ü-pieh.—*CCSY* 1981:1, 79–82. [A brief discussion on the differences between modern character dictionaries and word dictionaries.]
任遠：略論現代字典與詞典的區別

2990   Liu, Hou-ch'un: Tzu-shu yü tzu-hui.—*CKYT* 47:2, 1980, 74–78. [Character dictionaries and vocabularies.]
劉厚醇：字書與字彙

2991   Yang, Hsin-an: *Hsien-tai Han-yü* (1352), Pt. IV, Chap. VII: Character dictionaries and word dictionaries. [Modern Chinese.]
楊欣安：現代漢語／第四編，第七章：字典和詞典

2.2.4. Chinese Dictionaries and Their Uses (2992–3017)

2.2.4.1. Chinese Dictionaries (2992–3001)

2992   Chang, Shou-pai: Chung-kuo tzu-tien t'ung-lun.—*Ta-hsüeh tsa-chih* 1:6, 1934, 205–208. [A general introduction to Chinese (character) dictionaries.]
張守白：中國字典通論

2993   Cheng, Heng-hsiung: Chung-kuo te tzu-tien yü tz'u-tien.—*T'u-shu-kuan-hsüeh yü tzu-hsün k'o-hsüeh* 7:2, 1981, 204–223, E.S. [Chinese character dictionaries and word dictionaries.]
鄭恆雄：中國的字典與辭典

2994   Ch'eng, Wei-chin: Tzu-tien man t'an chi chien tui Chung-wen tzu-tien te liang-tien ch'i-wang.—*SPSM* 81, 1980, 5–11. [A random discussion on (character) (and word) dictionaries and two expectations for Chinese character dictionaries.]
程維進：字典漫談及兼對中文字典的兩點期望

2995   Koshimizu, Masaru: Chūgokugo no jisho.—*Gakutō* 69:1, 1972, 36–39. [Lexicographical works of the Chinese language.]
輿水優：中國語の辭書

2996   Liu, Yeh-ch'iu: *Chung-kuo te tzu-tien.*—Peking: Shang-wu, 1960, 4, 129 p. [(Character and word) dictionaries in China.]
劉葉秋：中國的字典

2997   Liu, Yeh-ch'iu: *Ch'ang-yung tzu-shu shih chiang.*—Peking: Shang-wu, 1964, 1, 58 p.; *Yü-wen hui-pien* (0058), 15:59. [Ten lectures on commonly used dictionaries.] / Ancient and modern.
劉葉秋：常用字書十講

2998   Ōkawa, Kansaburō: Chūgokugo no jisho.—*Gengo* 9:5, 1980, 41. [Lexicographical works of the Chinese language.]
大川完三郎：中國語の辭書

2999   Orishikise, Akira: Chūgokugo jiten ni tsuite.—*Gengo Bunka* 14, 1977, 70–74. [On Chinese language dictionaries.]
折敷瀨興：中國語辭典について

3000   Sasaki, Toshio: Chūgokugo jiten ni tsuite.—*TSKZ* 67:2, 1973, 28–31. [On Chinese language dictionaries.]
佐佐木敏雄：中國語辭典について

3001   Taishūkan Henshūbu: Chūgoku no jisho.—*Gengo* 4:5, 1975, 31–37, pl. [Lexicographical works of China.]
大修館編輯部：中國の辭書

2.2.4.2. Methods of Using Dictionaries (3002–3017)

3002   Ch'en, Hung-t'ien: Tsen-yang shih-yung tzu-tien ho tz'u-tien.—*Yü-wen chi-ch'u chih-shih* (0076), 63–73. [How to use character dictionaries and word dictionaries.]
陳宏天：怎樣使用字典和詞典

3003   Ch'en, Kang: *Tsen-yang ch'a tzu-tien.*—Shanghai: Hua-tung jen-min, 1952, [ii], 28 p.; *Yü-wen hui-pien* (0058), 13:52. [How to consult a (character) dictionary.]
陳剛：怎樣查字典

3004   Chi, Wei: Ch'a tzu-tien.—*CKYT* 33:5, 1973, 104–105. [Consulting (character) dictionaries.]
季薇：查字典

3005   Chou, Kan: Ch'ing k'ao-lü chien-shao ch'a tzu te chou-che.—*TSYC* 1981:1, 242–243. [Please consider the reduction of trouble in looking up characters (in a dictionary).]
周幹：請考慮減少查字的周折

3006   Ch'üeh, Hsün-wu: *Tsen-yang shih-yung li-shih kung-chü shu* (2891), 83–92: Several methods of consulting character dictionaries and word dictionaries. [How to use reference books on history.]
闕勛吾：怎樣使用歷史工具書／83–92：字典、詞典的幾種查法

3007   Hou, Ch'uan-hsün: *Chung-kuo yü-wen chin-liang.*—Taipei: Wei-hsin shu-chü, 1978, 4, 309 p./ Chap. 2: Methods of consulting dictionaries with radical indexing systems. [A guide to Chinese language and writing.]
侯傳勛：中國語文津梁／第二篇：部首字典檢查法

3008   Hsüan, Ch'ang: T'an-t'an tzu-tien te yung-ch'ü.—*YWHH* 1956: 6, 40–41. [A discussion on the use of (character) dictionaries.]
玄常：談談字典的用處

3009   Hu, K'o-meng: *Tsen-yang yung ni-te kung-chü shu—tzu-tien.*—Hong Kong: Shang-hai shu-chü, 1956, 82 p. [How to use your reference books—(character) dictionaries.]
胡軻蒙：怎樣用你的工具書——字典

3010   Li, Hsüeh: Tsen-yang ch'a tzu-tien.—*YWHH* 1955:6, 39–40. [How to consult a (character) dictionary.]
李學：怎樣查字典

3011   Li, Jui-ch'ing: Chien chieh chi-pen ch'ang-chien te tzu-tien tz'u-shu chi ch'i

shih-yung fang-fa.—*YWTC* 1, 1979, 34–40. [A brief introduction to several commonly seen (character) dictionaries and lexicographical works and their methods of usage.]
李銳清：簡介幾本常見的字典辭書及其使用方法

3012   P'an, Shu-kuang: Tz'u-shu te shih-yung ho ch'uan-po.—*TSYC* 1982:1, 85–91. [The use and dissemination of lexicographical works.]
潘樹廣：辭書的使用和傳播

3013   Pao, K'o-i: *Tsen-yang ch'a tz'u-tien.*—Shanghai: Shang-hai chiao-yü, 1981, 2, 2, 142 p. [How to consult a word dictionary.]
鮑克怡：怎樣查詞典

3014   P'eng, Lang-ping: Chiao hsüeh-sheng ch'a tzu-tien te shou-huo ho ching-yen.—*FCCY* 1961:10, 18. [My gains and experiences from teaching students to consult (character) dictionaries.]
彭浪兵：教學生查字典的收穫和經驗

3015   Wang, Wen-t'ai: Tzu-tien ho tz'u-tien li-yung fa.—*TSCW* 2:5, 1937, 45–50. [Methods in using character dictionaries and word dictionaries.]
王文泰：字典和辭典利用法

3016   Wei, Sheng & Chao, Tseng: T'an-t'an ch'a tzu-tien.—*YWCS* 1954:4, 41. [A discussion on consulting (character) dictionaries.]
渭生、肇曾：談談查字典

3017   Yün, Chuang: Tsen-yang fan-ch'a tzu-tien tz'u-shu.—*KWTCK* 2:5, 1943, 25–27. [How to consult (character) dictionaries and lexicographical works.]
蘊莊：怎樣翻查字典辭書

2.3.   Encyclopedias (3018–3041)

3018   Chang, Ch'en-shih: *Yung-lo ta-tien* man

hua.—*TS* 1979:3, 78–86. [A random discussion on *Yung-lo ta-tien* ('Yung-lo encyclopedia').]

張忱石：『永樂大典』漫話

3019 Chang, Chin-lang: Lei-shu pai-k'o ch'üan-shu.—*Chung-wen ts'an-k'ao . . . chih-yin* (2889), 327–387. [Ancient and modern encyclopedias.]

張錦郎：類書百科全書

3020 Ch'ang, Cheng: Pai-k'o ch'üan-shu san t'i.—*TSYC* 1980:4, 22–34. [Three subjects in encyclopedias.]

常政：百科全書三題

3021 Ch'ang, Cheng: Pai-k'o ch'üan-shu kai-lun.—*TSYC* 1982:5, 21–36. [An introduction to encyclopedias.]

常政：百科全書概論

3022 Ch'en, Hung-t'ien: Chung-kuo li-tai lei-shu.—*Pai-k'o chih-shih* 1979:3, 27–29. [Chinese ancient encyclopedias throughout the ages.]

陳宏天：中國歷代類書

3023 Chiang, Ch'un-fang: Chung-kuo ti-i pu pai-k'o ch'üan-shu.—*TSYC* 1980:4, 1–6, 21. [The first Chinese encyclopedia.] / The forthcoming *Chung-kuo ta pai-k'o ch'üan-shu* ('The great Chinese encyclopedia'); See (3024).

姜椿芳：中國第一部百科全書

3024 Ch'ien, Chung-lien, et al.; *Chung-kuo ta pai-k'o ch'üan-shu* shih hsieh t'iao-mu hsüan k'an.—*TSYC* 1980:4, 58–80. [Selected sample entries from *Chung-kuo ta pai-k'o ch'üan-shu* ('The great Chinese encyclopedia').]

錢鍾聯等：『中國大百科全書』試寫條目選刊

3025 Enoki, Kazuo: Kūringu to Morison—Shina hyakka jiten no hensan o chūshin toshite.—*Nagasawa Sensei Koki Kinen Toshogaku Ronshū* (Tokyo: Sanseidō, 1973), 187–228. [Samuel Couling and George E. Morrison—with special focus

on the compilation of *Encyclopedia Sinica*.]

榎一雄：クーリングとモリソン―― 支那百科辭典の編纂を中心として――『長澤先生古稀記念圖書學論集』

3026 Fang, Jen: Wo kuo tsui tsao tsui ta te pai-k'o ch'üan-shu—*Yung-lo ta tien.* —*TSYC* 1982:2, 190. [The earliest and largest Chinese encyclopedia—*Yung-lo ta tien.*] / See (3018).

方人：我國最早最大的百科全書――『永樂大典』

3027 Ho, To-yüan: Lei-shu pai-k'o ch'üan-shu.—*Chung-wen ts'an-k'ao shu chih-nan* (2892), 99–133. [Ancient and modern encyclopedias.]

何多源：類書百科全書

3028 Hsing, Kuang-tsu: Lun pien-tsuan *Chien-ming Chung-hua min-kuo pai-k'o ch'üan-shu.*—*Tung-hsi wen-hua* 17, 1968, 60–61. [On the compilation of *Chien-ming Chung-hua min-kuo pai-k'o ch'üan-shu* ('A concise encyclopedia of the Republic of China').] / A letter to Mr. Chang Ch'i-yün.

邢光祖：論編纂『簡明中華民國百科全書』（張其昀）

3029 Hu, Tao-ching: Shih-ch'i shih-chi i-k'o nung-yeh pai-k'o te ming chu—*Nung cheng ch'üan-shu.*—*TSYC* 1980:4, 221–229. [A brilliant pearl among the agricultural encyclopedias of the seventeenth century—*Nung cheng ch'üan-shu* ('An encyclopedia of agriculture').] / By Hsü Kuang-ch'i (1562–1633).

胡道靜：十七世紀一顆農業百科的明珠――『農政全書』（徐光啓著）

3030 Hu, Tao-ching: K'o chi pai-k'o *Meng-hsi pi-t'an* ho t'a-te tso-che Shen K'uo.—*TSYC* 1981:2, 226–233. [The scientific and technological encyclopedia *Meng-hsi pi-t'an* ('Meng-hsi's talks on paper')—and its author Shen K'uo (1029–1093).]

胡道靜：科技百科『夢溪筆談』和它的作者沈括

3031 Hu, Tao-ching: *Chung-kuo ku-tai te lei-shu.*—Peking: Chung-hua, 1982, 2, 154 p., pl. [Encyclopedias of ancient China.]
胡道靜：中國古代的類書

3032 Li, Chih-chung & Wang, Yin-lan: Lei-shu, pai-k'o ch'üan-shu.—*Chung-wen ts'an-k'ao . . . chih-nan* (2894), 147–162. [Ancient encyclopedias, modern encyclopedias.]
李志鍾、汪引蘭：類書、百科全書

3033 Lin, Feng: *Pen-ts'ao kang-mu* te chu-che Li Shih-chen.—*TSYC* 1982:2, 165–170. [The author of *Pen-ts'ao kang-mu* ('A compendium of materia medica')—Li Shih-chen (1518–1593).]
林峯：『本草綱目』的著者李時珍

3034 Liu, Yeh-ch'iu: *Lei-shu chien shuo.*—Shanghai: Shang-hai ku-chi, 1980, [iii], 2, 2, 70 p. [A brief discussion on ancient encyclopedias.]
劉葉秋：類書簡說

3035 Liu, Yeh-ch'iu: Lei-shu ch'ang t'an.—*TSYC* 1982:6, 132–138. [Plain talk on ancient encyclopedias.]
劉葉秋：類書常談

3036 P'an, Shu-kuang: *I-wen lei-chü* kai shuo.—*TSYC* 1980:1, 163–173. [A general discussion on *I-wen lei-chü* ('An encyclopedia of arts and letters').]
潘樹廣：『藝文類聚』概說

3037 Sung, Ta-jen: Ku-tai i-yao pai-k'o ch'üan-shu—*Pen ts'ao kang-mu.*—*TSYC* 1982:2, 107–112. [An ancient medical encyclopedia—*Pen-ts'ao kang-mu* ('A compendium of materia medica').]/ By Li Shih-chen; See (3033).
宋大仁：古代醫藥百科全書——『本草綱目』

3038 Teng, Ssu-yü & Biggerstaff, Knight: Encyclopedias.—*An annotated . . . reference works* (2898), 83–128.

3039 Wang, Fu-tseng: Fa-chan wo kuo pai-k'o ch'üan-shu shih-yeh te i-t'iao t'u-ching.—*TSYC* 1979:1, 155–159. [A way of developing the enterprise of (publication of) Chinese encyclopedias.]
王福曾：發展我國百科全書事業的一條途徑

3040 Yang, Chia-lo: Hsüeh-tien yü tz'u-tien.—*TSKHK* 1, 1967, 21–46. [Encyclopedias and word dictionaries.]
楊家駱：學典與辭典

3041 Yü, Kuang-yüan: Kuan-yü pien hao pai-k'o ch'üan-shu te chi-ko wen-t'i.—*TSYC* 1980:4, 7–21. [Several problems concerning good compilation of encyclopedias.]
于光遠：關於編好百科全書的幾個問題

3.   DICTIONARY COMPILATION (3042–3479)

3.1.   General Methods of Compiling Dictionaries (3042–3075)

3.1.1.   General Studies and Problems (3042–3075)

3.1.1.1.   General Studies (3042–3061)

3042   Ch'en, Kuang-yü: Pien tz'u-shu ho ch'a tzu-liao.—*TSYC* 1979:2, 40–42. [The compilation of lexicographical works and the examination of (lexicographical) materials.]
陳光裕：編辭書和查資料

3043   Ch'en, Yüan: Hua ch'ing tz'u-tien kung-tso chung te jo-kan shih fei chieh-hsieh.—*CKYW* 1978:1, 42–51; *Hsien-tai Han-yü . . . tzu-liao* (0064), 434–451. [One should clearly draw several correct and incorrect boundaries in the compilation of word dictionaries.]
陳原：劃清詞典工作中的若干是非界限

3044   Ch'en, Yüan: Pien-hsieh tz'u-shu te ching-shen ho t'ai-tu.—*TSYC* 1981:2, 11–29. [The spirit and attitude of compiling lexicographical works.]
陳原：編寫辭書的精神和態度

3045   Chi, Ch'ang-hung: Kuan-yü tz'u-tien hsi-shou yen-chiu ch'eng-kuo te i-hsieh hsiang-fa.—*YWYC* 1, 1981, 106–110. [A few views concerning the absorption of (previous) research achievements in (the compilation of) word dictionaries.]
吉常宏：關於詞典吸收研究成果的一些想法

3046   Chung-kuo k'o-hsüeh-yüan Shao-shu min-tsu yü-yen yen-chiu-so: *Tz'u-tien pien-tsuan fa lun-wen hsüan i (Ti-i-chi).*—Peking: K'o-hsüeh, 1959, 129 p. [Selected translation of essays on methods of compiling word dictionaries (Vol. I).]
中國科學院少數民族語言研究所：辭典編纂法論文選譯（第一輯）

3047   Han, Ta-hsin: Tzu-tien te fen-pu wen-t'i.—*YWCS* 1954:7, 40. [The problems in the divisions of (character) dictionaries.]
韓大鑫：字典的分部問題

3048   Hang, Wei: T'an ts'ung shih-chi ch'u-fa pien-hsieh tz'u-shu te t'i-hui.—*TSYC* 1983:2, 52–54. [A discussion on personal experiences from the actual situation of setting out to compile lexicographical works.]
杭葦：談從實際出發編寫辭書的體會

3049   Hsieh, Tzu-li: P'i-p'an yü-wen tz'u-tien pien-tsuan kung-tso chung hsing-erh-shang-hsüeh te miu lun.—*CKYW* 1978:3, 215–219. [The fallacious statement of metaphysics in and appraisal of the work of compiling language and writing word dictionaries.]
謝自立：批判語文詞典編纂工作中形而上學的謬論

3050   Huang, Ch'ih-kang: Tz'u-tien te pien-tsuan ho yü-wen yen-chiu te ch'eng-kuo.—*TSYC* 1983:1, 98–102. [The compilation of word dictionaries and the achievements in the study of language and writing.]
黃持剛：詞典的編纂和語文研究的成果

3051   Huang, Chien-hua: Tz'u-tien pien-tsuan wen-t'i.—*TSYC* 1980:2, 97–104. [The problem of compiling word dictionaries.]
黃建華：詞典編纂問題

3052   Liao, Hsien-hui: Chung hsiao hsing tz'u-shu te p'ien-fu.—*TSYC* 1982:3, 124–125. [The length of middle-size and small-size lexicographical works.]
廖顯輝：中小型辭書的篇幅

3053   Lu, Tsung-ta: Ts'ung Tuan Yü-ts'ai te *Shuo-wen chieh-tzu chu* t'an tz'u-shu pien-tsuan.—*TSYC* 1982:3, 63–66. [On the compilation of lexicographical works (as viewed) from Tuan Yü-ts'ai's *Shuo-wen chieh-tzu chu* (3546).]
陸宗達：從段玉裁的『說文解字注』談辭書編纂

3054 Lü, Shu-hsiang: Tz'u-shu kung-tso te chien-k'u ho yü-yüeh.—*TSYC* 1981:2, 1–10. [The arduousness and delight of the work on lexicographical works.]
呂叔湘：辭書工作的艱苦和愉悅

3055 Ni, Li-min: Tz'u-hui yen-chiu yü tz'u-tien pien-tsuan ch'ien t'an.—*TYT* 4, 1982, 16–27. [A simple discussion of the study of lexicons and the compilation of word dictionaries.]
倪立民：詞滙研究與詞典編纂淺談

3056 Pu, Tung-hsin: Tz'u-tien pien-tsuan kung-i-hsüeh.—*TSYC* 1980:3, 123–133. [Technology for compiling word dictionaries.]
卜東新：詞典編纂工藝學

3057 T'ien, Hsi-an: Han-tzu kai-tsao chung tz'u-tien pien-tsuan-fa te chi-ko t'i-i.—*KYYK* 1:7, 1922, 151–153. [Several suggestions for ways of compiling word dictionaries during the reform of the Chinese script.]
田錫安：漢字改造中詞典編纂法的幾個提議

3058 Tu, Ting-yu: Min-chung tz'u-tien pien p'ai wen-t'i.—*CYYMC* 3:3, 1931, 453–460. [Problems in the compilation and arrangement of a popular word dictionary.]
杜定友：民衆詞典編排問題

3059 Wan, Hsiang-ch'eng: Chung-kuo tzu-shu te pien-chih.—*YNLH* 1:3, 1935, 9–23. [The compilation of Chinese (character) dictionaries.]
萬湘澂：中國字書的編製

3060 Wei, Chien-kung: Ts'an-chia tz'u-shu pien-chi ho ku-chi cheng-li kung-tso te t'i-hui.—*CKYW* 1961:3, 9–10; *HCS* 1961:1, 42–44. [Personal experiences from participation in compilation of lexicographical works and the work of putting ancient books in proper order.]
魏建功：參加辭書編輯和古籍整理工作的體會

3061 Yen, Ch'ing-lung: Tz'u-shu pien-tsuan chung te p'ing-heng wen-t'i.—*TSYC* 1979: 2, 35–38. [The problem of balance in the compilations of lexicographical works.]
嚴慶龍：辭書編纂中的平衡問題

3.1.1.2. Problems (3062–3075)

3062 Ch'ao, Feng: Shih lun tz'u-shu te cheng-chih-hsing.—*TSYC* 1979:2, 53–64. [A preliminary discussion on the political nature of lexicographical works.]
巢峯：試論辭書的政治性

3063 Ch'ih, Che: Tz'u-tien yao yu chien-ming-hsing.—*TSYC* 1979:2, 86–90. [Word dictionaries should have simplicity and clarity.]
池哲：辭典要有簡明性

3064 Feng, Ying-tzu: T'an tz'u-shu te wen-ting-hsing.—*TSYC* 1979:2, 81–85. [A discussion on the stability of lexicographical works.]
馮英子：談辭書的穩定性

3065 Han, Jung-shih: Tui shih-yung te tzu-tien tz'u-tien te p'o-ch'ieh yao-ch'iu.—*CKYW* 1956:3, 42–46. [The urgent demand for practical character dictionaries and word dictionaries.]
韓鎔石：對實用的字典詞典的迫切要求

3066 Ho, Mei-ts'en; Mo, Heng & Wu, Ch'ung-k'ang: Tz'u-tien li ju-ho piao-hsien szu-hsiang-hsing.—*CKYW* 1960:9, 401–406. [How to manifest ideology in word dictionaries.]
何梅岑、莫衡、吳崇康：詞典裏如何表現思想性

3067 Hsiao, Chin: To chiang-chiu tien shih-yung-hsing.—*TSYC* 1981:1, 236–237. [Be more particular on the point of practicality (in dictionaries).]
曉津：多講究點實用性

3068 Hsü, Ch'ing-k'ai: Chien-ch'ih tz'u-shu te

k'o-hsüeh-hsing.—*TSYC* 1979:2, 65–70. [The scientific nature of lexicographical works should be insisted upon.]

徐慶凱：堅持辭書的科學性

3069   Kao, Kuang-lieh: Lüeh t'an pien-hsieh tz'u-tien te k'o-hsüeh-hsing.—*CLTH* 1978: 2, 69–74. [A brief discussion on the scientific nature of the compilation of dictionaries.]

高光烈：略談編寫詞典的科學性

3070   Koshimizu, Masaru: Watashi no risō no jisho.—*Kyōgaku* 6, 1978, 2–4. [My ideal dictionary.]

興水優：わたしの 理想の辭書

3071   Koshimizu, Masaru. Transl. by Szu, Ying-ch'i: Li-hsiang te tz'u-shu.—*TSYC* 1981:2, 170–173. [An ideal dictionary.] (3070)

興水優著，斯英琦譯：理想的辭書

3072   Kuan, Szu-chiu: Min-chung tzu-tien te hsü-yao ho nei-jung.—*CHCYC* 23:12, 1936, 63–66. [The needs and contents of a popular (character) dictionary.]

管思九：民衆字典的需要和內容

3073   Ts'ao, Hsien-cho: Kuan-yü tz'u-shu te szu-hsiang-hsing wen-t'i.—*CKYW* 1978:3, 210–214. [Concerning the problem of idealogy in lexicographical works.]

曹先擢：關於詞書的思想性問題

3074   Wang, Li: Li-hsiang te tzu-tien.—*KWYK* 33, 1945, 2–27; *Chung-kuo yü-wen ts'an-k'ao tzu-liao hsüan-chi* (0079), 236–271; *Lung-ch'ung ping-tiao-chai wen-chi* (0086), 345–378. [The ideal (character) dictionary.]

王力：理想的字典

3075   Yang, Tsu-hsi: Chih-shih-hsing—tz'u-shu te chung-hsin.—*TSYC* 1979:2, 71–80. [Knowledge—the center of lexicographical works.]

楊祖希：知識性——辭書的中心

3.1.2. General Methods of Compiling Monolingual Dictionaries (3076–3116)
3.1.2.1. General Studies (3076–3109)

3076   Chang, Chih-i: T'ung-tz'u tz'u-tien pien-tsuan fa te chi-ko wen-t'i.—*CKYW* 1980:5, 353–362. [Several problems of the methods for compiling dictionaries of synonyms.]

張志毅：同義詞詞典編纂法的幾個問題

3077   Chang, Shih-t'ing: Lei-i tz'u-tien te t'e-shu kung-neng.—*TSYC* 1981:4, 150–154. [The special functions of dictionaries of synonymous words.]

張世挺：類義詞典的特殊功能

3078   Chang, Yeh: Ch'ien lun wen-yen hsü-tz'u tz'u-tien te pien-tsuan.—*TSYC* 1982:6, 76–82. [A simple discussion on the compilation of dictionaries of cenematic words from the literary langauge.]

章也：淺論文言虛詞詞典的編纂

3079   Ch'en, Liao: Wen-hsüeh hsing-hsiang tz'u-tien she-hsiang.—*TSYC* 1981:2, 270–272. [Assumptions for a dictionary on literary imagery.]

陳燎：文學形象詞典設想

3080   Ch'en, Liao: Ch'eng-yü tz'u-hui pien li shih tso.—*TSYC* 1982:5, 82–84. [Preliminary notes for compilation of a glossary of set-phrases.]/ Arrangement according to poetic rhymes.

陳燎：成語詞滙編例試作

3081   Ch'en, Ping-hsin: Ta-hsing yü-wen tz'u-tien hsi-shou ku wen-tzu-hsüeh ch'eng-kuo wen-t'i.—*TSYC* 1983:1, 91–97. [The problem of absorbing the achievements of paleography in (the compilation of) large-size language and writing dictionaries.]

陳秉新：大型語文詞典吸收古文字學成果問題

3082   Cheng, Tien, et al.: Chung hsing hsien-tai Han-yu tz'u-tien pien-tsuan fa (ch'u kao).—*CKYW* 1956:7, 31–36, 22; 8,

39–44; 9, 31–36; *Hsien-tai Han-yü . . . tzu-liao* (0064), 384–433. [Methods for the compilation of a middle-size Modern Chinese dictionary (first draft).]/ See (3103).

鄭奠等：中型現代漢語詞典編纂法（初稿）

3083 Ch'iu, Hsing-hsi: Hsiao-hsing yü-wen tz'u-tien ho ch'a-t'u.—*TSYC* 1983:2, 159. [Small-size language and writing dictionaries and their illustrations.]

裘星煕：小型語文詞典和插圖

3084 Chou, Chi-wu: Yin-yü tz'u-tien te tso-yung.—*TSYC* 1981:4, 155–160. [The functions of quotation dictionaries.]

周繼武：引語詞典的作用

3085 Chu, Chih-hsien: Erh-t'ung tzu-tien te yen-chiu.—*CHCYC* 18:3, 1–19. [A study of children's (character) dictionaries.]

朱智賢：兒童字典的研究

3086 Ho, Wei: Kuan-yü pien-tsuan Han-yü fang-yen tz'u-tien te chi-ko wen-t'i.—*CKYW* 1960:7, 331–333. [Several problems concerning the compilation of Chinese dialect dictionaries.]

賀巍：關於編纂漢語方言詞典的幾個問題

3087 Huang, Ching-ming: Wen-yen hsü-tz'u tz'u-shu shuo-lüeh.—*YWHH* 1979:5, 63–64. [A brief discussion of lexicographical works on cenematic words in literary Chinese.]

黃敬明：文言虛詞辭書説略

3088 Liao, Ting-wen: Chien-i pien-hsieh hsien-tai Han-yü fen-lei tz'u-tien.—*TSYC* 1980:4, 244–250. [Suggestions for the compilation of a classified Modern Chinese dictionary.]

廖定文：建議編寫現代漢語分類詞典

3089 Lin, Yü-t'ang: Fen-lei ch'eng-yü tz'u-shu pien-tsuan fa.—*Yü-yen-hsüeh lun-ts'ung* (0072), 307–313. [Methods for compiling a classified dictionary of set-phrases.]

林語堂：分類成語辭書編纂法

3090 Lin, Yü-t'ang: Pien-tsuan i-tien chi-hua shu.—*Yü-yen-hsüeh lun-ts'ung* (0072), 314–324. [A prospectus for compiling a semantic dictionary.]

林語堂：編纂義典計劃書

3091 Liu, Cheng-t'an: Kuan-yü pien-tsuan Han-yü wai-lai tz'u tz'u-tien te i-hsieh wen-t'i.—*TSYC* 1979:1, 104–117. [A few problems concerning the compilation of a dictionary of foreign loan-words in the Chinese language.]

劉正埮：關於編纂漢語外來詞詞典的一些問題

3092 Liu, Shu-hsin: Lun t'ung-i tz'u-tien te pien-tsuan yüan-tse.—*TSYC* 1982:1, 55–65. [On the principles for the compilation of a dictionary of synonyms.]

劉叔新：論同義詞典的編纂原則

3093 Lo, Chu-feng: Shih lun yü-wen tz'u-tien pien-tsuan kung-tso.—*TSYC* 1981:2, 58–73. [A preliminary discussion on the work in compiling language and writing dictionaries.]

羅竹鳳：試論語文詞典編纂工作

3094 Lu, Chi-ch'un: Shih pien i-pu yu yün tz'u-tien.—*TSYC* 1982:1, 51–53. [A preliminary compilation of a dictionary with rhymes.]

陸繼椿：試編一部有韻詞典

3095 Lü, Shu-hsiang: Kuan-yü Han-yü tz'u-tien te pien-chi kung-tso.—*HCS* 1961:1, 12–13; *CKYW* 1961:3, 8–9. [Concerning the work of compiling Chinese word dictionaries.]

呂叔湘：關於漢語詞典的編輯工作

3096 P'an, Cheng: Hsi-wang yu ni-hsü-shih Han-yü tz'u-tien.—*TSYC* 1981:1, 223–234. [Hoping to have Chinese word dictionaries with conversely arranged patterns.]

潘征：希望有逆序式漢語詞典

3097   Ping, Jen: Kuan-yü pien-hsieh t'ung-su tzu-tien te chi-tien i-chien.—*YWHH* 1952:8, 56—58. [Several opinions concerning the compilation of popular (character) dictionaries.]
秉仁：關於編寫通俗字典的幾點意見

3098   Schafer, Edward H.: Thoughts about a students dictionary of Classical Chinese. —*MS* 25, 1966, 197—206.

3099   Shu, Ch'ih: Tsung-ho-hsing tz'u-tien ch'ien t'an.—*TSYC* 1979:2, 33—35. [A simple discussion on integrated word dictionaries.]
舒池：綜合性辭典淺談

3100   T'o, Mu: Yin hsü tzu-tien te yu-yüeh-hsing.—*WTKK* 1960:5, 11—12. [The superiority of phonetically arranged (character) dictionaries.]
拓牧：音序字典的優越性

3101   Ueno, Keiji. Transl. by Lang, Sheng: Pien-chi Han-yü ni-hsü tz'u-tien te kou-szu.—*TSYC* 1981:2, 174—175. [A concept for the compilation of a conversely arranged Chinese word dictionary.] / A partial translation without giving the original source.
上野惠司著，郎生節譯：編輯漢語逆序辭典的構思

3102   Wang, Keng-t'ang: Pien-hsieh yen-yü tz'u-tien te chi-ko wen-t'i.—*TSYC* 1980:4, 236—243. [Several problems in the compilation of a dictionary of proverbs.]
王賡唐：編寫諺語詞典的幾個問題

3103   Wang, Shih-hsiang: Tui *Chung-hsing hsien-tai Han-yü tz'u-tien pien-tsuan fa* te i-chien.—*CKYW* 1957:3, 49. [An opinion on *Chung-hsing hsien-tai Han-yü tz'u-tien pien-tsuan fa* (3082).]
王士襄：對『中型現代漢語詞典編纂法』的意見

3104   Wang, Te-ch'un: Fan-ying shih-tai mai-

po te tz'u-tien—t'an-t'an hsin-tz'u tz'u-tien te pien-tsuan.—*TSYC* 1981:1, 184—189. [Dictionaries which reflect the pulse of the times—a discussion on the compilation of dictionaries of new words.]
王德春：反映時代脈搏的詞典——談談新詞詞典的編纂

3105   Wang, Tzu-ch'iang: Pien-tsuan tsung-ho-hsing tz'u-shu te chi-ko wen-t'i.—*CYTH* 1978:2, 1—8. [Several problems in the compilation of integrated dictionaries.]
王自強：編纂綜合性辭書的幾個問題

3106   Wei, Chü-hsien: Tzu-yüan te pien-tsuan chi-hua.—*SWYK* 1:1, 1939, 3—16; 2, 1—7; 3, 1—14; 4, 1—28; 5—6, 1—18; 7, 1—2; 8, 1—2; 9, 1—2. [Plans for the compilation of an etymological dictionary.]
衛聚賢：字源的編纂計劃

3107   Yang, Yin-shen: Shih t'an pien-hsieh chung-hsing tz'u-shu.—*TSYC* 1980:3, 181—184. [A preliminary discussion on compiling middle-size dictionaries.]
楊蔭深：試談編寫中型辭書

3108   Yen, Shuang & Wang, Tzu-ch'iang: Tsung-ho-hsing tz'u-shu te t'i-li.—*TSYC* 1979:2, 94—99. [The form and arrangement of integrated dictionaries.]
嚴霜、王自強：綜合性辭書的體例

3109   Yü, Yün-hsia: Ni-yin tz'u-tien te i-i ho tso-yung.—*TSYC* 1981:2, 217—221, 251. [The significance and use of a conversely indexed dictionary.]
余雲霞：逆引詞典的意義和作用

3.1.2.2. Cited Monolingual Dictionaries (3110—3116)

3110   Ch'iu, K'o-an: Kuan-yü pien-hsieh *Han-yü pai-hua wen tz'u-tien* te chien-i. —*TSYC* 1979:2, 257—258. [Suggestions concerning the compilation of *Han-yü pai-hua wen tz'u-tien* ('A dictionary of Chinese vernacular literature').]

裘克安：關於編寫『漢語白話文詞典』的建議

3111 Hsü, Tsun: *Kuo-yü ta tz'u-tien* chih
k'ai-mo.—*Pien-ts'e . chou-k'an* 2:1, 1932,
9–11. [A model for *Kuo-yü ta tz'u-tien*
('A comprehensive dictionary of the
National Language').]

須尊：『國語大辭典』之楷模

3112 Liu, Chieh-hsiu: *Han-yü ch'eng-yü k'ao-
shih tz'u-tien* hsüan li.—*CKYW* 1981:6,
432–437. [Selected sample entries from
Han-yü ch'eng-yü k'ao-shih tz'u-tien ('A
dictionary of the sources of Chinese
set-phrases').]

劉潔修：『漢語成語考實詞典』選例

3113 Liu, Fu: Pien-tsuan *Chung-kuo ta tzu-
tien* chi-hua kang-yao.—*TSYC* 1979:1,
83–96. [A projected outline for the
compilation of *Chung-kuo ta tzu-tien*
('A comprehensive Chinese character
dictionary').]

劉復：編纂『中國大字典』計劃綱要

3114 Mei, Chia-chü, et al.: Pien-tsuan Han-yü
lei-i tz'u-tien te ch'ang-shih—*T'ung-i tz'u
tz'u-lin* chien chieh.—*TSYC* 1983:1, 133–
138, 47. [An attempt to compile a
Chinese dictionary of synonymous words
—A brief introduction to *T'ung-i-tz'u
tz'u-lin* ('A grove of synonymous words').]/
See (3115).

梅家駒等：編纂漢語類義詞典的嘗試——『同
義詞詞林』簡介

3115 Pao, K'o-i: Han-yü lei-i tz'u-tien t'an-so
—*T'ung-i-tz'u tz'u-lin* pien hou.—*TSYC*
1983:2, 64–70, 152. [A look into a
Chinese dictionary of synonymous words
—after the compilation of *T'ung-i-tz'u
tz'u-lin* ('A grove of synonymous words').]/
See (3114).

鮑克怡：漢語類義詞典探索——『同義詞詞林』
編後

3116 Wang, Liao-i: *Liao-i hsiao tzu-tien*
ch'u-kao.—*KWYK* 43–44, 1946, 40–52;
Lung-ch'ung ping-tiao-chai wen-chi (0086),

379–406. [A first draft of *Liao-i hsiao
tzu-tien* ('Liao-i's small (character)
dictionary').]

王了一：『了一小字典』初稿

3.1.3. General Methods of Compiling Bilingual Dictionaries (3117–3151)
3.1.3.1. General Studies (3117–3131)

3117 Chang, Chüan-yün: T'an-t'an shuang-yü
tz'u-tien chung te so-lüeh tz'u.—*TSYC*
1981:1, 173–179. [A discussion on
contracted and abbreviated words in
bilingual dictionaries.]

張娟雲：談談雙語詞典中的縮略詞

3118 Ch'en, Ch'u-hsiang: Shuang-yü tz'u-
tien chung te shih i ho fan-i.—*TSYC*
1979:2, 193–201. [The explanation of
meanings and translation in a bilingual
dictionary.]

陳楚祥：雙語詞典中的釋義和翻譯

3119 Ch'en, Chung-ch'eng: Shuang-yü tz'u-
tien chung fa-hsüeh shu-yü te fan-i.—
TSYC 1981:4, 173–180. [The translation
of legal terminology in a bilingual
dictionary.]

陳忠誠：雙語詞典中法學術語的翻譯

3120 Chiang, Hsi-ho: Shuang-yü tz'u-tien i i
wen-t'i.—*TSYC* 1982:3, 35–42. [The
problem of translating meanings in a
bilingual dictionary.]

江希和：雙語詞典譯義問題

3121 Chiang, Hsi-ho: Shuang-yü tz'u-tien
pu-k'o-huo-ch'üeh te tz'u-mu nei-jung.—
TSYC 1982:4, 11–18, 37. [Indispensable
entry content in a bilingual dictionary.]

江希和：雙語詞典不可或缺的詞目內容

3122 Chu, I-ming: Shuang-yü tz'u-tien ju-ho
p'ei li.—*TSYC* 1982:4, 26–29. [How to
pair (equivalent) examples in a bilingual
dictionary.]

竺一鳴：雙語詞典如何配例

3123 Hsiao, Chia-ch'eng: Shuang-yü tui shih

yü-wen tz'u-tien te t'e-tien ho fang-fa. —*TSYC* 1981:3, 208–216. [Special features and methods of contrasting explanations in bilingual language and writing dictionaries.]

蕭家成：雙語對釋語文詞典的特點和方法

3124   Huang, Chien-hua: Shuang-yü tz'u-tien lei-hsing ch'u i.—*TSYC* 1982:4, 1–10. [A preliminary discussion on the types of bilingual dictionaries.]

黃建華：雙語詞典類型初議

3125   Li, Hsi-yin: Shuang-yü tz'u-tien te ling-hun—yü-i tui-pi.—*TSYC* 1980:2, 68–86. [The soul of a bilingual dictionary —contrasting of lexical meanings.]

李錫胤：雙語詞典的靈魂——語義對比

3126   Li, Hsi-yin: Shuang-yü tz'u-tien chung ming-wu tz'u te shih i.—*TSYC* 1982:4, 19–25. [The explanation of the meanings of words for the names of objects in a bilingual dictionary.]

李錫胤：雙語詞典中名物詞的釋義

3127   Li, Nan-ch'iu: Chung-kuo shuang-yü tz'u-tien shih-hua.—*TSYC* 1982:1, 166–172. [A historical account of bilingual dictionaries in China.]

黎難秋：中國雙語詞典史話

3128   Wang, Shu-hsing: Shuang-yu tz'u-tien chung ch'eng-yü yen-yü te fan-i.—*TSYC* 1980:2, 87–96. [The translation of set-phrases and proverbs in a bilingual dictionary.]

王淑馨：雙語詞典中成語、諺語的翻譯

3129   Wei, Kuang-hua: Shuang-yü tz'u-tien chung te tz'u-yu fu-hsien wen-t'i.—*TSYC* 1979:2, 202–210. [The problem of recurrence of words and phrases in a bilingual dictionary.]

韋光華：雙語詞典中的詞語復現問題

3130   Wu, Ying: Shuang-yü tz'u-tien te shou tz'u.—*TSYC* 1982:1, 27–33. [The inclusion of words in a bilingual dictionary.]

吳瑩：雙語詞典的收詞

3131   Yü, Ch'iung-sha (transl.): Shuang-yü tz'u-tien pien-tsuan chung te jo-kan wen-t'i.—*TSYC* 1981:1, 165–172./ Adapted partial translation from Ali M. Al-kasimi's *Linguistics and bilingual dictionaries.* [Several problems in the compilation of bilingual dictionaries.]

于瓊沙譯：雙語詞典編纂中的若干問題

3.1.3.2. Chinese-Foreign Dictionaries (3132–3139)

3132   Beal, Edwin G. Jr.: CETA's response to Chinese-English dictionary needs.— *JCLTA* 11:1, 1976, 58–61.

3133   Chao, Yuen Ren: Problems in Chinese-English-Chinese lexicography.—*JCLTA* 7:3, 1972, 96–102; *Aspects of Chinese sociolinguistics* (0048), 170–179.

3134   Eide, Elling O.: New hope for a Chinese-Enlgish dictionary?—*JCLTA* 10:2, 1975, 36–47.

3135   Ku, Pai-lin: Shuang-yü tz'u-tien te fan-i ho p'ei li wen-t'i—*Han-O tz'u-tien* pien-hsieh te i-hsieh jen-shih.—*TSYC* 1980:2, 58–67. [The problems of translation and pairing of examples in a bilingual dictionary —Some knowledge from compiling *Han-O tz'u-tien* ('A Chinese-Russian dictionary').]

顧柏林：雙語詞典的翻譯和配例問題——『漢俄詞典』編寫的一些認識

3136   Liebenthal, W.: The problem of a Chinese-Sanskrit dictionary.—*MS* 1, 1935–1936, 168–172.

3137   Spies, Gottfried: Die Arbeiten am Chinesisch-deutschen Wörterbuch.—*MIO* 14, 1968, 128–131.

3138   Wang, Tsung-yen: Chao Yüan-jen lun Han-Ying Ying-Han tz'u-tien pien-tsuan fa.—*TSYC* 1982:4, 38–46. [Chao Yuen Ren's discussion on methods of compiling Chinese-English and English-Chinese dictionaries.] / See (3133).

王宗炎：趙元任論漢英、英漢辭典編纂法

3139   Werner, Edward Theodore Chalmers: *A suggestion for the compilation of an alphabetical Chinese-English dictionary.* — Shanghai: Shanghai Times, 1941, 80 p.

3.1.3.3. Foreign-Chinese Dictionaries (3140–3151)

3140   Arita, Tadahiro: Nichi-Kan jiten no mondaiten. — *CGGG* 1959:8, 3–9, 18. [The central problem of Japanese-Chinese dictionaries.]

有田忠弘：日漢字典の問題點

3141   Ch'en, Yü-lun: *Ying-Han hsiao tz'u-tien* te pien-hsieh. — *TSYC* 1981:1, 74–79. [The compilation of *Ying-Han hsiao tz'u-tien* ('A small English-Chinese dictionary').]

陳羽編：『英漢小詞典』的編寫

3142   Chiang, Hsi-ho: Ying-Han tz'u-tien pien-hsieh shih-to. — *TSYC* 1981:4, 213–221. [Tidying up the compilation of English-Chinese dictionaries.]

江希和：英漢詞典編寫拾掇

3143   Hsü, Hsi-hsiang: *Fa-Han tz'u-tien* pien hou so t'an. — *TSYC* 1980:2, 51–57. [Small talk after compilation of *Fa-Han tz'u-tien* (4147).]

徐錫祥：『法漢詞典』編後瑣談

3144   Hu, Tseng-i: Shih lun shuang hsü-lieh cheih-kou te min-tsu-yü — Han-yu tz'u-tien. — *CKYW* 1978:4, 260–264. [A preliminary discussion on the double alignment of arrangement in minority language-Chinese dictionaries.]

胡增益：試論雙序列結構的民族語——漢語詞典

3145   Huang, Chien-hua: Fa-Han tz'u-tien hsüan-tz'u, shih-i, tz'u-li wen-t'i ch'u t'an. — *TSYC* 1979:1, 143–154. [A preliminary investigation into the problems of lexical selection, semantic explanation, and lexical examples for a Franch-Chinese dictionary.]

黃建華：法漢詞典選詞、譯義、詞例問題初探

3146   Kao, Sen: Wai-Han yü-wen tz'u-tien te hsien-tai-hua. — *TSYC* 1980:3, 48–56. [The modernization of foreign-Chinese language and writing dictionaries.]

高森：外漢語文詞典的現代化

3147   Kratochvíl, Pavel, et al.: Some problems of a Czech-Chinese dictionary. — *AO* 30, 1962, 258–313.

3148   P'an, An-jung: Liu Tse-jung ho O-Han tz'u-tien. — *TSYC* 1981:2, 234–244. [Liu Tse-jung and Russian-Chinese dictionaries.] / See (4136), (4137).

潘安榮：劉澤榮和俄漢詞典

3149   Tan, Han-yüan: Ying-Han tz'u-tien te hsiu-ting. — *TSYC* 1981:3, 217–221. [The revision of English-Chinese dictionaries.]

但漢源：英漢詞典的修訂

3150   Wu, Ying: Shih p'ing *Hsin Ying-Han tz'u-tien.* — *TSYC* 1979:1, 134–138, 142. [A preliminary review of *Hsin Ying-Han tz'u-tien* (4103).]

吳瑩：試評『新英漢詞典』

3151   Yen, Ch'ing-hsi: Pien-tsuan *Te-Han tz'u-tien* te i-hsieh t'i-hui. — *TSYC* 1980:2, 42–50. [Some personal experiences in compiling *Te-Han tz'u-tien* (4127).]

嚴慶禧：編纂『德漢詞典』的一些體會

3.1.4. General Methods of Compiling Technical and Special-subject Dictionaries (3152–3171)

3.1.4.1. General Studies (3152–3164)

3152   Chiang, Yü: Chuan-k'o tz'u-tien tsen-yang li mu? — *TSYC* 1982:6, 17–21. [How to establish headings in technical dictionaries?]

江宇：專科詞典怎樣立目？

3153   Fang, Tsu: Chuan-k'o tz'u-tien te

chu-yin.—*TSYC* 1982:6, 46–47. [The phonetic notations of technical dictionaries.]
方祖：專科詞典的注音

3154   Hsiao, Lan: Chuan-k'o tz'u-tien tsen-yang hsüan tz'u?—*TSYC* 1982:1, 34–38. [How to select words for technical dictionaries?]
蕭嵐：專科詞典怎樣選詞？

3155   Hsü, Ch'ing-k'ai: Pien-hsieh chuan-k'o tz'u-tien te jo-kan wen-t'i.—*TSYC* 1981:2, 114–128. [Several problems of compiling technical dictionaries.]
徐慶凱：編寫專科詞典的若干問題

3156   Juan, Chih-fu: Chuan-k'o tz'u-tien t'i-li chung te chi-ko wen-t'i.—*TSYC* 1982:6, 38–45. [Several problems in the general form of technical dictionaries.]
阮智富：專科詞典體例中的幾個問題

3157   K'o, Ch'i: K'o-chi tz'u-t'iao te ch'u-li.—*TSYC* 1981:3, 54–62. [The handling of scientific and technological word entries (in *Hsien-tai Han-yü tz'u-tien*) (1356).]
柯琦：科技詞條的處理

3158   K'o, Jan: K'o-chi chuan-k'o tz'u-tien shih-wen te pien-hsieh.—*TSYC* 1982:6, 30–37. [The compiling of entry explanations in scientific and technological dictionaries.]
柯然：科技專科詞典釋文的編寫

3159   Lin, Feng: K'o-chi chuan-k'o tz'u-tien te ch'a-t'u.—*TSYC* 1982:6, 48–49. [Illustrations in scientific and technological dictionaries.]
林峯：科技專科詞典的插圖

3160   Ni, Chi-kuang: K'o-chi chuan-k'o tz'u-tien te hsüan tz'u ho shih i.—*TSYC* 1981:2, 129–137. [Lexical selection and semantic explanation in scientific technological dictionaries.]
倪繼光：科技專科詞典的選詞和釋義

3161   Pao, K'o-i: Yü-tz'u tz'u-tien chung chuan-k'o shu-yü te hsüan tz'u yü shih i.—*TSYC* 1982:6, 68–75. [Lexical selection and semantic explanation of technical terms in word and phrase dictionaries.]
鮑克怡：語詞詞典中專科術語的選詞與釋義

3162   Yang, Tsu-hsi: Chuan-k'o tz'u-tien pien-tsuan fa ch'u t'an.—*TSYC* 1981:2, 97–113. [A preliminary investigation into methods of compilation for technical dictionaries.]
楊祖希：專科詞典編纂法初探

3163   Yang, Tsu-hsi: Chung-kuo-shih chuan-k'o tz'u-tien te shih i.—*TSYC* 1982:6, 59–67. [Semantic explanations in Chinese-style technical dictionaries.]
楊祖希：中國式專科辭典的釋義

3164   Yen, Ch'ing-lung: Chuan-k'o tz'u-tien te t'e-tien ho yao-ch'iu.—*TSYC* 1982:6, 9–16. [Special features and demands of technical dictionaries.]
嚴慶龍：專科詞典的特點和要求

3.1.4.2. Cited Technical and Special-subject Dictionaries (3165–3171)

3165   Ch'en, Kuang-yü: *Shih-chieh ti-ming tz'u-tien* te pien-hsieh ho ting kao.—*TSYC* 1980:3, 266–271. [The compilation and final draft of *Shih-chieh ti-ming tz'u-tien* ('A dictionary of world place names').]
陳光裕：『世界地名辭典』的編寫和定稿

3166   *Cheng-chih ching-chi-hsüeh tz'u-tien* pien-chi-pu: *Cheng-chih ching-chi-hsüeh tz'u-tien* te pien-hsieh kung-tso.—*TSYC* 1980:3, 257–262. [The work in the compilation of *Cheng-chih ching-chi-hsüeh tz'u-tien* ('A dictionary of political science and economics').]
『政治經濟學詞典』編輯部：『政治經濟學詞典』的編寫工作

3167 Kuo, Ch'ang-sheng & Huang, Chih-hsüeh: *Hua-kung tz'u-tien* te pien-chi. —*TSYC* 1981:1, 198–200. [The compilation of *Hua-kung tz'u-tien* ('A dictionary of the chemical engineering').]
郭長生、黃志學：『化工辭典』的編輯

3168 Liu, K'ang: Pien-hsieh *Shih-chieh ti-ming tz'u-tien* te i-hsieh t'i-hui.—*TSYC* 1979:1, 127–133. [Some personal experiences in compiling *Shih-chieh ti-ming tz'u-tien* ('A dictionary of world place names').]
劉优：編寫『世界地名詞典』的一些體會

3169 Su, Yen-pin & Lin, P'iao-liang: *Fang-chih tz'u-tien* te pien-tsuan yao-ch'iu.—*TSYC* 1981:1, 190–197. [The demands for the compilation of *Fang-chih tz'u-tien* ('A dictionary of the textile industry').]
蘇延賓、林飄涼：『紡織詞典』的編纂要求

3170 Wei, Ch'i-yü, et al.: *Shui-yün chi-shu tz'u-tien* te pien-hsieh.—*TSYC* 1980:1, 139–146. [The compilation of *Shui-yün chi-shu tz'u-tien* ('A dictionary of water transportation technology').]
魏啓宇等：『水運技術詞典』的編寫

3171 Yüan, K'o: *Chung-kuo shen-hua tz'u-tien* t'i ch'i.—*TSYC* 1979:1, 118–126, 47. [A summary note on *Chung-kuo shen-hua tz'u-tien* ('A dictionary of Chinese mythology').]
袁珂：『中國神話辭典』題記

3.2. Lexicographical Entry (3172–3268)
3.2.1. Entry Selection (3172–3190)

3172 Chang, Kung-kuei: Tz'u te t'ung-i-hsing ho tz'u-mu te fen-li wen-t'i.—*TSYC* 1979:1, 60–74. [The problems of idendity of words and separation of lexical headings.]
張拱貴：詞的同一性和詞目的分立問題

3173 Chao, Chen-to: Ta-hsing tzu-tien shou lieh fu-yin-tz'u ch'u i.—*TSYC* 1982:1, 9–15, 26. [My personal opinions on the inclusion and arrangement of disyllabic words in a large-size dictionary.]
趙振鐸：大型字典收列複音詞芻議

3174 Chao, En-chu: Yü-wen tz'u-tien t'iao-mu te shou lieh wen-t'i.—*TSYC* 1982:2, 77–84. [The problem of inclusion and arrangement of entries in a language and writing dictionary.]
趙恩柱：語文詞典條目的收列問題

3175 Ch'en, Yüan: Shih i—Kuan-yü tz'u-tien shou tz'u shih-i te jo-kan sui-hsiang.—*TSYC* 1980:2, 1–19. [Explaining the meanings of *i* ('one')—Several thoughts brought to mind concerning lexical inclusion and semantic explanations in a dictionary.]
陳原：釋『一』——關於詞典收詞、釋義的若干隨想

3176 Chiang, Ch'un-fang & Chin, Ch'ang-cheng: Pai-k'o ch'üan-shu shih tsen-yang hsüan t'iao te?—*TSYC* 1982:1, 1–8. [How the entries of an encyclopedia are selected?]
姜椿芳、金常政：百科全書是怎樣選條的？

3177 Ch'ien, Chien-fu: *Ku chin chien shou, yüan-liu ping chung* sui-hsiang.—*TSYC* 1981:1, 48–52. [Thoughts brought to mind on "Include both old and new, lay equal stress on origin and development."]
錢劍夫：『古今兼收，源流並重』隨想

3178 Kao, Chen-yeh: Ta-hsing Han-yü tzu-tien chung ch'u-li fu-yin-tz'u te chi-tien i-chien.—*TYT* 3, 1981, 65–73. [Several opinions on the handling of disyllabic words in a large-size Chinese dictionary.]
高振業：大型漢語字典中處理複音詞的幾點意見

3179 Li, Fu-keng: Kuan-yü niao pu tzu chung fu-yin tz'u te shou lieh wen-t'i.—*TYT* 2, 1981, 131–138. [Concerning the problems of inclusion and arrangement of disyllabic words in the 'bird' radical section (of a dictionary).]
李福賡：關於鳥部字中複音詞的收列問題

3180   Liu, Ch'ing-lung: *Hsien-tai Han-yü tz'u-tien* te shou tz'u.—*TSYC* 1982:1, 16–26. [Lexical inclusion in *Hsien-tai Han-yü tz'u-tien* (1356).] / See (3183).
劉慶隆：『現代漢語詞典』的收詞

3181   Liu, Shu-hsin: Tz'u-mu te ch'üeh-ting ho tz'u-hui te fan-wei.—*Yü-yen yen-chiu lun-ts'ung* (0074), 162–188. [The determination of lexical headings and the scope of lexical items.]
劉叔新：詞目的確定和詞滙的範圍

3182   Lo, Wei-li: T'an hsiang-kuan t'iao-mu te ch'u-li.—*TSYC* 1981:1, 44–47. [A discussion on the handling of related entries.]
駱偉里：談相關條目的處理

3183   Min, Chia-chi: Lüeh t'an shou tz'u. —*TSYC* 1981:3, 20–29, 41. [A short discussion on the inclusion of words (in *Hsien-tai Han-yü tz'u-tien* (1356).] / See (3180).
閔家驥：略談收詞

3184   Min, Chia-chi: Shou-lu fang-yen tz'u shih yü-wen tz'u-tien te i-hsiang jen-wu. —*TSYC* 1982:6, 97–103. [To collect and record dialect words is one of the tasks of language and writing dictionaries.]
閔家驥：收錄方言詞是語文詞典的一項任務

3185   Mu, Wu-hsiang: Yü-yen huan-ching chung te tz'u ho tz'u-tien t'iao-mu chung te tz'u.—*TSYC* 1981:1, 111–112, 150. [Words in the environs of language and words in the entries of dictionaries.]
穆武祥：語言環境中的詞和詞典條目中的詞

3186   Ning, Chü: Lüeh-t'an tz'u-tien pien-tsuan kung-tso ju-ho ch'u-li tz'u-hui te wen-t'i.—*CKYW* 1956:3, 42–46. [A brief discussion on the problem of how to handle lexical items in the work of dictionary compilation.]
寧榘：略談詞典編纂工作如何處理詞滙的問題

3187   Sun, Ch'ung-i: Kuan-yü tz'u-tien te hsüan tz'u kung-tso.—*CKYW* 1955:12, 28–29; *Hsien-tai Han-yü kuei-fan* . . . *wen-chien hui-pien* (0063), 159–161. [Concerning the work of lexical selection for a dictionary.]
孫崇義：關於詞典的選詞工作

3188   Wang, Chih-fen: Hsüan tz'u shih chi. —*TSYC* 1979:2, 91–93. [Ten taboos in lexical selection.]
王芝芬：選詞十忌

3189   Wang, Chih-i: Yü-wen tz'u-tien chung te pai-k'o tz'u-mu.—*TSYC* 1982:2, 85–92. [Encyclopedic lexical headings in a language and writing dictionary.]
王知伊：語文詞典中的百科詞目

3190   Yen, Ho: Man t'an kuo-le-shih te yü-tz'u.—*TSYC* 1981:3, 126–128. [A random discussion on obsolete words and phrases.]
彥和：漫談過了時的語詞

3.2.2. Character Entry (3191–3201)

3191   Chang, Hsüeh-ming: Lun ta-hsing tzu-tien te ku wen-tzu hsing-t'i chieh-shih. —*TSYC* 1982:3, 77–84. [On the explanation of the forms for ancient writing in a large-size character dictionary.]
張雪明：論大型字典的古文字形體解釋

3192   Ch'eng, Erh-ju: Pien-hsieh ta-hsing Han-yü tzu-tien yao tan-fu-ch'i ch'ing-li wen-tzu te tse-jen.—*TYT* 3, 1981, 22–27. [In compiling large-size Chinese character dictionaries, one should bear the responsibility of putting the writing in order.]
程二如：編寫大型漢語字典要擔負起清理文字的責任

3193   Ho, Ming-yüan: Kuan-yü pien-hsieh sheng p'i tzu.—*TYT* 3, 1981, 109–119. [Conerning the compilation of rarely seen characters.]
賀明元：關於編寫生僻字

3194   Jan, Yu-ch'iao: *Han-yü ta tzu-tien* wei-shen-ma hai yao yung chiu pi-hsing te fan-t'i tzu?—*TYT* 3, 1982, 6–9. [Why *Han-yü ta tzu-tien* ('A comprehensive Chinese character dictionary') still should use the complete characters (= non-simplified characters) of the old-stroke form?]
再友僑：『漢語大字典』爲甚麼還要用舊筆形的繁體字？

3195   Liu, Shu-hsin: Tz'u-tien tzu-t'ou te hsing-chih chi ch'i chu-shih.—*TSYC* 1979: 2, 136–147. [The nature of character headings in dictionaries and their annotations.]
劉叔新：詞典字頭的性質及其注釋

3196   Liu, Yu-hsin: Ta-hsing Han-yü tzu-tien chung te i-t'i tzu, t'ung-chia tzu wen-t'i. —*CKYW* 1979:4, 253–259, 309. [The problem of variant characters and interchangeable loan characters in a large-size Chinese character dictionary.]
劉又辛：大型漢語字典中的異體字，通假字問題

3197   Liu, Yu-hsin: Kuan-yü cheng-li i-t'i tzu te she-hsiang.—*TSYC* 1980:3, 20–35. [Assumptions concerning arrangement of variant characters.]
劉又辛：關於整理異體字的設想

3198   Ma, T'ien-hsiang: Ch'ien i yü-wen tz'u-shu ju-ho ch'u-li t'ung-chia tzu.—*TSYC* 1982:5, 135–140. [A simple discussion on how to handle interchangeable loan characters in a language and writing dictionary.]
馬天祥：淺議語文辭書如何處理通假字

3199   T'ang, Tso-fan: P'o-tu yin te ch'u-li wen-t'i.—*TSYC* 1979:2, 148–158. [The problems in the handling of polyphonous pronunciations (in dictionaries).]
唐作藩：破讀音的處理問題

3200   Ts'ao, Nai-mu: Han-yü tzu-tien, tz'u-tien chung ch'ing-sheng tzu te ch'u-li wen-t'i.—*CYTH* 1979:1–2, 49–51. [The problems in the handling of neutral-tone characters in Chinese character dictionaries and word dictionaries.]
曹乃木：漢語字典、詞典中輕聲字的處理問題

3201   Wu, Ch'i-hsing: T'an t'an tz'u-tien chung te ku chin tzu.—*TSYC* 1982:5, 146–150. [A discussion on ancient and modern characters in a dictionary.]
吳琦幸：談談詞典中的古今字

3.2.3. Semantic Entry (3202–3268)
3.2.3.1. Semantic Heading (3202–3216)

3202   Chang, Ching-shu: Yeh t'an i-hsiang te chien-li yü fen ho.—*TYT* 3, 1981, 74–86. [Also discussing the establishment and the separation and reunion of semantic entries.]
張靜書：也談義項的建立與分合

3203   Chang, Ch'ing-yüan: T'an i-hsiang te chien-li yü fen ho.—*TYT* 1, 1980, 34–68. [A discussion on the establishment and the separation and reunion of semantic entries.]
張清源：談義項的建立與分合

3204   Chang, Hung-fan: Kuan-yü tz'u-shu te lei mu.—*TSYC* 1981:2, 259–269. [Concerning the (semantic) category headings of dictionaries.]
張閎凡：關於辭書的類目

3205   Chao, Chen-to: I-hsiang so t'an—*T'an i-hsiang te chien-li yü fen ho* tu hou.—*TYT* 1, 1980, 69–87. [Small talk on semantic entries—(Notes) after reading *T'an i-hsiang te chien-li yü fen ho* (3203).]
趙振鐸：義項瑣談——『談義項的建立與分合』讀後

3206   Chao, Ying-to: Kuan-yü ch'üeh-li i-hsiang te chi-ko wen-t'i.—*AHTH* 1979:3, 88–96. [Several problems concerning firmly establishing semantic entries (in dictionaries).]
趙應鐸：關於確立義項的幾個問題

3207 Fu, Huai-ch'ing: I-hsiang te hsing-chih
ho fen ho.—*TSYC* 1981:3, 86–94, 112.
[The nature and the separation and reunion
of semantic entries.]
符淮青：義項的性質和分合

3208 Lu, Tsun-wu: Yü-wen tz'u-tien te hu
hsün wen-t'i.—*TSYC* 1982:4, 68–78.
[The problem of (semantic) cross reference
in language and writing dictionaries.]
陸尊梧：語文詞典的互訓問題

3209 P'an, Shu-yang: To i-hsiang kai ju-ho
p'ai-lieh?—*TYT* 1, 1980, 91–94. [How
polysemous entries should be arranged?]
潘述羊：多義項該如何排列？

3210 Shih, An-shih & Wang, Li-chia: Tz'u te
i-hsiang yu-wu yü fen ho wen-t'i.—*YLT*
6, 1980, 210–221. [The problems of the
presence or absence and the separation
and reunion of semantic entries of words.]
石安石、王理嘉：詞的義項有無與分合問題

3211 Tsou, Feng: Lun i-hsiang te kai-k'uo
yü fen ho.—*TSYC* 1980:4, 197–208.
[On the generalization and the separation
and reunion of semantic entries.]
鄒酆：論義項的概括與分合

3212 Tsou, Feng: Yü-wen tzu-tien te i-hsiang
p'ai-lieh.—*TSYC* 1981:3, 95–104. [The
arrangements of semantic entries in language
and writing dictionaries.]
鄒酆：語文字典的義項排列

3213 Wang, Te-ch'un: Yung fen-hsi ta-p'ei
te fang-fa hua-fen i-hsiang.—*Shan-tung
wai-yü chiao-hsüeh* 1981:1, 38–42.
[Delineate semantic entries by using the
methods of investigation of analysis and
collocation.]
王德春：用分析搭配的方法劃分義項

3214 Wang, Yao-nan: To-i-tz'u i-hsiang
te kai-k'uo yü ch'ü-fen.—*TSYC* 1982:2,
99–106. [The generalization and
differentiation of semantic entries for
polysemous words.]

王耀楠：多義詞義項的概括與區分

3215 Wu, Ch'i-hsing: I-hsiang kai shuo.—
TSYC 1982:3, 94–100. [A general
discussion on semantic entries.]
吳琦幸：義項概說

3216 Yeh, Ch'u-ch'iang: T'an i-hsü.—*TSYC*
1980:3, 248–250. [A discussion on the
order of meanings.]
葉楚強：談義序

3.2.3.2. Semantic Explanation (3217–3256)

3217 Chang, Lü-hsiang: Shih lun yü-wen
tz'u-tien chung te pi-yü i.—*TSYC* 1982:3,
101–108. [A preliminary discussion on
metaphorical meanings in a language and
writing dictionary.]
張履祥：試論語文詞典中的比喻義

3218 Chang, Shih-t'ing: Ch'eng-yü shih-i lüeh
i.—*TSYC* 1982:3, 48–55. [A brief
discussion on the explanation of meanings
of set-phrases.]
張世挺：成語釋義略議

3219 Chao, Ying-to: An yü-yen she-hui-hsing
yüan-tse shih-i.—*TSYC* 1982:2, 97–98,
121. [Explaining the meanings according
to sociolinguistic principles.]
趙應鐸：按語言社會性原則釋義

3220 Ch'en, Chung-ch'eng: Man t'an shih-i
te ch'i-i.—*TSYC* 1980:1, 125–127. [A
random discussion on the divergence of
semantic explanations.]
陳忠誠：漫談釋義的歧異

3221 Ch'en, Yüan: Shih i—Kuan-yü tz'u-tien
shou tz'u shih-i te jo-kan sui-hsiang
(3175). [Explaining the meanings of *i*
('one')—Several thoughts brought to mind
concerning lexical inclusion and semantic
explanation in a dictionary.]
陳原：釋『一』——關於詞典收詞、釋義的若
干隨想

3222 Cheng, Yüan-han: T'an t'ung-hsün.—

TSYC 1980:2, 193–198. [A discussion on 'identical (semantic) reference'.]

鄭遠漢：談『同訓』

3223   Chiang, Ch'un-fang & Chin, Ch'ang-cheng: Pai-k'o ch'üan-shu shih wen te chuan-hsieh.—*TSYC* 1982:3, 19–26. [Writing of the entry explanations in an encyclopedia.]

姜椿芳、金常政：百科全書釋文的撰寫

3224   Chiang, Li-hung: Shuo t'ung.—*TSYC* 1980:1, 47–52. [A discussion on *t'ung* ('same as').]

蔣禮鴻：說『通』

3225   Chu, Chu-hsien: Chun-ch'üeh shih-i man t'an.—*TSYC* 1981:1, 134–140. [A random discussion on accurate explanations of meanings.]

祝注先：準確釋義漫談

3226   Chu, Min-ch'e: T'an-t'an t'ung yü t'ung.—*TSYC* 1980:3, 184–186. [A discussion on *t'ung* ('identical') and *t'ung* ('same as').]

祝敏徹：談談『同』與『通』

3227   Fang, Fu-jen: Shih-i wen-t'i sui-hsiang.—*TSYC* 1980:3, 186–188. [Thoughts brought to mind on the problem of semantic explanation.]

方福仁：釋義問題隨想

3228   Fu, Huai-ch'ing: Tz'u te shih-i fang-shih.—*TSYC* 1980:2, 158–169. [Methods for explaining the meanings of words.]

符淮青．詞的釋義方式

3229   Fu, Huai-ch'ing: Ming-wu tz'u te shih-i.—*TSYC* 1982:3, 85–93. [The explanation of the meanings of words for the names of objects.]

符淮青：名物詞的釋義

3230   Han, Ching-t'i: T'ung-i tz'u-yu chi ch'i chu-shih.—*TSYC* 1981:3, 42–53. [Synonymous words and phrases and their annotations (in *Hsien-tai Han-yü tz'u-tien*) (1356).]

韓敬體：同義詞語及其注釋

3231   Hsü, Ch'ing: Tz'u te yü-i-yü ho tz'u-tien.—*TSYC* 1981:1, 87–97. [The semantic field of words and dictionaries.]

徐青：詞的語義域和詞典

3232   Hsü, Ch'ing-k'ai: Ting-i san i.—*TSYC* 1980:3, 57–64. [Three discussion on definitions.]

徐慶凱：定義三議

3233   Hsü, Ch'ing-k'ai: Shih-i shen-hua te t'u-ching.—*TSYC* 1982:6, 22–29. [The path (leading) to a deepening of the explanation of meanings.]

徐慶凱：釋義深化的途徑

3234   Hsü, Kuang-lieh: Kuan-yü yü pu tzu shih-i te chi-ko wen-t'i.—*TYT* 2, 1981, 92–103. [Several problems concerning the explanation of meanings in the 'fish' radical section (of a dictionary).]

徐光烈：關於『魚』部字釋義的幾個問題

3235   Hsu, Kuo-ch'iang: Shih-i ho yü-fa chieh-kou.—*TSYC* 1982:4, 168–169. [Explanation of meanings and grammatical structure.]

徐國強：釋義和語法結構

3236   Hu, Chao-yen: T'an wang-wen sheng-i.—*TSYC* 1980:3, 76–79. [A discussion on *wang-wen sheng-i* ('to misconstrue the meaning of words prima facie').]

胡昭諺：談『望文生義』

3237   Huang, Hung-sen: Ting-i ho ting-hsing hsü-shu.—*TSYC* 1980:4, 35–43. [Definition and qualitative description (for encyclopedic entries).]

黃鴻森：定義和定性叙述

3238   Huang, Li-yeh: Shih-i te k'o-hsüeh-hsing chü-li.—*TSYC* 1980:4, 182–196. [Examples of the scientific nature of semantic explanation.]

黃立業：釋義的科學性舉例

3239   Huang, Yüeh-chou: Ts'ung i tao wan
—shu-yü chung shu-tz'u te ch'ou-hsiang
i.—*TSYC* 1980:4, 209–220. [From one
to ten thousand—the abstract meanings
of numerals in idioms.]
黃岳洲：從一到萬 —— 熟語中數詞的抽象義

3240   Li, Ching-pai: Ts'ung chan tzu te shih-
i k'an chiu tzu-tien te ch'üeh-tien.—*TYT*
1, 1980, 21–33. [The shortcomings of
old (character) dictionaries as seen from
the explanations of meanings of the
character *chan*.]
李景白：從『颭』字的釋義看舊字典的缺點

3241   Li, Hsing-chien: P'ien ho p'ien-ma
chien shuo—tz'u-tien pien-chi ho tz'u
i k'ao-shih chung te i-hsieh wen-t'i.—
Yü-yen yen-chiu lun-ts'ung (0074), 189–
196. [A brief discussion on *p'ien* and
p'ien-ma—a few problems in the compilation of dictionaries and the explanation
of lexical meanings.]
李行健：『騙』和『騙馬』簡說——詞典編輯
和詞義考釋中的一些問題

3242   Li, Hsing-chien: Kai-nien i-i ho i-pan
tz'u-i.—*TSYC* 1981:2, 43–49. [Conceptual
meaning and general lexical meaning.]
李行健：概念意義和一般詞義

3243   Liang, Shih-chung: Lüeh t'an chun-
ch'üeh shih i wen-t'i.—*TSYC* 1980:1,
60–67. [A brief discussion on the
problem of accurately explaining (lexical)
meanings.]
梁式中：略談準確釋義問題

3244   Liang, Shih-chung: Hsiao-hsing tzu-tien
shih-i te chi-ko wen-t'i.—*TSYC* 1982:3,
56–62. [Several problems concerning the
explanation of meanings in a small-size
character dictionary.]
梁式中：小型字典釋義的幾個問題

3245   Liu, Ch'ing-lung: T'an-t'an *Hsien-tai
Han-yü tz'u-tien* te chu-shih hsing-shih.—
YWYC 1982:2, 50–68. [A discussion
on the annotational forms in *Hsien-tai

Han-yü tz'u-tien (1356).]
劉慶隆：談談『現代漢語辭典』的注釋形式

3246   Lu, Fu-ch'ing & Chang, Li-mao: T'an
yü-wen tz'u-shu t'ung ho t'ung te ch'u-li.
—*TSYC* 1982:5, 131–134. [A discussion
on the handling of *t'ung* ('identical') and
t'ung ('same as') in language and writing
dictionaries.]/ See (3224) and (3226).
陸福慶、張立茂：談語文辭書『同』和『通』
的處理

3247   Lu, Tsung-ta & Wang, Ning: Wen-hsien
yü-i-hsüeh yü tz'u-shu pien-tsuan—ku-tai
wen-hsien tz'u-i te t'an-ch'iu.—*TSYC* 1982:
2, 18–28. [Documentary semantics and
the compilation of lexicographical works
—in search of the lexical meanings of
ancient documents.]
陸宗達、王寧：文獻語義學與辭書編纂——古
代文獻詞義的探求

3248   Sheng, Chiu-ch'ou: Tz'u te i-i ho tz'u
te yung-fa.—*TSYC* 1982:2, 93–96. [The
meanings and the uses of words.]
盛九疇：詞的意義和詞的用法

3249   Su, Yüan-lei: Shih-i ting-i chu-i szu
chi.—*TSYC* 1980:1, 124–125. [Four
taboos to pay attention to in semantic
explanations and definitions.]
蘇淵雷：釋義定義注意四忌

3250   Sun, Te-hsüan: Lun shih-i te k'o-hsüeh-
hsing.—*TSYC* 1981:3, 30–41. [On the
scientific nature of semantic explanation
in *Hsien-tai Han-yü tz'u-tien* (1356).]
孫德宣：論釋義的科學性

3251   T'ang, Ch'ao-ch'ün: Shih-i ho li-cheng
te i-chih.—*TSYC* 1982:4, 166–167. [The
uniformity between the semantic explanations and illustrative examples.]
唐超羣：釋義和例證的一致

3252   Wang, Li: Pen ho t'ung.—*TSYC* 1980:1,
50–51. [*Pen* ('original') and *t'ung* ('same
as').]
王力：『本』和『通』

3253   Wang, Yao-nan & Chu, Chu-hsien: Ta hsing yu-wen tz'u-tien shih-i te t'e-tien ho yao-ch'iu.—*TSYC* 1982:3, 27–34. [The special features and demands of semantic explanation in a large-size language and writing dictionary.]
汪耀楠、祝注先：大型語文詞典釋義的特點和要求

3254   Wen, Ta-sheng: Tz'u-tien te k'uo-chu hsing-shih.—*TSYC* 1982:3, 109–116. [The form of parenthetical annotations in a dictionary.]
文大生：詞典的括注形式

3255   Wu, Ch'ung-k'ang: T'an yü-wen tz'u-tien te shih-i.—*CKYW* 1978:3, 220–222, 209. [A discussion on the explanations of meanings in language and writing dictionaries.]
吳崇康：談語文詞典的釋義

3256   Yen, Hsien-chüeh: Tzu-tien li chü ch'u i.—*TYT* 2, 1981, 104–122. [My personal opinion on the illustrative sentences in a character dictionary.]
鄢先覺：字典例句芻議

3.2.3.3. Semantic Source (3257–3264)

3257   Chang, Hsi-liang: Lüeh lun ch'eng-yü tien-ku tsai tz'u-shu chung te li-mu ho shu-cheng.—*CSSY* 1979:3, 54–57. [A brief discussion on the establishment of headings and documented proof of set-phrases and literary allusions in dictionaries.]
章錫艮：略論成語典故在辭書中的立目和書證

3258   Ch'en, Ju-fa: Ch'eng-yü yin yüan wen-t'i lüeh shuo.—*TSYC* 1981:4, 122–124. [A brief discussion on the problem of citing the sources of set-phrases.]
陳汝法：成語引源問題略說

3259   Ch'en, Ju-fa: Tz'u-yü yin yüan wen-t'i erh san chih.—*TSYC* 1982:5, 85–91. [Two or three notes on the problem of citing the sources of words and phrases.]
陳汝法：詞語引源問題二三識

3260   Ch'en, Lin-mao: Yü-wen tz'u-tien shu-cheng shih-tang fen-lei li chü.—*TSYC* 1980:3, 80–87. [Classified examples of inappropriate documented proof in language and writing dictionaries.]
陳林茂：語文詞典書證失當分類例舉

3261   Ch'ien, Chien-fu: *Ku chin chien shou, yüan-liu ping chung* sui-hsiang (3177). [Thoughts brought to mind on 'Include both old and new, lay equal stress on origin and development.']
錢劍夫：『古今兼收，源流並重』隨想

3262   Liang, Chih-i: Ch'eng-yü yin yüan san lun.—*TSYC* 1980:1, 33–46. [A diffuse discussion on citing the sources of set-phrases.]
梁之抑：成語引源散論

3263   Wang, Yao-nan: Ta-hsing tz'u-shu chu-shu ts'ai-liao te yün-yung.—*TSYC* 1981:1, 141–150. [Utilization of materials for annotation and commentary in large-size lexicographical works.]
汪耀楠：大型辭書注疏材料的運用

3264   Yüan, Yü-hsin: Lüeh t'an tz'u-shu te chieh-shuo ho shu-cheng.—*TSYC* 1980:2, 170–180. [A brief discussion on explanation and documented proof of lexicographical works.]
苑育新：略談辭書的解說和書證

3.2.3.4. Grammatical Indication (3265–3268)

3265   Chung, Ch'in: Han-yü tz'u-tien piao-chu tz'u hsing wen-t'i.—*TSYC* 1980:1, 68–93. [The problem of marking lexical nature in a Chinese dictionary.]
鍾梫：漢語詞典標注詞性問題

3266   Lu, Ping-fu: Tung-tz'u ming-tz'u chien lei wen-t'i—yeh t'an Han-yu tz'u-tien piao-chu tz'u-hsing.—*TSYC* 1981:1, 151–155. [The problem of words having functions both as verbs and as nouns—also discussing the marking of lexical nature in Chinese dictionaries.]

陸丙甫：動詞名詞兼類問題──也談漢語詞典
標注詞性

3267   Švarný, Oldřich: Grammatikalische und
phonetische Anzeigen im chinesischen
Wörterbuch.—*Probleme der Lexikographie*
(2968), 53–58; E.S.

3268   Wang, T'ao: Tz'u ts'eng hua-fen yü
ta-hsing Han-yü tz'u-tien te pien-tsuan.
—*TSYC* 1981:2, 74–84. [Division and
delimitation of lexical layer and the compilation of large-size Chinese dictionaries.]
王濤：詞層劃分與大型漢語詞典的編纂

3.3. Phonetic Notation (3269–3357)
3.3.1. General Problems (3269–3278)

3269   Chan, Po-hui: Han-yü tzu-tien tz'u-tien
chu-yin chung te chi-ko wen-t'i.—*CKYW*
1979:1, 72–77. [Several problems in
the phonetic notation of Chinese character
dictionaries and word dictionaries.]
詹伯慧：漢語字典詞典注音中的幾個問題

3270   Hsü, Chin-chih: Tz'u-shu chu-yin hsiao
i.—*TSYC* 1980:1, 130–131. [A brief
discussion on the phonetic notation of
lexicographical works.]
徐近之：辭書注音小議

3271   Huang, Ch'ih-kang: Hsiao t'an hsing-
shih te chu-yin.—*TSYC* 1982:2, 144–145.
[A brief discussion on the phonetic
notation of surnames.]
黃持剛：小談姓氏的注音

3272   Li, Hsin-ti: Chu-yin cha chi.—*TYT*
3, 1981, 95–108. [Notes on phonetic
notation.]
黎新第：注音札記

3273   Min, Chia-chi: Tz'u-tien chu-yin te fen
tz'u lien-hsieh wen-t'i.—*TSYC* 1980:3,
103–115. [The problems of dividing words
and joining syllables in the phonetic
notation of dictionaries.]
閔家驥：詞典注音的分詞連寫問題

3274   Pai, Ti-chou: Han-tzu piao-yin fang-fa
chih yen-chin.—*KHCK* 4:4, 1935, 87–119.
[The evolution of the methods for phonetic
notation of Chinese characters.]
白滌洲：漢字標音方法之演進

3275   Shen, Shih-ying: Han-tzu chu-yin te
li-shih fa-chan.—*HYHH* 1982:2, 50–55.
[The historical development of phonetic
notation for Chinese characters.]
沈士英：漢字注音的歷史發展

3276   T'ien, Kuang-ming: P'u-t'ung-hua ch'ing-
ju te kuei-tiao wen-t'i.—*TSYC* 1981:1,
156–160. [The problem of tonal classification of the (ancient) voiceless entering
tone in the Common Language.]
田光明：普通話『清入』的歸調問題

3277   Ts'ai, Chien-fei: Tzu-tien te chu-yin.
—*CNC* 5:5, 1948, 31–33. [Phonetic
notation of (character) dictionaries.]
蔡劍飛：字典的注音

3278   Yen, Hsüeh-ch'ün: Tsen-yang chu-yin,
ting-yin ho cheng-yin.—*TSYC* 1980:3,
36–47. [How to note pronunciation,
determine pronunciation, and correct
pronunciation.]
嚴學宭：怎樣注音、訂音和正音

3.3.2. *Tu-jo* Method (3279–3286)

3279   Chou, Ho: *Shuo-wen chieh-tzu* tu-jo
wen-tzu t'ung-chia k'ao.—*TSST* 6, 1962,
1–217. [A study on the interchangeability
of the *tu-jo* ('read as') characters in *Shuo-
wen chieh-tzu.*]
周何：『說文解字』讀若文字通假考

3280   Chu, K'ung-chang: Shih *Shuo-wen* tu-jo
li.—*Kuo-ts'ui hsüeh-pao* 7th year, 7:80,
1911, 1–3. [Explanations of the *tu-jo*
('read as') examples in *Shuo-wen.*]
朱孔彰：釋『說文』讀若例

3281   Coblin, W. South: The initials of Xu
Shen's language as reflected in the *Shuowen*
duruo glosses.—*JCL* 6, 1978, 27–75.

〔柯蔚南：『說文』讀若〕

3282 Coblin, W. South: The finals of Xu Shen's language as reflected in the *Shuowen duruo* glosses.—*JCL* 7, 1979, 181–245; C.S.
〔柯蔚南：許慎的韻母系統〕

3283 Lu, Chih-wei: *Shuo-wen chieh-tzu* tu-jo yin ting.—*YCHP* 30, 1946, 135–278. [Collation of the *tu-jo* ('read as') pronunciations in *Shuo-wen chieh-tzu*.]
陸志韋：『說文解字』讀若音訂

3284 Takahashi, Shun: *Setsumon kaiji* doku-jaku kō.—*KGKZ* 4:2, 1936, 92–100. [A study on *tu-jo* ('read as') in *Shuo-wen chieh-tzu*.]
高橋峻：『說文解字』讀若考

3285 Yang, Chien-ch'iao: *Shuo-wen chieh-tzu* te tu-jo.—*TSYC* 1983:3, 87–92. [The *tu-jo* ('read as') in *Shuo-wen chieh-tzu*.]
楊劍橋：『說文解字』的讀若

3286 Yang, Shu-ta: *Shuo-wen* tu-jo t'an yüan.—*Hsüeh-yüan* 1:5, 1947, 71–84; 1:6, 55–68; *Chi-wei-chü hsiao-hsüeh shu-lin* (0091), 109–152. [Tracing the origins of *tu-jo* ('read as') in *Shuo-wen*.]
楊樹達：『說文』讀若探源

3.3.3. *Fan-ch'ieh* Method (3287–3313)

3287 Chao, Lan-t'ing: Tzu-tien tz'u-shu chung chih fan-ch'ieh wen-t'i.—*KYCKN* 3, 1941, 1–2. [The problem with *fan-ch'ieh* in dictionaries and lexicographical works.]
趙藍庭：字典辭書中之反切問題

3288 Chao, Shao-hsien: T'an fan-ch'ieh.—*Han-yü lun-ts'ung* (0087), 50–77. [A discussion on *fan-ch'ieh*.]
趙少咸：談反切

3289 Chou, Ping-chün: *Ku Han-yü kang-yao* (1042), 164–171: *Fan-ch'ieh*. [An outline of Ancient Chinese.]
周秉鈞：古漢語綱要／164–171：反切

3290 Chung, En-t'ai: Fan-ch'ieh lüeh shuo.—*Wen-hsüeh ts'ung-k'an* 1929, 71–77. [A brief discussion on *fan-ch'ieh*.]
鍾恩泰：反切略說

3291 Downer, G.B.: Traditional Chinese phonology.—*TPS* 1964, 127–142./ Centers on the *fan-ch'ieh* method.

3292 Fu, Mao-chi: Fan-ch'ieh chih kou-ch'eng yü shih-yung.—*Wen-hua yüeh-k'an* 1:4, 1942, 31–35. [The structure and usage of *fan-ch'ieh*.]
傅懋勣：反切之構成與使用

3293 Kao, Ming: Fan-ch'ieh ch'i-yüan lun.—*Wen-chiao lun-ts'ung* (Taipei: Cheng-chung, 1971), 153–169. [On the origins of *fan-ch'ieh*.]
高明：反切起源論——『文教論叢』

3294 Li, Wei-fen: Fan-yü ch'i-yüan hsin cheng.—*TCHP* 5, 1966, 85–92; 92: E.S. [New evidence on the origins of *fan-yü* (*fan-ch'ieh* words).]
李維棻：反語起源新證

3295 Liao: Fan-ch'ieh.—*YYWH* 1960:1, 16–17. [*Fan-ch'ieh*.]
廖：反切

3296 Lin, Chin: Fan-ch'ieh shih tsen-ma hui shih?—*YWHH* 1957:4, 26. [What is *fan-ch'ieh*?]
林瑾：反切是怎麼回事？

3297 Liu, P'an-sui: Fan-ch'ieh pu shih yü Sun Shu-jan pien.—*Wen-tzu li-shih-kuan yü ko-ming lun* (0069), 111–122. [*Fan-ch'ieh* did not begin with Sun Shu-jan.]/ Sun Shu-jan or Sun Yen (fl. 200–260 A.D.).
劉盼遂：反切不始於孫叔然辨

3298 Lo, Hsin-t'ien [Lo, Ch'ang-p'ei]: Fan-ch'ieh te fang-fa chi ch'i ying-yung.—*KWYK* 27, 1944, 2–14. [The method of *fan-ch'ieh* and its usage.]
羅莘田〔羅常培〕：反切的方法及其應用

3299   Lu, Chih-wei: Ku fan-ch'ieh shih tsen-yang kou-tsao te?—*CKYW* 1963:5, 349–385. [How were ancient *fan-ch'ieh* constructed?]
陸志韋：古反切是怎樣構造的？

3300   Lung, Hsiao-yün: Fan-ch'ieh ch'i-yüan k'ao lüeh.—*Hsüeh-feng* 2:8, 1932, 26–29. [A brief study on the origins of *fan-ch'ieh*.]
龍笑雲：反切起原考略

3301   Lung, Yü-ch'un: Li-wai fan-ch'ieh te yen-chiu.—*BIHP* 36, 1965, 331–373. [A study of exceptions to *fan-ch'ieh*.]
龍宇純：例外反切的研究

3302   Ogawa, Tamaki: Hansetsu no kigen to shisei oyobi goon.—*GK* 19–20, 1951, 35–42; E.S. [The origins of *fan-ch'ieh* and the four tones and the five sounds (in Chinese).]
小川環樹：反切の起源と四聲及び五音

3303   Ōtaki, Yukiko: Hansetsu hō.—*Kanji no jōshiki* 2, 1981, 44–52. [*Fan-ch'ieh* methods.]
大瀧幸子：反切法

3304   P'an, Tsun-hsing: Fan-yü fan-yin pien.—*CSWS* 1:2, 1932, 275–306. [The distinctions between *fan-yü* ('*fan-ch'ieh* words') and *fan-yin* ('*fan-ch'ieh* phonetic spelling').]
潘尊行：反語反音辨

3305   Shen, Ch'ang-chih: Sheng yün fan-ch'ieh ch'ien shuo.—*Wei-hsing* 1:4, 1937, 3–6; 5, 3–9; 6, 3–8. [A simple discussion on the initials and finals (used) in *fan-ch'ieh*.]
沈昌直：聲韻反切淺說

3306   Shen, Ch'un: Fan-ch'ieh shang hsia tzu ch'ing cho yü sheng-tiao chih kuan-hsi.—*KWYK* 81, 1949, 4–7. [The relationships between voicelessness and voicedness of (initials of) the first and last characters in *fan-ch'ieh* and tones.]
沈純：反切上下字清濁與聲調之關係

3307   Shih, Ts'un-chih: Shuo fan-ch'ieh.—*YWLT* 1, 1981, 51–69. [A discussion on *fan-ch'ieh*.]
史存直：說反切

3308   Ts'ao, Hsien-cho: T'an-t'an fan-ch'ieh.—*TSYC* 1981:4, 125–133, 172. [A discussion on *fan-ch'ieh*.]
曹先擢：談談反切

3309   Wang, Tsu-yu: *Fan-ch'ieh shih-li.*—Peking: Wen-tzu kai-ko, 1957, vi, 60 p./ *CKYW* 1957:12, 46–47, Mi Ch'ing. [Explanations for examples of *fan-ch'ieh*.]
王祖佑：反切釋例／米青評

3310   Yin, Huan-hsien: Fan-ch'ieh shih-li.—*CKYW* 1962:8–9, 384–392. [Explanations for examples of *fan-ch'ieh*.]
殷煥先：反切釋例

3311   Yin, Huan-hsien: Fan-ch'ieh hsü shih.—*STTH* 1963:4, 84–96. [A continuation of explanations (for examples) of *fan-ch'ieh* (3310).]
殷煥先：反切續釋

3312   Yin, Huan-hsien: *Fan-ch'ieh shih yao.*—Chinan: Ch'i-lu shu-she, 1979, [iv], 4, 111 p. [Explanations of the essentials of *fan-ch'ieh*.]
殷煥先：反切釋要

3313   Yü, Ch'ao-yüan: Sheng-yün-hsüeh shang fan-ch'ieh chih yen-chiu.—*WSHK* 1:2, 1935, 161–176. [A study of *fan-ch'ieh* in Chinese historical phonology.]
余超原：聲韻學上反切之研究

3.3.4. Phonetic Symbols and Romanization Systems (3314–3357)

3.3.4.1. Historical Development (3314–3317)

3314   Hu, Ying: San-pai-wu-shih nien lai tsai Chung-kuo te Lo-ma-tzu p'in-yin chi-lüeh.—*KYCK* 105, 1933, Sept. 30; 106, Oct. 7. [A brief record on the romanized spelling in China of the past 350 years.]
胡英：三百五十年來在中國的羅馬字拼音記略

3315   Hu, Ying. Transl. by Shimada, Takashi: Shina ni okeru Shinago romaji kion shi. —*SOS* 2:11, 1940, 2–10. [A history of the romanization of the Chinese language in China.] (3314)
胡英著，島田隆譯：支那に於ける支那語ローマ字記音史

3316   Lo, Ch'ang-p'ei: *Kuo-yin tzu-mu yen-chin shih.*—Shanghai: Shang-wu, 1934; 1947, 4th ed., 5, 4, 80, tab./ 4–9: Bibliography; *Yu-wen hui-pien* (0058), 5:22. [A history of the evolution of the National Phonetic Alphabet.]
羅常培：國音字母演進史

3317   Lo, Ch'ang-p'ei: *Han-yü p'in-yin tzu-mu yen-chin shih.*—Peking: Wen-tzu kai-ko, 1959, 59 p., tab. [A history of the evolution of the Chinese Phonetic Alphabet.]/ A reprint of (3316).
羅常培：漢語拼音字母演進史

3.3.4.2. General Studies (3318–3326)

3318   Anderson, Olov Bertil: *A concordance to five systems of transcription for standard Chinese.*—Lund: Studentlitteratur, 1970, 228 p./ Wade, Simplified Wade, *Gwoyeu Romatzyh*, Pinyin, Yale; *AM* 17:1, 1971, 90, G. Weys.

3319   Chung, Lu-sheng: *Kuo-yü yü-yin-hsüeh.* —Taipei: Yü-wen, 1966; 1970, 5th ed., 11, 486 p./ Chap. 14: Various phonetic symbols for the National Language pronunciation, including Phonetic Symbols and National Language Romanization. [Phonetics of the National Language.]
鍾露昇：國語語音學／第十四章：各式國音符號，包括注音符號、國語羅馬字等

3320   Deeney, John J.: *Style manual and transcription tables for Mandarin.*—Taipei: Western Literature Research Institute, Tamkang College of Arts and Sciences, 1973, v, 190, 46 p.; Taipei: T'ien Audio-Visual Center, 1978, 2nd rev. ed., [iv], 190 p./ Pinyin, Wade-Giles, Yale, *Chu-yin*

fu-hao, Gwoyeu Romatzyh, Simplified *Gwoyeu Romatzyh,* International Phonetic Alphabet; 185–190: Annotated bibliography.

3321   Kuo-li T'ai-wan shih-fan ta-hsüeh Kuo-yin chiao-ts'ai pien-chi wei-yüan hui: *Kuo-yin-hsüeh.*—Taipei: Cheng-chung, 1982, 4, 8, 619 p./ Chap. 12: Various phonetic symbols, including *Gwoyeu Romatzyh* ('National Language Romanization'). [The study of National Pronunciation.]
國立臺灣師範大學國音教材編輯委員會：國音學／第十二章：各式譯音符號，包括國語羅馬字

3322   Legeza, Ireneus László: *Guide to transliterated Chinese in the Peking dialect.* —Leiden: E.J. Brill, 2 vols., 1968–1969, viii, 176; 262 p./ Including *Chu-yin tzu-mu* ('Phonetic Alphabet') system and *Gwoyeu Romatzyh* ('National Language Romanization') system.

3323   Ohio State U., East Asian Languages and Literatures: *Comparative table of Pinyin, Yale, Wade-Giles, Zhuyin zimu and Gwoyeu Romatzyh* (Tonal Spelling) *systems.*—Columbus: Ditto, 1967, 13 p.; repr. in *Current trends in linguistics* (0078), 927–938.

3324   Rygaloff, Alexis: *Tables de concordances pour l'alphabet phonétique chinois.*—The Hague & Paris: Mouton, 1967, 116 p./ Pinyin, *Gwoyeu Romatzyh* ('National Language Romanization'), *Chu-yin fu-hao* ('Phonetic Symbols') in French, German, and Russian transcription systems.

3325   Tien, H.C.; Hsia, Ronald & Penn, Peter: *A guide to the new Latin spelling of Chinese.*—Hong Kong: Oriental Book Co., 1962, 64 p./ Pinyin, *Gwoyeu Romatzyh* ('National Language Romanization'), Wade-Giles and Yale systems.

3326   Yee, Dennis K.: *Chinese romanization self-study guide.*—Honolulu: U. Press of

Hawaii, 1975, vii, 55 p./ Subtitle: Comparison of Yale and Pinyin romanizations; comparison of Pinyin and Wade-Giles romanizations./ PALI Language Texts: Chinese; *JCLTA* 12:2, 1977, 175, R.A. Juhl.

3.3.4.3. *Chu-yin fu-hao* (3327–3339)

3327   Chiao-yü-pu: *Chu-yin fu-hao ch'uan-hsi hsiao ts'e.*—Shanghai: Chung-hua, 1930, (not seen). [A pamphlet for promulgating and learning the Phonetic Symbols.]
教育部：注音符號傳習小冊

3328   Feng, Ch'ang-ch'ing: *Chu-yin fu-hao chiang-i.*—Taipei: Ditto, 1962, 87 p.; 3 tab. [Lectures on the Phonetic Symbols.]
馮長青：注音符號講義

3329   Ho, Jung, et al.: *Kuo-yü chu-yin fu-hao kai-lun.*—Taipei: Kuo-fang-pu tsung cheng-chih-pu, 1956, 206 p. [An introduction to the Phonetic Symbols of the National Language.]
何容等：國語注音符號概論

3330   Hsü, Shih-jung & Sun, Ch'ung-i: *Chu-yin fu-hao chiang-hua.*—Peking: Ta-chung shu-tien, 1952, 2, 2, 2, 76 p. [Lectures on the Phonetic Symbols.]
徐世榮、孫崇義：注音符號講話

3331   Kuan, Yü-shu: *Chu-yin fu-hao k'o-pen.*—Macao: Szu-li ta-yung Kuo-yü chiang-hsi-so, 1937; 1939, 2nd ed., 28 p. [A textbook on the Phonetic Symbols.]
關玉書：注音符號課本

3332   Li, Chin-hsi & Pai, Ti-chou: *Chu-yin tzu-mu wu shih tzu t'ung.*—Peiping: Pei-p'ing wen-hua hsüeh-she, 1929; 1930, 2nd ed., 20 p. [The Phonetic Alphabet self-taught.]
黎錦熙、白滌洲：注音字母無師自通

3333   Lo-shan yeh-jen: Fan-ch'ieh yü chu-yin tzu-mu.—*Kuo-hsüeh tsa-chih* 1, 1933, 1–2; 2, 6–7; 3, 10–11; 4, 14–15. [*Fan-ch'ieh* and the Phonetic Alphabet.]
羅山野人：反切與注音字母

3334   Pai, Yün-hsiang: Chu-yin fu-hao te li-shih.—*TCFY* 28:11, 1973, 5–16. [A history of the Phonetic Symbols.]
白雲祥：注音符號的歷史

3335   T'ai-wan-sheng Kuo-yü t'ui-hsing wei-yüan-hui: *Chu-yin fu-hao.*—Taipei: T'ai-wan shu-tien, 1955, 2, 36 p.; 1960, repr. [The Phonetic Symbols.]
臺灣省國語推行委員會：注音符號

3336   Wan, Ch'ien: *Tsen-yang chiao hsüeh chu-yin tzu-mu.*—Shanghai: Shang-wu, 1952, 2, 22, 8 p. [How to teach and learn the Phonetic Alphabet.]
萬茜：怎樣教學注音字母

3337   Wang, T'ien-ch'ang: Tu-yin t'ung-i-hui yü chu-yin fu-hao.—*SHJ* 350, 1978, 1–7. [The Committee on Unification of Pronunciation and the Phonetic Symbols.]
王天昌：讀音統一會與注音符號

3338   Wang, Yü-ch'uan: *Chu-yin fu-hao te li-shih jen-wu.*—Taipei: T'ai-wan-sheng Kuo-yü t'ui-hsing wei-yüan-hui, 1952, [i], 31 p. [The historical tasks of the Phonetic Symbols.]
王玉川：注音符號的歷史任務

3339   Wu, Chih-hui: Chu-yin fu-hao te lai-yüan yü kung-yung.—*Chiang-su hsün-k'an* 60, 1930, 1–7. [The origins and functions of the Phonetic Symbols.]
吳稚暉：注音符號的來源與功用

3.3.4.4. *Gwoyeu Romatzyh* (National Language Romanization) (3340–3350)

3340   Chang, Shih-lu: Ts'ung fan-ch'ieh tao Kuo-yü Lo-ma-tzu-mu.—*Hsüeh-sheng tsa-chih* 18:11, 1931, 29–40. [From *fan-ch'ieh* to National Language Romanization.]
張世祿：從反切到國語羅馬字母

3341   Chao, Yüan-jen: Kuo-yü Lo-ma-tzu te yen-chiu.—*KYYK* 1:7, 1922, 87–117. [A study of National Language Romanization.]
趙元任：國語羅馬字的研究

3342   Chao, Yüan-jen: *Kuo-yü Lo-ma-tzu ch'ang-yung tzu piao.*—Peiping: Pei-p'ing wen-hua hsüeh-she, 1930, 38 p. [A list of commonly used characters in National Language Romanization.]
趙元任：國語羅馬字常用字表

3343   Chao, Yüan-jen: Kuo-yü Lo-ma-tzu.—*Kuang-po chou-pao* 74, 1936, 37–46. [National Language Romanization.]
趙元任：國語羅馬字

3344   Chao, Yuen Ren: *Mandarin primer.*—Cambridge, Mass.: Harvard U. Press, 1948, viii, 336 p.; *Character text,* 142 p./ *Lg* 25, 1949, 210–215 p.; Chap. 2: Pronunciation and romanization (*Gwoyeu Romatzyh*).
〔趙元任：國語入門〕

3345   Ch'i, T'ieh-hen: *Kuo-yü Lo-ma-tzu.*—Shanghai: Shang-wu, 1930; 1933, 2nd ed., 89 p. [National Language Romanization.]
齊鐵恨：國語羅馬字

3346   Chiang, Ching-fu: *Kuo-yü Lo-ma-tzu.*—Shanghai: Chung-hua, 1936, 52 p. [National Language Romanization.]
蔣鏡夫：國語羅馬字

3347   Hsiao, Chia-lin: *Kuo-yü Lo-ma-tzu ju-men.*—Peiping: Kuo-yü Lo-ma-tzu ts'u-chin-hui, 1932, (not seen). [A primer of National Language Romanization.]
蕭家霖：國語羅馬字入門

3348   Kuo-yü chou-k'an-she (comp.): *Kuo-yü Lo-ma-tzu sheng-tiao p'in-fa piao.*—Shang-hai: Shang-wu, 1936, 6 p. [A table of the methods of spelling tones in National Language Romanization.]
國語週刊社編：國語羅馬字聲調拼法表

3349   Li, Chin-hsi: Kuo-yü Lo-ma-tzu kung-pu ching-kuo shu-lüeh.—*STKT* 1:3, 1932, 1–19. [A brief account of the course of the promulgation of National Language Romanization.]
黎錦熙：國語羅馬字公佈經過述略

3350   Simon, Walter: *The new official Chinese Latin script—Gwoyeu Romatzyh.*—London: A. Prosthain, 1942, 63 p./ With tables, rules, illustrative examples.

3.3.4.5. *Pinyin* (3351–3357)

3351   Chung-kuo wen-tzu kai-ko wei-yüan-hui t'ui-kuang-ch'u: *Han-yü p'in-yin kuang-po chiang-tso.*—Peking: Wen-tzu kai-ko, 1965, [ii], 22 p.; 1974, new ed., 32 p.; Hong Kong: San-lien, 1974, repr. [A broadcast lecture on Chinese Pinyin.]
中國文字改革委員會推廣處：漢語拼音廣播講座

3352   Hsü, Shih-jung: *Han-yü p'in-yin tzu-mu chiao-hsüeh kuang-po chiang-tso.*—Peking: Wen-tzu kai-ko, 1958, [v], 24 p. [A broadcast lecture on the teaching and learning of the Chinese Pinyin Alphabet.]
徐世榮：漢語拼音字母教學廣播講座

3353   Kuo-wu yüan: *Han-yü p'in-yin fang-an.*—Peking: Wen-tzu kai-ko, 1958, [ii], 18 p. [A scheme for a Chinese Pinyin.]
國務院：漢語拼音方案

3354   San-lien shu-tien: *Han-yü p'in-yin chien-i tu-pen.*—Hong Kong: Ditto, 1976, [ii], 28 p. [A simple and easy reader of Chinese Pinyin.]
三聯書店：漢語拼音簡易讀本

3355   Shang-hai chiao-yü ch'u-pan-she: *Han-tzu p'in-yin chien-tzu.*—Shanghai: Ditto, 1958; 1963, rev. ed.; 1973, repr.; 1980, new 3rd ed., 20, 281 p./ 3–5: A scheme for a Chinese Pinyin. [A Pinyin index to Chinese characters.]
上海教育出版社：漢字拼音檢字／3-5：漢語拼音方案

3356   Stimson, Hugh M.: *Introduction to Chinese pronunciation and the Pinyin romanization.*—New Haven: Far Eastern Publications, Yale U., 1975, iii, 36 p./ *JCLTA* 12:2, 1977, 175, R.A. Juhl.

3357   T'ang, Hung: *Pei-ching-hua yü Han-yü p'in-yin.*—Hong Kong: Shangh-hai shu-chü, 1974, 1979, 5th print., 2, 101 p. [The Peking dialect and Chinese Pinyin.]
唐宏：北京話與漢語拼音

3.4. Character Indexing (3358–3479)
3.4.1. Historical Development (3358–3361)

3358   Chiang, I-ch'ien: Han-tzu chien-tzu-fa yen-ko shih lüeh chi chin-tai ch'i-shih-ch'i chung hsin fa piao.—*TSKC* 7:4, 1933, 631–654; 8:1, 1934, 75–133. [A short history of the development of indexing systems for Chinese characters and a table of seventy-seven new methods in recent times.]
蔣一前：漢字檢字法沿革史略及近代七十七種新法表

3359   Fukuda, Jōnosuke: *Setsumon kaiji* ni kanrenshita kenji no sho.—*OKHB* 21, 1964, 32–38. [Lexicographical works related to the character indexing (system) of *Shuo-wen chieh-tzu.*]
福田襄之介：『説文解字』に關連した檢字の書

3360   Su, Shang-yao: T'an chien-tzu-fa te yen-chin.—*HWSC* 25, 1981, 24–31. [A discussion on the evolution of character indexing systems.]
蘇尚耀：談檢字法的演進

3361   Sun, Kung-wang: Han-tzu ch'a-tzu-fa te hui-ku.—*TSYC* 1980:3, 240–247. [A retrospective view of character indexing systems for Chinese characters.]
孫公望：漢字查字法的回顧

3.4.2. General Studies (3362–3380)

3362   Chang, Hsi-kuo: Chu-yin chien-tzu ho Chung-wen chi-suan-chi.—*CKYT* 32:1, 1973, 4–9. [Phonetic indexing of characters and Chinese language computers.]
張系國：注音檢字和中文計算機

3363   Ch'eng, Yang-chih: Kuan-yü t'ung-i kai-ko ch'a-tzu-fa te chien-i.—*YPTH* 1977:4, 81–85. [Suggestions concerning unified reform of character indexing systems.]
程養之：關於統一改革查字法的建議

3364   Ch'ien, Ya-hsin: P'ai-chien-fa te yüan-li.—*WHTS* 4:1, 1932, 7–12. [The principles of arrangement of indexing systems.]
錢亞新：排檢法的原理

3365   Dougherty, Ching-yi; Lamb, Sydney M. & Martin, Samuel E.: *Chinese character indexes:* 1. *Telegraphic code index;* 2. *Romanization index;* 3. *Radical index;* 4. *Total stroke count index;* 5. *Four Corner system index.*—Berkeley & Los Angeles: U. of California Press, 1963, xxxi, 364; 364; 364; 264; 364 p./ *Lg* 39, 1963, 681–684, H.M. Stimson; *GK* 45, 1963, 78–81, Tōdō Akiyasu.
藤堂明保評

3366   Hsia, Yün-chung: Han-tzu pi-hua pi-hsing chien-tzu-fa ying-kai kuei-fan-hua.—*TSYC* 1980:3, 251–254. [The stroke and form character indexing systems for Chinese characters should be standardized.]
夏允中：漢字筆劃筆形檢字法應該規範化

3367   Hsieh, San-pao: Chien-tzu wen-t'i yen-chiu ts'ai-liao.—*CHCY* 1, 1934, 100–102. [Materials for the study of the problems in character indexing.]
謝三寶：檢字問題研究材料

3368   Kang, Kuo: Han-tzu ch'a-tzu-fa te kuei-fan wen-t'i.—*WTKK* 1961:8–9, 50–52. [The problem of standardization of Chinese character indexing systems.]
剛果：漢字查字法的規範問題

3369   Liu, Ju-shui: Han-tzu ch'a-tzu-fa ying-kai t'ung-i.—*TSYC* 1980:1, 131–132.

[The character indexing systems for Chinese characters should be unified.]
劉如水：漢字查字法應該統一

3370 Shih, Ts'un-chih: Shih lun Han-tzu p'ai-chien wen-t'i.—*HTST* 1960:1, 101–116. [A preliminary discussion on the problems of arrangement and indexing of Chinese characters.]
史存直：試論漢字排檢問題

3371 Sui, Shu-sen: Ch'ang-yung tzu-tien tz'u-tien ho chien-tzu-fa.—*Yü-wen hsüeh-hsi te chi-ch'u* (0055), 267–314. [Commonly used character and phrase dictionaries and character indexing systems.]
隋樹森：常用字典詞典和檢字法

3372 Ts'ai, Chien-fei: Lueh t'an chien-tzu-fa.—*CNC* 4:3, 1947, 21–22. [A brief discussion on character indexing systems.]
蔡劍飛：略談檢字法

3373 Ts'ai, Yung-fei: Lun tang-ch'ien Han-tzu chien-tzu-fa yen-chiu te chung-ta i-i—chien chien chieh Han-tzu k'uai-su ch'a-tzu-fa.—*YPTH* 1977:4, 86–87. [On the significant meaning of current research on character indexing systems for Chinese characters—also a brief introduction to the 'Fast Character Indexing System for Chinese Characters'.]
蔡勇飛：論當前漢字檢字法研究的重大意義—兼簡介『漢字快速查字法』

3374 Ts'ao, Shu-chün: Chung-wen tzu-tien fen-pu ch'a-tzu-fa chih · hsin yen-chiu.—*Kuo-li pien-i-kuan kuan-k'an* 1:3, 1972, 220–230. [A new study on the character indexing systems in Chinese (character) dictionaries with (radical) divisions.]
曹樹鈞：中文字典分部查字法之新研究

3375 Tu, Ting-yu: Min-chung chien-tzu hsin-li lun lüeh.—*CYYMC* 6:9, 1935, 1759–1768. [A brief discussion on the popular psychology of character indexing.]
杜定友：民眾檢字心理論略

3376 Ushijima, Tokuji: Kanji no kensakuhō.—*KBKS* 36, 1958, 44–56. [Indexing systems for Chinese characters.]
牛島德次：漢字の檢索法

3377 Wan, Kuo-ting: Ko-chia chien-tzu hsin fa shu p'ing.—*TSKC* 2:4, 1928, 545–579. [Explanation and comment on various new character indexing systems.]
萬國鼎：各家檢字新法述評

3378 Wang, Ching-ch'un: Hsin Han-tzu chien-tzu-fa.—*TFTC* 38:12, 1941, 33–36. [A new character indexing system for Chinese characters.]
王景春：新漢字檢字法

3379 Wu, Hung-chih: Chien-tzu-fa chih yen-chiu.—*WTKC* 2:1, 1930, 37–62. [A study of character indexing systems.]
吳鴻志：檢字法之研究

3380 Yang, Fu-yao: Han-tzu chien-tzu-fa chih tsung-ho te chieh-shao yü p'ing-chia.—*CHCYC* 1:8, 1947, 42–50; 9, 25–34. [A general introduction and evaluation of character indexing systems for Chinese characters.]
楊復耀：漢字檢字法之綜合的介紹與評價

3.4.3. Radical Systems (3381–3421)
3.4.3.1. Ancient Radical Systems (3381–3397)

3381 Ch'en, Chien-hsin & Ch'ien, Hsüan-t'ung: *Shuo-wen pu-shou t'i-yao yü chin tu.*—Taipei: I-wen, 1977, 2, 102 p. [A synopsis and the modern readings of the *Shuo-wen* radicals.] / See (3384).
陳建信、錢玄同：說文部首提要與今讀

3382 Ch'en, Ch'ing-ling: *Pu-shou chiang-chieh.*—Tainan: Piao-chun, 1968, 58 p. [Explanations of the radicals (of *Shuo-wen chieh-tzu*).] / A repr. of (3387).
陳清凌：部首講解

3383 Chiang, Lu-sen: *Shuo-wen pu-shou hsi.*—*Chung-wen hsüeh-hui hsüeh-pao* 7, 1966, 20–26. [An analysis of the *Shuo-wen*

radicals.]
江祿森：『說文』部首析

3384   Ch'ien, Hsüan-t'ung: *Shuo-wen pu-shou chin tu.*—Shanghai: Hsin chih-shih, 1958, 15, 22 d.p.; with a postscript by his son Ch'ien Ping-hsiung./ A posthumous publication. [Modern readings of the *Shuo-wen* radicals.]
錢玄同遺著：說文部首今讀　錢秉雄：後記

3385   Hsiang, Ch'in-ko: *Shuo-wen pu-shou chien cheng* hsü.—*KHYK* 23, 1924, 51–55. [A preface to *Shuo-wen pu-shou chien cheng* ('Exegetical corrigenda to the *Shuo-wen* radicals').]
向琴閣：『說文部首箋正』序

3386   Hsü, Shao-chen: *Shuo-wen pu-shou shu-i.* Fu *Liu-shu pien.*—Taipei: Hsin wen-feng, 1975, v.p. [Explanations of the meanings of the *Shuo-wen* radicals. With Differentiation of the Six Scripts.]
徐紹楨：說文部首述義　附六書辨

3387   Huang, Ch'i: *Pu-shou chiang-chieh.*—Tientsin: T'ien-chin jen-min, 1957, [iii], 58 p.; Hong Kong: T'ai-p'ing shu-chü, 1963, repr. [Explanations of the radicals (of *Shuo-wen chieh-tzu*).]/ See (3382).
黃綺：部首講解

3388   Hun, Jan: *Shuo-wen* pu-shou chin-yü chieh.—*Chiao-yü chin-yü tsa-chih* 5–6, 1911, 9–44. [Explanations of the *Shuo-wen* radicals in the modern language.]
渾然：『說文』部首今語解

3389   K'ang, Yin: *Shuo-wen pu-shou.* Fu *Chien shih.*—Peking: Jung-pao chai, 1980, [ii], 132 p. [The *Shuo-wen* radicals. With brief explanations.]
康殷：說文部首　附簡釋

3390   Kuei, Wen-ts'an: *Shuo-wen* pu-shou chü-tou.—*Wen-feng hsüeh-pao* 1, 1947, 1–18. [Punctuation of the *Shuo-wen* radicals.]
桂文燦：『說文』部首句讀

3391   Li, Ch'iao: *Shuo-wen* chien-shou hsi piao.—*CSTY* 10:109, 1929, 1–25. [A systematic table of the *Shuo-wen* radicals.]
李翹：『說文』建首系表

3392   Meng, Ch'ing-chang: *Pu-shou t'an yüan.*—Hualien: Kuang-hua shu-chü, 1962, 61 p. [Tracing the origins of the (*Shuo-wen*) radicals.]
孟慶璋：部首探原

3393   Pao, Ming-shu: *Tu Shuo-wen kai-lun.* Fu *Pu-shou t'ung shih yang p'ien.*—Taipei: Ditto, 1963, 104 p. [An introduction to the reading of *Shuo-wen*. With a sample section for a general explanation of the radicals.]
包明叔：讀說文概論　附部首通釋樣篇

3394   Pao, Ming-shu: *Shuo-wen* pu-shou pien-ch'ien.—*CKYT* 19:5, 1966, 22–23; 6, 32–34. [Evolution of the *Shuo-wen* radicals.]
包明叔：『說文』部首變遷

3395   Pao, Ming-shu: *Shuo-wen pu-shou t'ung shih.*—Taipei: Ditto, 1967, [i], 2, 2, 4, 2, 2, 2, 2, 8, 16, 426, 4, 2, 2 p. [General explanations of the *Shuo-wen* radicals.]
包明叔：說文部首通釋

3396   Shih, An-ch'ang: T'ang jen tui *Shuo-wen chieh-tzu* pu-shou te kai-ko.—*TSYC* 1981:4, 224–231. [The reformation of the radicals of *Shuo-wen chieh-tzu* by the scholars of the T'ang (dynasty).]
施安昌：唐人對『說文解字』部首的改革

3397   T'ang, Yü-shu: *Shuo-wen pu-shou chiang-i.*—Peking: Printed by the Hsiang-shan Orphanage, 1935, ii, 270 p. [Lecture handouts on the *Shuo-wen* radicals.]
唐玉書：說文部首講義

3.4.3.2. Modern Radical Systems (3398–3421)

3398   Anderson, Olov Bertil: *The "radicals" of the Chinese script: traditional and new:*

a teaching aid.—Lund: Studentlitteratur, 1976, 113 p.
〔康熙部首・現代部首〕

3399 Astor, Wally G.: Chinese radical frequency.—*JCLTA* 4:1, 1969, 20–30.

3400 Carr, Michael: Pedagogy, radicals, and grapho-semantic fields.—*JCLTA* 16:3, 1981, 51–66.

3401 Chang, Cheng-fu: Hsin pu-shou ch'a-tzu-fa.—*WTKK* 1961:8–9, 36–37. [A new radical system of character indexing.]
張正夫：新部首查字法

3402 Ch'en, P'ei-chi: Pu-shou hao-ma ch'a-tzu-fa.—*WTKK* 1961:8–9, 33–34. [The radical-numerical system of character indexing.]
陳培基：部首號碼查字法

3403 Chih, Hsin: Pu-chou ch'a-tzu-fa hsü-yao t'ung-i.—*TSYC* 1982:2, 146–147. [The radical systems of character indexing need to be unified.]
知辛：部首查字法需要統一

3404 Chou, Yen-mou: T'an tzu-tien pu-shou chien-tzu-fa te ko-hsin.—*CHWH* 8:8, 1975, 18–20. [A discussion on the reformation of the radical systems of character indexing in dictionaries.]
周燕謀：談字典部首檢字法的革新

3405 Cohen, Alvin P.: Efficient study of the 214 classifiers ("radicals").—*JCLTA* 11:3, 1976, 192–193.

3406 Ho, S. H.: An analysis of the two Chinese radical systems.—*JCLTA* 13:2, 1978, 95–109.

3407 Hou, Ch'uan-hsün: *Chung-kuo yü-wen chin-liang.*—Taipei: Wei-hsin shu-chü, 1978, [i], 4, 308 p./ Chap. 2: Radical systems of indexing in dictionaries. [A guide to Chinese language and writing.]
侯傳勛：中國語文津梁／第二章：部首字典檢

查法

3408 Huang, C. C.: The "radical system" of character indexing in Chinese dictionaries. —*JCLTA* 2:3, 1967, 104–108.

3409 Jenner, Thomas: *Tsze-teen piao-muh: a guide to the dictionary.*—Rochester: Ditto, 1904, vii, 153 p.; London: Luzac, 1907, 2nd ed., xi, 122 p., 2 maps./ Subtitle: An essay exhibiting the 214 radicals of the Chinese written language.
〔字典標目〕

3410 Kaden, Klaus: Ist das chinesische Radikalsystem noch aktuell? Zur Problematik der Einordnung der vereinfachten Schriftzeichen.—*Probleme der Lexikographie* (2968), 39–52; E.S.

3411 Ku, Lin-sen & Li, Chin-hsi: Kuo-tzu hsin pu-shou.—*KYCKL* 40:3, 1945, 1–2. [The new radicals of Chinese characters.]
顧林森、黎錦熙：國字新部首

3412 Li, Chin-hsi: Han-tzu hsin pu-shou tsung ko-chüeh.—*KYCK* 195, 1935, June 22; 196, 1935, June 29; *WHYC* 59, 1935, 1–9. [Complete rhymes for the new radicals of Chinese characters.]
黎錦熙：漢字新部首總歌訣

3413 Li, Chin-hsi: Han-tzu hsin pu-shou. —*KYCK* 198, 1935, July 13; 199, July 20; 200, July 27; *WHYC* 60, 1935, 1–13. [The new radicals of Chinese characters.]
黎錦熙：漢字新部首

3414 Li, Chin-hsi: Li Chin-hsi ni Han-tzu hsin pu-shou.—*Hsin Chung-hua* 3:14, 1935, 73–80; 3:15, 75–80; 3:16, 73–78; 3:17, 75–78. [New radicals for Chinese characters proposed by Li Chin-hsi.]
黎錦熙：黎錦熙擬漢字新部首

3415 Li, Chin-hsi: Szu-shih-to nien lai ch'uang-ni Han-tzu hsin pu-shou te hui-i. —*WTKK* 1961:8–9, 26–28. [A look back to the creations and proposals in the past forty years for new radicals for Chinese characters.]

黎錦熙：四十多年來創擬漢字新部首的回憶

3416　Lin, Shu-ling: Pu-shou chien-hua ho lien-hsi.—*CKYT* 45:5, 1979, 23–25. [The simplification of radicals with exercises.]

林樹嶺：部首簡化和練習

3417　Lo, Shao-sen: *Hsin-hua tzu-tien* pu-shou nan chien-tzu ch'a-fa shih li piao.—*HCYY* 1980, 133–142. [A table showing examples for methods of looking up characters with difficult (to find) radicals in *Hsin-hua tzu-tien* (3829).]

羅邵森：『新華字典』部首難檢字查法示例表

3418　Ma, Kuo-ch'üan: Han-tzu pu-shou lüeh lun.—*CSTH* 1979:2, 105–110. [A brief discussion on the radicals of Chinese characters.]

馬國權：漢字部首略論

3419　P'ing, Ko: *Pu-shou chien-tzu hsin fa.*—Taipei: Ch'i-ming shu-chü, 1953, 2, 30 p. [A new radical system of character indexing.]

平閣：部首檢字新法

3420　T'ai-pei yü-wen hsüeh-yüan: *Ch'ang-yung Han-tzu pu-shou.*—Taipei: Ditto, 1970, 15 p. [Fifty common Chinese radicals.]

臺北語文學院：常用漢字部首

3421　Watanabe, Seiichi: Kanji bushu no kōyō.—*Gakudai Kokubun* 12, 1968, 115–123. [The utilization of the radicals of Chinese characters.]

渡邊清一：漢字部首の効用

3.4.4. Stroke and Number Systems (3422–3455)
3.4.4.1. Stroke Systems (3422–3431)

3422　Ch'en, Li-fu: Chung-kuo wen-tzu chih k'o-hsüeh te hsü-li—Ch'en Li-fu wu-pi chien-tzu fa.—*CWCC* 2:1, 1935, 59–62; *K'o-hsüeh te Chung-kuo* 5:4, 1935, 3–5. [An example of the scientific order of

Chinese characters—Ch'en Li-fu's five-stroke character indexing system.]

陳立夫：中國文字之科學的序例——陳立夫五筆檢字法

3423　Ch'en, Li-fu: *Wu-pi chien-tzu-fa.*—Taipei: Chung-kuo yü-wen yen-chiu chung-hsin, 1971, 18, 90, [20] p. [A five-stroke character indexing system.]

陳立夫：五筆檢字法

3424　Cheng, I-li: Liu-pi pu-shou ch'a-tzu-fa.—*WTKK* 1961:8–9, 28–32. [A six-stroke radical system of character indexing.]

鄭易里：六筆部首查字法

3425　Huang, Yu-hsiung: Pi-shun ch'a-tzu-fa.—*WTKK* 1961:8–9, 41–42. [A stroke-sequence character indexing system.]

黃幼雄：筆順查字法

3426　Lin, Yü-t'ang: Mo-pi chien-tzu-fa.—*Yü-yen-hsüeh lun-ts'ung* (0072), 283–287. [A final-stroke character indexing system.]

林語堂：末筆檢字法

3427　Pao, Chih-i: Fen-pi ch'a-tzu-fa.—*WTKK* 1961:8–9, 40. [A stroke-divisional character indexing system.]

包稚頤：分筆查字法

3428　Sung, Kuo-pin: Un nouveau système de lexicographie chinoise.—*CCS* 5, 1932, 598–600./ In French and Chinese; four-stroke system.

〔宋國賓：直斜彎點檢字法〕

3429　Tu, Hsüeh-chih: *Han-tzu shou-wei erh-pu p'ai-chien-fa.*—Tainan: Hsüeh-lin, 1962, 4, 270 p. [The head (initial stroke)-tail (final stroke) two stroke indexing system for Chinese characters.]

杜學知：漢字首尾二部排檢法

3430　Wan, Kuo-ting: Han-tzu mu-pi p'ai-lieh-fa.—*TFTC* 23:2, 1926, 75–90. [A method for arrangement of Chinese characters by original strokes.]

萬國鼎：漢字母筆排列法

3431　Wu, C. K. & Wu, K. S.: Initial three-stroke index system.—*JCLTA* 8:2, 1973, 99–103.

3.4.4.2. Four-corner Numerical System (3432–3441)

3432　Duyvendak, J.J.L.: Wong's system for arranging Chinese characters: The revised four-corner numeral system.—*TP* 28, 1931, 71–77./ See (3441).

3433　Ferguson, J. C.: Hunting characters in Chinese dictionaries: four-corner number system.—*CJ* 10, 1929, 68–71.

3434　Gillis, Irvin Van Gorder: Wong's four-corner system.—*CJ* 11, 1929, 10–17./ See (3441).

3435　Li, Chao-ch'üan: Man t'an szu-chiao hao-ma chi ch'i chiao-hsüeh fa.—*Yü-wen* 2, 1976, 32–38. [A random discussion on the 'four-corner numerical system' and its methods of teaching and learning.]
李兆權：漫談『四角號碼』及其教學法

3436　Nash, Vernon: Numerical conversion: a key to the maze of Chinese literature (4-corner system).—*Pacific Affairs* 9, 1936, 358–369.

3437　Proulx, A.: Essai de lexicographie chinoise, système des 'Traits numérotés'.—*BUA* 2:11, 1925–1926, 34–39.

3438　Ting, Mu & Chung, Yün: *Tsen-yang hsüeh-hui szu-chiao hao-ma chien-tzu-fa.*—Shanghai: Shang-wu, 1955, 1st ed.; 1956, 3rd print., [i], 80 p.; Hong Kong: Shang-wu, 1966, repr.; *Yü-wen hui-pien* (0058), 49:160. [How to study the four-corner numerical indexing system.]
丁木、仲芸：怎樣學會四角號碼檢字法

3439　Trittel, W.: Das 4-Ecken-Aufschlagesystem und die amtliche Lateinumschrift der Reichssprache.—*MSOS* 40, 1937, 94–148.

3440　Wang, Yün-wu: *Szu-chiao hao-ma chien-tzu fa.*—Shanghai: Shang-wu, 1934; 1935, 2nd ed., [iv], 5, 69, 75, 2, [6], 2, [4], [6] p.; Taipei: Shang-wu, 1975, repr. [The four-corner numerical (indexing) system.]
王雲五：四解號碼檢字法

3441　Wong, Y.W. [Wang, Yün-wu]: *Wong's system for arranging Chinese characters—the revised four-corner numerical system.*—Shanghai: The Commerical Press, 1928, 143 p.
〔王雲五：改訂四角號碼檢字法〕

3.4.4.3. Other Stroke and Number Systems (3442–3455)

3442　Chang, Feng: Chang Feng hsing-shu chien-tzu-fa.—*MTTC* 9:5, 1928, 1–16. [Chang Feng's form-number character indexing system.]
張鳳：張鳳形數檢字法

3443　Ch'eng, Yang-chih: Tui-yü *T'ung-ch'ou-fa tsai Han-tzu tzu-tien p'ai-lieh yu chien-tzu-fa kai-ko chung te ying-yung te i-chien.*—*YPTH* 1977:3, 63–64, 103. [Opinions concerning Lei & Fu's article (3449).]
程養之：對於『統籌法在漢字字典排列與檢字法改革中的應用』的意見

3444　Chuang, Wei-chi: Liang-tuan hao-ma-fa te chien-tzu yü so-yin te shuo-ming shu.—*HMTH* 1954:1, 40–47. [Illustrated notes on character indexing of the two part numeral system and indexes.]
莊爲璣：兩段號碼法的檢字與索引的說明書

3445　Hsieh, Ch'i-wen: Wo shih ch'uang te i-chung Han-tzu chien-tzu-fa—szu-pi tai-hao chien-tzu-fa chieh-shao.—*TCSY* 1978:3, 91–92. [A character indexing system for Chinese characters that I tentatively created—an introduction to 'a four-stroke numerical character indexing system.']
謝啓文：我試創的一種漢字檢字法——『四筆代號檢字法』介紹

3446   Hsieh, Ch'ing-chün: Chung-wen tzu-ken hsing-ma so-yin-fa.—*CKYT* 45:6, 1979, 26–32; 46:1, 1980, 27–33; 46:2, 35–38. [A root-form-numerical indexing system for Chinese characters.]
謝清俊：中文字根形碼索引法

3447   Hsü, Shih-ying: Chien-tzu-fa te ko-hsin —szu-pi tai-hao chien-tzu-fa p'ing hsi. —*TCSY* 1978:3, 93–96. [The reformation of character indexing systems—a critique and analysis of the 'four-stroke numerical character indexing system.']
徐世英：檢字法的革新——『四筆代號檢字法』評析

3448   Kwei, C. S.: *Kwei's video codes for Chinese characters.*—Hong Kong: The Chinese U. Press, 1979, xi, 203 p./ Two 4-digit codes: the structure code (is an improved version of the four-corner numerical system) and the pronouncing code.
〔桂中樞：桂氏漢字形聲碼〕

3449   Lei, Yu-wu & Fu, Yü-chu: T'ung-ch'ou-fa tsai Han-tzu tzu-tien p'ai-lieh yü chien-tzu-fa kai-ko chung te ying-yung—chieh-shao san-chung hsin-shih hao-ma chien-tzu-fa.—*YPTH* 1977:1, 96–107. [The uses of an overall unified method in the arrangement of Chinese (character) dictionaries and a revision of character indexing systems—an introduction to three new types of numerical character indexing systems.]/ See (3443).
雷友梧、傅玉珠：統籌法在漢字字典排列與檢字法改革中的應用——介紹三種新式號碼檢字法

3450   Li, Chin-k'ai & Li, I-min: Pi-hsiang hao-ma ch'a-tzu-fa.—*WTKK* 1961:8–9, 48–50. [The stroke-direction numerical character indexing system.]
李金鎧、李毅民：筆向號碼查字法

3451   Liu, Chung-ho: Liu Chung-ho te wu wei hao-ma chien-tzu-fa.—*CKYT* 33:3, 1973, 36–44. [Liu Chung-ho's five-position numerical character indexing system.]

劉中龢：劉中龢的『五位號碼檢字法』

3452   Shang, Fang: Ting-ti ho-ma chiu-pu ch'a-tzu-fa.—*WTKK* 1961:8–9, 3 & back cover page. [A top-bottom combined-number nine-division character indexing system.]
尚芳：頂底合碼九部查字法

3453   Sun, Kung-wang: Han-tzu piao-ma ch'a-tzu-fa.—*Hua-chung shih-yüan hsüeh-pao* 1980:1, 99–104. [A mark-number character indexing system for Chinese characters.]
孫公望：漢字『標碼』查字法

3454   Tsou, Ta-yen: Yeh t'an Han-tzu chien-tzu-fa te wen-t'i—chien chieh i-chung pi-shun hao-ma chien-tzu-fa.—*YPTH* 1978: 1, 42–46. [Also discussion the problem of Chinese character indexing systems—with an introduction to a type of stroke-sequence numerical character indexing system.]
鄒大炎：也談漢字檢字法的問題——兼介一種『筆順號碼檢字法』

3455   Yeh, I-t'ing: Szu-pi hao-ma ch'a-tzu-fa. —*WTKK* 1961:8–9, 42. [The four-stroke numerical character indexing system.]/ See (3445).
葉怡庭：四筆號碼查字法

3.4.5. Form and Position Systems (3456–3465)

3456   Chai, Chien-hsiung: Tso-shang ch'üan pu-wei ch'a-tzu-fa (ch'i-shih-ko pu-shou piao).—*WTKK* 1961:8–9, 46. [An upper-left complete-position character indexing system (a table of 70 radicals).]
翟健雄：左上全部位查字法（七十個部首表）

3457   Chao, Yu-p'ei: Ting-wei fen-pu chien-tzu-fa shih li.—*CKYT* 32:5, 1973, 56–74. [Practical examples of the headings for the fixed-position divided-radical character indexing system.]
趙友培：定位分部檢字法實例

3458 Chao, Yu-p'ei: *Ting wei fen pu chien-tzu-fa.*—Taipei: Chung-kuo yü-wen, 1973 (?), (not seen). [A fixed-position divided-radical character indexing system.]
趙友培：定位分部檢字法

3459 Kuei, Chung-shu: *The three-positional system.*—New Haven: (?), 1954, 8 p./ See (3461).
〔桂中樞〕

3460 P'eng, Tao-chen: Chiang shan ch'ien ku hung—Han-tzu ting-wei chien-tzu-fa. —*WTKK* 1961:8–9, 38–40. [The rivers and mountains endure forever as red— A fixed-position character indexing system for Chinese characters.]
彭道眞：江山千古紅——漢字定位查字法

3461 Tseng, Shen: Kuei Chung-shu ch'uang pien te hsin-shih Chung-wen tzu-tien.— *Chung-kuo i-chou* 504, 1959, 21–22. [A new-style Chinese character dictionary created and compiled by Kuei Chung-shu.]/ Based on the three-positional system (3459), printed at Yale U., but never circulated.
曾燊：桂中樞創編的新式中文字典

3462 Tu, Ting-yu: Han-tzu hsing-wei p'ai-chien-fa chih ta-yao.—*CHCYC* 18:10, 1930, 43–44. [An outline of a form-position arrangement and indexing system for Chinese characters.]
杜定友：漢字形位排檢法之大要

3463 Tu, Ting-yu: Tzu-hsing chien-tzu-fa.— *YWCS* 1954:6, 24–26. [A character-form character indexing system.]
杜定友：字形檢字法

3464 Tu, Ting-yu: Tzu-hsing p'ai-chien-fa. —*WTKK* 1961:8–9, 43–45. [A character-form arrangement and indexing system.]
杜定友：字形排檢法

3465 Wang, Yin-sheng: Tzu-hsing tzu-mu chieh-ho ch'a-tzu-fa.—*WTKK* 1961:8–9, 34–36. [A combination character-form and alphabetical character indexing system.]
王蔭聖：字形字母結合查字法

3.4.6. Methods of Compiling Indexes and Concordances (3466–3479)

3466 Chang, Chin-lang: *Chung-wen ts'an-k'ao . . . chih-yin* (2889), Chap. 3: Indexes./ Meaning, history, and categories of indexes. [A guide to Chinese reference books.]
張錦郎：中文參考用書指引／第三章：索引

3467 Ch'iao, Yen-kuan: So-yin man t'an. —*SMCK* 2:4, 1968, 19–28. [A random discussion on indexes.]
喬衍琯：索引漫談

3468 Ho, Feng-t'ai: Tsa-chih, shu, pao-k'an, lun-wen so-yin tien-nao-hua.—*Jen yü she-hui* 6:2, 1978, 49–50. [The computerization of indexes for magazines, books, periodicals, and articles.]
何鳳台：雜誌、書、報刊、論文索引電腦化

3469 Huang, En-chu: Chung-kuo ku-tai so-yin lüeh shu.—*TSYC* 1983:1, 54–60. [A brief account of indexes in ancient China.]
黃恩祝：中國古代索引略述

3470 Huang, Yün: So-yin chien lun.—*TSYC* 1981:3, 113–119. [A brief discussion on indexes.]
黃筼：索引簡論

3471 Hung, Yeh: Yin-te shuo.—Peiping: Yen-ching University Library, 1932; Taipei: Ch'eng-wen, 1966, repr., 69 p., 1 pl./ Harvard-Yenching Institute Sinological Index Series. Supplement, 4. [On indexing.]
洪業：引得說

3472 Lin, Yü-t'ang: Hsin yün chien-i (Fu T'u-shu so-yin chih i-hsin fa).—*KHMC* 1:9, 1925, 1–3; *Yü-yen-hsüeh lun-ts'ung* (0072), 297–306, with two more articles on the same subject. [Suggestions for new rhymes (With A new method of indexing for books).]
林語堂：新韻建議（附圖書索引之一新法）

3473   Lin, Yü-t'ang: T'u-shu so-yin chih i-hsin
fa.—*Yü-yen-hsüeh lun-ts'ung* (0072), 288–
296. [A new method of indexing for
books.] / A rev. version of (3472).
林語堂：圖書索引之一新法

3474   Mei, Kung: ABC k'uai-su so-yin.—
WTKK 1962:5, 4–5. [Fast ABC indexes.]
湄公：ＡＢＣ快速索引

3475   P'an, Shu-kuang: Wen-hsien chien-so
yü yü-wen yen-chiu.—*TSYC* 1979:1, 248–
259. [The indexing of documents and
the study of language and writing.]
潘樹廣：文獻檢索與語文研究

3476   P'an, Shu-kuang: Chen-hsien, ch'uan-chu
yü tz'u-shu.—*TSYC* 1980:4, 230–235,
277. [The terms *chen-hsien* ('needle and
thread'), *ch'uan-chu* 'stringed pearls'), and
(ancient) lexicographical works.] / *chen-
hsien* means 'index', *ch'uan-chu* means
'concordance'.
潘樹廣：『針線』、『串珠』與辭書

3477   Talbot, H.D.: The indexing of Chinese
names.—*Indexer* 2, 1961, 99–103.

3478   Wang, Fang-yu: Report on Chinese
language concordances made by computer.
—*JCLTA* 1, 1966, 74–76.

3479   Yü, Chün-li: Tui pien-chih tz'u-tien
so-yin te liang-t'iao chien-i.—*CYTH* 1978:
2, 8–10. [Two suggestions on compiling
dictionary indexes.]
俞君立：對編製詞典索引的兩條建議

4. PRE-MODERN STANDARD CHINESE-CHINESE DICTIONARIES (3480–3814)

4.1. Character Dictionaries (3480–3597)

4.1.1. *Shuo-wen chieh-tzu* (3480–3563)

4.1.1.1. Life and Work of Hsü Shen (3480–3485)

3480   A, Hsiang: Hsü Shen te sheng-p'ing ho szu-hsiang.—*TSYC* 1981:1, 267–270. [The life and thought of Hsü Shen.]
阿祥：許慎的生平和思想

3481   Chou, Tsu-mo: Hsü Shen ho t'a-te *Shuo-wen chieh-tzu.*— *CKYW* 1956:9, 26–30; repr. in *Wen-hsüeh chi* (0054), 710–722, under the title of Hsü Shen chi ch'i *Shuo-wen chieh-tzu.* [Hsü Shen and his *Shuo-wen chieh-tzu.*]
周祖謨：許慎和他的（＝及其）『說文解字』

3482   Hung, Tu-jen: *Shuo-wen chieh-tzu* te tso-che Hsü Shen.—*TSYC* 1981:3, 222–238. [Hsü Shen, author of *Shuo-wen chieh-tzu.*]
洪篤仁：『說文解字』的作者許慎

3483   Kao, Ming: Hsü Shen sheng-p'ing hsing-chi k'ao.—*CCTH* 18, 1968, 1–27. [A study on the life and manner of Hsü Shen.]
高明：許慎生平行跡考

3484   Wang, Hsien: Chiu tui Hsü Shen chi ch'i *Shuo-wen* te chih-tse t'an i-tien k'an-fa.—*CKYW* 1978:4, 271–275. [A few viewpoints on the criticism of Hsü Shen and his *Shuo-wen.*]
王顯：就對許慎及其『說文』的指責談一點看法

3485   Yao, Hsiao-sui: *Hsü Shen yü Shuo-wen chieh-tzu.*—Peking: Chung-hua, 1983, 48 p. [Hsü Shen and (his) *Shuo-wen chieh-tzu.*]
姚孝遂：許慎與說文解字

4.1.1.2. *Shuo-wen* Editions (3486–3492)

3486   Hsü, Shen. Ed. by Hsü, Hsüan: *Shuo-wen chieh-tzu.*—Shanghai: Shang-wu, 1914, repr., 15 *chüan;* Taipei: Wen-hua t'u-shu, 1956, repr., 143 p.; Taipei: I-wen, 1959, repr., 4 *ts'e./* Szu-k'u shan-pen ts'ung-shu, 1. [Discussion of simple characters and explanation of compound characters.]
許慎著，徐鉉校：說文解字「四庫善本叢書」初集

3487   Hsü, Shen. Ed. by Ch'en, Ch'ang-chih: *Shuo-wen chieh-tzu.* Fu *Chien-tzu.*—Peking: Chung-hua, 1963, repr., 5, 328, (index) 62 p.; Hong Kong: Chung-hua, 1972, 1974, 1975, repr. [Discussion of simple characters and explanation of compound characters. With An index.]
許慎著，陳昌治刊：說文解字　附檢字

3488   Chou, Tsu-mo: *Shuo-wen chieh-tzu* chih ch'uan pen.—*KHCK* 5:1, 1935, 107–117. [Various editions of *Shuo-wen chieh-tzu.*]
周祖謨：『說文解字』之傳本

3489   Chou, Tsu-mo: Sun Hsing-yen P'ing-chin kuan ch'ung k'an Sung pen *Shuo-wen chieh-tzu* chiao k'an chi.—*KHCK* 5:1, 1935, 119–142. [Critical notes on *Shuo-wen chieh-tzu* reprinted by Sun Hsing-yen from a Sung edition (kept) in the P'ing-chin kuan.]
周祖謨：孫星衍平津館重刊宋本『說文解字』校勘記

3490   Chou, Tsu-mo: *Shuo-wen chieh-tzu* chih Sung k'o pen.—*Wen-hsüeh chi* (0054), 760–800. [A Sung wood-block edition of *Shuo-wen chieh-tzu.*]
周祖謨：『說文解字』之宋刻本

3491   Fukuda, Jōnosuke: *Setsumon kaiji* no shoon.—*OKHB* 30, 1969, 243–261. [Various editions of *Shuo-wen chieh-tzu.*]
福田襄之介：『說文解字』の　諸本

3492   Kao, Ming: *Shuo-wen chieh-tzu* ch'uan pen k'ao.—*THHP* 16, 1975, 1–18; *Kao Ming hsiao-hsüeh lun-ts'ung* (0067), 20–50. [A study of the various editions of *Shuo-wen chieh-tzu.*]
高明：『說文解字』傳本考

4.1.1.3. Methods of Studying *Shuo-wen* (3493–3496)

3493 Ch'en, Chin: *Shuo-wen yen-chiu fa.*— Shanghai: Shang-wu, 1934, 4, 4, 2, 189 p. [Methods for the study of *Shuo-wen.*]
陳晉：說文研究法

3494 Liu, Jui & Chiang, Jen-chieh: *Shuo-wen chieh-tzu* yen-chiu ch'u i.—*TSYC* 1980:3, 232–239. [Our opinion on the study of *Shuo-wen chieh-tzu.*]
劉銳、蔣人杰：『說文解字』研究芻議

3495 Lo, Chün-t'i: Wo tsen-yang yen-chiu *Shuo-wen chieh-tzu.*—*TSYC* 1982:5, 76–79. [How I study *Shuo-wen chieh-tzu.*]
羅君惕：我怎樣研究『說文解字』

3496 Ma, Hsü-lun: *Shuo-wen chieh-tzu yen-chiu fa.*—Shanghai: Shang-wu, 1933; 1955, repr., 4, 121 p.; Hong Kong: T'ai-p'ing, 1964, repr. [Methods for the study of *Shuo-wen chieh-tzu.*]
馬叙倫：說文解字研究法

4.1.1.4. General Studies (3497–3522)

3497 Chang, Hsing-fu: *Shuo-wen fa-i.*—N. p.: 1884, 6 *chüan.* [Dispel doubts about *Shuo-wen.*] / A general introduction.
張行孚：說文發疑

3498 Chiang, Chü-ch'ien: *Shuo-wen chieh-tzu tsung-ho yen-chiu.*—Taichung: Tung-hai U., 1970, 2, 22, 594 p. [An integrated study of *Shuo-wen chieh-tzu.*]
江舉謙：說文解字綜合研究

3499 Ch'ien, Chien-fu: *Shuo-wen chieh-tzu kai shu.*—*TSYC* 1979:1, 229–247. [A general explanation of *Shuo-wen chieh-tzu.*]
錢劍夫：『說文解字』概述

3500 Chu, Min-shen: Shih lun *Shuo-wen chieh-tzu* chi Hsü Shen hsüeh-shu szu-hsiang te chin-pu-hsing.—*FTHP* 1979:2, 50–57. [A preliminary discussion on *Shuo-wen chieh-tzu* and the progressive-

ness of the thoughts of Hsü Shen on learning.]
祝敏申：試論『說文解字』及許慎學術思想的進步性

3501 Fukuda, Jōnosuke: *Setsumon kaiji* chū-shaku hon no kenkyū—Chūgoku jishoshi kenkyū no ikkan.—*OKHB* 33, 1973, 28–38. [A study of commentaries on *Shuo-wen chieh-tzu*—A link in the study of the history of Chinese character dictionaries.]
福田襄之介：『說文解字』注釋本の研究——中國字書史研究の一環

3502 Fukuda, Jōnosuke: *Setsumon kaiji setsukai no keishiki*—Chūgoku jishoshi kenkyū no ikkan toshite.—*Obi hakase taikyū kinen Chūgoku bungaku ronshū* (Hiroshima: Daiichi gakushūsha, 1976), 161–189. [The patterns of explanations in *Shuo-wen chieh-tzu*—A link in the study of the history of Chinese character dictionaries.]
福田襄之介：『說文解字』說解の形式——中國字書史研究の一環として——『小尾博士退休記念中國文學論集』

3503 Hsiang, Hsi: *Shuo-wen* yüeh-tu i te.—*YLT* 1, 1957, 98–112. [Some insights from the reading of *Shuo-wen.*]
向熹：『說文』閱讀一得

3504 Huang, K'an: *Shuo-wen lüeh shuo.*—*Chih-yen* 15, 1936, 47 s.p.; *Huang K'an lun-hsüeh tsa-chu* (0066), 1–49. [A short discussion on *Shuo-wen.*]
黃侃：『說文』略說

3505 Hulsewé, A.F.P.: The *Shuo-wen* dictionary as a source for ancient Chinese law.—*Studia Serica Bernhard Karlgren dedicata* (Ed. by Egerod, Søren & Glahn, Else.—Copenhagen: Ejnar Munksgaard, 1959), 239–258.

3506 Hung, Tu-jen: *Shuo-wen* tui tz'u-shu pien-tsuan fa te kung-hsien.—*TSYC* 1982: 1, 77–84. [Contributions of *Shuo-wen* to the methods of compiling lexicographical works.]

洪篤仁：『說文』對辭書編纂法的貢獻

3507 Kao, Ming: Lun *Shuo-wen chieh-tzu chih pien tz'u.—JWHP* 5, 1976, 187—213; *Kao Ming hsiao-hsüeh lun-ts'ung* (0067), 93—128. [On the order of (entry) arrangement in *Shuo-wen chieh-tzu.*]
高明：論『說文解字』之編次

3508 Kao, Ming: Tui *Shuo-wen chieh-tzu chih hsin p'ing-chia.—Kao Ming hsiao-hsüeh lun-ts'ung* (0067), 1—19. [A new critical evaluation of *Shuo-wen chieh-tzu.*]
高明：對『說文解字』之新評價

3509 Ku, Chin-ch'en: *Shuo-wen tsung-ho-te yen-chiu.*—Shanghai: Shih-chieh, 1931, 2 vols., [xiii], 350 p.; 271 p.; Taipei: Wen-hai, 1971, repr. in one vol. [An integrated study of *Shuo-wen.*]
顧藎臣：說文綜合的研究

3510 Li, Ching-kao: *Hsü-hsüeh k'ao.*—Taipei: Hua-wen shu-chü, 1970, repr., 26 *chüan*, 1794 p./ First ed., publ. in 1927 by the author. [A study on Hsüology.]/ An annotated bibliography.
黎經誥：許學考

3511 Lin, Ming-po: Ch'ing-tai Hsü-hsüeh k'ao. —*TSST* 5, 1961, 1—192; Taipei: Chia-hsin shui-ni kung-szu, 1964, 8, [iii], 283 p. [A study of the Hsüology of the Ch'ing period.]/ An annotated bibliography.
林明波：清代許學考

3512 Liu, Yeh-ch'iu: *Shuo-wen chieh-tzu.— Chung-kuo ku-tai te tzu-tien* (2927), 6—23; *Chung-kuo te tzu-tien* (2996), 12—21. [*Shuo-wen chieh-tzu.*]
劉葉秋：『說文解字』

3513 Lu, Tsung-ta: *Shuo-wen chieh-tzu t'ung-lun.*—Peking: Pei-ching, 1981, 2, 3, 232 p. [A general introduction to *Shuo-wen chieh-tzu.*]
陸宗達：說文解字通論

3514 Miller, Roy A.: *Problems in the study of Shuo-wen chieh-tzu.* New York: Columbia U., 1953, xvi, 351 p./ Unpubl. doc. diss.; *DA* 14:1215; UM 6673.

3515 Nishijima, Teisei: *Setsumon.—Sekai dai hyakka jiten* (0042) 17, 486. [*Shuo-wen.*]
西嶋定生：『說文』

3516 Ozaki, Yūjirō: *Setsumon kaiji.—Ajia rekishi jiten* (0040), 5:255, pl. [*Shuo-wen chieh-tzu.*]
尾崎雄二郎：『說文解字』

3517 P'an, Ch'ung-kuei: *Shuo-wen yüeh lun.* —*HYSY* 5, 1963, 247—272. [A short discussion on *Shuo-wen.*]
潘重規：『說文』約論

3518 San-chia-ts'un hsüeh-chiu: *Chien-tzu i-kuan-san.*—Taipei: I-wen, 1955, repr., 33 *chüan*, 429 p./ First publ. ca. 1890. [A single index for the characters of three works.]/ Index to *Shuo-wen t'ung-hsün ting-sheng* (3530), *Shuo-wen chieh-tzu chu* (3546), and *Ching-chi tsuan-ku* (3690).
三家村學究：檢字一貫三

3519 Simon, Walter: Das erste etymologische wörterbuch der Chinesischen sprache.— *Deutsche Literaturzeitung* 1, 1924, 1905—1910.

3520 Ting, Fu-pao: *Shuo-wen tsung lun.* —*Shuo-wen chieh-tzu ku-lin* (3542), Vol. I, pt. 3, 234—279. [A general introduction to *Shuo-wen.*]
丁福保：『說文』總論

3521 Tōdō, Akiyasu: *Setsumon kaiji.—Sekai meicho daijiten* (0041) 4, 29—30. [*Shuo-wen chieh-tzu.*]
藤堂明保：『說文解字』

3522 Wei, Chü-hsien: *Wen-tzu-hsüeh.*—Taipei: Li-ming, 1979, 2, 4, 400 p./ 243—261: *Shuo-wen chieh-tzu.*/ A general introduction. [Chinese logography.]

衞聚賢：文字學／243-261：『說文解字』

4.1.1.5. Studies on the Preface of *Shuo-wen* (3523–3526)

3523 Chiang, Chü-ch'ien: Hsü Shen *Shuo-wen chieh-tzu* hsü ch'üan shu.—*THHP* 6:1, 1964, 21–39; E.S. [An exegesis to the preface of Hsü Shen's *Shuo-wen chieh-tzu.*]

江擧謙：許愼『說文解字』叙詮疏

3524 Feng, Chen-hsin: Hsü Shen *Shuo-wen chieh-tzu* hsü chiang chi.—*HITC* 12:1, 1933, 37–52. [Lecture notes on the preface of Hsü Shen's *Shuo-wen chieh-tzu.*]

馮振心：許愼『說文解字』叙講記

3525 Li, Ch'eng-ch'üan: *Shuo-wen chieh-tzu hsü chiang shu.*—Shanghai: Shang-wu, 1935, 3, 146 p./ 145–146: Bibliography. [Explanatory exegesis to the preface of *Shuo-wen chieh-tzu.*]

酈承銓：說文解字敍講疏

3526 Thern, K.L.: *Postface of the Shuo-wen chieh-tzu.*—Madison: Dept. of East Asian Languages and Literature, U. of Wisconsin, 1966, viii, 110 p./ Wisconsin China Series, 1.

〔說文解字敍英譯〕

4.1.1.6. Special Studies (3527–3545)

3527 Chang, Jih-sheng & Lin, Chieh-ming: *Shuo-wen t'ung-hsün ting-sheng mu-lu Chou Fa-kao yin.*—Taipei: Chou Fa-kao, 1973, [iii], 261 p. [A catalogue of (the characters of) *Shuo-wen t'ung-hsün ting-sheng* (3530) with Chou Fa-kao's (Archaic/Ancient/Mandarin/Cantonese) phonetic transcriptions.]

張日昇、林潔明：說文通訓定聲目錄周法高音

3528 Chou, Tsu-mo: Hsü K'ai te *Shuo-wen-hsüeh.*—*Wen-hsüeh chi* (0054), 843–851. [Hsü K'ai's study of *Shuo-wen.*]

周祖謨：徐鍇的『說文』學

3529 Chou, Ts'ung-chün: *Shuo-wen i-yüeh*

yen-chiu.—Taipei: Shih-fan ta-hsüeh, 1978, 9, 380, (bibliography:) 19 p.; *TSST* 23, 1979, 225–366./ 351–366: Bibliography; publ. M.A. thesis. [A study of the *i-yüeh* ('another interpretation') in *Shuo-wen.*]

周聰俊：說文一曰研究

3530 Chu, Chün-sheng: *Shuo-wen t'ung-hsün ting-sheng.*—Shanghai: Shih-chieh, 1936, repr., 18 *chüan*, 845 p.; Taipei: Shih-chieh, 1956, repr., 3 vols., 26, 46, 845 p.; Taipei: Shih-chieh, 1966, repr., 2 vols., 26, 46, 845, 28, 54, 30 p.; Appendices./ P'u-hsüeh ts'ung-shu, 1:2. [*Shuo-wen chieh-tzu* (rearranged and studied) according to semantic and phonetic affinities.]

朱駿聲：說文通訓定聲 「樸學叢書」第一集，第二冊

3531 Chu, Hsing: P'ing *Shuo-wen t'ung-hsün ting-sheng.*—*PCST* 5, 1978, 45–49. [A critique of *Shuo-wen t'ung-hsün ting-sheng* (3530).]

朱星：評『說文通訓定聲』

3532 Hsieh, I-min: *Shuo-wen chieh-tzu chien-cheng.*—Taipei: Lan-t'ai shu-chü, 1964, 326 p. [Exegetical corrigenda to *Shuo-wen chieh-tzu.*]

謝一民：說文解字箋正

3533 Hsü, K'ai: *Shuo-wen chieh-tzu hsi chüan.*—Shanghai: Shang-wu, 1936, repr., 40 *chüan*, 2 vols., 333 p., Szu-pu ts'ung-k'an, 017–018; Taipei: Hua-wen, 1971, repr., 2 vols., 1574 p.; Appendices. [A related commentary on *Shuo-wen chieh-tzu.*]

徐鍇：說文解字繫傳 「四部叢刊」初編 017-018

3534 Kuan, Kuo-hsüan: Ting Fu-pao hsien-sheng hsiao chüan.—*TLTC* 27:2, 1963, 31. [A short biography of Mr. Ting Fu-pao.]／ See (3542).

關國暄：丁福保先生小傳

3535 Kuei, Fu: *Shuo-wen chieh-tzu i cheng.* —Wuchang: Ch'ung-wen shu-chu, 1869, repr., 50 *chüan.* [Semantic evidence for *Shuo-wen chieh-tzu.*]

桂馥：說文解字義證

3536   Li, Kuo-ying: *Shuo-wen lei-shih.*—Taipei: Chang Meng-sheng, 1975, 4, 4, 547 p. [A categorical explanation of *Shuo-wen.*]/ According to the principles of the Six Scripts.

李國英：說文類釋

3537   Li, Yung-ch'un: *Shuo-wen t'ung-chien.*—Shanghai: Chung-hua, 1927–1935, 14 *chüan,* v.p./ Szu-pu pei-yao ed. [A general index to *Shuo-wen.*]

黎永春：說文通檢　「四部備要」本

3538   Ma, Hsü-lun: *Shuo-wen chieh-tzu liu-shu shu-cheng.*—Peking: K'o-hsüeh, 1957, 3 vols., 30 *chüan,* v. p.; Taipei: Ting-wen, 1975, repr., 5 vols., 4006, 42 p./ *RBS* 3, 1957, 546, M. Kaltenmark. [Exegetical evidence for the Six Scripts in *Shuo-wen chieh-tzu.*]

馬叙倫：說文解字六書疏證

3539   Sha, Ch'ing-yen: *Shuo-wen ta tz'u-tien.*—Tientsin: T'ien-chin ku-chi shu-tien, 1980, 2 vols., 8 *chüan,* v. p. [A comprehensive dictionary of *Shuo-wen.*]

沙青巖：說文大辭典

3540   Shirakawa, Shizuka: *Setsumon shingi.*—Kyoto: Goten shoin, 1969–1971, 15 vols., 12, 3325 p.; Extra vol. 16, 2, 116, 152 p./ Vol. 16, 1–50: A catalogue of important works on *Shuo-wen.* [New meanings for *Shuo-wen.*]

白川靜：說文新義／卷十六，1-50：說文解字文獻要目

3541   Teng, Ssu-yü & Biggerstaff, Knight: *Shuo-wen chieh-tzu ku-lin.—An annotated bibliography . . . reference works* (2898), 141–142.

〔說文解字詁林〕

3542   Ting, Fu-pao: *Shuo-wen chieh-tzu ku-lin.*—Shanghai: I-hsüeh, 1928, 66 *ts'e.*

Shuo-wen chieh-tzu ku-lin pu-i.—Shanghai: I-hsüeh, 1932, 16 *ts'e;* Taipei: Shang-wu, 1959, repr., 13 vols.; Supplement 3 vols.; Taipei: Kuo-min, 1966, repr./ *TP* 29, 1933, 245–246, P. Pelliot [A collection of commentaries on *Shuo-wen chieh-tzu.*]/ Arranged in the original order of *Shuo-wen.*

丁福保：說文解字詁林　說文解字詁林補遺

3543   Tōdō, Akiyasu: *Setsumon tsūkun teisei.*—*Sekai meicho daijiten* (0041) 4, 30. [*Shuo-wen t'ung-hsün ting-sheng* (3530).]

藤堂明保：『說文通訓定聲』

3544   Wang, Yün: *Shuo-wen chieh-tzu chü-tou.*—Szechwan: Tsun-ching shu-chü, 1882, 30 *chüan,* with *Pu-cheng* [Addenda and corrigenda]. [*Shuo-wen chieh-tzu* punctuated.]

王筠：說文解字句讀　補正

3545   Wang, Yün: *Shuo-wen shih li.*—Taipei: Shih-chieh, 1961, repr., 30 *chüan,* with *Pu-cheng* [Addenda and corrigenda] 20 *chüan.*/ Wang Yün (1784–1854). [Explanations with examples of *Shuo-wen.*]

王筠：說文釋例　補正

4.1.1.7. Tuan's Commentary on *Shuo-wen* (3546–3563)

3546   Hsü, Shen. Comment. by Tuan, Yü-ts'ai: *Shuo-wen chieh-tzu chu.*—Shanghai: Chung-hua, 1937, 15 *chüan,* 16 *ts'e,* v.p., Szu-pu pei-yao ed.; Shanghai: Shang-hai ku-chi, 1981, repr., 15 *chüan,* 1, 7, 1, 2, 867, (character index) 1, 48 p./ Tuan Yü-ts'ai (1755–1815). [A commentary on *Shuo-wen chieh-tzu.*]

許慎撰，段玉裁注：說文解字注　「四部備要」本

3547   Hsü, Shen. Comment. by Tuan, Yü-ts'ai: *Shuo-wen chieh-tzu chu. Fu Shuo-wen cheng-pu, Chien-tzu so-yin.*—Taipei: Li-ming, 1975, 1, 877, 83, (index) 100 p. [A commentary on *Shuo-wen chieh-tzu.* With A supplement to *Shuo-wen* and A character index.]

許慎撰，段玉裁注：說文解字注　附說文正補檢字索引

3548   Ch'en, Sheng-ch'ang: *Shuo-wen Tuan-chu ti-wu k'ao.*—Hong Kong: Hsiang-kang Chung-wen ta-hsüeh Chung-kuo yü-yen wen-hsüeh-hui & Wan-yu t'u-shu kung-szu, 1970, 281 p. [A study on the conflicts (found) in Tuan's commentary on *Shuo-wen.*]
陳勝長：說文段注牴牾考

3549   Chou, Tsu-mo: Lun Tuan-shih *Shuo-wen chieh-tzu chu.*—*Wen-hsüeh chi* (0054), 852–884. [On Mr. Tuan's *Shuo-wen chieh-tzu chu.*]
周祖謨：論段氏『說文解字注』

3550   Fu, Tung-hua: Lüeh t'an *Shuo-wen chieh-tzu* Tuan-chu te chü-hsien-hsing.—*CKYW* 1961:10–11, 58–61. [A brief discussion on the limitations of Tuan's commentary on *Shuo-wen chieh-tzu.*]
傅東華：略談『說文解字』段注的局限性

3551   Huang, Jan-wei: *Shuo-wen chieh-tzu* Tuan-chu k'ao-cheng chiao-pu.—*Chung-kuo wen-tzu* 18, 1965, 1–18; 19, 1966, 1–8. [A supplement to the study and correction of Tuan's commentary on *Shuo-wen chieh-tzu.*]
黃然偉：『說文解字』段注考正校補

3552   Kimura, Eiichi: Dan Gyokusai no *Setsumon kaijichū* ni tsuite.—*Shinagaku* 7:3, 1934, 105–116. [On Tuan Yü-ts'ai's *Shuo-wen chieh-tzu chu.*]
木村英一：段玉裁 の『說文解字注』に 就いて

3553   Kuo, Tsai-i: Ts'ung *Shuo-wen Tuan-chu* k'an Chung-kuo ch'uan-t'ung yü-yen-hsüeh te yen-chiu fang-fa.—*Yü-yen wen-tzu . . . chuan-chi* (0089), 302–322. [Methods of traditional linguistic study in China as seen from *Shuo-wen Tuan chu.*]
郭在貽：從『說文段註』看中國傳統語言學的研究方法

3554   Lin, Ch'ing-hsün: Tuan Yü-ts'ai nien-piao.—*KMHP* 40, 1980, 227–260. [A chronology of Tuan Yü-ts'ai.]
林慶勳：段玉裁年表

3555   Liu, P'an-sui: Tuan Yü-ts'ai hsien-sheng nien-p'u.—*CHHP* 7:2, 1932, 52 s.p. [A chronological biography of Tuan Yü-ts'ai.]
劉盼遂：段玉裁先生年譜

3556   Lü, Ching-hsien: *Shuo-wen Tuan-chu chih li.*—Shanghai: Cheng-chung, 1946; Taipei: Cheng-chung, 1953, repr., 4, 98 p. [Topics in Tuan's commentary on *Shuo-wen.*]
呂景先：說文段注指例

3557   Pao, Kuo-shun: *Tuan Yü-ts'ai chiao kai Shuo-wen chih yen-chiu.*—Taipei: Kuo-li Cheng-chih ta-hsüeh, 1974, 4, 10, 580 p./ Publ. M.A. thesis. [A study of the corrections to *Shuo-wen* by Tuan Yü-ts'ai.]
鮑國順：段玉裁校改說文之研究

3558   San-chia-ts'ün hsüeh-chiu: *Chien-tzu i-kuan-san* (3518). [A single index for the characters of three works.]/ An index to (3530), (3546), and (3690).
三家村學究：檢字一貫三

3559   Shen, Ch'iu-hsiung: *Shuo-wen chieh-tzu Tuan-chu chih i.*—Taipei: Wen-shih-che, 1973, 18, 810 p./ 789–810: Bibliography. [Doubtful problems in *Shuo-wen chieh-tsu Tuan-chu.*]
沈秋雄：說文解字段注質疑

3560   Teng, Ssu-yü & Biggerstaff, Knight: *Shuo-wen chieh-tzu chu.*—*An annotated bibliography . . . reference works* (2898), 140.
〔說文解字注〕

3561   Wei, Yü-chang: *Tuan-chu Shuo-wen chieh-tzu chiao wu.*—Shanghai: Shang-wu, 1935, 2 vols., 2, 4, 3, 2, 49 p.; 4, 92 p. [Corrigenda to Tuan's commentary on *Shuo-wen chieh-tzu.*]
衛瑜章：段注說文解字斠誤

3562 Yin, Meng-lun: *Tuan Yü-ts'ai ho t'ate Shuo-wen chieh-tzu chu.*—*CKYW* 1961: 8, 43–49. [Tuan Yü-ts'ai and his *Shuo-wen chieh-tzu chu.*]
殷孟倫：段玉裁和他的『說文解字注』

3563 Ying, Yü-k'ang & Hsieh, Yün-fei: *Shuo-wen chieh-tzu chu.*—*Chung-wen kung-chü shu chih-yin* (2908), 7–9. [*Shuo-wen chieh-tzu chu.*]
應裕康、謝雲飛：『說文解字注』

4.1.2. *Yü-p'ien* (3564–3572)

3564 Ku, Yeh-wang. Rev. by Ch'en, P'engnien, et al.: *Ta-kuang i-hui Yü-p'ien.*—Shanghai: Shang-wu, 1936, repr., 30 *chüan*, 5 vols., 4, 672 p.; Shanghai: Chung-hua, 1937, repr., 30 *chüan*, 3 vols., v.p., Szu-pu pei-yao edition; Taipei: Hsin-hsing, 1963, repr., 432 p./ Ku Yeh-wang (A.D. 519–581). [An expanded and enlarged (edition of) *Jade chapters.*]
顧野王撰，陳彭年等重修：大廣益會玉篇 「四部備要」本

3565 Huang, Hsiao-te: *Yü-p'ien te ch'engchiu chi ch'i pan-pen hsi-t'ung.*—*TSYC* 1983:2, 145–152. [The achievements of *Yü-p'ien* and its system of edition.]
黃孝德：『玉篇』的成就及其版本系統

3566 Liu, Yeh-ch'iu: *Yü-p'ien.*—*Chung-kuo ku-tai te tzu-tien* (2927), 23–28; *Chung-kuo te tzu-tien* (2996), 21–23. [*Yü-p'ien.*]
劉葉秋：『玉篇』

3567 Okai, Shingo: *Gyokuhen no kenkyū ni tsuite.*—*Shibun* 15:7, 1933, 14–19. [On the study of *Yü-p'ien.*]
岡井慎吾：『玉篇』の研究について

3568 Okai, Shingo: *Gyokuhen no kenkyū.*—Tokyo: Tōyō Bunko, 1933, xiv, 430, 178, 6, 22 p., 20 pl./ Tōyō Bunko Ronsō, 19; *Shibun* 16:5, 1934, 17–23, Kanda Kiichirō & Hamano Chizaburō. [A (bibliographical and lexicographical) study of *Yü-p'ien.*]

岡井慎吾：玉篇の研究　「東洋文庫論叢」十九／神田喜一郎、濱野知三郎評

3569 Shiba, Rokurō: *Gyokuhen.*—*Ajia rekishi jiten* (0040), 2:422–423. [*Yü-p'ien.*]
斯波六郎：『玉篇』

3570 Tōdō, Akiyasu: *Gyokuhen.*—*Sekai meicho daijiten* (0041), 2:76. [*Yü-p'ien.*]
藤堂明保：『玉篇』

3571 Ueda, Tadashi: *Gyokuhen zankan ronkō.*—*KBJGD* 17:1, 1970, 21–37. [A study on the fragments of *Yü-p'ien.*]
上田正：『玉篇』殘卷論考

3572 Wang, Kuei-nien: *Yü-p'ien fan-ch'ieh k'ao.*—Tientsin: I-wen hsüeh-hui, 1935, 101 p. [A study on the *fan-ch'ieh* (system) of *Yü-p'ien.*]
汪桂年：玉篇反切考

4.1.3. *K'ang-hsi tzu-tien* (3573–3597)

3573 Chang, Yü-shu; Ch'en, T'ing-ching; et al.: *K'ang-hsi tzu-tien.*—Peking: Palace block-print ed., 1716, 40 *ts'e;* Peking: Chung-hua, 1958, 71, 1562, 2, 47 p.; Taipei: I-wen, 1965, 2 vols., 6, 3598 p.; Hong Kong: Chung-hua, 1958; 1977, repr., 6, 4, 2, 28, 31, 1562, 2, 47 p.; Peking: Chung-hua, 1981, 4th print.; Tainan: Tsung-ho, 1980, repr. [The K'ang-hsi dictionary.]/ See (3590).
張玉書、陳廷敬等：康熙字典

3574 Chang, Yü-shu; Ling, Shao-wen & Kao, Shu-fan: *Hsin hsiu K'ang-hsi tzu-tien.*—Taipei: Ch'i-yeh shu-chü, 1979, 2 vols., 71, 2424, (appendices) 276 p. [A newly revised (edition of) *K'ang-hsi tzu-tien.*]/ Rearranged with new phonetic annotations, etc.
張玉書（總閱）、凌紹雯（纂修）、高樹藩（重修）：新修康熙字典

3575 Chang, Chin-lang: *K'ang-hsi tzu-tien.*—*Chung-wen ts'an-k'ao . . . chih-yin* (2889), 219–220. [*K'ang-hsi tzu-tien.*]

張錦郎：『康熙字典』

3576   Chang, P'u, et al.: Yeh t'an *K'ang-hsi tzu-tien* te shou tzu tsung-shu.—*CYTH* 1981:3. 22–23. [Also discussing the total number of characters entered in *K'ang-hsi tzu-tien.*]
張普等：也談『康熙字典』的收字總數

3577   Chang, Ti-hua: Lun *K'ang-hsi tzu-tien.* —*Chiang-huai hsüeh-k'an* 1962:1 49–55; 2, 57–68. [On *K'ang-hsi tzu-tien.*]
張滌華：論『康熙字典』

3578   Chao, Yin-t'ang: *K'ang-hsi tzu-tien Tzu-mu ch'ieh-yün yao-fa* k'ao-cheng.—*BIHP* 3:1, 1931, 93–120. [Textual verification of the principal methods for *fan-ch'ieh* spelling (found) of in *K'ang-hsi tzu-tien.*]
趙蔭棠：『康熙字典字母切韻要法』考證

3579   Courant, M.A.: A propos du "système unique de transcription en lettres latines des caractères du dictionnaire de K'ang-hi".—*TP* 10, 1899, 53–67.

3580   Fu, Pao-shen: Kai-liang *K'ang-hsi tzu-tien* te chien-i yü pien-chi min-chung shih-yung tzu-tien te shang-ch'üeh. —*CYYMC* 2:4, 1930, 1–15. [Suggestions on revising *K'ang-hsi tzu-tien* and a discussion of the compilatio of a people's practical (character) dictionary.]
傅葆琛：改良『康熙字典』的建議與編輯民眾實用字典的商榷

3581   Hsiao, Hsien: Tien k'o t'ung-pan *K'ang-hsi tzu-tien.*—*Ch'ang liu* 20:8, 1959, 16. [The palace copperplate engraved edition of *K'ang-hsi tzu-tien.*]
蕭閒：殿刻銅版『康熙字典』

3582   Huang, Chi-kang: Lun *K'ang-hsi tzu-tien* chih fei.—*Chih-yen* 40, 1937, 1–2. [On errata (found) in *K'ang-hsi tzu-tien.*]
黃季剛：論『康熙字典』之非

3583   Huang, Yün-mei: *K'ang-hsi tzu-tien* yin shu cheng wu.—*CLHP* 6:2, 1936, 173–

181. [Evidence of errata in citations in *K'ang-hsi tzu-tien.*]
黃云眉：『康熙字典』引書證誤

3584   Kao, Ming: Tzu-shu yü hsin hsiu *K'ang-hsi tzu-tien.*—*HWSC* 16, 1979, 16–20. [Character dictionaries and the newly revised (edition of) *K'ang-hsi tzu-tien* (3574).]
高明：字書與新修『康熙字典』

3585   Kao, Ming: Tzu-shu yü *K'ang-hsi tzu-tien.*—*Chiang-su wen-hsien* 10, 1979, 72–75. [Character dictionaries and *K'ang-hsi tzu-tien.*]
高明：字書與『康熙字典』

3586   Kao, Ming: Hsin pien *K'ang-hsi tzu-tien* hsü.—*CHHY* 23, 1980, 6–9. [A preface to the newly edited *K'ang-hsi tzu-tien* (3574).]
高明：新編『康熙字典』序

3587   Kurata, Junnosuke: *Kōki jiten.*—*Sekai dai hyakka jiten* (0042) 10, 81. [*K'ang-hsi tzu-tien.*]
倉田淳之助：『康熙字典』

3588   Li, Hsin-k'uei: *K'ang-hsi tzu-tien* te liang chung yün t'u.—*TSYC* 1980:1, 174–182. [Two types of rhyme tables in *K'ang-hsi tzu-tien.*]
李新魁：『康熙字典』的兩種韵圖

3589   Liu, Yeh-ch'iu: *K'ang-hsi tzu-tien.*—*Chung-kuo ku-tai te tzu-tien* (2927), 50–56; *Chung-kuo te tzu-tien* (2996), 35–39; *Ch'ang-yung tzu-shu shih chiang* (2997), 10–13. [*K'ang-hsi tzu-tien.*]
劉葉秋：『康熙字典』

3590   Nash, Vernon: *Trindex: An index to three dictionaries.*—Peiping: Index Press, Yenching U., 1936, i, lxx, 576 p.; Taipei: Ch'eng-wen, 1967, repr., i, lxx, 584, 6, 10 p./ Index to Giles' *Chinese-English dictionary* (4048), *K'ang-hsi tzu-tien* (3573), and *P'ei-wen yün-fu* (3709).
〔三字典引得〕

3591 Teng, Ssu-yü & Biggerstaff, Knight: *K'ang-hsi tzu-tien.—An annotated bibliography . . . reference works* (2898), 129–130.

〔康熙字典〕

3592 Tōdō, Akiyasu: *Kōki jiten.—Sekai meicho daijiten* (0041) 2, 340. [*K'ang-hsi tzu-tien.*]

藤堂明保：『康熙字典』

3593 Tsuchihashi, Yachita: Sur la correction du dictionnaire chinois *K'ang-hi-tse-tien* 康熙字典*.—MN* 5:2, 1942, 46–60.

〔土橋八千太〕

3594 Tung, Tso-pin: *K'ang-hsi tzu-tien te ting-cheng.—TLTC* 15:2, 1957, 1–4. [Corrigenda to *K'ang-hsi tzu-tien.*]

董作賓：『康熙字典』的訂正

3595 Wang, Yin-chih: *Tzu-tien k'ao cheng.* —Wuchang: Ch'ung-wen shu-chü, 1876, 6 vols., 12 pts., v.p.; Taipei: I-wen, 1959, repr., 284 p. [Textual verification of *K'ang-hsi tzu-tien.*]

王引之：字典考證

3596 Watabe, Atsushi: *Kōki jiten kōi seigo.* —Tokyo: Ida shoten, 1943, 423 p./ First publ. in 1887. [A study of (lexical) differences and correction of errors in *K'ang-hsi tzu-tien.*]

渡部溫：康熙字典考異正誤

3597 Wu, Hsiao-ju & Chuang, Ming-ch'üan: *K'ang-hsi tzu-tien.— Chung-kuo wen-shih . . . chü-yao* (2903), 41–48. [*K'ang-hsi tzu-tien.*]

吳小如、莊銘權：『康熙字典』

4.2. Word and Phrase Dictionaries (3598–3668)
4.2.1. *Erh-ya* and *Kuang-ya* (3598–3634)
4.2.1.1. *Erh-ya* (3598–3630)

3598 Anonymous. Kuo, P'u (comment.): *Erh-ya chu.*—Taipei: Shang-wu, 1963, 3 *chüan*, 30 p./ Szu-pu ts'ung-k'an ch'u-pien, 010; Kuo P'u (A.D. 276–324). [A commentary on *Approaching elegance and refinement.*]

無名氏著，郭璞注：爾雅注 「四部叢刊」初編 010

3599 Anonymous. Kuo, P'u & Hsing, Ping (comment.): *Erh-ya chu shu.*—Taipei: I-wen, 1965, repr., 10 *chüan*, 206 p./ Shih-san ching chu shu, Vol. 8; Hsing Ping (A.D. 932–1010). [Notes and commentary on *Erh-ya.*]

無名氏著，郭璞注，邢昺疏：爾雅注疏 「十三經注疏」第八冊

3600 Carr, Michael Edward: *A linguistic study of the flora and fauna sections of the Erh-ya.*—Tucson: The U. of Arizona, 1979, 616 p./ Unpubl. doc. diss. *DAI* 40:2035–2036–A; UM 7920598.

3601 Chang, Wei-szu: *Erh-ya i lei.—Chih-hsüeh yüeh-k'an* 1, 1942, 11–13; 2, 16–19. [Semantic categories of *Erh-ya.*]

張維思：『爾雅』義類

3602 Chang, Yung-yen: Lun Hao I-hsing te *Erh-ya i-shu.—CKYW* 1962:11, 502–509, 495. [On Hao I-hsing's *Erh-ya i-shu* (3610).]

張永言：論郝懿行的『爾雅義疏』

3603 Chou, Tsu-mo: *Erh-ya* chih tso-che chi ch'i ch'eng-shu chih nien-tai.—*Wen-hsüeh chi* (0054), 670–675. [The author of *Erh-ya* and its period of completion.]

周祖謨：『爾雅』之作者及其成書之年代

3604 Chou, Tsu-mo: *Erh-ya* Kuo-chu ku-pen pa.—*Wen-hsüeh chi* (0054), 676–682, 1 pl. [A postscript to the ancient edition of Kuo's commentary on *Erh-ya.*]

周祖謨：『爾雅』郭注古本跋

3605 Chou, Tsu-mo: Kuo P'u *Erh-ya chu* yü *Erh-ya yin-i.—Wen-hsüeh chi* (0054), 683–686. [Kuo P'u's commentary on *Erh-ya* and *Erh-ya yin-i* ('Pronunciations and meanings in *Erh-ya*').]

周祖謨：郭璞『爾雅注』與『爾雅音義』

3606   Chou, Yin-meng: Po-wen ch'iang-chi te Kuo P'u.—*CKYW* 1956:7, 39–43. [Kuo P'u: A learned scholar and man of good memory.]
周因夢：博聞強記的郭璞

3607   Coblin, Weldon South Jr.: *An introductory study of textual and linguistic problems in Erh-ya.*—Seattle: U. of Washington, 1972, ix, 574 p.; 559–574: Bibliography./ Unpubl. doc. diss.; *DAI* 33:4, 1972, 2353–A; UM 72–28,584.

3608   Fang, Yen: Shih-chieh tsui-tsao te pai-k'o ch'üan-shu—*Erh-ya.*—*Hsüeh-hsi yü t'an-so* 1979:4, 95– (not seen). [The world's earliest encyclopedia—*Erh-ya.*]
方衍：世界最早的百科全書——『爾雅』

3609   Fukuda, Jōnosuke: *Jiga no seikaku*—Chūgoku jishoshi no ikkan toshite.—*OKHB* 36, 1975, 29–36. [The characteristics of *Erh-ya*—as a link in the history of Chinese character dictionaries.]
福田襄之介：『爾雅』の 性格——中國字書史 の一環として

3610   Hao, I-hsing: *Erh-ya i-shu.*—Taipei: Fu-hsing shu-chü, 1961, repr., 20 *chüan*, v.p./ Huang Ch'ing ching-chieh, Vol. 1257–1276. [An exegesis of *Erh-ya.*]
郝懿行：爾雅義疏   「皇清經解」本

3611   Harvard-Yenching Institute: *Erh-ya yin-te.*—Peking: Harvard-Yenching Institute, 1941, xxxii, 129 p.; Taipei: Ch'eng-wen, 1966, repr./ Harvard-Yenching Institute Sinological Index Series. Supplement, 18. [An index to *Erh-ya.*]/ Preceded by a standard text.
哈佛燕京學社：爾雅引得

3612   Ho, Wen-kuang: *Erh-ya* chieh t'i.—*Wen-hsüeh* 2, 1948, 12–14. [Explanation of *Erh-ya.*]
何文廣：『爾雅』 解題

3613   Huang, K'an: *Erh-ya* lüeh shuo.—*Chung-yang ta-hsüeh wen-i ts'ung-k'an* 2:2, 1936, 1–36; *Huang K'an lun-hsüeh tsa-chu* (0066), 361–401. [A brief discussion on *Erh-ya.*]
黃侃：『爾雅』略說

3614   Kao, Ming: *Erh-ya* chih tso-che chi ch'i chuan-tso chih shih-tai.—*CHHY* 14, 1974, 11–30; *Kao Ming hsiao-hsüeh lun-ts'ung* (0067), 445–465. [The author of *Erh-ya* and its period of compilation.]
高明：『爾雅』 之作者及其撰作之時代

3615   Kondō, Hideyoshi: *Jiga kō*—*Shiko teiyō* yakuchū.—*Daitō Bunka Daigaku Kangakkaishi* 12, 1973, 44–60. [A study of *Erh-ya*—Translation and commentary on *Szu k'u t'i-yao.*]
近藤英幸：『爾雅』考——『四庫提要』譯註

3616   Kondō, Mitsuo: *Jiga.*—*Ajia rekishi jiten* (0040), 4, 126–127. [*Erh-ya.*]
近藤光男：『爾雅』

3617   Kuraishi, Takeshirō: *Jiga.*—*Sekai dai hyakka jiten* (0042) 13, 53. [*Erh-ya.*]
倉石武四郎：『爾雅』

3618   Li, Fa-pai: *Erh-ya* shih tz'u ts'o li.—*CTHP* 1963:4, 85–112. [Extracts of explanations of words in *Erh-ya.*]
李法白：『爾雅』 釋詞撮例

3619   Liu, Shih-p'ei: *Erh-ya* ch'ung ming chin shih.—*Kuo-ts'ui hsüeh-pao* 3rd year: 6:29, 1907, 7–11; 30, 1–3; 33, 1–2; 34, 1–2; 37, 6–8; 5th year: 1:50, 1909, 1–3; 2:51, 1–3; 4:53, 5–6. [Modern explanations of insect names in *Erh-ya.*]
劉師培：『爾雅』 蟲名今釋

3620   Liu, Yeh-ch'iu: *Erh-ya.*—*Chung-kuo ku-tai te tzu-tien* (2927), 81–90; *Chung-kuo te tzu-tien* (2996), 78–82. [*Erh-ya.*]
劉葉秋：『爾雅』

3621   Lu, Tien: *Erh-ya hsin-i.*—Shanghai: Shang-wu, 1937, repr., 20 *chüan*, 3 vols.,

616 p./ Lu Tien (1042–1102). [The new meanings of *Erh-ya*.]
陸佃：爾雅新義

3622   Rosthorn, Arthur von: Das *Er-ya* und andere Synonymiken.—*WZKM* 49, 1942, 126–144.

3623   Rosthorn, Arthur von. Transl. by Ernst Wolff: The *Erh-ya* and other synonymicons (3622).—*JCLTA* 10:3, 1975, 137–145.

3624   Tōdō, Akiyasu: *Jiga.—Sekai meicho daijiten* (0041) 3, 8. [*Erh-ya*.]
藤堂明保：『爾雅』

3625   Ts'ai, Sheng-yung: *Erh-ya* yü pai-k'o ch'üan-shu.—*TSYC* 1981:1, 244–259, 243. [*Erh-ya* and encyclopedias.]
蔡聲鏞：『爾雅』與百科全書

3626   Wang, Yün-shih: *Erh-ya* cheng ming. —*Chih-yen* 18, 1936, 1–63; 19, 65–132. [Rectification of the name '*Erh-ya*'.]
汪芸石：『爾雅』正名

3627   Wei, Tzu-ming: *Erh-ya*-hsüeh.—*Pei-ch'iang yüeh-k'an* 2:1, 1935, 1–14. [*Erh-ya* studies.]
魏紫銘：『爾雅』學

3628   Wu, Chi-hui: *Erh-ya* yü liu ching te kuan-hsi.—*Wen-hsüeh yen-chiu* 1:3, 1939, 197–204. [The relationship between *Erh-ya* and the Six Classics.]
吳繼輝：『爾雅』與六經的關係

3629   Yang, Shu-ta: *Erh-ya* lüeh li.—*Chi-wei-chü hsiao-hsüeh shu-lin* (0091), 240–241. [Examples in general from *Erh-ya*.]
楊樹達：『爾雅』略例

3630   Yüan, Yü-hsin: Tien-chi chu-shih-chia Kuo P'u.—*TSYC* 1982:2, 171–174. [Kuo P'u: Commentator on classical texts.]
苑育新：典籍注釋家郭璞

4.2.1.2 *Kuang-ya* (3631–3634)

3631   Chang, I. Comm. by Wang, Nien-sun: *Kuang-ya shu-cheng.*—Taipei: Wu-chou, n.d., 10 *chüan*, 415 p.; Taipei: Ting-wen shu-chü, 1972, repr., 2, 398 p. [Exegetical evidence for *Erh-ya* expanded.]
張揖撰，王念孫疏證：廣雅疏證

3632   Chou, Fa-kao (ed. in chief): *Kuang-ya so-yin.*—Hong Kong: Hsiang-kang Chung-wen ta-hsüeh ch'u-pan-she, 1977, 50, 675 p. [An index to *Kuang-ya*.]
周法高主編：廣雅索引

3633   Chu, T'ien-chün & Ch'en, Hung-t'ien: *Kuang-ya shu-cheng.*—*Wen-k'o kung-chü shu chien chieh* (2890), 23–25. [*Kuang-ya shu-cheng*.]
朱天俊、陳宏天：『廣雅疏證』

3634   Liang, Ch'un-hua: *Kuang-ya k'ao.*—Taipei: Kuo-li Cheng-chih ta-hsüeh Chung-wen yen-chiu-so, 1975, [i], 7, 131 p./ 127–131: Bibliography; publ. M.A. thesis. [A study of *Kuang-ya*.]
梁春華：廣雅考

4.2.2. *Shih-ming* (3635–3646)

3635   Liu, Hsi: *Shih-ming.*—Shanghai: Shang-wu, 1936, repr., 8 *chüan*, 35 p./ Szu-pu ts'ung-k'an ch'u-pien, 015. [Explanations of names.]
劉熙：釋名 「四部叢刊」初編015

3636   Liu, Hsi. Comment. by Pi, Yüan: *Shih-ming shu-cheng.*—Taipei: Kuang-wen, 1971, 8 *chüan*, 3, 70 p. [Exegetical evidence for *Shih-ming*.]
劉熙撰，畢沅疏證：釋名疏證

3637   Ch'i, P'ei-jung: *Shih-ming* yin-hsün chü-li chi ch'i tsai yü-yen-hsüeh shang chih kung-hsien (0849). [Examples of sound glosses in *Shih-ming* and its contribution to (Chinese) linguistics.]
齊佩瑢：『釋名』音訓舉例及其在語言學上之貢獻

3638   Chou, Tsu-mo: Shu Liu Hsi *Shih-ming*

hou.—*Wen-hsüeh chi* (0054), 885—888. [A postscript to Liu Hsi's *Shih-ming.*]

周祖謨：書劉熙『釋名』後

3639   Fang, Chün-chi: *Shih-ming k'ao shih* (0840)./ Chap. 7: Works related to *Shih-ming.* [A study and explanation of *Shih-ming.*]

方俊吉：釋名考釋／第七章：『釋名』有關之著述

3640   Hu, Ch'u-sheng: *Shih-ming* k'ao.—*TSST* 8, 1964, 139—361. [The study of *Shih-ming.*]/ A classified and annotated bibliography.

胡楚生：『釋名』考

3641   Kondō, Mitsuo: *Shakumei.*—*Ajia rekishi jiten* (0040) 4, 233. [*Shih-ming.*]

近藤光男：『釋名』

3642   Li, Wei-fen: *Shih-ming yen-chiu* (0851). [A study of *Shih-ming.*]

李維棻：釋名研究

3643   Liu, Yeh-ch'iu: *Shih-ming.*—*Chung-kuo ku-tai te tzu-tien* (2927), 90—94; *Chung-kuo te tzu-tien* (2996), 82—84. [*Shih-ming.*]

劉葉秋：『釋名』

3644   Sun, Te-hsüan: Liu Hsi ho t'a-te *Shih-ming.*—*CKYW* 1956:11, 26—30. [Liu Hsi and his *Shih-ming.*]

孫德宣：劉熙和他的『釋名』

3645   Tōdō, Akiyasu: *Shakumei.*—*Sekai meicho daijiten* (0041) 3, 188. [*Shih-ming.*]

藤堂明保：『釋名』

3646   Wang, Hsien-ch'ien: *Shih-ming shu-cheng pu.*—Taipei: Shang-wu, 1968, 2 vols., 8 *chüan,* 474 p./ Kuo-hsüeh chi-pen ts'ung-shu, 112. [A supplement to *Shih-ming shu-cheng* (3636).]

王先謙：釋名疏證補　「國學基本叢書」112

4.2.3. *Fang-yen* (3647—3668)

3647   Yang, Hsiung. Comment. by Kuo, P'u

& Tai, Chen: *Yu-hsüan shih-che chüeh-tai yü shih pieh-kuo fang-yen.*—Shanghai: Shang-wu, 1937, repr., 13 *chüan,* 2 vols., ix, ii, 326, 4, 2 p./ Yang Hsiung (53 B.C.—A.D. 18). [Dialect words of other states in times immemorial (collected and) explained by the Light-Carriage Messenger.]

揚雄撰，郭璞注，戴震疏證：輶軒使者絕代語釋別國方言

3648   Chao, Chen-to: Yang Hsiung *Fang-yen* shih tui *Erh-ya* te fa-chan.—*SKY* 1969:4, 116—119. [Yang Hsiung's *Fang-yen* in relation to the development of *Erh-ya.*]

趙振鐸：揚雄『方言』是對『爾雅』的發展

3649   Chou, Tsu-mo & Wu, Hsiao-ling: *Fang-yen chiao-chien chi t'ung-chien.*—Peking: K'o-hsüeh, 1956, xxii, 95, 1 map; lx, 249 p./ *CKYW* 1957:3, 47, Chang Ch'i-hua; *CKYW* 1963:5, 428—431, Hu Chih-fan; *Orbis* 15, 1966, 97—98, Paul Yang. [Critical notes and a general index to *Fang-yen.*]

周祖謨、吳曉鈴：方言校箋及通檢／張其華評，胡芷藩評

3650   Chou, Yin-meng: Yang Hsiung ho t'a-te *Fang-yen.*—*CKYW* 1956:5, 37—40. [Yang Hsiung and his *Fang-yen.*]

周因夢：揚雄和他的『方言』

3651   Fukuda, Jōnosuke: Yō Yū *Hōgen* no seiritsu ni tsuite.—*Tōhōgakkai sōritsu nijūgoshūnen kinen Tōhōgaku ronshū* (Tokyo: Tōhōgakkai, 1972), 739—753. [On the formation of Yang Hsiung's *Fang-yen.*]

福田襄之助：揚雄『方言』の成立について──『東方學會創立二十五周年紀念東方學論集』

3652   Huang, Tien-ch'eng: *Fang-yen* chi ch'i chu pen.—*TSYC* 1982:3, 162—171. [*Fang-yen* and its commentaries.]

黃典誠：『方言』及其注本

3653   Knechtges, David R.: The Liu Hsin/ Yang Hsiung correspondence on the *Fang Yen.*—*MS* 33, 1977—1978, 309—325.

3654   Knechtges, David R. (transl. & annot.): *The Han shu biography of Yang Xiong* (53 B.C.–A.D. 18).—Tempe, Arizona: Center for Asian Studies, Arizona State U., 1982, ix, 179 p./ 148–161: Bibliography; Center for Asian Studies, Occasional Paper, 14.
〔『漢書』揚雄傳〕

3655   Li, Hsien: Yang Hsiung sheng-p'ing k'ao shu.—*THHP* 17, 1976, 15–31. [An account of the life of Yang Hsiung.]
李鋟：揚雄生平考述

3656   Liu, Yeh-ch'iu: *Fang-yen.*— *Chung-kuo ku-tai te tzu-tien* (2927), 109–117; *Chung-kuo te tzu-tien* (2996), 92–96. [*Fang-yen.*]
劉葉秋：『方言』

3657   Lo, Ch'ang-p'ei: Yang Hsiung *Fang-yen* tsai Chung-kuo yü-yen-hsüeh shih shang te ti-wei.—*Lo Ch'ang-p'ei yü-yen-hsüeh lun-wen hsüan-chi* (Peking: Chung-hua, 1963), 177–179. [The position of Yang Hsiung's *Fang-yen* in the history of Chinese linguistics.]
羅常培：揚雄『方言』在中國語言學史上的地位──『羅常培語言學論文選集』

3658   Ma, Kuang-yü: *Fang-yen chiao shih.* —Taipei: Shang-wu, 1970, ii, 92 p. [Critical notes and explanations on *Fang-yen.*]
馬光宇：方言校釋

3659   Nishida, Taiichirō: *Hōgen.*—*Ajia rekishi jiten* (0040) 8, 261. [*Fang-yen.*]
西田太一郎：『方言』

3660   Serruys, Paul L-M.: *Prolegomena to the study of Chinese dialects of Han times according to Fang-yen.*—Berkeley: U. of California, 1956, xi, 605 p./ Unpubl. doc. diss.

3661   Serruys, Paul L-M.: *The Chinese dialects of Han Time according to Fang Yen.*—Berkeley and Los Angeles: U. of California Press, 1959, xix, 350 p., maps./ *JAOS* 79, 1959, 309–310, Li Fang-kuei; *RBS* 5, 1959, 483, N.C. Bodman; *TP* 47, 1959, 435–441, M.J. Künstler; *BSOAS* 23, 1960, 165–167, G.B. Downer; *Lingua* 9, 1960, 306–309, A.F.P. Hulsewé; *MS* 19, 1960, 518–523; *Chūgokugogaku ken-kyū* (0075), 339–351, Ogawa Tamaki; *TYGH* 43:3, 1960, 86–91, Kōno Rokurō; *AOH* 13, 1961, 333–335, B. Csongor; *Orbis* 15, 1966, 98, Paul Yang.

3662   Tagawa, Kazumi: Yō Yū to sono cho *Hōgen* ni tsuite.—*DBDK* 14, 1976, 141–147. [On Yang Hiung and his work *Fang-yen.*]
田川一巳：揚雄とその著『方言』について

3663   Tōdō, Akiyasu: *Hōgen.*—*Sekai meicho daijiten* (0041) 5, 479–480. [*Fang-yen.*]
藤堂明保：『方言』

3664   Ts'ai, Feng-ch'i: Wu *Ya* chi *Fang-yen* te fen-lei.—*SWYK* 1:1, 1939, 22–28; 1:2, 1939, 17–18. [The classifications of the Five *Ya* and *Fang-yen.*]
蔡鳳圻：五雅及『方言』的分類

3665   Tung, Tso-pin: Fang-yen-hsüeh-chia Yang Hsiung nien-p'u.—*CSTY* 8:85–87, 1929, 82–88. [A chronological biography of the dialectologist Yang Hsiung.]
董作賓：方言學家揚雄年譜

3666   Wang, Te-chao: Yang Hsiung.—*Chung-kuo wen-hsüeh shih lun-chi* (Ed. by Chang, Ch'i-yün. Taipei: Chung-hua wen-hua, 1958), 79–112. [(A biography of) Yang Hsiung.]
王德昭：揚雄──張其昀編：『中國文學史論集』

3667   Yang, Shu-ta: Tu *Fang-yen* shu-hou. —*Chi-wei-chü hsiao-hsüeh shu-lin* (0091), 271–272. [A postscript after reading *Fang-yen.*]
楊樹達：讀『方言』書後

3668   Yuan, Yü-hsin: Hsin-ch'in pien-hsieh

Fang-yen te Yang Hsiung.—*TSYC* 1982:3, 172–175. [Yang Hsiung: The diligent compiler of *Fang-yen*.]
苑育新：辛勤編寫『方言』的揚雄

4.3. Exegetical and Grammatical Dictionaries (3669–3708)

4.3.1. *Ching-tien shih-wen* (3669–3677)

3669   Lu, Te-ming. Rev. by Lu, Wen-ch'ao: *Ching-tien shih-wen.*—Shaghai: Shang-wu, 1936, repr., 30 *chüan*, 18 vols., 1732, 4 p.; Taipei: Han-ching wen-hua, 1980, repr., 4, 546 p.; Shanghai: Shang-hai ku-chi, 1981, repr./ T'u-shu chi-ch'eng ed.; Lu Te-ming (?–A.D. 630); Lu Wen-ch'ao (1717–1795). [Textual explanations of Chinese classics.]
陸德明撰，盧文弨校正：經典釋文
「圖書集成本」

3670   Chao, Shao-hsien: Ju-ho tu *Ching-tien shih-wen.*—*SCTH* 1959:5, 1–10. [How to read *Ching-tien shih-wen.*]
趙少咸：如何讀『經典釋文』

3671   Chou, Fa-kao: Chi chu-chia chiao-pen *Ching-tien shih-wen.*—*TLTC* 11:11, 1955, 1–4; *Chung-kuo yü-wen lun-ts'ung* (0052), 351–369. [Notes on various authors' revised editions of *Ching-tien shih-wen.*]
周法高：記諸家校本『經典釋文』

3672   Huang, Liu-p'ing: Lu Wen-ch'ao *Ching-tien shih-wen Mao-shih yin-i k'ao-cheng ting-pu.*—*JOS* 8:2, 1970, 289–301; E.S. [Revised supplements to Lu Wen-ch'ao's *Mao-shih yin-i k'ao-cheng* in *Ching-tien shih-wen.*]
黃六平：盧文弨『經典釋文』『毛詩音義考證』訂補

3673   Lin, T'ao: *Ching-tien shih-wen* i-wen chih fen-hsi.—*YCHP* 38, 1950, 1–102; Lu, Chih-wei: Pu-cheng.—*YCHP* 40, 1951, 64–88. [An analysis of textual variants (quoted) in *Ching-tien shih-wen.* Supplementary corrigenda.]
林燾：『經典釋文』異文之分析 陸志韋：補正

3674   Lin, T'ao: Lu Te-ming te *Ching-tien shih-wen.*—*CKYW* 1962:3, 132–136. [Lu Te-ming's *Ching-tien shih-wen.*]
林燾：陸德明的『經典釋文』

3675   Liu, Yeh-ch'iu: *Ching-tien shih-wen.*—*Chung-kuo ku-tai te tzu-tien* (2927), 56–60; *Chung-kuo te tzu-tien* (2996), 47–50. [*Ching-tien shih-wen.*]
劉葉秋：『經典釋文』

3676   Lu, Wen-ch'ao: *Ching-ten shih-wen k'ao-cheng.*—Shanghai: Shang-wu, 1935, repr., 4 vols., 386 p./ First ed., 1791. [Textual verification of *Ching-tien shih-wen.*]
盧文弨：經典釋文考證

3677   Wu, Hsiao-ju & Chuang, Ming-ch'üan: *Ching-tien shih-wen.*—*Chung-kuo wen-shih . . . chü-yao* (2903), 186–188. [*Ching-tien shih-wen.*]
吳小如、莊銘權：『經典釋文』

4.3.2. *I-ch'ieh-ching yin-i* (3678–3689)

3678   Hsüan, Ying. Rev. by Chuang, Hsin; Ch'ien, Tien & Sun, Hsing-yen: *I-ch'ieh-ching yin-i.*—Shanghai: Shang-wu, 1936, repr., 25 *chüan*, 6 vols., 1158 p./ Hsüan Ying (?–ca. A.D. 663). [Sound and meaning of all Sutras.]
玄應撰，莊炘、錢坫、孫星衍校：一切經音義

3679   Hui, Lin. Supplement by Hsi, Lin: *I-ch'ieh-ching yin-i.*—Shanghai: Shang-wu, 1938, repr., 100; 10 *chüan*, 3 vols., 2114, 79 p.; Taipei: Ta-t'ung, 1970, repr./ Hui Lin (A.D. 737–820); Hsi Lin (fl. A.D. 987). [Sound and meaning of all Sutras.]
慧琳撰，希麟續：一切經音義

3680   Ch'en, Ting-min: Hui Lin *I-ch'ieh-ching yin-i* chung chih i-t'i tzu.—*CFTH* 3:1, 1933, 13–36; 3:2–3, 101–118; 3:4–5, 141–154; 4:4, 1934, 115–121. [Logographic variants in Hui Lin's *I-ch'ieh-ching yin-i.*]
陳定民：慧琳『一切經音義』中之異體字

3681   Chou, Fa-kao (ed.): *Hsüan Ying I-ch'ieh-ching yin-i. Fu So-yin mu-lu.*—Taipei: Academia Sinica, 1962, 16, 97, 87 p. [Hsüan Ying's *I-ch'ieh-ching yin-i.* With An index of contents.]
周法高編：玄應一切經音義　附索引目錄

3682   Chou, Tsu-mo: Chiao-tu Hsüan Ying *I-ch'ieh-ching yin-i* hou chi.—*Wen-hsüeh chi* (0054), 192–212, 1 pl. [Notes after proofreading Hsüan Ying's *I-ch'ieh-ching yin-i.*]
周祖謨：校讀玄應『一切經音義』後記

3683   Liu, Yeh-ch'iu: *I-ch'ieh-ching yin-i.*—*Chung-kuo ku-tai te tzu-tien* (2927), 60–67. [*I-ch'ieh-ching yin-i.*]
劉葉秋：『一切經音義』

3684   Pei-ching ta-hsüeh Yen-chiu-yüan Wen-shih-pu: *Hui Lin I-ch'ieh-ching yin-i yin-yung shu so-yin.*—Shanghai: Shang-wu, 1938, 5 vols., 3, 1548, 3 p.; Taipei: Ta-t'ung, 1970, repr., 2 vols./ Pei-ching ta-hsüeh Wen-hsüeh-yüan Wen-shih ts'ung-k'an, 6. [An index to the works quoted in Hui Lin's *I-ch'ieh-ching yin-i.*]
北京大學研究院文史部：慧琳一切經音義引用書索引　「北京大學文學院文史叢刊」第六種

3685   Ueda, Tadashi: Gen Ō *Ongi* shohon ronkō.—*TYGH* 63, 1981, 1–28; E.S. [A study of the various editions of Hsüan Ying's *I-ch'ieh-ching yin-i.*]
上田正：玄應『音義』諸本論考

3686   Wu, Hsiao-ju & Chuang, Ming-ch'üan: *I-ch'ieh-ching yin-i.*—*Chung-kuo wen-shih . . . chü-yao* (2903), 188–190. [*I-ch'ieh-ching yin-i.*]
吳小如、莊銘權：『一切經音義』

3687   Wu, Huan-jui: *Hui Lin Hsi Lin I-ch'ieh-ching yin-i cheng hsü pien yin Erh-ya k'ao.*—Taipei: Wen-chin, 1976, 8, 2, 138 p. [A study on the citations from *Erh-ya* in Hui Lin and Hsi Lin's first and second volumes of *I-ch'ieh-ching yin-i.*]
吳煥瑞：慧琳希麟一切經音義正續編引爾雅考

3688   Yamada, Yoshio: *Issaikyō ongi sakuin.*—Tokyo: Saitō shobō, 1963, rev. ed., xvii, 722, 21 p./ First ed., 1925. [An index to *I-ch'ieh-ching yin-i.*]
山田孝雄：一切經音義索引

3689   Yen, Pei-ming: I pu ku Fo-chiao tz'u-tien—*I-ch'ieh-ching yin-i.*—*TSYC* 1980: 3, 173–180. [An old Buddhist dictionary —*I-ch'ieh-ching yin-i.*]
嚴北溟：一部古佛教辭典——『一切經音義』

4.3.3.   *Ching-chi tsuan-ku* (3690–3699)

3690   Juan, Yüan, et al.: *Ching-chi tsuan-ku.*—Shanghai: Kuo-hsüeh cheng-li-she, 1936, repr., [82], 1072 p.; Taipei: Shih-chieh, 1956, repr., [82], 1072 p.; Peking: Chung-hua, 1982, repr./ Completed in 1798; Juan Yüan (1764–1849). [Classical books collected and explained.]
阮元等：經籍纂詁

3691   Chang, Chin-lang: *Ching-chi tsuan-ku.*—*Chung-wen ts'an-k'ao . . . chih-yin* (2889), 221–222. [*Ching-chi tsuan-ku.*]
張錦郎：『經籍纂詁』

3692   Liu, Yeh-ch'iu: *Ching-chi tsuan-ku.*—*Chung-kuo ku-tai te tzu-tien* (2927), 67–70; *Chung-kuo te tzu-tien* (2996), 53–54; *Ch'ang-yung tzu-shu shih chiang* (2997), 53–54. [*Ching-chi tsuan-ku.*]
劉葉秋：『經籍纂詁』

3693   San-chia-ts'un hsüeh-chiu: *Chien-tzu i-kuan-san* (3518). [A single index for the characters of three works.]/ An index to (3530), (3546), and (3690).
三家村學究：檢字一貫三

3694   Teng, Ssu-yü & Biggerstaff, Knight: *Ching-chi tsuan-ku.*—*An annotated bibliography . . . reference works* (2898), 135–136.
〔經籍纂詁〕

3695   Tōdō, Akiyasu: *Keiseki sanko.—Sekai meicho daijiten* (0041) 2, 242. [*Ching-chi tsuan-ku.*]
藤堂明保：『經籍纂詁』

3696   Wang, Yao-nan: Tsuan-chi-pai hsün-ku chu-tso *Ching-chi tsuan-ku.—TSYC* 1982: 4, 155–162. [*Ching-chi tsuan-ku*—a traditional semantic work by the School of Compilation and Collection.]
汪耀楠：纂集派訓詁著作『經籍纂詁』

3697   Wu, Hsiao-ju & Chuang, Ming-ch'üan: *Ching-chi tsuan-ku.—Chung-kuo wen-shih . . . chü-yao* (2903), 190–193. [*Ching-chi tsuan-ku.*]
吳小如、莊銘權：『經籍纂詁』

3698   Ying, Yü-k'ang & Hsieh, Yün-fei: *Ching-chi tsuan-ku.—Chung-wen kung-chü shu chih-yin* (2908), 52–53. [*Ching-chi tsuan-ku.*]
應裕康、謝雲飛：『經籍纂詁』

3699   Yuasa, Yukihiko: *Keiseki sanko.—Ajia rekishi jiten* (0040) 3, 107–108. [*Ching-chi tsuan-ku.*]
湯淺幸孫：『經籍纂詁』

4.3.4. *Ching-chuan shih-tz'u* (3700–3708)

3700   Wang, Yin-chih: *Ching-chuan shih-tz'u* (1109). [Explanations of words (found) in the Classics and commentaries.]/ Explanations of 160 particles.
王引之：經傳釋詞

3701   Chang, I-jen: *Ching-chuan shih-tz'u* chu-shu hsün-chieh chi yin-cheng fang-mien te chien-t'ao.—*Chung-kuo . . . lun-chi* (0774), 125–156. [A thorough discussion of the aspects of semantic explanation and the citation of supporting evidence in *Ching-chuan shih-tz'u* and other works.]
張以仁：『經傳釋詞』諸書訓解及引證方面的檢討

3702   Chang, I-jen: *Ching-chuan shih-tz'u* chu-

shu so-yung ts'ai-liao te shih-tai wen-t'i. —*Chung-kuo . . . lun-chi* (0774), 157–163. [The problem of the dates of materials used in *Ching-chuan shih-tz'u* and other works.]
張以仁：『經傳釋詞』諸書所用材料的時代問題

3703   Chu, T'ien-chün & Ch'en, Hung-t'ien: *Ching-chuan shih-tz'u.—Wen-k'o kung-chü shu chien chieh* (2890), 31–32. [*Ching-chuan shih-tz'u.*]
朱天俊、陳宏天：『經傳釋詞』

3704   Liu, Yeh-ch'iu: *Ching-chuan shih-tz'u.* —*Chung-kuo ku-tai te tzu-tien* (2927), 74–79; *Chung-kuo te tzu-tien* (2996), 58–62. [*Ching-chuan shih-tz'u.*]
劉葉秋：『經傳釋詞』

3705   Sun, Ching-shih: *Ching-chuan shih-tz'u pu* & *Ching-chuan shih-tz'u tsai pu.*— Changchow: Chiang Feng-tsao hsin-chü-chai, 1888 & 1895, 1 *chüan* & 1 *chüan*, v.p.; Peking: Chung-hua, 1956, repr. together with (1109). [Addenda to *Ching-chuan shih-tz'u* & additional addenda to *Ching-chuan shih-tz'u.*]
孫經世：經傳釋詞補，經傳釋詞再補

3706   Teng, Ssu-yü & Biggerstaff, Knight: *Ching-chuan shih-tz'u.—An annotated bibliography . . . reference works* (2898), 143–144.
〔經傳釋詞〕

3707   Wu, Hsiao-ju & Chuang, Ming-ch'üan: *Ching-chuan shih-tz'u.—Chung-kuo wen-shih . . . chü-yao* (2903), 195–198. [*Ching-chuan shih-tz'u.*]
吳小如、莊銘權：『經傳釋詞』

3708   Ying, Yü-k'ang & Hsieh, Yün-fei: *Ching-chuan shih-tz'u.—Chung-wen kung-chü shu chih-yin* (2908), 20. [*Ching-chuan shih-tz'u.*]
應裕康、謝雲飛：『經傳釋詞』

4.4. Rhetorical and Allusive Dictionaries (3709–3724)

4.4.1. *P'ei-wen yün-fu* (3709–3718)

3709 Chang, Yü-shu, et al.: *P'ei-wen yün-fu* (1057). [The *P'ei-wen* thesaurus of rhyming phrases.]
張玉書等：佩文韻府

3710 Chang, Chin-lang: *P'ei-wen yün-fu.— Chung-wen ts'an-k'ao . . . chih-yin* (2889), 351–352. [*P'ei-wen yün-fu.*]
張錦郎：『佩文韻府』

3711 Kondō, Mitsuo: *Haibun inpu.—Ajia reki-shi jiten* (0040), 7:327. [*P'ei-wen yün-fu.*]
近藤光男：『佩文韻府』

3712 Liu, Yeh-ch'iu: *P'ei-wen yün-fu.— Chung-kuo ku-tai te tzu-tien* (2927), 128–130; *Ch'ang-yung tzu-shu shih chiang* (2997), 55–56. [*P'ei-wen yün-fu.*]
劉葉秋：『佩文韻府』

3713 Nash, Vernon: *Trindex: An index to three dictionaries* (3590)./ Giles' *A Chinese-English dictionary* (4048), *K'ang-hsi tzu-tien* (3573), and *P'ei-wen yün-fu* (3709).
〔三字典引得〕

3715 Teng, Ssu-yü & Biggerstaff, Knight: *P'ei-wen yün-fu.—An annotated biblio-graphy . . . reference works* (2898), 97–98.
〔佩文韻府〕

3714 Ōkubo, Shibutsu: *Haibun inpu ryōin benran.*—Japan: 1805, (not seen). [A two-rhyme handbook of *P'ei-wen yün-fu.*]/ *P'ing* and *tse* rhymes.
大窪詩佛：佩文韻府兩韻便覽

3716 Wu, Hsiao-ju & Chuang, Ming-ch'üan: *P'ei-wen yün-fu.— Chung-kuo wen-shih . . . chü-yao* (2903), 218–221. [*P'ei-wen yün-fu.*]
吳小如、莊銘權：『佩文韻府』

3717 Ying, Yü-k'ang & Hsieh, Yün-fei: *P'ei-wen yün-fu.— Chung-wen kung-chü shu chih-yin* (2908), 88–90. [*P'ei-wen yün-fu.*]
應裕康、謝雲飛：『佩文韻府』

3718 Zach, Erwin von: Über Fehler im *P'eiwenyünfu.—AM* 2, 1925, 170–175.
〔佩文韻府〕

4.4.2. *P'ien-tzu lei-pien* (3719–3724)

3719 Chang, T'ing-yü, et al.: *P'ien-tzu lei-pien* (1056). [A classified collection of paired-character phrases.]
張廷玉等：駢字類編

3720 Chang, Chin-lang: *P'ien-tzu lei-pien.— Chung-kuo ts'an-k'ao . . . chih-yin* (2889), 352–353. [*P'ien-tzu lei-pien.*]
張錦郎：『駢字類編』

3721 Chuang, Wei-szu: *P'ien-tzu lei-pien yin-te* (1058). [An index to *P'ien-tzu lei-pien.*]
莊爲斯：駢字類編引得

3722 Teng, Ssu-yü & Biggerstaff, Knight: *P'ien-tzu lei-pien.—An annotated biblio-graphy . . . reference works* (2898), 98–99.
〔駢字類編〕

3723 Wu, Hsiao-ju & Chuang, Ming-ch'üan: *P'ien-tzu lei-pien.—Chung-kuo wen-shih . . . chü-yao* (2903), 221–223. [*P'ien-tzu lei-pien.*]
吳小如、莊銘權：『駢字類編』

3724 Ying, Yü-k'ang & Hsieh, Yün-fei: *P'ien-tzu lei-pien.—Chung-wen kung-chü shu chih-yin* (2908), 90–91. [*P'ien-tzu lei-pien.*]
應裕康、謝雲飛：『駢字類編』

4.5. Rhyme Books (3725–3814)

4.5.1. *Ch'ieh-yün* (3725–3757)

4.5.1.1. General Studies on *Ch'ieh-yün* (3725–3748)

3725 Lu, Fa-yen, et al.: *Ch'ieh-yün.*— completed in A.D. 601/ See (3733) and (3749); Lu Fa-yen (A.D. 581–617). [Spelling rhymes.]/ Rhyme classification

of characters.
陸法言等：切韻

3726   Chao, Chen-to: Ts'ung *Ch'ieh-yün* hsü lun *Ch'ieh-yün.*—*CKYW* 1962:10, 467–476. [A discussion of *Ch'ieh-yün* from its preface.]
趙振鐸：從『切韻』序論『切韻』

3727   Chao, Ch'eng: *Ch'ieh-yün.*—*Chung-kuo ku-tai yün-shu* (2919), 21–31. [*Ch'ieh-yün.*]
趙誠：『切韻』

3728   Ch'en, Yin-k'o: Ts'ung shih-shih lun *Ch'ieh-yün.*—*LNHP* 9: 2, 1949, 1–18. [A discussion on *Ch'ieh-yün* from historical facts.]
陳寅恪：從史實論『切韻』

3729   Chou, Tsu-mo: *Ch'ieh-yün* te hsing-chih ho t'a-te yin-hsi chi-ch'u.—*YLT* 5, 1963, 39–70; *Wen-hsüeh chi* (0054), 434–473./ *TYGH* 47, 1964, 133–140, Sakai Ken'ichi. [The nature of *Ch'ieh-yün* and the basis of its phonological system.]
周祖謨：『切韻』的性質和它的音系基礎／坂井健一評

3730   Chou, Tsu-mo. Transl. by Malmqvist, Göran: Chou Tsu-mo on the *Ch'ieh-yün.*—*BMFEA* 40, 1968, 33–78. [*Ch'ieh-yün* te hsing-chih ho t'a-te yin-hsi chi-ch'u.] (3729)

3731   Huang, Tien-ch'eng: *Ch'ieh-yün* te tso-che—Lu Fa-yen.—*TSYC* 1981:4, 232–242. [The author of *Ch'ieh-yün*—Lu Fa-yen.]
黃典誠：『切韻』的作者——陸法言

3732   Li, Yü-p'ing: Lu Fa-yen te *Ch'ieh-yün.*—*CKYW* 1957:2, 28–36. [Lu Fa-yen's *Ch'ieh-yün.*]
李于平：陸法言的『切韻』

3733   Liu, Fu; Lo, Ch'ang-p'ei & Wei, Chien-kung: *Shih-yün hui-pien.*—Peking:

Pei-ching ta-hsüeh, 1937, 3 vols., 90, 494 p.; Taipei: T'ai-wan hsüeh-sheng, 1963, repr., 1 vol./ Pei-ching ta-hsüeh Wen-hsüeh shih-hsüeh ts'ung-k'an, 5; *SWYK* 1, 1941, 810–813, Ch'en Chih-liang. [A collection of ten rhyme books.]/ Fragments of *Ch'ieh-yün, T'ang-yün, Kuang-yün,* etc.
劉復、羅常培、魏建功：十韻彙編　「北京大學文學史學叢刊」第五／陳志良評

3734   Lo, Ch'ang-p'ei: *Ch'ieh-yün* hsü chiao-shih.—*CSTY* 25–27, 1928, 6–25. [Revised explanations on the preface of *Ch'ieh-yün.*]
羅常培：『切韻』序校釋

3735   Lo, Ch'ang-p'ei: *Ch'ieh-yün* t'an tse.—*CSTY* 25–27, 1928, 26–56. [An investigation into the profoundity of *Ch'ieh-yün.*]
羅常培：『切韻』探賾

3736   Lung, Yü-ch'un: Ying Lun ts'ang Tun-huang *Ch'ieh-yin* ts'an-chüan chiao chi.—*BIHPEV* 4, 1961, 803–825, 8 pl. [Critical notes on the fragments of *Ch'ieh-yün* from Tunhuang kept in (the British Museum of) London, England.]
龍宇純：英倫藏敦煌『切韻』殘卷校記

3737   Misawa, Junjirō: *Setsuin* kaitai nishō.—*KNKB* 16, 1969, 48–56. [Two chapters of bibliographical introduction to *Ch'ieh-yün.*]
三澤諄治郎：『切韻』解題二章

3738   Ozaki, Yūjirō: *Setsuin* kei insho ni okeru in no hairetsu ni tsuite.—*NCGH* 22, 1970, 34–51. E.S. [On the arrangement of rhymes in rhyme books of the *Ch'ieh-yün* system.]
尾崎雄二郎：『切韻』系韻書における韻の排列について

3739   Ozaki, Yūjirō: *Setsuin* no kihansei ni tsuite.—*JB* 17, 1971, 57–76. [On the nature of the standards of *Ch'ieh-yün.*]
尾崎雄二郎：『切韻』の規範性について

3740   Ting, Shan: Lu Fa-yen chuan lüeh. —*CSTY* 3:25–27, 1939, 1–5. [A short biography of Lu Fa-yen.]
丁山：陸法言傳略

3741   Tōdō, Akiyasu: *Setsuin.—Sekai meicho daijiten* (0041) 4, 25–26. [*Ch'ieh-yün.*]
藤堂明保：『切韻』

3742   Tung, Tso-pin: *Ch'ieh-yün* nien-piao. —*CSTY* 25–27, 1928, 141–142. [A chronology of *Ch'ieh-yün.*]
董作賓：『切韻』年表

3743   Wang, Hsien: *Ch'ieh-yün* te ming-ming ho *Ch'ieh-yün* te hsing-chih.—*CKYW* 1961:4, 16–25. [The naming and the nature of *Ch'ien-yün.*]
王顯：『切韻』的命名和『切韻』的性質

3744   Shao, Jung-fen: *Ch'ieh-yün yen-chiu.* —Peking: Chung-kuo she-hui k'o-hsüeh, 1982, 2, 1, 167 p. [A study of *Ch'ieh-yün.*]
邵榮芬：切韻研究

3745   Ueda, Tadashi: *Setsuin zanken shohon hosei.*—Tokyo: Tōyōgaku Bunken Sentā Kankō Iinkai, Tōkyō Daigaku Tōyō Bunka Kenkyūjo, 1973, 277 p. [Addenda and corrigenda to various editions of *Ch'ieh-yün* fragments.]
上田正：切韻殘卷諸本補正

3746   Ueda, Tadashi: *Setsuin shohon hansetsu sōran.*—Kyoto: Insha, Kyōto Daigaku Bungakubu Chūbun Kenkyūshitsu, 1975, [ii], 222 p. [A conspectus of the *fan-ch'ieh* in various editions of *Ch'ieh-yün.*]
上田正：切韻諸本反切總覽

3747   Wei, Chien-kung: Lu Fa-yen *Ch'ieh-yün* i-ch'ien te chi-chung yün-shu.—*KHCK* 3:2, 1932, 201–235. [Several rhyme books before Lu Fa-yen's *Ch'ieh-yün.*]
魏建功：陸法言『切韵』以前的幾種韻書

3748   Wei, Chien-kung: *Shih-yün hui-pien tzu-liao pu ping shih.*—Peking: Pei-ching ta-hsüeh, 1948, 72 p., 11 pl./ Kuo-li

Pei-ching ta-hsüeh wu-shih chou-nien chi-nien lun-wen chi, 15. [Additional materials and explanations of *Shih-yün hui-pien* (3733).]
魏建功：　十韻彙編資料補並釋　「國立北京大學五十週年紀念論文集」十五

4.5.1.2. *K'an-miu pu-ch'üeh Ch'ieh-yün* (3749–3757)

3749   Wang, Jen-hsü. Ed. by T'ang, Lan: *T'ang hsieh-pen Wang Jen-hsü K'an-miu pu-ch'üeh Ch'ieh-yün.*—Peiping: Ku-kung po-wu-yüan, 1947, no pagination; Taipei: Kuang-wen, 1964, repr./ Wang Jen-hsü (fl. A.D. 684–709); see (3752). [Wang Jen-hsü's T'ang manuscript of the revised and augmented edition of *Ch'ieh-yün.*]
王仁昫撰，唐蘭刊：唐寫本王仁昫刊謬補缺切韻

3750   Chao, Ch'eng: *K'an-miu pu-ch'üeh Ch'ieh-yün.—Chung-kuo ku-tai yün-shu* (2919), 31–36. [*K'an-miu pu-ch'üeh Ch'ieh-yün.*]
趙誠：『刊謬補缺切韻』

3751   Chiang, Ching-pang: Tun-huang pen Wang Jen-hsü *K'an-miu pu-ch'üeh Ch'ieh-yün* pa.—*KHCK* 4:3, 1934, 417–428. [A postscript to the Tunhuang edition of Wang Jen-hsü's *K'an-miu pu-ch'üeh Ch'ieh-yün.*]
蔣經邦：敦煌本王仁昫『刊謬補缺切韻』跋

3752   Chou, Tsu-mo: Wang Jen-hsü *Ch'ieh-yün* chu-tso nien-tai shih i.—*Wen-hsüeh chi* (0054), 483–493. [Dispel doubts concerning the dates of the compilation of Wang Jen-hsü's *Ch'ieh-yün.*]/ During A.D. 684–709.
周祖謨：王仁昫『切韻』著作年代釋疑

3753   Chuang, Hui-fen: Ch'üan-pen Wang Jen-hsü *K'an-miu pu-ch'üeh Ch'ieh-yün fan-ch'ieh* shang tzu te yen-chiu.—*TCHP* 3, 1964, 97–114. [A study of the first characters in the *fan-ch'ieh* from the complete manuscript of Wang Jen-hsü's

K'an-miu pu-ch'üeh Ch'ieh-yün.]

莊惠芬：全本王仁昫『刊謬補缺切韻』反切上
字的研究

3754 Lung, Yü-ch'un: *T'ang hsieh ch'üan-pen Wang Jen-hsü K'an-miu pu-ch'üeh Ch'ieh-yün chiao chien.*—Hong Kong: Hsiang-kang Chung-wen ta-hsüeh, 1968, 6, 3, text, 725 p., pl./ *TYGH* 52:3, 1969, 79–85, Sakai Ken'ichi; *JOS* 7, 1969, 294–302, Huang Liu-p'ing. [Critical notes on the T'ang complete manuscript of Wang Jen-hsü's *K'an miu pu-ch'üeh Ch'ieh-yün.*]

龍宇純：唐寫全本王仁昫刊謬補缺切韻校箋／
坂井健一評，黃六平評

3755 Tung, T'ung-ho: Ch'üan-pen Wang Jen-hsü *K'an-miu pu-ch'üeh Ch'ieh-yün te fan-ch'ieh* hsia-tzu.—*BIHP* 19, 1948, 549–588. [The second characters in the *fan-ch'ieh* from the complete manuscript of Wang Jen-hsü's *K'an-miu pu-ch'üeh Ch'ieh-yün.*]

董同龢：全本王仁昫『刊謬補缺切韵』的反切
下字

3756 Tung, T'ung-ho: Ch'üan-pen Wang Jen-hsü *K'an-miu pu-ch'üeh Ch'ieh-yün te fan-ch'ieh* shang-tzu.—*BIHP* 22, 1952, 511–522. [The first characters in the *fan-ch'ieh* from the complete manuscript of Wang Jen-hsü's *K'an-miu pu-ch'üeh Ch'ieh-yün.*]

董同龢：全本王仁昫『刊謬補缺切韻』反切的
上字

3757 Wang, Lien-tseng: Un dictionnaire phonologique des T'ang Le *Ts'ie Yun corrigé et complété* de Wang Jen-hiu.—*TP* 45, 1957, 51–150./ *RBS* 3, 1957, 559, R.A. Miller.

〔王聯曾：唐王仁昫撰刊謬補闕切韻〕

4.5.2. *Kuang-yün* (3758–3781)

3758 Ch'en, P'eng-nien, et al.: *Ta Sung ch'ung-hsiu Kuang-yün.*—Peking: Lai-hsün ko, 1934, repr., 5 *chüan*, v.p.; Shanghai: Shang-wu, 1936, repr., 162 p./ Szu-pu ts'ung-k'an, 020; Ch'en P'eng-nien (A.D. 961–1017). [The great Sung (dynasty) revised and expanded *Ch'ieh-yün.*]

陳彭年等：大宋重修廣韻「四部叢刊」初編
020

3759 Ch'en, P'eng-nien, et al. Rev. & ed. by Lin, Yin: *Hsin chiao-cheng fan-ch'ieh Sung-pen Kuang-yün. Fu Ch'ieh-yün-hsi yün-shu fan-ch'ieh i-wen piao, Chien tzu so-yin.*—Taipei: Li-ming, 1976, 2, 5, 554; 12, 183; 2, 225 p. [The Sung (dynasty) edition of *Kuang-yün* with new corrigenda on the *fan-ch'ieh*. With A table of *fan-ch'ieh* variants in the rhyme books of the *Ch'ieh-yün* system and A character index.]

陳彭年等，林尹訂校：新校正反切宋本廣韻附
切韻系韻書反切異文表，檢字索引

3760 Chang, Shih-lu: *Kuang-yün yen-chiu.*—Shanghai: Shang-wu, 1933, v, 274 p.; Hong Kong: T'ai-p'ing, 1964, repr.; Taipei: Shang-wu, 1969, repr., 2, v, 274 p.; 1973, repr. [A study of *Kuang-yün.*]

張世祿：廣韻研究

3761 Chao, Ch'eng: *Kuang-yün.*—*Chung-kuo ku-tai yün-shu* (2919), 46–56. [*Kuang-yün.*]

趙誠：『廣韻』

3762 Chin, Chou-sheng: *Kuang-yün i-tzu to-yin hsien-hsiang ch'u t'an.*—Hsinchuang: Fu-jen U., 1979, 2, 327, 2 p./ Publ. M.A. thesis. [A preliminary investigation into the phenomenon of one character having multiple pronunciations in *Kuang-yün.*]

金周生：廣韻一字多音現象初探

3763 Chou, Tsu-mo: *Kuang-yün chiao-pen.*—Peking: Chung-hua, 1960, 2 vols., I. *Sung-pen Kuang-yün*, vi, 563 p.; II. *Kuang-yün chiao-k'an chi*, 616 p./ First ed. of the *Kuang-yün chiao-k'an chi.*—Shanghai: Shang-wu, 1938, 5 vols.;

Academia Sinica Special Publication, 16. [A revised edition of *Kuang-yün*: I. The Sung (dynasty) edition of *Kuang-yün;* II. Critical notes on *Kuang-yün.*]
周祖謨：廣韻校本　（上）宋本廣韻
　　　　　　　　　（下）廣韻校勘記

3764　Chou, Tsu-mo: *Kuang-yün szu-sheng yün-tzu chin-yin piao.*—Peking: Chung-hua, 1980, 8, 79 p. [A table of the modern pronunciations for the characters with four tones in *Kuang-yün.*]
周祖謨：廣韻四聲韻字今音表

3765　Chuang, Hui-fen: *Kuang-yün ch'ieh-yü chin-tu piao.*—Taipei: Kuang-wen, 1964, 256 p. [A table of the modern readings of the *fan-ch'ieh* words of *Kuang-yün.*]
莊惠芬：廣韻切語今讀表

3766　Harada, Taneshige: *Kōin hansetsu sakuin.*—Tokyo: Mukyūkai Tōyō Bunka Kenkyūjo, 1966, 85 p.; *Seigohyō* ('A table of corrigenda').—*Tōyō Bunka* 17, 1968, 69. [An index to the *fan-ch'ieh* in *Kuang-yün.*]/ According to *Kuang-yün chiao-pen* (3763).
原田種成：廣韻反切索引　正誤表

3767　Kuang-wen pien-i-so: *Ch'ung-chiao Sung-pen Kuang-yün.* Fu *So-yin.*—Taipei: Kuang-wen, 1960; 1961, 2nd ed., (index) 106, 534 p. [A revised Sung (dynasty) edition of *Kuang-yün.* With An index.]
廣文編譯所：重校宋本廣韻　附索引

3768　Li, Jung: *Kuang-yün te fan-ch'ieh ho chin-yin.*—*CKYW* 1964:2, 89–100; *Yin-yün ts'un kao* (Peking: Shang-wu, 1982), 93–106./ First publ. under the pseudonym: Ch'ang Hou. [The *fan-ch'ieh* of *Kuang-yün* and the modern pronunciations.]
李榮：『廣韻』的反切和今音──『音韻存稿』
／（筆名：昌厚）

3769　Lin, Wei-fen: Chieh-shao *Kuang-yün sheng-hsi.*—*CWFY* 12:3, 1979, 71–76. [An introduction to *Kuang-yün sheng-hsi*

(3777).]
林維棻：介紹『廣韻聲系』

3770　Liu, P'an-sui: *Kuang-yün* hsü-lu chiao-chien.—*Wen-tzu yin-yün-hsüeh lun-ts'ung* (0073), 251–274. [Critical notes on the preface of *Kuang-yün.*]
劉盼遂：『廣韻』叙錄校箋

3771　Liu, Yeh-ch'iu: *Kuang-yün.*—*Chung-kuo ku-tai te tzu-tien* (2927), 135–137; *Chung-kuo te tzu-tien* (2996), 124–125. [*Kuang-yün.*]
劉葉秋：『廣韻』

3772　Mabuchi, Kazuo: *Inkyō kyōhon to Kōin sakuin.*—Tokyo: Nihon Gakujutsu Shinkōkai, 1954, 466 p.; Tokyo: Gannandō, 1970, rev. ed., 481 p. [A revised edition of *Yün-ching* and an index to *Kuang-yün.*]
馬淵和夫：韻鏡校本と廣韻索引

3773　Okai, Shingo: *Chōshū Kōin izen no Kōin.*—*Hattori* [*Unokichi*] *sensei koki shukuga kinen ronbunshū* (Tokyo: Fuzanbō, 1936), 227–241. [*Kuang-yün* before *Ch'ung-hsiu Kuang-yün* (3758).]
岡井慎吾：『重修廣韻』以前の『廣韻』──
『服部〔宇之吉〕先生古稀祝賀記念論文集』

3774　Pai, Ti-chou: *Kuang-yün t'ung chien.*—Taipei: T'ien-i, 1975, 3, 1004, 36, [6] p. [A general index to *Kuang-yün.*]
白滌洲：廣韻通檢

3775　P'eng, Hsüeh-hsüan: Sui T'ang yün-shu yü *Kuang-yün* chih kuan-hsi.—*KMWH* 2:1, 1935, 41–45. [The relationships between Sui and T'ang (dynasty) rhyme books and *Kuang-yün.*]
彭學選：隋唐韻書與『廣韻』之關係

3776　Sakai, Ken'ichi: *Kōin sakuin.*—Tokyo: Tōkyō Kyōiku Daigaku Chūgoku Bunka Kenkyūkai, 1953, mimeogr., 180 p./ *CGKK* 1953:9, 8, Anonymous. [An index to *Kuang-yün.*]
坂井健一：廣韻索引

3777 Shen, Chien-shih: *Kuang-yün sheng-hsi.*—Peking: Fu-jen ta-hsüeh, 1945; Peking: Wen-tzu kai-ko, 1960, repr., xliii, 1106, 89, 16 p.; Taipei; Chung-hua, 1969, repr./ *MS* 11, 1946, 123–149, Achilles Fang; *CFHY* 2, 1946, 162–163, Anonymous. [*Kuang-yün* rearranged according to the phonological system of Ancient Chinese.]
沈兼士：廣韻聲系

3778 Teng, Ssu-yü & Biggerstaff, Knight: *Kuang-yün.—An annotated bibliography . . . reference works* (2898), 146–147.
〔廣韻〕

3779 Tu, Hsüeh-chih (ed.): *Ku-yin ta tzu-tien.*—Taipei: Shang-wu, 1982, 4, 6, 35, 10, 1272, 2, 2, 87 p. [A comprehensive dictionary of ancient sounds.]/ Rearranged and augmented ed. of *Kuang-yün sheng-hsi* (3777).
杜學知編：古音大字典

3780 Yü, Hsing-ta: Kuan-yü *Kuang-yün* te chi-ko wen-t'i.—*CKYW* 1961:9, 1–9; 1962:4, 189–190. [Several problems concerning *Kuang-yün.*]
余行達：關於『廣韻』的幾個問題

3781 Yü, Nai-yung (ed.): *Hu-chu chiao-cheng Sung-pen Kuang-yün.*—Taipei: Lien-kuan, 1974, 10, 5, 554, (character index) 151 p. [Annotation and corrigenda to the Sung (dynasty) edition of *Kuang-yün.*]
余迺永校：互註校正宋本廣韻

4.5.3. *Chi-yün* (3782–3788)

3782 Ting, Tu, et al.: *Chi-yün.*—Taipei: Chung-hua, 1966, repr., 10 *chüan*, v.p./ Szu-pu pei-yao ed. [A collection of rhymes.]
丁度等：集韻　「四部備要」本

3783 Chao, Ch'eng: *Chi-yün.—Chung-kuo ku-tai yün-shu* (2919), 56–61. [*Chi-yün.*]
趙誠：『集韻』

3784 Ch'iu, Ch'i-yang: *Chi-yün yen-chiu.*

—Taipei: Cho Shao-lan, 1974, 1234, [3] p., pl., illus., E.S. [A study of *Chi-yün.*]
邱樂鍚：集韻研究

3785 Huang, Chi-kang: Tu *Chi-yün* cheng su-yü.—*Chih-yen* 24, 1936, 1–29. [Verification of popular sayings by reading *Chi-yün.*]
黃季剛：讀『集韻』證俗語

3786 Huang, Kuei-lan: *Chi-yün yin Shuo-wen k'ao.*—Taipei: Wen-shih-che, 1973, [ii], 1590 p./ 1587–1590: Bibliography. [A study on the citations of *Shuo-wen* in *Chi-yün.*]
黃桂蘭：集韻引說文考

3787 Liu, Yeh-ch'iu: *Chi-yün.—Chung-kuo ku-tai te tzu-tien* (2927), 137–139; *Chung-kuo te tzu-tien* (2996), 125–126. [*Chi-yün.*]
劉葉秋：『集韻』

3788 Teng, Ssu-yü & Biggerstaff, Knight: *Chi-yün.—An annotated bibliography . . . reference works* (2898), 147.
〔集韻〕

4.5.4. *Chung-yüan yin-yün* (3789–3805)

3789 Chou, Te-ch'ing: *Chung-yüan yin-yün.* Fu *Chiao-k'an chi.—Chung-kuo ku-tien hsi-ch'ü lun-chu chi-ch'eng* (Peking: Chung-kuo hsi-chü, 1959) Vol. 1, 167–285./ Completed in 1324. [The phonology of the Central Plains. With Critical notes.]
周德清：中原音韻　附校勘記　「中國古典戲曲論著集成」第一集

3790 Chou, Te-ch'ing: *Chung-yüan yin-yün.*—Taipei: I-wen, 1970, repr., 148 p. [The phonology of the Central Plains.]
周德清：中原音韻

3791 Chou, Te-ch'ing; Hsü, Shih-ying (ed.) & Liu, Te-chih (phonetic transcription): *Yin-chu Chung-yüan yin-yün.*—Taipei: Kuang-wen, 1962, 5, 55 p. [*Chung-yüan* *yin-yün* with phonetic transcription.] / In I.P.A.

周德清著，許世瑛校訂，劉德智注音：音注中原音韻

3792   Chou, Te-ch'ing. Rev. & ed. by Li, Tien-k'uei: *Chiao-ting pu-cheng Chung-yüan yin-yün chi Cheng-yü tso-tz'u ch'i-li.* Fu *So-yin.*—Taipei: Hsüeh-hai, 1978, 148, 75, [2] p. [Revision and corrigenda to *Chung-yüan yin-yün* and examples of the correct words to use in writing *tz'u* poetry. With An index.]

周德清著，李殿魁校訂：校訂補正中原音韻及正語作詞起例　附索引

3793   Chao, Ch'eng: *Chung-yüan yin-yün.*—*Chung-kuo ku-tai yün-shu* (2919), 85–88. [*Chung-yüan yin-yün.*]

趙誠：『中原音韻』

3794   Chao, Yin-t'ang: *Chung-yüan yin-yün yen-chiu.*—Shanghai: Shang-wu, 1936; 1956, repr., 1, 22, 4, 339 p. [A study of *Chung-yüan yin-yün.*]

趙蔭棠：中原音韻研究

3795   Ch'en, Hsin-hsiung: *Chung-yüan yin-yün kai-yao.*—Taipei: Hsüeh-hai, 1976, [ii], ii, 148 p. [Essentials of *Chung-yüan yin-yün.*]

陳新雄：中原音韻概要

3796   Hattori, Shirō & Tōdō, Akiyasu: *Chūgen on'in no kenkyū. Kōhonpen.*—Tokyo: Kōnan shoin, 1958, 3, 11, 2, 266 p./ *RBS* 4, 1958, 546, W. Simon. [A study of *Chung-yüan yin-yün.* Vol. I. *Textual criticism.*] / With a reproduction of the Yüan dynasty text from the T'ieh-ch'in t'ung-chien-lou edition.

服部四郎、藤堂明保：中原音韻の研究：校本篇　鐵琴銅劍樓刊本

3797   Ishiyama, Fukuji: *Kōtei Chūgen on'in.*—Tokyo: Tōyō Bunko, 1925, 5, 6, 402, 99 p./ Tōyō Bunko Ronsō, 1. [A revised *Chung-yüan yin-yün.*]/ By collection of different editions, with

an intorduction and notes.

石山福治：攷定中原音韻　「東洋文庫論叢」第一

3798   Kanai, Yasuzō: *Chūgen on'in* ni tsukite.—*TYGH* 3:3, 1913, 405–428. [On *Chung-yüan yin-yün.*]

金井保三：『中原音韻』につきて

3799   Lan-t'ai shu-chü: *Chung-yüan yin-yün.*—Taipei: Ditto, 1970, 360 p. [*Chung-yüan yin-yün.*]/ Wtih I.P.A. transcriptions.

蘭臺書局：中原音韻

3800   Lung, Liang-tung: Ku-chin t'u-shu chi-ch'eng so shou Hsiao Yü-p'u pen *Chung-yüan yin-yün* chiao-k'an chi.—*Han-hsüeh lun-wen chi* (by Huang, Chin-hung, et al., Taipei: Ching-sheng wen-wu, 1970), 323–300. [Critical notes on the Hsiao Yü-p'u edition of *Chung-yüan yin-yün* collected in *Ku-chin t'u-shu chi-ch'eng.*]

龍民棟：「古今圖書集成」所收「嘯餘譜」本『中原音韻』校勘記――黃錦鋐等：『漢學論文集』

3801   Stimson, Hugh M.: *Jongyuan inyunn—A guide to Old Mandarin pronunciation.*—New Haven: Far Eastern Publications, Yale U., 1966, v, 485 p.; 1–4: Bibliography./ Sinological Series, 12; *AO* 37, 1969, 300, O. Švarný; *AM* 17:1, 1971, 123–124, Nicholas C. Bodman.

3802   T'ang, Tso-fan: P'ing Yang Nai-szu *Chung-yüan yin-yün yin-hsi.*—*YWYC* 1982:2, 111–115. [A critique of Yang Nai-szu's *Chung-yüan yin-yün yin-hsi* (3805).]

唐作藩：評楊耐思『中原音韻音系』

3803   Wang, Ching-ch'ang: *Chung-yüan yin-yün chiang shu.*—Taipei: Kuang-wen, 1961, 9, 37, 3 p. [Explanatory exegesis of *Chung-yüan yin-yün.*]

王經昌：中原音韻講疏

3804   Yang, Nai-szu: Chou Te-ch'ing te *Chung-yüan yin-yün.*—*CKYW* 1957:11, 33–37. [Chou Te-ch'ing's *Chung-yüan yin-yün.*]

楊耐思：周德清的『中原音韻』

3805 Yang, Nai-szu: *Chung-yüan yin-yün yin-hsi.*—Peking: Chung-kuo she-hui k'o-hsüeh, 1981, 6, 186 p. [The phonetic system of *Chung-yüan yin-yün.*]

楊耐思：中原音韻音系

4.5.5. *Hsi-ju erh-mu tzu* (3806–3814)

3806 Chin, Ni-ko [Trigault, Nicholas]: *Hsi-ju erh-mu tzu.*—Hangchow, 1626, 3 vols., 274; 322; 322 p.; Peking: Pei-ching ta-hsüeh and Pei-ching ta-hsüeh t'u-shu-kuan, 1933, repr.; Peking: Wen-tzu kai-ko, 1957, repr. [An audio-visual aid to Western scholars.]

金尼閣：西儒耳目資

3807 Chang, Feng-chen: Ming-mo Ch'ing-ch'u T'ien-chu-chiao ch'uan-chiao-shih te san-chung yü-yin-hsüeh chu-tso.—*Chung-hua hsüeh-shu-yüan T'ien-chu-chiao hsüeh-shu yen-chiu-so hsüeh-pao* 1, 1969, 109–116./ 110–114: Nicholas Trigault's *Hsi-ju erh-mu tzu.* [Three phonetic works by Catholic missionaries of the late Ming and early Ch'ing (dynasties).]

張奉箴：明末清初天主教傳教士的三種語音學著作／110-114：金尼閣的『西儒耳目資』

3808 Chang, Shih-lu: *Chung-kuo yin-yün-hsüeh shih* (2909), Vol. II, 330–332: *Hsi-ju erh-mu tzu.* [A history of Chinese phonological studies.]

張世祿：中國音韻學史（下）330-332：『西儒耳目資』

3809 Li, Hsin-k'uei: Chi piao-hsien Shan-hsi fang-yin te *Hsi-ju erh-mu tzu.*—*YWYC* 1982:1, 126–129. [A note on *Hsi-ju erh-mu tzu* which manifests the dialect sounds of Shansi.]

李新魁：記表現山西方音的『西儒耳目資』

3810 Lo, Ch'ang-p'ei: Yeh-su-hui-shih tsai yin-yün-hsüeh shang te kung-hsien.—*BIHP* 1, 1930, 267–338. [Contributions to (Chinese) phonological studies by the Jesuits.]/ A phonological study on Matteo Ricci's romanization and Trigault's *Hsi-ju erh-mu tzu.*]

羅常培：耶穌會士在音韻學上的貢獻

3811 Lu, Chih-wei: Chin Ni-ko *Hsi-ju erh-mu tzu* so-chi te yin.—*YCHP* 33, 1947, 115–128; 318: E.S. [The sounds recorded in Nicholas Trigault's *Hsi-ju erh-mu tzu.*]

陸志韋：金尼閣『西儒耳目資』所記的音

3812 Matsumoto, Akira: *Saiju jimokushi.*—*Sekai meicho daijiten* (0041) 2, 510–511. [*Hsi-ju erh-mu tzu.*]

松本昭：『西儒耳目資』

3813 Yang, Paul Fu-mien, S.J.: The Catholic missionary contribution to the study of Chinese dialects.—*Orbis* 9:1, 1960, 158–185./ 163–165: Nicholas Trigault's *Hsi-ju erh-mu tzu.*

3814 Yang, Tao-ching: T'an *Hsi-ju erh-mu tzu.*—*CKYW* 1957:4, back cover. [A discussion on *Hsi-ju erh-mu tzu.*]

楊道經：談『西儒耳目資』

5. MODERN STANDARD CHINESE-CHINESE DICTIONARIES (3815–4024)

5.1. Character Dictionaries (3815–3851)

5.1.1. *Chung-hua ta tzu-tien* (3815–3822)

3815 Hsü, Yüan-kao, et al.: *Chung-hua ta tzu-tien.*—Shanghai: Chung-hua, 1915, 4 vols.; 1927, repr., 325, 2997, 42 p.; Peking: Chung-hua, 1958, repr., 3262 p.; Taipei: Chung-hua, 1960, repr., 2 vols., 224, 3044 p.; 1977, repr.; Peking: Chung-hua, 1981, 2 vols., 6, 14, 4, 3044 p. [A comprehensive Chinese character dictionary.]
徐元誥等：中華大字典

3816 Chang, Chin-lang: *Chung-hua ta tzu-tien.—Chung-wen ts'an-k'ao . . . chih-yin* (2889), 220–221. [*Chung-hua ta tzu-tien.*]
張錦郎：『中華大字典』

3817 Chu, T'ien-chün & Ch'en, Hung-t'ien: *Chung-hua ta tzu-tien.—Wen-k'o kung-chü shu chien-chieh* (2890), 16–17. [*Chung-hua ta tzu-tien.*]
朱天俊、陳宏天：『中華大字典』

3818 Liu, Yeh-ch'iu: *Chung-hua ta tzu-tien.—Chung-kuo te tzu-tien* (2996), 63–67; *Ch'ang-yung tzu-shu shih chiang* (2997), 13–17. [*Chung-hua ta tzu-tien.*]
劉葉秋：『中華大字典』

3819 Lu, Fei-k'uei, et al.: *Chung-hua ta-tzu-tien hsü-wen.—TCH* 1:1, 1915, 1–8; 2, 1–2; 3, 1. [A preface to *Chung-hua ta tzu-tien.*]
陸費達等：『中華大字典』序文

3820 Teng, Ssu-yü & Biggerstaff, Knight: *Chung-hua ta tzu-tien.—An annotated bibliography . . . reference works* (2898), 131–132.
〔中華大字典〕

3821 Tu, Tao-sheng: *Chung-hua ta tzu-tien chiao yüeh so chi.—TYT* 1, 1980, 129–169. [Miscellaneous notes on examining *Chung-hua ta tzu-tien.*]

杜道生：『中華大字典』校閱瑣記

3822 Wu, Hsiao-ju & Chuang, Ming-ch'üan: *Chung-hua ta tzu-tien.—Chung-kuo wen-shih . . . chü-yao* (2903), 48–50. [*Chung-hua ta tzu-tien.*]
吳小如、莊銘權：『中華大字典』

5.1.2. *Kuo-yin tzu-tien* (3823–3824)

3823 Chung-kuo ta tz'u-tien pien-tsuan-ch'u: *Kuo-yin tzu-tien.*—Shanghai: Shang-wu, 1949, 18, 12, 399, 2, 3, 8, 93, 20 p.; Taipei: Shang-wu, 1965, repr., 3, 2, 2, 4, 2, 9, 73, 399, [2] p.; 1976, 6th print./ [A character dictionary of the National Language Pronunciation.]
中國大辭典編纂處：國音字典

3824 Ying, Yü-k'ang & Hsieh, Yün-fei: *Kuo-yin tzu-tien.—Chung-wen kung-chü shu chih-yin* (2908), 7. [*Kuo-yin tzu-tien.*]
應裕康、謝雲飛：『國音字典』

5.1.3. *Cheng-chung hsing-yin-i tsung-ho ta tzu-tien* (3825–3828)

3825 Kao, Shu-fan & Wang, Hsiu-ming: *Cheng-chung hsing-yin-i tsung-ho ta tzu-tien* (0540). [Cheng-chung's integrated comprehensive dictionary of forms, sounds and meanings (of Chinese characters).]
高樹藩、王修明：正中形音義綜合大字典

3826 Chang, Chin-lang: *Cheng-chung hsing-yin-i tsung-ho ta tzu-tien.—Chung-wen ts'an-k'ao . . . chih-yin* (2889), 222. [*Cheng-chung hsing-yin-i tsung-ho ta tzu-tien.*]
張錦郎：『正中形音義綜合大字典』

3827 Li, Chih-chung & Wang, Yin-lan: *Cheng-chung hsing-yin-i tsung-ho ta tzu-tien.—Chung-wen ts'an-k'ao . . . chih-nan* (2894), 169–170. [*Cheng-chung hsing-yin-i tsung-ho ta tzu-tien.*]
李志鍾、汪引蘭：『正中形音義綜合大字典』

3828   Ying, Yü-k'ang & Hsieh, Yün-fei: *Cheng-chung hsing-yin-i tsung-ho ta tzu-tien.* —*Chung-wen kung-chü shu chih-yin* (2908), 5–7. [*Cheng-chung hsing-yin-i tsung-ho ta tzu-tien.*]
應裕康、謝雲飛：『正中形音義綜合大字典』

5.1.4. *Hsin-hua tzu-tien* (3829–3838)

3829   Hsin-hua tz'u-shu-she: *Hsin-hua tzu-tien.*—Peking: Jen-min chiao-yü, 1953; 1954, 4th print., 4, 700, 132, 46 p., illus.; Peking: Shang-wu, 1971, rev. ed., 84, 618 p.; 1972, repr., 1979, repr./ Arranged according to Pinyin system. [A new China character dictionary.]/ See (4043).
新華辭書社：新華字典

3830   Chou, Tsu-mo: *Hsin-hua tzu-tien.*— *CKYW* 1954:4, 31–33. [A critical introduction to *Hsin-hua tzu-tien.*]
周祖謨：『新華字典』

3831   Chu, T'ien-chun & Ch'en, Hung-t'ien: *Hsin-hua tzu-tien.*—*Wen-k'o kung-chü shu chien-chieh* (2890), 2–3. [*Hsin-hua tzu-tien.*]
朱天俊、陳宏天：『新華字典』

3832   Enomoto, Hideo: *Shinka jiten* ni tsuite no ichi kōsatsu.—*MGRS* 253, 1977, 55–86. [An examination on *Hsin-hua tzu-tien.*]
榎本英雄：『新華字典』についての 一考察

3833   Hsiung, Hsiao-meng: *Hsin-hua tzu-tien* pien-hsieh shang te chi-ko t'e-se.—*TSYC* 1981:1, 64–68. [Several special features in the compilation of *Hsin-hua tzu-tien.*]
熊效孟『新華字典』編寫上的幾個特色

3834   Hsiung, Hsiao-meng: Yung *Hsin-hua tzu-tien* cheng yin pien hsing ch'iu i.— *YCT* 1, 1981, 43–51. [Using *Hsin-hua tzu-tien* to correct pronunciations, distinguish forms, and find meanings.]
熊效孟：用『新華字典』正音辨形求義

3835   Hsü, Li-p'ing: *Hsin-hua tzu-tien* erh t'i.—*YWTC* 3, 1980, 70–72. [Two notes on *Hsin-hua tzu-tien.*]
許禮平：『新華字典』二題

3836   Liu, Yeh-ch'iu: *Hsin-hua tzu-tien.*— *Chung-kuo te tzu-tien* (2996), 71–73. [*Hsin-hua tzu-tien.*]
劉葉秋：『新華字典』

3837   Matsumoto, Akira: Shōkai *Shinka jiten.* —*Chūgokugo* 6, 1955, (not seen). [Introducing *Hsin-hua tzu-tien.*]
松本昭：紹介『新華字典』

3838   Wu, Hsiao-ju & Chuang, Ming-ch'üan: *Hsin-hua tzu-tien.*—*Chung-kuo wen-shih . . . chü-yao* (2903), 53–55. [*Hsin-hua tzu-tien.*]
吳小如、莊銘權：『新華字典』

5.1.5. Other Chinese-Chinese Character Dictionaries (3839–3845)

3839   Lu, Erh-k'uei, et al.: *Hsin tzu-tien.* —Shanghai: Shang-wu, 1914; 1947, 33rd ed., 2, 4, 3, 6, 44, 569, 15 p. [A new (Chinese) character dictionary.]
陸爾奎等：新字典

3840   Teng, Ssu-yü & Biggerstaff, Knight: *Hsin tzu-tien.*—*An annotated bibliography . . . reference works*, 1950 ed. (2898), 188.
〔新字典〕

3841   Ts'ai, Yüan-p'ei: Shang-wu yin-shu-kuan *Hsin tzu-tien* hsü.—*TFTC* 9:4, 1912, 7. [A preface to the *Hsin tzu-tien* published by the Commercial Press.]
蔡元培：商務印書館『新字典』序

3842   Wu, Ching-heng: Shang-wu yin-shu-kuan *Hsin tzu-tien* shu-hou.—*TFTC* 9:4, 1912, 7–8. [A postscript to the *Hsin tzu-tien* published by the Commercial Press.]
吳敬恒：商務印書館『新字典』書後

3843 Chang, Ch'i-yün (ed. in chief); Lin, Yin & Li, Tien-k'uei (eds.): *Ta-hsüeh tzu-tien.*—Yangmingshan: Hua-kang, 1973, 4, 5, 2, 65, 2179, 52 p. [The university character dictionary.]/ Based on *Chung-wen ta tz'u-tien* (3976).
張其昀監修，林尹主編，李殿魁總編纂：大學字典

3844 Chang, Chin-lang: *Ta-hsüeh tzu-tien.*—*Chung-wen ts'an-k'ao . . . chih-yin* (2889), 222–223. [*Ta-hsüeh tzu-tien.*]
張錦郎：『大學字典』

3845 Li, Cho-min: *Li shih Chung-wen tzu-tien.*—Hong Kong: Hsiang-kang Chung-wen ta-hsüeh, 1980, 2, 22, 62, 86, 370, 138 p./ Hsing-sheng pu-shou, Kuo-yin Yüeh-yin. Fu Ch'ui-shan chien-tzu-fa; *China Quarterly* 91, 1982, 534–535, R.P. Sloss. [Li's Chinese character dictionary.]/ Phonetic radicals, National and Cantonese pronunciations. With 'Hanging Fan' character indexing system.
李卓敏：李氏中文字典／形聲部首，國音粵音附垂扇檢字法

5.1.6. Projected *Han-yü ta tzu-tien* (3846–3851)

3846 *Han-yü ta tzu-tien* pien-tsuan wei-yüan-hui: *Han-yü ta tzu-tien.*—A projected work started in 1975 in Szechwan and Hupei. Forthcoming. [A comprehensive character dictionary of the Chinese language.]
『漢語大字典』編纂委員會：漢語大字典

3847 Chao, Chen-to: Kuan-yü *Han-yü ta tzu-tien* te pien-hsieh kung-tso.—*TSYC* 1979:1, 97–103. [Concerning the work in the compilation of *Han-yü ta tzu-tien.*]
趙振鐸：關於『漢語大字典』的編寫工作

3848 Chao, Chen-to & Tso, Ta-ch'eng: *Han-yü ta tzu-tien* te pien-hsieh kung-tso.—*TSYC* 1983:2, 10–16, 167. [The work in the compilation of *Han-yü ta tzu-tien.*]

趙振鐸、左大成：『漢語大字典』的編寫工作

3849 Ch'eng, Yü-szu: *Han-yü ta tzu-tien* i-hsiang wen-t'i ch'u t'an.—*TSYC* 1980:3, 9–19. [A preliminary investigation into the problem of the semantic entries in *Han-yü ta tzu-tien.*]
成於思：『漢語大字典』義項問題初探

3850 Li, Ching-pai: Kuan-yü *Han-yü ta tzu-tien* te shou-tz'u wen-t'i.—*TYT* 4, 1982, 1–15. [Concerning the problem of lexical inclusions in *Han-yü ta tzu-tien.*]
李景白：關於『漢語大字典』的收詞問題

3851 Li, Ko-fei & Chao, Chen-to: *Han-yü ta tzu-tien* pien-hsieh kung-tso.—*TSYC* 1980:3, 3–8. [The work in the compilation of *Han-yü ta tzu-tien.*]
李格非、趙振鐸：『漢語大字典』編寫工作

5.2. Word and Phrase Dictionaries (3852–4024)
5.2.1. *Tz'u-yüan* (3852–3877)
5.2.1.1. Old Editions (3852–3863)

3852 Lu, Erh-k'uei, et al.: *Tz'u-yüan* & *Tz'u-yüan hsü-pien* (1082). [The sources of words] and [A supplement to *Tz'u-yüan.*]
陸爾奎等：辭源
方毅：辭源續編

3853 Chang, Chin-lang: *Tz'u-yüan.*—*Chung-wen ts'an-k'ao . . . chih-yin* (2889), 253–254. [*Tz'u-yüan.*]
張錦郎：『辭源』

3854 Chou, Hou-yü: *Tz'u-yüan* cheng-wu.—*Su-chung hsiao-k'an* 81, 1933, 5–7. [Corrigenda to *Tz'u-yüan.*]
周侯于：『辭源』正誤

3855 Chu, T'ien-chun & Ch'en, Hung-t'ien: *Tz'u-yüan* (cheng hsü ho-ting pen).—*Wen-k'o kung-chü shu chien-chieh* (2890), 13. [*Tz'u-yüan* (Vols. I and II combined ed.]/ 1949 edition.
朱天俊、陳宏天：『辭源（正續合訂本）』

3856 Chü, Jun-min: *Tz'u-Yüan* cheng-wu.
—*WHNP* 6, 1940, 157–168. [Corrigenda
to *Tz'u-yüan.*]
瞿潤緡：『辭源』正誤

3857 Liu, Yeh-ch'iu: *Tz'u-yüan.— Chung-kuo
te tzu-tien* (2996), 101–105; *Ch'ang-yung
tzu-tien shih chiang* (2997), 18–22.
[*Tz'u-yüan.*]
劉葉秋：『辭源』

3858 Lu, Erh-k'uei: *Tz'u-yüan* shuo-lüeh.
—*TFTC* 12:4, 1915, 13–16. [A brief
discussion of *Tz'u-yüan.*]
陸爾奎：『辭源』說略

3859 Teng, Ssu-yü & Biggerstaff, Knight:
*Tz'u-yüan.—An annotated bibliography . . .
reference works* (2898), 132–133.
〔辭源〕

3860 Ting, Hsiao-han: *Tz'u-yüan* chien
p'ing.—*Wen-hua chien-she yüeh-k'an* 1:10,
1935, 127–140. [A brief review of
Tz'u-yüan.]
丁霄漢：『辭源』簡評

3861 Tōdō, Akiyasu: *Jigen.—Sekai meicho
daijiten* (0041) 6, 455–456. [*Tz'u-yüan.*]
藤堂明保：『辭源』

3862 Wu, Hsiao-ju & Chuang, Ming-ch'üan:
*Tz'u-yüan.— Chung-kuo wen-shih . . .
chü-yao* (2903), 56–58. [*Tz'u-yüan.*]
吳小如、莊銘權：『辭源』

3863 Zach, Erwin von: Zum Shanghaier
Tz'u-yüan.—TP 24, 1926, 384–386;
MSOS 30, 1927, 123–146.

5.2.1.2. Mainland New Editions (3864–3873)

3864 Shang-wu yin-shu-kuan pien-shen-pu:
Tz'u-yüan (kai-pien pen).—Shanghai:
Shang-wu, 1950; 1953, 2nd ed., [i], 2,
2, 2, 4, 981, 10, 6 p. [The sources of
words (rearranged ed.)]/ With a Four-
corner system index.
商務印書館編審部：辭源（改編本）

3865 Shang-wu yin-shu-kuan pien-chi-pu: *Tz'u-
yüan* (hsiu-ting pen).—Peking: Shang-wu,
1979, Vol. I; 1980, Vol. II; 1981, Vol.
III; 1984, Vol. IV, 3620, (Four-corner
and Pinyin system indexes:) 123 p. [The
sources of words (rev. ed.).]
商務印書館編輯部：辭源（修訂本）

3866 Chao, K'o-ch'in: T'an *Tz'u-yüan* shih-i.
—*TSYC* 1980:1, 19–25. [A discussion
on the explanations of meanings in
Tz'u-yüan.]
趙克勤：談『辭源』釋義

3867 Chao, K'o-ch'in: *Tz'u-yüan* yü *Tz'u-hai.*
—*WSCS* 1981:3, 55–60. [*Tz'u-yüan* and
Tz'u-hai (1083).]
趙克勤：『辭源』與『辭海』

3868 Ch'üeh, Hsün-wu: *Tz'u-yüan, Tz'u-hai.*
—*Tsen-yang . . . kung-chü shu* (2891),
96–98. [*Tz'u-yüan* and *Tz'u-hai* (1083).]
闕勛吾：『辭源』、『辭海』

3869 Liu, Yeh-ch'iu: Chiu miu, pu ch'üeh,
ch'ung shih—*Tz'u-yüan* hsiu-ting san chi.
—*TSYC* 1981:4, 15–27. [Correct the
errors, supply the deficiencies, and
enrich the contents—Miscellaneous notes
on the revision of *Tz'u-yüan.*]
劉葉秋：糾謬、補缺、充實——『辭源』修訂
散記

3870 Lo, Wei-li: Shih p'ing *Tz'u-yüan* hsiu-
ting pen.—*TSYC* 1980:1, 26–32. [A
preliminary review of the revised edition
of *Tz'u-yüan.*]
駱偉里：試評『辭源』修訂本

3871 Sheng, Chiu-ch'ou: Chih liang ch'ou
yang fen-hsi.—*TSYC* 1981:4, 35–40. [An
analysis of quality and quantity from
a sampling (of *Tz'u-yüan*).]
盛九疇：質量抽樣分析

3872 Shu, Pao-chang: Ch'ien-chin te chiao
yin—*Tz'u-yüan* hsiu-ting kung-tso te shih-
chien.—*TSYC* 1981:4, 5–14. [Footprints
of advance—The realization of the work

on revision of *Tz'u-yüan.*]
舒寶璋：前進的腳印——『辭源』修訂工作的
實踐

3873　Wu, Tse-yen: I-pei jen chieh i-pei jen
te shih-yeh—T'an *Tz'u-yüan* te hsiu-ting.
—*TSYC* 1981:4, 1—4. [One generation
inherits another generation's undertaking
—A discussion on the revision of *Tz'u-*
yüan.]
吳澤炎：一輩人接一輩人的事業——談『辭源』
的修訂

5.2.1.3. Taiwan New Editions (3874—3877)

3874　T'ai-wan Shang-wu yin-shu-kuan pien-
shen-pu: *Tz'u-yüan* (hsiu-ting cheng hsü
ho-pien, Fu Pu-pien).—Taipei: Ditto,
1970, [iv], 6, 1862, (Four corner system
index:) 216, 11 p. [The sources of words
(rev. ed., Vols. I & II combined. With
A supplement).]
臺灣商務印書館編審部：辭源（修訂正續合編
，附補編）

3875　T'ai-wan Shang-wu yin-shu-kuan pien-
shen wei-yüan-hui: *Tseng-hsiu Tz'u-yüan.*
Fu *Szu-chiao hao-ma so-yin* (1082).
[A revised and enlarged *Tz'u-yüan.* With
A Four-corner numerical character
index.]
臺灣商務印書館編審委員會：增修辭源　附四
角號碼索引

3876　Chu, T'ien-chun & Ch'en, Hung-t'ien:
Tz'u-yüan (hsiu-ting pen).—*Wen-k'o kung-*
chü shu chien-chieh (2890), 14. [*Tz'u-yüan*
(rev. ed.).]/ 1979 ed.
朱天俊、陳宏天：『辭源（修訂本）』

3877　Wang, Yün-wu: Tseng-hsiu *Tz'u-yüan*
hsü.—*THHP* 12:2, 1978, 16—25. [A
preface to the revised and enlarged *Tz'u-*
yüan.]
王雲五：增修『辭源』序

5.2.2. *Tz'u-hai* (3878—3909)
5.2.2.1. Old Editions (3878—3889)

3878　Shu, Hsin-ch'eng, et al.: *Tz'u-hai*
(1083). [A sea of words.]
舒新城等：辭海

3879　Chang, Chin-lang: *Tz'u-hai.*—*Chung-wen*
ts'an-k'ao . . . chih-yin (2889), 254—255.
[*Tz'u-hai.*]
張錦郎：『辭海』

3880　Chu, T'ien-chun & Ch'en, Hung-t'ien:
Tz'u-hai (ho-ting pen).—*Wen-k'o kung-chü*
shu chien-chieh (2890), 9—11. [*Tz'u-hai*
(combined 1 volume ed.).]/ 1949 ed.
朱天俊、陳宏天：『辭海（合訂本）』

3881　Chuang, Sheng: P'ing *Tz'u-hai.*—
Chung-kuo kung-lun 1:2, 1939, 114—117.
[A review of *Tz'u-hai.*]
戀生：評『辭海』

3882　Fang, Hui-sheng: *Tz'u-hai* pu-pien (su
yen chih pu).—*KWTC* 3:1, 1944, 39—45;
2, 36—42; 3, 1945, 35—41; 4, 35—43.
[A supplement to *Tz'u-hai* (A section
of popular proverbs).]
方輝繩：『辭海』補編（俗諺之部）

3883　Kennedy, George A.: *ZH guide, an*
introduction to Sinology.—New Haven:
Yale Sinological Seminar, 1953, 171 p.;
New Haven: Far Eastern Publications,
1965, 185 p./ *Lg* 29, 1953, 568—576,
E.H. Schafer; *FEQ* 13, 1954, 88—90,
A.W. Hummel.
〔辭海〕

3884　Li, Chin-hsi: *Tz'u-hai* hsü.—*KYCK* 268,
1936, Nov. 21; 269, Nov. 28. [A preface
to *Tz'u-hai.*]
黎錦熙：『辭海』序

3885　Liu, Yeh-ch'iu: *Tz'u-hai.*—*Chung-kuo*
te tzu-tien (2996), 105—107; *Ch'ang-*
yung tzu-shu shih chiang (2997), 22—23.
[*Tz'u-hai.*]
劉葉秋：『辭海』

3886　Shu, Ch'ih: Shu Hsin-ch'eng ho *Tz'u-*
hai.—*TSYC* 1982:1, 178—186. [Shu
Hsin-ch'eng and (his) *Tz'u-hai.*]
舒池：舒新城和『辭海』

3887   Teng, Ssu-yü & Biggerstaff, Knight: *Tz'u-hai.—An annotated bibliography* . . . *reference works* (2898), 133—134.
〔辭海〕

3888   Tōdō, Akiyasu: *Jikai.—Sekai meicho daijiten* (0041) 6, 455. [*Tz'u-hai.*]
藤堂明保：『辭海』

3889   Wu, Hsiao-ju & Chuang, Ming-ch'üan: *Tz'u-hai.— Chung-kuo wen-shih* . . . *chü-yao* (2903), 58—61. [*Tz'u-hai.*]
吳小如、莊銘權：『辭海』

5.2.2.2. Mainland New Editions (3890–3905)

3890   *Tz'u-hai* pien-chi wei-yüan-hui: *Tz'u-hai* (1087). [A sea of words.]
『辭海』編輯委員會：辭海

3891   Chang, Ch'ün-hsien: Lüeh t'an hsin *Tz'u-hai* te chien-tzu she-chi.—*YWTC* 3, 1980, 20. [A brief discussion on the character indexing design of the new (edition of) *Tz'u-hai.*]
張羣顯：略談新『辭海』的檢字設計

3892   Chang, Ti-hua: Tu hsin-pan *Tz'u-hai* ou chih.—*TSYC* 1981:1, 229—232, 278. [Occasional notes on reading the new edition of *Tz'u-hai.*]
張滌華：讀新版『辭海』偶識

3893   Chang, Yeh-lu: Hsin-pan *Tz'u-hai* chih i.—*CCSY* 1981:4, 105—110. [Doubtful questions about the new edition of *Tz'u-hai.*]
張葉蘆：新版『辭海』質疑

3894   Ch'en, Tseng-chieh: Tu hsin-pan *Tz'u-hai Tz'u-yüan* cha chi.—*Wen-chou shih-chuan hsüeh-pao* 1981:2, 84— (not seen). [Notes on reading the new editions of *Tz'u-hai* and *Tz'u-yüan.*]
陳增傑：讀新版『辭海』、『辭源』劄記

3895   Chu, T'ien-chün & Ch'en, Hung-t'ien: *Tz'u-hai.—Wen-k'o kung-chü shu chien-chieh* (2890), 11—12. [*Tz'u-hai.*]/ 1979

rev. edition.
朱天俊、陳宏天：『辭海』

3896   Chung-hua shu-chü *Tz'u-hai* pien-chi-so: Wo-men shih tsen-yang ch'ung pien *Tz'u-hai* te?—*HSYK* 1958:12, 59—60. [How did we recompile *Tz'u-hai?*]
中華書局『辭海』編輯所：我們是怎樣重編『辭海』的？

3897   Hang, Wei: T'i-kao chih-liang ho chieh-chüeh mao-tun—pien-hsieh *Tz'u-hai* wei-ting kao te t'i-hui.—*TSYC* 1980:2, 20—31. [Improve the quality and resolve the contradications—my personal experiences from compiling the first draft of *Tz'u-hai.*]
杭葦：提高質量和解決矛盾——編寫『辭海』未定稿的體會

3898   Hsü, Ch'ing-k'ai: Hsin Chung-kuo ti-i-pu ta-hsing tz'u-shu kung-k'ai ch'u-pan—*Tz'u-hai* shih-hua.—*SL* 1979:1, 33—34. [The official publication of the first large-size dictionary in New China—a historical account of *Tz'u-hai.*]
徐慶凱：新中國第一部大型辭書公開出版——『辭海』史話

3899   Li, Chün-ying: Hsin-pan *Tz'u-hai* yin i wen-t'i p'ing i.—*CKYT* 47:5, 1980, 30—38, 16. [A critical discussion on the problems of pronunciations and meanings in the new edition of *Tz'u-hai.*]
李俊英：新版『辭海』音義問題評議

3900   Lo, Chu-feng: *Tz'u-hai* shih tsen-yang hsiu-ting te?—*TSYC* 1979:2, 5—15. [How was *Tz'u-hai* revised?]
羅竹風：『辭海』是怎樣修訂的？

3901   Mao, P'ei-lei: Wo ho *Tz'u-hai.—TSYC* 1982:2, 72—73. [I and *Tz'u-hai.*]/ Old and new editions.
毛蓓蕾：我和『辭海』

3902   Shang-hai tz'u-shu ch'u-pan-she: *Tz'u-hai szu-chiao hao-ma ch'a-tzu piao.*—Shanghai: Ditto, 1982, 4, 192 p. [A Four-corner numerical character index table to *Tz'u-hai*.]

上海辭書出版社：辭海四角號碼查字表

3903 Shu, Jen-ch'iu & Hsü, Shou-ming: Chieh-fang szu-hsiang shih chia su *Tz'u-hai* ch'u-pan te t'ui-tung li.—*TSYC* 1979:2, 16—23. [Liberation of thought was the motive for speeding up the publication of *Tz'u-hai*.]

束紉秋、徐壽明：解放思想是加速『辭海』出版的推動力

3904 T'ang, Wen: Ch'ien p'ing *Tz'u-hai yü-tz'u fen-ts'e.*—*CSSY* 1978:2, 55—63. [A simple review of *Tz'u-hai tz'u-yü fen-ts'e.*]

唐文：淺評『辭海・語詞分册』

3905 Wang, Ying-hsüan: P'ing *Tz'u-hai* (hsiu-ting kao) jen tzu t'iao.—*CYTH* 1979:1—2, 15—16, 48. [A review of the character entry *jen* of *Tz'u-hai* (revised draft).]

王應瑄：評『辭海』（修訂稿）『仁』字條

5.2.2.3. Taiwan New Editions (3906—3909)

3906 T'ai-wan Chung-hua shu-chü *Tz'u-hai* pien-chi wei-yüan-hui: *Tsui-hsin tseng-ting pen Tz'u-hai* (1085). [A newly revised edition of A sea of words.]

臺灣中華書局『辭海』編輯委員會：最新增訂本辭海

3907 Ch'ü, Shou-yüeh: *Tz'u-hai* pu cheng. —*YSHP* 2:1, 1959, 1—64. [Addenda and corrigenda to *Tz'u-hai*.]

曲守約：『辭海』補正

3908 T'ang, Yün: P'ing ting *Tz'u-hai.*—*Hsin shih-tai* 2:11, 1962, 29—31. [A critique of the revised (editon of) *Tz'u-hai*.]

唐允：評訂『辭海』

3909 Tso, Hsiu-ling: Tsai t'an hsiu-ting pen *Tz'u-hai* te ts'o-wu.—*SPSM* 38, 1976, 28—33. [Another discussion on the errata of the revised edition of *Tz'u-hai*.]

左秀靈：再談修訂本『辭海』的錯誤

5.2.3. *Tz'u-t'ung* (3910—3925)

3910 Chu, Ch'i-feng: *Tz'u-t'ung* (1064). [A thoroughfare of words.]/ Ancient and literary polysyllabic words and phrases.

朱起鳳：辭通

3911 Chang, Chin-lang: *Tz'u-t'ung.*—*Chung-wen ts'an-k'ao . . . chih-yin* (2889), 258. [*Tz'u-t'ung.*]

張錦郎：『辭通』

3912 Chi, Wei-lung: Chu Ch'i-feng wei-ho fa-fen pien *Tz'u-t'ung?*—*SHST* 1979:4, 96. [Why did Chu Ch'i-feng make a firm resolution to compile *Tz'u-t'ung?*]

季維龍：朱起鳳爲何發憤編『辭通』？

3913 Ch'ien, Hsüan-t'ung: *Tz'u-t'ung* hsü.— *STYK* 10, 1934, 164—169. [A preface to *Tz'u-t'ung.*]

錢玄同：『辭通』序

3914 Chin, Wen-ming; Wang, T'ao & Szu, Ying-ch'i: T'an *Tz'u-t'ung.*—*TSYC* 1980:4, 197—207. [A discussion on *Tz'u-t'ung.*]

金文明、王濤、斯英琦：談『辭通』

3915 Chu, T'ien-chün & Ch'en, Hung-t'ien: *Tz'u-t'ung.*—*Wen-k'o kung-chü shu chien-chieh* (2890), 18—19. [*Tz'u-t'ung.*]

朱天俊、陳宏天：『辭通』

3916 Hu, Shih: *Tz'u-t'ung* hsü.—*CHS* 44, 1934, 61—70. [A preface to *Tz'u-t'ung.*]

胡適：『辭通』序

3917 Hu, Shih: The *Tz'u-t'ung*, a new dictionary of classical polysyllabic words and phrases.—*QBCB* 1, 1934, 55—58.

3918 Liu, Ta-pai: *Tz'u-t'ung* hsü.—*PPTS* 6:6, 1932, 11—17. [A preface to *Tz'u-t'ung.*]

劉大白：『辭通』序

3919 Liu, Yeh-ch'iu: *Tz'u-t'ung.*—*Chung-kuo te tzu-tien* (2996), 107—109; *Ch'ang-yung tzu-shu shih chiang* (2997), 27—29. [*Tz'u-t'ung.*]

劉葉秋：『辭通』

3920   Teng, Ssu-yü & Biggerstaff, Knight: *Tz'u-t'ung.—An annotated bibliography . . . reference works* (2898), 137.
〔辭通〕

3921   Tōdō, Akiyasu: *Jitsū.—Sekai meicho daijiten* (0041) 6, 456. [*Tz'u-t'ung.*]
藤堂明保：『辭通』

3922   Tu, Ming-fu: P'ing Chu Ch'i-feng *Tz'u-t'ung* shang ts'e.—*TSCK* 1:2, 1934, 81–87. [A critique of the first volume of Chu Ch'i-feng's *Tz'u-t'ung.*]
杜明甫：評朱起鳳『辭通』上冊

3923   T'u, Chi-chih: I-wei k'o-ching te hsün-ku-hsüeh-chia—Chu Ch'i-feng.—*TSYC* 1980:3, 208–214. [A venerable Chinese traditional semanticist—Chu Ch'i-feng.]
屠基治：一位可敬的訓詁學家──朱起鳳

3924   Wu, Hsiao-ju & Chuang, Ming-ch'üan: *Tz'u-t'ung.— Chung-kuo wen-shih . . . chü-yao* (2903), 224–226. [*Tz'u-t'ung.*]
吳小如、莊銘權：『辭通』

3925   Wu, Wen-ch'i: Chieh-shao Chu Tan-chiu hsien-sheng chu *Tz'u-t'ung.*—*PPTS* 7:2, 1933, 23–36. [An introduction to Mr. Chu Tan-chiu's *Tz'u-t'ung.*]
吳文祺：介紹朱丹九先生著『辭通』

5.2.4. *Lien-mien tzu-tien* (3926–3934)

3926   Fu, Ting-i: *Lien-mien tzu-tien* (0977). [A dictionary of sound-correlated disyllabic words.]
符定一：聯綿字典

3927   Chu, T'ien-chün & Ch'en, Hung-t'ien: *Lien-mien tzu-tien.— Wen-k'o kung-chü shu chien-chieh* (2890), 19–20. [*Lien-mien tzu-tien.*]
朱天俊、陳宏天：『聯綿字典』

3928   Fu, Ting-i: *Lien-mien tzu-tien* shu-p'ing te ting-wu.—*TSCW* 3, 1947, 20–24. [Revision of the mistakes of book reviews on *Lien-mien tzu-tien* (0977).]

符定一：『聯綿字典』書評的訂誤

3929   Jen, Hsin-shu: *Lien-mien tzu-tien.— TSCW* 2, 1947, 12–14. [*Lien-mien tzu-tien.*]
任心叔：『聯綿字典』

3930   Liu, Yeh-ch'iu: *Lien-mien tzu-tien.— Chung-kuo te tzu-tien* (2996), 109–110; *Ch'ang-yung tzu-shu shih chiang* (2997), 29–32. [*Lien-mien tzu-tien.*]
劉葉秋：『聯綿字典』

3931   Lo, Chih-ch'ien: Yü Fu Yü-cheng hsien-sheng lun *Lien-mien tzu-tien* shu. —*KHLH* 6, 1935, 3–4. [A letter to Mr. Fu Yü-cheng on (his) *Lien-mien tzu-tien.*]
羅植乾：與符宇澂先生論『聯綿字典』書

3932   Sun, Fu-yüan: P'ing *Lien-mien tzu-tien.*—*SCCY* 23, 1947, 2–6. [A review of *Lien-mien tzu-tien.*]
孫伏園：評『聯綿字典』

3933   Tun, Weng: *Lien-mien tzu-tien.—Han-hiue* 1, 1944, 231–241. [*Lien-mien tzu-tien.*]
鈍翁：『聯綿字典』

3934   Wu, Hsiao-ju & Chuang, Ming-ch'üan: *Lien-mien tzu-tien.— Chung-kuo wen-shih . . . chü-yao* (2903), 226–227. [*Lien-mien tzu-tien.*]
吳小如、莊銘權：『聯綿字典』

5.2.5. *Kuo-yü tz'u-tien* and *Han-yü tz'u-tien* (3935–3953)

5.2.5.1. *Kuo-yü tz'u-tien* (Old Edition) (3935–3945)

3935   Chung-kuo ta-tz'u-tien pien-tsuan-ch'u: *Kuo-yü tz'u-tien* (1357). [A dictionary of the National Language.]
中國大辭典編纂處：國語辭典

3936   Chang, Chin-lang: *Kuo-yü tz'u-tien.— Chung-wen ts'an-k'ao . . . chih-yin* (2889), 263–264. [*Kuo-yü tz'u-tien.*]
張錦郎 ：『國語辭典』

3937 Chang, Po-yü: Chung-kuo ta tz'u-tien pien-tsuan-ch'u ho *Kuo-yü tz'u-tien* te pien-tsuan ken pan-pen.—*SHJ* 268, 1975, 1–8. [The Editorial Bureau of *Chung-kuo ta tz'u-tien* and the compilation and editions of *Kuo-yü tz'u-tien*.]
張博宇：中國大辭典編纂處和『國語辭典』的編纂跟版本

3938 Kuraishi, Takeshirō: *Kokugo jiten* o mukaete.—*CGGG* 4, 1947, (not seen). [Welcoming *Kuo-yü tz'u-tien*.]
倉石武四郎：『國語辭典』を迎えて

3939 Kuraishi, Takeshirō: *Kokugo jiten* o kakomu zadankai.—*CGGG* 6, 1947, (not seen). [A round-table discussion on *Kuo-yü tz'u-tien*.]
倉石武四郎：『國語辭典』を圍む座談會

3940 Kuraishi, Takeshirō: *Kokugo jiten.—Chūgoku Bunka* 4, 1948, (not seen). [*Kuo-yü tz'u-tien*.]
倉石武四郎：『國語辭典』

3941 Li, Chin-hsi: *Kuo-yü tz'u-tien* pien-tsuan te ching-kuo.—*KYCK* 275, 1937, Jan. 16; 276, Jan. 23. [The compilatory processes of *Kuo-yü tz'u-tien*.]
黎錦熙：『國語辭典』編纂的經過

3942 Teng, Ssu-yü & Biggerstaff, Knight: *Kuo-yü tz'u-tien.—An annotated bibliography . . . reference works* (2898), 134.
〔國語辭典〕

3943 Tōdō, Akiyasu: *Kokugo jiten.—Sekai meicho daijiten* (0041) 6, 452. [*Kuo-yü tz'u-tien*.]
藤堂明保：『國語辭典』

3944 Wan, Grace: *A guide to Gwoyeu tzyrdean.*—San Francisco: Chinese Materials and Research Aids Service Center, 1970, 43 p./ *JCLTA* 6:2, 1971, 86–88, C.K. Wu.
〔國語辭典〕

3945 Ying, Yü-k'ang & Hsieh, Yün-fei: *Kuo-yü tz'u-tien.—Chung-wen kung-chü shu chih-yin* (2908), 33–34. [*Kuo-yü tz'u-tien*.]
應裕康、謝雲飛：『國語辭典』

5.2.5.2. *Kuo-yü tz'u-tien* (New Edition) (3946–3948)

3946 Chiao-yü-pu *Ch'ung-pien Kuo-yü tz'u-tien* pien-chi wei-yüan-hui: *Ch'ung-pien Kuo-yü tz'u-tien* (1354). [A recompiled edition of a dictionary of the National Language.]
教育部『重編國語辭典』編輯委員會：重編國語辭典

3947 Lin, I-t'ung: K'o kung ta-chung ts'an-yüeh te tzu-tien——*Ch'ung-pien Kuo-yü tz'u-tien.—CKYT* 50:6, 1982, 61–66. [A readable reference dictionary for the public—*Ch'ung-pien Kuo-yü tz'u-tien*.]
林以通：可供大衆參閱的字典——『重編國語辭典』

3948 Sabban, Françoise: *Chongbian Guoyu cidian.—CLAO* 11:2, 1982, 103–104./ A review.
〔重編國語辭典〕

5.2.5.3. *Han-yü tz'u-tien* (3949–3953)

3949 Chung-kuo ta tz'u-tien pien-tsuan-ch'u: *Han-yü tz'u-tien* (1358). [A dictionary of the Chinese language.]
中國大辭典編纂處：漢語辭典

3950 Chung-kuo ta tz'u-tien pien-tsuan-ch'u: *Hua-yü ta tz'u-tien.*—Hong Kong: Shanghai, 1967, [i], 7, [4], 35, 1241, 179, 4, 34 p./ An adapted repr. of (1358) using the radical system. [A comprehensive dictionary of the Chinese language.]
中國大辭典編纂處：華語大辭典

3951 Chu, T'ien-chun & Ch'en, Hung-t'ien: *Han-yü tz'u-tien.—Wen-k'o kung-chü shu chien-chieh* (2890), 8–9. [*Han-yü tz'u-tien*.]
朱天俊、陳宏天：『漢語辭典』

3952 Liu, Yeh-ch'iu: *Han-yü tz'u-tien.—*
Chung-kuo te tzu-tien (2996), 110–113;
Ch'ang-yung tzu-shu shih chiang (2997),
24–26. [*Han-yü tz'u-tien.*]
劉葉秋：『漢語辭典』

3953 Wu, Hsiao-ju & Chuang, Ming-ch'üan:
Han-yü tz'u-tien.— Chung-kuo wen-shih . . .
chü-yao (2903), 61–64. [*Han-yü tz'u-tien.*]
吳小如、莊銘權：『漢語辭典』

5.2.6. Wang Yün-wu's Four-corner System
 Dictionaries (3954–3962)

3954 Wang, Yün-wu: *Wang Yün-wu ta tz'u-*
*tien.—*Shanghai: Shang-wu, 1928; 1930,
2nd ed., [ii], 2, 3, 2, 1384, 154,
45, 53, [3] p.; Hong Kong: Wan-t'ung
shu-tien, 1963, repr., 5, 1384, 40, 44,
53 p./ *TSPL* 2:12, 1934, 3–24, Chao
Jui-sheng. [Wang Yün-wu's comprehensive
dictionary.]
王雲五：王雲五大辭典／趙瑞生評

3955 Wang, Yün-wu: *Wang Yün-wu hsiao*
*tz'u-tien.—*Shanghai: Shang-wu, 1931;
1948, 41st ed., 835 p. [Wang Yün-wu's
small dictionary.]
王雲五：王雲五小辭典

3956 Wang, Yün-wu: *Wang Yün-wu hsin-*
*tz'u-tien.—*Chungking: Shang-wu, 1943;
Taipei: Shang-wu, 1965; 1977, 2nd ed.,
4, 254, 17 p. [Wang Yün-wu's dictionary
of new terms.]/ See (3957).
王雲五：王雲五新詞典

3957 Wang, Yün-wu: Hsin ming-tz'u su yüan
—Wang Yün-wu hsin tz'u-tien hsü.—*TFTC*
39:15, 1943, 48–50. [Tracing the origins
of new terms—A preface to *Wang Yün-wu*
hsin-tz'u-tien (3956).]
王雲五：新名詞溯源——『王雲五新詞典』序

3958 Wang, Yün-wu: *Wang Yün-wu tsung-ho*
*tz'u-tien.—*Taipei: Hua-kuo, 1950; 1954,
rev. ed.; 1968, rev. 4th ed., [xii], 1000,
23, 63, 2 p.; 1970, repr. [Wang Yün-wu's
integrated dictionary.]/ Combination of

(3954) & (3955).
王雲五：王雲五綜合詞典

3959 Wang, Yün-wu: *Szu-chiao hao-ma*
*Wang Yün-wu kuo-min tzu-hui.—*Taipei:
Hua-kuo, 1953, 6, [7], 300 p. [Wang
Yün-wu's A citizen's Four-corner system
character glossary.]
王雲五：四角號碼王雲五國民字彙

3960 Chao, Jui-sheng: *Wang Yün-wu ta*
tz'u-tien.—TSPL 2:12, 1934, 3–24.
[*Wang Yün-wu ta tz'u-tien.*]
趙瑞生：『王雲五大辭典』

3961 Li, Chih-chung & Wang, Yin-lan: *Wang*
Yün-wu tsung-ho tz'u-tien.— Chung-wen
ts'an-k'ao . . . chih-nan (2894), 173–174
(AJ 15). [*Wang Yün-wu tsung-ho tz'u-tien*
(3958).]
李志鍾、汪引蘭：『王雲五綜合詞典』

3962 Teng, Ssu-yü & Biggerstaff, Knight:
Wang Yün-wu ta tz'u-tien.—An annotated
bibliography . . . reference works (2898),
134–135.
〔王雲五大詞典〕

5.2.7. Shang-wu's New Four-corner System
 Dictionary (3963–3965)

3963 Shang-wu yin-shu-kuan: *Szu-chiao hao-*
*ma hsin tz'u-tien.—*Peking: Ditto, 1958;
1979, 8th ed., 10, 688, 18, 102 p.;
Hong Kong: Shang-wu, 1972, repr.,
14, 576, 12, 64 p. [A new Four-corner
system dictionary.]
商務印書館：四角號碼新詞典

3964 Chu, T'ien-chün & Ch'en, Hung-t'ien:
Szu-chiao hao-ma hsin tz'u-tien.— Wen-
k'o kung-chü shu chien-chieh (2890),
6–7. [*Szu-chiao hao-ma hsin tz'u-tien.*]
朱天俊、陳宏天：『四角號碼新詞典』

3965 Hai, Heng: Tu *Szu-chiao hao-ma hsin*
tz'u-tien.—CKYW 1978:4, 310–313. [On
reading *Szu-chiao hao-ma hsin tz'u-tien.*]
海恒：讀『四角號碼新詞典』

5.2.8. *Dai Kan-Wa jiten* (3966—3975)

3966 Morohashi, Tetsuji: *Dai Kan-Wa jiten.* —Tokyo: Taishūkan, 1955—1960, 13 vols., text 13757 p., indexes 1101 p.; 1966, reduced ed./ *RBS* 2, 1956, 377, I.M. Oshanin; *RBS* 6, 1960, 402, D. Holzman. [A comprehensive Sino-Japanese dictionary.]
諸橋轍次：大漢和辭典

3967 Chang, Chin-lang: *Dai Kan-Wa jiten.*— *Chung-wen ts'an-k'ao . . . chih-yin* (2889), 255—256. [*Dai Kan-Wa jiten.*]
張錦郎：『大漢和辭典』

3968 Chiang, Ying-lung: *Ta Han-Ho tz'u-tien chi ch'i tso-che.*—*Weng hsing* 7:4, 1961, 14—16. [*Dai Kan-Wa jiten* and its author.]
江應龍：『大漢和辭典』及其作者

3969 Kondō, Haruo: *Dai Kan-Wa jiten* to goshoku no koto nado.—*Zeirin* 27, 1979, 12—15. [Misprints, etc. found in *Dai Kan-Wa jiten.*]
近藤春雄：『大漢和辭典』と誤植のことなど

3970 Li, Chih-chung & Wang, Yin-lan: *Dai Kan-Wa jiten.—Chung-wen ts'an-k'ao . . . chih-nan* (2894), 194—195. [*Dai Kan-Wa jiten.*]
李志鍾、汪引蘭：『大漢和辭典』

3971 Liang, Jung-jo: Chu-ch'iao Ch'e-tz'u chu *Han-Ho ta tz'u-tien.*—*THHP* 10:2, 1969, 1—13; E.S. [Morohashi Tetsuji's *Dai Kan-Wa jiten.*]
梁容若：諸橋轍次著『漢和大辭典』（should be：『大漢和辭典』）

3972 Morohasi, Tetsuji: *Dai Kan-Wan jiten* kankan ni saishite.—*Aoyama Gakuin Joshi Tanki Daigaku Kiyō* 13, 1960, (not seen). [At the time of the completion of the publication of *Dai Kan-Wa jiten.*]
諸橋轍次：『大漢和辭典』完刊に際して

3973 Teng, Ssu-yü & Biggerstaff, Knight: *Dai Kan-Wa jiten.—An annotated biblio-*

graphy . . . reference works (2898), 133. 〔大漢和辭典〕

3974 T'ien, Tsung-yao: *Ta Han-Ho tz'u-tien che wu.*—*Szu yü yen* 3:6, 1966, 47—48. [Corrigenda to *Dai Kan-Wa jiten.*]
田宗堯：『大漢和辭典』摘誤

3975 Yü, Chia-ch'i & Hsü, Yung-chen: Hsien shen *Ta Han-Ho tz'u-tien* pien-tsuan te Chu-ch'iao Ch'e-tz'u.—*TSYC* 1982:4, 177—180. [Morohashi Tetsuji in dedicating himself to the compilation of *Dai Kan-Wa jiten.*]
于家齊、徐永眞：獻身『大漢和辭典』編纂的諸橋轍次

5.2.9. *Chung-wen ta tz'u-tien* (3976—3993)

3976 Chang, Ch'i-yün (ed. in chief), Lin, Yin & Kao, Ming (eds.): *Chung-wen ta tz'u-tien.*—Yangmingshan: Chung-kuo wen-hua yen-chiu-so, 1962—1968, (text:) 38 vols., (index:) 2 vols., 8, 9, 17244 p.; 397 p.; 364 p., illus.; Yangmingshan: Chung-kuo wen-hua hsüeh-yüan, 1980, 5th rev. ed., 10 vols; 1982, repr./ Based on *Dai Kan-Wa jiten* (3966). [A comprehensive dictionary of the Chinese language.]
張其昀主編，林尹、高明編：中文大辭典

3977 Chang, Chin-lang: *Chung-wen ta tz'u-tien.—Chung-wen ts'an-k'ao . . . chih-yin* (2889), 256—258. [*Chung-wen ta tz'u-tien.*]
張錦郎：『中文大辭典』

3978 Ch'en, Ping-chao: T'ai-wan-sheng *Chung-wen ta tz'u-tien* (hsiu-ting pan) ch'u-pan. —*CYTH* 1979:4, 23—24. [The publication of *Chung-wen ta tz'u-tien* (rev. ed.) in Taiwan province.]
陳炳昭：臺灣省『中文大辭典』（修訂版）出版

3979 Ch'en, Ping-chao: Ku chin tz'u-shu chih chi ta-ch'eng che, *Chung-wen ta tz'u-tien.*—*SHST* 1979:3, 110. [A great consumation of ancient and modern lexicographical works—*Chung-wen ta tz'u-tien*.]

陳炳昭：古今辭書之集大成者——『中文大辭典』

3980   Ch'en, Shih-fu: P'ing *Chung-wen ta tz'u-tien*.—*Chung-kuo i-chou* 679, 1963, 14. [A critique of *Chung-wen ta tz'u-tien*.]

陳石孚：評『中文大辭典』

3981   Ch'en, Tseng-chieh: *Chung-wen ta tz'u-tien* te yu-tien ho wen-t'i.—*TSYC* 1982:1, 92–103. [The merits and problems of *Chung-wen ta tz'u-tien*.]

陳增杰：『中文大辭典』的優點和問題

3982   Ch'ien, Chien-fu: Lüeh t'an T'ai-wan-sheng pien *Chung-wen ta tz'u-tien*.—*TSYC* 1980:1, 133–135. [A short discussion on the *Chung-wen ta tz'u-tien* compiled in Taiwan province.]

錢劍夫：略談臺灣省編『中文大辭典』

3983   Hsia, Wei-wen: Yin i wei chien—tui *Chung-wen ta tz'u-tien* wu t'iao shih wen te t'an-t'ao.—*TSYC* 1980:1, 136–138. [Take warning from it—an investigation into the explanations of the contents in five entries of *Chung-wen ta tz'u-tien*.]

夏蔚文：引以為鑒——對『中文大辭典』五條釋文的探討

3984   Hsüeh, K'o: T'ai-wan *Chung-wen ta tz'u-tien* o-wu chü li.—*HCTH* 1981:4, 42–47. [Examples of errata in Taiwan's *Chung-wen ta tz'u-tien*.]

雪克：臺灣『中文大辭典』譌誤舉例

3985   Huang, Tien-ch'eng: P'ing *Chung-wen ta tz'u-tien* te chu-yin chi ch'i-t'a.—*TSYC* 1982:1, 104–110, 140. [A critique of the phonetic notations, etc. in *Chung-wen ta tz'u-tien*.]

黃典誠：評『中文大辭典』的注音及其他

3986   Hung, Po: P'ing *Chung-wen ta tz'u-tien* pien-tsuan chung te chi-ko wen-t'i.—*HCTH* 1981:2, (not seen). [A critique of several problems in the compilation of *Chung-wen ta tz'u-tien*.]

洪波：評『中文大辭典』編纂中的幾個問題

3987   Hung, Po: Lüeh t'an *Chung-wen ta tz'u-tien* te shih-i.—*TSYC* 1982:1, 111–115. [A brief discussion on explanations of meanings in *Chung-wen ta tz'u-tien*.]

洪波：略談『中文大辭典』的釋義

3988   Li, Chih-chung & Wang, Yin-lan: *Chung-wen ta tz'u-tien*.—*Chung-wen ts'an-k'ao . . . chih-nan* (2894), 168–169. [*Chung-wen ta tz'u-tien*.]

李志鍾、汪引蘭：『中文大辭典』

3989   Suzuki, Osamu: Shohyō *Chūbun dai jiten* sha-bu kaku-bu jakkan.—*Biburia* 1970:4, 39–43. [A review of *Chung-wen ta tz'u-tien*. Radicals *ch'e* and *ko* sections.]

鈴木治：書評『中文大辭典』車部，革部若干

3990   Teng, Ssu-yü & Biggerstaff, Knight: *Chung-wen ta tz'u-tien*.—*An annotated bibliography . . . reference works* (2898), 133.

〔中文大辭典〕

3991   T'ien, Shui: Ts'ung T'ai-wan-sheng pien *Chung-wen ta tz'u-tien* te chi-t'iao yung-li k'an tzu-liao te ho-tui ho li-yung wen-t'i.—*TYT* 3, 1981, 133–139. [The problems of verification and use of (lexicographical) materials as seen from several examples used in the *Chung-wen ta tz'u-tien* compiled in Taiwan province.]

天水：從臺灣省編『中文大辭典』的幾條用例看資料的核對和利用問題

3992   Wang, Chieh-yü: Hsin tu *Chung-wen ta tz'u-tien* ch'u-pan.—*TSYK* 1:1, 1966, 15–20. [On happily reading the publication of *Chung-wen ta tz'u-tien*.]

王潔宇：欣讀『中文大辭典』出版

3993   Ying, Yü-k'ang & Hsieh, Yün-fei: *Chung-wen ta tz'u-tien*.—*Chung-wen kung-chü shu chih-yin* (2908), 30–31. [*Chung-wen ta tz'u-tien*.]

應裕康、謝雲飛：『中文大辭典』

5.2.10. *Kuo-yü jih-pao tz'u-tien* (3994–3999)

3994   Ho, Jung: *Kuo-yü jih-pao tz'u-tien* (1360). [The National Language Daily News dictionary.]
何容：國語日報辭典

3995   Chang, Chin-lang: *Kuo-yü jih-pao tz'u-tien.—Chung-wen ts'an-k'ao . . . chih-yin* (2889), 259. [*Kuo-yü jih-pao tz'u-tien.*]
張錦郎：『國語日報辭典』

3996   Hu, Chi-chün: Fu shih *Kuo-yü jih-pao tz'u-tien* te wei tz'u.—*SPSM* 24, 1975, 67–70. [Stoop and pick up minor defects of *Kuo-yü jih-pao tz'u-tien.*]
胡基峻：俯拾『國語日報辭典』的微疵

3997   Liang, Jung-jo: K'an *Kuo-yü jih-pao tz'u-tien* pi-chi.—*SHJ* 269, 1975, 7–8. [Notes on reading *Kuo-yü jih-pao tz'u-tien.*]
梁容若：看『國語日報辭典』筆記

3998   Liu, Ch'ung-ch'un: P'ing *Kuo-yü jih-pao tz'u-tien.—SHJ* 269, 1975, 1–7. [A critique of *Kuo-yü jih-pao tz'u-tien.*]
劉崇純：評『國語日報辭典』

3999   Wang, Meng-wu: Wo k'an-le *Kuo-yü jih-pao tz'u-tien.—CKYT* 36:4, 1975, 70–71. [I read *Kuo-yü jih-pao tz'u-tien.*]
王孟武：我看了『國語日報辭典』

5.2.11. *Hsien-tai Han-yü tz'u-tien* and *Hsin-hua tz'u-tien* (4000–4011)
5.2.11.1. *Hsien-tai Han-yü tz'u-tien* (4000–4009)

4000   Chung-kuo k'o-hsüeh-yüan Yü-yen yen-chiu-so tz'u-tien pien-chi-shih: *Hsien-tai Han-yü tz'u-tien* (shih-yung pen).—Peking: Shang-wu, 1965; 1973, repr.; Hong Kong: Shang-wu, 1977, repr., [v], 88, 1400 p. [A dictionary of the modern Chinese language (preliminary edition).]
中國科學院語言研究所詞典編輯室：現代漢語詞典（試用本）

4001   Chung-kuo she-hui k'o-hsüeh-yüan Yü-yen yen-chiu-so tz'u-tien pien-chi-shih:

Hsien-tai Han-yü tz'u-tien (1356). [A dictionary of the modern Chinese language.]
中國社會科學院語言研究所詞典編輯室：現代漢語詞典

4002   Chang, Chih-i: *Hsien-tai Han-yü tz'u-tien* shih-i te yü-wen-hsing.—*TSYC* 1981:3, 79–85. [The linguistic nature of the explanations of meanings in *Hsien-tai Han-yü tz'u-tien.*]
張志毅：『現代漢語詞典』釋義的語文性

4003   Chao, Chi-chou: *Hsien-tai Han-yü tz'u-tien* yü Pei-ching fang-yen tz'u.—*TSYC* 1982:6, 104–109. [*Hsien-tai Han-yü tz'u-tien* and Peking dialect words.]
晁繼周：『現代漢語詞典』與北京方言詞

4004   Chou, Chung-ling: Lüeh lun *Hsien-tai Han-yü tz'u-tien* te shih-i.—*TSYC* 1980:1, 13–18. [A brief discussion on the explanation of meanings in *Hsien-tai Han-yü tz'u-tien.*]
周鍾靈：略論『現代漢語詞典』的釋義

4005   Han, Ching-t'i & Yü, Ken-yüan: Hsiang-kang ch'u-pan fa-hsing *Hsien-tai Han-yü tz'u-tien* ping fa-piao p'ing-lun wen-chang.—*YYHT* 1978:2, 79–80. [The publication of the Hong Kong edition of *Hsien-tai Han-yü tz'u-tien* and review articles.]
韓敬體、于根元：香港出版發行『現代漢語詞典』並發表評論文章

4006   Li, Shih: Kuan-yü tzu-liao.—*TSYC* 1981:3, 70–78. [Concerning materials (in *Hsien-tai Han-yü tz'u-tien*).]
李實：關於資料

4007   Liu, Ch'ing-lung: *Hsien-tai Han-yü tz'u-tien* pien-hsieh kung-tso erh-shih nien.—*TSYC* 1981:3, 1–19. [Twenty years of work in the compilation of *Hsien-tai Han-yü tz'u-tien.*]
劉慶隆：『現代漢語詞典』編寫工作二十年

4008   Sun, Te-hsüan: *Hsien-tai Han-yü tz'u-tien* pien-tsuan tsa chih.—*TSYC* 1980:1, 1–12. [Miscellaneous notes on the compilation of *Hsien-tai Han-yü tz'u-tien.*]

孫德宣：『現代漢語詞典』編纂雜識

4009   Wu, Hsiao-ju & Chuang, Ming-ch'üan: *Hsien-tai Han-yü tz'u-tien.*—*Chung-kuo wen-shih . . . chü-yao* (2903), 64–68. [*Hsien-tai Han-yü tz'u-tien.*]

吳小如　莊銘權：『現代漢語詞典』

5.2.11.2. *Hsin-hua tz'u-tien* (4010–4011)

4010   *Hsin-hua tz'u-tien* pien-tsuan-tsu: *Hsin-hua tz'u-tien* (1361). [A new China dictionary.]

『新華辭典』編纂組：新華辭典

4011   Morikawa, Kyūjirō: *Shinka jiten* o yomu.—*Tōhō* 18, 1981, 7–9. [On reading *Hsin-hua tz'u-tien.*]

森川久次郎：『新華詞典』を讀む

5.2.12.   Other Chinese-Chinese Word and Phrase Dictionaries (4012–4017)

4012   Ch'üan-kuo Kuo-yü chiao-yü ts'u-chin-hui shen-tz'u wei-yüan-hui: *Piao-chun Kuo-yü ta tz'u-tien.*—Shanghai: Shang-wu, 1935; 1938, 5th ed., 5, 638, 46 p. [A comprehensive dictionary of the standard National Language.]

全國國語教育促進會審詞委員會：標準國語大辭典

4013   *Han-yü hsiao tz'u-tien* pien-hsieh-tsu: *Han-yü hsiao tz'u-tien.*—Shanghai: Shanghai tz'u-shu, 1981, 2, 47, 695 p. [A small dictionary of the Chinese language.]

『漢語小詞典』編寫組：漢詞小詞典

4014   Hsü, Ch'ing-t'i (ed. in chief): *Tz'u-yüan.*—Taipei: Ta-hsin shu-chü, 1978, 2, 77, 2152, (appendices:) 197 p., illus. [A source of words.]

許清梯主編：辭淵

4015   Kuang-fu shu-chü pien-chi-pu: *Kuo-yü t'u-chieh tz'u-tien.*—Taipei: Ditto, 1976, [vi], 16, 1139 p., illus. [An illustrated

dictionary of the National Language.]

光復書局編輯部：國語圖解辭典

4016   Lu, Shih-ch'eng (ed. in chief): *Tz'u-hui.*—Taipei: Wen-hua t'u-shu, 1975, 2, 10, 2005, 75 p./ *SPSM* 42, 1976, 16–23, Lin Ch'ing-chang. [A dictionary of words.]

陸師成主編：辭彙／林慶彰評

4017   Wang, Yün-wu (ed. in chief): *Chung-shan ta tz'u-tien i tzu ch'ang-pien.*—Shanghai: Shang-wu, 1938; Taipei: Shang-wu, 1967, repr., [iv], 12, 478 p. [The Chung-shan comprehensive dictionary, a long section for the character *i* ('one').]

王雲五總編輯：中山大辭典『一』字長編

5.2.13.   Projected *Han-yü ta tz'u-tien* (4018–4024)

4018   Lo, Chu-feng (ed. in chief): *Han-yü ta tz'u-tien.*—Forthcoming. [A comprehensive dictionary of the Chinese language.]

羅竹風主編：漢語大辭典

4019   Anonymous: *Han-yü ta tz'u-tien* ch'u kao hsüan k'an.—*TSYC* 1981:1, 53–63. [Selected sample entries from the preliminary draft of *Han-yü ta tz'u-tien.*]

無名氏：『漢語大詞典』初稿選刊

4020   Chang, Lü-hsiang: Yü-wen tz'u-tien shih-i ch'u-t'an—*Han-yü ta tz'u-tien* pien-tsuan cha-chi.—*TSYC* 1981:1, 13–24. [A preliminary investigation into the explanation of meanings in language and writing dictionaries—Notes on the compilation of *Han-yü ta tz'u-tien.*]

張履祥：語文辭典釋義初探——『漢語大詞典』編纂札記

4021   Ch'en, Yüan: *Han-yü ta tz'u-tien* te li-shih shih-ming.—*TSYC* 1982:3, 4–11. [The historical mission of *Han-yü ta tz'u-tien.*]

陳原：『漢語大詞典』的歷史使命

4022   Chin, Wen-ming: Na-hsieh fang-mien yu so ch'u hsin—*Han-yü ta tz'u-tien*

pien-chi kung-tso shou chi.—*TSYC* 1981:
1, 25—32. [In what respect do features
appear as new?—Personal notes on the
work in the compilation of *Han-yü ta
tz'u-tien.*]

金文明：哪些方面有所出新？──『漢語大詞
典』編輯工作手記

4023   Lo, Chu-feng: *Han-yü ta tz'u-tien*
tsai shih-chien chung.—*TSYC* 1981:1,
4—12. [*Han-yü ta tz'u-tien* is now in
progress.]

羅竹風：『漢語大詞典』在實踐中

4024   Wang, T'ao: T'an shu cheng—*Han-yü
ta tz'u-tien* pu-fen ch'u kao pien-chi cha-
chi.—*TSYC* 1981:1, 33—42. [A discussion
on documented proofs—Notes on the
compilation of a partial preliminary draft
of *Han-yü ta tz'u-tien.*]

王濤：談書證──『漢語大詞典』部分初稿編
輯札記

6. MODERN STANDARD CHINESE AND ENGLISH DICTIONARIES (4025–4108)

6.1. Chinese-English Character Dictionaries (4025–4047)

6.1.1. Karlgren's Dictionaries (4025–4031)

4025 Karlgren, Bernhard: *An analytic dictionary of Chinese and Sino-Japanese.* —Paris: Geuthner, 1923, 436 p.; Taipei: Ch'eng-wen, 1970, repr.; New York: Dover, 1974, repr./ *BSOS* 3, 1923–1925, 362–365, Arthur Waley.

4026 Karlgren, Bernhard: *Grammata Serica —Script and phonetic in Chinese and Sino-Japanese* (1068).

4027 Karlgren, Bernhard: *Grammata Serica recensa* (1071).

4028 Karlgren, Bernhard. Transl. by Chang Shih-lu: Kao Pen-han *Chung-wen chieh-hsi tzu-tien* hsü.—*CYTK* 1, 1933, 62–67. [The preface of Bernhard Karlgren's *An analytic dictionary of Chinese and Sino-Japanese* (4025).]
高本漢著，張世祿譯：高本漢『中文解析字典』序

4029 Gil, Avishai: *Character index to Grammata Serica recensa.*—Cambridge: U. of Cambridge, 1974, [i], 92 p.

4030 Tanikawa, Hidenori: *Kao Pen-han chu Chung-Jih Han-tzu hsing-sheng lun tzu-huei yin-te.*—N.p.: Ditto, 1952, [ii], 162, 9 p. [An index to the characters in Karlgren's *Grammata Serica* (4026).]
谷川英則：高本漢著『中日漢字形聲論』字彙引得

4031 Wilkinson, Endymion: Bernhard Karlgren's *Grammata Serica recensa* (4027).— *The history of imperial China* (2901), 6.

6.1.2. Fenn's Dictionary (4032–4034)

4032 Fenn, Courtenay H. & Chin, Hsien-tseng: *The five thousand ·dictionary.*—

Shanghai: Mission Book Company, 1926, 578, 49 p.; Peiping: North China Union Language School, cooperating with California College in China, 1932, 2, 2, 578, 50, 7 [2] p.; Cambridge, Mass.: Harvard U. Press, 1942, rev. American ed., xxxviii, 694 p.; 1971, 11th print., xxxviii, 696 p.; Taipei: Chung-shan, 1969, repr./ Subtitle: *A Chinese-English pocket dictionary and index to the character cards of the College of Chinese Studies, California College in China.*
〔金憲增〕

4033 Dunn, Robert: Fenn's *The five thousand dictionary.—Chinese-English . . . in the Library of Congress* (2872), 79 (No. 408).

4034 Li, Chih-chung & Wang, Yin-lan: *The five thousand dictionary.—Chung-wen ts'an-k'ao . . . chih-nan* (2894), 190.
李志鍾、汪引蘭：[The five thousand dictionary.]

6.1.3. Chao's Dictionary (4035–4038)

4035 Chao, Yüen Ren & Yang, Lien-sheng: *Concise dictionary of spoken Chinese.* —Cambridge, Mass.: Harvard U. Press, 1947, xxxix, 291 p./ *Gwoyeu Romatzyh* (*romanization*); *HJAS* 10, 1947, 432–436, Lo Ch'ang-p'ei; *FEQ* 7, 1948, 447–448, John De Francis; *BSL* 45, 1949, 281–283, Paul-Demiéville; *JA* 237, 1949, 159–160, E. Gaspardone; *AM*, 1, 1949, 137, Walter Simon.
〔趙元任、楊聯陞：國語字典〕／羅常培評

4036 Ijichi, Yoshitsugu: *Concise dictionary of spoken Chinese* ni tsuite.—*Tōyō Bunka,* 3, 1954, 112–116. [On *Concise dictionary of spoken Chinese.*]
伊地智繼善：Concise dictionary of spoken Chinese について

4037 Lü, Hsiang: Chao Yüan-jen Yang Lien-sheng ho-pien (Han-Ying) *Kuo-yü tzu-tien* p'ing chieh.—*CWYH* 7, 1947, 251–258. [A critical introduction to Chao

Yüan-jen and Yang Lien-sheng's jointly published (Chinese-English) *Concise dictionary of spoken Chinese.*]
呂湘：趙元任楊聯陞合編（漢英）『國語字典』
評介

4038 Tōdō, Akiyasu: *Kokugo jiten.—Sekai meicho daijiten* (0041) 6, 452–453.
藤堂明保：『國語字典』（趙元任、楊聯陞）

6.1.4. Other Chinese-English Character Dictionaries (4039–4047)

4039 Goodrich, Chauncey S.: *A pocket dictionary, Chinese-English, and Pekingese syllabary. Sixth thousand.*—Shanghai: American Presbyterian Mission Press, 1907, vii, 237, 70 p.; Shanghai: Kwang Hsüeh Publ. House, 1933, repr.; New York: Columbia U. Press, 1944, repr.; Hong Kong: Hong Kong U. Press, 1965, xviii, 252, 70 p., with a supplement of new abbreviated characters in official use./ *BSOS* 11, 1943–1946, 898, Lionel Giles; *AM* 13, 1967, 240, Walter Simon; *AcOr* 31, 1968, 138–140, Kristina Lindell.

4040 Dunn, Robert: Goodrich, Chauncey. *A pocket dictionary, Chinese-English, and Pekingese syllabary.—Chinese-English . . . in the Library of Congress* (2872), 80 (No. 411).

4041 Herring, J.A.: *The foursquare dictionary.*—Taipei: Ditto, 1969, 12, 431, 135, 39 p./ Chinese-English.
〔漢英四角號碼字典〕

4042 Dunn, Robert: Herring, James A. *The foursquare dictionary in Chinese and English.—Chinese-English . . . in the Library of Congress* (2872), 80 (No. 412).

4043 Hsin-hua tz'u-shu-she. Transl. by C.K. Wu, et al.: *Chinese to English dictionary.*—Presidio: Chinese Language Research Association, 1976, viii, 357 p.
〔漢英字典〕/ English translation of (3829).

4044 Simon, Walter: *A beginners' Chinese-English dictionary of the National Language (Gwoyeu).*—London: Percy Lund, Humphries, & Co., 1964, cxlix, 880, 194 p./ lxxvii–xci: The Wang Yün-wu Four-corner system; *Gwoyeu Romatzyh* (romanization); *BSOS* 12, 1947–1948, 481–482, L. Giles; *HJAS* 11, 1948, 221–223, Fang-kuei Li.
〔初級中英國語字典〕

4045 Dunn, Robert: Simon, Walter. *A beginners' Chinese-English dictionary of the National Language (Gwoyeu).—Chinese-English . . . in the Library of Congress* (2872), 84 (No. 431).

4046 Soothill, William E.: *The student's four thousand* 字 *and general pocket dictionary.*—Shanghai: Presbyterian Mission Press, 1899, 3, xxvii, 358, lxxxv p.; 1903, 3rd ed., xxxv, 429 p.; London: Kegan Paul, Rench, Trubner, 1943; 1949, 9th ed., xxxv, 428 p.

4047 Dunn, Robert: Soothill, William E. *The student's four thousand [characters] and general dictionary.—Chinese-English . . . in the Library of Congress* (2872), 84 (No. 432).

6.2. Chinese-English Word and Phrase Dictionaries (4048–4096)
6.2.1. Giles' Dictionary (4048–4055)

4048 Giles, Herbert A.: *A Chinese-English dictionary.*—London: Quaritch, & Shanghai: Kelly & Walsh, 1892, 3 vols.; Shanghai & Hong Kong: Kelly & Walsh, 1919, 2nd rev. & enl. ed., 3 vols., xviii, 84, 1711 p.; Taipei: Ch'eng-wen, 1967, repr., 1 vol., xviii, 84, 1711 p./ Includes dialect pronunciations; see (3590).

4049 Dunn, Robert: Giles' *A Chinese-English dictionary.—Chinese-English . . . in the Library of Congress* (2872), 79–80 (No. 410).

4050 Moule, A.C.: Questions on some points in Giles' dictionary.—*NCR* 4, 1922, 128–133.

4051　Nash, Vernon: *Trindex: An index to three dictionaries* (3590)./ Giles' *Chinese-English dictionary* (4048), *K'ang-hsi tzu-tien* (3573), and *P'ei-wen yün-fu* (3709).
〔三字典引得〕

4052　Wilkinson, Endymion: H. A. Giles. *Chinese-English dictionary.—The history of imperial China* (2901), 6.

4053　Woitsch, L.: Beiträge zur lexikographie des Chinesischen.—*AcOr* 2, 1924 218–234./ Addenda to Giles' *Chinese-English dictionary* (4048).

4054　Woitsch, L.: Lexicographical contributions.—*AM* 4, 1927, 447–457./ Addenda to Giles' *Chinese-English dictionary* (4048).

4055　Woitsch, L.: Lexikographische Beiträge. —*AcOr* 6, 1928, 279–287; 8, 1930, 163–176, 280–287./ Addenda to Giles' *Chinese-English dictionary* (4048).

6.2.2. Matthews' Dictionary (4056–4063)

4056　Matthews, Robert H.: *Matthews' Chinese-English dictionary.*—Shanghai: China Mainland Mission & Presbyterian Mission Press, 1931; Cambridge, Mass.: Harvard U. Press, 1943, rev. American ed., xxiv, 1226 p.; 1975, 13th print./ Introduction by Chao Yuen Ren.

4057　Anderson, Olov Bertil: *A companion volume to R.H. Matthew's Chinese-English dictionary.*—Lund: Studentlitteratur, 1972, 210 p.; 1978, 335 p./ *AM* 18, 1973, 220, George Weys; *AO* 42, 1974, 176–177, Zdenka Heřmanová-Novotná.

4058　Astor, Wally G.: A content analysis of two Chinese-English dictionaries.— *JCLTA* 4:2, 1969, 55–60./ Analysis being of *Matthews' Chinese-English dictionary* and a *Chinese-English current political phrases and terms dictionary* (1620).

4059　Branch, Harry M.: *Matthews and Fenn re-indexed Five willows system.*—Amityville: Five Willows Press, 1973, 51 p./ Index to (4056) & (4032).

4060　Chow, Tse-tsung: *A new index to Matthews' Chinese-English dictionary.*— Madison: U. of Wisconsin, 1972, 26, 314 p./ Based on *Chung* character seven stroke character indexing system.
〔周策縱：麥氏漢英大字典新索引／"衷"字七筆檢字法〕

4061　Dunn, Robert: *Matthews' Chinese-English dictionary.—Chinese-English . . . in the Library of Congress* (2872), 82 (No. 422).

4062　Harvard-Yenching Institute: *Matthews' Chinese-English dictionary revised English index.*—Cambridge, Mass.: Harvard U. Press, 1963, 186 p., with Errata of Matthews.

4063　Wilkinson, Endymion: R.H. Matthews' *A Chinese-English dictionary.—The history of imperial China* (2901), 6.

6.2.3. Liang's Dictionary (4064–4067)

4064　Liang, Shih-ch'iu (ed. in chief): *Tsui-hsin shih-yung Han-Ying tz'u-tien.*—Taipei: Yüan-tung, 1971, [ii], xxxv, 1381, [2] p.; 1972, repr.; 1973, repr. [A new practical Chinese-English dictionary.]
梁實秋主編：最新實用漢英辭典

4065　Chien, Ch'ing-kuo: P'ing Liang Shih-ch'iu teng chu *Tsui-hsin shih-yung Han-Ying tz'u-tien.*—*SPSM* 82, 1980, 2–9. [A critique of Liang Shih-ch'iu et al.'s *Tsui-hsin shih-yung Han-Ying tz'u-tien.*]
簡清國：評梁實秋等著『最新實用漢英辭典』

4066　Huang, Hsüan-fan: T'an liang-pu Han-Ying tz'u-tien.—*Yü-yen-hsüeh yen-chiu lun-ts'ung* (0065), 129–142. [A (critical) discussion of two Chinese-English dictionaries.]/ Liang Shih-ch'iu's *A new practical Chinese-English dictionary* (4064) and Lin Yutang's *Chinese-English dictionary of modern usage* (4068).

黃宣範：談兩部漢英詞典

4067   Walton, Ronald A.: Two recent Chinese-English dictionaries.—*JCLTA* 11:3, 1976, 204—208./ A review of Liang Shih-ch'iu's *A new practical Chinese-English dictionary* (1972 ed.) and *Lin Yutang's Chinese-English dictionary of modern usage* (4068).

6.2.4. Lin's Dictionary (4068—4075)

4068   Lin Yutang: *Lin Yutang's Chinese-English dictionary of modern usage.*— The Chinese U. of Hong Kong, 1972, lxvi, 1720 p.; 1982, 3rd print.; *Supplementary index* to *Lin Yutang's Chinese-English dictionary of modern usage,* comp. by The Chinese U. Press, 1978, [iii], 105 p.; 1982, 3rd print./ Wade-Giles romanized index and radical index.

〔林語堂：當代漢英詞典〕

〔中文大學出版社：林語堂當代漢英詞典增編索引〕

4069   Chang, Chin-lang: Lin Yü-t'ang pien *Tang-tai Han-Ying tz'u-tien.*—*Chung-wen ts'an-k'ao . . . chih-yin* (2889), 240—241. [Lin Yutang's *Chinese-English dictionary of modern usage.*]

張錦郎：林語堂編『當代漢英辭典』

4070   Ching, Eugene: *Chinese-English dictionary of modern usage* (by Lin Yutang).—*JAS* 34:2, 1975, 521—524.

〔荊允敬〕

4071   Dunn, Robert: *Lin Yutang's Chinese-English dictionary of modern usage.*— *Chinese-English . . . in the Library of Congress* (2872), 81—82 (No. 419).

4072   Huang, Hsüan-fan: P'ing-hsin lun Lin Yü-t'ang *Tang-tai Han-Ying tz'u-tien.*—*Yü-yen-hsüeh yen-chiu lun-ts'ung* (0065), 143—160. [A fair discussion of Lin Yutang's *Chinese-English dictionary of modern usage.*]

黃宣範：平心論林語堂『當代漢英詞典』

4073   Liu, Ts'un-yan: Some thoughts on *Lin Yutang's Chinese-English dictionary of modern usage.*—*Chinese language in use* (0062), 103—122.

〔柳存仁〕

4074   Pollard, David E.: *Lin Yutang's Chinese-English dictionary of modern usage.*—*China Quarterly* 56, 1973, 786—788./ A review.

4075   Walton, Ronald A.: Two recent Chinese-English dictionaries (4067)./ A review of Liang Shih-ch'iu's *A new practical Chinese-English dictionary* (4064) and *Lin Yutang's Chinese-English dictionary of modern usage* (4068).

6.2.5. Pei-ching wai-yü hsüeh-yüan's Dictionary (4076—4081)

4076   Pei-ching wai-kuo-yü hsüeh-yüan Ying-yü-hsi *Han-Ying tz'u-tien* pien-hsieh-tsu: *Han-Ying tz'u-tien.*—Peking: Shang-wu, 1978; Hong Kong: Shang-wu, 1979, repr., 37, 976 p.; San Francisco: Pitman Advanced Publishing Program, 1979, repr. with changed title: *The Pinyin Chinese-English dictionary.* [The Chinese-English dictionary.]

北京外國語學院英語系『漢英詞典』編寫組：漢英詞典

4077   Ch'en, Chung-ch'eng: *Han-Ying tz'u-tien* yü *Han-O tz'u-tien* te i-hsieh pi-chiao. —*TSYC* 1981:2, 213—216. [A few comparisons of *Han-Ying tz'u-tien* (4076) and *Han-O tz'u-tien* (4134).]

陳忠誠：『漢英詞典』與『漢俄詞典』的一些比較

4078   Ch'en, Shih-min & T'ang, Jen-kuang: Shih p'ing *Han-Ying tz'u-tien* te ch'eng-yü shih-i.—*HMTH* 1979:3, 116—123. [A preliminary critique of the semantic explanations of set-phrases in *Han-Ying tz'u-tien.*]

陳世民、唐仁光：試評『漢英詞典』的成語釋義

4079   Ch'iu, K'o-an: Nei-jung ch'ung-shih te *Han-Ying tz'u-tien.*—*TS* 1979:2, 75–76. [*Han-Ying tz'u-tien* with substantial contents.]
裘克安：內容充實的『漢英詞典』

4080   Wu, Ching-jung: Pien-hsieh *Han-Ying tz'u-tien* te ching-yen yü chiao-hsün.—*TSYC* 1980:2, 32–41. [The experience and lesson learned from the compilation of *Han-Ying tz'u-tien.*]
吳景榮：編寫『漢英詞典』的經驗與教訓

4081   Wu, Ching-jung: Wo-men tsou-kuo te tao-lu—pien-hsieh *Han-Ying tz'u-tien* te hui-ku.—*WCYY* 1979:3, 1–13. [The road we have gone over—retrospection of the compilation of *Han-Ying tz'u-tien.*]
吳景榮：我們走過的道路——編寫『漢英詞典』的回顧

6.2.6. Liu's Dictionary (4082–4084)

4082   Liu, Ta-jen: *Liu-shih Han-Ying tz'u-tien.*—Taipei: Hua-ying, 1978, xxxi, 1554 p., illus. [Liu's Chinese-English dictionary.]/ Uses Liu's Rapid Radical indexing system.
劉達人：劉氏漢英辭典／採用劉氏快檢部首

4083   Liu, Ta-jen: *Liu-shih Han-Ying tz'u-tien* hsü.—*HHYK* 78, 1978, 22–25. [A preface to *Liu-shih Han-Ying tz'u-tien.*]
劉達人：『劉氏漢英辭典』序

4084   Chang, Chin-lang: Liu Ta-jen pien *Liu-shih Han-Ying tz'u-tien.*—*Chung-wen ts'an-k'ao . . . chih-yin* (2889), 242. [Liu Ta-jen's *Liu-shih Han-Ying tz'u-tien.*]
張錦郎：劉達人編『劉氏漢英辭典』

6.2.7. Other Chinese-English Word and Phrase Dictionaries (4085–4096)

4085   Chung-hua shu-chü: *T'ung-yung Han-Ying tz'u-tien.*—Hong Kong: Ditto, 1967,

2nd ed., [iv], 903, 22, 23 p.; Taipei: Chung-hua, 1968, repr., with changed title: *Chung-hua Han-Ying tz'u-tien.* [General Chinese-English dictionary. Chunghua Chinese-English dictionary.]/ A repr. of (4090).
中華書局：通用漢英辭典 （臺灣版：中華漢英辭典）

4086   Chung-mei ch'u-pan chung-hsin: *Chung-mei hsin Han-Ying tz'u-tien.*—Taipei: Ditto, 1979, 6, 605 p. [A Chung-mei new Chinese-English dictionary.]/ A repr. of (4088).
中美出版中心：中美新漢英詞典

4087   Cosmos Books: *A current Chinese-English dictionary.*—Hong Kong: (Ditto, 1978, 30, 750 p.
〔現代漢英詞典〕

4088   Hsiang-kang Ch'ing-nien ch'u-pan-she: *Hsin Han-Ying tz'u-tien.*—Hong Kong: Ditto, 1979, [ii], 6, 718 p. [A new Chinese-English dictionary.]/ See (4086).
香港青年出版社：新漢英詞典

4089   Lee, S. T. [Li, Shih-te] (ed. in chief): *A new complete Chinese-English dictionary.*—Kowloon: Chung-kuo t'u-shu ch'u-pan, 1956, repr., [iii], 1511, 63 p./ A repr. of (4093).
〔李仕德主編：最新漢英大辭典〕

4090   Lu, Fei-chih, et al.: *Chung-hua Han-Ying ta tz'u-tien.*—Shanghai: Chung-hua, 1931, 30, 25, 2, 758, 2, 18 p.; 1934, rev. ed., 758, 70 p.; Taipei: Chung-hua, 1967, rev. ed., 22, 903, 23 p. [The Chung Hwa Chinese-English dictionary.]/ See (4085).
陸費執等：中華漢英大辭典

4091   Luc, Kynh: *Chinese-English-French dictionary.* Featuring a modern practical Chinese script.—[Shanghai]: Ditto, 1945, xxii, 702 p./ Uses the 'Interdialectal Romanization system'.
〔盧謹〕

4092 Pai-ling ch'u-pan-she: *A new complete Chinese-English dictionary.*—Taipei: Ditto, 1970, [ii] , 6, 1938 p.

〔百齡出版社：漢英求解、名詞、辨義、成語四用辭典〕

4093 Tsang, O.Z. [Chang, P'eng-yün] : *A complete Chinese-English dictionary.*—Shanghai: Hsin Chung-kuo, 1920; 1923, 7th ed., 964, xxxvii, 30 p.; 1926, rev. ed., iv, 1511, (index:) 64 p.; Hong Kong: Kuo-chi shu-tien, 1956, repr., 964, xxxvii, 30 p.; Taipei: Wen-hua t'u-shu, 1969, repr., 946, 413 p., with changed title: *Tsung-ho Han-Ying tz'u-tien.*/ Wade-Giles romanization; see (4089).

〔張鵬雲：漢英大辭典〕（臺灣版：）〔綜合漢英大辭典〕

4094 Wang, Fred Fangyu: *Mandarin Chinese dictionary, Chinese-English.*—South Orange: Seton Hall U. Press, 1967, xix, 660 p.

〔王方宇〕

4095 Williams, Samuel Wells: *A syllabic dictionary of the Chinese language arranged according to the Wu-fang yüan yin, with the pronunciation of the characters as heard in Peking, Canton, Amoy, and Shanghai.*—Shanghai: American Presbyterian Mission Press, 1874; 1903, repr., lxxxiv, 1254 p.; Tungchow: North China Union College, 1909, rev. ed., lxxxiv, 1056 p.

〔衞三畏廉士：漢英韻府〕

4096 Yale U., Institute of Far Eastern Languages: *Dictionary of spoken Chinese.*—New Haven: Yale U. Press, 1966, xxxix, 1071 p.; Taipei: Mei Ya Publications, 1966, repr./ Yale romanization; *JCLTA* 2, 1967, 28−34, Tsu-lin Mei; *MIO* 13, 1967, 304−307, Gunnar Richter; *NAA* 1969:5, 198−200, S. Ch. Ioffe; *OLZ* 64, 1967, 394−396, Klaus Kaden; *AO* 38, 1970, 126−127, Dana Heroldová.

〔梅祖麟評〕

6.3.　English-Chinese Dictionaries (4097−4108)

4097 Chang, Ch'i-ch'un & Ts'ai, Wen-ying: *Chien-ming Ying-Han tz'u-tien.*—Peking: Shang-wu, 1963, 22, 1252 p.; 1972, 4th print., 18, 1211 p. [A concise English-Chinese dictionary.]

張其春、蔡文縈：簡明英漢詞典

4098 Chang, Meng-k'ai & Ou-yang, Ch'eng: *Tsung-ho Ying-Hua Hua-Ying ta tz'u-tien.*—Taipei: Chung-kuo t'u-shu, 1975, 14, 2137 p. [A new integrated comprehensive English-Chinese and Chinese-English dictionary.]/ A repr. of (4100).

張夢憩、歐陽承：綜合英華華英大辭典

4099 Chang, Shih-liu: *Ying-Han mo-fan tzu-tien.*—Hong Kong: Shang-wu, 1965, rev. ed., 1687, 67 p.; Taipei: Shang-wu, 1969, rev. ed., 1396, 150 p. [A model English-Chinese dictionary.]

張世鎏：英漢模範字典

4100 Cheng, I-li & Ts'ao, Ch'eng-hsiu: *Ying-Hua ta tz'u-tien. Fu Chung-wen so-yin.*—Peking: Sheng-huo, Tu-shu, Hsin chih-shih san-lien shu-tien, 1950; Peking: Shih-tai, 1957, 3, 15, 1542 p.; Hong Kong: Tsung-ho shu-tien, 1957, repr., 13, 2143 p.; Hong Kong: Kuang-t'ai shu-chü, 1965, repr./ See (4098). [A comprehensive English-Chinese dictionary. With A Chinese index.]

鄭易里、曹成修：英華大辭典　附中文索引

4101 Ch'i-ming shu-chü: *International dictionary, English-Chinese.*—Taipei: Ditto, 1961, [v], 2, 1852 p., illus./ Based on *Webster's International dictionary*, 2nd ed.

〔啓明書局：國際英漢雙解大辭典〕

4102 Hemeling, Karl E.G.: *English-Chinese dictionary of the standard Chinese spoken language* (官話) *and handbook for translators, including scientific, technical, modern and documentary terms.*—Shanghai: Statistical Department of the Inspectorate General of Customs, 1916, vi, 1726 p.; Freeport, N.Y.: Books for Libraries Press, 1973, repr., 3 vols./ Based on George Carter Stent's *A dictionary from English to colloquial Mandarin Chinese* (1905 ed.).

4103 *Hsin Ying-Han tz'u-tien* pien-hsieh-tsu: *Hsin Ying-Han tz'u-tien.*—Shanghai: Shang-hai jen-min, 1975; Hong Kong: San-lien, 1975, repr., [ii], 2, 12, [3], 1688 p., tab.; Shanghai: I-wen, 1978, rev. ed./ *TSYC* 1979:1, 134–138, 142, Wu Ying. [A new English-Chinese dictionary.]

『新英漢詞典』編寫組：新英漢詞典／吳瑩評

4104 Huang, Shih-fu & Chiang, T'ieh (eds. in chief): *Tsung-ho Ying-Han ta tz'u-tien.*—Shanghai: Shang-wu, 1928, 2 vols.; 1936, 1 vol.; 1948, rev. ed., xvi, 1502, 63, 172 p., illus; Taipei: Shang-wu, 1954; 1957; 1974, repr. [An integrated comprehensive English-Chinese dictionary.]

黃士復、江鐵主編：綜合英漢大辭典

4105 Liang, Shih-ch'iu: *Tsui-hsin shih-yung Ying-Han tz'u-tien.*—Taipei: Yüan-tung, 1960, 18, 1428, 12 p.; 1970, rev. &

enl. ed., 18, 2401, 11 p., with changed title: *Yüan-tung Ying-Han wu-yung tz'u-tien;* 1979, repr. [A new practical English-Chinese dictionary.], [A Far East five-usage English-Chinese dictionary.]

梁實秋：最新實用英漢辭典
遠東英漢五用辭典

4106 Shih-chieh shu-chü pien-chi-pu: *A daily use English-Chinese dictionary.*—Hong Kong: Shih-chieh, 1959, 17th ed., [iii], ii, [ii], 1950, 20, 4 p.; Taipei: Shih-chieh, 1964, repr., with Supplement, ii, 1950, 202 p.

〔世界書局編輯部：英漢求解作文文法辨義四用辭典　附補編〕

4107 Wang, Fred Fangyu: *Mandarin Chinese dictionary, English-Chinese.*—South Orange: Seton Hall U. Press, 1971, xxi, 779 p.; Taipei: Mei Ya Publications, 1971, repr. 〔王方宇〕

4108 Wu, Ping-chung, et al.: *Continental's concise English-Chinese dictionary.*—Taipei: Ta-lu shu-chü, 1973, xv, 1324 p. 〔吳炳鐘等：大陸簡明英漢辭典〕

7. MODERN STANDARD CHINESE AND OTHER FOREIGN LANGUAGE DICTIONARIES (4109–4165)

7.1. Chinese and Japanese Dictionaries (4109–4121)

7.1.1. Chinese-Japanese (4109–4117)

4109 Aichi Daigaku *Chū-Nichi daijiten* hensansho: *Chū-Nichi daijiten.*—Tokyo: Daian, 1968, 11, (index:) 88, 1947, 68, 19 p./ *OE* 17, 1970, 225–228, Wolfgang Lippert. [A Chinese-Japanese comprehensive dictionary.]
愛知大學『中日大辭典』編纂處：中日大辭典

4110 Inoue, Midori: *Inoue Shinago chūjiten.* —Tokyo: Bunkyūdō, 1941, 1388, 65 p./ *Chūgoku gogaku jiten* (0037), 424, Murao Tsutomu. [Inoue's medium-size Chinese-Japanese dictionary.]
井上翠：井上支那語中辭典／尾村力評

4111 Inoue, Midori: *Inoue Chūgokugo shinjiten.*—Tokyo: Kōnan shoin, 1954, 1111, 65 p./ *Chūgoku gogaku jiten* (0037), 421–422, Murao Tsutomu. [Inoue's new Chinese language dictionary.]
井上翠：井上中國語新辭典／尾村力評

4112 Ishiyama, Fukuji: *Saishin Shinago daijiten.*—Tokyo: Daiichi shobō, 1938, 2, 2, 4, 5, 51, 1746, 20, 26 p./ *Chūgoku gogaku jiten* (0037), 424, Murao Tsutomu. [A new comprehensive Chinese-Japanese dictionary.]
石田福治：最新支那語大辭典／村尾力評

4113 Kanegae, Nobumitsu: *Chūgokugo jiten.* —Tokyo: Daigaku shorin, 1960, viii, 1157 p./ *CGGG* 1960:6, 13–15, Sakamoto Ichirō; *Sekai meicho daijiten* (0041), 6, 464–465, Tōdō Akiyasu. [A Chinese language dictionary.]
鍾ヶ信光：中國語辭典／坂本一郎評，藤堂明保評

4114 Kōsaka, Jun'ichi & Ōta, Tatsuo: *Gendai Chū-Nichi jiten.*—Tokyo: Kōseikan, 1965, 12, 924, 54 p., illus. [A modern Chinese-Japanese dictionary.]
香坂順一、太田辰夫：現代中日辭典

4115 Kōsaka, Jun'ichi & Ōta, Tatsuo: *Kijun Chū-Nichi jiten.*—Tokyo: Kōseikan, 1966, 4, 6, 344, 42 p. [A standard Chinese-Japanese dictionary.]
香坂順一、太田辰夫：基準中日辭典

4116 Kuraishi, Takeshirō: *Iwanami Chūgokugo jiten.*—Tokyo: Iwanami shoten, 1963, 25, 926 p.; 1975, 11th repr./ *AO* 32, 1964, 495–496, Z. Novotná; *KBKS* 67, 1964, 31–33, Togawa Yoshio; *OE* 12:2, 1965, 255–256, W. Franke. [Iwanami's Chinese language dictionary.]
倉石武四郎：岩波中國語辭典／戶川芳郎評

4117 Ōbunsha: *Ka-Nichi daijiten.*—Tokyo: Ditto, 1950, 1412, 47 p.; Taipei: Wen-ching t'u-shu, 1971; 1973, repr./ *Chūgoku gogaku jiten* (0037), 425, Murao Tsutomu. [A comprehensive Chinese-Japanese dictionary.]
旺文社：華日大辭典／村尾力評

7.1.2. Japanese-Chinese (4118–4121)

4118 Ch'en, T'ao (ed. in chief): *Jih-Han tz'u-tien.*—Peking: Shang-wu, 1959; 1962, 3rd print., 2 vols., 8, 2587 p.; Tokyo: Daian, 1964, abridged ed., 5, 2213, [6] p./ *CGGG* 1959:8, 1–9, 18, Arita Tadahiro; *Sekai meicho daijiten* (0041), 6, 469., Tōdō Akiyasu. [A Japanese-Chinese dictionary.]
陳濤主編：日漢辭典／有田忠弘評，藤堂明保評

4119 Hiraoka, Ryūjō, et al.: *Nichi-Ka daijiten.*—Tokyo: Tōyō Bunka Mikan Tosho Kankōkai, 1936, 3 vols., [iii], 2537 p., illus.; Taipei: Kuang-hung-wen, 1965, repr./ *Chūgoku gogaku jiten* (0037), 426, Murao, Tsutomu. [A Japanese-Chinese comprehensive dictionary.]
平岡龍城等：日華大辭典／村尾力評

4120 Kuraishi, Takeshirō & Orishikise, Akira: *Iwanami Nichi-Chū jiten.* —Tokyo: Iwanami shoten, 1983, vi, 1250 p. [Iwanami's Japanese-Chinese dictionary.]
倉石武四郎、折敷瀬興：岩波日中辭典

4121 Ta-lien wai-kuo-yü hsüeh-yüan *Hsin Jih-Han tz'u-tien* pien-chi-tsu: *Hsin Jih-Han tz'u-tien.* —Talien: Liao-ning jen-min, 1979; Hong Kong: San-lien, 1980, repr., vii, 2690 p. [A new Japanese-Chinese dictionary.]
大連外國語學院『新日漢辭典』編輯組：新日漢辭典

7.2. Chinese and German Dictionaries (4122–4130)
7.2.1. Chinese-German (4122–4123)

4122 Pei-ching wai-kuo-yü hsüeh-yüan Te-yü-hsi: *Han-Te tz'u-tien.* —Peking: Shang-wu, 1959; 1964, repr., [iv], 789, 14, (index:) 27 p. [Chinesisch-deutsch Wörterbuch.] / See an English conversion (1632).
北京外國語學院德語系：漢德詞典

4123 Rüdenberg, Werner: *Chinesische-deutsches Wörterbuch.* —Hamburg: Friederichsen, De Gruyter & Co., 1924, ix, 686 p.; Hamburg: Cram, De Gruyter, 1958–1963, rev. by Hans Otto Heinrich Stange, xx, 821 p., with *Deutscher Index zu Rüdenberg-Stange Chinesische-deutsches Wörterbuch.* —Berlin: Walter de Gruyter, 1971, [ii], 742 p.; Taipei: Chin-shan t'u-shu, n.d., repr. / *MSOS* 29, 1926, 233–237, F. Lessing; *TP* 25, 1928, 364–365, E. von Zach; *TP* 47, 1959, 107–128, D.R. Jonker; *OLZ* 56, 1961, 303–304, Paul Kratochvíl; *Sinologica* 8, 1965, 175–176, H. Köster; *OE* 13, 1966, 243–256, Wolfgang Franke; *HJAS* 27, 1967, 324–326, Wolfgang Franke; *AM* 18, 1973, 242–244, George Weys.
〔華德辭典〕

7.2.2. German-Chinese (4124–4130)

4124 Chung-shan ta-hsüeh wai-yü-hsi Te-yü chuan-yeh: *Chien-ming Te-Han tz'u-tien.* —Peking: Shang-wu, 1964, 629 p. [Deutsch-chinesisches Handwörterbuch.]
中山大學外語系德語專業：簡明德漢詞典

4125 Huang, Po-ch'iao (ed. in chief): *Te-Hua piao-chun ta tzu-tien.* —Shanghai: Chung-kuo k'o-hsüeh t'u-shu i-ch'i, 1950; 1953, 3rd ed., ix, 1364 p.; Taipei: Tung-ya shu-she, 1958, repr., without author's name; Hong Kong: San-lien, 1979, repr. [Deutsch-chinesisches Standard-Handwörterbuch.] / See (4129).
黃伯樵主編：德華標準大字典

4126 Kuang-chou wai-yü hsüeh-yüan: *Chien-ming Te-Han tz'u-tien.* —Peking: Shang-wu, Canton: Kuang-tung jen-min, 1979, v, 1197 p. [Deutsch-chinesisches Handwörterbuch.]
廣州外語學院：簡明德漢詞典

4127 Kuang-chou wai-kuo-yü hsüeh-yüan *Te-Han tz'u-tien* tsu: *Te-Han tz'u-tien.* —Peking: Shang-wu, 1979; Hong Kong: Shang-wu, 1980, v, 1197 p. [Deutsch-chinesisches Handwörterbuch.] / See (3151).
廣州外國語學院『德漢詞典』組：德漢詞典

4128 Stenz, George M., S.V.D.: *Deutsch-chinesisches Wörterbuch.* —Yenchowfu: Verlag der Katholischen Mission, 1929, 2nd ed., vi, 773 p.; Shanghai: (Sole agent) Van Chong Book. Co., 1947, repr.
〔德華字典〕

4129 Tung-ya shu-she: *Te-Hua piao-chun ta tzu-tien.* —Taipei: Ditto, 1965, ix, 1364 p. [Deutsch-chinesisches Standard-Handwörterbuch.] / A repr. of (4125).
東亞書社：德華標準大字典

4130 Wilhelm, Hellmut: *Deutsch-chinesisches Wörterbuch.* —Shanghai: Max Nössler & Co., 1945, x, 1256 p.; Hidlesheim & New York: G. Olms, 1970, repr.; 1973, repr.
〔衛德明：德華大辭典〕

7.3. Chinese and Russian Dictionaries (4131–4142)

7.3.1. Chinese-Russian (4131–4134)

4131 Kotov, A.V.: *Kitaisko-Russkii slovar'-minimum.*—Moscow: Izdatel'stvo "Russki Yazik", 1974, 429, [2] p./ *JazA* 12, 1975, 185–186, Sáva Heřman./ A Chinese-Russian minimum dictionary.
〔科托夫：漢俄常用字滙〕

4132 O-yü wen-chai-she: *Hua-O ta tz'u-tien.*—Taipei: Ditto, 1973, 2nd ed., 898, 206 p. [Kitaisko-Russkii slovar'.]/ A comprehensive Chinese-Russian dictionary.
俄語文摘社：華俄大辭典

4133 Oshanin, I.M. (ed. in chief): *Kitaisko-Russkii slovar'.*—Moscow: Gosudarstvennoe Izdatel'stvo Inostrannykh i Natsional'nykh Slovarei, 1959, 3rd ed., 1100 p./ *Chūgoku gogaku jiten* (0037), 437–445, Hashimoto Mantarō./ A Chinese-Russian dictionary.
〔鄂山蔭主編：華俄辭典〕／橋本萬太郎評

4134 Shang-hai wai-kuo-yü hsüeh-yüan *Han-O tz'u-tien* pien-hsieh-tsu: *Han-O tz'u-tien.*—Peking: Shang-wu, 1977, 29, 1235 p. [Kitaisko-Russkii slovar'.]/ A Chinese-Russian dictionary.
上海外國語學院『漢俄詞典』編寫組：漢俄詞典

7.3.2. Russian-Chinese (4135–4142)

4135 Ch'en, Ch'ang-hao; Dubrovskii, A.G. & Kotov, A.V.: *Russko-Kitaiskii slovar'.*—Moscow: Gosudarstvennoe Izdatel'stvo Inostrannykh i Natsional'nykh Slovarei, 1953, xvi, 975 p.; Peking: Shih-tai, 1953, 736 p./ *Chūgoku gogaku jiten* (0037), 446–447, Hashimoto Mantarō./ A Russian-Chinese dictionary.
〔陳昌浩、杜布洛夫斯基、科托夫：俄華辭典〕／橋本萬太郎評

4136 Liu, Tse-jung (ed. in chief): *O-Han hsin tz'u-tien.*—Peking: Shih-tai, 1956–

1958, 2 vols., 1059, 1411 p./ *Chūgoku gogaku jiten* (0037), 447–449, Hashimoto Mantarō. [Novyi Russko-Kitaiskii slovar'.]/ A new Russian-Chinese dictionary.
劉澤榮主編：俄漢新詞典／橋本萬太郎評

4137 Liu, Tse-jung (ed. in chief): *O-Han ta tz'u-tien.*—Peking: Shang-wu, 1961, viii, 1384 p. [Bol'shoi Russko-Kitaiskii slovar'.]/ A comprehensive Russian-Chinese dictionary.]
劉澤榮主編：俄漢大辭典

4138 Liu, Tsung-i (rev.): *O-Han ta tz'u-tien.*—Taipei: Shuang-yeh shu-lang, 1968, repr., x, 2229 p. [Russko-Kitaiskii slovar'.]/ A Russian-Chinese dictionary.
劉宗怡校訂：俄漢大辭典

4139 Palei, Ia. B. & Iustov, V.K.: *Kratkii Russko-Kitaiskii slovar'.*—Moscow: Gosudarstvennoe Izdatel'stvo Inostrannykh i Natsional'nykh Slovarei, 1960, 3rd ed., 516 p.; 1963, rev. ed., 590 p./ A concise Russian-Chinese dictionary.
〔俄華簡明辭典〕

4140 Shen, Feng-wei, et al.: *Chien-ming O-Han tz'u-tien.*—Peking: Shang-wu, 1965, x, 1156 p. [Kratkii Russko-Kitaiskii slovar'.]/ A concise Russian-Chinese dictionary.
沈鳳威等：簡明俄漢詞典

4141 Shih-tai ch'u-pan-she: *O-Hua ta tz'u-tien.*—Peking: Ditto, 1956, xiii, 1220 p. [Russko-Kitaiskii slovar'.]/ A Russian-Chinese dictionary.
時代出版社：俄華大辭典

4142 Wen, Shu-te: *O-Chung tzu-tien.*—Taipei: Ta Chung-kuo t'u-shu, 1971, xi, 443 p. [Russko-Kitaiskii slovar'.]/ A Russian-Chinese dictionary.
溫樹德：俄中字典

7.4. Chinese and French Dictionaries (4143—4150)

7.4.1. Chinese-French (4143—4146)

4143   Couvreur, F. Séraphin, S.J.: *Petit dictionnaire chinois-français.*—Ho Kien Fou: Imprimerie de la Mission Catholique, 1903, xiv, 736 p., illus./ *TP* 4:5, 1903, 418, Henri Cordier.

4144   Couvreur, F. Séraphin, S.J.: *Dictionnaire classique de la langue chinoise.*—Ho Kien Fou: Imprimerie de la Mission Catholique, 1904; 1911, 2nd print., xii, 1144 p.; 1931, 2nd ed., xii, 1080 p.; Taichung: Kuang-ch'i, 1966, repr.; Taipei: Wen-hsing, 1966, repr., vi, 1080 p./ *TP* 6, 1905, 242—249, Ed. Chavannes; *BEFEO* 4, 1904, 761—762, Paul Pelliot; *Revue Critique* 5, 1905, Henri Cordier; *CCS* 5, 1932, 646, Anonymous.
〔法文註釋中國古文大辭典〕

4145   Institut Ricci: *Dictionnaire de la langue chinoise.*—Taipei: Ditto; Taichung: Kuang-ch'i, 1976, xii, 1135, 186 p.
〔利氏學社：漢法綜合辭典〕

4146   Pei-ching ta-hsüeh Hsi-yü-hsi Fa-yü chuan-yeh: *Han-Fa tz'u-tien.*—Peking: Shang-wu, 1964, [iii], 646, 27 p. [Dictionnaire chinois-français.]
北京大學西語系法語專業：漢法詞典

7.4.2. French-Chinese (4147—4150)

4147   *Fa-Han tz'u-tien* pien-hsieh-tsu: *Fa-Han tz'u-tien.*—Shanghai: I-wen, 1979, xi, 1493 p.; Hong Kong: San-lien, 1981, repr. with a new title: *Hsin Fa-Han tz'u-tien,* xi, 1499 p. [(Nouveau) dictionnaire français-chinois.]
『法漢詞典』編寫組：法漢詞典　（香港版：新法漢詞典）

4148   Hsiao, Tzu-ch'in, et al.: *Mo-fan Fa-Hua tzu-tien.*—Shanghai: Shang-wu, 1923; 1933, reduced ed.; 1937, 4th ed., 2, 846 p.; Taipei: Shang-wu, 1958, repr.

[Nouveau dictionnaire français-chinois.]
蕭子琴等：模範法華字典

4149   Hsin-lu shu-chü pien-chi-pu: *Piao-chun Fa-Hua ta tzu-tien.*—Taipei: Ditto, 1966, ix, 956 p. [A new standard French-Chinese dictionary.]/ A repr. of (4150).
新陸書局編輯部：標準法華大字典

4150   Kao, Ta-kuan & Hsü, Chung-nien: *Chien-ming Fa-Han tz'u-tien.*—Peking: Shang-wu, 1963, x, 956 p. [Petit dictionnaire français-chinois.]
高達觀、徐仲年：簡明法漢詞典

7.5. Chinese and Spanish Dictionaries (4151—4154)

7.5.1. Chinese-Spanish (4151—4152)

4151   Mateos, Fernando, S.J.; Otegui, Miguel, S.J. & Arrizabalaga, Ignacio, S.J.: *Diccionario español de la lengua china.*—Madrid: Espasa-Calpe, 1977, [iii], xxxviii, 1140, 179 p.; Taipei: Li-te, 1981, repr./ A Chinese-Spanish dictionary.
〔沈起元、梅格、李清鍾：漢西綜合辭典〕

4152   Nieto, Luis Maria, S.J.: *Diccionario manual chino-castellano.*—Shanghai: Zika-wei, 1929, x, 941 p.; 1933, 2nd. ed., xiv, 852, 47 p./ *BAEO* 13, 1977, 86, Fernando Mateos, S.J./ A Chinese-Castilan (Spanish) dictionary.
〔嚴毅：華班字典〕

7.5.2. Spanish-Chinese (4153—4154)

4153   Nieto, Luis Maria, S.J.: *Diccionario manual castellano-chino.*—Shanghai: Zika-wei, 1931, xvii, 802, 39 p./ *BAEO* 13, 1977, 86, Fernando Mateos, S.J./ A Castilan (Spanish)-Chinese dictionary.
〔嚴毅：班華字典〕

4154   Pei-ching wai-kuo-yü hsüeh-yüan Hsi-pan-ya-yü-hsi: *Hsi-Han tz'u-tien.*—Peking: Shang-wu, 1959, 8, 888 p.; 1961, 2nd print. [Diccionario español-chino.]
北京外國語學院西班牙語系：西漢辭典

7.6. Chinese and Italian Dictionaries (4155—4159)

7.6.1. Chinese-Italian (4155—4157)

4155   De Nino, Generoso: *Piccolo vocabolario cinese-italiano.*—Peking: Typografia dei Lazaristi, 1925, viii, 325 p.

4156   Valle, Benedetto: *Dizionario cinese-italiano.*—Hong Kong: Nazareth Press, 1948, xii, 1139 p./ *Anthropos* 1951, 1031—1032, L. Vannicelli; *RSO* 26, 1951, 187—195, P. D'Elia.
〔華義辭典〕

4157   Valle, Benedetto: *Piccolo vocabolario cinese-italiano.*—Hong Kong: Catholic Truth Society, 1949, [ii], 317, [2] p.
〔華義袖珍字典〕

7.6.2. Italian-Chinese (4158—4159)

4158   Landi, F.: *Piccolo dizionario italiano-cinese.*—Shanghai: T'ou-sè-wè, 1939, x, 655 p.
〔義華字典〕

4159   Valle, Benedetto: *Dizionario italiano-cinese.*—Hong Kong: Catholic Truth Society, 1967, xiv, 809, [2] p.
〔義華辭典〕

7.7. Chinese and Latin Dictionaries (4160—4165)

7.7.1. Chinese-Latin (4160—4161)

4160   Couvreur, F. Séraphin, S.J.: *Dictionarium Sinicum et Latinum, ex radicum ordine dispositum, selectis variorum scriptorum sententiis firmatum ac illustratum.*—Ho Kien Fou: Ex Missione Catholica S.J., 1892, xiv, 1200 p.; 1932, 3rd ed., xviii, 1200 p./ A Chinese-Latin dictionary in the order of radicals.

4161   Mittler, Theodor, S.V.D.; Böhm, Ernest, S.V.D.; Chang, Vitus, S.V.D. & Kan, Joseph: *Magnum lexicon Sinico-Latinum.*—Hong Kong: Catholic Mission, St. Paul's Press, 1957; 1983, 2nd ed., xxiii, 1981 p./ *MS* 16, 1957, 497—499, H. Busch, S.V.D.; *AAHG* 11, 1958, 233—238, A. Pluta./ A great Chinese-Latin lexicon.
〔苗德秀、彭加德編，張維篤、甘增佑校：中華拉丁大辭典〕

7.7.2. Latin-Chinese (4162—4165)

4162   Gonçalves, Joaquim Alfonso, C.M.: *Lexicon manuale Latino-Sinicum continens omnia vocabula utilia, et primitiva, etiam scripturae sacrae.*—Macao: In Collegio S. Joseph, ab Emmanuele Rosa typis mandatum, 1839, vii, 498 p.; Hokien, 1863, repr. with two appendices, 498, 47 p.; Peking: Pé-t'ang, 1892, 3rd ed., viii, 571 p./ A Latin-Chinese hand-lexicon containing all the useful and primitive vocabulary, also (vocabulary of) the Holy Scripture.
〔辣丁中華合璧字典〕

4163   Gonçalves, Joaquim Alfonso, C.M.: *Lexicon magnum Latino-Sinicum ostendens etymologiam, prosodiam, et constructionem vocabulorum.*—Macao: In Collegio S. Joseph, ab Emmanuele Rosa typis mandatum, 1841, iv, 779 p.; Peking: Typis Congregationis Missionis, 1892, 2nd ed., [iii], 779 p.; Taipei: Ts'ai Wen-hsing, 1970, repr./ A great Latin-Chinese dictionary, showing etymology, prosody, and construction of vocabulary.
〔辣丁中華合璧字典〕

4164   Pétillon, Corentin, S.J.: *Dictionarium Latino-Sinicum.*—Shanghai: T'ou-sè-wè, 1907; 1951, 2nd ed., [iii], 569 p./ A Latin-Chinese dictionary.
〔貝迪榮：辣丁中華字典〕

4165   Wu, Peter Chin-jui, S.J.: *Dictionarium Latino-Sinicum.*—Taichung: Kuang-ch'i, 1965, [vii], 1497, [22] p., illus.; 1980, 3rd print./ A Latin-Chinese dictionary.
〔吳金瑞：拉丁漢文詞典〕

List of Chinese and Japanese Publishers

Ajia-Afurika gengo bunka kenkyūjo.　Tokyo.
アジア・アフリカ言語文化研究所　東京

Ajia Kenkyūjo.　Tokyo.
アジア研究所

An-hui jen-min—ch'u-pan-she.　Hofei.
安徽人民出版社　合肥

Bunkyō shoin.　Tokyo.
文京書院　東京

Bunkyūdō.　Tokyo.
文求堂　東京

Bunshōkaku.　Tokyo.
文章閣　東京

Chang Meng-sheng.　Taipei.
張孟生　臺北

Ch'ang-ch'ing—ch'u-pan-she.　Taipei.
長青出版社　臺北

Ch'ang-ch'un shu shu-fang.　Taipei.
常春樹書坊　臺北

Ch'ao-feng—ch'u-pan-she.　Shanghai.
潮峯出版社　上海

Che-chiang jen-min—ch'u-pan-she.　Hangchow.
浙江人民出版社　杭州

Che-chiang-sheng min-chung chiao-yü shih-yen hsüeh-hsiao.　Hangchow.
浙江省民衆教育實驗學校　杭州

Che-chiang t'u-shu-kuan.　Hangchow.
浙江圖書館　杭州

Cheng-chung—shu-chü.　Shanghai,　Chungking, Taipei.

正中書局　上海、重慶、臺北

Cheng-yen—ch'u-pan-she.　Tainan.
正言出版社　臺南

Ch'eng-wen—ch'u-pan yu-hsien kung-szu.　Taipei.
成文出版有限公司　臺北

Chi-lin jen-min—ch'u-pan-she.　Changchun.
吉林人民出版社　長春

Ch'i-lu shu-she.　Chinan.
齊魯書社　濟南

Ch'i-ming hsüeh-she.　Shanghai.
啓明學社　上海

Ch'i-ming shu-chü.　Taipei.
啓明書局　臺北

Ch'i-yeh shu-chü.　Taipei.
啓業書局　臺北

Chia-hsin shui-ni kung-szu wen-hua chi-chin hui.　Taipei.
嘉新水泥公司文化基金會　臺北

Chia-shu shan-fang.
嘉樹山房

Chiang Feng-tsao hsin-chü-chai.　Changchow.
蔣風藻心矩齋　長州

Chiang-hsi jen-min—ch'ü-pan-she.　Nanchang.
江西人民出版社　南昌

Chiang-men—ch'u-pan-she.　Tainan.
將門出版社　臺南

Chiang-su jen-min—ch'u-pan-she.　Nanking.
江蘇人民出版社　南京

Chiao-yü—ch'u-pan-she.　Hong Kong.

教育出版社　香港

Chiao-yü-pu min-chung tu-wu pien-she wei-yüan-hui.　Chungking (?).
教育部民衆讀物編審委員會　重慶（？）

Chiao-yü-pu she-hui chiao-yü-szu.　Taipei.
教育部社會教育司　臺北

Chiao-yü shu-tien.　Hong Kong.
教育書店　香港

Ch'iao-kuang shu-tien.　Hong Kong.
僑光書店　香港

Ch'iao-liang—ch'u-pan-she.　Taipei.
橋梁出版社　臺北

Ch'iao-wu wei-yüan-hui Chung-hua han-shou hsüeh-hsiao.　Taipei.
僑務委員會中華函授學校　臺北

Chih-ta t'u-shu—wen-chü chiao-yü p'in ku-fen yu-hsien kung-szu.　Taipei.
至大圖書文具教育品股份有限公司　臺北

Chin-ch'uan—ch'u-pan-she.　Tainan.
金川出版社　臺南

Chin-hsiu—ch'u-pan-she.　Hong Kong.
進修出版社　香港

Chin-ling ta-hsüeh nung-lin hsin-pao-she.　Nanking.
金陵大學農林新報社　南京

Chin-wen—t'u-shu kung-szu.　Taipei.
金文圖書公司　臺北

Ching-shan shu-she.　Peking.
景山書社　北京

Ching-sheng wen-wu kung-ying kung-szu.　Taipei.
驚聲文物供應公司　臺北

Ching-wei shu-chü.　Shanghai.
經緯書局　上海

Ch'ing-hai jen-min—ch'u-pan-she.　Hsining.
青海人民出版社　西寧

Ch'ing-liu—ch'u-pan-she.　Taipei.
清流出版社　臺北

Chiu-chiu ch'u-pan-she.　Taipei.
久久出版社　臺北

Cho Shao-lan.　Taipei.
卓少蘭　臺北

Chu-che shu-tien.　Peiping.
著者書店　北平

Chu-i-t'ang shu-fang.　Shanghai.
著易堂書房　上海

Chuang-chia—ch'u-pan-she.　Tainan.
莊稼出版社　臺南

Chūgoku Chūse Bungaku Kenkyūkai.　Hiroshima.
中國中世文學研究會　廣島

Ch'un-ming shu-tien.　Shanghai.
春明書店　上海

Ch'ün-chung t'u-shu—kung-szu.　Shanghai.
羣衆圖書公司　上海

Ch'ün-feng—ch'u-pan-she.　Taipei.
羣豐出版社　臺北

Chung-chou shu-hua-she.　Chengchow.
中州書畫社　鄭州

Chung-hsi wen-hua—ch'u-pan-she.　Hong Kong.
中西文化出版社　香港

Chung-hua—shu-chü.　Shanghai, Peking, Hong Kong, Taipei.
中華書局　上海、北京、香港、臺北

Chung-hua ts'ung-shu—pien-shen wei-yüan-hui.　Taipei.
中華叢書編審委員會　臺北

Chung-hua wen-hua ch'u-pan shih-yeh wei-yüan-hui.　Shanghai, Taipei.
中華文化出版事業委員會　上海、臺北

Chung-hua wen-k'u. Hong Kong.
中華文庫　香港

Chun-hua yin-shu-chü. Peiping.
中華印書局　北平

Chung-kuo ch'ing-nien—ch'u-pan-she. Peking.
中國青年出版社　北京

Chung-kuo—ch'u-pan kung-szu. Hong Kong, Taipei.
中國出版公司　香港、臺北

Chung-kuo jen-min ta-hsüeh—ch'u-pan-she. Peking.
中國人民大學出版社　北京

Chung-kuo k'o-hsüeh t'u-shu i-ch'i kung-szu. Taipei.
中國科學圖書儀器公司　臺北

Chung-kuo k'o-hsüeh-yüan. Peking.
中國科學院　北京

Chung-kuo shao-nien erh-t'ung—ch'u-pan-she. Peking.
中國少年兒童出版社　北京

Chung-kuo she-hui k'o-hsüeh—ch'u-pan-she. Peking.
中國社會科學出版社　北京

Chung-kuo she-hui k'o-hsüeh-yüan Min-tsu yen-chiu-so yü-yen yen-chiu-shih. Peking.
中國社會科學院民族研究所語言研究室　北京

Chung-kuo ta tz'u-tien pien-tsuan-ch'u. Peking.
中國大辭典編纂處　北京

Chung-kuo t'u-shu ch'u-pan—kung-szu. Kowloon.
中國圖書出版公司　九龍

Chung-kuo t'u-shu k'an-ch'uan hui.
中國圖書刊傳會

Chung-kuo t'u-shu—kung-szu. Kowloon, Taipei.
中國圖書公司　九龍、臺北

Chung-kuo wen-hua hsüeh-yüan. Yangmingshan.
中國文化學院　陽明山

Chung-kuo wen-hua yen-chiu-so. Taipei.
中國文化研究所　臺北

Chung-kuo yü-wen hsüeh-she. Hong Kong.
中國語文學社　香港

Chung-kuo yü-wen yen-chiu chung-hsin. Taipei.
中國語文研究中心　臺北

Chung-kuo yü-wen yen-chiu-hui. Hong Kong.
中國語文研究會　香港

Chung-kuo yü-wen yen-chiu-she. Taipei.
中國語文研究社　臺北

Chung-liu—ch'u-pan-she. Hong Kong.
中流出版社　香港

Chung-mei ch'u-pan chung-hsin. Taipei.
中美出版中心　臺北

Chung-shan ta-hsüeh. Canton.
中山大學　廣州

Chung-yang wen-wu kung-ying-she. Taipei.
中央文物供應社　臺北

Chung-yang yen-chiu-yüan. Taipei.
中央研究院　臺北

Chung-yu wen-hua shih-yeh—ku-fen yu-hsien kung-szu. Taipei.
中友文化事業股份有限公司　臺北

Ch'ung-chi shu-tien. Hong Kong.
崇基書店　香港

Ch'ung-ch'ing jen-min—ch'u-pan-she. Chung-king.
重慶人民出版社　重慶

Ch'ung-ming—ch'u-pan-she. Hong Kong.
崇明出版社　香港

Ch'ung-wen shu-chü. Hupei.
崇文書局　湖北

Ch'ung-wen shu-tien. Hong Kong.
崇文書店　香港

Daian. Tokyo.
大安　東京

Daigaku shorin. Tokyo.
大學書林　東京

Daiichi gakushūsha. Hiroshima.
第一學修社　廣島

Daiichi shobō. Tokyo.
第一書房　東京

Dōhōsha. Kyoto.
同朋社　京都

Eiwa gogaku shuppan. Tokyo.
永和語學出版　東京

Erh-ya—ch'u-pan-she. Hong Kong.
爾雅出版社　香港

Fan T'ai-p'ing-yang shu-yeh—szu-jen yu-hsien kung-szu. Singapore.
汎太平洋書業私人有限公司　新嘉坡

Feng-hsing—ch'u-pan-she. Hong Kong.
風行出版社　香港

Fu-chien chiao-yü—ch'u-pan-she. Foochow.
福建教育出版社　福州

Fu-chien jen-min—ch'u-pan-she. Foochow.
福建人民出版社　福州

Fu-chien jen-min chiao-yü—ch'u-pan-she. Foochow.
福建人民教育出版社　福州

Fu-chien k'o-hsüeh chi-shu—ch'u-pan-she. Foochow.
福建科學技術出版社　福州

Fu-han—ch'u-pan-she. Tainan.
復漢出版社　臺南

Fu-hsing shu-chü. Taipei.
復興書局　臺北

Fu-jen ta-hsüeh. Peking, Taipei.
輔仁大學　北京、臺北

Fu-ming ch'an-yeh ti-li yen-chiu-so. Taipei.
敷明產業地理研究所　臺北

Fu-tan—ch'u-pan kung-szu. Shanghai.
復旦出版公司　上海

Fu-wen—shu-chü. Tainan.
復文書局　臺南

Fuji shuppansha. Tokyo.
不二出版社　東京

Fukuinkan. Tokyo.
福音館　東京

Fuzanbō. Tokyo.
富山房　東京

Gaigokugo Gakuin shuppansha. Tokyo.
外國語學院出版社　東京

Gakushūsha. Tokyo.
學習社　東京

Gakutōsha. Tokyo.
學燈社　東京

Gannandō—shoten. Tokyo.
嚴南堂書店　東京

Gengensha. Tokyo.
元元社　東京

Goten shoin. Kyoto.
五典書院，京都

Guoji shudian.   Peking.
國際書店   北京

Gyōsei.   Tokyo.
ぎょうせい   東京

Hakushuisha.   Tokyo.
白水社   東京

Han-ching wen-hua—shih-yeh yu-hsien kung-szu.
Shulinchen (Taipei).
漢京文化事業有限公司   樹林鎮（臺北）

Han-lin—ch'u-pan-she.   Tainan.
翰林出版社   臺南

Han mo-lin,   Nantung.
翰墨林   南通

Han-ying shu-chü.   Hong Kong.
漢英書局   香港

Hao-wang—shu-tien.   Peking.
好望書店   北京

Hei-lung-chiang jen-min—ch'u-pan-she.   Harbin.
黑龍江人民出版社   哈爾濱

Heibonsha.   Tokyo.
平凡社   東京

Heigo shuppansha.   Tokyo.
丙午出版社   東京

Hiroshima Daigaku Bungakubu.   Hiroshima.
廣島大學文學部   廣島

Ho-nan jem-nin—ch'u-pan-she.   Kaifeng.
河南人民出版社   開封

Ho-pei jen-min—ch'u-pan-she.   Paoting, Tientsin,
Shihchiachuang.
河北人民出版社   保定、天津、石家莊

Hōbunkan.   Tokyo.
寶文館   東京

Hōyū shoten.   Kyoto.

朋友書店   京都

Hsi-ch'üan nung-k'o chih-yeh hsüeh-hsiao.   Hsi-
chuan.
喜泉農科職業學校   喜泉

Hsi-pei—ch'u-pan-she.   Tainan.
西北出版社   臺南

Hsiang-kang   ch'ing-nien—ch'u-pan-she.   Hong
Kong.
香港青年出版社   香港

(Hsiang-kang) Chung-wen ta-hsüeh—ch'u-pan-she.
Hong Kong.
（香港）中文大學出版社   香港

Hsiang-kang   Chung-wen   ta-hsüeh   Ch'ung-chi
hsüeh-yüan.   Hong Kong.
香港中文大學崇基學院   香港

Hsiang-kang hung-yeh—shu-chü.   Hong Kong.
香港宏業書局   香港

Hsiang-kang   P'u-t'ung-hua   yen-hsi-she.   Hong
Kong.
香港普通話研習社   香港

Hsiang-kang Shang-hai—shu-chü.   Hong Kong.
香港上海書局   香港

Hsiang-kang t'u-shu—kung-szu.   Hong Kong.
香港圖書公司   香港

Hsiang-kang wen-hua yen-chiu-she.   Hong Kong.
香港文化研究社   香港

Hsiang-sheng ch'u-pan-she.   Taipei.
祥生出版社   臺北

Hsiang-ts'ao-shan—ch'u-pan kung-szu.   Taipei.
香草山出版公司   臺北

Hsin-chiang jen-min—ch'u-pan-she.   Urumchi.
新疆人民出版社   烏魯木齊

Hsin chih-shih—ch'u-pan-she.   Shanghai.
新知識出版社   上海

Hsin Chung-kuo—yin-shu-kuan.   Shanghai.
新中國印書館   上海

Hsin-feng wen-hua—shih-yeh kung-szu.   Hong Kong.
新風文化事業公司   香港

Hsin-hsing—shu-chü.   Taipei.
新興書局   臺北

Hsin-hua—shu-tien.   Peking.
新華書店   北京

Hsin-lu shu-chü.   Taipei.
新陸書局   臺北

Hsin-lu shu-tien.   Shanghai.
新魯書店   上海

Hsin‑sheng—ch'u-pan-she.   Taipei.
新生出版社   臺北

Hsin sheng-ming shu-chü.   Shanghai.
新生命書局   上海

Hsin shih-chi—ch'u-pan kung-szu.   Tainan.
新世紀出版公司   臺南

Hsin shih-tai—ch'u-pan-she.   Hong Kong.
新時代出版社   香港

Hsin-ta ch'u-pan-she.   Taipei.
欣大出版社   臺北

Hsin wen-feng—ch'u-pan-she.   Taipei.
新文風出版社   臺北

Hsin Ya-chou—ch'u-pan-she.   Hong Kong.
新亞洲出版社   香港

Hsing-chou shih-chieh shu-chü.   Singapore.
星洲世界書局   新嘉坡

Hsing-kuang—ch'u-pan-she.   Taichung, Taipei.
星光出版社   臺中、臺北

Hsing-t'ai wen-hua—ch'u-pan-she.   Fenshan.
興臺文化出版社   鳳山

Hsing-yeh t'u-shu—kung-szu.   Tainan.
興業圖書公司   臺南

Hsüeh-hai—ch'u-pan-she.   Taipei.
學海出版社   臺北

Hsüeh-lin—ch'u-pan-she.   Tainan.
學林出版社   臺南

Hsüeh-lin—shu-tien.   Hong Kong.
學林書店   香港

Hsüeh-sheng ch'u-pan-she.   Taipei.
學生出版社   臺北

Hsüeh-sheng—shu-chü.   Taipei.
學生書局   臺北

Hsüeh-yu t'u-shu—ch'u-pan-she.   Taipei.
學友圖書出版社   臺北

Hu-nan chiao-yü—ch'u-pan-she.   Changsha.
湖南教育出版社   長沙

Hu-nan jen-min—ch'u-pan-she.   Changsha.
湖南人民出版社   長沙

Hu-nan-sheng t'u-shu-kuan.   Changsha.
湖南省圖書館   長沙

Hu-pei jen-min—ch'u-pan-she.   Wuhan.
湖北人民出版社   武漢

Hua-cheng shu-chü.   Taipei.
華正書局   臺北

Hua-ch'iao yü-wen—ch'u-pan-she.   Hong Kong.
華僑語文出版社   香港

Hua-chung kung-hsüeh-yüan.   Wuhan.
華中工學院   武漢

Hua-hsing—ch'u-pan-she.   Panchiao.
華星出版社   板橋

Hua-kang—ch'u-pan yu-hsien kung-szu.   Taipei.
華岡出版有限公司   臺北

Hua-kuo—ch'u-pan-she. Taipei.
華國出版社 臺北

Hua-lien—ch'u-pan-she. Taipei.
華聯出版社 臺北

Hua-ming—shu-chü. Taipei.
華明書局 臺北

Hua-tung jen-min—ch'u-pan-she. Shanghai.
華東人民出版社 上海

Hua-wen shu-chü. Taipei.
華文書局 臺北

Hua-ying—ch'u-pan-she. Taipei.
華英出版社 臺北

Hui-t'ung shu-tien. Hong Kong.
滙通書店 香港

Hung-tao wen-hua shih-yeh—yu-hsien kung-szu.
Taipei.
弘道文化事業有限公司 臺北

Hung-yeh shu-chü. Taipei.
宏業書局 臺北

I-chih—shu-chü. Taipei.
益智書局 臺北

I-hsüeh—shu-chü. Shanghai.
醫學書局 上海

I-lin—ch'u-pan-she. Hong Kong.
藝林出版社 香港

I-pan—shu-chü. Taipei.
一般書局 臺北

I-wen—ch'u-pan-she. Shanghai.
譯文出版社 上海

I-wen hsüeh-hui. Tientsin.
藝文學會 天津

I-wen—yin-shu-kuan. Taipei, Hong Kong.
藝文印書館 臺北、香港

Ida shoten. Tokyo.
井田書店 東京

Iwanami shoten. Tokyo.
岩波書店 東京

Jen-min chiao-yü—ch'u-pan-she. Peking.
人民教育出版社 北京

Jen-min chiao-t'ung—ch'u-pan-she. Peking.
人民交通出版社 北京

Jen-min—ch'u-pan-she. Peking.
人民出版社 北京

Jen-min yu-tien—ch'u-pan-she. Peking.
人民郵電出版社 北京

Jen-wen shu-tien. Peiping.
人文書店 北平

Jiji tsūshinsha. Tokyo.
時事通信社 東京

Jui-ch'ang ko.
瑞昌閣

Jui-ch'eng shu-chü. Taichung.
瑞成書局 臺中

Jung-pao chai. Peking.
榮寶齋 北京

Kadogawa shoten. Tokyo.
角川書店 東京

K'ai-ming—shu-tien. Shanghai, Peking, Taipei.
開明書店 上海、北京、臺北

Kaikōsha. Tokyo.
偕行社 東京

Kan-su jen-min—ch'u-pan-she. Lanchow.
甘肅人民出版社 蘭州

Kang-ch'ing—ch'u-pan-she. Hong Kong.
港青出版社 香港

Kazama shobō.   Tokyo.
風間書房　東京

Kinokuniya—shoten.   Tokyo.
紀伊國書店　東京

Ko-hsin wen-hua—ch'u-pan-she.   Kaohsiung.
革新文化出版社　高雄

K'o-hsüeh chi-shu—ch'u-pan-she.   Shanghai.
科學技術出版社　上海

K'o-hsüeh—ch'u-pan-she.   Peking.
科學出版社　北京

K'o-hsüeh shu-tien.   Shanghai.
科學書店　上海

K'o-wen—ch'u-pan-she.   Taipei.
科文出版社　臺北

Kōbundō shoten.   Tokyo.
光文堂書店　東京

Kōdansha.   Tokyo.
講談社　東京

Kokusho kankōkai.   Tokyo.
國書刊行會　東京

Komazawa Daigaku Zenshū Jiten Hensanjo.
駒澤大學禪宗辭典編纂所

Kōnan shoin.   Tokyo.
江南書院　東京

Kōseikan.   Tokyo.
光生館　東京

Ku-chi—ch'u-pan-she.   Peking.
古籍出版社　北京

Ku-hsiang—ch'u-pan-she.   Taipei.
故鄉出版社　臺北

Ku-tien wen-hsüeh—ch'u-pan-she.   Shanghai.
古典文學出版社　上海

Kuan-yüan shan-fang.   Hong Kong.
觀遠山房　香港

Kuang-ch'eng—ch'u-pan-she.   Taipei.
廣城出版社　臺北

Kuang-ch'i—ch'u-pan-she.   Taichung.
光啓出版社　臺中

Kuang-fu shu-chü.   Taipei.
光復書局　臺北

Kuang-hsi jen-min—ch'u-pan-she.   Nanning.
廣西人民出版社　南寧

Kuang-hua shu-chü.   Hualien.
光華書局　花蓮

Kuang-hung-wen—ch'u-pan-she.   Taipei.
廣鴻文出版社　臺北

Kuang-lu—shu-tien.   Hong Kong.
光祿書店　香港

Kuang-ming shu-chü.   Shanghai.
光明書局　上海

Kuang-po—ch'u-pan-she.   Peking.
廣播出版社　北京

Kuang-t'ai shu-chü.   Hong Kong.
廣泰書局　香港

Kuang-t'ien—ch'u-pan-she.   Tainan.
光田出版社　臺南

Kuang-tung jen-min—ch'u-pan-she.   Canton.
廣東人民出版社　廣州

Kuang-wen—shu-chü.   Taipei.
廣文書局　臺北

Kuang-wen t'u-shu kung-szu.   Hong Kong.
廣文圖書公司　香港

Kuei-chou jen-min—ch'u-pan-she.   Kweiyang.
貴州人民出版社　貴陽

Kuo-chi shu-tien.　Hong Kong.
國際書店　香港

Kuo-chi wen-hua shih-yeh—yu-hsien kung-szu. Taipei.
國際文化事業有限公司　臺北

Kuo-fang kung-yeh—ch'u-pan-she.　Peking.
國防工業出版社　北京

Kuo-fang-pu tsung cheng-chih-pu.　Taipei.
國防部總政治部　臺北

Kuo-hsüeh cheng-li-she.　Shanghai.
國學整理社　上海

Kuo-hsüeh—ch'u-pan-she.　Taipei.
國學出版社　臺北

Kuo-kuang shu-chü.　Shanghai.
國光書局　上海

Kuo-li Cheng-chih ta-hsüeh.　Taipei.
國立政治大學　臺北

Kuo-li Cheng-chih ta-hsüeh Chung-wen yen-chiu-so.　Taipei.
國立政治大學中文研究所　臺北

Kuo-li Chung-yang t'u-shu-kuan.　Taipei.
國立中央圖書館　臺北

Kuo-li Hua-pei pien-i-kuan.　Peking.
國立華北編譯館　北京

Kuo-li Pei-p'ing yen-chiu-yüan.　Peiping.
國立北平研究院　北平

Kuo-li T'ai-wan shih-fan ta-hsüeh Kuo-wen yen-chiu-so.　Taipei.
國立臺灣師範大學國文研究所　臺北

Kuo-li T'ai-wan ta-hsüeh t'u-shu-kuan.　Taipei.
國立臺灣大學圖書館　臺北

Kuo-yü jih-pao-she.　Taipei.
國語日報社　臺北

Kuo-yü Lo-ma-tzu ts'u-chin-hui.　Peiping.
國語羅馬字促進會　北平

Kyōto Daigaku Bungakubu Chūbun Kenkyūshitsu. Kyoto.
京都大學文學部中文研究室　京都

Kyōto Daigaku Bungakubu Tōyōshi Kenkyūshitsu. Kyoto.
京都大學文學部東洋史研究室　京都

Kyōto Daigaku Jinbunkagaku Kenkyūjo.　Kyoto.
京都大學人文科學研究所　京都

Kyūko shoin.　Tokyo.
汲古書院　東京

Lai-hsün-ko shu-tien.　Peking.
來薰閣書店　北京

Lan-t'ai shu-chü.　Taipei.
蘭臺書局　臺北

Lan-teng wen-hua shih-yeh—ku-fen yu-hsien kung-szu.　Taipei.
藍燈文化事業股份有限公司　臺北

Li-ming—wen-hua shih-yeh ku-fen yu-hsien kung-szu.　Taipei.
黎明文化事業股份有限公司　臺北

Li-ta—ch'u-pan-she.　Tainan.
利大出版社　臺南

Liang-yu—t'u-shu kung-szu.　Hong Kong.
良友圖書公司　香港

Liao-ning jen-min—ch'u-pan-she.　Shenyang.
遼寧人民出版社　瀋陽

Lien-ching—ch'u-pan shih-yeh kung-szu.　Taipei.
聯經出版事業公司　臺北

Lien-kuan—ch'u-pan-she.　Taipei.
聯貫出版社　臺北

Liu-kuo—ch'u-pan-she.　Taipei.
六國出版社　臺北

Lo-t'o—ch'u-pan-she. Hong Kong.
駱駝出版社　香港

Lung-men shu-tien. Hong Kong.
龍門書店　香港

Maki shobō. Tokyo.
牧書房　東京

Mao-yü—ch'u-pan-she. Taipei.
茂育出版社　臺北

Maruzen. Tokyo.
丸善　東京

Mei-mei—t'u-shu kung-szu. Hong Kong.
美美圖書公司　香港

Meicho kankōkai. Tokyo.
名著刊行會　東京

Meiji shoin. Tokyo.
明治書院　東京

Meizendō—shoten. Tokyo.
明善堂書店　東京

Min-chien ch'u-pan-she. Shaohsing.
民間出版社　紹興

Min-chu—ch'u-pan-she. Taipei.
民主出版社　臺北

Min-lo—ch'u-pan-she. Taipei.
民樂出版社　臺北

Min-sheng-pao she. Taipei.
民生報社　臺北

Min-sheng—shu-chü. Hong Kong.
民生書局　香港

Min-Shin Bungaku Gengo Kenkyūkai. Osaka.
明淸文學言語研究會　大阪

Ming-hua shu-tien. Hong Kong.
明華書店　香港

Ming-jen—ch'u-pan-she. Taipei.

名人出版社　臺北

Ming-yüan—ch'u-pan-she. Taipei.
名遠出版社　臺北

Morie shoten. Tokyo.
森江書店．東京

Mukyūkai Tōyō Bunka Kenkyūjo. Tokyo.
無窮會東洋文化研究所　東京

Nan-ch'iang shu-chü. Shanghai.
南強書局　上海

Nan-ching—ch'u-pan-she. Taipei.
南京出版社　臺北

Nan-k'ai ta-hsüeh. Kunming.
南開大學　昆明

Nan-kuo—ch'u-pan-she. Hong Kong.
南國出版社　香港

Nan-yang ta-hsüeh Hua-yü yen-chiu chung-hsin.
Singapore.
南洋大學華語研究中心　新嘉坡

Nei Meng-ku jen-min—ch'u-pan-she. Huhehot.
內蒙古人民出版社　呼和浩特

Nichinichi no shūyōsha. Taipei.
日日之修養社　臺北

Nichinichi Shinbunsha. Dairen (Talien).
日日新聞社　大連

Nihon Gakujutsu Kaigi. Tokyo.
日本學術會議　東京

Nihon Gakujutsu Shinkōkai. Tokyo.
日本學術振興會　東京

Ning-hsia jen-min—ch'u-pan-she. Yinchuan.
寧夏人民出版社　銀川

Nippon Gaiji Kyōkai. Tokyo.
日本外事協會　東京

Nung-yeh—ch'u-pan-she. Peking.
農業出版社　北京

O-yü wen-chai-she. Taipei.
俄語文摘社　臺北

Ōbunsha. Tokyo.
旺文社　東京

Ōsaka Daigaku Chūgokugo Kenkyūshitsu.
Osaka.
大阪大學中國語研究室　大阪

Ōsaka Shiritsu Daigaku Bungakubu Chūgokugo
Chūgoku Bungaku Kenkyūshitsu. Osaka.
大阪市立大學文學部中國語中國文學研究室
大阪

Ōsakayago shiten. Lüshun.
大阪屋號支店　旅順

Ōsakayago shoten. Tokyo.
大阪屋號書店　東京

Pa-t'i shu-chü. Taipei.
拔提書局　臺北

Pai-ch'eng—shu-chü. Kaohsiung.
百成書局　高雄

Pai-ch'üan hsiang-shih shih-yen yen-chiu-so. Paichüan.
百泉鄉師實驗研究所　百泉

Pai-ling ch'u-pan-she. Taipei, Kowloon.
百齡出版社　臺北、九龍

Pao-wen-t'ang T'ung-chi shu-p'u. Peiping.
寶文堂同記書鋪　北平

Pei-ching—ch'u-pan-she. Peking.
北京出版社　北京

Pei-ching wai-yü hsüeh-yüan. Peking.
北京外語學院　北京

Pei-ching Shih-fan ta-hsüeh ch'u-pan-pu. Peking.
北京師範大學出版部　北京

Pei-ching ta-hsüeh—ch'u-pan-pu. Peking.
北京大學出版部　北京

Pei-hsin—shu-chü. Shanghai.
北新書局　上海

Pei-p'ing ta-hsüeh nung-hsüeh-yüan. Peiping.
北平大學農學院　北平

Pei-p'ing wen-hua hsüeh-she. Peiping.
北平文化學社　北平

Piao-chun—ch'u-pan-she. Tainan.
標準出版社　臺南

P'ing-p'ing—ch'u-pan-she. Sanchung (Taipei).
平平出版社　三重（臺北）

Po-wen—shu-chü. Hong Kong.
波文書局　香港

Po-wen-t'ang—wen-hua shih-yeh yu-hsien kung-
szu. Taipei.
博文堂文化事業有限公司　臺北

Ryūkei shosha. Tokyo.
龍溪書社　東京

Ryūmon shokyoku. Tokyo.
龍門書局　東京

Saika shorin. Nagoya.
采華書林　名古屋

Saitō shobō. Tokyo.
西東書房　東京

San-lien—shu-tien. Shanghai, Peking, Hong Kong.
三聯書店　上海、北京、香港

San-yü—t'u-shu wen-chü kung-szu. Hong Kong.
三育圖書文具公司　香港

Sankibō. Tokyo.
三喜房　東京

Sanseidō. Tokyo.

三省堂　東京

Shakai shisōsha.　Tokyo.
社會思想社　東京

Shan-hsi jen-min—ch'u-pan-she.　Taiyüan.
山西人民出版社　太原

Shan-hsi jen-min—ch'u-pan-she.　Sian.
陝西人民出版社　西安

Shan-hsi-sheng chiao-yü-t'ing.　Sian.
陝西省教育廳　西安

Shan-tung jen-min—ch'u-pan-she.　Chinan.
山東人民出版社　濟南

Shang-hai chiao-yü—ch'u-pan-she.　Shanghai.
上海教育出版社　上海

Shang-hai jen-min—ch'u-pan-she.　Shanghai.
上海人民出版社　上海

Shang-hai ku-chi—ch'u-pan-she.　Shanghai.
上海古籍出版社　上海

Shang-hai shu-chü.　Hong Kong.
上海書局　香港

Shang-hai t'u-shu—kung-szu.　Shanghai.
上海圖書公司　上海

Shang-hai tz'u-shu—ch'u-pan-she.　Shanghai.
上海辭書出版社　上海

Shang-hai wai-yü chiao-hsüeh—ch'u-pan-she.
Shanghai.
上海外語教學出版社　上海

Shang-hai wen-i—ch'u-pan-she.　Shanghai.
上海文藝出版社　上海

Shang-hai yin-shu-kuan.　Hong Kong.
上海印書館　香港

Shang-wu—yin-shu-kuan.　Shanghai, Peking,

Hong Kong, Taipei.
商務印書館　上海、北京、香港、臺北

Shao-hua wen-hua fu-wu-she.　Hong Kong.
邵華文化服務社　香港

Shao-nien erh-t'ung—ch'u-pan-she.　Shanghai.
少年兒童出版社　上海

Shen-chou—t'u-shu kung-szu.　Hong Kong.
神州圖書公司　香港

Sheng-huo, Tu-shu, Hsin chih-shih San-lien su-tien.
(See San-lien shu-tien). Shanghai, Peking,
Hong Kong.
生活、讀書、新知識三聯書店（見三聯書店）
上海、北京、香港

Shih-chieh—shu-chü.　Shanghai, Hong Kong, Taipei, Singapore.
世界書局　上海、香港、臺北、新嘉坡

Shih-fan ta-hsüeh.　Taipei.
師範大學　臺北

Shih-huo—ch'u-pan-she.　Taipei.
食貨出版社　臺北

Shih-i—shu-chü.　Tainan.
世一書局　臺南

Shih-tai—ch'u-pan-she.　Shanghai, Peking.
時代出版社　上海、北京

Shih-tai t'u-shu—kung-szu.　Hong Kong.
時代圖書公司　香港

Shih-tzu hsün-lien hsüeh-yüan.　Singapore.
師資訓練學院　新嘉坡

Shih-yung—shu-chü.　Kowloon.
實用書局　九龍

Shinchōsha.　Tokyo.
新潮社　東京

Shōgakkan.　Tokyo.
小學館　東京

Shu-mu wen-hsien—ch'u-pan-she.　Peking.
書目文獻出版社　北京

Shuang-yeh shu-lang.　Taipei.
雙葉書廊　臺北

Shun'yōdō.　Tokyo.
春陽堂　東京

Sōbunsha.　Tokyo.
創文社　東京

Sōgensha.　Tokyo, Osaka.
創元社　東京、大阪

Sui-ch'ang chien-i shih-fan.　Swichang.
遂昌簡易師範　遂昌

Szu-ch'uan jen-min—ch'u-pan-she.　Chengtu.
四川人民出版社　成都

Szu-ch'uan-sheng　chiao-yü　k'o-hsüeh-kuan.
Chengtu.
四川省教育科學館　成都

Szu-k'u shu-chü.　Taipei.
四庫書局　臺北

Szu-li ta-yung Kuo-yü chiang-hsi-so.　Macao.
私立達用國語講習所　澳門

Ta Chung-kuo—t'u-shu kung-szu.　Taipei.
大中國圖書公司　臺北

Ta Chung-kuo yin-shua-ch'ang.　Taiyüan (?).
大中國印刷廠　太原（？）

Ta-chung shu-chü.　Kaohsiung.
大衆書局　高雄

Ta-chung shu-tien.　Peking.
大衆書店　北京

Ta-fang—ch'u-pan-she.　Yunghochen.
大方出版社　永和鎮

Ta fu-ch'eng—ch'u-apn-she.　Tainan.
大府城出版社　臺南

Ta-hsia—ch'u-pan-she.　Tainan.
大廈出版社　臺南

Ta-hsin shu-chü.　Taipei.
大新書局　臺北

Ta-hsüeh wen-hsüan-she.　Hsinchuang.
大學文選社　新莊

Ta-hua shu-chü.　Taipei.
大化書局　臺北

Ta-lu tsa-chih-she.　Taipei.
大陸雜誌社　臺北

Ta-lu t'u-shu—kung-szu.　Shanghai.
大陸圖書公司　上海

Ta-ti—ch'u-pan-she.　Taipei.
大地出版社　臺北

Ta-ti shu-tien.　Shanghai.
大地書店　上海

Ta-tung—shu-chü.　Shanghai.
大東書局　上海

Ta-t'ung—shu-chü.　Taipei, Hong Kong.
大通書局　臺北、香港

Ta wu-t'ai shu-yüan.　Kaohsiung.
大舞臺書苑　高雄

T'ai-hua yin-shua-ch'ang.　Sian.
泰華印刷廠　西安

T'ai-pei-shih lien-ho ch'ing-wu tsung szu-ling-pu
ts'e-liang-ch'u.　Taipei.
臺北市聯合勤務總司令部測量處　臺北

T'ai-pei yü-wen hsüeh-yüan.　Taipei.
臺北語文學院　臺北

T'ai-p'ing—shu-chü.　Hong Kong.
太平書局　香港

T'ai-p'ing-yang—ch'u-pan-she.　Shanghai.
太平洋出版社　上海

T'ai-tung shu-chü.   Shanghai.
泰東書局　上海

T'ai-tung yin-shua-chü.   Yentai.
臺東印刷局　烟臺

T'ai-wan hsüeh-sheng—shu-tien.   Taipei.
臺灣學生書店　臺北

T'ai-wan sheng-cheng-fu yin-shua-ch'u.   Taichung.
臺灣省政府印刷處　臺中

T'ai-wan-sheng Kuo-yü t'ui-hsing wei-yüan-hui.
Taipei.
臺灣省國語推行委員會　臺北

T'ai-wen sheng-li Hsin-chu she-hui chiao-yü-kuan.
Hsinchu.
臺灣省立新竹社會教育館　新竹

T'ai-wan Shih-fan ta-hsüeh Kuo-wen yen-chiu-so.
Taipei.
臺灣師範大學國文研究所　臺北

T'ai-wan—shu-tien.   Taipei.
臺灣書店　臺北

T'ai-wan Ying-wen—ch'u-pan-she.   Taipei.
臺灣英文出版社　臺北

Taishūkan.   Tokyo.
大修館　東京

Taiwan gogaku kenkyūkai.   Taipei.
臺灣語學研究會　臺北

Taiwan keisatsu kyōkai.   Taipei.
臺灣警察協會　臺北

Taiwan sōtokufu gakumubu.   Taipei.
臺灣總督府學務部　臺北

T'ang-ti—ch'u-pan-she.   Shanghai.
棠棣出版社　上海

Te-hsin shih—ch'u-pan-she.   Kaohsiung.
德馨室出版社　高雄

Tenri Daigaku Chūgoku Gakka Kenkyūshitsu.
Tenri.
天理大學中國學科研究室　天理

Tenri Daigaku shuppansha.   Tenri.
天理大學出版社　天理

Ti-t'u ch'u-pan-she.   Peking.
地圖出版社　北京

T'ien-chin jen-min—ch'u-pan-she.   Tientsin.
天津人民出版社　天津

T'ien-chin ku-chi shu-tien.   Tientsin.
天津古籍書店　天津

T'ien-i—ch'u-pan-she.   Taipei.
天一出版社　臺北

T'ien-ma shu-tien.   Shanghai.
天馬書店　上海

T'ien-ti—t'u-shu yu-hsien kung-szu.   Hong Kong.
天地圖書有限公司　香港

T'ien-t'ien t'u-shu—fa-hsing kung-szu.   Hong
Kong.
天天圖書發行公司　香港

Times shuppansha.   Tokyo.
タイムス出版社　東京

Ting-wen shu-chü.   Taipei.
鼎文書局　臺北

Tōhō Bunka Gakuin Kyōto Kenkyūjo.   Kyoto.
東方文化學院京都研究所　京都

Tōhō Bunka Gakuin Tōkyō Kenkyūjo.   Tokyo.
東方文化學院東京研究所　東京

Tōhō Gakkai.   Tokyo.
東方學會　東京

Tōhō shoin.   Tokyo.
東方書院　東京

Tōhō shoten.   Tokyo.

東方書店　東京

Tōkyō Bunrika Daigaku Chūbun Kokubungaku Kenkyūshitsu.　Tokyo.
東京文理科大學中文國文學研究室　東京

Tōkyō Bunrika Daigaku Chūgoku Bungaku Kenkyūshitsu.　Tokyo.
東京文理科大學中國文學研究室　東京

Tōkyō Bunrika Daigaku Kanbungaku Daini Kenkyūshitsu.　Tokyo.
東京文理科大學漢文學第二研究室　東京

Tōkyō Daigaku Tōyō Bunka Kenkyūjo.　Tokyo.
東京大學東洋文化研究所　東京

Tōkyō Kyōiku Daigaku Chūgoku Bunka Kenkyūkai.　Tokyo.
東京教育大學中國文化研究會　東京

Tōkyōdō.　Tokyo.
東京堂　東京

Tōto shoseki—kabushikigaisha.　Taipei.
東都書籍株式會社　臺北

T'ou-sè-wè.　Shanghai.
土山灣　上海

Tōyō Bunka Kenkyūjo.　Tokyo.
東洋文化研究所　東京

Tōyō Bunka Kenkyūjo Fuzoku Tōyō Bunken Sentā.　Tokyo.
東洋文化研究所附屬東洋文獻センター　東京

Tōyō Bunka Mikan Tosho Kankōkai.　Tokyo.
東洋文化未刊圖書刊行會　東京

Tōyō Bunko.　Tokyo.
東洋文庫　東京

Tōyō Bunko Kindai Chūgoku Kenkyū Sentā.　Tokyo.
東洋文庫近代中國研究センター　東京

Tōyō Daigaku Chūtetsubun Kenkyūshitsu.　Tokyo.
東洋大學中哲文研究室　東京

Tōyōgaku Bunken Sentā Kankō Iinkai.　Tokyo.
東洋學文獻センター刊行委員會　東京

Ts'ai-cheng ching-chi—ch'u-pan-she.　Peking.
財政經濟出版社　北京

Ts'e-hui—ch'u-pan-she.　Peking.
測繪出版社　北京

Tseng-wen ch'u-pan-she.　Taichung.
曾文出版社　臺中

Tso-chia—ch'u-pan-she.　Peking.
作家出版社　北京

Tsun-ching shu-chü.　Szechwan.
尊經書局　四川

Tsung-ho—ch'u-pan-she.　Tainan.
綜合出版社　臺南

Tu Yüan-ch'ing.　Shupu.
杜元清　淑浦

Tung-fang ch'u-pan-she.　Taipei.
東方出版社　臺北

Tung-fang—shu-tien.　Shanghai.
東方書店　上海

Tung-fang wen-hua kung-ying-she.　Taipei.
東方文化供應社　臺北

Tung-hai—ch'u-pan-she.　Tainan.
東海出版社　臺南

Tung-pei shi-ta.　Changchun.
東北師大　長春

Tung-sheng—ch'u-pan shih-yeh yu-hsien kung-tzu.　Taipei.
東昇出版事業有限公司　臺北

Tung-ya t'u-shu-kuan.　Shanghai.
東亞圖書館　上海

T'ung-nien shu-tien.   Hong Kong.
童年書店　香港

T'ung-su tu-wu—ch'u-pan-she.   Shanghai.
通俗讀物出版社　上海

T'ung-wen shu-chü.   Shanghai.
同文書局　上海

Wai-wen—ch'u-pan-she.   Peking.
外文出版社　北京

Wai-yü chiao-hsüeh yü yen-chiu—ch'u-pan-she.
Peking.
外語教學與研究出版社　北京

Wan-feng—ch'u-pan-she.   Hong Kong.
萬豐出版社　香港

Wan-jen—ch'u-pan-she.   Taipei.
萬人出版社　臺北

Wan-t'ung shu-tien.   Hong Kong.
萬通書店　香港

Wan-yu t'u-shu kung-szu.   Hong Kong.
萬有圖書公司　香港

Wan-yüan t'u-shu kung-szu.   Hong Kong.
萬源圖書公司　香港

Waseda Daigaku Gogaku Kyōiku Kenkyūjo.
Tokyo.
早稻田大學語學教育研究所　東京

Wei-ch'ing—shu-tien.   Hong Kong.
偉青書店　香港

Wei-hsin shu-chü.   Taipei.
維新書局　臺北

Wei-wen t'u-shu—ch'u-pan-she.   Taipei.
偉文圖書出版社　臺北

Wen-chih—ch'u-pan-she.   Taipei.
文致出版社　臺北

Wen-chin—ch'u-pan-she.   Taipei.

文津出版社　臺北

Wen-ching t'u-shu—kung-szu.   Taipei.
文京圖書公司　臺北

Wen-hai—ch'u-pan-she.   Yunghochen (Taipei).
文海出版社　永和鎮（臺北縣）

Wen-hsin shu-wu.   Hong Kong.
文新書屋　香港

Wen-hsing—shu-chü.   Taipei.
文星書局　臺北

Wen-hua chiao-yü—ch'u-pan-she.   Shanghai,
Peking.
文化教育出版社　上海、北京

Wen-hua shu-chü.   Canton.
文華書局　廣州

Wen-hua t'u-shu—kung-szu.   Taipei.
文化圖書公司　臺北

Wen-i lien-ho—ch'u-pan-she.   Shanghai.
文藝聯合出版社　上海

Wen-shih-che—ch'u-pan-she.   Taipei.
文史哲出版社　臺北

Wen-t'ung—shu-chü.   Kweiyang.
文通書局　貴陽

Wen-t'ung—yin-shu-kuan.   Taipei.
文通印書館　臺北

Wen-tzu kai-ko—ch'u-pan-she.   Peking.
文字改革出版社　北京

Wen-yu shu-chü.   Chiayi.
文友書局　嘉義

Wen-yüan shu-tien.   Hong Kong.
文淵書店　香港

Wu-chou—ch'u-pan-she.   Taipei.
五洲出版社　臺北

Wu-kuei-t'ang. Canton.
五桂堂　廣州

Wu-ling—ch'u-pan-she. Taipei.
武陵出版社　臺北

Wu-shih nien-tai—ch'u-pan-she. Peking.
五十年代出版社　北京

Yang-yang—ch'u-pan-she. Tainan.
洋洋出版社　臺南

Yen-ch'en-she. Peiping.
燕塵社　北平

Yen-pien chiao-yu—ch'u-pan-she. Yenchi.
延邊教育出版社　延吉

Ying-hua—ch'u-pan-she. Hong Kong.
英華出版社　香港

Ying-hua shu-yüan. Hong Kong.
英華書院　香港

Yu-shih wen-hua shih-yeh kung-szu. Taipei.
幼獅文化事業公司　臺北

Yüan-tung—t'u-shu kung-szu. Hong Kong, Taipei.
遠東圖書公司　香港、臺北

Yūhōdō. Tokyo.
有朋堂　東京

Yün-hsüan ch'u-pan-she. Shanghai.
雲軒出版社　上海

Yün-nan jen-min—ch'u-pan-she. Kunming;
雲南人民出版社　昆明

Yung-chi—ch'u-pan-she. Chingshuichen.
永吉出版社　清水鎮

Yung-hsin shu-chü. Taipei.
永新書局　臺北

Romanized Index of Authors

Chao, I-po 趙憛伯   1517

Chao, Jui-sheng 趙瑞生   3954, 3960

Chao, Jung-kuang 趙榮光   2582

Chao, K'o-ch'in 趙克勤   1014, 3866, 3967

Chao, Lan-t'ing 趙藍庭   3287

Chao, Meng-mei 趙夢梅   2595

Chao, Shao-hsien 趙少咸   3288, 3670

Chao, Sheng-ming 趙生明   2813

Chao, Shih-ch'en 趙實宸   2514

Chao, Shih-k'ai 趙世開   0112

Chao, Shun 趙順   2022

Chao, T'ien-li 趙天吏   0596

Chao, Tseng 肇曾   3016

Chao, Ya-po 趙雅博   0415

Chao, Yin-t'ang 趙蔭棠   3578, 3794

Chao, Ying-to 趙應鐸   3206, 3219

Chao, Yu-p'ei 趙友培   0187, 3457, 3458

Chao, Yüan-jen 趙元任   See Chao, Yuen Ren
0117, 0118, 0407, 0417, 3341, 3342, 3343

Chao, Yuen Ren 趙元任   0048, 0119, 0142,
0143, 0179, 0254, 0255, 0320, 0323, 0340,
0348, 0382, 0408, 0416, 0659, 1068, 1518,
1610, 1664, 1691, 1765, 3133, 3344, 4035,
4056

Chao-ch'ing shih-fan chuan-k'o hsüeh-hsiao Chung-
wen-hsi 肇慶師範專科學校中文系   1436

Ch'ao, Feng 巢峯   2954, 3062

Ch'ao, T'ien 超天   2023

Char, Tin-yuke 謝廷玉   2334

Chavannes, Edouard   4144

Che-chiang-sheng chiao-yü-t'ing 浙江省教育廳
0687

Chen, Charles K.H.   0959

Chen, Fu 振甫   0383, 0436

Chen, Shang-ling 甄尙靈   0877

Chen, T.S.   1680

Chen, Tsu-lung 陳祚龍   1138, 1146

Chen, Yuvoon   0485

Ch'en, Ai-wen 陳愛文   0219

Ch'en, Chan 陳鱣   1252

Ch'en, Chang-huan 陳章煥   0304

Ch'en, Ch'ang-chih 陳昌治   3487

Ch'en, Ch'ang-hao 陳昌浩   4135

Ch'en, Chao-jung 陳昭容   0804

Ch'en, Cheng-hsiang 陳正祥   1766, 1785, 1786

Ch'en, Ch'eng-chih 陳澄之   2024, 2121, 2284,
2335

Ch'en, Ch'eng-tse 陳承澤   0805

Ch'en, Chi-kang 陳紀綱   2025

Ch'en, Ch'i-p'ing 陳啓平   2122

Ch'en, Chien 陳堅   2264

Ch'en, Chien-ch'iu 陳劍秋   1438

Ch'en, Chien-hsin 陳見昕   2026

Ch'en, Chien-hsin 陳建信   3381

Ch'en, Chien-min 陳建民   0400, 1767

Ch'en, Chih-liang 陳志良   3733

Ch'en, Chin 陳晉   3493

Ch'en, Ching-jen 陳靜仁   2123

Ch'en, Ching-t'ang 陳鏡堂   2515

Ch'en, Ch'ing-ling 陳淸凌   1964, 3382

Ch'en, Cho-min 陳卓民   2435

Ch'en, Chu-tsun 陳柱尊   0549

Ch'en, Ch'u-hsiang 陳楚祥   3118

Ch'en, Ch'üan-wang 陳泉汪   2583

Ch'en, Chün-an 陳君安   1059

Ch'en, Chung 陳忠   1519

Ch'en, Chung-ch'eng 陳忠誠   3119, 3220 4077

Ch'en, Chung-fang 陳中方   2285

Ch:en, Fa-wei 陳法衞   1520

Ch'en, Hsiao-ying 陳孝英   2814

Ch'en, Hsin-hsiang 陳欣向   0706

Ch'en, Hsin-hsiung 陳新雄   3795

Ch'en, Hsüan 陳玄   0713

Ch'en, Hui-chih 陳徽治   0793

Cheng-chih ching-chi-hsüeh tz'u-tien pien-chi-pu 『政治經濟學詞典』編輯部 3166

Cheng-yen ch'u-pan-she 正言出版社   1965

Ch'eng, Chia-shu 程家樞 1351

Ch'eng, Chih-wei 成志偉 2287

Ch'eng, Ch'ui-ch'eng 程垂成 1315

Ch'eng, Erh-ju 程二如 3192

Ch'eng, Fa-jen 程發軔 0050, 1759, 1760, 1761

Ch'eng, Hsiang-hui 程祥徽 1398

Ch'eng, Jung 承融 0238

Ch'eng, Kuan-lin 程觀林 0778

Ch'eng, Ta-ming 程達明 1307, 2656

Ch'eng, Tseng-hou 程曾厚 0401

Ch'eng, Wei-chin 程維進 2994

Ch'eng, Yang-chih 程養之 0714, 3363, 3443

Ch'eng, Ying-chang 程瀛章 1809

Ch'eng, Yü-szu 成於思 3849

Ch'eng-tu-shih ch'un-chung i-shu-kuan 成都市羣眾藝術館 2548, 2702

Ch'eng-yü hsüan chu tsu 『成語選注』組 2029

Chesterman, A.P.C. 2786

Chi, Ch'ang-hung 吉常宏 3045

Chi, Ch'eng-chia 季成家 2288, 2461

Chi, Hsien-lin 季羨林 1567

Chi, Lin 紀林 1739

Chi, Wei 季薇 3004

Chi, Wei-lung 季維龍 3912

Chi, Wen-shen 1303

Chi, Wen-shun 1610

Chi-lin shih-fan ta-hsüeh Chung-wen-hsi 吉林師範大學中文系 1320

Ch'i, Ch'ung-t'ien 齊冲天 0211, 1397

Ch'i, Hsüeh-ch'u 齊學初 0670, 0715

Ch'i, I 齊翼 2172

Ch'i, Ju-shan 齊如山 2369

Ch'i, Nai-ch'eng 祁乃成 2481

Ch'i, P'ei-jung 齊佩瑢 0826, 0839, 0849, 0862, 3637

Ch'i, Su-chen 齊素貞 0716

Ch'i, T'ieh-hen 齊鐵恨 0188, 0220, 0597, 0598, 0701, 0702, 0717, 0718, 1471, 2743, 2744, 2745, 3345

Ch'i-ming shu-chü 啓明書局 4101

Chia, Ch'i-ming 賈啓明 1437

Chia, Shuang-hu 賈雙虎 2794

Chia, Yen-te 賈彥德 1682

Chiang, Ch'eng-k'un 蔣成坤 1433

Chiang, Ching-fu 蔣鏡夫 3346

Chiang, Ching-pang 蔣經邦 3751

Chiang, Chü-ch'ien 江擧謙 3498, 3523

Chiang, Ch'un-fang 姜椿芳 3023, 3176, 3223

Chiang, Hsi-ho 江希和 3120, 3121, 3142

Chiang, I-ch'ien 蔣一前 3358

Chiang, Jen-chieh 蔣人杰 3494

Chiang, Ker Chiu 蔣克秋 2125

Chiang, K'un-wu 姜昆武 1886

Chiang, Li-hung 蔣禮鴻 1063, 1138, 2921, 3224

Chiang, Liang-fu 姜亮夫 0550, 0910, 2922

Chiang, Lu-sen 江祿森 3383

Chiang, Shao-yü 蔣紹愚 1023, 1024, 1041, 1139, 1046, 1140, 2787

Chiang, Shui 江水 0551

Chiang, T'ieh 江鐵 4104

Chiang, Yin-nan 蔣蔭楠 2030

Chiang, Yin-tan 蔣蔭枬 2794

Chiang, Ying-lung 江應龍 3968

Chiang, Yü 江羽 2683

Chiang, Yü 江宇 3152

Chiang, Yüeh-ch'iao 蔣月樵 1966, 2031

Chiang-hsi Shih-yüan Chung-wen-hsi 江西師院中文系 1967

Chiang-su chiao-yü-she 江蘇教育社 2753

Chiao, J.W. 0749

Chiao-yü ch'u-pan-she pien-chi-pu 教育出版社編輯部 1414

Chiao-yü-pu 教育部 1473, 3327

Kroll, J.L.   2728

Kryukov, M.V.   1715

Ku, Chih-chien 顧志堅   1578

Ku, Chin-ch'en 顧藎臣   3509

Ku, Hsin-ling 古信凌   1988

Ku, Hsing-hua 顧星華   1485

Ku, Kuang-yü 谷光宇   2072

Ku, Lin-sen 顧林森   3411

Ku, Mu 古牧   2688

Ku, Pai-lin 顧柏林   3135

Ku, Yeh-wang 顧野王   3564

Ku, Yüeh 顧越   0541, 0692, 0956

Kuan, Chen-hsiung 關辰雄   2186

Kuan, Hsieh-ch'u 管燮初   0957

Kuan, Kuo-hsüan 關國暄   3534

Kuan, Szu-chiu 管思九   3072

Kuan, Yü-shu 關玉書   3331

Kuang-chou wai-yü hsüeh-yüan 廣州外語學院
4126

Kuang-chou wai-kuo-yü hsüeh-yüan *Te-Han tz'u-tien* tsu   廣州外國語學院『德漢詞典』組
4127

Kuang-fu shu-chü pien-chi-pu 光復書局編輯部
4015

Kuang-hsi jen-min ch'u-pan-she 廣西人民出版社
2710

Kuang-hsi shih-fan hsüeh-yüan Chung-wen-hsi
廣西師範學院中文系   1446

Kuang-wen pien-i-so 廣文編譯所   3767

Kubler, Cornelius C.   1372

Kuei, Chung-shu 桂中樞   3459

Kuei, Fu 桂馥   3535

Kuei, I 瓊一   0571, 1890, 2161, 2205

Kuei, Wen-ts'an 桂文燦   3390

Kumagai, Yoshimasa 熊谷良正   2625

Kung, Chao-p'ing 宮兆平   2764

Kung, Hsiang-p'ing 龔湘萍   2424

Kung, Hsiu-shih 龔秀石   0174

Kung, Jen-nien 貢仁年   0572

Kung, Ju-hsü 龔汝緒   2765

Kung, Ta-ch'ing 龔達清   0627

Künstler, M.J.   0066, 0706, 0818, 0923, 2932,
3661

Kuo, Ch'ang-sheng 郭長生   3167

Kuo, Chao-mu 郭昭穆   1028

Kuo, Ch'eng-mou 郭成謀   2564

Kuo, Chien-chang 郭建章   2766

Kuo, Hou-chüeh 郭後覺   0155, 2073

Kuo, Hsi-liang 郭錫良   0531, 1029

Kuo, Hsiu-mei 郭秀梅   2132

Kuo, Hua-lun 郭華倫   See Kuo, Warren

Kuo, Jung-i 郭榮一   0363

Kuo, Ku-hsi 郭谷兮   1916

Kuo, Kuo-ying 郭國英   0606

Kuo, Liang-fu 郭良夫   0424, 2859

Kuo, Ming-k'un 郭明昆   1694, 1695

Kuo, Nai-ts'en 郭乃岑   0393

Kuo, P'u 郭璞   3598, 3599, 3647

Kuo, Shao-yü 郭紹虞   0425, 2187

Kuo, Tsai-i 郭在貽   1030, 1117, 1118, 1150,
1174, 3553

Kuo, Warren 郭華倫   1623

Kuo, Wen-jui 郭文瑞   2914

Kuo-li Chung-yang t'u-shu-kuan 國立中央圖書館
0015, 0016, 0017

Kuo-li Pei-ching ta-hsüeh yen-chiu-so Wen-shih-pu 國立北京大學研究所文史部   3684

Kuo-li pien-i kuan 國立編譯館   1486, 1671,
1849

Kuo-li T'ai-wan shih-fan ta-hsüeh Kuo-yin chiao-ts'ai pien-chi wei-yüan-hui 國立臺灣師範大學國
音教材編輯委員會   3321

Kuo-li T'ai-wan ta-hsüeh t'u-shu-kuan 國立臺灣大學
圖書館   0018

Kuo-wu yüan 國務院   3353

Kuo-yü chou-k'an-she 國語週刊社   3348

Mei, Kung 淝公　3474

Mei, Tsu-lin 梅祖麟　4096

Meng, Ch'i 孟起　0159

Meng, Ch'ing-chang 孟慶璋　3392

Meng, Ch'uan-ming 蒙傳銘　0450, 0490

Meng, Hsiang 夢湘　0371

Meng, Keng-yeh 蒙耕野　2489

Meng, Yüan 孟原　1322

Métaille, Georges　1672

Mi, Ch'ing 米青　3309

Mi, Sung-i 彌松頤　1260

Miao, Hsin-cheng 繆鑫正　1795

Miao, Mu 苗木　2862

Miao, Shu-ch'eng 繆樹晟　0295

Miao, T'ien-hua 繆天華　2086

Miller, Robert P.　1201

Miller, Roy A.　0308, 0836, 0915, 0984, 1333, 3514, 3757

Milsky, Constantin　0260

Min, Chia-chi 閔家驥　3183, 3184, 3273

Min-Shin Bungaku Gengo Kenkyūkai 明清文學言語研究會　1227

Ming 明　2445

Misawa, Junjirō 三澤諄治郎　3737

Mittler, Theodor, S.V.D. 苗德秀　4161

Miwa, Noritsugu 三輪典嗣　1995

Miyahara, Minpei 宮原民平　0742

Miyakoshi, Kentarō 宮越健太郎　1421

Miyata, Ichirō 宮田一郎　0160, 1258, 1261, 1262, 1263

Miyoshi, Seibi 三好成美　1851

Mizukami, Shizuo 水上靖夫　1987

Mō Dakutō Chosaku Gengo Kenkyūkai 毛澤東著作言語研究會　1374

Mo, Heng 莫衡　3066

Mo, Ju-pan 莫如邦　0292

Mochizuki, Shinchō 望月眞澄　0558

Mochizuki, Yasokichi 望月八十吉　0161, 0271, 0272, 0332, 0695, 1368, 1369

Mogi, Ichirō 茂木一郎　2523

Mohr, P.　1616

Morgan, Evan　1582

Morgan, Harry Titterton　2354

Morikawa, Kyūjirō 森川久次郎　0396, 4011

Morino, Shigeo 森野繁夫　1130, 1131, 1132, 1133

Morohashi, Tetsuji 諸橋轍次　3966, 3972

Morris, Peter Thomas 潘敏賢　1952

Motte, Joseph, S.J. 穆啓蒙　2355

Mou, Kou-yüan 牟构垣　0333

Moule, A.C.　4050

Moule, A.E.　2404

Mu, Liu-sen 穆柳森　1741

Mu, Tun-mo 穆敦謨　0334

Mu, Wu-hsiang 穆武祥　3185

Murakami, Futeki 村上不適　2386

Muramatsu, Kazuya 村松一彌　1264

Murao, Tsutomu 村尾力　2878, 2882, 4110, 4111, 4112, 4117, 4119

Murata, Ryōa 村田了阿　2322

Nagasawa, Kikuya 長澤規矩也　1225, 1228, 2276

Nai, Fan 耐煩　0335

Nakagawa, Jūan 中川涉庵　1154

Nakagawa, Tōshi 中川登史　0372

Nakajima, Motoki 中嶋幹起　2953

Nakanishi, Jirō 中西次郎　2323

Nakano, Yoshihei 中野吉平　2324

Nakazawa, Shinzō 中澤信三　1527

Nan, Hai 南海　0815

Nan-ching ta-hsüeh t'u-shu-kuan, Chung-wen-hsi, Li-shih-hsi 南京大學圖書館、中文系、歷史系　2895

Nan-ching ta-hsüeh wai-wen-hsi 南京大學外文系　2140

Wang, Hsien-ch'ien 王先謙   3646

Wang, Hsien-en 王顯恩   1434

Wang, Hsien-sheng 王憲生   1633

Wang, Hsing-hua 王星華   0698

Wang, Hsiu-ming 王修明   0540, 3825

Wang, Huan 王還   1309, 1313, 1314, 1365

Wang, Hung-chi 王鴻基   2569

Wang, I 王毅   2197

Wang, I-hsin 王一心   2100

Wang, Jen-hsü 王仁昫   3749

Wang, Jen-lu 王仁祿   0819

Wang, Keng-t'ang 王賡唐   3102

Wang, K'o-chung 王克仲   0707, 2101, 2062

Wang, Kuang 王光   1658

Wang, Kuang-ch'ing 王廣慶   0985, 0986, 0987, 2782

Wang, Kuei-hua 王桂華   0515, 1898

Wang, Kuei-nien 汪桂年   3572

Wang, Kuo-chang 王國璋   1454

Wang, Kuo-chung 王國忠   2363

Wang, Li 王力   0086, 0103, 0104, 0105, 0177, 0235, 0820, 0821, 0945, 0946, 0947, 0948, 0949, 1004, 1052, 1053, 1298, 1349, 1928, 2972, 2983, 3074, 3252

Wang, Li-chia 王理嘉   0588, 3210

Wang, Li-hua 王麗華   0960

Wang, Li-ta 王立達   0106, 1564, 1565

Wang, Li-t'ing 王力廷   1334

Wang, Liao-i 王了一   See Wang, Li   0198, 0498, 0545, 0546, 0822, 0936, 1021, 1832, 3116

Wang, Lien-tseng 王聯曾   3757

Wang, Lun 王綸   0460, 0547, 0823, 1247, 1248, 1249

Wang, Meng-hsiung 王夢熊   2506

Wang, Meng-wu 王孟武   1360, 3999

Wang, Ming-ken 王明根   2900

Wang, Nien-sun 王念孫   3631

Wang, Ning 王寧   0557, 0787, 1033, 3247

Wang, P'ei-chien 王佩劍   2570

Wang, Sen-jan 王森然   1005

Wang, Shih-chün 王士均   2718

Wang, Shih-hsiang 王士襄   3103

Wang, Shih-hsieh 王士燮   1659

Wang, Shih-shih 王士湜   2102

Wang, Shih-tzu 王石子   2328

Wang, Shou-chen 王守珍   1411

Wang, Shu-hsin 王淑馨   3128

Wang, Shu-min 王叔民   1108

Wang, Sou-pi 汪漱碧   2166

Wang, Su-ts'un 王素存   1746

Wang, Sung-mao 王松茂   2868, 2869

Wang, Ta-ch'ang 王大昌   2103, 2312

Wang, T'ao 王濤   1064, 3268, 3914, 4024

Wang, Te-chao 王德昭   3666

Wang, Te-ch'un 王德春   2984, 3104, 3213

Wang, Te-hsin 王德新   2698

Wang, Ti-p'ing 王砥平   1006

Wang, Tien-chieh 王黜潔   2507

Wang, T'ien-ch'ang 王天昌   1498, 2611, 3337

Wang, T'ien-shih 王天石   2679

Wang, Ting-chün 王鼎鈞   2840

Wang, Tso-liang 王佐良   0461

Wang, Tsu-yu 王祖佑   3309

Wang, Tsung-chieh 王宗傑   2167, 2313

Wang, Tsung-hu 汪宗虎   1727

Wang, Tsung-yen 王宗炎   3138

Wang, Tzu-ch'iang 王自强   1455, 1634, 3105, 3108

Wang, Wei-hsien 王維賢   0473

Wang, Wei-yung 王偉勇   1947

Wang, Wen-hsin 王文新   1396

Wang, Wen-t'ai 王文泰   3015

Wang, Wen-yü 王問漁   1882

Wang, William S-Y. 王士元   0030, 0031, 0114